The
and
into
by
clas
forı
epi
of
myı
app
froı
and
to
valu
sch
and

Ro
sics
Un
and
tioı
Dr.
Languages, which received a CHOICE Outstanding Academic Title
award in 2006.

THE CAMBRIDGE COMPANION TO

GREEK
MYTHOLOGY

Edited by

ROGER D. WOODARD

Andrew V. V. Raymond Professor of the Classics
Professor of Linguistics
University of Buffalo (The State University of New York)

CAMBRIDGE
UNIVERSITY PRESS

CAMBRIDGE UNIVERSITY PRESS

Cambridge, New York, Melbourne, Madrid, Cape Town, Singapore, São Paulo, Delhi

Cambridge University Press
32 Avenue of the Americas, New York, NY 10013-2473, USA

www.cambridge.org
Information on this title: www.cambridge.org/9780521845205

First published 2007

Printed in the United States of America

A catalog record for this publication is available from the British Library.

Library of Congress Cataloging in Publication Data

The Cambridge companion to Greek mythology / edited by Roger D. Woodard.
p.   cm.
Includes bibliographical references and index.
ISBN   978-0-521-84520-5 (hardback) – ISBN   978-0-521-60726-1 (pbk.)
1. Mythology, Greek.   I. Woodard, Roger D.   II. Title.
BL783.C36   2007
292.1′3 – dc22   2007005451

ISBN   978-0-521-84520-5 hardback
ISBN   978-0-521-60726-1 paperback

Contents

List of Illustrations   *page* vii
List of Contributors   ix
Acknowledgments   xiii
List of Abbreviations   xv

Introduction: *Muthoi* in Continuity and Variation   1
ROGER D. WOODARD

PART I: SOURCES AND INTERPRETATIONS   15

1   Lyric and Greek Myth   19
     GREGORY NAGY

2   Homer and Greek Myth   52
     GREGORY NAGY

3   Hesiod and Greek Myth   83
     ROGER D. WOODARD

4   Tragedy and Greek Myth   166
     RICHARD BUXTON

5   Myth in Aristophanes   190
     ANGUS BOWIE

6   Plato Philomythos   210
     DISKIN CLAY

7   Hellenistic Mythographers   237
     CAROLYN HIGBIE

CONTENTS

PART 2: RESPONSE, INTEGRATION, REPRESENTATION   255

8   Greek Myth and Greek Religion   259
    CLAUDE CALAME

9   Myth and Greek Art: Creating a Visual Language   286
    JENIFER NEILS

10 Mythic Landscapes of Greece   305
    ADA COHEN

11 Politics and Greek Myth   331
    JONATHAN M. HALL

12 Ovid and Greek Myth   355
    A. J. BOYLE

PART 3: RECEPTION   383

13 Women and Greek Myth   387
    VANDA ZAJKO

14 Let Us Make Gods in Our Image: Greek Myth in
    Medieval and Renaissance Literature   407
    H. DAVID BRUMBLE

15 'Hail, Muse! *et cetera*': Greek Myth in English and
    American Literature   425
    SARAH ANNES BROWN

16 Greek Myth on the Screen   453
    MARTIN M. WINKLER

    Bibliography   481
    Index   511

ILLUSTRATIONS

FIGURES

Figures follow page 304

1 A Fox Telling Aesop Fables. Red-figure kylix of the Bologna Painter from Vulci.
2 The Charioteer of the Phaedrus. Andrea Sansovino.
3 Deeds of Theseus. Attic red-figure cup attributed to the Codrus Painter from Vulci.
4 Tyrannicides. Casts of Roman marble copies after bronze originals by Kritios and Nesiotes.
5 Departure of a Hero. Attic Late Geometric spouted crater from Thebes.
6 Death of Priam; Attic black-figure amphora by Lydos from Vulci.
7 Return of Hephaestus. Attic red-figure skyphos attributed to the Curti Painter.
8 Return of Hephaestus. Attic red-figure volute-crater by Polion from Spina.
9 Heracles and the Nemean Lion. Metope from the Temple of Zeus at Olympia.
10 Birth of Erichthonius. Attic red-figure squat lekythos attributed to the Meidias Painter.
11 Battle of Athena and a Giant. Attic red-figure lekythos attributed to Douris.
12 Naval Fresco from Akrotiri.
13 Nymphs and Pan. Marble votive relief.
14 The Blinding of Polyphemus. Fragment from a vase.
15 Meeting of Odysseus and Nausicaa. Lid of a red-figure pyxis attributed to Aison.
16 Abduction of the Leucippides by the Dioscuri and the Garden of the Hesperides. Attic red-figure hydria by the Meidias Painter.

17 Odysseus' Descent to the Underworld. Drawing of Attic red-figure pelike attributed to the Lykaon Painter.

18 The Suicide of Ajax. Black-figure amphora by Exekias.

19 Book 2, Emblem 2, in Frances Quarles, *Emblemes*.

20 "*Venus*," from *The Copenhagen Planet Book*. See Filedt Kok (1985) for a similar blockbook by the Master of the Amsterdam Cabinet.

21 *Clash of the Titans*. Zeus and the "Arena of Life."

22 *Jason and the Argonauts*. Hera observing Jason and Medea on the Olympian screen.

23 *Jason and the Argonauts*. Talos towering above the Argonauts.

24 *Hercules*. Our hero at the climax of the film that made him immortal on the screen.

25 *Hercules Conquers Atlantis*. Hercules, descended from his twelve-horse chariot, discovers massacre victims at the palace of Atlantis. Note the panther reliefs on the wall.

TABLES

3.1 Comparison of Indo-Iranian Traditions: Cosmogonic and Cosmologic — *page* 132

3.2 Comparison of Greek and Indic Traditions — 142

CONTRIBUTORS

ANGUS BOWIE is Fellow of The Queen's College, Oxford, and the Lobel Praelector in Classics. His publications include *The Poetic Dialect of Sappho and Alcaeus* (1981) and *Aristophanes: Myth, Ritual and Comedy* (1993). Dr. Bowie also serves as editor of the *Journal of Hellenic Studies*.

A. J. BOYLE is professor of classics at the University of Southern California. His recent publications include *Tragic Seneca* (1997), *Ovid's Fasti* (with R. D. Woodard 2000), *Flavian Rome* (with W. J. Dominik 2003), *Ovid and the Monuments* (2004), and *Roman Tragedy* (2006).

Professor SARAH ANNES BROWN is professor of English at Anglia Ruskin University, Cambridge. She is the author of *The Metamorphosis of Ovid: From Chaucer to Ted Hughes* (1999) and the coeditor (with Charles Martindale) of Nicholas Rowe's translation of Lucan's *Pharsalia* (1997). She has also published numerous shorter pieces on various aspects of classical reception, including articles on its relationship with queer theory and science fiction. She is currently editing a collection of essays, *Tragedy in Transition* (with Catherine Silverstone).

H. DAVID BRUMBLE is professor of English at the University of Pittsburgh. Among his scholarly works are *Classical Myths and Legends in the Middle Ages and Renaissance: A Dictionary of Allegorical Meanings* (1998) and *Street Gangs and Warrior Tribes* (forthcoming).

RICHARD BUXTON is professor of Greek language and literature at the University of Bristol. Among the works he has authored are *Persuasion in Greek Tragedy* (1982), *Sophocles* (1984; reprinted with Addenda 1995),

Imaginary Greece: The Contexts of Mythology (1994), and *The Complete World of Greek Mythology* (2004). Professor Buxton is editor of *From Myth to Reason?* (1999) and *Oxford Readings in Greek Religion* (2000). Since 2006, Professor Buxton has been President of the *Fondation pour le Lexicon Iconographicum Mythologiae Classicae*.

CLAUDE CALAME is Director of Studies at the École des Hautes Études en Sciences Sociales in Paris and Honorary Professor of Greek Language and Literature at the University of Lausanne. In English, he has published *The Craft of Poetic Speech in Ancient Greece* (1995), *The Poetics of Eros in Ancient Greece* (1999), *Choruses of Young Women in Ancient Greece* (second edition 2001), *Myth and History in Ancient Greece* (2003), *Masks of Authority. Fiction and Pragmatics in Ancient Greece* (2005), and, on Greek mythology, *Thésée et l'imaginaire athénien. Légende et culte en Grèce classique* (second edition 1996) and *Poétique des mythes dans la Grèce antique* (2000).

DISKIN CLAY is professor of classical studies at Duke University. His interests have focused on the intersection of ancient poetry and philosophy. He is the author of many studies of the Platonic dialogues, *Lucretius and Epicurus* (1983), *Platonic Questions: Dialogues with the Silent Philosopher* (2000), and *Archilochos Heros: The Cult of Poets in the Greek Polis* (2004). At present he is working on a study of *The Art of Hell: Reflections of Dante's Inferno in the Religious Art of Tuscany from the Early Trecento to 1579.*

ADA COHEN is an associate professor of art history at Dartmouth College. She has written essays on various aspects of Greek art, including gender and sexuality, myth, and landscape. She is author of *The Alexander Mosaic: Stories of History and Defeat* (1997) and coeditor of and contributor to *Constructions of Childhood in the Greek and Roman Antiquity* (2007). She recently completed a book on masculinity and power in late Classical and Hellenistic art titled *Paradigms of Manhood: Art and Culture in the Times of Alexander the Great* and is working on a study of feminine beauty in ancient Greece.

JONATHAN M. HALL is the Phyllis Fay Horton Professor in the Humanities, professor and chair of classics, and professor of history at the University of Chicago. He is the author of *Ethnic Identity in Greek Antiquity* (1997), *Hellenicity: Between Ethnicity and Culture* (2002), and *A History of the Archaic Greek World* (2007).

CAROLYN HIGBIE is professor of classics at the University of Buffalo (The State University of New York). Her scholarly work includes the book *The Lindian Chronicle and the Greek Creation of Their Past* and the recent articles "The Bones of a Hero, the Ashes of a Politician: Athens, Salamis, and the Usable Past" (*Classical Antiquity* 16 (1997) 279–308) and "Craterus and the Use of Inscriptions in Ancient Scholarship" (*TAPA* 129 (1999) 43–83).

GREGORY NAGY has been the Director of the Harvard Center for Hellenic Studies in Washington, DC, since 2000, while continuing to teach half-time at the Harvard campus in Cambridge, Massachusetts as the Francis Jones Professor of Classical Greek Literature and professor of comparative literature. Among the books he has authored are *Greek Mythology and Poetics* (1990), *Pindar's Homer: The Lyric Possession of an Epic Past* (1990), *Poetry as Performance: Homer and Beyond* (1996), *Homeric Questions* (1996), *The Best of the Achaeans: Concepts of the Hero in Archaic Greek Poetry* (2nd ed., with new Introduction, 1999), *Homeric Responses* (2003), *Homer's Text and Language* (2004), and *Homer the Classic* (2007). Forthcoming in 2008 is *Homer the Preclassic*.

JENIFER NEILS is the Ruth Coulter Heede Professor of Art History and Classics at Case Western Reserve University. She is the author of *The Youthful Deeds of Theseus* (1987) and *The Parthenon Frieze* (2001) and has organized two major exhibitions of Greek art: *Goddess and Polis: The Panathenaic Festival in Ancient Athens* (1992) and *Coming of Age in Ancient Greece: Images of Childhood from the Classical World* (2003, with John Oakley). Professor Neils has contributed several major entries to the *Lexicon Iconographicum Mythologiae Classicae* and recently edited *The Parthenon from Antiquity to the Present* (2005).

MARTIN M. WINKLER is professor of classics at George Mason University. He has published books and articles on Roman literature, the classical tradition, and classical and medieval mythology in film. He has edited the essay collections *Classical Myth and Culture in the Cinema* (2001), *Gladiator: Film and History* (2004), *Troy: From Homer's Iliad to Hollywood Epic* (2006), and *Spartacus: Film and History* (2007).

ROGER D. WOODARD is the Andrew V. V. Raymond Professor of the Classics and professor of linguistics at the University of Buffalo (The State University of New York). Among his more recent publications are *Greek Writing from Knossos to Homer: A Linguistic Interpretation of the Origin of the Greek Alphabet and the Continuity of Ancient Greek Literacy* (1997), *The Cambridge Encyclopedia of the World's Ancient Languages* (2004), *Ovid: Fasti* (with A. J. Boyle, revised edition, 2004), and *Indo-European Sacred Space: Vedic and Roman Cult* (2006).

VANDA ZAJKO is senior lecturer in classics at the University of Bristol, UK. She has wide-ranging interests in the reception of classical myth and literature, particularly in the twentieth century. Recent publications include "Homer and Ulysses" in *The Cambridge Companion to Homer* (2004), "Narratives of Tragic Predicaments: *Frankenstein* and *Prometheus Bound*" in *The Blackwell Companion to Tragedy* (2007), and "What Difference Was Made? Feminist Models of Reception" in *A Companion to Classical Receptions* (2007). She is coeditor of *Laughing with Medusa: Classical Myth and Feminist Thought* (2006).

ACKNOWLEDGMENTS

The editor would like to express his appreciation first and foremost to the contributors to *The Cambridge Companion to Greek Mythology*, distinguished scholars all, without whose dedicated and expert efforts this volume could not have taken shape. I wish too to thank Beatrice Rehl and her staff at the New York office of Cambridge University Press for their characteristic efficiency and professionalism. Thanks go also to Professor Amy Graves for assisting Calame and Woodard in producing an English translation of Chapter 8.

ABBREVIATIONS

ANET   *Ancient Near Eastern Texts. See* Pritchard 1969
AJA   *American Journal of Archaeology*
AJP   *American Journal of Philology*
Ant. Class.   *L'Antiquité Classique*
BA   *See* Nagy 1979
BABesch   *Bulletin Antieke Beschaving*
BICS   *Bulletin of the Institute of Classical Studies*
Cl. Ant.   *Classical Antiquity*
CJ   *Classical Journal*
C Phil.   *Classical Philology*
CQ   *Classical Quarterly*
CVA   *Corpus Vasorum Antiquorum*
EH   *See* Nagy 2005
ETCSL   The Electronic Text Corpus of Sumerian Literature (etcsl.orinst.ox.ac.uk)
FGrH   *Fragmente der Griechischen Historiker*
GM   *See* Nagy 1990b
Harv. Stud.   *Harvard Studies in Classical Philology*
HC   *See* Nagy 2007
HPC   *See* Nagy 2008
HQ   *See* Nagy 1996b
HR   *See* Nagy 2003
HTL   *See* Nagy 2004b
JAOS   *Journal of the American Oriental Society*
JHS   *Journal of Hellenic Studies*
JNES   *Journal of Near Eastern Studies*
LIMC   *Lexicon Iconographicum Mythologiae Classicae* (Zurich 1981–1997)
PCPS   *Proceedings of the Cambridge Philological Society*
PH   *See* Nagy 1990a
PP   *See* Nagy 1996a

PR	*See* Nagy 2002
Rev. Ét. Grec.	*Revue des études grecques*
TAPA	*Transactions of the American Philological Association*
YClS	*Yale Classical Studies*
ZPE	*Zeitschrift für Papyrologie und Epigraphik*

For additional abbreviations the reader might wish to consult, *inter alia,* *L'Année philologique* and the *Oxford Classical Dictionary.*

INTRODUCTION: *MUTHOI* IN CONTINUITY AND VARIATION

Roger D. Woodard

> But as a rule the ancient myths [*palaious muthous* (παλαιοὺς μύθους)] are not found to yield a simple and consistent story, so that nobody need wonder if details of my recension cannot be reconciled with those given by every poet and historian.

The editor trusts that he will be forgiven the presumptuousness (or audacity, as the case may be) of beginning with Robert Graves's translation of Diodorus Siculus 4.44.5–6 – the lines that Graves prefixed to the preface of his work *The Golden Fleece* – lines that seem no less relevant here than at the outset of Graves' novelistic retelling (influenced by his experiences in the trenches of the Great War, no less than by Frazer's *Golden Bough*) of the ancient mythic tradition of the young hero Jason and his band of warrior comrades, who sailed from Greece on board the Argo to recover the fleece of a golden ram from distant Colchis. What we call "Greek myth" is no featureless monolith, but multifaceted, multifarious and multivalent, a fluid phenomenon, as was obvious to the historian Diodorus in the first century BC, and as is made plain by the essays that make up this *Cambridge Companion*.

The chapters that follow are divided into three major parts. *Sources and Interpretations*, the first part of the three, consists of seven essays examining the forms and uses of Greek mythic traditions in Greek texts, ranging in period and genre from eighth-century BC oral poetry to encyclopedic prose compilations of the early centuries AD – from an era rich in a spontaneous performative creativity to one seemingly more concerned with documenting the mythic traditions of a glorious literary past. Yet even in the earliest attested periods, there is, as we shall see, evidence of a concern for preserving still more ancient forms and notions about gods and heroes.

Part One begins with Gregory Nagy's examination of the lyric poets, followed by his essay on Homer. If from a chronological perspective the order might seem unorthodox – it should not. As Nagy reminds his readers, "Lyric did not start in the archaic period. It is just as old as epic, which clearly pre-dates the archaic period. And the traditions of lyric, like those of epic, were rooted in oral poetry, which is a matter of performance as well as composition." In the archaic period, composition and performance are inextricably linked. Nagy explores occasions of performance for his readers by examining, *inter alia*, a "primary test case" – the lyric works of the Lesbian poets Sappho and Alcaeus, jointly representing "the repertoire of the myths and rituals of the people of Lesbos as expressed in lyric performance." The place of such performance was the sacred ritual space of Messon – the space for the celebration of the *Kallisteia*, a festival featuring choral singing and dancing by Lesbian women – a ritual space that can be "figured . . . in mythological terms."

In oral lyric poetry, Nagy demonstrates, the interaction of performance with composition parallels "the interaction of myth with ritual. The same can be said about the epic poetry attributed to Homer: to perform this epic is to activate myth, and such activation is fundamentally a matter of ritual." The performance of epic poetry is a matter of producing "speech-acts" – the doing of something by the act of the speaking of something (in the sense of Austin 1962): "In Homeric poetry, the word for such a performative act is *muthos*, ancestor of the modern term *myth*." Drawing upon Martin 1989, Nagy offers "a working definition of *muthos* as it functions within the epic frame of Homeric poetry: 'a speech-act indicating authority, performed at length, usually in public, with a focus on full attention to every detail.'" The truth-value of such speech-acts – 'myths' – is a function of their performative framing. From the perspective of the lyric poet Pindar, for example, the 'truth' (*alētheia*) of local myths, set in local rituals, concerning Odysseus and Ajax becomes 'falsehoods' (*pseudea*) when incorporated into the delocalized "master myth" of the epic *Odyssey*, "controlled by the master narrator" of that epic poem: "Under such control, the myths about Odysseus in the Odyssey lose the grounding they once had in their local contexts. Once *muthoi* 'myths' are delocalized, they become relative and thus multiple in application, to be contrasted with the *alētheia* 'truth' claimed by lyric."

In his chapter on Greek lyric, Nagy writes of the orientalizing of Lesbian traditions under the influence of the Lydians of Asia Minor. At the end of "Homer and Greek Myth," he takes note of Homer's Indo-European antecedents, while again reminding his readers of the orientalizing factor – "the lateral influence of Near Eastern languages and civilizations." These two formative elements – Indo-European inheritance and Near Eastern influence – lie at the heart of Chapter 3, the editor's treatment of myth in Hesiod's epic poems, the *Theogony* and *Works and Days*. Hesiod's poetic compositions, no less bound up with performance than lyric and Homeric epic, attest a particular, even unique, saliency and transparency for the formative history, documentation, and study of Greek myth and for that reason are examined in close detail. The so-called kingship-in-heaven tradition of the *Theogony* is one well attested among various Near Eastern peoples of Asia Minor and Mesopotamia and is reported to have existed in a Phoenician form as well. Hesiod's kingship-in-heaven account, though a primitive and core component of the "ancient myths" of the Greeks, was almost certainly taken over from one or another of these Near Eastern cultures and not inherited from the Greeks' own Indo-European ancestors. Hesiod's *Works and Days* is a didactic poem that is itself of a sort commonly encountered in the Near East (the Biblical book of Proverbs perhaps being the most familiar example), and Near Eastern influence in this case is also undeniable. For some scholars in fact, such as Georges Dumézil, precious little of Greek myth appears to be inherited from earlier Indo-European periods. Yet, I argue, following in part Jean-Pierre Vernant, there are indeed primitive Indo-European elements present – and conspicuously so – in *Works and Days* (as well as in the *Theogony*): "The playful, creative use to which Hesiod puts these inherited notions and conventions and the freedom that he displays in restructuring them on the surface, while preserving what we may term underlying structures, suggests to us that this 'Hesiod' is fully conversant with traditions of his Indo-European ancestors."

With Richard Buxton's chapter on tragedy and Greek myth, we move some 300 years beyond Homer and Hesiod, squarely into the world of classical Greek literature. The performative element of myth is, however, still central: "At the annual festival of the City Dionysia, myths were reembodied in performances by members of the citizen group. In these reembodiments, as heroes and divinities walked the stage, myths were not just narrated as past events: they were actualised as present happenings. Then and there, but also now and here; remote enough to allow room for pity, but close enough to inspire awe." Among core issues explored by Buxton is that of the locality of this tragic reembodiment of *muthoi* – political, social, topographical, and psychological spaces of liminality: "the distinctive location of tragic myths is in the gaps between certainties. Tragedy is a place of edges and margins, an in-between territory where boundaries – literal and metaphorical – are ripe for exploration and contestation." The gods of the *muthoi* form the "framework" or "backdrop" of competitive tragic performance, Buxton demonstrates: "Each playwright staged his own version of the mythological past, striving to be adjudged superior to his rivals." The result was typically one in which the gods appear in conflict with one another and in which there is displayed a "readiness to tolerate overt criticism of the gods' behaviour" – "one feature of ancient Greek religion which can be particularly difficult to comprehend for a modern observer."

Such a willingness to scorn the gods is no less an element of myth-in-comedy, as Angus Bowie shows us in his essay "Myth in Aristophanes." Considering first the few remains of mythological Old Comedy generally – best evidenced by a summary of Cratinus' *Dionysalexandrus*, in which the story of the Trojan War "is reworked so that Dionysus becomes as it were a failed actor in the role of Paris" – Bowie observes that comedy "was a genre in which the gods were not spared mockery, even the god in whose honour the festival was being held. Indeed, Dionysus [celebrated by the City Dionysia] is the most frequent butt of humour in the comedies as far as we can tell: the god features regularly in his own festival." Indeed, from the fragmentary texts mythological Old Comedy looks to be a genre that "could take considerable liberties with mythology" and one that could frequently use a "mythical story for political purpose." Turning to Aristophanes, Bowie notes that "one not infrequent category of comedy is that which parodies earlier tragic performances of myth. The difficulty here is that it is not always clear whether Aristophanes is producing a parodic version of a myth or a parody of a particular tragic version of that myth." Beyond this, Bowie argues, comedy can imitate the structure of myth and its affiliated framing festivals, as in Aristophanes' *Thesmophoriazusae*, structured in such a way that "the comedy . . . has (allegedly) the same benefit to the city as the Thesmophoria," the Eleusinian festival of Demeter.

Diskin Clay next examines Plato and myth in "Plato Philomythos." Clay captures the essential if sometimes unrecognized *otherness* of Greek "myth" for modern peoples and contextualizes it nicely for us – and this is very important – as he writes: "The luxuriant varieties of definitions of Greek 'myth' are a symptom of the remoteness of our culture from the culture of ancient Greece. We have no real equivalent for the traditional stories and histories that circulated among the Greeks (and Romans) concerning their origins, the origins of their world, their gods and the progeny of their gods, the relation between humans and animals, and the fate awaiting mortals after death." Among the issues that Clay addresses is the contrastiveness not uncommonly set up between *mythos* (i.e., *muthos*) and *logos* ("the myth of *logos* versus *mythos*"). "In Homer, *mythos* is a word that describes something said in epic. But already in Herodotus the word *mythos* had come to describe an idle and unbelievable tale. . . . Yet Herodotus' predecessor, Hecataeus of Miletus, can describe his own history as a *mythos* . . . and, conversely, traditional but misleading historical accounts as *logoi*. . . . Thucydides rejected what he called the poets' 'tendency to myth' . . . but, in his narrative of speeches . . . *logoi* were often the equivalent of myths." And what of Plato? "Because of the deliberate ambiguity he has created in his dialogues as to what constitutes a *mythos* and what qualifies as a *logos*, Plato has contributed to our modern confusion over what can be described as a 'myth.'" Though he can use *mythos* to denote 'fable' and *logos* a 'noble and true account', as in the *Gorgias*, "the distinction does not hold. Elsewhere in Plato, what we would regard as his seriously meant truth is often treated as a *mythos*, and fictions, based on traditional accounts, are called *logoi*." Clay further observes, "Whether a narrative is called a *mythos* or *logos* depends on the viewpoint of the teller of the tale (usually Socrates) and his audience." More than that, Plato is capable of the "simultaneous dismissal and use of Greek myth." And Plato is himself a mythmaker – an artisan "weaving the strands of Greek myth into a fabric of his own design": "It has been said that myth died in Plato's youth. It did not. Of all Greek philosophers, Plato is most mythopoeic" (and "the most notorious of Plato's myths is the myth of Atlantis . . . the most impressive philosophical fiction ever written"). "Plato's real quarrel," Clay shows us, "is not with Greek myth; it is with the poetry of the Greek polis and its false and debasing representations of reality."

Part One comes to an end with Carolyn Higbie's contribution on the "Hellenistic Mythographers": "from sometime in the fourth century BC on, Greeks developed an interest in collecting, documenting, and interpreting the important literary works of their past." Scholarly devotion to the written records of performative traditions led to the production of interpretative aids and an acute awareness of the particular body of information preserved within these traditions: "from this double opportunity . . . developed at least two genres, mythography and paradoxography" – "stories about the gods and heroes" and "stories about the weird or unusual," respectively. Higbie notes that "myths certainly appeared in prose texts before the Hellenistic world, but they lack, so far as one can tell from the fragmentary remains, the flavor of a compilation, of time spent in libraries gathering stories from different sources." Of such "mythological compendia," "the most famous and influential, in modern times, . . . is the *Bibliotheca* – 'Library'" authored by Apollodorus in, perhaps, the first century AD.

Part Two, *Response, Integration, Representation*, begins with Claude Calame's discussion of "Greek Myth and Greek Religion." The position occupied by Calame's work – at the midpoint of the volume – is metaphorically significant: it is a work that intersects in crucial ways with several of the contributions that precede and several that follow. Opening with the claim that "neither 'myth' nor 'religion' constitutes a category native to Greek thought," Calame challenges the very existence of what we are given to conceptualize as *Greek mythology* – "unless considered in the form of manuals of mythography, such as the one in the *Library* attributed to Apollodorus." His examination of the relationship of Greek "myth" and "religion" takes the form of five case studies: in each, he observes, "we can see how an individual heroic tale is called upon to legitimate a particular cult practice through an intermediary poetic form that influences both the narrative and semantic characteristics of the account and the religious and political conception underlying the ritual concerned." Calame's conclusion from the fivefold examination – "Supported by poetic genre, this or that episode of the divine and heroic past of the Greek communities is inserted into both a specific cult institution and a form of ritual poetry, most often choral. These poetic forms make from narratives, appearing to us as mythic, an active history, inscribed in a collective memory realized through ritual." And, he continues, "The ensemble of the myths of the Hellenic tradition is characterized by a certain plasticity that allows the poetic creation of versions constantly readapted for cult and for religious and ideological paradigms offered by a polytheism that varies within the multifarious civic space and time of the cities of Greece."

In "Myth and Greek Art: Creating a Visual Language," Jenifer Neils begins by reminding the reader that, with respect to myth, "Greek narrative art displays an amazing degree of imagination, ingenuity, and originality" (echoing Calame and many of the contributors that the reader has by now encountered) and goes on to expound manageably for the reader the vast domain of Greek myth and art by focusing on two essential – one might say "performative" – elements: "First, what devices did the artist employ for depicting a myth and how did this visual language come about? Second, how did the artist make his chosen theme relevant to a particular audience at a specific point in time?" Special attention is given to the example of a wine cup decorated by the Codrus painter on which are depicted "the seven deeds of the local hero Theseus." Harbingering Jonathan Hall's discussion of Athenian usage of Theseus for political ends (Chapter 11), Neils reveals how, when the symbolism of the object is properly parsed, "this cycle cup does much more than recount some of the deeds of the hero Theseus; it rewrites history by associating Athens's glorious Bronze Age hero with its glorious present. For the Athenians their myths were their history, and they saw no problem in embellishing them for the greater glory of the *polis*."

Treatment of the visual aspect of the presentation of Greek myth continues in Ada Cohen's "Mythic Landscapes of Greece"; Cohen offers an insightful look at the use of landscape – caves, countryside, the Underworld, mountains, and so on – vis-à-vis mythic representation in both literature and art, exploring the "intersection of narrative and description in light of common as well as rarely depicted myths in painting and sculpture." Pausanias, the second-century AD periegetic (travel) author, is an important literary source for Cohen and other scholars of mythic landscape – a source with a retrospective view: "When invoking landmark single trees and groves as noteworthy spatial markers . . . Pausanias, to whom we owe much of our knowledge of ancient sites and now-lost monuments, did not linger on their greenery or on the flowers and fruits they produced, but on their cultic associations as well as associations with important events of the classical past." The use of landscape in ancient Greek art is surprisingly limited; when landscape elements are depicted, it is by utilizing "a restrained repertoire and a symbolic employment of landscape." Even so, Cohen argues, there is in Greek art "a rich and viable conception of landscape." She concludes that "in all cases artists took for granted their audiences' deep familiarity with the Greek landscape and asked the imagination to fill the voids. This situation is in the end not so different from that of mythical discourse itself, whose multiple versions were the result of traditions colliding with individual tellers' points of view and emphases."

It is with a contrastive reference to this Roman-era Greek sanias, and the "matrix of myth and memories" that Pausani for the various *poleis* he visits, that Jonathan Hall begin "Politics and Greek Myth" ("The fact is that myth i entirely different to the Greeks of Pausanias' generation than it had to their ancestors"). The political uses of myth that Hall addresses – "myth's capacity to charter and justify changing political circumstances" – are, he argues, grounded in myth's ideological character and its existence as a productive symbolic system (analogous to the system of *langue* and *parole* of Saussurian structural linguistics): "Through the dynamic dialectic between narrator and audience, traditional materials could be reconfigured and modulated to stake claims about the natural order and to advance partisan interests and it is precisely myth's ideological character that made it so effective in the practice of ancient Greek politics." The mutability and adaptability of myth is foregrounded, again, as Hall presents his readers with three case studies: these involve the Spartan and Argive use of "mythical prototypes of alliances to justify their own claims to Peloponnesian hegemony in the mid-sixth century"; the Athenian Pisistratus' capitalizing upon Theseus as "an attractive prototype of the strong, wise, and just leader" and his elevation of "Theseus to Panathenaic status"; and the fifth-century "orientalization" of the Trojans, consequent, chiefly, to the second Persian War.

A. J. Boyle's "Ovid and Greek Myth," the concluding chapter of Part Two, which moves the reader squarely into Imperial Rome, brings this aspect of Greek myth into the sharpest focus yet: "Much of the discursive and political use of Greek myth was made possible by its separation from Roman ritual, its function in Roman intellectual life as an instrument of thinking. By Roman intellectuals Greek myth was generally regarded as *fabulae*, a collection of fictions." "[Ovid] is fully aware of the contemporary categorisation of myth as fiction. . . . His interest in myth is neither religious nor ritualistic, but poetic." With regard specifically to Ovid's sardonic literary response to Augustus' moral legislation ("The transformation of adultery and other forms of transgressive fornication [*stuprum*] into crimes with severe penalties imposed by a special permanent court [*quaestio perpetua*] suddenly made sexual morality and practice subject to political control"), Boyle observes, "The poet develops his subversion of Augustan sexual codes by turning to Greek myth – to the famous adulteress Helen"; that Ovid should have invoked the unfaithful wife of Menelaus "not as a denunciation of adulterers but rather as a text pontificating on the excusability, even innocence, of certain kinds of adultery, astonishes": thus, Boyle concludes, "Myth's paradigmatic function dissolves into political and social critique." Ovid's stinging political critiques can, already in the first century, make recourse to the *otherness* of Greek myth: "What Ovid presents in *Metamorphoses* is a world of unaccountable otherness, in which controllers of that world and the putative guardians of its morality exemplify the vices they condemn."

A work of central interest to Boyle is *Heroides*, "an early work of Ovid and a self-proclaimed revolutionary one (*Ars* 3.346), in which a whole collection of poems focusses on the female voice, female memory, and female desire." These, in turn, are issues on which the first chapter of section three, *Reception*, has direct bearing – "Women and Greek Myth" by Vanda Zajko, an essay that explores "some of the tensions surrounding the descriptions of stories about women as being 'pro' or 'anti' women and the ideological entailments of such descriptions." One of the issues with which Zajko deals is central to all of the chapters of Part Three, and indeed one that we have repeatedly encountered in the first two Parts – that of the "rewriting of myth." At what point does the "rewriting" of a myth create something that is fundamentally different from that myth? Is the result of the "rewriting" still "myth" – still *muthos*? These are questions with which the reader of this *Companion* will have to grapple. Zajko herself chooses to paint with the broader stroke: "But tradition can be seen as a less static concept that is, and always has been, reshaped and reenergised by continual retellings. Doherty's statement that 'the modern rewritings of myths is a continuation of ancient practice' [(2001) 10] subscribes to this kind of notion and emphasises that ancient poets and artists freely imported the issues of their own times into their treatments of myth."

"Let Us Make Gods in Our Image," David Brumble's contribution on Greek myth in Medieval and Renaissance literature, follows. Allegorical interpretation of the ancient myths is the hallmark of these materials, whose authors and readers often assume a composite and variegated profile of Greek mythic figures – the product of the deposition of layers of interpretative accretion, one upon another: "Theseus appears in the 'Knight's Tale.' A good classical dictionary would not tell us that Chaucer's readers might have interpreted Theseus as a wisdom figure; as an example of perfect friendship, of the ideal ruler, of the unfaithful lover; as a type for God or Christ; as an allegorical figure for the balance of the active and contemplative lives." In keeping with the Medieval Christian tradition of interpreting Old Testament figures typologically (i.e., as "types"), "Deucalion was a type of Noah"; "Hippolytus...could be a type of Joseph"; "Hippolytus, Theseus, Hercules, Orpheus, and many others served as types of Christ." Among interpretative methods utilized was that one dubbed "fourfold allegory," involving allegorical readings at different levels simultaneously – a method readily associated with Dante; though, Brumble reminds his

9

readers, "fourfold allegory is just one expression of the Medieval and Renaissance inclination to multiple interpretation."

Sarah Brown treats the literary response to Greek myth from the seventeenth century onward in her "Hail Muse! *et cetera*: Greek Myth in English and American Literature": "Many of the most interesting responses to Greek myth register its polyvalency, and display a corresponding ambivalence towards their sources, a combination of reverence and antagonism." The interpretative tradition of this era is clearly heir to the past, but is also, one might say, "reactive" (the editor's term, not the author's): "Mythology is central to the works of Pope, Keats, Pound, Toni Morrison, and Carol Ann Duffy, *inter alia*, but each of these writers figures his or her relationship with the classical past in a distinctive way." Brown demonstrates that the pendulum has oscillated between what she aptly likens to the Protestant and Catholic aspects of Christianity: "Whereas some writers appear to seek an unmediated correspondence with an 'authentic' and pristine past, wherever possible sloughing off intervening layers of adaptation and reception, for others Greek myth represents a continuous tradition whose origins may certainly be traced back to Homer, Hesiod, Euripides, et al., but which owes at least as crucial a debt to such mediating forces as Chaucer, Shakespeare, and Milton." In part, these oscillations reflect a resurgence of literary awareness of and interest in Greek-language, as opposed to Latinized, mythic materials: "Gradually, over the course of the eighteenth and nineteenth centuries, interest in Greek antiquities, literature and society intensified, and a movement away from Roman culture towards Greek can be identified, although the shift was not stark or absolute." Still – the pendulum has momentum; in commenting on the monologues in Duffy's *The World's Wife*, Brown observes: "They emerge from the strong late-twentieth-century reawakening of interest in classical myth, in part a response to Ted Hughes's much praised *Tales from Ovid*. (We seemed to have returned to the Renaissance preference for Latinised mythology.)"

The *Companion* concludes with Martin Winkler's treatment of the portrayal of myth in cinema, "Greek Mythology on the Screen." The interpretative dimension of Greek mythic tradition is perhaps nowhere more pronounced than here: "Cinema and its offspring, television, have proven the most fertile ground for reimagining and reinventing antiquity." As Winkler tells us – and as the reader will have by now observed many times over – "the tradition of imagining alternatives to well-attested and even canonical versions of myth goes back to antiquity itself.... This tradition has never ceased." The phenomenon of contemporary cinematic reinterpretation, Winkler continues, citing Italian director Vittorio Cottafavi, has been dubbed "neomythologism." Just how far removed such neomythologism can be from acts and contexts of *muthoi* that the reader encountered in the early chapters of this volume – and especially in Calame's myth and religion chapter – is revealed, for example, by comments made by director Wolfgang Petersen regarding his film *Troy* (2004): "I think that, if we could consult with him up there, Homer would be the first today to advise: 'Get rid of the gods.'" For some readers such a claim will be received with disbelief, revealing, as it does, an inverted state of affairs consequent to a full denuding of the framing contexts of *muthoi*; but, Winkler contends, "filmmakers follow their own rules when they make mythological films and do not consider themselves bound by their sources. In the process they become adaptors of stories comparable to the ancient poets themselves, who took the materials for their epics or dramas from older versions of myth." Thus, Winkler continues, "Cottafavi's film [*Hercules Conquers Atlantis* (1961)] is a prime example of neomythologism, but it is more. It exemplifies a society's understanding of the past in modern terms. The Atlantis from whose sinister threat Hercules saves the world reflects the twentieth century in two major aspects": the potential for a nuclear apocalypse and the threat of extermination posed by totalitarian ideologies.

The editor has chosen – revealingly, one hopes, if, admittedly, a bit idiosyncratically – to preface each section with a few pertinent lines from *A Wonder Book*[1] and *Tanglewood Tales*,[2] together Hawthorne's mid-nineteenth-century retelling of various Greek myths, ostensibly for children – a creative adaptation of the remotely other, penned in a Transcendentalized New England in the decade that preceded that Rubiconic upheaval that tore a nation apart and metamorphosed its children – making ghosts of its sons, widows of its daughters. Following each selection from Hawthorne is an ancient Greek text, two from Apollodorus, one from Hesiod.[3] These juxtapositions – Hawthorne, Greek authors, contemporary essays – are intended to serve several ends: to demonstrate the malleability of the Greek traditions, for one; for another, to remind ourselves of both the enchanting romantic familiarity of these materials, and of their utter foreignness in a world from which their formative frame vanished long ago. Perhaps the reader will recognize others.

> These old legends, so brimming over with everything that
> is most abhorrent to our Christianised moral sense – some
> of them so hideous, others so melancholy and miserable,
> amid which the Greek tragedians sought their themes, and

moulded them into the sternest forms of grief that ever the world saw; was such material the stuff that children's play-things should be made of! How were they to be purified? How was the blessed sunshine to be thrown into them?

But Eustace [Eustace Bright – Hawthorne's Williams College narrator] told me that these myths were the most singular things in the world, and that he was invariably aston-ished, whenever he began to relate one, by the readiness with which it adapted itself to the childish purity of his audi-tors. The objectionable characteristics seem to be a parasiti-cal growth, having no essential connection with the original fable. They fall away, and are thought of no more, the instant he puts his imagination in sympathy with the innocent little circle, whose wide-open eyes are fixed so eagerly upon him. Thus the stories (not by any strained effort of the narrator's, but in harmony with their inherent germ) transform them-selves, and reassume the shapes which they might be sup-posed to possess in the pure childhood of the world. When the first poet or romancer told these marvelous legends (such is Eustace Bright's opinion), it was still the Golden Age. Evil had never yet existed; and sorrow, misfortune, crime, were mere shadows which the mind fancifully created for itself, as a shelter against too sunny realities; or, at most, but prophetic dreams, to which the dreamer himself did not yield a waking credence. Children are now the only representatives of the men and women of that happy era; and therefore it is that we must raise the intellect and fancy to the level of childhood, in order to recreate the original myths.

Nathaniel Hawthorne; from the Preface to
Tanglewood Tales (1853)

Toward contextualizing Hawthorne himself (though only in part – and Hawthorne could only dubiously be described as a "mythologist"), Graf's remarks are helpful:

The mythologists of the eighteenth and nineteenth cen-turies clung to the notion that to explain myth one had to discover its origin, which, they believed, lay in the child-hood of mankind. Accordingly, the interpretation of myth always seemed to involve reconstructing the life of early man. Requiring a basis for this reconstruction, the theorists of this period turned to the so-called primitive peoples of their own day, to children, and to the simplest peasants of Europe, all of whom, it was thought, resembled early man in some respects.[4]

The reader will find more discussion of such matters in Chapters 14 and 15.

And so we begin.

NOTES

1   The text of *A Wonder Book* quoted herein is that of 1883 Riverside Edition published by Houghton Mifflin and reprinted by Ægypan Press.

2   The text of *Tanglewood Tales* quoted herein is that of the 1918 edition published by Hodder and Stoughton and reprinted by The Folio Society.

3   The translations of Apollodorus and Hesiod are those of the editor, adapted from Woodard, in press.

4   Graf (1993) 33.

PART ONE

SOURCES AND
INTERPRETATIONS

Gleaming among the venerable oaks, there was a radiance, not like the moonbeams, but rather resembling the golden glory of the setting sun. It proceeded from an object, which appeared to be suspended at about a man's height from the ground, a little farther within the wood.

'What is it?' asked Jason.

'Have you come so far to seek it,' exclaimed Medea, 'do you not recognise the meed of all your toils and perils, when it glitters before your eyes? It is the Golden Fleece.'

Jason went onward a few steps farther, and then stopped to gaze. Oh, how beautiful it looked, shining with a marvellous light of its own, that inestimable prize, which so many heroes had longed to behold, but had perished in the quest of it, either by the perils of their voyage, or by the fiery breath of the brazen-lunged bulls.

'How gloriously it shines!' cried Jason, in a rapture. 'It has surely been dipped in the richest gold of sunset. Let me hasten onward, and take it to my bosom.'

'Stay,' said Medea, holding him back. 'Have you forgotten what guards it?'

To say the truth, in the joy of beholding the object of his desires, the terrible dragon had quite slipped out of Jason's memory. . . .

'Stay, foolish youth,' said Medea, grasping his arm. 'Do not you see you are lost, without me as your good angel? In this gold box I have a magic potion, which will do the dragon's business far more effectually than your sword.'

The dragon had probably heard the voices; for, swift as lightning, his black head and forked tongue came hissing among the trees again, darting full forty feet at a stretch. As it approached, Medea tossed the contents of the gold box right down the monster's wide-open throat. Immediately, with an outrageous hiss and a tremendous wriggle – flinging his tail up to the tip-top of the tallest tree, and shattering all its branches as it crashed heavily down again – the dragon fell at full length upon the ground, and lay quite motionless.

'It is only a sleeping potion,' said the enchantress to Prince Jason. 'One always finds a use for these mischievous creatures, sooner or later; so I did not wish to kill him outright. Quick! Snatch the prize, and let us begone. You have won the Golden Fleece.'

Jason caught the fleece from the tree, and hurried through the grove, the deep shadows of which were illuminated, as he passed, by the golden glory of the precious object that he bore along. . . .

As Jason drew near, he heard the Talking Image calling to him with more than ordinary eagerness, in its grave, sweet voice:

'Make haste, Prince Jason! For your life, make haste!'

With one bound he leaped aboard. At sight of the glorious radiance of the Golden Fleece, the nine-and-forty heroes gave a mighty shout, and Orpheus, striking his harp, sang a song of triumph, to the cadence of which the galley flew over the water, homeward bound, as if careering along with wings!

Nathaniel Hawthorne; from "The Golden Fleece,"
Tanglewood Tales (1853)

---

[16]Jason was the son of Aeson, the son of Cretheus and Polymede, the daughter of Autolycus. He lived in Iolcus, where Pelias ruled as king, following the reign of Cretheus. When Pelias consulted the oracle concerning his kingship, the god declared that he should beware of the one-sandaled man. At first he could make no sense of the oracle, but later he came to understand it; for offering a sacrifice to Poseidon by the sea, he sent for Jason and many others to come and take part. Jason was staying out in the country because of his passion for farming, so he had to hurry to the sacrifice. Wading through the river Anaurus, he came out with only one sandal, having lost the other shoe in the stream. Upon seeing him and putting together the meaning of the oracle, Pelias approached Jason and asked what he would do if he were in a position of authority and an oracle revealed to him that he would be murdered

by one of the citizens. Whether by the wrath of Hera – so that Medea would turn out to be the bane of Pelias (for he was not in the habit of honoring Hera) – or whatever, Jason said, "I would command him to bring the golden fleece." Once Pelias heard this, he immediately commanded him to go after the fleece, which was in Colchis in a grove sacred to Ares, hanging upon an oak tree, guarded by a dragon that never slept.

Being sent on this expedition, Jason summoned for help the son of Phrixus, Argus, who, advised by Athena, built a ship of fifty oars, named after its builder the "Argo." On the prow, Athena fitted a talking piece of wood from the oak of Dodona. When the ship had been built, Jason consulted the oracle and was instructed by the deity to set sail after he had brought together the best and bravest of the heroes of Greece. . . .

[23]The Argonauts came to the land of the Mariandyni, and there Lycus the king welcomed them with kindness. There Idmon the prophet died after a boar attacked him. Tiphys also died, and Ancaeus took over the task of steering the ship.

After sailing past Thermodon and the Caucasus, they came to the Phasis River, which is found in the region of Colchis. Once the ship had been tied up at anchor, Jason found Aeetes, and telling him what Pelias had ordered, urged him to part with the fleece. Aeetes promised he would deliver it, if Jason could, on his own, yoke together the bronze-hoofed bulls. He owned two wild bulls of exceptional size, a gift from Hephaestus; they had hooves of bronze, and fire would bellow out of their mouths. Aeetes commanded that after Jason had yoked these bulls, he was then to sow dragon's teeth; for Aeetes had received from Athena half of the teeth that Cadmus had sown in Thebes. While Jason agonized over how he could possibly yoke the bulls together, Medea was nursing a passion for him. She was a sorceress, a daughter of Aeetes and Eidyia, daughter of Oceanus. Being afraid that he might be destroyed by the bulls, she promised – without her father's knowledge – to help him yoke the bulls together and to hand over the fleece, if he would swear to marry her and to take her with him on the return voyage to Greece. After Jason swore to do this, she gave him a drug and told him to rub his shield, spear and body with it just before he yoked the bulls; for, she said, when he had done so he could not be harmed by either fire or by steel for a period of one day. And she explained to Jason that when the teeth were planted, armed men would spring up out of the ground and turn against him; and, she said, whenever he saw a crowd of them, to throw stones among them from a distance, and when, because of this, they began to fight one another, to kill them. Jason listened to her advice, applied the drug and approached the grove of the temple, looking for the bulls; though they charged at him with massive flames, he yoked them together. And after he sowed the teeth, armed men came growing up out of the ground; where he saw a lot of them together, he threw stones without letting them see him, and while they battled each other, he came upon them and killed them. Even though the bulls stood yoked together, Aeetes steadfastly refused to surrender the fleece; he wanted to torch the Argo and kill the crew. But acting first, Medea brought Jason to the fleece by night, and putting the dragon that guarded it into a drug-induced sleep, and holding the fleece she made her way to the Argo with Jason; and her brother, Apsyrtus, followed her. With these on board, the Argonauts put out to sea in the night.

[24]When Aeetes discovered what brash things Medea had done, he set off in pursuit of the Argo; and she, spying him approaching, murdered her brother, dismembered his body, and threw it overboard into the deep. Aeetes, fishing the limbs of his son from the sea, trailed off from the pursuit; for that reason he turned back, buried the recovered limbs and called the place "Tomi." But he sent out many of the Colchians in search of the Argo and threatened that if they did not bring back Medea, they would suffer the fate that awaited her. They split up, some searching in one place, others in another.

Apollodorus, Bibliotheca 1.9.16, 23–24

1: Lyric and Greek Myth

Gregory Nagy

In the history of Greek literature, poets of "lyric" are conventionally associated with the *archaic period*. Some would go so far as to call this period a "lyric age," to be contrasted with an earlier age represented by *Homer* and *Hesiod*, poets of "epic." There is in fact a book about the archaic period bearing the title *The Lyric Age of Greece* (Burn 1960). The archaic period ended around the second half of the fifth century BCE, to be followed by the so-called *classical period*. The archaic period is thought to have ended with the lyric poet Pindar, while the classical period is thought to have begun with the tragic poet Aeschylus, even though these two literary figures were roughly contemporaneous.

There is a lack of precision in the general use of the term *lyric*. It is commonly associated with a variety of assumptions regarding the historical emergence of a "subjective I," as represented by the individual poet of lyric, who is to be contrasted with the generic poet of epic, imagined as earlier and thus somehow less advanced. By extension, *the subjective I* is thought to be symptomatic of emerging notions of authorship. Such assumptions, it is argued here, cannot be sustained.

Lyric did not start in the archaic period. It is just as old as epic, which clearly pre-dates the archaic period. And the traditions of lyric, like those of epic, were rooted in *oral poetry*, which is a matter of *performance* as well as *composition* (Lord 1995: 22–68, "Oral Traditional Lyric Poetry").

These two aspects of oral poetry, composition and performance, are interactive, and this interaction is parallel to the interaction of myth and ritual. In oral poetry, the performing of a composition is an activation of myth, and such activation is fundamentally a matter of ritual (Nagy 1994/1995).

During the archaic period, the artistic production of lyric involved performance as well as composition. The performance was executed either by a single performer or by a group that was actually or at least notionally participating in the performance. The most prominent Greek word referring to such a group is *khoros* 'chorus', which designates not just singing, like its derivative *chorus* in English, but dancing as well. *Choral lyric* could be sung and danced, or just sung or just danced. To be contrasted is *monody*, which means 'solo singing'.

Lyric could be sung to the accompaniment of a string instrument, ordinarily the *kithara*, which is conventionally translated as 'lyre'. This English noun *lyre* and its adjective *lyric* are derived from *lura* (*lyra*), which is another Greek word for a string instrument. Lyric could also be sung to the accompaniment of a wind instrument, ordinarily the *aulos* 'reed'. Either way, whether the accompaniment took the form of string or wind instruments, a more precise term for such lyric is *melic*, derived from the Greek noun *melos* 'song'. English *melody* is derived from Greek *melōidia*, which means 'the singing of *melos*'.

Lyric could also be sung without instrumental accompaniment. In some forms of unaccompanied lyric, the melody was reduced and the rhythm became more regulated than the rhythm of melic. In describing the rhythm of these forms of unaccompanied lyric, it is more accurate to use the term *meter*. And, in describing the performance of this kind of lyric, it is more accurate to speak of *reciting* instead of *singing*. Recited poetry is typified by three meters in particular: *dactylic hexameter*, *elegiac couplet*, and *iambic trimeter*. In ancient Greek poetic traditions, the dactylic hexameter became the sole medium of epic. As a poetic form, then, epic is far more specialized than lyric (PH [= Nagy 1990a] 1§§1–16, 55–64).

In the classical period, the solo performance of lyric poetry, both melic and nonmelic, became highly professionalized. Melic poetry was sung by professional soloists – either *kitharōidoi* 'citharodes' (= 'kithara-singers') or *aulōidoi* 'aulodes' (= 'aulos-singers') – while nonmelic poetry was recited by professional soloists called *rhapsōidoi* 'rhapsodes'. Such solo performance was *monody*. In classical Athens, the primary occasion for citharodic, or aulodic, or rhapsodic solo performance was the festival of the Panathenaia, which was the context of competitions called *mousikoi agōnes* 'musical contests'. These Panathenaic *agōnes* 'contests' were *mousikoi* 'musical' only in the sense that they were linked with the goddesses of poetic memory, the Muses (HC [= Nagy 2007] 3§4). They were not 'musical' in the modern sense, since the contests featured epic as well as lyric poetry. The epic repertoire was restricted to the Homeric *Iliad* and *Odyssey*, competitively performed by rhapsodes,

20

while the lyric repertoire was restricted to melic poetry, competitively performed by citharodes and aulodes.

In the classical period of Athens, melic poetry was also sung *and danced* by nonprofessional choruses. The primary occasion for such performances was the festival of the City Dionysia, the official venue of Athenian state theater. The actors who delivered their lines by reciting the verses of nonmelic poetry embedded in the dramas of Athenian state theater were professionals, while the choruses who sang and danced the melic poetry also embedded in these dramas were nonprofessional, recruited from the body politic of citizens; theatrical choruses became professionalized only after the classical period, toward the end of the fourth century BCE (PP [= Nagy 1996a] 157, 172–6).

The performances of nonprofessional choruses in Athenian state theater represent an essential aspect of melic poetry that transcends the classical period. Not only in Athens but throughout the Greek-speaking world of the classical period and beyond, the most authoritative context of melic poetry was choral performance. The *khoros* 'chorus' was in fact a basic social reality in all phases of archaic Greek prehistory and history, and this reality was essential in the evolution of lyric during these phases (Calame 2001).

An important differentiation becomes evident in the course of this evolution. It is an emerging split between the composer and the performer of lyric. Before this split, the authorship of any lyric composition was closely linked to the authority of lyric performance. This authority played itself out in a dramatized relationship between the *khoros* 'chorus' and a highlighted *khorēgos* 'leader of the chorus', as idealized in the relationship of the Muses as chorus to Apollo as their choral leader (PH 12§29). In lyric, as we will see, such authority is linked to the articulation of myth itself.

The *khoros*, as an institution, was considered the most authoritative medium not only for the performance of lyric composition but also for its transmission in the archaic period. As we see from the wording of choral lyric poetry, the poet's voice is transmitted and notionally perpetuated by the seasonally recurring choral performances of his or her poetry. A most prominent example is Song 1 of Alcman (PH 12§18). The voices of the performers who sing and dance such poetry can even speak of the poet by name in the third person, identifying him as the one who composed their song. An example is Song 39 of Alcman. In other situations, the choral lyric composer speaks in the first person by borrowing, as it were, the voices of those who sing and dance in his choral compositions. In Song 26 of Alcman, for example, the speaker declares that he is too old and weak to dance with the chorus of women who sing and dance his song: by implication, he continues to sing as their lead singer (PH 12§32).

For an understanding of authority and authorship in lyric poetry, more needs to be said about the actual transmission of lyric from the archaic into the classical period. The lyric traditions of the archaic period became an integral part of *liberal education* for the elites of the classical period. In leading cities such as Athens, the young were educated by professionals in the nonprofessional singing, dancing, and reciting of songs that stemmed from the archaic period – songs that had become the classics of the classical period. As we see in the *Clouds* of Aristophanes (1355–6), a young man who had the benefit of such an education could be expected to perform the artistic feat of singing solo a choral song composed by the archaic poet Simonides (F 507) while accompanying himself on the lyre. Elsewhere in the *Clouds* (967), we see a similar reference to a similar solo performance of a choral song composed by the even more archaic poet Stesichorus (F 274).

Among the elites of the classical period, the primary venue for the nonprofessional performance of archaic lyric songs that youths learned through such a liberal education was the *sumposion* 'symposium'. Like the chorus, the symposium was a basic social reality in all phases of archaic Greek prehistory and history. And, like the chorus, it was a venue for the nonprofessional performance of lyric in all its forms.

The poets of lyric in the archaic period became the models for performing lyric in the classical period. And, as models, these figures became part of a canon of melic poets (Wilamowitz 1900: 63–71). This canon, as it evolved from the archaic into the classical period and beyond, was composed of the following nine figures: Sappho, Alcaeus, Anacreon, Alcman, Stesichorus, Ibycus, Simonides, Pindar, and Bacchylides. To this canonical grouping we may add a tenth figure, Corinna, although her status as a member of the canon was a matter of dispute in the post-classical period (PH 3§2n3). Other figures can be classified as authors of nonmelic poetry: they include Archilochus, Callinus, Hipponax, Mimnermus, Theognis, Tyrtacus, Semonides, Solon, and Xenophanes.

One of these figures, Xenophanes, can be classified in other ways as well. He is one of the so-called pre-Socratic thinkers whose thinking is attested primarily in the form of poetry. Two other such figures are Empedocles and Parmenides. Since the extant poetry of Xenophanes is composed in elegiac couplets, he belongs technically to the overall category of lyric poetry, whereas Empedocles and Parmenides do not, since their extant poetry is composed in dactylic hexameters, which are the medium of epic.

Such taxonomies are imprecise in any case. A case in point is Simonides, whose attested compositions include nonmelic poetry (like the *Plataea Elegy*, F 11 W²) as well as melic poetry. Simonides is credited with the composition of epigrams as well (*Epigrammata* I–LXXXIX, edited by Page). Conversely, the poetry of Sappho was evidently not restricted to melic: she is credited with the composition of elegiac couplets, iambic trimeters, and even epigrammatic dactylic hexameters (T 2; F 157–159D). A comparable phenomenon in the archaic period is the perception of Homer as an epigrammatist (as in the Herodotean *Life of Homer* 133–40 Allen; HPC [= Nagy 2008] 1§§8–9).

On the basis of what we have seen so far, it is clear that a given lyric composition could be sung or recited, instrumentally accompanied or not accompanied, and danced or not danced. It could be performed solo or in ensemble. Evidently, all these variables contributed to a wide variety of genres, but the actual categories of these genres are in general difficult to determine (Harvey 1955). Moreover, the categories as formulated in the postclassical period and thereafter may be in some respects artificial (M. Davies 1988). Such difficulties can be traced back to the fact that the actual writing down of archaic lyric poetry blurs whatever we may know about the occasion or occasions of performance. The genres of lyric poetry stem ultimately from such occasions (Nagy 1994/1995).

In the postclassical period, antiquarians lost interest in finding out about occasions for performance, and they assumed for the most part that poets in the archaic period composed by way of writing. For example, Pausanias (7.20.4) says that Alcaeus *wrote* (*graphein*) his *Hymn to Hermes* (F 308c). A similar assumption is made about Homer himself: Pausanias (3.24.11, 8.29.2) thinks of Homer as an author who *wrote* (*graphein*) his poetry.

In the classical period, by contrast, the making of poetry by the grand poets of the past was not equated with the act of writing (HPC 1§8). As we see from the wording of Plato, for example (*Phaedo* 94d, *Hippias Minor* 371a, *Republic* 2.378d, *Ion* 531c-d), Homer is consistently pictured as a poet who 'makes' (*poieîn*) his poetry, not as one who 'writes' (*graphein*) it. So also Herodotus says that Homer and Hesiod 'make' (*poieîn*) what they say in poetry (2.53.2); and he says elsewhere that Alcaeus 'makes' (*poieîn*) his poetry (5.95).

In any case, the basic fact remains that the *composition* of poetry in the archaic period came to life in *performance*, not in the reading of something that was written. Accordingly, the *occasions* of performance need to be studied in their historical contexts.

In this chapter, the primary test case for studying occasions of performance is the lyric poetry attributed to Sappho and Alcaeus. The historical context of this poetry is relatively better known than the contexts of other comparable poetry. The place in question is the island of Lesbos, off the northern coast of Asia Minor. The time in question is around 600 BCE. That rough date matches a reference in a song of Alcaeus (F 49.12) to a contemporary event that can be dated independently, the destruction of Ascalon by Nebuchadnezzar, King of Babylon, in 604 BCE (Alcaeus T 1).

The lyric poetry of Sappho and Alcaeus, taken together, represents the repertoire of the myths and the rituals of the people of Lesbos as expressed in lyric performance. Their poetry, and its transmission, goes back to a period when the city-states of the island of Lesbos were confederated into a single state. This federal state, the political term for which was *sunoikisis* (Thucydides 3.3.1), was dominated by Mytilene, the city of Sappho and Alcaeus. There was a single communal place reserved for the festivals of this island federation, and that place was named *Messon*, the 'middle space', as Louis Robert (1960) has demonstrated, primarily on the basis of relevant epigraphical evidence. Songs 129 and 130 of Alcaeus show explicit references to this federal space, which is described as sacred to three divinities: Zeus, Hera, and Dionysus. Also relevant is a reference to the *teikhos basilēion* 'wall of kings' (Alcaeus 130A.15), which is equated with 'the [precinct-]wall of Hera' (according to a scholion in the relevant papyrus fragment).

The same federal space is mentioned in Song 17 of Sappho (also T 59), where the woman who is the main speaker is represented as praying to the goddess Hera: as this speaker says, it was *tuide* 'here' (line 7) at this federal space that the heroes Agamemnon and Menelaos made a stop after their destruction of Troy; and it was here, the speaker continues, that these Achaean heroes prayed to Zeus and Hera and Dionysus (lines 9–10), asking the gods to reveal to them the best way to sail back home. There is a related reference in *Odyssey* 3, where the story is told how Menelaos (but not Agamemnon) and his men joined Nestor and Diomedes in Lesbos (line 169) after the destruction of Troy in order to consult an unnamed god about the best way to sail back home (lines 173–4).

In the words of Alcaeus, this federal space was called the *temenos theōn* 'sacred precinct of the gods' (F 130B.13). It was the designated place for celebrating a seasonally recurring festival, described in the words of Alcaeus as the occasion for the seasonally recurring assemblies or 'comings together' of the people of Lesbos (F 130B.15 *sunodoisi*; Nagy 1993: 22).

This festival featured as its main spectacle the choral singing and dancing of the *Lesbiades* 'women of Lesbos', described as 'exceptional in their beauty' (130B.17 *krinnomenai phuan*). The reality of such a festival in Lesbos featuring the choral performances of women is independently verified by a scholion attached to a passage in the Homeric *Iliad* (9.130): from this scholion we learn that the name of the festival was the *Kallisteia*, which can be translated as 'pageant of beauty'. In the relevant Iliadic passage, as well as elsewhere in the *Iliad*, there are references to the women of Lesbos, described as exceptional in their beauty, who were captured by Achilles in the years that preceded the final destruction of Troy (9.128–31, 270–73). These direct references in the *Iliad* can be analyzed as indirect references to the festival of the *Kallisteia* in Lesbos (HPC 2§16, 18). Another reference to the *Kallisteia* is attested in a poem from the *Greek Anthology* (9.189), which says that this festival takes place within the *temenos* 'sacred precinct' of Hera: this festival, it also says, was the occasion for choral singing and dancing by the women of Lesbos, with Sappho herself pictured as the leader of their *khoros* 'chorus' (Page 1955: 168n4).

Sappho in her songs is conventionally pictured as the lead singer of a chorus composed of the women of Lesbos, and she speaks as their main choral personality (PH 12§60). As we see in the *Greek Anthology*, she is figured as the prima donna of this chorus of women who sing and dance in the federal space of the people of Lesbos. Sappho's songs are pictured as taking place within this sacred place, marked by the deictic marker *tuide* 'here', as we saw earlier in Sappho's Song 17 (line 7).

In Song 96 of Sappho, this same federal space of the people of Lesbos is once again marked by the deictic marker *tuide* 'here' (line 2) as the sacred place of choral performance, and the noun *molpa* (line 5) makes it explicit that the performance takes the form of choral singing and dancing. In archaic poetry, the verb for 'sing and dance in a chorus' is *melpesthai* (PH 12§29n62 and n64).

In Song 96 of Sappho, such performance within the common choral ground of Lesbos is being nostalgically contrasted with the choral performance of a missing prima donna who is imagined as performing somewhere else at that same moment: she is now in an alien choral ground, as the prima donna of "Lydian women" who are singing and dancing in the moonlight (lines 4–9). The wording here refers to a seasonally recurring choral event known as the "Dance of the Lydian

Maidens," performed by the local women of the Ionian city of Ephesus at a grand festival held in their own sacred place of singing and dancing (PH 10§31). There are comparable "Lydian" themes embedded in the seasonally recurring choral festivities of Sparta: one such event was known as the "Procession of the Lydians" (Plutarch *Life of Aristides* 17.10). And just as Sappho's Song 96 represents the women of Lydia as singing and dancing their choral song in a moonlit setting, so too are the women of Lesbos singing and dancing their own choral song *tuide* 'here' in their own sacred space. There is a comparable setting in Song 154 of Sappho, where we see women pictured as poised to sing and dance around a *bōmos* 'altar' in the moonlight.

There is another such reference to the common choral ground of Lesbos, as marked by the deictic *tuide* 'here', in the most celebrated song of Sappho, Song 1:

> You with the varied pattern-woven flowers, immortal Aphrodite, | child of Zeus, weaver of wiles, I implore you, | do not devastate with aches and sorrows, | Mistress, my heart. | But come *here* [*tuide*], if ever at any other time | hearing my voice from afar, | you heeded me and, leaving the palace of your father that is | golden, you came, | and golden is the chariot you harnessed; beautiful they were as they carried you along, | those swift sparrows, high above the dark earth, | swirling with their dense plumage all the way down from the sky through the | midst of the aether, | and right away they arrived. Then you, O holy one, | smiling with your immortal looks, | kept asking *what* is it *once again this time* [*dē'ute*] that has happened to me and for *what* reason | *once again this time* [*dē'ute*] do I invoke you, | and *what* is it that I want more than anything to happen | to my frenzied heart? "Whom am I *once again this time* [*dē'ute*] to persuade, | setting out to bring her back to your love? Who is doing you, | Sappho, wrong? | For if she is fleeing now, soon she will pursue. | If she is not taking gifts, soon she will be giving them. | If she does not love, soon she will love | against her will." | Come to me even now, and free me from harsh | anxieties, and however many things | my heart yearns to get done, *you* do for me. *You* | become my ally in battle.
>
> Sappho F 1

As we will see in due course, Sappho is being pictured here as the lead singer of a choral performance. She leads off by praying to

Aphrodite to be present, that is, to manifest herself in an epiphany. The goddess is invoked from far away in the sky, which is separated from the earth by the immeasurably vast space of "aether." Despite this overwhelming sense of separation, Aphrodite makes her presence felt in a single moment once she is invoked. The goddess appears, that is, she is now present in the sacred space of performance, and her presence becomes an epiphany for all those who are present. Then, once Aphrodite is present, she exchanges roles with the prima donna who figures as the leader of choral performance. In the part of Song 1 that we see enclosed within quotation marks in the visual formatting of modern editions (lines 18–24), the first-person "I" of Sappho is now replaced by Aphrodite herself, who has been a second-person "you" up to this point. We see here an exchange of roles between the first-person "I" and the second-person "you." The first-person "I" now becomes Aphrodite, who proceeds to speak in the performing voice of Sappho to Sappho herself, who has now become the second-person "you." During Aphrodite's epiphany inside the sacred space of the people of Lesbos, a fusion of identities takes place between the goddess and the prima donna who leads the choral performance "here," that is, in this sacred space (PP 97–103).

Sappho prays to Aphrodite to give her the power that the goddess has to make love happen. She prays that she may 'get done' whatever it is that Aphrodite 'gets done' in the active voice of the verb meaning 'to get something done', *telessai* (Sappho F 1.26), which is to be contrasted with the passive voice *telesthēn* applying to a passive lover who simply lets love happen (Sappho F 5.4). To be granted that power is to be the lead singer of the song that has the power to make love happen. Such is the power of song in the songs of Sappho.

Within the archaic context of the myths and rituals of the people of Lesbos, as framed by the sacred space of their federal precinct "here" in the middle ground of their political space, Song 1 of Sappho can be seen as a *prayer* in the sense of *a totalizing formula* for authorizing choral performances of women at the festival of the *Kallisteia*. The seasonal recurrences of the festival are signaled by the triple deployment of the adverb *dē'ute* 'once again this time' in Sappho's prayer. Every time in the past when Sappho has invoked Aphrodite by offering to her this prayer that we now hear, the goddess has heeded the prayer and has manifested herself in an ever-new epiphany. And now, once again this time, the goddess appears to Sappho, who will once again this time speak for the whole chorus as she speaks first for herself and then for Aphrodite and then once again this time for herself.

In the postclassical era of literary critics like Menander the Rhetorician, the description of compositions like Song 1 of Sappho as 'prayers' (Sappho T 47) fails to capture the meaning of an act of prayer in the context of a choral performance. The modern mind, seizing on such descriptions, is quick to infer that such 'prayers' must be mere literary conceits. This is to ignore the dimension of performance, which complements the dimension of composition in the lyric poetry of the archaic period. It is also to ignore the ritual background of such performance, which complements the mythological background of the composition (Yatromanolakis 2003).

What appears to be a private prayer uttered by Sappho is at the same time a public act of worship that is notionally sung and danced by the people of Lesbos as represented by a chorus of their women, legendary as they are for their beauty, and as led by the figure of Sappho as their prima donna. What appears to be the most deeply personal experience of Sappho is at the same time the most widely shared communal experience of the people of Lesbos.

Comparable examples can be found in other forms of song in the repertoire of Sappho. One such form is the *hymenaeus* or 'wedding song'. Most revealing in this regard is the standard word that we translate as 'bride' – *numphē* (pronounced *numpha* in the poetic dialect of Lesbos, as in Sappho F 116). This word, as we can see from its Homeric usage, means not only 'bride' but also 'goddess' – in the sense of *a local goddess as worshipped in the rituals of a given locale*. And, as we can see from the wedding songs of Sappho, the *numphē* is perceived as both a bride and a goddess at the actual moment of the wedding. Similarly, the bridegroom is perceived as a god at that same moment. These perceptions are mythologized in the description of Hector and Andromache at the moment of their wedding in Song 44 of Sappho: the wedded couple are called *i[keloi theoi[s* (line 21) and *theoeikeloi* (line 34), both meaning 'equal to the gods'.

It remains to ask what gods are models for wedded couples. In the poetics of Sappho, two figures who fill the role of such a divine pair are Ares and Aphrodite. In the case of Ares, he is a model for the *gambros* 'bridegroom', who is explicitly described as *isos Areui* 'equal to Ares' (Sappho F 111.5). In the case of Aphrodite, there are many instances of implicit equations of the bride with this goddess: in one song, for example, the bridegroom is said to be infused with the divine charisma of Aphrodite, evidently by way of his direct contact with the bride (Sappho F 112).

Typical of such contact with divinity is this celebrated wedding song of Sappho:

> He *appears* [*phainetai*] to me, that one, *equal to the gods* [*isos theoisin*], | that man who, facing you | is seated and, up close, that sweet voice of yours | he hears, | and how you laugh a laugh that brings desire. It just | makes my heart flutter within my breast. | You see, the moment I look at you, right then, for me | to make any sound at all won't work any more. | My tongue has a breakdown and a delicate | − all of a sudden − fire rushes under my skin. | With my eyes I see not a thing, and there is a roar | my ears make. | Sweat pours down me and a trembling | seizes all of me; paler than grass | am I, and a little short of death | do I *appear* [*phainomai*] to myself.
>
> Sappho F 31, first four of five stanzas

It is said that the bridegroom *phainetai* 'appears' to be *isos theoisin* 'equal to the gods'. Appearances become realities, however, since *phainetai* means not only 'he appears' but also 'he is manifested in an epiphany', and this epiphany is felt as real (PH 7§2n10). In the internal logic of this song, seeing the bridegroom as a god for a moment is just as real as seeing Sappho as a goddess for a moment in the logic of Song 1 of Sappho.

The sense of reality is evident in the wording we have just seen, *phainetai moi kēnos isos theoisin | emmen' ōnēr* 'he appears [*phainetai*] to me, that one, equal to the gods, | the man who. . . . '. The first-person *moi* here in Song 31 of Sappho refers to the speaker, who is "Sappho." In another song of Sappho, we find the wording *phainetai woi kēnos isos theoisin* 'he appears [*phainetai*] to her, that one, equal to the gods' (F 165). In this song, the third-person *woi* 'to her' may perhaps refer to the bride. Or perhaps the speaker of this wording is imagined as Aphrodite herself.

In the first of these two songs of Sappho (F 31), the subjectivity is linked to the first-person speaker, who is the vicarious participant; in the second song (F 165), on the other hand, the subjectivity is linked to the third person, who is the immediate participant. There is a shifting of referents that accompanies the shifting of pronouns from "I" to "she." We saw another shifting of referents in Song 1 of Sappho, from "you" to "I." In that case, the shift in the ownership of pronouns involves the second-person "you" of Aphrodite and the first-person "I" of Sappho. During the epiphany of Aphrodite, Sappho exchanges identities with the goddess herself. It is a moment of personal fusion with Aphrodite. Similarly in the wedding song (F 31), the vicariousness of Sappho links the "I" with the "you" of the bride.

The exchange between the "I" and the "you" of Sappho and Aphrodite in Song 1 is reflected also in the wording of another song of Sappho (F 159), where Aphrodite is imagined once again as speaking to Sappho and addressing her by name. In yet another song of Sappho (F 134), the speaker says she is dreaming she has a dialogue (*dialegesthai*) with Aphrodite.

The erotic experience shared by the "he" who is the bridegroom and by the "you" who is the bride in Song 31 of Sappho is communalized in the reaction of the "I" who figures as the vicarious participant in the experience. And this reaction is an epiphany in itself. In this song, the subjectivity is linked to the first-person speaker who is Sappho. When we hear *phainetai moi kēnos isos theoisin* 'he appears [*phainetai*] to me, that one, equal to the gods', it is the first-person speaker who is feeling the erotic sensations experienced by the bride in the second person and by the bridegroom in the third person. At the climax of the erotic experience as spoken by the first-person speaker, she says about her feelings: *tethnakēn d'oligō 'pideuēs phainom' emautāi* 'and a little short of death | do I *appear* [*phainomai*] to myself.' The verb *phainomai* 'I appear' here signals again an epiphany – an epiphany that manifests itself to the self, to the speaking "I."

This appearance of the self to the self, as an epiphany, signals the divine presence of Aphrodite. In one sense, then, what is seen is the epiphany of Aphrodite, since she is the goddess of the occasion. In another sense, however, what is seen is the epiphany of the bride, whose identity fuses with that of Aphrodite at the moment of her wedding. And, in still another sense, what is seen is the epiphany of the speaking "I" who identifies with Aphrodite by virtue of identifying with the "you" of the bride who is Aphrodite at this very moment. For Sappho, then, what is seen is an auto-epiphany.

The epiphany of Song 31 induces a near-death experience, and such a stylized personal death is modeled on a realized mythical death. As we will see, death in myth is a prototype for whatever it is that the first-person speaker experiences vicariously in her interaction with the second-person bride and with the third-person bridegroom, who are respectively the vision of Aphrodite and the corresponding vision of Ares.

To start with the third person, it is essential to recall that the bridegroom is visualized as *isos Areui* 'equal to Ares' in another song of Sappho (F 111.5). Comparable to the bridegroom who gets married in lyric is the warrior who gets killed in epic. As we will see, he too is visualized as *isos Arēi* 'equal to Ares'. And, as we will also see, the bridegroom can be visualized as Achilles himself in the songs of Sappho.

In the Homeric *Iliad*, warriors are conventionally called the *therapontes* of Ares as the god of war (2.110, 6.67, 15.733, 19.78). This word *therapōn* (plural *therapontes*) means both 'attendant' and 'ritual substitute' in epic. When a warrior is killed in war, he becomes a 'ritual substitute' who dies for Ares by becoming identical to the war god at the moment of death; then, after death, the warrior is eligible to become a cult hero who serves as a sacralized 'attendant' of the war god (BA [= Nagy 1979] 17§§5–6). As an epic warrior, Achilles is a *therapōn* 'ritual substitute' for Ares by virtue of becoming identical to the war god at the moment of death. In the *Iliad*, however, this relationship between Achilles and Ares is expressed only by way of an intermediary, who is Patroklos. This warrior is described not as the *therapōn* of Ares but rather as the *therapōn* of Achilles, and, as such, he is not only that hero's 'attendant' but also his 'ritual substitute', since he actually dies for Achilles (BA 17§§5–6). So Achilles dies only indirectly as the *therapōn* of Ares through the intermediacy of Patroklos, who dies as the *therapōn* of Achilles.

As an epic warrior, Achilles also qualifies as *isos Arēi* 'equal to Ares'. This description suits Achilles in the *Iliad* – though it applies to him only vicariously by way of Patroklos, who takes upon himself the role of a ritual substitute for Achilles. Patroklos is actually called *isos Arēi* (11.604) at the exact moment when the story of his fatal impersonation of Achilles begins (BA 2§8, 17§5).

So a missing link for understanding Song 31 of Sappho is the vision of the hero Achilles as a model warrior at the moment of his death in epic, when he, too, like the model bridegroom in lyric, is 'equal to Ares'. This link is verified by ancient sources, which make it explicit that Sappho conventionally imagined the model bridegroom as Achilles himself (F 105b).

Such a lyric convention in the songs of Sappho can be explained as an organic correlation of myth and ritual. In the logic of myth, Achilles never becomes a model husband because War personified cuts him down like a flower in the bloom of his youth. In the logic of ritual, on the other hand, Achilles is the perfect model for a bridegroom precisely because he is cut down in war and thus cannot ever became a husband.

For love to find its self-expression in the ritual of a wedding, it needs someone to die for love.

Such a ritual need is expressed in the relationship of Eros, personified as the god of erotic love, with Aphrodite, the goddess of erotic love. As we see from the imagined dialogue between Sappho and Aphrodite in a song of Sappho mentioned earlier, the goddess says in her own words that Eros is her *therapōn* (F 159). As in epic, this word in lyric means not only 'attendant' but also 'ritual substitute', that is, someone who ritually dies for the sake of the one he attends. Pictured as a pubescent (not prepubescent) boy, Eros is doomed to die for the sake of Aphrodite. In the poetics of Sappho, as later ancient sources tell us (F 172), the death of erotic Love personified is a most persistent theme.

The death of Eros could be pictured as a martial death resulting from the warfare of love. We see clearly the language of love as war in Song 1 of Sappho, where Aphrodite is invoked in prayer to become a *summakhos* 'ally in battle' for Sappho in speaking the words of lyric love poetry (1.28). Conversely, Sappho as the speaker of lyric love poetry is offering herself as an 'ally in battle' for Aphrodite, thus crossing over into the themes of epic. Similarly in the *Iliad*, Aphrodite crosses over into the themes of epic by intervening in the epic action – and she gets wounded in doing so, as if she were a mortal (5.327–54).

Parallel to the wounding of the goddess Aphrodite are the two woundings of the god Ares in the *Iliad*: he too gets wounded as if he were a mortal (5.855–63, 21.401–8). More than that, the woundings of Ares are in both cases described as mortal woundings, and the *Iliad* actually shows Ares in the act of going through the motions of a stylized martial death. Such an epic experience is for Ares a mock death (EH [= Nagy 2005] §76). Similarly, the lyric experience of Eros in dying for love can be viewed as a mock death, and such ritualized mockery is typical of "divine burlesque," which represents one of the oldest features of Greek myth. There are striking parallels to be found in Near Eastern sources dating back to the second millennium BCE (Burkert 1960: 132).

The stylized death of the god Ares in the *Iliad* is an extreme case of divine mirroring: the immortal god of war gets involved not only in the martial actions of heroes but even in their martial deaths. And he gets so involved because god and hero mirror each other at the moment of a hero's death, which is the climax of the inherent antagonism between them (EH §§105, 108, 110, 115).

At the moment when he dies a warrior's death in place of Achilles, Patroklos is vicariously experiencing such a moment of mirroring between Achilles as warrior and Ares as god of warriors: that is why Patroklos looks just like Ares at that moment (BA 2§8, 17§5).

As mutual antagonists, the hero and the god match each other in life as well as in death. In the case of Achilles, as we see from surviving traces in the Epic Cycle, this hero was imagined as an irresistible lover by lovelorn girls hoping to make him their husband (EH §56). In the case of Ares, as we see from the second song of Demodocus in the Homeric *Odyssey*, this god is imagined as an irresistible lover by the goddess of sexuality herself, Aphrodite (8.266–366).

Among other related characteristics shared by the hero Achilles and the god Ares is their superhuman speed. In the case of Achilles, his success in war is closely connected with the use of such epithets as *podōkēs* 'swift-footed' in the *Iliad*. In the case of Ares, his own swiftness of foot is pictured as ideal for success in courtship as well as in warfare. In the song of Demodocus about the love affair of Ares and Aphrodite in the *Odyssey*, we find that one of the war god's most irresistible attributes is his nimbleness of foot in choral lyric dancing (HPC 1§17). And yet, despite his irresistible attractiveness in courting Aphrodite, the dashing young Ares will never marry. Like the dashing young Achilles, Ares is eternally the bridegroom and never the husband.

Having started with the third-person bridegroom in Song 31 of Sappho, I now continue with the second-person bride. Just as the bridegroom looks like a local cult hero, so also the bride looks like a local cult heroine. In Aeolic traditions, such heroines figured in myths about the conquests of Achilles – not only martial but also amorous conquests – in the years that preceded the destruction of Troy. These myths told of beautiful Aeolic girls of Asia Minor and the outlying island of Lesbos who had once been immune to love and thus unreachable to their frustrated suitors. But then they fall helplessly in love with Achilles – that dashing young Aeolic hero who had sailed across the sea from his home in Hellas to attack their people (HPC 2§§7, 18).

Comparable to these once-unreachable Aeolic girls is a prize apple, unreachable to the apple-pickers, which "blushes" enticingly from the heights of a "shooter-branch" in a song of Sappho (F 105a; on the cultivation of apples in ancient and modern Lesbos, see Mason 2004). It is no coincidence that the brides of Sappho's songs are conventionally compared to apples (F 105b). Like Sappho's prize apple, these contemporary brides are imagined as unreachable. But they are unreachable only up to the moment when they take the place of Aeolic heroines who had once upon a time fallen in love with Achilles, that eternal bridegroom. These Aeolic girls of the heroic past are imagined as throwing themselves at

Achilles. That is, they throw a metonymic extension of themselves at Achilles by throwing an apple at him: such a theme is attested in the bittersweet story of a lovelorn girl from the Aeolic city of Pedasos (Hesiod F 214; BA 7§29n6). In the logic of myth, the love felt by such heroines is doomed from the start, and, in the end, they die for their love. In the logic of ritual, however, that same love promises to be requited. Such is the love expressed by girls pictured in the act of throwing apples at their prospective lovers in the songs of Sappho (F 214A).

Just as the hero Achilles stands in for a god at moments that center on the ritual of a wedding, so also various Aeolic heroines can stand in for a goddess. A case in point is the captive woman Briseis in the *Iliad*, who is overtly associated with the women of Lesbos whom Achilles captured as beauty-prizes in the years that preceded the destruction of Troy (9.128–31, 270–73; 19.245–6). The *Iliad* quotes, as it were, Briseis in the act of singing a choral lyric song of lament for the death of Patroklos (19.287–300); this quotation of Briseis, along with the framing narrative concerning the antiphonal response of the women attending Briseis (19.301–2), reenacts most accurately the morphology of a genuine choral lyric lament (Dué 2002: 70–71; HPC 2§18). As she begins to sing her choral lyric song of lament for Patroklos, Briseis is likened to Aphrodite (19.282). In her lament, Briseis sings her bittersweet sorrow not only over the death of Patroklos but also over the death of her own fondest hope: when he was alive, Patroklos had promised to arrange for her a marriage to Achilles, but, now that he is dead, the hope of that promise is gone forever (19.295–300). So the *Iliad* pictures Patroklos as a ritual substitute for Achilles in courtship as well as in war.

In the logic of myth, from what we have seen so far, a hero's identity at the moment of death can merge with a god's identity. In the logic of ritual, on the other hand, such a merger of identity leads only to a stylized death (PP 87–97). Death in ritual is not physical but psychic. For example, from crosscultural surveys of rituals of initiation as practiced in traditional societies around the world, it becomes evident that initiands who are identified with divinities at the moment of initiation are imagined as dying to their old selves as members of a given age-class and being reborn to their new selves as members of the next age-class (PP 101–3).

In the ritual of a wedding as celebrated by the songs of Sappho, there is the prospect of a happy ending as the identity of the Aeolic *numpha* 'bride' shifts from girl to goddess to woman. In the process of becoming a goddess for a moment, the bride dies to her old self as a girl and is reborn to her new self as a woman. In the corresponding myth, by contrast, there is the prospect of a sad but compellingly erotic ending to the story. The bride-to-be will never get married to the eternal bridegroom, imagined as Achilles.

The death of Achilles himself in war is the climax of his erotic charisma. In general, the martial death of heroes is eroticized as the beautiful death, *la belle mort*; even the body of the dead hero is eroticized – as the beautiful corpse, *le beau mort* (Tyrtaeus F 10; Vernant 1982; HC 4§18, HPC 2§24). Achilles is pictured as a *beau mort* in the *Iliad*, as when the goddess Thetis and her fellow Nereids lament the future death of her beloved son in war; in this context, the hero is compared to a beautiful plant that dies in full bloom (18.54–60; BA 10§11). In a song of Sappho (F 105c), we see a comparable image of a beautiful plant at the moment of death (also comparable is the image of a bridegroom as a beautiful plant in F 115).

Such themes of eroticized death are relevant to the near-death experience of the "I" in Song 31 of Sappho. Having started with the third-person bridegroom in this song and having continued with the second-person bride, I conclude with this first-person speaker. The woman who speaks in the first person here is vicariously speaking for the whole group that attends the wedding. The whole group is notionally participating in the stylized deaths of the male and the female initiands – in this case, of the bridegroom and the bride.

The stylized death of the bridegroom in a wedding as described by Sappho matches the realized death of Achilles in war. Premarital death in ritual marks the transition from bridegroom to husband, while martial death in myth marks an eternal deferral of such a transition. By dying in war, Achilles becomes the very picture of the ultimate bridegroom in eternally suspended animation, forever on the verge of marrying. In the logic of ritual, what is needed for female initiands, especially for brides, is such an eternal bridegroom (Dué 2006: 82–3). A comparable model of unfulfilled desire and unrequited love is the hero Hippolytus in the *Hippolytus* of Euripides: at the end of this drama (1423–30), we find an anthropologically accurate description of a ritual of female initiation featuring a chorus of girls performing a lament for the death of Hippolytus as their local cult hero (PP 94–6). As this drama illustrates, the identity of the female initiand depends on the program, as it were, of the ritual of initiation. The nuptial Aphrodite and the prenuptial/postnuptial Artemis reveal different phases of erotic engagement in the life cycle of a woman, determining when she is attainable – and when she is unattainable.

In compensation for his being cut down in the bloom of his youth, Achilles is destined to have a *kleos* 'glory' that is *aphthiton* 'unwilting': that is what the hero's mother foretells for him, as Achilles himself is quoted as saying (*Iliad* 9.413). The word *kleos* expresses not only the idea of *prestige* as conveyed by the translation 'glory' but also the idea of *a medium that confers this prestige* (BA 1§§2–4). And this medium of *kleos* is not only epic, as represented by the Homeric *Iliad*, but also lyric, as best represented in the historical period by the poet Pindar. In the praise poetry of Pindar, the poet proudly proclaims his mastery of the prestige conferred by *kleos* (as in *Nemean* 7.61–3; PH 6§3). As for the word *aphthiton* 'unwilting', it is used as an epithet of *kleos* not only in epic but also in lyric, as we see from the songs of Sappho (F 44.4) and Ibycus (F 282.47). This epithet expresses the idea that the medium of *kleos* is a metaphorical flower that will never stop blossoming. As the words of a song by Pindar predict, the hero who is glorified by the *kleos* will die and will thus stop blossoming, that is, he will 'wilt', *phthinein*, but the medium that conveys the message of death will never wilt: that medium is pictured as a choral lyric song eternally sung by the Muses as they lament the beautiful wilted flower that is Achilles, the quintessential *beau mort* (*Isthmian* 8.56a–62; PH 7§6). This song of the Muses is parallel to the choral lyric song that is sung by Thetis accompanied by her fellow Nereids as they lament in the *Iliad* the future death of her beloved son: here again, as we saw earlier, Achilles is figured as a beautiful flower cut down in full bloom (18.54–60; BA 10§11). In the *Odyssey*, we find a retrospective description of the lament sung by Thetis and her fellow Nereids at the actual funeral of Achilles, followed by the lament of the Muses themselves (24.58–59, 60–62).

The idea of *kleos aphthiton* 'unwilting glory' as conferred by poetry applies not only to the epic theme of a hero's death in war, as in the case of Achilles in the *Iliad* (9.413), but also to the lyric theme of a wedding, as in the case of Hector as bridegroom and Andromache as bride in Song 44 of Sappho (line 4). The expression *kleos aphthiton* links the doomed warrior in epic with the wedded couple in lyric. Parallel to the linking effected by this expression is the linking effected by the god Apollo himself: he too links Achilles in epic with Hector and Andromache in lyric. The celebrants at the wedding in Song 44 of Sappho sing Apollo by invoking his epithet *Paean* (*Paōn* in the local dialect) when they celebrate Hector and Andromache as bridegroom and bride (line 33). To sing a paean is to sing a song from Lesbos, as we see from the wording of Archilochus (F 121). To sing a paean in the *Iliad* is to sing Apollo as Paean, though Paean is a god in his own right in more archaizing contexts of the *Iliad* (as at 5.401 and 5.899–901). Elsewhere in the *Iliad*, Achilles calls on the Achaeans to sing a paean, that is, to sing Apollo as Paean when they celebrate the death of Hector in war (22.391).

There are also other linkings of the doomed warrior in epic with the wedded couple in lyric. Achilles is *theoeikelos* 'just like the gods' as a warrior in the *Iliad* (1.131, 23.155), and so too Hector and Andromache as bridegroom and bride are *theoeikeloi* 'just like the gods' at the moment of their wedding in Song 44 of Sappho (at line 34; also *i]keloi theoi[s* 'just like the gods' at line 21). Now Achilles is in fact the only recipient of the epithet *theoeikelos* in the Homeric *Iliad*. So the warrior who kills Hector attracts the same epithet in epic that Hector attracts in lyric.

It remains to ask about the god with whom Achilles is identified in epic and with whom Hector and Andromache are identified in lyric. For this god, epic and lyric are undifferentiated, just as the *kleos aphthiton* of Achilles as warrior in epic is undifferentiated from the *kleos aphthiton* of Hector and Andromache as bridegroom and bride in lyric. This god is Apollo.

At the moment of his death, the hero Achilles is destined to confront not only the god Ares as the generic divine antagonist of warriors but also the god Apollo as his own personal divine antagonist. This personalized destiny of Achilles is explicit in the Epic Cycle, that is, in the *Aithiopis*, but only implicit in the *Iliad*, where Patroklos substitutes for Achilles in his antagonism with Apollo just as he substitutes for him in his antagonism with Ares.

What makes this destiny of Achilles so personalized is his special connection with poetry, a medium signaled as *kleos aphthiton* 'unwilting glory'. The god of this medium is Apollo, who is the god of poetry. And this poetry is conceived as lyric. To put it another way, *this poetry is a form of epic that is not yet differentiated from lyric* (PH 12§§44–5). Apollo is the god of an older form of epic that is still sung to the accompaniment of the lyre.

Correspondingly, Achilles is the hero of such an older form of epic. In this role, he is imagined as looking exactly like Apollo – beardless and wearing long hair. Like Apollo, Achilles is the essence of a beautiful promise in the making, of a *telos* or 'fulfillment' realized only in performance, only when the song is fully performed (HTL [= Nagy 2004b] 138–43). There is a visual signature of this shared role of god and hero in the *Iliad*. Achilles, like Apollo, is pictured in this epic as singing to the tune of a lyre that he himself is playing (9.186–9). Achilles had plundered this lyre from the Aeolic city of Thebe, ruled by the king Eëtion (9.186–9), whom he killed when he captured that city – and who was the father of that greatest singer of lamentations in the *Iliad*, Andromache (6.414–16). What Achilles sings to the tune of this Aeolic lyre is an echo of the loves and bittersweet sorrows heard in lyric song (HPC 2§17). An example of such lyric in historical times is the song of Sappho about the wedding of Hector and Andromache (F 44): the lyric *kleos aphthiton* 'unwilting glory' of this Aeolic song (F 44.4) is cognate with the epic *kleos aphthiton* 'unwilting glory' that Achilles is promised in the *Iliad* (9.413), which is metonymically linked with the epic *klea andrōn* 'glories of heroes' that Achilles is singing on the Aeolic lyre (9.189).

Such a lyrical image of Achilles evokes a correspondingly lyrical image of Apollo. Even in epic, this god is conventionally pictured as a lyric personality. In fact, Apollo controls the medium of lyric, of choral lyric. A prime example is the conventional description of Apollo as the *Mous(h)ēgētēs*, that is, as the choral leader of the Muses (PH 12§29). Such a description is attested in lyric (an example is Song 208 of Sappho) and even in epic (*Iliad* 1.603–4). Apollo accompanies himself on the lyre as he sings and dances, while the Muses in the chorus also sing and dance (*Homeric Hymn to Hermes* 475–6).

The god Apollo controls not only lyric. He controls all song and poetry, and he is ultimately in control of all occasions for the performance of song and poetry. In this overarching role, he embodies the authority of poets, that is, of craftsmen who compose song and poetry. This authority transcends such categories as epic and lyric. And it transcends the genres that figure as subcategories of epic and lyric, as well as the occasions that shape those genres. This authority is linked to the authorship of song and poetry.

An ancient term that refers to the exercising of such divine authority and authorship in performance is *exarkhein* (as in Archilochus F 120), which can be pragmatically translated this way: 'to emerge [in the act of performance] as the choral leader'; Aristotle uses the participle *exarkhōn* (*Poetics* 1449a 10–11) in building his evolutionary model of the emergent choral leader. The image of Apollo in choral lyric performance, in the act of singing and dancing as he accompanies himself on the lyre, captures the essence of the *exarkhōn* as the 'emergent choral leader'. As the divine *exarkhōn*, Apollo is the source of authority for the making of song and poetry. As for human *exarkhontes* in the act of performance, they are the makers of this song and poetry. In effect, they are historical authors in the making (HC 2§9).

An ancient term that refers to the medium of exercising such authority and authorship is the noun *humnos*, which is usually translated by way of a word derived from it, 'hymn'. To understand *humnos* merely as 'hymn' in the current sense of the word is inadequate, however, since this sense conveys not much more than a mere literary conceit. In the ancient sense of the term, however, as attested in both epic and lyric, the *humnos* is a notionally perfect beginning of any poetic composition because it is a notionally perfect invocation of the god who presides over the occasion of performing that composition. The god invoked in the *humnos* absolutizes not only the *humnos* but also everything that the *humnos* introduces. Moreover, the totality of everything introduced by the *humnos* is then subsumed by the *humnos* itself, which is totalizing by virtue of being absolutely authoritative. When a *humnos* calls itself a *humnos*, the word refers not only to the *humnos* but also to everything in the performance that follows the *humnos* (HC 2§§2–4).

The immediate referent of the *humnos* is the god or goddess to whom the speaker prays on a given occasion of performance. As the absolute authority who is being invoked by the prayer, that god or goddess makes the performance absolutely authoritative. But the referent of the *humnos* is also the one who reenacts the god or goddess by virtue of performing the *humnos*. The technical term for such reenactment is *mimēsis* (PP 54–58). That is what we see happening in Song 1 of Sappho. At the climax of her performance as a prima donna, Sappho notionally becomes Aphrodite when she sings with the voice of the goddess – and with the authority of the goddess. Sappho herself, by speaking with the voice of the speaker in the *humnos*, becomes absolutely authoritative (PP 87–103).

And to be authoritative in this way requires a group to respond to the authority of the speaker. That group is ideally a chorus of singers and dancers, and, by extension, the entire community of those attending the singing and dancing. As noted before, such authority is played out in the dramatized relationship between the *khoros* 'chorus' and a highlighted *khorēgos* 'leader of the chorus', as mythologized in the relationship of the Muses to Apollo as their choral leader (PH 12§29). Apollo shows the way to celebrate a god in a *humnos* by performing in his own right the perfect performance of such a celebration.

To repeat, the primary referent of the *humnos* is the given divinity who presides over the given festival. The primary participant in the reference system of the *humnos* is the human performer who reenacts a given divine figure in the sacred moment of performance. There is a fusion of identities in that sacred moment, and this fusion is the essence of the *humnos*. That is why the *humnos* becomes the instrument of authority and authorization and authorship. Such is the theology, as it were, of the *humnos*. And such is the theology of the transcendent author, which extends into the reality of the historical author.

We have already seen such a historical author in the personalized figure of the prima donna in Song 1 of Sappho, where the author is actually named. Or, more precisely, Aphrodite names the author, authorizes her, as Sappho. As the *khorēgos* 'leader of the chorus', Sappho is notionally equated with and thus authorized by the goddess she invokes in her prayer, which is the *humnos* she performs.

Regarding examples of ritual occasions for choral performance, I have concentrated so far on the wedding. But there are also many other such occasions having to do with various forms of initiation, that is, with formal transitions from one social status to another, including political inaugurations of various kinds. It is often difficult to pinpoint the historical settings of such occasions. Some of them, such as weddings, are ad hoc, while others seem to be seasonally recurrent, timed to coincide with festivals.

Song 1 of Sappho may be an example of a recurrent occasion: it seems to be an inaugural *humnos* that showcases the Panhellenic prestige of the seasonally recurring festival of the *Kallisteia* in the federal space of Lesbos. Another such example is Song 1 of Alcman, which highlights the double debut of two female *khorēgoi* 'chorus-leaders' stemming from the two royal lineages of the dual kingship of Sparta (PH 12§§17–25). The two Spartan debutantes as celebrated in Song 1 of Alcman are in many ways analogous to the brides of Lesbos as celebrated in the songs of Sappho: for example, the girls from Sparta are compared to horses (Alcman 1.45–54) in much the same way as a bride from Lesbos is compared to a haughty mare (Sappho F 156 via Gregorios of Corinth: also with reference to Anacreon) – or as a bridegroom is compared to a prize-winning steed (Sappho F 194A).

In Song 1 of Alcman, the two female *khorēgoi* 'chorus-leaders' perform as surrogates of the *Leukippides* 'Shining Horses', envisioned as twin female celestial divinities (PH 12§§19–20). There are analogous celestial associations in the songs of Sappho. We have already seen how her identification with Aphrodite makes it possible for Sappho's songs to make personalized contact with the roles of the goddess in the world of myth. One of these roles is the identification of Aphrodite with the planet Venus, which is imagined as the celestial force that makes the sun rise (GM [= Nagy 1990b] 258). Accordingly, Sappho imagines herself as falling in love with a hero called *Phaōn* just as the goddess

Aphrodite in her role as the planet Venus falls in love with the same hero. The name *Phaōn*, stemming from the dialect of Lesbos, is the local Aeolic equivalent of *phaethōn* 'shining', which is the epithet of the sun in Homeric diction (PP 90, 102–103).

Sappho not only identifies with Aphrodite in loving this hero Phaon: *she* can even speak with the voice of Aphrodite in addressing Phaon (T 19), just as she speaks with the voice of Aphrodite when the goddess is pictured as speaking to her in Song 1. In speaking to Phaon, as also in speaking to Aphrodite, Sappho is authorized by Aphrodite. And she thereby authorizes herself. Just as Aphrodite undergoes a mock death by executing a "lover's leap" from the heights of a white rock into the dark sea below for the love of Phaon, so also Sappho can picture herself as undergoing an erotic death for the love of the same solar hero (T 23). The myth tells how Aphrodite disguised herself as an old woman and persuaded the old ferryman Phaon to ferry her across a strait separating the mainland of Asia Minor from the island of Lesbos (Sappho F 211). Sappho pictures herself in the place of Aphrodite as the goddess turns young again while making Phaon young as well – in fond hopes of turning him into her lover. Similar themes recur elsewhere, as in a mention of Eos the goddess of dawn and her mortal lover Tithonus (Sappho F 58).

Despite such hopeful projections of divine identity, the gap between the divine and the human can lead to bittersweet feelings of sadness. Such is the theme of a song of Sappho (F 168B) that pictures the Moon, personified as the local Aeolic goddess *Selanna* (Ionic *Selēnē*), at the moment when it sets beneath the horizon: the goddess is now on her way to meet the beautiful hero Endymion in his secret lair, and there she will sleep with him. We know of the tryst of Selanna with Endymion from a second such song of Sappho (F 199). In the first song (F 168B), the tryst of the goddess with the beautiful hero is signaled by the particle *men*, to be answered by the contrastive particle *de* highlighting the sad loneliness of the lamenting first-person speaker as she says *egō de monā katheudō* 'but I sleep alone' (Clay 1970). Such feelings of sadness are balanced against hopes of identification with the celestial realm: as we saw in a third song of Sappho, the prima donna of an all-night choral lyric performance in the moonlight is pictured as looking just like the moon (F 96.7–9). In that moment, she is identical to the goddess Selanna (F 96.4–6 *se theāi s'ikelan arignōtāi*).

The songs of the queenly Sappho, in all their celestial loveliness, appear worlds apart from the songs of the down-to-earth Alcaeus, which appear downright profane by comparison. The basic context of his songs is the *sumposion* 'symposium', which is conventionally understood to be a drinking party organized by a group of like-minded *(h)etairoi* 'comrades' who sing drinking songs. In terms of such an understanding, Alcaeus is a historical personality who sings in the context of such a group (Rösler 1980). In the symposium, the *(h)etairoi* act out in their songs a whole gamut of social and antisocial behavior, good and bad characters, noble and base feelings. In so doing, they replay the history and even the prehistory of their community.

The medium of these drinking songs shows both *positive* and *negative* ways of speaking, what Aristotle calls *en-kōmion* and *psogos*, loosely translated as '*praise*' and '*blame*' (*Poetics* 1448b27; BA 14 §§1–5). Dominant are the themes of peace and war, statesmanship and factional strife, the joys of civic solidarity and the sorrows, hatreds, and angers of alienation culminating in civic exile. In brief, the medium of such drinking songs recaptures the look and feel of political rhetoric in the polis or 'city state'. If you removed the meter from the drinking songs of Alcaeus, says Dionysius of Halicarnassus (*On Imitation* 421f), what you would have left over is political rhetoric pure and simple (Alcaeus T 20). In terms of this observation, the message of this medium is the medium itself.

It is as if we were looking at some vast unbridgeable gap separating these songs of Alcaeus from the songs of Sappho. And the poetry attributed to Alcaeus even draws attention to such a gap. In one song of Alcaeus (F 384), he is pictured as addressing Sappho in words fit for a divine queen: *ioplok' agna mellikhomeide Sapphoi* 'you with strands of hair in violet, O holy [*(h)agna*] one, you with the honey-sweet smile, O Sappho!'. And the wording is actually fit for a goddess. For example, the epithet *(h)agna* 'holy' is applied to the goddess Athena (Alcaeus F 298.17) and to the *Kharites* 'Graces' as goddesses (Sappho F 53.1, 103.8; Alcaeus F 386.1). As for the epithet *ioplokos* 'with strands of hair in violet', it is applied as a generic epithet to the Muses themselves (Bacchylides 3.17).

Behind the appearances of such disconnectedness between the songs of Alcaeus and Sappho is a basic pattern of connectedness in both form and content. This pattern is a matter of *symmetry*. In archaic Greek poetry, symmetry is achieved by balancing two opposing members of a binary opposition, so that one member is *marked* and the other member is *unmarked*; while the marked member is *exclusive* of the unmarked, the unmarked member is *inclusive* of the marked, serving as the actual *basis of inclusion* (PH 0§15). Such a description suits the working relationship between the profane and the sacred in the songs of Alcaeus and Sappho. What is sacred about these songs is the divine basis of their performance in a festive setting, that is, at festivals sacred to gods. What is profane about these songs is the human basis of what they express in that same setting. We see in these songs genuine expressions of human experiences, such as feelings of love, hate, anger, fear, and pity. These experiences, though they are unmarked in everyday settings, are marked in festive settings. In other words, the symmetry of the profane and the sacred in the songs of Alcaeus and Sappho is a matter of balancing the profane as the marked member against the sacred as the unmarked member in their opposition to each other; while the profane is exclusive of the sacred, the sacred is inclusive of the profane, serving as the actual basis of inclusion.

On the island of Lesbos, the sacred space of Messon was the festive context in which this symmetry of the profane and the sacred could be played out. It was here at Messon that the sacred could serve as the basis for including the profane. Not only the songs of Sappho, which tended toward the sacred side of the symmetry, were marked by the "here" that was Messon. So too the songs of Alcaeus, which tended toward the profane side, were marked by the same "here." A case in point is a song of Alcaeus that begins as a formal hymn to the Dioskouroi, where the divine twins are formally invoked to come "here," that is, to the place where the song is being performed (F 34.1).

Thus even the songs of Alcaeus, which appear to represent the profane side of the symmetry between the profane and the sacred, are worthy of inauguration by way of a *humnos*, which as we have seen sacralizes not only the beginning of performance but also whatever follows the beginning all the way to the end. Whatever that may be includes the drinking song at the symposium. And the god who presides over the drinking at the symposium and over the drinking songs performed there is Dionysus, whose essence is not only sympotic but also mimetic. After all, Dionysus is not only the god who presides over the drinking of wine in a symposium: he is also the god of theater. Conversely, Dionysus is not only the god of mimesis in the theater (PH 13§§6–46): he is also the god of mimesis in the symposium (PP 218).

The mimetic essence of Dionysus is most evident in his role as the presiding god of the City Dionysia of Athens, which must be seen as a parallel to his role as the presiding god of the symposium. The symposium of Dionysus, like the theater of Dionysus, is a stage for mimesis. The stage that is the symposium is the notional "here" that marks the place of performance for the songs of Alcaeus. This "here" is a festive place, that is, the sacred space of a festival. Such a place is the federal district of Messon in Lesbos, which as we have seen is sacred to Dionysus as well as to Hera and to Zeus.

In the state of mind that is this sacred space of Messon, there are two kinds of mimesis represented symmetrically by the choral performances of Sappho and by the sympotic performances of Alcaeus. Each of these two figures plays out a variety of roles. For their primary roles they speak with the authority of the lead singer, of the author in the making. In these roles, the "I" represents the speaker of the inaugurating *humnos* who is speaking by way of praying to a presiding divinity. Or the "I" may represent that divinity speaking to the lead singer or even to the whole group attending and participating in the performance of the song. Beyond this incipient authorial role, the "I" of both Sappho and Alcaeus stands ready to exchange identities with the "you," the "he," the "she," or the "they" that populate the world reflected by the song culture of Lesbos. So all three persons of the personal pronoun in Greek lyric take on the role of *shifters* (for applications of this technical term, see PH0§17n30).

In the songs of Sappho, for example, the "I" who speaks may be Sappho speaking in the first person to the bride or to the bridegroom in the second person – or about them in the third person. Or it may be the bridegroom or the bride speaking to each other – or even to Sappho. So also in the songs of Alcaeus, the "I" may play out a variety of roles. The "I" is not only the speaker who is Alcaeus speaking in the first person to his comrades in the second person – or about them in the third person. In one song of Alcaeus, for example, the song starts with the "I" of a female speaker, who speaks of the sound of a mating-call from a stag that lingers in the heart of a hind (F 10B).

The "I" of Alcaeus can act as the crazed lover of a young boy or girl. His "I" can even be Sappho herself, transposed from the protective context of the chorus into the unprotected context of the symposium. Aristotle (*Rhetoric* 1.1367a) quotes the relevant wording of a duet featuring, on one side, Alcaeus in the act of making sly sexual advances on Sappho and, on the other side, Sappho in the act of trying to protect her honor by cleverly fending off the predatory words of Alcaeus:

He: I want to say something to you, but I am
prevented by shame . . .
She: But if you had a desire for good and beautiful things
and if your tongue were not stirring up something bad to say
then shame would not seize your eyes
and you would be speaking about the just and honorable thing
  to do.

Sappho F 137

Such symmetry between Alcaeus and Sappho was perpetuated in the poetic traditions of the symposium well beyond the old historical setting of festive celebrations at Messon in Lesbos. A newer historical setting was Athens during the sixth and the fifth centuries BCE. Here the songs of Alcaeus and Sappho continued to be performed in two coexisting formats of monodic performance: one of these was the relatively small-scale and restricted format of the symposium, while the other was the spectacularly large-scale and public format of citharodic concerts at the musical competitions of the festival of the Panathenaia (Nagy 2004a).

In the context of this Athenian reception, the symmetry between Alcaeus and Sappho is still visible. On a red-figure vase made sometime in the decade of 480–470 BCE (Munich, Antikensammlungen no. 2416), we see on one side of the vase a painting that features the roguish Alcaeus and the demure Sappho: the two are pictured as concert performers, each playing on a specialized lyre known as the barbiton. On the other side of the vase, we see a painting that features the god Dionysus and a maenad in a stylized sympotic scene. The stylized musical duet between Alcaeus and Sappho in this red-figure painting matches in its symmetry the stylized musical duet between the same singers as quoted by Aristotle.

The symmetry between Alcaeus and Sappho as exponents of sympotic and choral performance is already framed within the sympotic poetry of Alcaeus. It happens in his Song 130, which is the same context in which we saw him referring to the choral performance of women at the festival of the *Kallisteia* at Messon. The ritual space of Messon is figured here in mythological terms. At the mythologized moment when the poet speaks in Song 130, this space is imagined as a "no man's land" serving as a place of refuge for the alienated Alcaeus, exiled from his native city of Mytilene. Such a view of this ritual space is a mythologized way of looking at an "everyman's land" serving as a place of integration for the poetry of Alcaeus in the festive here-and-now of this poetry as it continues to be performed in this ritual space. To conceive of this poetry as having a life of its own, beyond the lifetime of the poet himself, is a ritualized way of looking at the ongoing performance of the songs of Alcaeus, which are imagined as worthy of universal acceptance by all who take part in the festivals held at Messon, the sacred space of the federation of Lesbos (Nagy 1993).

Such a poetic gesture is an epigrammatic way for the figure of Alcaeus to foretell the reception of his poetry within the overall community. There are similar epigrammatic gestures to be found in the poetry of Thegonis (19–24): in that case as well, the mythologized rejection of the poet by his own community in his own lifetime is predicated on the ritualized acceptance of his poetry after he dies (PP 220–23). In the poetics of such epigrammatic gestures, the ongoing reception of a poet's poetry is expressed by the disembodied voice of the poet imagined as speaking from the dead, as if from an epigram (Theognis 1209–10; Wickersham 1986 and Nagy 1993). There are similar gestures attested in archaic epigrams attributed to Homer (HPC 1§9). But the disembodied voice of an archaic lyric poet such as Alcaeus needs no such epigram: his songs are reactivated every time they are sung by live voices at the festivals of Messon in Lesbos.

The sympotic poetry of Alcaeus, framing the choral poetry of Sappho, was hardly isolated in its native Aeolian setting on the island of Lesbos. It was strongly influenced by contacts with the neighboring empire of the Lydians on the mainland of Asia Minor. The orientalization of the musical traditions of Lesbos was in fact a pattern common to the song cultures of all Hellenes native to Asia Minor and to the outlying islands, most notably Lesbos, Chios, and Samos. This pattern of orientalization was especially apparent in the Greek institution of the symposium, as reshaped by the exotic fashions of the Lydian empire. Among these fashions, marked by ostentatious signs of luxury, was the new Greek custom of reclining on couches on the occasion of a symposium. A most flamboyant musical example of such Lydian orientalism was the lyric virtuoso Anacreon, court poet of Polycrates, who was tyrant of Samos. Although Anacreon and his patron Polycrates flourished in a period when the Persian empire had already replaced the Lydian empire, the exotic themes of Lydian musical orientalism persisted: as a performer of lyric, Anacreon was associated with such paraphernalia as turbans, parasols, and sympotic couches. Herodotus pictures Anacreon in the act of singing his lyric poetry at a symposium hosted by Polycrates, who is shown reclining on a sympotic couch (3.121).

The Lydian musical orientalism of drinking and singing while reclining on a couch at a symposium extends to representations of Dionysus as god of the symposium: he too is conventionally pictured as drinking and singing while reclining on a couch. He too is orientalized – and orientalizing. To those who are notionally uninitiated in the traditions of the symposium – and of theater – Dionysus appears to be more of a Lydian than a Hellene. That is how the god appears to the uninitiated Pentheus in the *Bacchae* of Euripides.

The orientalizing of the symposium and of sympotic singing was fundamentally a sign of political power, modeled on the imperial power of a Lydian *turannos* (PH 10§§6–22). A Greek tyrant like Polycrates of Samos was defined by the Lydian musical orientalism of his court poet Anacreon, whose sympotic poetry served to express the power of his patron. The personal love of the tyrant for a beautiful boy like Bathyllus became a public expression of his political power as mediated by the sympotic love poetry of Anacreon.

Even before Anacreon, there are already clear signs of Lydian musical orientalism in the earlier lyric traditions of Alcaeus and Sappho, as also in the even earlier traditions of Terpander. And there is a wealth of references to exotic Lydian fashions not only in sympotic but also in choral lyric contexts. Such a context is Sappho's self-professed love of *(h)abrosuna* 'luxury' (F 58.25), which is a lyric theme fit for Lydian kings and queens (Xenophanes 3.1; PH 10§§18–19). Moreover, we have already noted such Greek choral lyric events as the "Dance of the Lydian Maidens" at a festival in Ephesus and the "Procession of the Lydians" at a festival in Sparta.

A vital point of contact between earlier and later phases of such orientalizing features in the making of Greek lyric was the Ionian island empire of Polycrates, tyrant of Samos. The sympotic love poetry of his court poet Anacreon was closely related to older forms of sympotic love poetry native to Lesbos. Like the older poetry of Alcaeus, the newer poetry of Anacreon refers even to Sappho herself as a stylized love interest (Nagy 2004a).

After the island empire of Polycrates imploded in the course of its rivalry with the mainland empire of the Persians, there was a massive shift from East to West in the history of Greek lyric traditions. A most fitting symbol of this shift was the gesture made by Hipparchus, tyrant of Athens, in sending a warship to Samos to rescue the lyric virtuoso Anacreon and bring him to his city ("Plato" *Hipparkhos* 228c). Around this time, Athens became a vitally important new center for the development and diffusion of lyric poetry as performed nonprofessionally at symposia and professionally at public concerts. At the most prestigious Athenian festival of the Panathenaia, professional citharodes and aulodes competed with each other in spectacular performances of melic poetry originating from poets such as Alcaeus, Sappho, Anacreon, and Simonides, while professional rhapsodes competed in performing nonmelic poetry originating from Archilochus, Hipponax, Callinus, Mimnermus, and so on.

Such melic and nonmelic traditions, in becoming an integral part of the Athenian song culture, strongly influenced the corresponding traditions of another most prestigious festival of Athens, the City Dionysia.

That is how the melic and the nonmelic traditions of Athenian state theater became eventually merged with the older lyric traditions of the Aeolic and Ionic worlds as once mediated by the island empire of Polycrates. And the resulting network of cross-influences and cross-references can be seen in the themes of Athenian comedy, which mirrored the negative as well as the positive themes of the older sympotic traditions. These themes, dealing with such special topics of interest as the behavior of women in love or of men at war, naturally led to the comic ridicule of influential lyric models such as Sappho and Archilochus.

Further to the west of Athens, there were other vitally important new centers for the development and diffusion of lyric poetry as performed in symposia or in larger-scale public contexts of choral performance. The Panhellenism of this diffusion is evident from the prestige of early masters of Aeolian lyric such as Terpander in Sparta or Arion in Corinth. Even further to the west, the art of such early masters eventually became merged with the art of other early masters such as Stesichorus in Italy and Sicily. Later on, with the implosion of the island empire of Polycrates in the east, the shift of lyric traditions to the west became most pronounced in Italy and Sicily. Just as Anacreon left behind the luxurious orientalizing world of the tyrant Polycrates in Samos, so too did Ibycus. Whereas Anacreon left for Athens, however, Ibycus left for Italy and Sicily, infusing with new life the old lyric traditions represented there by Stesichorus. The *kleos aphthiton* 'unwilting glory' promised by the lyric poetry of Ibycus to the tyrant Polycrates (F 282.47) had sadly wilted in the East. But that *kleos* 'glory' was to blossom again in the West, as we see from the poetry of lyric virtuosi such as Ibycus, Lasus, Pindar, Simonides, and Bacchylides.

The idea that the medium of *kleos* is a metaphorical flower that will never stop blossoming was understood by Pindar. As we saw earlier from the wording of one of his songs, Achilles as the hero who is the message glorified by the *kleos* will die and thus stop blossoming, as expressed by the verb *phthinein* 'wilt', but the medium that conveys the message will never die (*Isthmian* 8.56a–62; PH 7§6). As a master of this medium of *kleos*, Pindar presents himself as a poet who controls the lyric present as well as the epic past:

> I am a guest [*xenos*]. Keeping away dark blame [*psogos*] and bringing genuine glory [*kleos*], like streams of water, to a man who is near and dear [*philos*], I will praise [*aineîn*] him.
>
> Pindar *Nemean* 7.61–63

We see here the authority of Pindar as a master of *kleos*. In this passage, which comes from one of his *epinikia* 'epinicians, victory songs', the poet refers to himself in an authoritative setting, which is the choral lyric celebration of an athletic victory.

Pindar's self-references in his victory songs are so stylized, however, that no one can be sure of even the most basic circumstances of artistic production. For example, there is continuing controversy over whether such songs were actually performed by a solo singer, who is maybe Pindar himself, or by a *khoros* or 'chorus', that is, by a singing and dancing ensemble that was trained by Pindar or by a delegate of Pindar. In terms of this controversy, there is a bifocal interest in the first-person singular "I" of Pindar (Lefkowitz 1988) and in a notionally performing ensemble that is called the *kōmos* by the poetry itself (Heath 1988).

As the celebrant, the speaker of the victory song oscillates between the singular and the plural of the first person, "I" or "we," in referring to himself in the act of performance. In the singular, the celebrant is the poet, Pindar himself. He is the *xenos* or guest of honor who is giving praise to his host at a feast celebrating the athletic victory. In the plural, on the other hand, the "we" of Pindar's epinicians is the voice of the *kōmos*, that is, of 'a group of celebrants'.

In fact, there is no such thing as an *audience* in such situations of celebration. Everyone who attends is notionally a member of the *group* of celebrants. Sometimes the group speaks as a group, and sometimes the main speaker speaks as a soloist for the group.

The concept of a group is essential for understanding Greek lyric in general (Rösler 1980). Unlike an audience, the group is not distinguished from those who actually perform in and for the group. The whole group notionally takes part in the performance.

The interpretation of Pindaric references to a group of celebrants depends on analysis of the conventions that made such references possible. For example, even if the Pindaric references to the *kōmos* as a group of celebrants do not fit our own notion of the *khoros* as a chorus, that is, a singing and dancing ensemble, it is still possible to interpret the Pindaric *kōmos* as a stylization of the *khoros* in the specific context of a victory celebration (Nagy 1994/1995).

Of course there are other forms of Pindaric compositions, such as the *paean* or the *partheneion*, where it is obvious that the speaker is a group. Moreover, in the choral lyric poetry of both Pindar and Bacchylides, the celebrating group of the here-and-now is interwoven with celebrating groups of the mythical past (Power 2000).

Conversely, myth is interwoven with the here-and-now of its reenactment by the group participating in lyric performance. A particularly
striking example is Pindar's *Olympian* 1, a song that recapitulates a complex of myths that notionally motivate the entire complex of rituals
known as the Olympic Games (PH 4§§1–26). By way of such interweaving, the lyric performance becomes a myth in and of itself. By
linking itself with past mythical *exempla*, the lyric performance becomes
a mythical *exemplum* of its own.

The myths of lyric, however, need not be universal. The *muthoi*
that are believed by some may not be believable to the poet himself:

> Yes, there are many wondrous things [*thaumata*]. And the
> words that men tell, *myths* [*muthoi*] embellished with varied
> pattern-woven [*poikila*] *falsehoods* [*pseudea*], beyond wording
> [*logos*] that is *true* [*alēthēs*], are deceptive. But *charisma* [*kharis*],
> which makes everything pleasurable for mortals, brings it
> about, by way of giving honor, that even the unbelievable
> oftentimes becomes believable.
>
> Pindar *Olympian* 1.28–32

The myths that Pindar's song marks as falsehoods have to do with
things *heard* about the hero Pelops during a time when he was not
to be *seen* (*Olympian* 1.46–48). The myths that Pindar's song marks
as falsehoods here are falsehoods not because they are myths but only
because they are myths that differ from the master myth privileged as the
truth by Pindar. In this case, the "false" myths represent rejected versions
of the story of the hero Pelops, while the "true" myth represents the
official version as integrated into the complex of rituals known as the
Olympic Games (PH 4§24). While the myths that are "falsehoods" can
merely be *heard*, the myth that is "true" can actually be *seen*: the visibility
of the myth is captured in the moment when Pelops emerges from
the purifying caldron, resplendent with his ivory shoulder (*Olympian*
1.26–27).

The Greek word *kharis*, which I have translated for the moment
as 'charisma', is imagined here as a superhuman force giving power to
the myths of lyric; it is parallel to the Latin word *gratia*, which refers
simultaneously to the *beauty* ('grace') and the *pleasure* ('gratification') of
any *exchange* (PH 2§27n72). In the poetry of lyric, such an exchange
takes place between the lyric performer and everyone who participates
in the lyric performance – including the gods and heroes who figure
in the lyric composition. So the charisma of *kharis* is the essence of

lyric performance and composition. This charisma is what gives myth the "'honor'" it deserves, making people believe what myth says – even when the things that are said transcend the believable.

SUGGESTED READING

On myth in lyric as distinct from epic, the observations of Martin 1997 are seminal. On the common heritage of Greek epic and lyric: Bergren 1975; also Petropoulos 1994. Bundy 1986 shows how myth comes to life in the context of lyric conventions; also Kurke 1991. On myth in choral lyric, Calame 2001 is foundational. On the subtleties of myth in lyric, Carson 1986 offers an engaging essay.

2: HOMER AND GREEK MYTH

Gregory Nagy

I n the classical period of Greek literature, *Homer* was the primary
representative of what we know as *epic*. The figure of Homer as a
poet of epic was considered to be far older than the oldest known
poets of lyric, who stemmed from the archaic period. It was thought that
Homer, acknowledged as the poet of the *Iliad* and the *Odyssey*, stemmed
from an earlier age. Herodotus (second half of the fifth century BCE)
says outright that Homer and Hesiod were the first poets of the Greeks
(2.53.1–3). It does not follow, however, that the myths conveyed by
the poetry of Homer and Hesiod are consistently older than the myths
conveyed by the poetry of lyric. In fact, the traditions of Greek lyric are
in many ways older than the traditions of Greek epic, and the myths conveyed by epic are in many ways newer than the myths conveyed by lyric.

As we saw in the previous chapter, the traditions of Greek lyric
were rooted in *oral poetry*. If, then, Homer as a poet of epic was thought
to have lived in an even earlier era than the era of the earliest known
poets of lyric, it follows that the traditions of epic as represented by
Homer were likewise rooted in oral poetry.

The oral traditional basis of Homeric poetry can be demonstrated
by way of comparative as well as internal analysis. The decisive impetus
for comparative research comes from the evidence of living oral traditions. The two most prominent names in the history of this research
are Milman Parry (collected papers published posthumously in Parry
1971) and Albert Lord (definitive books published in 1960, 1991, 1995).
Although Parry had started his own research by analyzing the internal
evidence of Homeric poetry, as reflected in the texts of the *Iliad* and
the *Odyssey*, he later set out to observe first-hand the living oral poetic
traditions of the former Yugoslavia (first in the summer of 1933, and
then from June 1934 to September 1935).

On the basis of his comparative analysis, Parry found that oral poetry was not restricted to epic, which had seemed, at first, to be the prototypical poetic genre in the prehistory of Greek literature. Parry's finding has been reinforced by the cumulative evidence of ongoing comparative research, which shows that oral poetry and prose span a wide range of genres in large-scale as well as small-scale societies throughout the world; further, epic is not a universal type of poetry, let alone a privileged prototype (PH [= Nagy 1990a] 14§§2–3).

On the basis of internal evidence as well, Parry found that epic was not the only extant form of ancient Greek poetry that derived directly from oral traditions. Parry's own work (1932) on the poetry of Sappho and of Alcaeus showed that oral traditions shaped the ancient Greek traditions of lyric as well as epic. The work of Lord (1995: 22–68) has provided comparative evidence to reinforce Parry's internal evidence about Greek lyric. As we see from the combined work of Parry and Lord, to draw a line between Homer and the rest of ancient Greek literature is to risk creating a false dichotomy. There is a similar risk in making rigid distinctions between oral and written aspects of early Greek poetry in general (Lord 1995: 105–6).

In the history of research on ancient Greek literature, the single most important body of internal evidence showing traces of oral traditions has been the text of Homeric poetry, in the form of the *Iliad* and the *Odyssey*. For some (such as Adam Parry 1966: 193), the artistry of an epic such as the *Iliad* is living proof that the text is "the design of a single mind." By implication, the artistic organization and cohesiveness of Homeric poetry must be indicative of individual creativity, achievable only in writing. We see here the makings of another false dichotomy (as restated by Finkelberg 2000): what is "unique" and therefore supposedly *literary* is contrasted with what is "multiform" and therefore supposedly *oral*. The fact is that multiformity, as a characteristic of oral poetry, is a matter of degrees and historical contingencies: for example, even if "our" *Iliad* is less multiform than, say, a poem of the so-called Epic Cycle such as the *Cypria*, it does not follow that Homeric poetry is absolutely uniform while "Cyclic" poetry is multiform (HTL [= Nagy 2004b] 25–39).

In the oral poetics of lyric, we saw that *composition* interacts with *performance*, and such interaction is parallel to the interaction of *myth* with *ritual*. The same can be said about the epic poetry attributed to Homer: to perform this epic is to activate *myth*, and such activation is fundamentally a matter of *ritual*.

Homeric poetry actually demonstrates how myth is activated. It does this by quoting, as it were, the performance of poetry within its own poetry. The performers of such poetry are characters of epic, human and divine alike, represented as speaking within the epic, and what they speak – that is, what they perform – is poetry embedded within the poetry of epic. What they speak is "speech-acts" (Martin 1989). This term *speech-act* designates a special way of speaking in situations where you are actually *doing* something by way of *speaking* something (Austin 1962). In Homeric poetry, the *making* of poetry is itself an act of *doing* by way of *speaking*, and that act of doing is an act of *performance* (HQ [= Nagy 1996b] 119). In Homeric poetry, the word for such a performative act is *muthos*, ancestor of the modern term *myth*.

This word *muthos* refers to the following kinds of speech-acts as quoted by Homeric poetry: *boasts, threats, invectives, laments, prophecies,* and *prayers* (Martin 1989: 12–42). Such speech-acts, in and of themselves, need not be poetry, but they become poetry once they are framed by poetry. And, in the act of framing, the poetry of epic demonstrates that it, too, like the poetry it frames, is a speech-act. The *making* of Homeric poetry, that is, the *composing* of this poetry, is notionally the same thing as *doing* something, which is the *performing* of this poetry. Just as the making of boasts, threats, invectives, laments, prophecies, and prayers is literally a matter of *doing* these things, that is, of ritually performing speech-acts, so also the *making* of Homeric poetry is a matter of ritually performing the epic that frames these same speech-acts. Just as the speech-acts framed by Homeric poetry are *muthoi*, so also Homeric poetry is itself an overall *muthos*.

Here is a working definition of *muthos* as it functions within the epic frame of Homeric poetry: it is "a speech-act indicating authority, performed at length, usually in public, with a focus on full attention to every detail" (Martin 1989: 12). This working definition applies also to the epic frame itself, that is, to Homeric poetry as defined by the *Iliad* and *Odyssey* (HQ 120–21, 128–38).

In Homeric poetry, to speak a *muthos* is to perform it from memory. *A muthos is a speech-act of recollection* (Martin 1989: 44). In the *Iliad*, for example, when the old hero Nestor is trying to make a point by way of recalling the story of the battle of the Centaurs and the Lapiths (1.260–74), he says that the point he is making is a *muthos* (1.273). In making his point, directed at Agamemnon and Achilles, Nestor is recalling his own participation in the older story, which he says happened in an era pre-dating the era of the present story, that is, the era of the *Iliad*.

So the *muthos* of Nestor here is embedded within the overall *muthos* of Homeric poetry – in this case, of the *Iliad*.

In Homeric poetry, the recalling of a memory is not necessarily an act of recalling a personal experience, as in the case of Nestor. In other epic situations, the speaker may recall something that happened in the experience of others. Such is the case when the old hero Phoenix tells a story directed at the young hero Achilles. He introduces his story by saying:

> *memnēmai tode ergon egō palai ou ti neon ge*
> *hōs ēn. en d' humin ereō pantessi philoisi*
> I *totally recall* [*me-mnē-mai*] this action that happened a long time
>   ago – it is not something new –
> exactly how it was. I will tell it in your company – since you are
>   all near and dear to me.
>
> Iliad 9.527–8

When the verb *mnē-*, in the sense of 'recall', takes a direct object in the accusative case, as here, then the act of recalling is total and absolute; when, on the other hand, this verb takes an object in the genitive case, then the act of recalling is only partial and therefore not at all absolute (HQ 152n13). Phoenix says that he had learned his story from others (9.524). So the question is, how can you recall an epic action that you did not personally experience?

The answer is to be found in the word *kleos* 'glory', the abbreviated plural form of which is *klea* 'glories', which refers to the story told by Phoenix. This story, which is about the hero Meleager, is intended by its narrator as a model for the story about the hero Achilles, which is a story-in-progress while it is being performed. The *klea* 'glories' of heroic predecessors are being set up as a model for the main hero of the *Iliad*:

> This is the way [*houtōs*] that we [= I, Phoenix] learned it, the
>   glories [*klea*] of men of an earlier time
> who were heroes – whenever one of them was overcome by
>   tempestuous anger . . .
>
> Iliad 9.524–5

The expression *klea andrōn*, which I have translated here as 'glories of men (of an earlier time)', applies not only to the epic story about

Meleager. As we will see, it applies also to the epic story about Achilles. That is how the heroic song of Homeric poetry refers to itself.

The word *kleos* applies to Homeric poetry as performed by the master narrator of that poetry. Etymologically, *kleos* is a noun derived from the verb *kluein* 'hear' and means 'that which is heard'. In the *Iliad*, the master narrator declares that the epic he narrates is something he 'hears' from the Muses (2.486: *akouein*), who *know* everything *because they were present when everything happened* (2.485). What the omniscient Muses *see* and what they *hear* is a *total recall*: they recall everything that has ever happened, whereas the narrator only *hears* the *kleos* from the Muses (BA [= Nagy 1979] 1§§2–4). The narrator of epic depends on these goddesses to tell him exactly what they *saw* and to quote for him exactly what they *heard*.

So *the omniscient Muses are goddesses of total recall*, and their absolute power of recall is expressed by an active form of the verb *mnē-* in the sense of 'remind' (2.492). The master narrator of the *Iliad* receives the same absolute power of total recall when he prays to the goddesses to tell him everything about the Achaean forces that sailed to Troy (2.484, 491–2). Inspired by the omniscient Muses, he becomes an omniscient narrator. Although he says he will not exercise the option of telling everything in full, deciding instead to tell only the salient details by concentrating on the names of the leaders of the warriors who sailed to Troy and on the precise number of each leader's ships (2.493), the master narrator insists on his power of total recall (HTL 175n78; cf. 80n75). The very idea of such mental power is basic to Homeric poetry.

So when Phoenix says he has total recall, totally recalling the epic action he narrates, his power of memory depends on the power of the omniscient narrator who tells the framing story of the *Iliad*, and that power in turn depends on the power of the omniscient Muses themselves, who are given credit for controlling the master narrative.

Phoenix has total recall because he uses the medium of poetry and because his mind is connected to the power source of poetry. He expresses himself in the meter of epic, dactylic hexameter, because he is speaking inside a medium that expresses itself that way. He is "speaking" in dactylic hexameter just like the master narrator who is quoting him. When Phoenix says *memnēmai*, he is in effect saying: "I have total recall *by way of speaking in the medium of poetry*."

As we have seen, Phoenix refers to his story as *klea andrōn | hērōōn* 'the glories [*kleos* plural] of men of an earlier time who were heroes' (9.524–5). It is a story about the hero Meleager and his anger against his people, parallel to the framing story about the hero Achilles and his anger against his own people, the Achaeans (also known as the Argives or the Danaans). The telling of the story by Phoenix is an activation of epic within epic.

Phoenix is a hero in the epic of the Homeric *Iliad*, and this epic is a narrative about the distant heroic past – from the standpoint of listeners who live in a present tense devoid of contemporary heroes. But Phoenix here is narrating to listeners who live in that distant heroic past tense. And his narrative-within-a-narrative is about heroes who lived in an even more distant heroic past tense.

Just as the framing epic about the anger of Achilles is technically a speech-act, a *muthos*, so too is the framed epic about the anger of Meleager. Conversely, just as the framed epic about Meleager is a poetic recollection of the *klea* 'glories' of heroes of the past, so too is the framing epic about Achilles. That framing epic, which is the *Iliad*, is a poetic recollection by the Muse whom the master narrator invokes to sing the story of the anger of Achilles (1.1). As the narrator of a framed epic, Phoenix does not have to invoke the goddesses of memory, the Muses, since the narrator of the framing epic has already invoked them for him.

Technically, everything in Homeric poetry is said by the Muse invoked at the beginning of the *Iliad* and, again, at the beginning of the *Odyssey*. And everything is heard by the master narrator, who then says it all to those who hear him, just as characters say what they say to the characters who hear them within the master narrative. Those who hear the master narrator include the characters inside the action of his master narrative: they too are assumed to be listening to the master narration, and that is why Homeric characters, such as Menelaus, Patroklos, and Eumaeus, can be addressed in the second person by the master narrator (Martin 1989: 235–6).

All poetry embedded within the outer frame of Homeric narrative is epic poetry – to the extent that the outer frame is epic poetry. But the embedded poetry can also take on a vast variety of forms other than epic. An example is lament. The quotations of laments performed by women in the *Iliad* show a poetic form that belongs to the general category of lyric, not epic, as we saw in the previous chapter. Still, when epic as *muthos* refers to lament, it can call this lyric form a *muthos*, as in the case of a lament performed for the hero Hector by his grieving mother Hecuba in the *Iliad* (24.200). Such a lament is a *muthos* not because it is in fact a lament but simply because it is framed and regulated by the master *muthos* that is epic (Martin 1989: 87–8).

The regulatory power of epic as a master *muthos* leads poets who are outside of epic to question the veracity of *muthoi* in epic. For a lyric poet, such as Pindar, the problem with Homeric *muthoi* is the fact that they are framed by epic and therefore controlled and regulated by epic. Such control and regulation lead to *pseudea* 'falsehoods' that go far beyond the truth, as in the case of Homeric stories about Odysseus:

> I think that the things said about Odysseus outnumber the things he experienced – all because of *Homer*, the one with the sweet words, whose *falsehoods* [*pseudea*] and winged inventiveness have a kind of majesty hovering over them; *poetic craft* [*sophia*], misleading by way of its *myths* [*muthoi*], is deceptive. *Blind* in heart are most men. For if they could have *seen* the *truth* [*alētheia*], never would great Ajax, angered over the armor [of Achilles], have driven the burnished sword through his own heart.
>
> Pindar Nemean 7.20–27

The lyric setting of this song of Pindar is defined by local rituals as well as local myths connected to the hero Ajax: the song was meant to be performed in the island-state of Aegina, culturally dominated by elites who claimed to be descended from a heroic lineage that included Ajax (PH 6§§56–58, 8§10n41). In Pindar's words, the local fame of Ajax in Aegina is defended by the singular *alētheia* 'truth' of lyric – while it is assaulted by the multiple *muthoi* 'myths' of epic (PH 14§22). Whereas the perspective of lyric is localized and thus grounded, enabling the listener to visualize – literally, to *see* – the integrated singularity of *alētheia* 'truth', the perspective of epic is delocalized and thus ungrounded, allowing the listener only to *hear* a disintegrated multiplicity of *muthoi* 'myths'.

Whereas the singular 'truth' of Pindar's lyric highlights the integrity of Ajax, the multiple 'myths' of Homer's epic shade it over. In this way, epic allows Odysseus to seize the advantage at the expense of Ajax. The epic focus of interest shifts from the integrity of Ajax to the craftiness of Odysseus, and this shift blurs the moral focus of Homer. From the retrospective vantage point of the moral high ground claimed by the lyric poetry of Pindar, this shift in interest causes the despair that led to the suicide of Ajax. This despair is tied to the epic story that tells how Ajax, consistently marked as the second-best of the Achaeans after Achilles in the *Iliad*, failed to win as his prize the armor of Achilles after the martial death of that hero, who is consistently marked as the best of the Achaeans (BA 2§§1–6). The despair of Ajax is tied also to his failure to become the next hero in line to be the best of the Achaeans and thus to continue the epic of Homer after the *Iliad*. This failure is pointedly mentioned in the Homeric *Odyssey* (11.541–567; PH 8§33n110).

The epic failure of Ajax is a foil for the epic success of Odysseus, which is made possible by the poetic craft of Homer's *Odyssey*. Just as the craftiness of Odysseus prevents Ajax from inheriting the armor of Achilles, so also the craft of Homer prevents Ajax from inheriting the epic status of 'the best of the Achaeans' after the death of Achilles. In the *Odyssey*, that epic status is earned by Odysseus through his own epic experiences after the death of Achilles (BA 2§§12–18).

As we have seen from Pindar's *Nemean 7*, the *muthoi* 'myths' about the experiences of Odysseus are to some extent falsehoods. They are falsehoods, however, not because they are myths but only because they are controlled by a master myth that differs from the master myth privileged as the truth by Pindar. That different master myth is controlled by the master narrator of the *Odyssey*. Under such control, the myths about Odysseus in the *Odyssey* lose the grounding they once had in their local contexts. Once *muthoi* 'myths' are delocalized, they become relative and thus multiple in application, to be contrasted with the *alētheia* 'truth' claimed by lyric, which is supposedly absolute and unique (PH 7§5n17).

As we are now about to see from Pindar's *Olympian 1*, *muthoi* 'myths' can be imagined as additions to the kernel of truth as expressed by wording that is *alēthēs* 'true'. Such additional myths stand for an undifferentiated outer core, where various versions from various locales may contradict each other, while the wording that is *alēthēs* 'true' stands for a differentiated inner core of myth that tends to avoid the conflicts of localized versions (PH 2§28):

> Yes, there are many wondrous things [*thaumata*]. And the words that men tell, myths [*muthoi*] embellished with varied pattern-woven [*poikila*] *falsehoods* [*pseudea*], beyond wording [*logos*] that is *true* [*alēthēs*], are deceptive. But *charisma* [*kharis*], which makes everything pleasurable for mortals, brings it about, by way of giving honor, that even the unbelievable oftentimes becomes believable.
>
> Pindar *Olympian* 1.28–32

A multiplicity of 'false' myths is being contrasted here with a singular master myth described as *logos* 'wording' that is *alēthēs* 'true'. So even some *muthoi* 'myths' retold by Pindar can be rejected as falsehoods in the process of retelling those myths. There is a comparable idea of *pseudea* 'false things' as told by the Muses in addition to the *alēthea* 'true things' they tell in the poetics of Hesiod (*Theogony* 27–28; PH 2§32).

The myths that Pindar's song marks as 'false' have to do with things *heard* and not *seen* (*Olympian* 1.46–48). As we saw in the previous chapter, such myths are 'false' not because they are myths but only because they are myths that differ from the master myth privileged by Pindar, and that master myth is notionally the only myth that can be 'true' at the moment of telling it. While the myths that are 'false' can merely be *heard*, details from the alternative myth that is 'true' can actually be visualized, that is, literally *seen* (*Olympian* 1.26–27).

The conceit of lyric poetry is that it can see the truth that it tells, whereas epic poetry only hears what it tells, and what epic hears may or may not be true. A prime example is a song known as the *palinode* or *recantation* of the lyric poet Stesichorus (F 193): in this song, the poet rejects the myths that tell how Helen allowed herself to be abducted by Paris from her home in Sparta, substituting another myth that claims she never left Sparta. This alternative myth about Helen, which highlights her status as a goddess, is grounded in local Dorian traditions (Pausanias 3.19.11; PH 14§§13–21), and it is complemented by a myth about Stesichorus himself: according to this complementary myth, the poet had been blinded by the goddess for having defamed her by perpetuating myths affirming her abduction by Paris – but then the goddess restored the eyesight of Stesichorus in order to reward the poet for unsinging, as it were, his previous song by way of singing his palinode or recantation (Isocrates *Helen* 64; Conon FGrH 26 F 1.18; Plato *Phaedrus* 243a).

There is a parallel myth about Homer: this poet too had been blinded by Helen for having defamed her by perpetuating myths affirming her abduction by Paris (*Life of Homer* 6.51–7 ed. Allen); unlike the lyric poet Stesichorus, however, the epic poet Homer never recants and he stays blind forever (Plato *Phaedrus* 243a). Unlike lyric poetry, which privileges the metaphor of *seeing* the true myth, the epic poetry of Homer privileges the metaphor of *hearing* from the Muses the *kleos* 'glory' of the myths that he tells (*Iliad* 2.486); as we have seen, even the word *kleos*, derived from *kluein* 'hear', proclaims the privileging of this metaphor of hearing (PH 14§19).

As we see from such contrasts between *lyric master myths* that are seen and *epic myths* that are just heard, not all myths qualify as the truth in any single telling of myths. Whereas all myths count as *muthoi* in Homeric poetry, including the epic master myth told by the master narrator himself, a master myth told in other media need not to be called a *muthos*. Not all *muthoi* count as myths in the positive sense of the word *muthos* as used in Homeric poetry.

Even in Homeric poetry, where *muthos* is used consistently in a positive sense, not all *muthoi* are myths of and by themselves. Such is the case in situations where the word *muthos* functions as a synonym of the expression *epea pteroenta* 'winged words': in each of these epic situations, the one who is speaking to the one who is listening succeeds in making a speech-act that makes that listener do something that is specially significant to the plot of epic (Martin 1989:30–37, HQ 122). Such a speech-act is a myth only to the extent that it gets to be told within the framework of a master narrative that counts as a *muthos*, that is, as the Homeric master myth.

Even those Homeric speech-acts that are not marked by the word *muthos* or by a synonym have the power of complementing and enhancing the telling of the Homeric master myth. Such is the case with the telling of Homeric similes, which serve the purpose of advancing the epic action by intensifying its vitality (on the telling of a simile as an act of divination, see Muellner 1990). The point of entry for these similes tends to be situated either before or after the occurrence of climactic moments in the epic action (Martin 1997:146). The power of the Homeric simile in driving the narrative forward is a matter of performance.

For the Homeric tradition in general, it can be said that the intensity of maintaining the epic narrative was correlated with the intensity of physically performing that narrative. There is a striking example in the commentary tradition preserved by the scholia for the Townley codex of the *Iliad* (at 16.131), where we read that the verses telling about the arming of Patroklos needed to be performed in an intensely rushed tempo: *speudonta dei propheresthai tauta, epipothēsin tēs exhodou mimoumenon* 'one must produce this in a rush, re-enacting the desire for the outcome [of the epic action]' (Martin 1997:141).

The strong visual component of Homeric similes stems mainly from lyric traditions that are still evident in later poetry, especially in the choral songs of Pindar and in the sympotic poetry of Theognis (Martin 1997: 153–66). A most vivid example is a simile that visualizes the Achaeans at a moment of defeat in battle in the *Iliad* by comparing them to a blighted population suffering from the conflagration caused by a thunderstorm (17.735–9). The wording in this simile is evidently cognate with the wording that describes a cosmic flood caused by Zeus in a song of Pindar (*Olympian* 9.49–53; Martin 1997: 160–61). In general, the *Iliad* is pervaded by similes centering on the complementary themes of *cosmic flood* and *cosmic conflagration*, that is, of *cataclysm* and *ecpyrosis* respectively, and these themes are initiated by what is called the Will of Zeus at the beginning of the *Iliad* (1.5): ecpyrosis applies to both the Trojans and the Achaeans, while cataclysm applies only to the Achaeans (EH [= Nagy 2005] §§63–4; PR [= Nagy 2002] 66). In the *Iliad*, the fire of the Achaeans menacing the Trojans and, conversely, the fire of the Trojans menacing the Achaeans are both pervasively compared to a cosmic conflagration expressing the *mēnis* 'anger' of Zeus (BA 20§§13–20; Muellner 1996). Similarly, when it is foretold that the rivers of the Trojan plain will erase all traces of the Achaean Wall at Troy, the flooding of the plain is described in language that evokes a cosmic cataclysm (*Iliad* 12.17–33; EH §64).

The power of the Homeric simile in advancing the plot of epic is evident in the *Odyssey* as well. A most striking example is the simile that describes the blinding of the Cyclops called Polyphemus: when Odysseus and his men thrust into the single eye of the monster the fire-hardened tip of a wooden stake they had just crafted, the sound produced by this horrific act is compared to the sound produced when a blacksmith is tempering steel as he thrusts into cold water the red-hot edge of the axe or adze he is crafting (9.390–94). From a crosscultural survey of myths that tell how a hero who stands for the civilizing forces of *culture* blinds a monster who stands for the brutalizing forces of *nature*, it becomes clear that such myths serve the purpose of providing an aetiology for *the invention of technology* (Burkert 1979: 33–4). (On the concept of *aetiology*, see BA 16§2n2.) It is no coincidence that the *three Cyclopes* in the Hesiodic *Theogony* (139–46) are imagined as exponents of technology: they are identified as the *three blacksmiths* who crafted the thunderbolt of Zeus (Burkert 1979: 156n23). Thus the simile about the tempering of steel in the Homeric narration of the blinding of Polyphemus serves the purpose of contextualizing and even advancing that narration by way of highlighting aspects of an underlying myth that is otherwise shaded over.

In considering the function of similes in the narrating of the master myth in Homeric narrative, we have seen that their formal features are distinct from those of epic, and that they follow their own distinct rules. To that extent, the simile may be classified as a genre distinct from the genre of epic as represented by Homeric poetry. Still, as we have also seen, the internal rules of the simile mesh with the external rules of the epic that frames it. So instead of saying that the *framed form* of the simile is a *subgenre* of epic, it is more apt to say that the *framing form* of the epic is a *supergenre* (Martin 1997: 166).

Besides the simile, there are also other genres framed within the supergenre of epic, and each of these genres affects in its own way the narration of the master myth. To take a premier example, let us return to the story told by the old hero Phoenix to the young hero Achilles in the *Iliad*. At first sight, this story seems to be simply an epic in its own right. A second look, however, shows much more. This story follows rules of its own, some of which differ from the rules of epic.

As Achilles contemplates the decisions he has to make in the making of an epic that centers on his own epic actions, he is invited by Phoenix to contemplate the decisions made by an earlier hero in the making of an earlier epic. As we saw earlier, that hero is Meleager, who figures in an earlier epic called the *klea* 'glories' of heroes (9.524–5). The framed epic about Meleager, quoted as a direct speech by the framing epic, is introduced by way of a special word *houtōs* 'thus', signaling the activation of a special form of speech otherwise known as the *ainos* (PH 7§1n4). Technically, *an ainos is any performance conveying a meaning that needs to be interpreted and then applied in moments of making moral decisions* (PH 7§§1–4).

The actual form of the *ainos* varies enormously in the classical and postclassical periods. At one extreme are the ostentatiously lofty victory songs of the choral lyric master Pindar, which mark the occasions for celebrating athletic victories – and which convey to the celebrants various lessons that myth teaches about the making of moral decisions in one's own life (BA 12§§14–19). At the other extreme are the ostensibly lowly fables of Aesop in the carnivalesque *Life of Aesop*, where the "moral of the story" is implicit in the context of actually telling the story to those who are actually listening to the performance of the fable (BA 16§5–6).

The *ainos* that Phoenix tells in the *Iliad*, drawing on myths concerning the hero Meleager, is intended to persuade Achilles to accept an offer made by Agamemnon. That is the short-range intention of Phoenix as a narrator narrating within the master narration that is the *Iliad*. But the long-range intention of the master narrator is quite different from the short-range intention of Phoenix. The master narrative shows that the embedded narrative of Phoenix was misguided – that is, misguided by hindsight. If Achilles had accepted the offer of Agamemnon, as Phoenix had intended, this acceptance would have undermined the epic reputation of Achilles (HQ 142–3).

So the reaction of Achilles to the *ainos* performed by Phoenix needs to be viewed within the framework of the master narrative performed by the master narrator. From the standpoint of Achilles as a character who takes shape within the plot of the overall epic that is the *Iliad*, the consequences of his decisions in reacting to the subplot of the epic about Meleager are still unclear at the moment when he makes these decisions. From the standpoint of the master narrator who narrates the plot of the *Iliad*, on the other hand, the consequences are quite clear, since the master narration takes shape by way of an interaction between the framed myth about the anger of Meleager and the framing myth about the anger of Achilles (Walsh 2005). The short-range agenda of Phoenix and Achilles will be transformed into the long-range agenda of the master myth, which will ultimately correspond to what actually happens to Achilles in his own heroic life. *In the world of epic, heroes live out their lives by living the myths that are their lives.*

The point of the story as told by Phoenix is that Achilles must identify with those who are *philoi* 'near and dear' – and must therefore rejoin his comrades in war. Phoenix himself, along with Odysseus and Ajax, is a representative of these comrades by virtue of being sent as a delegate to Achilles. More must be said about the word *philos* (singular) / *philoi* (plural), which means 'friend' as a noun and 'near and dear' as an adjective. The translation 'dear' conveys the fact that this word has an important *emotional* component. As we will see, the meaning of the framed narrative of Phoenix emerges from the framing narrative of the *Iliad*. As we will also see, the central theme has to do with the power of emotions, and the central character turns out to be someone who is not mentioned a single time in the framed narrative: that someone is Achilles' best friend, the hero Patroklos.

From the standpoint of Phoenix as narrator, the word *philoi* applies primarily to these three delegates at the moment when he begins to tell his story (9.528). But this word applies also to the whole group of epic characters who are listening to the telling of this story. This group is composed of (1) Odysseus and Ajax, who are the other two delegates besides Phoenix; (2) the two heralds who accompany the three delegates; (3) Achilles himself; and (4) Patroklos. Inside the story told by Phoenix, the comrades who approach Meleager as delegates are the *philtatoi*, that is, those persons who are 'nearest and dearest' to the hero (9.585–7). So, from the short-range perspective of Phoenix as the narrator of the *ainos* about Meleager, the three comrades who approach Achilles as delegates must be the persons who are nearest and dearest to him. From the long-range perspective of the master narrator, however, it is not Phoenix and the two other delegates but Patroklos who must be nearest and dearest to Achilles. Later on in the *Iliad*, after Patroklos is killed in battle, Achilles recognizes this hero as the one who was all along the *philtatos*, the 'nearest and dearest' of them all (17.411, 655; BA 6§15).

The story about Meleager as narrated by Phoenix is already anticipating such a long-range recognition, since there is someone even nearer and dearer to Meleager than the comrades, who are described by Phoenix as *philtatoi*, the 'nearest and dearest' (9.585–7): in the logic of the story, that someone who is even nearer and dearer turns out to be the wife of Meleager (9.588–596). In Meleager's *ascending scale of affection* (the term is explained in BA 6§15), the wife of the hero ultimately outranks even the comrades approaching him as delegates. Likewise, in Achilles' ascending scale of affection, there is someone who ultimately outranks the comrades approaching him as delegates. For Achilles that someone is Patroklos, who was all along the *philtatos*, the 'nearest and dearest' of them all (17.411, 655). The name of this hero in its full form, *Patrokleēs*, matches in meaning the name given to the wife of Meleager in the *ainos* narrated by Phoenix: she is *Kleopatra* (9.556). These two names, *Patrokleēs/Kleopatra*, both mean 'the one who has the glory [*kleos*] of the ancestors [*pateres*]' (BA 6§§15, 17–19). Both these names amount to a periphrasis of the expression *klea andrōn | hērōōn* 'the glories [*kleos* plural] of men of an earlier time who were heroes' (9.524–5), which refers to the *ainos* narrated by Phoenix to a group of listeners including not only the delegates approaching Achilles but also Achilles and Patroklos themselves (9.527–8). Phoenix is presuming that all his listeners are *philoi* 'near and dear' to him (9.528).

Even before the arrival of the delegates, Achilles himself is pictured as singing the glories of heroes, the *klea andrōn* (9.189). At this moment, he is alone except for one person. With him is Patroklos, who is intently listening to him and waiting for his own turn to sing, ready to start at whatever point Achilles leaves off singing (9.190–91). As Patroklos stands ready to continue the song sung by Achilles, the song of Achilles stands ready to become the song of Patroklos. So the hero whose name conveys the very idea of *klea andrōn* is figured here as the personal embodiment of the *klea andrōn* (PP [= Nagy 1996a] 72–3, PR 17).

The *ainos* as told by Phoenix, to which he refers as *klea andrōn* (9.524), connects with the song of Achilles, to which the master narrator refers likewise as *klea andrōn* (9.189). The *ainos* also connects with Patroklos as the one person who is nearest and dearest to Achilles. Patroklos is at the very top of that hero's ascending scale of affection.

What must mean more than anything else to Achilles is not only Patroklos himself but also the actual meaning of the name *Patrokleēs*, which conveys the idea of the *klea andrōn*. For Achilles, the words *klea andrōn* represent the master myth in the actual process of being narrated in the epic of the *Iliad*. For Achilles, it is a myth of his own making. And it is myth in the making.

Just as the song of Achilles is identified with the master myth of the *Iliad*, so also the style of this hero's language is identified with the overall style of the master narrator. In other words, the language of Achilles mirrors the language of the master narrator. Empirical studies of the language of Homeric diction have shown that the language of Achilles is made distinct from the language of other heroes quoted in the *Iliad*, and this distinctness carries over into the language of the master narrator, which is thus made distinct from the language of other narrators of epic (Martin 1989: 225, 227, 233, 237). It is as if the *klea andrōn* as sung by Achilles – and as heard by Patroklos – were the model for the overall *klea andrōn* as sung by Homer.

The *ainos* as told by Phoenix, to which he refers as *klea andrōn* (9.524), connects with the overall *klea andrōn* as told by the master narrator. The connection is made by way of poetic conventions distinguishing the *ainos* from epic. One of these conventions is a set of three features characterizing the rhetoric of the *ainos*. Unlike epic, the *ainos* requires three qualifications of its listeners in order to be understood (PH 6§5):

1. The listeners must be *sophoi* 'skilled' in understanding the message encoded in the poetry. That is, they must be mentally qualified.
2. They must be *agathoi* 'noble'. That is, they must be morally qualified.
3. They must be *philoi* 'near and dear' to each other and to the one who is telling them the *ainos*. That is, they must be emotionally qualified. Communication is achieved through a special sense of community, that is, through recognizing "the ties that bind."

Each of these three features of the *ainos* is made explicit in the lyric poetry of Pindar, which as we have seen refers to itself as *ainos* (PH 6§§5–8). One of these features is also made explicit in the *ainos* narrated by Phoenix, that is, in the *klea andrōn | hērōōn*, 'the glories [*kleos* plural] of men of an earlier time who were heroes' (9.524–5). When it comes to the emotional qualifications required for understanding the *ainos* spoken by Phoenix, we have already seen that the speaker refers to his listeners as *philoi* 'near and dear' to him (9.528). So the emotional requirements of the *ainos* are made quite explicit. By contrast, when it comes to the moral requirements for understanding the *ainos*, they are merely implicit in the word *philoi*. The moral message as encoded in his *ainos* becomes explicit only at a later point, once the outcome of the master myth is clarified. That point is reached when Patroklos is killed while fighting for his comrades. It is only then that Achilles, for whom the story about the anger of Meleager was intended, ultimately recognizes the moral message of that story.

This kind of recognition, to borrow from the wording used in the lyric poetry of Pindar, shows that the listener has become *sophos* 'skilled' in understanding the message encoded in the *ainos*. In the story told by Phoenix, that message is conveyed by the figure of Kleopatra, who is nearest and dearest to Meleager in that hero's ascending scale of affection. In the logic of the embedded narrative, that figure promotes the moral principle of fighting for one's comrades, just as the figure of Patroklos, who is nearest and dearest to Achilles, promotes the same principle in the logic of the master narrative.

Patroklos not only promotes that principle: he exemplifies it through his own epic actions, thereby forfeiting his life. Then, responding to the lesson learned from the death of Patroklos, Achilles will express his willingness to forfeit his own life in order to avenge the death of Patroklos, thereby justifying the principle for which Patroklos had died (*Iliad* 18.90–126).

Plato shows his understanding of this moral principle as developed in the master myth of the *Iliad*: in the *Apology* (28c–d), we see a paraphrase of the relevant verses of the *Iliad* (18.90–104), along with some quotations of the original wording. Likewise in Plato's *Symposium* (179e–180a), we see another paraphrase of the same verses. In the case of this second paraphrase, however, the choice made by Achilles to forfeit his life in order to avenge the death of Patroklos appears to be conflated with another choice that faces the hero. At an earlier point in the *Iliad* (9.410–16), Achilles is saying to the delegates that he must decide between two *kēres* 'fates' (9.411): either he dies at a ripe old age after a safe *nostos* 'homecoming' to Phthia or he dies young on the battlefield in Troy – and thereby wins for himself a *kleos* 'glory' that is *aphthiton* 'unwilting' (9.413).

Plato's apparent conflation of two choices facing Achilles turns out to be justified: the two choices are in fact one choice. Earlier in the *Iliad*, when Achilles says he must choose between two *kēres* 'fates' (9.411), either a *nostos* 'homecoming' or a *kleos* 'glory' that is *aphthiton* 'unwilting' (9.413), he is actually not yet ready to make his choice: the two alternative fates have simply been foretold for him by his mother, the goddess Thetis (9.410–11). Later on, after Patroklos has been killed, Achilles is facing the same choice, but by now he has made his decision. He says there cannot be a homecoming for him (*nosteîn*: 18.90) because he must kill Hector in order to avenge the death of Patroklos, and, once he kills Hector, his own death in battle will become a certainty (18.90–93), just as his mother had foretold – and as she now foretells again (18.96–7). By choosing to kill Hector, Achilles chooses to die young on the battlefield, and he refers to this death as his inevitable *kḗr* 'fate' (18.115). As his compensation, however, he will now win *kleos* 'glory' for himself (18.121).

So, ultimately, Achilles decides to choose *kleos* over life itself. Earlier on, however, when the choice is first formulated, it is not yet clear which of the two *kḗres* 'fates' (9.411) will be chosen by the hero – whether it will be a *nostos* 'homecoming' or the *kleos* 'glory' that is *aphthiton* 'unwilting' (9.413). The hero is saying that he loves life more than any property he can win for himself by fighting in Troy, and such property is defined in terms of raiding cattle in particular and acquiring wealth in general (9.401–8). Still earlier on, at the very start of the *Iliad*, such property is being defined in terms of the women as well as the cattle and the general wealth that the hero has already acquired in the course of raiding the Aeolic territories in the vicinity of Troy. At the start, the hero's sense of *timḗ* 'honor' is simply a function of all the property he has acquired. The prime example is Briseis, a woman whom Achilles captured in one of his raiding expeditions in the Aeolic territories: at the beginning of the *Iliad*, when she is forcibly taken from Achilles by Agamemnon, Briseis is treated merely as a war-prize, a trophy, and the hero's loss is seen initially as a loss of property. At this point, the hero's honor is still being expressed exclusively in terms of property. Later on, however, Achilles rethinks the loss of Briseis as the loss of a personal relationship: he says he loves her like a wife (9.340–43).

So the *ainos* of Phoenix about Meleager, a hero who seems at first to love his wife more than he loves his own comrades, will now take on a special meaning for the hero of the master myth that is the *Iliad*. But there are vital questions that remain: does Achilles love his would-be wife more than he loves his comrades – or even more than life itself? Here is where the name of Meleager's wife, *Kleopatra*, becomes essential. The meaning of this character's name is parallel to the meaning of *Patrokleēs*, the name of the one character who means more to Achilles than anyone else in the whole world. After Patroklos is killed, this hero is recognized as the one single character who was nearest and dearest to Achilles. Achilles now says that he has all along valued Patroklos as much as he has valued his own life (18.80–82).

So the hero Ajax misses the point when he accuses Achilles of loving Briseis more than he loves his comrades (9.622–38). Achilles loves his would-be wife the same way that Meleager loves Kleopatra: for what she actually means to his comrades. What Achilles loves more than anything else in the whole world is what Kleopatra means to Meleager – and what his own nearest and dearest comrade Patroklos means to him. Just as Patroklos made the moral choice of loving his comrades more than life itself, actually giving up his life for them, so also Achilles will now make the moral choice of giving up his own life for his comrade Patroklos – and for the meaning of Patroklos. The meaning of the name of Patroklos, 'the one who has the glory [*kleos*] of the ancestors [*pateres*]', recapitulates the epic choice of Achilles, who ultimately opts for *kleos* over life itself. That is why the epic *kleos* chosen by Achilles must be *aphthiton* 'unwilting' forever (9.413): the *kleos* of Achilles is like a flower so beautiful that it must not ever lose its divine vitality.

This epic *kleos* chosen by Achilles is also a lyric *kleos*. Achilles is pictured as singing the *klea andrōn* 'glories of heroes' (9.189) while accompanying himself on a lyre he plundered when he captured the native city of that greatest singer of lamentations in the *Iliad*, Andromache (9.186–9). As we saw in the chapter on lyric and myth, this epic song of Achilles is like an echo of the loves and bittersweet sorrows heard in lyric song, and such lyrical feelings are typically linked not only with Achilles but also with that most celebrated pair of doomed lovers, namely, Andromache and the man who earns the ultimate hatred and fury of Achilles in the *Iliad*, Hector (HPC [= Nagy 2008] 2§17). The *kleos* of Achilles is a form of song that dwells on the hatred and the fury, the love and the sorrow – and on the power of song in expressing all these intensely lyrical feelings.

Unlike Achilles, who must choose between *kleos* and *nostos* in the *Iliad*, the epic hero Odysseus must have both *kleos* and *nostos* in the *Odyssey*. For Odysseus to live out the master myth of his own heroic life, he must have a *nostos* or 'homecoming'. For Odysseus to succeed in coming home to Ithaca, however, his *nostos* must be more than simply a 'homecoming': it must be also a 'song about a homecoming'. The *kleos* or epic glory of Odysseus depends on his *nostos*, that is, on the song about his homecoming, which is the *Odyssey*. By contrast, the *kleos* of Achilles must be divorced from the very idea of ever achieving a successful *nostos*: as we have seen, Achilles will win *kleos* by dying young at Troy, but he will lose this *kleos* if he has a *nostos* and dies old at home (*Iliad* 9.413). For Achilles, *nostos* would be merely a homecoming, not a song about a homecoming that wins him any *kleos*. And the *kleos* that he wins by dying young is the *Iliad* itself.

Although Odysseus is credited with the epic feat of destroying the city of Troy, as the *Odyssey* proclaims at the very beginning (1.2), his *kleos* in that epic does not and cannot depend on the story of Troy. It depends instead on the story of his homecoming to Ithaca. By contrast, although Achilles is never credited with the destruction of Troy, since he is killed well before that event takes place, his *kleos* nonetheless depends on the story of Troy. More than that, his *kleos* is in fact the story of Troy. The name of the *Iliad*, which equates itself with the *kleos* of Achilles, means literally 'the song of Ilion', that is, the song of Troy (EH §49). So, for Odysseus to get his own *kleos*, which is the story of his homecoming to Ithaca in the *Odyssey*, he must get over the *kleos* of Achilles, which is the story of Troy in the *Iliad*. He must get over the *Iliad* and get on with the *Odyssey*. In other words, he must get on with his *nostos*, which is not only his *homecoming* to Ithaca but also the *song about this homecoming*. That is the essence of the master myth of the *Odyssey* (BA Preface §§16–18; 2§§10–18).

For Odysseus to get over the *Iliad*, he must sail past it. His ongoing story, which is the *Odyssey*, must be about the sailor who is making his way back home, not about the warrior who once fought at Troy. The *kleos* of Odysseus at Troy cannot be the master myth of the *Odyssey*, since the *kleos* of Achilles at Troy has already become the master myth of the *Iliad*. The *kleos* of Achilles in the *Iliad* has preempted a *kleos* for Odysseus that centers on this rival hero's glorious exploits at Troy. For the hero of the *Odyssey*, the ongoing *kleos* of his adventures in the course of his *nostos* is actually threatened by any past *kleos* of his adventures back at Troy. Such a *kleos* of the past in the *Odyssey* could not rival the *kleos* of the more distant past in the *Iliad*. It would be a false *Iliad*. That is why Odysseus must sail past the Island of the Sirens. The Sirens, as false Muses, tempt the hero by offering to sing for him an endless variety of songs about Troy in particular and about everything else in general (*Odyssey* 12.184–91). The sheer pleasure of listening to the songs of the Sirens threatens not only the homecoming of Odysseus, who is tempted to linger and never stop listening to the endless stories about Troy, but also the ongoing song about that homecoming, that is, the *Odyssey* itself (BA Preface §17n; EH §50).

Just as Odysseus achieves his *kleos* by achieving his *nostos*, so also does his son, Telemakhos. When the son goes on a quest for the *kleos* of his father (*Odyssey* 3.83), this quest is also for the father's *nostos* (2.360; EH §53). To aid the young epic hero in this quest, the goddess Athena assumes the role of 'mentor' to him, and so she becomes personified as a fatherly epic hero, turning into *Mentēs* in Rhapsody 1 of the *Odyssey* and into *Mentōr* in Rhapsody 2 (GM [= Nagy 1990b] 113). (The *Iliad* and the *Odyssey* are each divided into twenty-four *rhapsōidiai* 'rhapsodies', sometimes called 'scrolls' or 'books', which are divisions based on traditions of performance: PR 63.)

The rivalry of Odysseus and Achilles in the story of Troy is formalized in a dispute between the two heroes: was the city to be destroyed by *biē* 'force', as represented by the hero Achilles, or by *mētis* 'craft', as represented by Odysseus? There are indirect references to this dispute in both the *Iliad* and the *Odyssey* (BA 3§§5, 7), and some of these references are relevant to the master myths of the two epics (as in *Iliad* 9.423–6 and in *Odyssey* 8.72–82 respectively). Ultimately, *the craft or craftiness of Odysseus in devising the stratagem of the Wooden Horse leads to the destruction of Troy*, as narrated by the disguised hero himself in the *Odyssey* (8.492–520). This validation of craft at the expense of force does not translate, however, into a validation of Odysseus at the expense of Achilles in the overall story of Troy. As we have just seen, that story is the *kleos* of Achilles in the *Iliad*, not the *kleos* of Odysseus in the *Odyssey*.

Even in situations where the *mētis* 'craft' of Odysseus helps advance the homecoming of the hero in the *Odyssey*, it does nothing to advance the *kleos* of his past epic exploits at Troy. A case in point is the decisive moment in the *Odyssey* when Odysseus devises the stratagem of calling himself *Outis* 'no one' (9.366) in order to deceive and then blind Polyphemus the Cyclops. The pronoun *ou tis* 'no one' used by the hero for the crafting of his false name deceives not only the Cyclops but also the monster's fellow Cyclopes when they use the same pronoun to ask the blinded Polyphemus this question: *perhaps someone has wronged you?* (9.405, 406). The syntax of the question, expressing the uncertainty of the questioners, requires the changing of the pronoun *ou tis* 'no one' into its modal byform *mē tis* 'perhaps someone', which sounds like the noun *mētis* 'craft'. The modal byform *mē tis* is intentionally signaling here the verbal craft used by Odysseus in devising this stratagem (BA 20§4n7). And this intentional act of signaling is made explicit later on when the narrating hero actually refers to his stratagem as a *mētis* (9.414). The same can be said about the hero's previous stratagem of blinding the Cyclops with a sharpened stake, an act of craftiness compared to the craft of blacksmiths (9.390–94). These and all other stratagems used by the hero against the Cyclops qualify as *mētis* 'craft' (9.422).

It goes without saying that the stratagem of crafting the false name *Outis* succeeds: when the blinded Cyclops answers the question of his fellow Cyclopes, *perhaps someone has wronged you?* (9.405, 406), he uses the nonmodal form of the pronoun, saying *ou tis* 'no one' *has wronged me* (9.408). Still, though this stratagem succeeds in rescuing Odysseus (and, for the moment, some of his comrades), it fails to rescue the hero's past *kleos* in Troy. In fact, the stratagem of Odysseus in calling himself *Outis* 'no one' produces just the opposite effect: it erases any previous claim to any *kleos* that the hero would have had before he entered the cave of the Cyclops. Such erasure is signaled by the epithet *outidanos* 'good-for-nothing', derivative of the pronoun *ou tis* 'no one': whenever this epithet is applied to a hero in the *Iliad*, it is intended to revile the name of that hero by erasing his epic identity (as in *Iliad* 11.390). Such erasure means that someone who used to have a name will now no longer have a name and has therefore become a *nobody*, a *no one*, *ou tis*. In the *Odyssey*, the Cyclops reviles the name of the man who blinded him by applying this same epithet *outidanos* 'good-for-nothing' to the false name *Outis* (9.460). The effect of applying this epithet completes the erasure of the hero's past identity that was started by Odysseus when he renamed himself as *ou tis* 'no one'. The name that the hero had heretofore achieved for himself has been reduced to nothing and must hereafter be rebuilt from nothing.

It is relevant that the annihilation of the hero's identity happens in the darkness of an otherworldly cave, in the context of extinguishing the light of the single eye of the Cyclops, thereby darkening forever the monster's power to see the truth unless he hears it. In the poetics of Greek myth, both epic and lyric, the identity or nonidentity of a hero matches the presence or absence of light: in the words of Pindar (*Pythian* 8.95–7), the difference between being *tis* 'someone' and being *ou tis* 'no one' becomes visible when a burst of *light and life* coming from Zeus himself illuminates the void of *darkness and death* (Nagy 2000: 110–11).

It is just as relevant that the master narrative of the *Odyssey* situates Odysseus in the darkness of another otherworldly cave at the very beginning of that narrative. At the point chosen for the beginning of the actual storytelling (1.11: *entha* 'there'), the first detail to be narrated is that Odysseus is at this moment being deprived of his *nostos* (1.13) by a goddess called Calypso (1.14) who is keeping him concealed in her cave (1.15). The feelings of attraction associated with the beautiful nymph Calypso are matched by feelings of repulsion evoked by her terrifying name *Kalupsō*, derived from the verb *kaluptein* 'conceal' (GM 254n108; Crane 1988): this verb is traditionally used in ritual formulas of burial,

72

and it conveys the idea of consigning the dead to concealment in the realm of darkness and death (as in *Iliad* 6.464, 23.91).

Of all the tales of homecomings experienced by the Achaean heroes after Troy, whether these homecomings succeed or fail, only the tale of Odysseus is still untold at the beginning of the *Odyssey*. Only his homecoming is still in doubt. This is the point being made at the very start of the tale: that the narrative is being kept in a state of suspension, and the cause of this suspension is said to be the goddess Calypso, who is preventing Odysseus from his *nostos* (1.13) by keeping him concealed in her cave (1.15). For the narrative to start, the *nostos* of Odysseus has to be activated, and so the Olympian gods intervene to ensure the eventual homecoming of Odysseus to Ithaca (1.16–17).

In Rhapsody 5 of the *Odyssey*, the Olympians send the god Hermes as their messenger to Calypso, and he tells her that she must allow Odysseus to make his way back home. So she must stop preventing Odysseus from getting started with the master myth of the *Odyssey*. That master myth is the *nostos* of Odysseus, which must be not only the hero's homecoming but also the song about his homecoming.

The role of the goddess Calypso in threatening to prevent the *nostos* of the hero Odysseus is reflected in the tales that she herself tells the god Hermes about other heroes who became lovers of other goddesses: the outcome of these tales is death (5.118–29). For example, the hero Orion is killed off by Artemis because he became the lover of Eos, the goddess of the dawn (5.121–4). And the narrative of the *Odyssey* actually foretells a similar death for Odysseus – if he had continued to be the lover of Calypso (5.271–5; BA 10§39).

The relationship of Odysseus and Calypso shows that the *nostos* of the hero is not only a 'homecoming' but also, more basically, a 'return'. That is, the *nostos* of the hero is not only a *return to Ithaca* but also, in a mystical sense, a *return to light and life* (Frame 1978). To return from the cave of Calypso at the end of Rhapsody 12 of the *Odyssey* is to return from the darkness and death of that cave. The same can be said about the return of Odysseus from the cave of the Cyclops Polyphemus at the end of Rhapsody 9 of the *Odyssey*.

Even more basically, the same can also be said about the return of Odysseus from Hades at the beginning of Rhapsody 12 of the *Odyssey*. Here too we see the theme of *returning to light and life* (Frame 1978).

This grand theme takes shape at the beginning of Rhapsody 11 of the *Odyssey*, when Odysseus starts to make his descent into Hades after a series of wanderings that take him farther and farther westward toward the outer limits of the world. The island of the goddess Circe, situated

73

at these outer limits in the Far West, becomes the point of departure for the hero's planned entry into Hades (11.1–12), but the actual point of entry is situated even farther west than that mystical island, since Odysseus has to cross the river Okeanos before he can cross over into Hades (11.13, 21). The Okeanos must be even farther west than the island of Circe. That is because the Okeanos is the absolute marker of the Far West.

The Okeanos is situated at the outermost limits of the world, which is encircled by its stream. The circular stream of the Okeanos flows eternally around the world and eternally recycles the infinite supply of fresh water that feeds upon itself (*Iliad* 14.246–246a, 18.399, 20.65; HC [= Nagy 2007] 2§§13–15, 18). This mystical river Okeanos, surrounding the earth and even the seas surrounding the earth, defines the limits of the known world. Every evening, as the sun sets at sunset, it literally plunges into the fresh waters of this eternally self-recycling cosmic stream (*Iliad* 8.485), and it is from these same fresh waters that the sun rises again every morning at sunrise (*Iliad* 7.421–3; *Odyssey* 19.433–4).

After his sojourn in Hades, which is narrated in Rhapsody 11 of the *Odyssey*, Odysseus finally emerges from this realm of darkness and death at the beginning of Rhapsody 12. But the island of Circe is no longer in the Far West. When Odysseus returns from Hades, crossing again the circular cosmic stream of Okeanos (12.1–2) and coming back to his point of departure, that is, to the island of the goddess Circe (12.3), we find that this island is not in the Far West: instead, it is now in the Far East, where Helios the god of the sun has his 'sunrises', *an(a)tolai* (12.4), and where Eos the goddess of the dawn has her own palace, featuring a special space for her 'choral dancing and singing', *khoroi* (12.3–4). Before the hero's descent into the realm of darkness and death, we saw the Okeanos as the absolute marker of the Far West; after his ascent into the realm of light and life, we see it as the absolute marker of the Far East (GM 237). *In returning to the island of Circe by crossing the circular cosmic river Okeanos for the second time, the hero has come full circle, experiencing sunrise after having experienced sunset.*

This return of the hero into the realm of light and life is *a journey of a soul*. The word that I translate for the moment as 'soul' is *psukhē*, which is used in Homeric poetry to refer to the *soul* of the dead – or to the *life* of the living (GM 87–93). The journey of the soul after death replicates the journey of the sun after sunset, as we see from the wording of a death wish expressed by Penelope in the *Odyssey*: after dying, she pictures herself as journeying to the Far West and, once there, plunging into the waters of the Okeanos (20.61–5; GM 99n61). As we saw earlier, the sun is imagined as plunging into these waters at sunset and then emerging from these same waters at sunrise. So also the soul of the hero can be imagined as replicating that same cycle (GM 90–91).

But the return of the hero's *psukhē* to light and life at sunrise is not made explicit in Homeric poetry. Instead, Odysseus himself personally experiences such a return when he returns from Hades at the beginning of Rhapsody 12 of the *Odyssey*. This experience of Odysseus, by way of replicating the mystical journey of the sun, is a substitute for the mystical journey of a soul. In this way, the *nostos* of Odysseus, as an epic narrative, becomes interwoven with a mystical subnarrative. While the epic narrative tells about the hero's return from Troy to Ithaca, the mystical subnarrative tells about the soul's return from darkness and death to light and life. In lyric traditions, the mystical subnarrative of the hero's *nostos* can even be foregrounded (as in Theognis 1123–4: Nagy 1985 §69).

At the beginning of the *Odyssey*, both the epic narrative about the hero's return to his home and the mystical subnarrative about the soul's return to light and life are recapitulated in the double meaning of *psukhē* as either 'life' or 'soul':

> That man, Muse, tell me the story of that man, the one
> who could change in many different ways who he was,
> the one who in many different ways
> veered from his path, once he destroyed the sacred citadel of Troy.
> Many different cities of many different people did he see, getting
> to know different ways of thinking [*noos*].
> Many were the pains [*algea*] he suffered in his heart while
> crossing the sea,
> struggling to win as his prize his own *psukhē* and *nostos* – as well
> as the *nostos* of his comrades,
> and he saved himself but could not save his comrades, though he
> very much wanted to.
>
> *Odyssey* 1.1–6

The hero's *noos* 'thinking' (verse 3) keeps changing just as he keeps changing, adapting to the different ways that different people in different places do their own 'thinking'. In the myth foretold by the seer Teiresias about the travels of Odysseus beyond the *Odyssey*, for example, Odysseus will have to change the way he is thinking about the oar he is told to carry on his shoulder as he journeys to highlands far removed from the sea: people whose life depends on travel by sea will think of what he carries on his shoulder as an *oar*, but people whose life depends on cultivating the land will think of the same thing as a *winnowing shovel* (11.121–37; 23.265–84). Only Odysseus will know that what he is carrying on his shoulder as he goes from city to city (23.267–8) means different things depending on where he is – *either* an oar *or* a winnowing shovel (GM 212–15).

The noun *noos* means *thinking* in the sense of *being conscious, not being unconscious*: like the noun *nostos*, it is derived from the root **nes–* in the mystical sense of *returning to light and life* (Frame 1978).

The hero's *nostos* 'return' (verse 5) connects with his *noos* 'thinking' (verse 3) not only in the explicit sense of *thinking about saving his own life* but also in the implicit sense of *being conscious of returning home*. This implicit sense is encoded in the telling of the myth of the Land of the Lotus-Eaters (9.82–104). When Odysseus visits that land, those of his comrades who eat the lotus lose their consciousness of home and therefore cannot return home. The verb *lēth-* 'forget', combined with *nostos* 'return' as its object, conveys the idea of such unconsciousness (9.97, 102). By contrast, the noun *noos* 'thinking' conveys the idea of being conscious of *nostos*.

The very idea of *consciousness* as conveyed by *noos* is derived from the metaphor of *returning to light from darkness*, as encapsulated in the moment of *waking up from sleep*, or of *regaining consciousness after losing consciousness*, that is, of "coming to." This metaphor of *coming to* is at work not only in the meaning of *noos* in the sense of *consciousness* but also in the meaning of *nostos* in the sense of *returning from darkness and death to light and life*. Remarkably, these two meanings converge at one single point in the master myth of the *Odyssey*. It happens when Odysseus finally reaches his homeland of Ithaca. He has been sailing home on a ship provided by the Phaeacians, against the will of the god Poseidon, and he falls into a deep sleep that most resembles death itself (13.79–80). This sleep makes him momentarily unconscious: he 'forgets', as expressed by the verb *lēth-* (13.92), all the *algea* 'pains' of his past journeys through so many different cities of so many different people (13.90–91). Then, at the very moment when the ship reaches the shore of the hero's homeland, the morning star appears, heralding the coming of dawn (13.93–5). The Phaeacians hurriedly leave Odysseus on the beach where they placed him, still asleep, when they landed (13.119), and, once they sail away, he wakes up there (13.187). So the moment of the hero's homecoming, which is synchronized with the moment of sunrise, is now further synchronized with a moment of awakening from a sleep that most resembles death.

From this moment on, now that Odysseus has succeeded in making his return from his journeys at sea, he must succeed also in making another kind of return. That is, he must now return to his former social status as king at home in Ithaca. In the course of the twenty years that elapsed since his departure for Troy, however, the hero's social status at home has been reduced to nothing. So now, most fittingly, he disguises himself as a beggar. Now he must work his way up from the bottom of the social scale, starting from nothing. He starts by being a nobody – that is, by being a somebody who has nothing and is therefore a nobody. As a beggar, he hides his social and moral nobility as king. In this way, his interaction with the suitors of his wife exposes them as lacking in interior moral nobility despite their exterior social nobility (Nagy 1985 §§68–70).

Earlier in the *Odyssey*, the status of Odysseus as a hero of epic had already been reduced to nothing. As we saw in the tale of his encounter with the Cyclops, the return of Odysseus from the monster's cave deprives him of his past identity at Troy. His epic fame can no longer depend on his power of *mētis* 'craft', which had brought about the destruction of Troy. After his encounter with the Cyclops, Odysseus must achieve a new epic identity as the hero of his own epic about homecoming, about his own *nostos*, but, for the moment, his confidence in his power to bring about this *nostos* is reduced to nothing. He has lost his confidence in the power of his own *mētis* to devise a stratagem for achieving a *nostos*. When he reaches the island of Circe and learns that this place, though it first seems familiar and reminiscent of his own island, is in fact strange and alien and antithetical to home, he despairs (10.190–202). The wording that expresses his desperation connects the hero's *mētis* with his *nostos*:

> My friends, I am speaking this way because I do not know
>> which place is west and which place is east
> – which is the place where the sun, bringing light for mortals,
>> goes underneath the earth
> and which is the place where it rises. Still, let us start thinking it
>> through, as quickly as we can,
> whether there is still any craft [*mētis*] left. I must tell you, though,
>> I think there is none.
>
> *Odyssey* 10.190–93

The hero feels he has no craft left in him to devise a stratagem for a successful homecoming, and his despair is expressed as a feeling of disorientation. He is no longer able to distinguish between orient and occident. In effect, the hero is experiencing a loss of orientation in his *noos* or 'thinking', and this loss is currently blocking his *nostos* 'homecoming'.

The hero's despair makes his comrades despair as well: as soon as they hear the news of their leader's disorientation, they break down and cry (10.198–202) as they recall Antiphates the Laestrygonian and Polyphemus the Cyclops (199–200). The recalling of these two monstrous figures evokes not only some of the worst moments experienced by Odysseus and his comrades since they left Troy, but also some of the worst moments experienced by all the Achaeans when they were still at Troy. Strangely, when the comrades of Odysseus recall Polyphemus, the monster is described by way of the epithet *megalētōr* 'great-hearted' (10.200), and this same description applies also to Antiphates in an alternative version of a verse attested elsewhere in the *Odyssey* (10.106). Beyond these two attestations, this epithet occurs nowhere else in the *Odyssey*, whereas it occurs regularly as a conventional description of generic warriors in the *Iliad* (BA 20§4n8). Why, then, are these two Odyssean monsters described by way of an Iliadic epithet? It is relevant that Antiphates, like Polyphemus, is an eater of raw human flesh in the *Odyssey* (10.116). In the *Iliad*, the urge to eat raw human flesh is experienced by heroes in their darkest moments of bestial fury, as when Achilles says he is sorely tempted to cut up and eat raw his deadliest enemy, Hector (22.346–7). So the heroic disorientation of Odysseus in the *Odyssey* evokes nightmarish memories of heroic dehumanization in the *Iliad* (BA 20§4).

Despite such moments of disorientation for Odysseus, his *noos* 'thinking' ultimately reorients him, steering him away from his Iliadic past and toward his ultimate Odyssean future. That is, the hero's *noos* makes it possible for him to achieve a *nostos*, which is not only his 'homecoming' but also the 'song about a homecoming' that is the *Odyssey*. For this song to succeed, Odysseus must keep adapting his identity by making his *noos* fit the *noos* of the many different characters he encounters in the course of his *nostos* in progress. In order to adapt, he must master many different forms of discourse, many different kinds of *ainos*. That is why he is addressed as *poluainos* 'having many different kinds of *ainos*' by the Sirens when he sails past their island (12.184; BA 12§19n1; PH 8§30).

Even the transparent meaning of *Polyphemus* (*Poluphēmos*), the name of the Cyclops blinded by Odysseus, foretells the hero's mastery of the *ainos*. As an adjective, *poluphēmos* means 'having many different kinds of prophetic utterance', derived from the noun *phēmē* 'prophetic utterance' (as in 20.100, 105; HR [= Nagy 2003] 55–9); this adjective is applied as an epithet to the singer *Phēmios* (22.376), portrayed in the *Odyssey* as a master of the *phēmē* 'prophetic utterance' (BA 1§4n1). In the case of Polyphemus, the very meaning of his name, which conveys the opposite of the meaning conveyed by the false name of Odysseus, *Outis* 'no one', foretells the verbal mastery of the hero who blinded the monster.

After the return of Odysseus from Hades, he finds his way to the island of the Phaeacians, where he starts the process of rebuilding his epic identity from nothing by retelling for them all his experiences since he left Troy. This retelling, which extends from the beginning of Rhapsody 9 to the end of Rhapsody 12, is coterminous with the telling of the *Odyssey* up to the point where Odysseus leaves the cave of Calypso. Then, after Odysseus finishes his narration, he leaves the island of the Phaeacians and finally comes back home to Ithaca, where his narration is taken over by the master narrator of the *Odyssey*. The process of rebuilding the hero's epic identity continues in the master narration, but now the direct mode of speaking used by Odysseus in retelling his ongoing *nostos* to the Phaeacians gives way to an indirect mode, analogous to the indirect mode of speaking that he had used earlier before he made contact with the Phaeacians. Now, after the Phaeacians, Odysseus becomes once again the master of the *ainos*.

From here on, the tales Odysseus tells are masterpieces of myth-making as embedded in the master myth of the *Odyssey*. One such tale is a "Cretan lie" told by the disguised Odysseus to the swineherd Eumaeus about the Trojan War (14.192–359; BA 7§26, 12§14); at a later point in their verbal exchanges, Eumaeus refers to another tale told by Odysseus about the Trojan War (14.462–506) by describing it as a faultless *ainos* (14.508; BA 12§§14–16). As a master of the *ainos*, Odysseus keeps on adapting his identity by making his *noos* fit the *noos* of the many different characters he encounters. And the multiple *ainoi* of Odysseus can thus be adapted to the master myth of the *Odyssey*.

By the time all is said and done in the master myth of the *Odyssey*, the character of Odysseus has become fully adapted to his ultimate role as the multiform central hero of this epic, a fitting counterpoint to the monolithic central hero of the *Iliad*, Achilles. This ultimate adaptation of Odysseus demonstrates his prodigious adaptability as a character in myth. He is the ultimate multiform. That is why he is called *polutropos* at the very beginning of the *Odyssey*, that is, 'the one who could change in many different ways who he was' (1.1).

Odysseus can be all things to all people. His character undergoes the most fantastic imaginable adventures of the mind during his journeys – and the most realistic personal experiences when he finally reaches his home in Ithaca. The psychological realism of this hero's character when we see him at home with himself tempts us to forget about the fantastic journeys of his *psukhē* in alien realms. Our sense of the familiar blocks our sense of the unfamiliar. Our mentality as modern readers invites us to see Odysseus at home as "reality" and Odysseus abroad as "myth," as if the myth of the hero contradicted the reality of the hero.

Such a split vision is a false dichotomy. The reality of Odysseus is in fact the myth of Odysseus, since that myth derives from the historical reality of Homeric poetry as a medium of myth. The reality of the myth is the reality of the medium that conveys the myth to its listeners over time.

Even the Ithaca of Odysseus is real only to the extent that it was recognized as real by those who heard epics about Odysseus over time. For listeners of the *Odyssey* in the classical period of the fifth century BCE, this Ithaca of Odysseus was the island then known as Ithakē. In earlier periods, on the other hand, the Ithaca of Odysseus may well have been what is now the western peninsula of the island now known as Kefalonia. This peninsula, now known as Paliki, had once been an island west of Kefalonia (Bittlestone 2005, Bordewich 2006), and such a prehistoric Ithaca fits the Homeric description of the hero's home as the westernmost of all the other islands nearby (*Odyssey* 9.25–6).

In their greatest moments of epic action, the heroes of Homeric poetry show their true nature. They are larger than life, superhuman, especially in their interactions with gods. Not only in Greek epics but also in cognate epics such as the Indic *Mahābhārata*, the superhuman status of heroes depends on their special relationship with divinity and with the sacred (EH §§70–73).

The age of epic heroes is a sacred world of myth that must be set apart from the everyday world of the present. The mythology of epic heroes must distance itself from the present by holding on to a remote past far removed from the world of listeners hearing the glories of heroes. To hold on to such a past, this mythology must show not only that an age of heroes existed once upon a time but also, just as important, that such an age does not exist any more. It must privilege what is past over what is present, and it must remake that past into a sacred age of heroes.

Homeric poetry, as the primary epic mediator of myth, remakes the perceived past into such a sacred age by way of deliberately privileging realities perceived as belonging to a past age of heroes. Such realities can be tested by comparing them with corresponding realities ascertained independently by way of empirical approaches.

One such empirical approach to Homeric poetry is provided by the discipline of archaeology (Snodgrass 1987). The external dating criteria provided by the existing archaeological evidence point to many centuries of evolution for the oral poetic tradition that culminated in the Homeric *Iliad* and *Odyssey*. A major point of convergence for archaeology and the study of Homeric poetry is the story of the Trojan War – or, more accurately, Trojan Wars – and the degree to which the *Iliad* and the *Odyssey* reflect the realities of the late second millennium BCE (Sherratt 1990).

Homeric poetry, in the process of evolving as an oral tradition, reflects the realities of Greek civilization all the way from the middle of the second millennium BCE to the seventh century BCE and perhaps even later. This formulation, which takes into account the testimony of 1) Homeric poetry as an ongoing system of communication and 2) the successive layers of archaeological evidence, represents an evolutionary model (Sherratt 1990).

The archaeological evidence is supplemented by the important testimony of the so-called Mycenaean Linear B tablets, the earliest attestation of the Greek language in writing (on the factor of writing in general, see Woodard 1997). It can be argued that the Linear B documents show a cross section, dating back to the Mycenaean civilization of the second millennium BCE, of a phase of overall Greek civilization that decisively shaped the evolution of the Homeric tradition (Palmer 1979; on the name of Achilles as a reflex of "Mycenaean epic," see HTL 131–7).

Another empirical approach to Homeric poetry is provided by the discipline of art history. The evolving traditions of visual arts, going as far back as the middle of the second millennium BCE and even beyond, can be compared as parallel to the evolving traditions of the verbal arts as represented by Homeric poetry. A most dramatic illustration is the cross section provided by the miniature frescoes of Thera (Morris 1989). In these frescoes (see Figure 12 for an example), which are dated well before the middle of the second millennium BCE, we can find representations of various themes that match corresponding themes in Homeric poetry, and the resulting visual–verbal correspondences can lead to the conclusion that at least some of these Homeric themes, such as the "tale of two cities" as represented on the Shield of Achilles in *Iliad* 18, were well over a thousand years old before they were finally recorded in written versions of the Homeric *Iliad* (for more on the Shield, see HR 72–87).

Yet another empirical approach to Homeric poetry is provided by the discipline of historical linguistics (Nagy 1974; Muellner 1976; Frame 1978; see in general Watkins 1995). The application of this approach to the diction of oral poetry yields new techniques of reconstruction, where the terminus of a given reconstruction backward in time can stop short of a "proto-language" phase. (See, for example, HTL 131–7 on the name of Achilles, where the terminus of the reconstruction stops short of "proto-Indo-European"; West 1988 and 1992 surveys the evidence provided by linguistics for the derivation of Homeric poetry from Indo-European poetic antecedents; for similar conclusions but different perspectives, see Nagy 1974, supplemented in PH Appendix.) Such reconstructions of Homeric poetry from Indo-European models need to take into account the lateral influence of Near Eastern languages and civilizations, especially in the eighth and seventh centuries BCE (EH §§21–30).

SUGGESTED READING

Of lasting value for the study of Homer and Greek myth are the chapters on the Homeric *Iliad* and *Odyssey* in Lord 1960. Also valuable are the elaborations to be found in Lord 1991 and 1995. On Homer and the myths of the Cycle: Burgess 1996. On the interweaving of Homeric poetry and myth: Frame 1978, Slatkin 1991, Muellner 1996, Lowenstam 1997, Levaniouk 2000, Dué 2002, Wilson 2002, and Walsh 2005.

3: HESIOD AND GREEK MYTH

Roger D. Woodard

For the goats of Nahunta's hill,
My sometime Muses unawares.

INTRODUCTION

Writing in the second century BC, the Roman playwright Lucius Accius advanced the case – as reported, though disapprovingly, by Aulus Gellius in his *Attic Nights* 3.11.3–5[1] – that Hesiod's work had preceded that of Homer. Accius based his argument on what he deemed to be certain Homeric assumptions predicated upon Hesiodic revelation. Modern scholarship, while commonly assigning Hesiod to Homer's eighth century BC, more typically – though not universally[2] – reverses Accius' relative chronological ordering.

Whether it be something approaching a real-world life description or, as a number of scholars are now more inclined to advocate, only the construction of a literary persona, a biographic sketch of the poet named Hesiod has emerged from antiquity – chiefly gleaned from the works attributed to him.[3] His father is said to have been a native of the Aeolian port city of Cyme on the northwest coast of Asia Minor. Economic deprivation led the father to resettle in Greece – in the Boeotian village of Ascra, lying in Mt. Helicon's Valley of the Muses – the place that Hesiod would call home. The poet Hesiod presents himself as a herder and farmer – indeed, he tells that it was while he shepherded his flock on the slopes of Mt. Helicon that the Muses came to him and first inspired him with poetic art.

Whatever we make of him biographically, Hesiod and his poems undeniably occupy a seminal position in the history of Greek mythic tradition. Not only does the epic poet called Hesiod stand at the onset of the literary recording of that tradition, but also, of all ancient authors, it is this Hesiod whose word-weaving reveals to us most clearly the warp and woof of that tapestry that Greek myth is. Two well-preserved epic poems are attributed to him – the *Theogony* and *Works and Days* – and these will occupy most of our attention in the pages that ensue.

There is a third work, likewise well-preserved, to which the name Hesiod has been attached since antiquity – to wit, the *Shield of Heracles*, a poem about the strongman Heracles, the design of his fabulous shield (seemingly influenced by Homer's description of the shield of Achilles in *Iliad* 18 [or both influenced by some other, unattested, tradition(s)]), and his combat with Cycnus, a notorious robber and son of Ares. Many present-day scholars, however, consider this work to be the product of a somewhat later and less talented literary hand.

Yet if we are inclined to view "Hesiod" in terms of literary persona and, more than that, as a poet whose works experienced myriad shiftings (recompositions) in oral performance, works that evolved as their performance was taken up by increasingly farther-flung performers – becoming Panhellenic[4] – then the evaluation of the "authenticity" of the *Shield* takes on new nuances. Nagy's observations in this regard are instructive and illuminating:

> With the important added factor of pan-Hellenic diffusion, the successive recompositions of Hesiodic poetry could in time become ever less varied, more and more crystallized, as the requirements of composition became increasingly universalized. Of course the rate of such crystallization, and even the date, could have been different in each poem or even in different parts of the same poem. From this point of view, we can in principle include as Hesiodic even a composition like the *Shield of Heracles*, though it may contain references to the visual arts datable to the early sixth century. Scholars are too quick to dismiss this poem as not a genuine work on the basis of the dating alone, and then it becomes all the easier for them to underrate its artistic qualities on the grounds that it is merely an imitation of Hesiod.[5]

For all too pragmatic reasons having to do with paper and ink, however, the *Shield of Heracles* will be excluded from examination in the present work. Other poems that have been assigned Hesiodic authorship – poems less well preserved – will be encountered in passing in the discussions that follow.

THE *THEOGONY*

Whence each of the gods came into existence, or whether all of them existed for all time, and what sort of form they had, the Greeks did not know until recently – "just yesterday or the day before", so to speak – for I suppose that the time of Hesiod and Homer was four hundred years before my own – and no more than that. It was they who taught the Greeks of the genealogy of the gods (*theogoniē* [θεογονίη]) and who gave to the gods their names, specified their honors and skills, and revealed their forms.

Herodotus 2.53

Hesiod's *Theogony* – as the historian Herodotus tells us – is a tale of the "genealogy of the gods." It was perhaps long after Hesiod's own day that the poem acquired the phylogenetic title by which we know it – in the Hellenistic era, a nomenclatural contribution of the Alexandrian scholars.[6] Regardless, it is indeed a work about origins, and no less a cosmogony (an account of the origin of the cosmos) than a theogony.

Hesiod's is not, however, the only *Theogony* known from ancient Greece. Theogonies and cosmogonies, composed in verse or prose, are attributed to several literati dating from the seventh century BC on. The earliest of these are preserved in fragments, if at all.[7] Especially significant is the theogonic tradition associated with Orpheus, earliest preserved in a remarkable document called the Derveni papyrus, a carbonized scroll recovered from the remains of a Macedonian funeral pyre, "our oldest surviving Greek manuscript."[8] The composition of the papyrus text appears to date to the late fifth century BC, but the Orphic theogony that it reports can probably be assigned to the sixth century.[9]

In the section that ensues, we will examine the structure and content of Hesiod's *Theogony* in some detail. There are fundamentally three reasons for lavishing this descriptive attention on the *Theogony* (and, to a lesser extent, on *Works and Days*). First, limitations of space and considerations of purpose necessarily prohibit the telling of most of the tales that constitute the primary source material for the interpretative essays contained within this volume – but the reader is due some first-hand exposure. Second – and following on from the first – the tale here related may justifiably be labeled the most fundamental of all Greek mythic traditions – the starting point, as it were, for all that follows. And third, for discerning the formative elements and processes of Greek myth – to the extent we are able to do so – the structural details are crucial.

Structure and Content of the Theogony

Hesiod's epic song of emerging gods and cosmos forms a twisting genealogical tree within which are nested numerous mythic traditions, some rehearsed at length, some merely mentioned. The poem's 1022 lines[10] unfold as follows.

Typical of early Greek performance poetry, the *Theogony* begins with a prefatory hymn (lines 1–115). The deities upon whom the poet calls in this instance are the Muses, goddesses of artistic inspiration, daughters of Zeus. Within this proem, Hesiod invokes the goddesses not once, but three times it seems: "Let us begin our singing with the Heliconian Muses, who possess the great and holy Mount Helicon" (lines 1–2); and then, as though after a false start, "O Hesiod, let us begin with the Muses, who hymning father Zeus on Olympus delight his great heart" (lines 36–7); and a third time, as he approaches the end of the proem, "Hail, children of Zeus, give me lovely song; praise the holy race of deathless gods who ever are" (line 104).[11]

As the theogony proper begins, Hesiod sings of the appearance of the first of the primeval beings (lines 116–22). "At the very first, Chaos came to be"; the Greek term *Chaos* (Χάος) denotes a gaping void – in this context, she is a massive emptiness of dark. Next appear Gaea, the 'Earth'; Tartarus, a murky nether space far beneath the earth; and Eros, 'Desire'.

Both Chaos and Gaea then spontaneously produce offspring (lines 123, 126–32). From Chaos are born Erebus 'Darkness', and Nyx 'Night', (who in turn couple to produce Aether, the bright upper air, and Hemera 'Day'; lines 124–25). Gaea gives birth to Uranus 'Heaven', Urea 'Mountains', and Pontus 'Sea'.

Hesiod now shifts his attention to the great primeval couple Earth and Heaven – for Gaea has taken her first-born son, Uranus, to be her consort – and begins his narration (lines 133–210) of a myth of divine sovereigns who in succession are dethroned. The children that Gaea and Uranus produce are many and diverse, beginning with the twelve Titans: Oceanus, Coeus, Crius, Hyperion, Iapetus, Theia, Rhea,

Themis, Mnemosyne, Phoebe, Tethys, and Cronus. Gaea then bears the three one-eyed Cyclopes and the three Hecatoncheires, hundred-armed and fifty-headed. But Uranus hates his children, and as they each are born he hides them away within the depths of Earth. Cronus comes to the aid of his mother, and brandishing a toothed sickle of adamant that Gaea has crafted, submissive to her schemes, Cronus emasculates his unsuspecting father, Uranus, as he prepares to have intercourse with Gaea. The blood that drips from the castrated Uranus impregnates Gaea, and she conceives the Erinyes, armored giants, and the tree nymphs called Meliae. Cronus tosses his father's severed genitals into the sea and from them will spring the goddess Aphrodite. With the emasculation of Uranus, Cronus moves to center stage as divine sovereign.

Hesiod returns to his genealogies. As Chaos had spontaneously produced offspring, now her daughter Nyx does likewise (lines 211–32). Among the fifteen children she bears – mostly fell creatures of dark and trouble – are numbered Cer 'Destiny', Geras 'Old Age', Moerae 'Fates', Nemesis 'Retribution', and Eris 'Strife', who herself parthenogentically produces fifteen similar beings – such as Ponus 'Toil', Machae 'Wars', Pseudea 'Lies', and Horkus 'Oath' "who brings the greatest ruin to men on earth, when willingly they swear falsely." Gaea also takes her son Pontus as a consort; and together they produce Nereus, an "Old Man of the Sea," as well as Thaumas, Phorcys, Ceto, and Eurybia (lines 233–9).

A long heterogeneous section follows next, framed by the genealogy of the descendants of Nereus and his siblings (i.e., the children of Gaea and Pontus), into which are fitted fleeting references to mythic heroic deeds (lines 240–336). Nereus and Doris (one of the Oceanids; see below) produce fifty sea-nymph daughters, the Nereids, whom Hesiod names individually. Notable among the other descendants of Gaea and Pontus are those in the lineage of Phorcys (another "Old Man of the Sea") and his sister Ceto, who together produce monstrous offspring – the Graeae, Gorgons, and Echidna, among others – from whom, in turn, many more monsters and fantastic beings descend: Pegasus, Geryoneus, Orthus, the Hydra, and the Sphinx, to name but a few of those enumerated in this Catalog of Monsters (lines 270–336).

The poet now turns our attention back to the Titans (children of Gaea and Uranus), to their mating with one another (or with some other divine being), and to the offspring they produce (lines 337–452). Oceanus and Tethys produce sons, the rivers of the world, and 3,000 nymph daughters, the Oceanids. To Hyperion and Theia are born a son, Helios (the sun), and two daughters, Selene (the moon) and Eos (the dawn). Crius and Eurybia (daughter of Gaea and Pontus) have children – Astraeus, Pallas, and Perses. Through the marriage of Eos and Astraeus, Hyperion/Theia and Crius/Eurybia possess grandchildren in common (among which are the winds, Zephyrus, Boreas, and Notus), as do Oceanus/Tethys and Crius/Eurybia through the marriage of Styx (an Oceanid) and Pallas. Here Hesiod briefly interrupts his genealogical strains to praise Styx and her children who will side with Zeus (not yet born) in his coming conflict with the Titans. An even briefer return to genealogy brings the record of the Titans Phoebe and Coeus' children – Leto and Asteria – and the latter's daughter by Perses, Hecate. The poet seizes upon the genealogical mention of Hecate to hymn her praises, and in thirty-eight lines sets out a remarkable theological description of the goddess – a beneficent deity providing many advantages to humankind, quite distinct from the threatening and infernal Hecate of a later period.[12]

"And Rhea submitted herself to Cronus and bore illustrious children": Hestia; Demeter; "golden-sandaled" Hera; Hades, "whose heart knows no pity"; "loud-rumbling Earthshaker" (i.e., Poseidon); and Zeus, "father of gods and men" – so Hesiod continues with his Titanic genealogy and sets the stage for the second episode in his succession myth (lines 453–506). As Rhea births each of her children, Cronus swallows the infants, having been warned by Gaea and Uranus that his fate is to be overthrown by his progeny, just as Cronus himself had toppled his own father. But just before Rhea delivers Zeus, her sixth child, Gaea and Uranus assist her in slipping away to Crete. There Zeus is born and placed in Gaea's care, while Rhea presents to the expectant Cronus a stone wrapped in infants' clothing, which he promptly swallows, thinking he has ingested Rhea's newest babe. When Zeus is grown up (seemingly in a year's time), Gaea tricks Cronus into vomiting up the five swallowed children – as well as the stone, which Zeus sets up at Pytho as an object of veneration (in the second century AD, the Greek author Pausanias [10.24.6] writes of seeing the stone at Delphi and of how the Delphians anoint it with olive oil daily and drape raw wool over it at festival times). Zeus then releases his "father's brothers," the Cyclopes, who had remained bound within earth, and in gratitude they present him with his distinctive weapon – thunder and lightning bolt.

Interrupting the succession myth, Hesiod briefly returns to genealogical strains to rehearse the offspring of the Titan Iapetus and his consort Clymene (an Oceanid) – Atlas, Menoetius, Prometheus, and Epimetheus – only to segue quickly into the tale of Prometheus, his deceit, and his fate (lines 507–616). Prometheus tries to trick Zeus by setting out two portions of a sacrificed ox – one of bones and one of rich meat, but each disguised to hide the actual contents, the lesser portion of bones appearing more sumptuous, and vice versa. Crafty Prometheus invites Zeus to choose the portion he desires; the other will go to mortal men. Zeus, seemingly duped (actually not, says Hesiod) chooses the bones; in his anger at the deception, Zeus withholds fire from humankind. But fire will be provided to humans nonetheless – Prometheus steals it for them, carrying it off in a fennel stalk. As punishment for the theft, Zeus has Hephaestus create the first woman, Pandora (whom Hesiod names in *Works and Days*,[13] not in *Theogony*), the matriarch of womankind and a great bane sent upon men, by Hesiod's misogynistic reckoning.

The poet switchbacks to his succession myth with the saga of the Titanomachy (lines 617–735). Hesiod's account begins in the tenth year of a war that Zeus and his siblings, the Olympians – "the gods, givers of good fortune," (*theoi, dōtēres eaōn* [θεοί, δωτῆρες ἐάων]) – are waging against the "Titan gods" (*Titēnes theoi* [Τιτῆνες θεοί]). By Gaea's counsel, Zeus releases the Hecatoncheires – still locked away within earth – reviving them with nectar and ambrosia. These enter the melee on the side of the Olympians and, launching gigantic boulders with their hundred arms, pound Mt. Othrys, the citadel of the Titans. In near apocalyptic language, Hesiod describes how the attack of the Olympians, the counterattack of the Titans, and, most conspicuously, Zeus's unrestrained lightning-bolt bombardment shake creation to its core. The *coup de grâce* is delivered by the Hecatoncheires, whose barrage of 300 boulders brings the Titans to their knees and their fate – imprisonment beneath the earth in murky Tartarus, as far from earth as earth is from heaven (namely, that space through which a bronze anvil would plummet in ten days' time).

Hesiod's verses on the Titans' place of confinement provide a bridge to a long description of the Netherworld (lines 736–819).[14] The poet tells, *inter alia*, of the alternating coming and going of Nyx 'Night' and Hemera 'Day' from that subterranean place; the children of Nyx who live therein and venture forth at night – Hypnos 'Sleep' and Thanatos 'Death'; and the hound, Cerberus, who guards the gates of Hades. Styx, river of the Netherworld, is here reintroduced, and the poet sings of her dread waters, by which the gods of Olympus swear their oaths (and the fate that befalls one who is untrue).

The Netherworld described, the poet returns to his narration of the Greek succession myth (lines 820–68). Tartarus fathers a child on Gaea – a monstrous hundred-headed dragon, Typhoeus. The creature has been conceived in order to usurp Zeus, so that he might claim for himself the kingship "of immortals and mortals"; their combat is furious, rivaling (if not surpassing) that of the Titanomachy in cosmic intensity as Zeus unleashes the full force of his lightning attack. In the end, like the Titans before him, Typhoeus is vanquished and cast into Tartarus.

Hesiod then turns to a short description of a particular set of the progeny of Typhoeus: the ill winds (lines 869–80; of the monster's multiheaded brood by Echidna – Orthus, Cerberus, the Lernaean Hydra, the Chimaera – Hesiod has already spoken [lines 304–22, a portion of the Catalog of Monsters]). Distinct from the favorable Zephyrus, Boreas, and Notus (the sons of Eos and Astraeus), these winds bring destruction on land and sea.

It is now, the poet recites, that the immortals – following the council of the seemingly fickle Gaea[15] – prevail upon Zeus to reign over them as sovereign god (lines 881–5). So he does, dividing "their honors among them." Here Hesiod must hint at a tradition similar to that one preserved by Homer (*Iliad* 15.187–93) – the cosmos (and honor) was divided by lot between Poseidon, Hades, and Zeus, who receive respectively the sea, the gloomy Netherworld, and the sky; all three share the earth and Olympus.[16]

With the succession myth all but completed, Hesiod segues again into genealogical strains, rehearsing the wives of the heavenly sovereign and their progeny (lines 886–929). Zeus' first wife is Metis, an Oceanid. But with her mention, the theme of usurpation and succession again arises: warned by Gaea and Uranus that Metis would bear a daughter strong and wise like her father, and a son who would become *theōn basileus kai andrōn* (θεῶν βασιλεὺς καὶ ἀνδρῶν) 'king of gods and men' in his place, Zeus preemptively swallows Metis. The daughter, however, Metis already carries within her womb; and that girl-child – Athena – will be born from Zeus' body, emerging from his head. Wife two by Hesiod's accounting is the Titan Themis, and among the children she produces with Zeus are the Horae 'Seasons'. Zeus' third wife is another Oceanid, Eurynome; their daughters are the Charities (or Graces), beauty embodied. Demeter, Zeus' sister, is his fourth wife; born to them is a daughter, Persephone. Zeus next weds Mnemosyne, and their children are the nine Muses. The twin deities Artemis and Apollo are borne by Zeus' sixth wife, Leto. Last of all, Zeus takes Hera as his wife; their children are Hebe, Ares, Eileithyia, and Hephaestus (the last-named conceived parthenogenetically).

Passing through the section of the *Theogony* described immediately above, the reader is commonly said to cross into the literary domain of an author other than Hesiod. Many scholars have contended that some later poet or poets (pseudo-Hesiod(s)) have reworked or replaced the original ending of the poem.[17] The exact location of the authorial boundary is, however, a matter of disagreement: West, for example, argues for drawing the line after the Metis passage (line 900); Northrup has contended for placing it at line 935.[18] But again, Nagy's words are instructive:

> Critics have also noticed that the conclusion of the *Theogony* at verses 901–1020 is formally and even stylistically distinct from the previous parts of the poem. But this part is also functionally distinct from the rest, and we may note in general that different themes in oral poetry tend to exhibit different trends in formal – even linguistic – development. To put it another way: different contexts are characterized by different language. An explanation along these lines is surely preferable to a favorite scenario of many experts, in which the *Theogony* was somehow composed by a combination of one Hesiod and a plethora of pseudo-Hesiods.[19]

To return to our survey of the *Theogony* – the verses following the narration of Zeus' wives constitute a genealogical miscellany, a matter-of-fact poetic enumeration of the marriages and amorous affairs of various deities, and of progeny born consequent thereto. Thus, Poseidon, Ares, Aphrodite, Zeus, among several other deities, make an appearance in the initial portion of this section (lines 930–62).[20] The inventory is then interrupted by six lines (963–8): the first two are crafted as a kind of broad conclusion to all that has preceded, while the next four form a new proem – an invoking of the Muses to sing of goddesses and mortal men whom they have loved. This is indeed the subject of the longish set of enumerations that then follows – the mortal paramours of Demeter, Eos, Thetis, Aphrodite, Circe, and several more – and their children, "appearing like the gods" – among them famed heroes such as Memnon, Achilles, and Aeneas (lines 969–1018). Another conclusion (lines 1019–20) then ends this inventory, and yet another invocation follows (lines 1021–2): a calling upon the Muses to sing of mortal women – providing an introduction to the ensuing *Catalog of Women*, a compendium of genealogic accounts of female mortals who joined in love with the gods and the offspring they produced. While the *Catalog* (or

Ehoiai) was appended to the *Theogony* in antiquity and Hesiod deemed to be its author, present-day scholarship, again, often dates the work to a post-Hesiodic period.[21]

HESIOD: A VIEW TO THE EAST, PART I

Scholars have long had some level of awareness of similarities and inter-action between the cultures of early Greece and those of the Near East (here defined broadly to include Egypt, in addition to Anatolia, Syria-Palestine, Mesopotamia, and Iran). Throughout the nineteenth and much of the twentieth century, however, Classics seemed to have lost sight of archaic Greece's situation within a Near Eastern world.[22] But with twentieth-century discoveries of large bodies of Near East-ern documentary evidence (and, in several cases, the decipherment of the languages in which they were composed); the recognition of an "orientalizing phase" in Greek art; and archaeological discoveries of a Greek presence in the east, and vice versa,[23] it became increasingly clear that early Greek culture had evolved, in part, under the influence of its neighbors at the eastern end of the Mediterranean, and beyond.

One of the most remarkable and compelling pieces of evidence demonstrating Near Eastern influences was provided by the discovery of "kingship-in-heaven" myths among, especially, the Hittites (/Hurri-ans) and Babylonians. The similarity of these accounts to the Uranus–Cronus–Zeus succession myth of Hesiod's *Theogony* is indisputable.[24]

The Hittite (/Hurrian) Kingship in Heaven Myth

Among the many thousands of documents recovered during twentieth-century excavations at the Turkish village of Boğazköy, site of ancient Ḫattuša, the Hittite capital,[25] is a set of clay tablets preserving an account of the storm-god Teššub's rise to power and attempts to unseat him from the throne of heaven. Though the texts are recorded in the Indo-European language of the Hittites, the traditions they preserve plainly show themselves to have been acquired from the non-Indo-European Hurrians of eastern Anatolia – the principal deities, such as Teššub, being in fact Hurrian.[26] Somewhat complicating the picture, however, is the presence of Mesopotamian gods and goddesses as well (Anu, Ea, et al.), to which we shall return below. Bearing in mind the Hurrian "origin" of this mythic cycle, the tradition will herein often simply be designated as "Hittite," for the sake of expediency.

The documentation of the Hittite myth spans several distinct texts, or "songs,"[27] the best known and best preserved (though still somewhat fragmentary) of which are Song of Kumarbi and Song of Ullikummi, and it is these that will occupy the focus of our attention here – though not exclusively so, for the entire cycle appears to consist of no fewer than five episodes. On the basis of various considerations internal to the text, Hoffner[28] argues the probable relative order of these to be (1) Song of Kumarbi; (2) Song of LAMMA; (3) Song of Silver; (4) Song of Ḫedammu; and (5) Song of Ullikummi. A summary telling of the Songs of Kumarbi and Ullikummi ensues in the next two paragraphs – and, following that, a brief look at the LAMMA, Silver, and Ḫedammu songs.

The Song of Kumarbi begins as follows: Long ago in the earliest ages, Alalu is king in heaven. In the ninth year of his reign he is deposed by his cupbearer, Anu, and flees down to the "dark earth." Anu then reigns as king in heaven for nine years, only to be deposed by his own cupbearer, Kumarbi, the son of Alalu. Anu flees up toward the sky but is chased and caught by Kumarbi, who bites off Anu's genitals. But having swallowed Anu's seed, Kumarbi is impregnated with several of Anu's offspring – most notably Teššub, the storm-god; his advisor, Tašmišu; and Aranzaḫ, the Tigris River. At "birth" these children exit from their confinement within Kumarbi's body. During the delivery process, Kumarbi cries out to Ea (Mesopotamian god of wisdom), demanding "his child" so that he may eat him: "I will eat up Teššub. I will smash him like a brittle reed."[29] Though the text is fragmented, a stone also plays a role in this episode, which Kumarbi seemingly attempts to ingest or (/and) spits out. The ending of the Song of Kumarbi is lost, but it most likely related Teššub's ascension to the heavenly throne. In any event, at the outset of the Song of Ullikummi, Teššub, the storm-god, is clearly presented as the reigning king of heaven.

As the Song of Ullikummi opens, Kumarbi is depicted as plotting to overthrow Teššub. A usurper is required, and Kumarbi contrives to engender one by copulating with a massive rock (with dimensions measured in miles). The offspring of this union is a stone child, born from the rock, delivered by the "fate goddesses and the mother goddesses," and given the name "Ullikummi" by his father. Kumarbi commands the gods called the Irširra-deities to take the newly born Ullikummi to the Netherworld (the "Dark Earth"), where they affix him to the right shoulder of Ubelluri, the giant who supports heaven and earth. Kumarbi's stone progeny grows at a remarkable rate (one *AMMATU* per day, one IKU per month[30]). By the fifteenth day of its life, the stone has grown to be a giant of cosmic proportions:

> When the fifteenth day arrived ... the Stone was high: it was standing like a shaft with the sea coming up to its knees. The Stone came out of the water. In height it was like a [...]. The sea reached to the place of its [...] belt like a garment. The Basalt was lifted up like a. ... In the sky above it meets temples and a *kuntarra*-shrine.[31]

The Sun God of the Sky sees the monster and reports his sighting to Teššub. Then accompanied by his brother Tašmišu and sister Šauška, Teššub goes out to see the stone giant for himself and is overwhelmed with despair. Šauška (written in Hittite texts with the Akkadogram[32] *IŠTAR*, the name of the Mesopotamian love-goddess) attempts to overcome the monster with her seductive charms and song – all to no avail: Ullikummi can neither see nor hear. Teššub and the other gods subsequently attack the stone giant but are defeated and routed. Counseled by Tašmišu, Teššub seeks out Ea, god of wisdom, and the "tablets bearing ancient words." In response, Ea pays a visit to the Atlas-like Ubelluri, and seeing the stone giant Ullikummi mounted on his right shoulder, Ea calls for the "primordial gods" to bring out of storage the copper cutting tool that had been used in the earliest ages to sever heaven from earth. With that tool, Ullikummi is now sawed from the shoulder of Ubelluri, and Teššub attacks the stone giant. The lost ending of the song undoubtedly recounted the final victory of the storm god over his challenger for the throne of heaven.

The intervening songs of the cycle, though fragmentary, would appear to follow fundamentally the same thematic pattern seen in the Song of Ullikummi: Kumarbi engenders offspring for the purpose of driving Teššub from the throne of heaven, but Teššub successfully defends (or regains) his throne. The pattern is not, however, fully attested in the surviving fragments of these texts, as we shall see.

The legible portion of the Song of LAMMA begins with the god LAMMA fighting against Šauška and Teššub and gaining the throne of heaven with the assistance of Ea and Kumarbi (who perhaps should be interpreted as LAMMA's father, in keeping with the blueprint of the cycle). Ea, however, finds the boastful and contemptuous LAMMA to be an unacceptable king and deposes him from the throne of heaven. As the tablet ends, Teššub and his vizier NINURTA are attacking and seemingly vanquishing LAMMA.

In the partially preserved Song of Silver,[33] a being that personifies silver is identified as a son of Kumarbi by (apparently[34]) a mortal woman. This Silver appears to have taken the throne of heaven from Teššub, who, as in the Song of Ullikummi, seems to be overwhelmed by despair at his formidable opponent. In the surviving fragments, there is no account of Teššub's return to the throne of heaven.

The Song of Ḫedammu survives only in several fragments. Ḫedammu, a monstrous serpent, appears to be the offspring of Kumarbi, probably borne by Šertapšuruḫi, daughter of the Sea God – who, in any event, seems to offer her to Kumarbi, describing her in terms reminiscent of the description of the great rock that Kumarbi impregnates with Ullikummi. Ḫedammu is a usurper – his purpose, the taking of the throne of heaven. Teššub seemingly intends to meet the serpent in combat; however, in the text as we have it, Šauška seduces the creature with song and beauty (the same strategy she employs against Ullikummi, though successfully so in this instance).

HITTITE AND GREEK PARALLELS   When the Kumarbi cycle – particularly the Song of Kumarbi and the Song of Ullikummi – is compared to Hesiod's succession myth, the overall parallel structure of the two traditions (Hittite [/Hurrian] and Greek) and the individual bits of parallelism are obvious. "Cognate" figures and events can be readily identified. (i) Greek Uranus, 'heaven', is matched by Hittite (/Hurrian) Anu – who is in origin the Sumerian (Mesopotamian) god of the sky. (ii) As Uranus is emasculated by Cronus, using a toothed sickle, so Anu is emasculated by Kumarbi, who uses his own teeth for the job; that is, Cronus equals Kumarbi.[35] (iii) Cronus swallows his children as Rhea bears them, holding them imprisoned within his gullet; Kumarbi carries within his own body several children, the offspring of Anu.[36] (iv) Cronus swallows a stone, intending to ingest his son Zeus; Kumarbi exclaims that he wants to eat his son Teššub, and soon after, in the damaged Hittite text, Kumarbi has a stone in his mouth, a stone that will be set up upon the ground as an object of worshipful adoration – like the Delphic stone set up by Zeus. (v) As Cronus regurgitates his offspring – it was mother Gaea's doing, says Hesiod – so Kumarbi "births" those gods entrapped within himself[37] (in the damaged text the "[ ] Fate Goddesses" assist in delivery; as the Fate Goddesses are routinely accompanied by the Mother Goddesses, we likely should restore their names in the gap preceding "Fate Goddesses"). (vi) Zeus – the sky-god, armed with thunderbolts – vanquishes Cronus to become divine sovereign; just so, Teššub, the storm-god, defeats Kumarbi

(= Cronus) and takes the throne of heaven: Teššub corresponds to Zeus.[38]

One subtle difference between the Greek and Hittite traditions involves the nature of sovereign succession. In Hesiod's account, the reigning king is overthrown by his own son; in the Hittite myth, the reigning king is overthrown by the son of the previous king – two families thus alternating on the throne (i.e., Alalu$_1$ – Anu$_2$ – Kumarbi$_1$ – Teššub$_2$).[39] This distinction leads on to another interesting observation. As Hoffner notes, the struggles for the throne in the Hittite account pit two fundamentally different types of beings against each other – celestial gods against netherworld gods:

> In Kumarbi's camp are Alalu, Kumarbi's vizier Mukišanu, the Great Sea God, the Sea God's vizier Impaluri, the Sea God's daughter Šertapšuruḫi, Ḫedammu, Daganzipa (Earth), Silver, Ullikummi, the Irširra-deities, and probably Ubelluri (who lives under the earth).
>
> In Teššub's camp are Anu, Tašmišu/Šuwaliyat, Ḫebat, Ḫebat's maidservant Takiti, Šuaška/ISHTAR, the divine bulls Šeri and Ḫurri, the Sun and Moon Gods, the War God Aštabi, Teššub's brother the Aranzaḫ River (= the Tigris), the Mountain God Kanzura, KA.ZAL, and NAM.ḪE.[40]

The structure is paralleled in Hesiod's Theogony: two different sorts of divine beings oppose each other – the gods of Mt. Olympus and the Titan gods. Olympus is already in Hesiod's work practically equated with the celestial realm of heaven,[41] as in the poet's description of Zeus' furious and decisive onslaught against the Titans (*Theogony* 687–99):

> No longer Zeus withheld his warrior-rage, but now at once
> His breast was filled with wrath, and all his might
> Revealed; and down *from heaven and Olympus* Zeus
> Came hurling lightning – time and time again; the bolts   690
> Flew thick from out his sturdy hand, with thunderbolt and
>   lightning,
> One – then another – rolling out a fearsome flame.
> And life-endowing earth did bellow – burning up all round,
> The boundless wood howled loud with fire all round.
> The ground all seethed, and boiling up were ocean's streams 695
> And fruitless sea. A torrid blast closed round
> The earth-born Titans; flame unspeakable stretched to

The upper air; though strong, their eyes went blind
From flashing glare of thunderbolt and lightning-flame.[42]

On the other hand, there are the Titans. In this same scene, Hesiod identifies them as "earth-born" – chthonian – the Titans who will become denizens of the Netherworld after being vanquished by Zeus. While the etymology of Greek *Titēnes* [Τιτῆνες] 'Titan' is uncertain,[43] the idea that they were originally chthonian in opposition to the "heavenly" Olympians is common; thus, West writes of the Titans:

> There can be no certainty that they were ever worshipped: they may have existed from the beginning as 'the former gods' 'or the gods of the underworld', a mythological antithesis to the gods of the present and of the upper world.[44]

This parallelism persists as the Hittite myth continues to unfold in the Song of Ullikummi. A mammoth rock conceives, impregnated by the netherworld Kumarbi, in order to bring forth a monstrous stone giant that will remove Teššub from the kingship of heaven. Hesiod tells how "gargantuan Earth" (*Gaia pelōrē* [Γαῖα πελώρη]; *Theogony* 821) conceives, impregnated by Tartarus – that primeval being and netherworld locale – in order to bring forth a monstrous dragon to depose Zeus and in his stead "rule over both mortals and immortals" (*Theogony* 837). In both traditions, the reigning king of heaven has a desperate fight on his hands, though the two differ in the telling of that tale. Hesiod speaks of Zeus' quick and definitive response to Typhoeus – a powerful, unrelenting attack that boils the seas and melts the earth. In the Hittite version, on the other hand, Teššub realizes victory only after he has suffered a great setback in battle, subsequent to which Ullikummi is weakened, being cut off from his perch on the shoulder of Ubelluri, by the intervention of other gods – notably Ea and the "primeval gods."

Though Hesiod makes no mention of it, there is, nonetheless, an interesting Greek comparandum at this point, if not strict parallelism. In his second-century compendium of Greek myth, the *Bibliotheca*, the mythographer Apollodorus (1.6.3) writes that in his fight against Typhon (as Apollodorus names the monster), Zeus brandishes a sickle of adamant, the same – or same type of – cutting implement that Cronus had used to castrate Uranus when he was joined in love with Gaea – a primordial severing of heaven (Uranus) from earth (Gaea). Just so, in the Song of Ullikummi, the same instrument – the primeval copper cutting tool – is used to undercut Teššub's enemy, Ullikummi, that had been used originally to divide heaven from earth. But while the use of the copper saw *follows* Teššub's setback, and somewhat evens the score, the adamantine sickle *results in* a setback for Zeus, as Typhon is able to wrestle it away from Zeus and with it cut the tendons from Zeus' hands and feet. The hobbled king of heaven is then helplessly imprisoned in the dragon's cave in Cilicia, but is saved through the intervention of other deities – Hermes and Aegipan, according to Apollodorus[45] (compare the intervention of Ea et al. in the Song of Ullikummi) – who recover the removed tendons and fit them back into Zeus' hands and feet. Zeus then renews his attack and vanquishes Typhon, though only after yet more divine intervention – those goddesses called the Fates trick the monster into tasting certain fruits that rob him of strength.[46]

The Hittite episodes of chthonic LAMMA, Silver, and Hedammu – intervening between Teššub's defeat of Kumarbi (= Zeus' defeat of Cronus and the Titans) and the appearance of the rock-born Ullikummi (= the appearance of Earth-born Typhoeus) have no counterpart in Hesiod's *Theogony*: Hesiod relates no repeated attempts to storm the throne of heaven and wrench kingship away from Zeus.[47] Once again, however, Apollodorus shows tighter agreement with the Hittite tradition than does Hesiod. Prior to the birth of Typhon, writes Apollodorus (1.6.1–2),[48] Zeus and heaven are attacked by yet other earthborn creatures:

> Vexed by the fate of the Titans, Gea gave birth to Giants, fathered by Uranus. They were without equal in the enormity of their bodies and were unbeatable in might; their appearance was terrible – hair fell long from their head and chin, and for feet they had the scales of dragons.[49]

The giants assail heaven, hurling rocks and flaming trees. A confederacy of Olympian deities and the mortal hero Heracles counterattack the giants. After relating several individual duels in this Gigantomachy, Apollodorus brings the episode summarily to a close with an affirmation of the victorious defense of heaven: "and all the others Zeus destroyed, hurling his thunderbolts; and Heracles shot them all with arrows as they perished."

The Babylonian Enūma Eliš

The earliest discovered fragments of the Babylonian creation account, the Enūma Eliš ('When on high' – the opening words of the epic), came to the attention of scholars late in the nineteenth century; the succeeding decades brought discoveries of additional cuneiform tablets containing portions of the work. The date of its composition remains a matter of disagreement: some scholars assign the work to the early second millennium BC, during the Old Babylonian period; currently, however, it is more commonly dated to the late second millennium, that period when the worship of Marduk, protagonist of the epic, became prominent. The Enūma Eliš was recited annually as a part of the Babylonian New Year's festival.

That portion of the tale most pertinent to the task at hand goes like this.[50] In the beginning only Apsu, the fresh waters (male), and Tiamat, the sea waters (female),[51] existed. But eventually, within their waters, the divine pair Laḫmu and Laḫamu ('silt', masculine and feminine) take shape; these then engender Anshar and Kishar. The latter pair produce a son Anu, said to be the equal of Anshar and the rival of his fathers. Continuing the crescendo of potent progeny, Anu in turn engenders a son, Ea, called the "master of his fathers." These most recent generations of the gods behave raucously, disturbing Tiamat ("they troubled Tiamat's belly," 1.23). Apsu and Tiamat take counsel; encouraged by his vizier, Mummu, Apsu determines that the offending deities must be destroyed. Ea, however, acts preemptively: he causes a sleep to come upon Apsu, whom he slays as Apsu slumbers, and he imprisons Mummu. Having vanquished his enemies, Ea and his wife Damkina produce a son, Marduk – a being of perfection, surpassing the members of previous generations.

Anu, Marduk's grandfather, then stirs up storms that distress Tiamat as well as certain other gods who have aligned themselves with her and who urge her to respond and to avenge her slain consort, Apsu. Preparations are made for war – preparations that include Tiamat (here [1.132] called "Mother Ḫubur," a name frequently applied to the river of the Netherworld[52]) producing eleven monstrous offspring (dragon and serpent, *inter alios*), and the appointing of the god Kingu (her consort) to be commander, to whom Tiamat gives the "Tablets of Fate" – a symbol of power.[53]

Discovering Tiamat's intentions, Ea becomes somber and angry, but then calming himself goes to his grandfather Anshar to alert him of the advancing army. Anshar's reaction is likewise one of despondence; he sends Ea and then Anu to try to stop Tiamat, but both in turn retreat before Tiamat's force. In deep distress, Anshar announces to the gods that Marduk shall be their deliverer. Marduk accepts the challenge upon the condition that he be given supremacy among the gods.

Being summoned, Laḫmu and Laḫamu join Anshar; and after a banquet, the gods set up for Marduk a throne and bestow on him kingship over all.

Marduk ventures out to meet Tiamat in battle. He ensnares her with a net, beside which the four winds (East, West, North, and South) have been stationed; and as Tiamat stretches wide her mouth, Marduk drives in a storm that prevents her mouth from shutting. As the winds distend her belly, Marduk shoots an arrow through Tiamat's gaping jaws and kills her. Marduk ensnares and imprisons the gods who had followed Tiamat – he binds the eleven monstrous creatures (which will later be transformed into statutes and stationed at the gate of Ea's house) and Kingu, from whom Marduk seizes the Tablets of Fate. He crushes Tiamat's skull, severs her arteries and splits her body into two halves, with one of which he creates the heavens, filling them with luminous bodies – constellations, moon, sun – demarcating night and day. From the remainder of her body he fashions features of earth: from her head he forms mountains, with the Euphrates and Tigris flowing from her eyes, and so forth. In a communal act of reaffirmation, all the gods then acknowledge Marduk as king.

After announcing plans for the construction of his city, Babylon, Marduk orchestrates the creation of humankind. The rebel Kingu is brought forth and executed. Out of the blood that flows from his severed veins, Ea creates the first humans.

Though the structures of the Babylonian epic clearly constitute a less strict parallel to Hesiod's *Theogony* than do those of the Kumarbi cycle, fundamental motifs common to the Greek and Hittite myths recur in the Enūma Eliš – with the Babylonian account showing, in some instances, even closer agreement with Hesiod. (i) In both the *Theogony* and the Enūma Eliš, for example, the first beings to exist are deified geophysical entities that will engender ensuing generations: Chaos, Gaea, Tartarus; Tiamat, Apsu. (ii) In all three traditions a series of divine sovereigns unfolds generationally – with each generation in some way surpassing the preceding, and the series culminating in the birth of the preeminent heavenly king: Zeus, Teššub, Marduk. (iii) All entail the mutilation or murder of some primeval male deity: Cronus and Kumarbi emasculate Uranus and Anu respectively; Ea slays Apsu; moreover, in the Greek and Babylonian traditions (a) the injured party is caught off guard (Uranus preparing to have intercourse with Gaea, Apsu asleep under Ea's spell) and (b) the perpetrator of the act (Cronus, Ea) is both the son of the Sky (Uranus, Anu) and the father of the protagonist

(Zeus, Marduk). (iv) Primeval mothers – Gaea and Tiamat – produce monstrous offspring that will battle against the preeminent rulers of heaven – Zeus and Marduk – in an effort to secure cosmic rule for the offspring or the consort of that mother – Typhoeus and Kingu; the monster(s) is/are defeated, after which the gods affirm, or reaffirm, the sovereignty of the vanquisher – the Olympians urge Zeus "to be king and to rule the immortals," the gods assembled round Marduk bestow on him the title *Lugaldimmerankia* ('king of the gods of heaven and the Netherworld'). Still other parallels can be adduced;[54] these are sufficient to give the reader the picture.

The Theogony of Dunnu

The Hittite Kumarbi cycle and the Babylonian Enūma Eliš are not the only examples of Near Eastern traditions paralleling Hesiod's kingship-in-heaven myth. Also from Babylonia comes the much shorter and only partially preserved theogony of the city of Dunnu, dated to the Late Babylonian period.[55] The work has been judged particularly interesting, vis-à-vis Hesiod's *Theogony*, for the order of appearance of certain of the primeval beings. " ... In the beginning ... " – so the fractured opening lines declare – there was Ḫain and Earth, who then produce two children: Sea, a daughter – who is created by an act of plowing – and Amakandu, a son, conceived through intercourse. After being seduced by his mother and killing his father (and so becoming sovereign of Dunnu), Amakandu marries Sea, his sister, and they produce a son, Laḫar. This Laḫar, who kills his own father – thus becoming the new sovereign – has intercourse with his mother as well, and by her engenders a son – whose name is lost – and a daughter, River. These two likewise consort incestuously, and the nameless son kills both of his parents – and so the generational saga of parent-killing and sibling-marrying continues.

Investigators have called attention to the fact that *Sea* – who is seemingly born out of the *Earth* (via ploughing) – appears in this theogony before *River*. In a similar fashion, Hesiod's *Theogony* presents Pontus, the *Sea*, as borne parthogenetically by Gaea 'Earth'; while Oceanus – the *River* that flows around the rim of earth and the father of rivers – is born afterward. The pronounced incestuousness of the Dunnu myth (extending beyond the generations enumerated here) has also been compared with the numerous incestuous sibling relations among the Titans; the Babylonian mother–son sexual unions are especially singled out, as both Greek Pontus ("Sea" again) and Uranus have intercourse with their mother Gaea.[56]

Sanchuniathon's Phoenician History

In some respects, this is the most intriguing of the Hesiodic *Theogony*'s Near Eastern counterparts. A purported Phoenician version of the kingship in heaven myth is recorded in Greek by Herennius Philo – commonly called Philo of Byblos (first/second century AD). Philo claims that his notably euhemeristic work is the translation of an ancient Phoenician account preserved by Sanchuniathon,[57] a "polymath and ardent researcher" (FGrH 790 F 1 §24),[58] reported to have lived prior to (or about the time of) the Trojan war. Prefacing his Phoenician tale, Philo makes mention of two sources (which are possibly intended to be one and the same) that this Sanchuniathon discovered and utilized: (i) the works of a still more ancient figure named Taautos (whom the Egyptians call Thoth and the Greeks Hermes), said to be the inventor of the symbols and practice of writing; and (ii) certain hidden texts of (the temples of?) Ammon, written in an arcane script.[59]

The fundamental structure of Sanchuniathon's theogony is, by now, a familiar one, involving four successive generations, stretching from a founding figure who plays a comparatively minor role to a sovereign storm-god. Philo begins his rendition of the Phoenician tradition with "a certain Elioun" ('high one', a term known from various Semitic documents, including the Hebrew Bible[60]) and his female partner Berouth. They produce a son Epigeios (the Autochthon), whom they would later call Uranus, and a daughter named Ge (i.e., Gaea). Upon the death of his father Elioun (killed in some encounter with wild beasts), Uranus replaces him as sovereign and takes Ge, his sister, to be his wife; together Uranus and Ge produce four children – El, Baitylos, Dagon, and Atlas, the first three of whom are independently known to be Phoenician gods.[61] El – whom Philo also names as Cronus – eventually turns against his father, Uranus, avenging his mother, Ge: Uranus has abused her sexually and tried to destroy her children. Cronus and his allies make war on Uranus and depose him; Cronus takes the throne. One of the trophies of this intergenerational war is the concubine of Uranus, whom Cronus gives to his brother Dagan for a wife. The concubine, already pregnant by Uranus, then gives birth to a son Demarous, whose name appears to occur in Ugaritic – the language of a West Semitic people closely related to the Phoenicians – as an epithet of the storm-god Baal, or Hadad.[62] The deposed Uranus eventually tries to regain his throne by trickery and by force, but his efforts are unsuccessful; in the thirty-second year of his reign, Cronus ambushes and emasculates Uranus, his father and former sovereign. In time, Cronus assigns sovereignty to Demarous – whom Philo at that point in his tale identifies as "Zeus Demarous or Hadad,[63] king of gods" – and to the goddess Astarte.

Even from this brief summary of the theogony attributed to Sanchuniathon, it is clear that Philo of Byblos was well acquainted with Greek mythic traditions. He, in fact, accuses the Greeks – and Hesiod explicitly – of having taken over their myths from other peoples – dramatically modifying adopted traditions for the sake of entertainment (FGrH 790 F 2 §40):

> Thus Hesiod and the celebrated poets of the epic cycle fabricated their own theogonies, gigantomachies, titanomachies and castrations, and in popularizing these they trumped truth.

Hesiod antedated Philo by almost a millennium; even so, this is not simply a case of Philo committing the same sort of literary pilfering of which he accuses the epic poets. While the *Phoenician History* is undeniably infused with Greek mythic influences, scholars currently tend to view Philos' theogony as resting upon a native Phoenician tradition,[64] though the form in which Philo knew that tradition perhaps dates to the Hellenistic period rather than the second millennium BC.[65] Especially noteworthy are the several points at which Philo's account departs from Hesiod's, and in doing so agrees with the other Near Eastern versions summarized above. For example – there are four generations of sovereign figures rather than three; El (= Cronus = Kumarbi) fights with and emasculates his predecessor Epigeios (= Uranus = Anu), paralleling the Hittite tradition, as opposed to the Greek with castration occurring without a physical struggle; and so on.[66]

Hesiod's Near Eastern Sources

I began the preceding section by noting that the Phoenician theogony is in some ways the most intriguing of the Near Eastern parallels to Hesiod's kingship-in-heaven tradition. How so?

The historical Greeks are descendants of Indo-Europeans who made their way into the Balkan Peninsula – probably arriving in the last quarter of the third millennium BC – relative newcomers to the Mediterranean and geographically positioned on the cusp of the ancient Near East. Hesiod's theogonic tale of a succession of divine sovereigns – Uranus, Cronus, Zeus – is almost certainly not an inherited Indo-European tradition, but, as various scholars have sought to demonstrate, one borrowed from the Near East (just as Philo of Byblos claims) – as seems practically self-evident in light of the above examination of widespread parallel traditions, attested from an early time.[67] The Hittites of Anatolia, possessing a well-attested version of this tradition, are themselves an Indo-European people, though, as we saw, the Hittites acquired their kingship-in-heaven tradition from their non-Indo-European neighbors to the east, the Hurrians, whose gods – the storm god Teššub et al. – play leading roles in the myth.

The cultural indebtedness of the Greeks to the Phoenicians is well known. Witness the alphabet: that most utilitarian – and, possibly, most significant – of Greek gifts to modernity is an adaptation of the consonantal script of the Phoenicians. In other words, it was the Phoenicians who, in a certain sense (and only in a certain sense), taught the Greeks how to write.[68] While we would doubtless look too myopically were we to seek a single conduit by which Near Eastern influence came upon the Greeks, the Phoenicians must be judged likely candidates in matters of cultural transference within and out of eastern Mediterranean regions. Of those places where the Greeks could have acquired the Phoenician script, Cyprus is probably the most likely locale.[69] With its permanent and thriving Greek and Phoenician presence in the early first millennium BC and its mercantile, cultural, and political intercourse with Anatolia, Egypt, Syria-Palestine, and Mesopotamia,[70] Cyprus must be considered a no less likely locale for the Greek acquisition of other Near Eastern ideas – including, especially, mythic traditions – and, hence, the Phoenicians of Cyprus the most active of catalysts in the process.[71] Perhaps Philo of Byblos was not so far off the mark when he imagined it was from the Phoenicians that Hesiod and the epic poets acquired their theogonies and castration tales.

THE *WORKS AND DAYS*

Consider how helpful the noble poets of old have been.
Orpheus taught us mystic rites and to abstain from bloodshed,
Musaeus showed us remedies for sickness – oracles too, and

Hesiod the working of the earth, the seasons of the crops, the
    turning of the soil.
And god-like Homer – by what did he gain honor and fame,
Except by the useful teaching of the deployment, valor, and
    arming of men?

Aristophanes, Frogs 1030–36

"The working of the earth"; "the seasons of the crops"; "the turning of the soil" – at least superficially, this is the stuff of which Hesiod's
Works and Days is made – though not uniquely so, in two respects. First,
the poet is credited with having also composed the *Great Works*, a poem,
preserved only in fragments, that must have similarly treated agricultural
matters, and the also fragmentary *Astronomy*, which self-evidently dealt
with astronomical and calendrical phenomena. Second, *Works and Days*
is not only a farmer's manual and almanac but also a repository of practical advice and moral precepts. The *Great Works* likewise contained such
admonitions, as did – and presumably even more so – Hesiod's all-but-
lost poem entitled the *Precepts of Chiron*, presented as the teachings of
the centaur Chiron to his young pupil Achilles.

The didactic *Works and Days*, composed in the same epic
hexameters familiar from the *Theogony* and Homer's *Iliad* and *Odyssey*,
is couched in the form of instructions ('I would speak [*mutheomai*
(μυθέομαι)] truth' [line 10]) to Perses, Hesiod's wayward brother –
profligate, greedy, lazy, and, thus, in danger of becoming (and perhaps
already) destitute – and to an anonymous body of kings,[72] who are
willing to manipulate justice for the sake of gain. At the heart of
Hesiod's expositions are the opposing fundamental notions of *dikē*
(δίκη) and *hubris* (ὕβρις)): *dikē* is often translated as 'justice' – the sense
of Hesiod's usage being a more specifically legal than general one –
or, in some Hesiodic contexts, the legal process of determining justice,
that is, 'judgment';[73] its oppositional term, *hubris*, denotes 'violence'
or, more concretely, 'an outrage'.

Hesiod portrays his advice and warnings to Perses as being occasioned by a conflict in which the two brothers are embroiled, a conflict
stemming from the division of their inheritance (lines 27–41). Perses
received his share but has thrown it after judges, "gift-gobbling kings,"[74]
seemingly hoping thereby to acquire greater wealth through litigation;
now he is on the threshold of impoverishment and has already been
begging from Hesiod, who will assist him no more (see lines 393–7).
Hesiod urges Perses to let the two of them settle their own differences
by that straight *dikē* which is from Zeus.[75]

Hesiod admonishes Perses to work – to avoid that Eris ('Strife', one of the parthenogenetically produced daughters of Nyx named in the *Theogony*) who leads to "evil war" and who entices Perses to loiter at the courts, gawking at legal wrangling – but to follow, instead, that other Eris (also a daughter of Nyx, contrastively paired with her homonymous sister) who moves humans to strive to labor gainfully (lines 11–41; Hesiod similarly knows a good and bad Zelos 'Envy' [see below]).

And why must humankind work? It is ultimately because, reveals the poet, Prometheus stole fire for mortals (*Works and Days* 42–9):

> The gods keep hid from men the means of life;
> For else in just a single day you'd easily do work to have
> What's needed even for a year – a year of indolence no less.
> And right away you'd hang the rudder up above the hearth;   45
> The fields by labor-hardy mules and oxen tilled would
>   disappear.
> But Zeus, instead, he hid it, roused to anger in his heart,
> Because Prometheus deceived him, crooked-cunning one;
> So Zeus wrought baneful sorrow on mankind.[76]

Hesiod has here returned to the misogynistic tale of his *Theogony* – the sending of the first woman, Pandora, to men as punishment for Prometheus' theft – though in the *Works and Days* he relates the myth in fuller form (lines 60–105), telling how Pandora opened a jar containing all ills and how these escaped into the world so that humankind's former life of Utopian ease was transmuted into one of suffering and toil.

Keeping to the theme of the deterioration of humanity, the poet immediately follows up his Pandora episode with the narrative, *logos* (λόγος), of the five ages of mankind (lines 106–201). The first was a golden age, a generation of mortals created by the gods in that time when heaven's king was Cronus: their long lives were idyllic – free of sorrow and toil, enjoying earth's spontaneous bounty, beloved of the gods. After the passing of this age, the gods created a silver generation of mortal beings, inferior to the first: their childhood was long – a hundred years – but as adults their lives were short, being given to deeds of wrongdoing and irreverence toward the gods. Zeus put an end to the silver-age beings and created a third generation – a bronze race, said not to be "the same as" the preceding silver age (though not explicitly identified as inferior). Theirs was a mighty race of bronze-armored warriors, but by their war-making they brought themselves to extinction. With their passing from the earth, Zeus created a fourth generation, one of heroic demigods (*hēmitheoi* [ἡμίθεοι]) – the warriors of the Theban and Trojan wars – some of whom had died in those conflicts, but others of whom Zeus blessed with an idyllic existence in the Elysian Isles (where Cronus, released from his imprisonment in Tartarus, ruled as their king, according to some manuscripts of *Works and Days*). These noble heroes were immediately succeeded by the race of iron, the people of Hesiod's own day – and he rues his lot, wishing he had either "died before or been born after" that age (line 175). Of the four metallic generations that Zeus created (setting aside the race of heroes), it is this one on which Hesiod lavishes the most attention.[77] The poet begins his description in the present tense, slipping quickly into a prophetic future. Their lot is one of labor and sorrow, though they will be a mixed group – good being mingled with evil, as the poet has been interpreted to say. In time they will experience yet greater degradation – the newborn will have gray locks; family member will turn against family member, and friend against friend; violence and wickedness will prosper and be praised. Zelos 'Envy' – that is, the bad Zelos, associated with the bad Eris (as opposed to the good Zelos, affiliated with the good Eris)[78] – will be ever present:

> And Zelos shall walk with each and every wretched man,   195
> Cacophonous and evil-reveling, and hateful-faced.
> And then Olympus bound, both Nemesis and Aidos,[79]
> Their lovely frames enrobed in cloaks of white,
> To join the race of deathless gods they'll pass
> From wide-stretched earth, and humankind forsake. . . .   200

In the end, the iron race will stand helpless in the face of evil and perish at Zeus's hand. The finality of Hesiod's prophecy is palpable: there is no suggestion that the race of iron will continue upon the earth; presumably, only gods last – yet Hesiod conceives of the possibility of having "been born after" (and to this we shall return).

Hesiod then appends to the myth of the five ages a tale meant for the unjust kings – the fable (*ainos* [αἶνος]) of the hawk and the nightingale (lines 202–12). There was a hawk that snared a nightingale within his claws. The hawk soared into the heavens with its prey; and as the helpless songbird shrieked, the hawk cruelly spoke a *muthos* (μῦθος):

> Oh why the screams, you wretch? One stronger holds you now.
> And you shall go where'er I take you, songstress though you be;

A meal of you I'll make – or maybe set you free – it's up to me.
That one's a fool who'd choose against the mightier to
    stand;   210
He goes in want of victory and suffers shame no less than pain.

The poet's message to the kings seems truncated; even so, his insinuation of their arrogant intimidations cannot have been lost on his
audience.[80]

HESIOD: A VIEW TO THE EAST, PART 2

Does Hesiod's *Works and Days* also bespeak a Greek indebtedness to
the Near East? Undoubtedly so – in both particulars and generalities.
West, Perry, and other scholars[81] have observed, for example, that Greek
fables, of which Hesiod's hawk-and-nightingale is the earliest known,
find parallels in older, Babylonian fables – even exact matches at times,
as in the case of the Babylonian fable of the gnat and the elephant,
about which Perry,[82] translating Ebeling,[83] writes, "In this case one
may almost speak of the translation of a Babylonian original into Greek
or at least of a paraphrase." The genre of the fable in Mesopotamia is
not, however, unique to the Babylonians; many are preserved among the
literary remains of the Sumerians, the first Mesopotamian civilization
to develop a means of writing. Among the Sumerian fables, Wolcot[84]
has identified two that are close in sense to Hesiod's: one tells of a lion
that has seized a squealing pig, the other of a butcher preparing a pig,
also squealing, for slaughter.

> A pig which was about to be slaughtered by the pig-butcher
> squealed. (The butcher said:) "Your ancestors and forebears
> walked this road, and now you too are walking it, so why (?)
> are you squealing?"[85]

In each instance the helpless pig's fate lies in the hands – or jaws – of its
captor, despite the victim's annoying cries. With Hesiod's hawk-and-
nightingale fable, addressed as it is to the kings, one might also compare
the Sumerian fable of *The Heron and the Turtle*.[86] A turtle, depicted as
a quarrelsome, trouble-making predator, upends the nest of a heron,
spilling her young into the water, and then tears at the bird's head with

his claws, so that blood streams down upon her breast. The heron cries and pleads her case before "the king," the god Enki:

> Let my king judge my case, and give me verdict! Let Enki
> judge my case, and give me verdict!

The bird lays out her complaint to the king, who responds by commanding his minister Isimud to build some device, presumably for the bird's protection.[87]

Fables constitute only one element of the broader genre of didactic, or wisdom, literature – a genre well known from the ancient Near East. This is not to suggest that it is a genre unknown elsewhere – certainly collections of gnomic sayings and ethical exhortations are widely attested among the world's peoples, both ancient and modern. West[88] (following in part Chadwick and Chadwick[89]) provides a succinct but illuminating survey of wisdom literature worldwide. While, as one would expect, fundamental cross-cultural similarities are detectable globally, *Works and Days* shows a particular closeness to ancient Near Eastern wisdom traditions. West observes:

> Hesiod's poem does...show closer formal similarities to
> Near Eastern texts than to any of those from other litera-
> tures that were surveyed.... If we did not know that it came
> from Greece, and we had to try and place it on the basis of
> its resemblances to other works of wisdom, we should be
> inclined to put it somewhere near the ancient Near East.[90]

Indeed, one familiar with the book of Proverbs in the Hebrew Bible – the Christian Old Testament – can hardly read *Works and Days* without being reminded of that Biblical text; this is most especially so of the long section that immediately follows Hesiod's hawk-and-nightingale fable, beginning with lines 213–214a,

> But you, O Perses, attend to *dikē*, and do not nurture *hubris*;
> For *hubris* is an evil to the lowly man

and extending through line 382,

> And if your heart within your breast should long for wealth,
> Then do these things and work – in work after work.

The book of Proverbs is quite likely the best known of Near Eastern wisdom texts to most readers of this *Companion*. Portions of the Biblical text appear to date to the eighth century BC – Hesiod's own century. There are, however, many far older, and generally less familiar, examples of wisdom literature from the Near East. The genre is well attested within the Sumerian literary corpus (dating as early as the mid-third millennium BC). Some examples are known from Sumerian-language texts, such as *The Instructions of Šuruppag*, a collection of proverbial instructions said to have been shared by an ancient man of wisdom, Šuruppag, with his son Zi-ud-sura, long, long ago. Consider, for instance, the partially preserved lines 22–7:

> You should not loiter about where there is a quarrel; you should not let the quarrel make you a witness. You should not let (?) yourself... in a quarrel. You should not cause a quarrel;... the gate of the palace.... Stand aside from a quarrel, ... you should not take (?) another road.[91]

Other Sumerian wisdom texts are preserved in Akkadian (the languages and dialects of the Assyrians and Babylonians) translations of Sumerian originals.

Among several Akkadian wisdom works that have not been demonstrated to be translations from Sumerian is the *Counsels of Wisdom* (second half of the second millennium BC), a text that is impressionistically close to the spirit of *Works and Days*, showing several particular similarities, though of a sort common to Near Eastern didactic tradition. Let us consider as a single example *Works and Days* 706, 717–21:

> Beware the vengeance of immortal gods.[92]   706
> Don't ever dare to mock a man for baneful soul-
> Destroying poverty, a thing that's given by immortal gods.
> A sparing tongue – it is the treasure best of mortal kind,
> And greatest pleasure, moving in a way that's measured.   720
> If evil you should speak, you yourself will soon be spoken
>   evil of.

With the above compare the following lines from *Counsels of Wisdom*:

> [ ] the lowly, take pity on him   (56)
> Do not despise the miserable and [ ],
> Do not wrinkle up your nose haughtily at them.

One's god will be angry with him for that,
It is displeasing to Šamaš,[93] he will requite him with evil.
Hold your tongue, watch what you say.   (26)
A man's pride: the great value on your lips.
Insolence and insult should be abhorrent to you.
Speak nothing slanderous, no untrue report.
The frivolous person is of no account.[94]

Similar maxims find expression in the Biblical book of Proverbs, as, for example, in the following verses:

He who oppresses the poor insults his Maker,   14:31
He who is generous to the needy honours him.
He who sneers at the poor insults his Maker;   17:5
And he who gloats over another's ruin will answer for it.
Gossip can be sharp as a sword,   12:18
But the tongue of the wise heals.
A clever man conceals his knowledge,   12:23
But a stupid man broadcasts his folly.
When you see someone over-eager to speak,   29:20
There will be more hope for a fool than for him.[95]

In Egypt, wisdom texts – constituting a well-developed genre, typically dubbed *Instructions* – span the vast gulf of time that stretches from the Old Kingdom (c. 2300 BC) to the beginning of the Christian era.[96] Compare with the several texts cited above the following lines (24.9–17 and 22.7–16, respectively) from the Egyptian wisdom text called the *Instruction of Amen-em-Opet*, a work (perhaps composed c. 1200–1000 BC) that shows particular closeness to both Hesiod's *Works and Days* and to the Biblical book of Proverbs:[97]

Do not laugh at a blind man nor tease a dwarf
Nor injure the affairs of the lame.   (10)
Do not tease a man who is in the hand of the god,[98]
Nor be fierce of face against him if he errs.
For man is clay and straw,
And the god is his builder.
He is tearing down and building up every day.   (15)
He makes a thousand poor men as he wishes,
(Or) makes a thousand men *as overseers*,
When he is in his hour of life.

Sit thou down at the hands of the god,
And thy silence will cast them[99] down. . . .
Empty not thy belly [of words] to everybody,
Nor damage (thus) the regard for thee.
Spread not thy words to the common people,
Nor associate to thyself one (too) outgoing of heart.
Better is a man whose talk (remains) in his belly   (15)
Than he who speaks it out injuriously.[100]

Another Egyptian didactic text that has close affinities with Hesiod's *Works and Days* is the *Instructions of Ankhsheshonqy*. Languishing in prison after being falsely accused of treason, Ankhsheshonqy, a priest of the sun-god Pre', etches lamentations and words of wisdom on potsherds that he regularly sends off to his son. The work is later than the *Instruction of Amen-em-Opet*: the papyrus document that preserves the Ankhsheshonqy text perhaps dates to the period of the Ptolemies (the Macedonian rulers of Egypt following the death of Alexander the Great in the fourth century BC); composition of the text would be somewhat earlier. In this instance, however, it could conceivably be the case that the similarities are due to the influence of *Works and Days*, or other Greek sources, on the Egyptian text; strains of influence from the wisdom text called the *Words of Ahiqar* can also be detected.[101]

A widely disseminated work known from versions preserved in various languages of the Near East, the *Words of Ahiqar* is earliest attested in a fifth-century BC Aramaic document.[102] It tells the tale of one Ahiqar – depicted as a minister of the Assyrian monarchs Sennacherib (eighth to seventh centuries BC) and, in turn, his son Esarhaddon – who was unjustly accused of sedition and sentenced to death. His life was secretly spared by his executioner for favors previously rendered, and he was eventually vindicated and restored. Not least of the ways in which the work is reminiscent of Hesiod's *Works and Days* is its blending of maxim and fable.

The Five Ages of Mankind, Part 1

Hesiod's story of the five ages requires a closer look. For some scholars, such as West, it belongs securely under the rubric of Near Eastern – or at least Asian – influence:

There is one major case of material in the *Works and Days* which must be supposed to have come to Greece from the east: the Myth of Ages. It is a myth that could be told for its own sake, or to serve different purposes, and though it suits Hesiod's purpose well enough, it has no necessary connection with wisdom literature.[103]

Abstracting from the Hesiodic tale its essence, West concludes:

> When we subtract from Hesiod's narrative all that seems to have been put in to do justice to "folk memory," we are left with the doctrine of four metallic races, each of which is more sinful than its predecessor and quicker to age. The account of the last race is largely cast in the form of a prophecy. The scheme has striking oriental parallels.[104]

Let us consider the parallel eastern traditions, which emanate from both southwest and south Asia.

THE BOOK OF DANIEL The second chapter of the Biblical Book of Daniel preserves an account of a disturbing vision that came to the Babylonian monarch Nebuchadnezzar (seventh to sixth centuries BC) in a dream. The king required not only that his own Chaldean wise men interpret the vision, but that they first clairvoyantly tell it to him. Unable to perform the preliminary assignment, the Babylonian sages were sentenced to death – though in the end they would be delivered through the actions of a young Jewish deportee to Babylon by the name of Daniel, to whom the interpretative task next fell. Daniel (2:32–6) announces the vision: Nebuchadnezzar had dreamed of a colossal statue:

> The head of the image was of fine gold, its breast and arms of silver, its belly and thighs of bronze, its legs of iron, its feet part iron and part clay. While you looked, a stone was hewn from a mountain, not by human hands; it struck the image on its feet of clay and shattered them. Then the iron, the clay, the bronze, the silver, and the gold, were all shattered to fragments and were swept away like the chaff before the wind from a threshing-floor in summer, until no trace of them remained. But the stone which struck the image grew into a great mountain filling the whole earth. That was the dream.

And what of the interpretation? The vision was prophetic: the head of gold symbolized king Nebuchadnezzar and, continues Daniel (2:39–41):

> After you [Nebuchadnezzar] there shall arise another king-dom, inferior to yours, and yet a third kingdom, of bronze, which shall have sovereignty over the whole world. And there shall be a fourth kingdom, strong as iron; as iron shat-ters and destroys all things, it shall break and shatter the whole earth. As, in your vision, the feet and toes were part potter's clay and part iron, it shall be a divided kingdom.

This last kingdom – which receives the most attention of all as Daniel continues to unfurl his prophecy – having feet mixed with clay, "shall be partly strong and partly brittle" (2:42): the interpretation – "so shall men mix with each other by intermarriage, but such alliances shall not be stable: iron does not mix with clay" (2:43). The kingdom that is symbolized by the hardest metal shall prove to be the weakest. It shall be destroyed by the stone, which, reveals Daniel, is the kingdom of God: "It shall shatter and make an end to all of these kingdoms, while it shall endure forever" (2:44).

The parallelism between the Daniel account and Hesiod's tale of the metallic generations is striking indeed – both in general outline and in particulars. A succession of kingdoms or generations – gold, silver, bronze, iron – will culminate in the prophetic destruction of the last. The silver stratum is explicitly stated to be weaker than the gold. To the last, the iron race or kingdom, most attention is paid: explicit reference is made to its "mixed" nature and to familial dysfunctionality. While the differences in theological particulars cannot be overstated, in both traditions the iron element will be doomed by divine intervention; what survives are the Olympian deities themselves in the prophetic tradition that Hesiod knows – it is the kingdom of God that will continue forever in Daniel's prophetic message. As West (1997) 319 insightfully observes: "The rhetorical treatment of the disasters of the last age implies that the myth came to Greece not just as a raw story outline but in literary form, that is to say in poetic form." The question that remains to be answered is, of course, "Whence came this *logos* to Greece?"

Before going on, we should take notice that there is no stratum in Daniel's account that corresponds to Hesiod's age of heroes, sandwiched between the bronze and iron ages. Practically all classical scholars are in agreement that the heroic age represents an interpolation – a structural component that Hesiod, or Hesiod's Greek source, introduced into the traditional tale of a sequence of metallic races in order to harmonize that *logos* with essential Greek traditions about the Theban and Trojan wars. The heroes of those great expeditions, as West puts it,

> ...had to be accommodated in any survey of man's past. The position they occupy in Hesiod follows from the view that they were the people that preceded us ([line] 160), coupled with an unwillingness to identify them with the Bronze race – perhaps because the epics showed them as users of iron.[105]

IRAN A similar Iranian account is preserved in two Zoroastrian works: the *Vahman Yašt* and the *Dēnkard*, Pahlavi (Middle Iranian) versions of two books of the *Avesta* (the collection of sacred Zoroastrian texts) that have not survived in their earlier Avestan (Old Iranian) form.[106] The prophet Zardušt (the Pahlavi form of the Avestan name *Zarathuštra*, the founding figure and namesake of the Zoroastrian religion), requested of his supreme deity Ohrmazd (Avestan *Ahura Mazdāh*) the gift of immortality, whereupon the god sent to Zardušt a dream-vision. As he slept the prophet saw "the root of a tree," and on this there grew four branches – one of gold, one of silver, one of steel and one of mixed iron. After Zardušt awoke, Ohrmazd revealed to him the meaning of the prophetic dream: the four branches represent four successive ages. According to the accounts of *Vahman Yašt* 1.2–5 and *Dēnkard* 9.8 (both based on the *Sūdkar Nask*), the golden branch symbolizes that period in which Zardušt and Ohrmazd converse with one another, a time when righteousness flourishes and demonic forces are held in check. The Pahlavi sources have woven brief historic details into the description of the silver and steel ages, and these differ between the two accounts, though in neither text are these periods presented as eras of moral decline. The age of mixed iron is one of gathering evil and of religious apostasy – a time when honor and wisdom (*Dēnkard* 9.8.5) will take their leave of Iran. With the passing of the fourth age, the "millennium of Zardušt" comes to an end.

A variant account of the metallic ages follows in chapter two of the *Vahman Yašt* (2.14–22). Again Zardušt is said to dream of a tree, but in this instance, one with seven branches representing the periods of the millennium: gold, silver, bronze, copper, tin, steel, and mixed iron.[107] The nature of the golden age is the same as before; and, fundamentally as in chapter one, the Pahlavi document here identifies the reigning figures of the silver through steel ages with various historical personages deemed faithful to Zoroastrianism. The final age of mixed iron is again a time of advancing darkness, with a lengthy description of its near-apocalyptic evils being set out following the dream narrative (*Vahman Yašt* 2.23–63). Among its myriad banes some are particularly reminiscent of the ills that Hesiod assigns to his own iron age: deceit and division will trump friendship, respect will leave the world, and parents will lose affection for their children (2.30). While in *Works and Days* iron-age people will be born with gray hair (line 181) and grow old quickly (line 185), in the Iranian account people are born smaller and weaker (2.32). Hesiod declares that there will be no appreciation for the one who keeps an oath or for the just (*dikaios* [δίκαιος]) or the good; instead, people will praise the evil-doer and the man of *hubris* (lines 190–92), and an evil man will make false claims against a more noble man and swear that those claims are true (lines 193–4). The *Vahman Yašt* (2.39) states that justice will not be rightly determined and people will believe the words of the ignoble and maligners who swear oaths falsely.

In the account of the *Vahman Yašt* human history continues beyond the last of the metallic ages, and hence beyond the millennium of Zardušt. Afterward, in the millennium of one called Ušēdar (the first of three prophetic figures, the *sōšyants*), religious order is restored (*Vahman Yašt* 3.1–51). Next follows the millennium of Ušēdarmah (the second of the *sōšyants*), in which humans are noted as making great strides in medical care, but evil again asserts itself with the release of the imprisoned evil dragon Až Dahāk. The dragon will, however, be destroyed when Ohrmazd causes the ancient dragon-slayer Karšāsp to be awakened; that millennium comes to an end (*Vahman Yašt* 3.52–61). The final prophetic figure, known only generically as Sōšyant, then appears and ushers in a renewed purity, and cosmic history is brought to fulfillment (*Vahman Yašt* 3.62).[108]

INDIA In Book Three of the *Mahābhārata*, that tome among ancient epics, the sons of Paṇḍu wander the wilderness spaces of northern India in their twelve-year exile. Bhima, second eldest of the Paṇḍavas, one day encounters Hanuman – the ape-lord better known from that second Sanskrit epic, the *Rāmāyaṇa* – who instructs Bhima in the four *yugas* – ages – of the world (3.148). Each *yuga* bears the name of a dice-throw; while there is no metallic symbolism, each age is marked by the god Viṣṇu (Kṛṣṇa) taking on a color particular to that *yuga*. The first age is that of the 'winning throw', the *kṛtayuga*, an idyllic era in which *dharma*[109] holds sway; it knows no death, it knows neither toil nor pain nor illness. The earth puts forth its fruits without cultivation. In this age the four social elements of Indo-Aryan society – the *brāhmaṇa*, *kṣatriya*, *vaiśya*, and *śudra* classes – are well defined and perform each their appropriate function. Viṣnu's color in the *kṛtayuga* is white – the color of the *brāhmaṇa* (priestly) class.

In the second age, that of the *tretāyuga*, sacrifice is introduced. Though *dharma* is reduced by one-fourth, mankind is nonetheless devoted to the observance of law and rites. In the *tretāyuga*, Viṣnu's color becomes red – the color of the *kṣatriya* (warrior) class.

The *dvāparayuga*, the third age, sees *dharma* reduced by half. Ritual proliferates as the knowledge of the Vedas becomes uneven and variable among humankind. There is a falling away from truth and a consequent suffering from disease and disaster. Viṣnu's color becomes yellow – the color of the *vaiśya* (worker) class.

The fourth and final age, the *kaliyuga*, is one that sees only one-quarter of *dharma* remaining. Ritual and sacrifice are forsaken; disease and disaster multiply; famine and sloth abound; humanity and the world spiral into decline. It is an age of discord and darkness; Viṣnu's color is black – the color of the *śudra* (slave) class.

Later in Book Three of the *Mahābhārata* (3.186), Yudhiṣthira, king among the Paṇḍavas, meets the ancient seer Mārkaṇḍeya and questions him concerning the nature of the recurring cosmic cycles of destruction and creation. The hermit then tells Yudhiṣthira of the four ages, how they grow progressively shorter, and how, after the completion of the last, the cycle of four begins anew – and so on and on. Mārkaṇḍeya's initial summary description of the four ages is succinct, much more so than Hanuman's earlier account of the same. Up to this point, Mārkaṇḍeya's account approximates in scope and details the description of the four *yugas* found in the ancient brahmin legal text called the *Mānavadharmaśāstra*, or *Laws of Manu*, 1.68–74 (to which we shall return below; note that certain of the characteristics of each age specified in the ape-lord Hanuman's disquisition are reflected just a few lines later at *Laws of Manu* 1.79–86). Then, however, for more than 50 stanzas, Mārkaṇḍeya waxes eloquent about what things will occur as the last of the four ages, the *kaliyuga*, comes to an end.

Just a bit further along in the epic text (*Mahābhārata* 3.188), Yudhiṣthira again questions the sage about the discordant *kaliyuga*; and, again, Mārkaṇḍeya responds with a litany of symptoms and woes that will mark the final age – a list extending over more than 65 stanzas: the *brāhmaṇa*, *kṣatriya*, and *vaiśya* classes will intermingle in marriage and become like the *śudra*; the classes will invert their proper orders; fathers and sons will turn against one another; brahmins will turn away from their vows and rites; agriculturalists will abandon sensible practices; justice will be perverted; the warriors will victimize the defenseless; kings will claim for themselves the property of others; people will turn gray at sixteen years – the maximum lifespan – having produced children when only a child's age themselves.[110] The similarity of these deficiencies to the ills of the final age of both the Iranian and Hesiodic traditions is self-evident, as is the extensive attention that is paid to the final age in each case.

EGYPT AND MESOPOTAMIA While Mesopotamia preserves traditions of human lifespan growing progressively shorter as time passes – West[111] cites the example of the Sumerian king list – there is nothing structurally comparable to the motif of four world ages found in Hesiod's *Works and Days*, the Book of Daniel, Iranian religious texts, and Indic epic and law. Egypt is equally silent.[112] The cultural and geographic distribution of the motif must itself be of some significance, leading us to return to a consideration of the myth of ages once more below.

HESIOD: KEEPER OF THE GATE

The ancient Greeks were an Indo-European people, descended ultimately from those yet more ancient people that scholars dub the Proto-Indo-Europeans. Linguistically and culturally the Greeks thus share a common heritage with the other Indo-European populations of Europe and Asia – Italic, Celtic, Germanic, Balto-Slavic, Anatolian, Indo-Iranian, Armenian, and so on. Comparative crosscultural investigation of shared mythic traditions attested among the historical Indo-European peoples allows the reconstructive identification of ancestral mythic elements of the parent Indo-European culture.

Attributing the epithet "keeper of the gate" to Hesiod is here intended to make reference to his preservation of Indo-European mythic motifs; but some might consider the attribution to be almost tongue-in-cheek, for, they might suggest, there seems to be precious little that the Greeks – even Hesiod in the eighth century BC – have preserved of their Indo-European mythic heritage. Georges Dumézil, the twentieth-century's preeminent investigator of comparative Indo-European myth, referred to the Greeks as his *amants ingrats* "ungrateful lovers."[113] "Greek mythology," he wrote, "escapes Indo-European categories."[114] As argued above, the Greeks – Hesiod in this instance – fell under the influence of Near Eastern traditions, and this is certainly one reason – perhaps the chief reason – that they may appear to have wandered far from the Indo-European mythic fold. Even so, Dumézil's pronouncements are likely unduly pessimistic; as various scholars have demonstrated,[115] including Dumézil himself,[116] one can indeed identify vestiges of an Indo-European heritage preserved in the structures of Greek myth.

The Five Ages of Mankind, Part 2

In a wonderfully insightful investigation, Jean-Pierre Vernant (1983a) examined Hesiod's myth of the ages and identified there what is for the comparatist an unmistakable expression of Indo-European tripartite ideology.[117] Proto-Indo-European society, as recognized independently by Dumézil and Émile Benveniste, was characterized by a three-part structural division, consisting of elements of sovereignty, war-making, and goods-production (pastoralism/agriculturalism).[118] The concept was more fully explored and developed by Dumézil, whose nomenclature for the three elements, or "functions" as he called them, became commonplace in the twentieth century: Dumézil spoke of the *first*, *second*, and *third* functions, respectively – with a common shorthand content-denotation being that of the *priestly*, *warrior*, and *worker* functions. The first function is characterized by two distinct aspects – to wit, those of law and religion. In the case of some early historically attested Indo-European cultures, these three functions find expression in an actual tripartite structuring of society (i.e., a dividing of society into three classes) – notably among the Indic and Iranian peoples in Asia and among the Celts in Europe. In the case of other Indo-European peoples, however, primitive Indo-European tripartition survives only as a vestigial ideology (at least during the periods from which documentary evidence of those cultures has survived), often finding expression in religious and mythic motifs. Conspicuous among this latter group are the Italic peoples, most especially the Romans.

Vernant observed that by interpolating an additional age – that of the heroes (on the interpolation, see West's remarks above) – into the structure of the metallic generations, Hesiod constructs a classic Indo-European tripartite structure – though we might say an apparently "unorthodox" one, to the extent that each expression of the three functions is internally dichotomous, displaying a +/− opposition. This binary feature is itself, however, quite in keeping with Hesiod, who clearly displays a penchant for dichotomies and ambivalence.[119]

Hesiod's use of diametric contrastiveness occurs at many levels. We have already noted, for instance, his opposition of the good Eris and the bad Eris, of the good Zelos and the bad Zelos; in *Works and Days* 317–19, the poet presents Aidos (αἰδώς, 'respect, shame') as similarly, though not identically, ambivalent: she "both greatly harms and greatly prospers men."[120] We find such contrastiveness at the phrasal level as well: thus, in the *Theogony* (line 585), Hesiod denotes Pandora with the alliterative, oxymoronic phrase *kalon kakon* (καλὸν κακόν), the 'beautiful bane' – a denotation that itself contrasts with the name that the poet assigns her in *Works and Days* (lines 80–81), Pandora (Πανδώρη) 'All-giving' – and, continuing the spiral of contrasts, that name, no less, connotes dichotomy; in Clay's words, "To be sure, that name is as ambiguous as she is: promising all, but in reality all-consuming."[121] The poet's playful contrastiveness is heightened when one considers that *Pandora* – the appellation of Hesiod's 'beautiful bane', she who was responsible for bringing evil upon mankind – was otherwise the name or epithet of a beneficent chthonic goddess endowing mortals with all of earth's delightful gifts.[122] Hesiod's Pandora-dichotomies are part and parcel of the distinction he develops between "appearance" and "reality" and his ambivalent depiction of womankind. Clay puts it this way:

> The wondrous exterior of this ancestress, or better, prototype of female women/wives is counterbalanced by the simile of the bees and the drones which depicts her inner nature, invisible to the naked eye. . . . The Woman is a semblance of a semblance, whose fair exterior stands in complete opposition to the bitter facts of her true nature.
>
> The dilemma that follows is exclusively a human dilemma and Zeus's *coup de grâce*. The trap so carefully laid now clangs shut: if a man manages to escape marriage, he will indeed have enough to eat, but he will have no one to look after him in his old age and, since he remains childless, distant relatives will divide his inheritance. If, however, he should marry and have the luck to find a good wife, even so misery will continually battle with good; but should he chance upon a bad one, then boundless and unremitting misery will fill his days (603–12).[123]

Hesiod's oppositional method comes to the fore in his catalog of fantastic hybrid creatures – the monsters (*Theogony* 270–336). For example, as Clay points out, in Hesiod's description of the Graeae (the three

'old-women' daughters of Phorcys and Ceto; lines 270–73) the poet
ignores their most salient feature – the sharing of a single eye and tooth
that they pass back and forth between them – "but emphasizes rather
their paradoxical combination of youth and age"; moreover, "the Gorgons encompass yet another fundamental dichotomy; for while two
of the sisters are immortal, Medusa is singled out as mortal"[124] (lines
274–8). These hybrid creatures as a group contrast with Hesiod's other
hybrids – those that render the former harmless – the heroes; in setting
the two against one another, Clay observes, "Hesiod calls attention to
the different kinds of μίξις [mixis, 'mingling'], the one positive and controlled, the other destructive and disordered."[125] Indeed, she further
advocates (emphasis is mine), "In a sense, the catalogue of monsters
represents an *anti-cosmos* that explodes the whole conception of the
Theogony."[126] Other scholars have argued that +/− oppositions are to
be found within certain empirically identified functional categories in
Hesiod's myths (à la Lévi-Strauss).[127] The list of dichotomies utilized by
Hesiod could undoubtedly be greatly extended, but this is sufficient to
give the reader an idea.

Now returning to Vernant – and summarizing his analysis very
succinctly – the first two ages, those of the golden and silver races,
are an expression of the Indo-European first function, the realm of
sovereignty, having no affiliation with war (second function) and none
with agrarian labor (third function). Gold, the element of the initial age,
is a symbol of sovereignty; and upon passing from this life, the members
of that golden race receive a *geras basilēion* (γέρας βασιλήιον), literally
a 'kingly privilege': becoming *daimones* (δαίμονες), 'divine spirits' who
dwell on the earth (*epikhthonioi* [ἐπιχθόνιοι]), they serve as guardians of
humankind (protecting justice, according to most manuscripts[128]) and
bestowers of wealth (lines 121–6). Hesiod linguistically links the golden
age beings with the just rulers of his own day, using the same or similar
language to describe both (they are both "like gods," cf. *Works and Days*
112 and *Theogony* 91; they both enjoy earth's bounty, cf. *Works and Days*
114–20 and 225–37).

The silver age is likewise symbolized by a precious metal, though
one inferior to gold; and, indeed, Hesiod explicitly states that the beings
of this race are inferior to those of the golden age – the silver age is,
in Vernant's words, "its exact counterpart and opposite."[129] After their
long childhood, the people of the silver age live only briefly as adults,
because of the *hubris* that they display toward one another and toward the
gods – they are impious, refusing to give the gods their rightful sacrifices.
Again, Hesiod's language links the silver-age beings to the kings of his

own day – to the unjust rulers who pervert *dikē* among humankind and give no thought to revering the gods (cf. *Works and Days* 134–7 and 249–51). Zeus destroys the silver race. But even so, becoming "blessed spirits" (but not the *daimones* that their predecessors became) that have an existence beneath the earth (*hupokhthonioi* [ὑποχθόνιοι]), they receive honor. Vernant points out that their subterranean existence brings them into the sphere of the Titans, also characterized by *hubris*, and he argues that Hesiod thus constructs a parallelism between the golden and silver races of the *Works and Days* and, respectively, the Olympians (who "represent the rule of order") and Titans (who "embody the rule of disorder and hubris"[130]) of the *Theogony*. In the case of the first two of Hesiod's metallic races, Vernant argues, the "dominant value is *dikē*, *hubris* is secondary";[131] and for *dikē* the golden race is valued positive, the silver negative: the two races contrast antithetically.

Hesiod's bronze age is militaristic; concerning this age the poet offers no word about justice, nothing about religious observance: "We have moved from the juridical and religious plane to that of manifestations of brute force . . . , physical energy . . . , and the terror which the warrior inspires."[132] The men of bronze have nothing to do with agriculture as well – Hesiod tells us that they eat no bread.

> . . . Ares' woeful works 145
> They used to love, and deeds of *hubris* too . . .
> . . . .
> A mighty force was theirs, and arms invincible 148
> From out their shoulders grew, such steely limbs

They live by the sword and die by the sword; and seized by death they go nameless into the cold darkness of Hades' realm. Theirs is the *hubris* of the warrior, which "consists in wishing to recognize nothing but the lance, and devoting oneself entirely to it."[133]

As the silver race is defined by the golden, so the age of heroes is defined by the bronze age, "as its counterpart in the same sphere of action."[134] The heroes are warriors no less than the bronze men, but Hesiod describes them as *dikaioteron kai areion* (δικαιότερον καὶ ἄρειον) 'more just (the comparative form of the adjective derived from *dikē*) and nobler' (*Works and Days* 158) – Vernant summarizes: "the warrior who is just, and . . . willing to submit to the superior order of *dikē*"; "the warrior who is the champion of order."[135] Though he makes no mention of it, the contrast that Vernant here perceives between the

warriors of the bronze age and those of the heroic age – between the
hubris-type warrior of brute and raging force and the noble warrior
subject to *dikē* – looks to be a reflection of a widely occurring Indo-
European structure. Dumézil identified two distinct warrior-types that
contrastively recur in early Indo-European traditions: on the one hand
there is the brutish warrior – savage and untamed, often using his arms
and hands as weapons (such as Indic Bhima, Greek Heracles, Scandinavian Starkaðr); on the other, the warrior who is intelligent, civilized,
noble (such as Indic Arjuna, Greek Achilles, Scandinavian Sigurðr).[136] In
Hesiod's presentation of the second duo of races – bronze and heroic –
Vernant observes, his principal concern is "with the manifestation of
the physical force and violence linked with *hubris*":[137] the two groups,
again, contrast antithetically – the heroes display a positive aspect within
this sphere of characterization, the bronze warriors a negative.

Hesiod's own iron age – before which he wishes he had died, or
else been born after – is itself dichotomous. Hesiod lives in an ambiguous
age that knows both a positive and negative *eris*, both *dikē* and *hubris*,
both good and ill – but in time ill will prevail; and all of these ills,
Vernant observes, have as their source the *kalon kakon* (the 'beautiful
bane'), the woman with whom Zeus punished man for Prometheus'
theft of fire – whose tale Hesiod tells and immediately segues to his
logos of the five ages. In *Works and Days* the poet assigns her a name –
Pandora – a name that, as we have seen, is otherwise given to a goddess
of earth; more than that, the two – the gods' gift-woman and the earth-
goddess – are equated – at times in an explicit way, at other times more
indirectly. The gift-woman's central affiliation with the fertility of earth
and of humankind is crucial for a right understanding of the iron age:

> There is no longer that spontaneous abundance which, dur-
> ing the age of gold, made living creatures and their sustenance
> spring up from the soil simply as a result of the rule of justice
> and nothing else. Now it is man who entrusts new life to
> the woman's womb, just as it is the farmer who works the
> land and makes the cereals grow in it.[138]

Hesiod depicts his iron age using concepts fundamental to the domain
of the Indo-European third function – the domain of the agriculturalist,
the domain of fertility.

As Hesiod has made plain to Perses, iron-age man must determine
to follow the good Eris, or else the bad – that one which urges the farmer
on to hard work and its fruits, or that one which keeps him from honest

labor and nourishes human strife. The former is the path to *dikē* for the farmer, the latter that of *hubris*. The diametric opposition within this age is that between the period in which *dikē* can (but will not universally) be attained in the midst of labor and sorrow (positive) and the future era of degeneration in which *hubris* alone will hold sway (negative):

> This picture of the farmer misled by *hubris*, which is presented in the age of iron in its decline, is essentially that of a revolt against order; an upside-down world where every hierarchy, rule, and value is inverted. The contrast with the image of the farmer who is subject to *dikē*, at the beginning of the age of iron, is complete.[139]

Hesiod skillfully preserves in his *Works and Days* – a work heavily influenced by Near Eastern tradition – an archaic Indo-European tripartite ideology, associating his several ages with the elements of sovereignty, war-making, and goods-production. He is able to do so – to create a parallel structure in triplicate out of five generations – by integrating dichotomous oppositions into the scheme of the ages – oppositions that reverberate with his fundamental contrast of *dikē* and *hubris*.[140]

Questions immediately arise. Whence comes this tripartition? That is to say, how and in what sense is Hesiod aware of it? What is the poet's source and inspiration for the use of the ancestral tripartite ideology in his myth of the ages? Is it an integral feature of this tradition, or one that Hesiod – or some Hesiodic predecessor – has imposed upon the tradition *de novo*?

AN INDO-EUROPEAN TRADITION

We have seen that West, among others, identifies Hesiod's metallic-races *logos* as one borne to Greece out of the east. Yet might this tale of the ages itself be of Indo-European origin? When considered collectively, the individual strands of evidence point unmistakably, I will argue, in the direction of an Indo-European provenance. The first and most fundamental consideration is that of the geographic and cultural distribution of the tradition outside of Greece. We have met with this tale of Earth's ages in three literary venues: in the Biblical Book of Daniel; in Iranian (Zoroastrian) religious documents; and in Indic epic and law – hardly the geographic distribution typical of the "Near Eastern" elements that surface in Hesiod's poems.

The Book of Daniel and Persian Influence

Biblical scholars seem bedeviled by the date and compositional history of the Book of Daniel. The Biblical story is set in the reign of the Babylonian monarch Nebuchadnezzar II, during that period of Jewish history called the Babylonian Exile (c. 586–535 BC) – a time when significant elements of Jerusalem's population had been deported and resettled in Mesopotamia following Nebuchadnezzar's subjugation of Judah and its capital.[141] Currently, Biblical scholars typically view the Book of Daniel, in the form in which we know it, as a product of the Hellenistic era – an apocalyptic work written during a period of Jewish persecution at the hands of the Seleucid king Antiochus Epiphanes in the second century BC. Regardless of when and under what circumstances Daniel acquired its present form, clearly there must lie behind that form traditions older than the Hellenistic period.

NABONIDUS Compare, in this regard, a Jewish tradition concerning the Babylonian king Nabonidus, the last king of Babylon prior to its capitulation to Cyrus and his Persians in 539 BC. One of the Qumran documents (the Dead Sea Scrolls) preserves the record of an encounter between Nabonidus and a Jewish diviner and of how this holy man counseled the king as he suffered from some affliction – an episode that is in several respects reminiscent of the Biblical stories of Nebuchadnezzar and Daniel.[142] Nabonidus – who is otherwise known as having a particular penchant for dream interpretation[143] (he states that he was called to kingship in a dream sent by Sin, the Moon-god[144]) and confrontations with Babylonian priests – ruled Babylonia from the Arabian town of Tema, more than 600 miles away from his capital, for ten years of his seventeen-year reign, leaving his son, Belshazzar, in Babylon to manage affairs of state in his absence.[145] It is in Tema that Nabonidus fell ill, according to the Qumran record, and in his affliction prayed to the God of the Jews. Nabonidus busied himself with various towns in the region of Tema;[146] that these same towns are known as sites of Jewish settlement from later Islamic documents might be taken to suggest a Jewish presence in these places in Nabonidus' own day.[147] A Jewish presence in Babylon in Nabonidus' day is, of course, beyond question.

CYRUS When the Persian army entered Babylon in mid-October 539 BC, the city capitulated quickly and seemingly with little opposition.[148] Arriving two weeks later, Cyrus is claimed to have been welcomed as a liberator of this cosmopolitan city.[149] Babylon, like all of Babylonia, was populated by ethnically diverse peoples: documents, for example, from the reign of Nebuchadnezzar refer to the presence at his court of "Elamites, Persians, Cilicians, Jews, various emigrants from Asia Minor ('Ionians'), 'fugitives from Media', and others."[150] The rapid surrender of Babylon to Cyrus can most likely be attributed to the presence of pro-Persian elements already present within the city, including Jewish contingents.[151] By 538, Cyrus had issued a decree permitting the Jewish exiles to return to Palestine and restore the Jerusalem temple. The decree was reconfirmed in 520 by Darius I, who had followed Cyrus' own successor (his son Cambyses) on the throne of Persia.[152] The prophet Isaiah can refer to the Persian Cyrus as the "anointed" of the Lord (Isaiah 45:1), called to be Yahweh's shepherd, to fulfill His purposes (Isaiah 44:28).

THE ARAMAIC LANGUAGE A salient feature that sets the Book of Daniel apart from other Biblical works is its particular linguistic complexity. While the language of the Old Testament is of course predominantly Hebrew, a large subset of Daniel's twelve chapters – 2:4b to 7:28 – is written, instead, in the Semitic language Aramaic. Aside from a couple of minor occurrences, Aramaic is otherwise used in the Bible only for portions of the Book of Ezra, 4:8 to 6:18 and 7:12–26: passages recording communiqués with the Persian court and a decree issued by the Persian monarch Cyrus, in which he gives approval for the rebuilding of the Jewish temple in Jerusalem. Ancient Aramaic survives in several distinct varieties.[153] That one found in Daniel is a form of Imperial or Official Aramaic (in use c. 600–200 BC), a *lingua franca* used in the Neo-Babylonian Empire and, subsequently, by the Persians. The Aramaic language of Daniel contains Akkadian and, more especially, Persian loanwords. The latter group of borrowings includes not only terms denoting Persian officials and vocabulary from the realm of government, but less specialized lexemes as well. For example, in Daniel 2:5, a verse in which Nebuchadnezzar threatens his Chaldean priests with dismemberment if they cannot reveal to him his dream and its interpretation, the words for 'make known' and 'limb' are Persian loans.[154]

Linguistic and sociopolitical considerations, taken together with the evidence provided by the Qumran tradition of Nabonidus, point to the Aramaic portions of Daniel having taken shape in Mesopotamia (as opposed to Palestine) during a period of Persian influence. Composition of the Aramaic text could itself be plausibly assigned to the sixth or fifth century BC, with subsequent updating of some Aramaic vocabulary by copyists.[155] In a careful and balanced study of Daniel chapter two – that chapter containing the account of Nebuchadnezzar's dream of the colossal metallic statue – Davies argues that the earliest form of the narrative is of sixth-century date and that the interpretation then assigned to the four metallic components of the statue was that each represented one of the last four Neo-Babylonian monarchs: Nebuchadnezzar, Amel-Marduk, Neriglissar, and Nabonidus – the last named being the feet of clay whose collapse brought an end to the Neo-Babylonian empire.[156]

PERSIAN INFLUENCE Biblical scholars have long acknowledged that the Persians exerted an influence on (Post)-Exilic Judaism, if they have disagreed concerning the extent and specific forms of such influence.[157] Nebuchadnezzar's dream vision – the gigantic statue of gold, silver, bronze, and iron mixed with clay – is practically unique among Biblical symbols; to identify anything roughly comparable one must "adduce the bizarre symbols of Zechariah, influenced, as is commonly recognized, by the Babylonian culture and art."[158] Daniel's colossus appears, *prima facie*, to be a probable instance of Persian influence, in light of the setting described above and given the occurrence of the similar Zoroastrian tradition. Indeed, some Biblical scholars have argued in favor of this position, others against it,[159] but the more typical ("safer") view seems to be that the motif of metallic ages was just something in the air that infected the Greeks, the Jews, and the Persians alike.[160] This is clearly not a satisfying solution; but, more than that, there is in fact an additional piece of evidence, one that appears heretofore to have been overlooked, that draws Daniel's account more securely into the realm of Iranian cultural influence, as we shall see.

Indo-Iranian Traditions and Hesiod

If the presence of the metallic world-ages motif in Daniel can be attributed to Persian (or, perhaps more carefully, Iranian) influence – a reasonable and *prima facie* compelling hypothesis – then, within a comparative Indo-European framework, the cultural and geographic distribution of the tradition takes on considerable significance, being attested among the Greeks, Iranians, and Indo-Aryans. Indic and Iranian languages belong to a single Indo-European linguistic subfamily, Indo-Iranian. Together with Greek and Armenian, Indo-Iranian forms a well-recognized cluster within the Indo-European language family, sharing several innovative linguistic features.[161] Such clustering reveals a period of linguistic and cultural commonality or intercourse in an early

Indo-European community whose descendants would become the historically attested Greek, Indo-Iranian and Armenian peoples. Little has survived in the way of archaic Armenian cultural usages, but the co-occurrence of the world-ages motif in Greek and Indo-Iranian lore may reveal that the origin of the tradition lies in the period of ancestral cultural commonality. Significant in this regard is the conspicuous presence in Hesiod of other features shared with Indo-Iranian tradition.

Thirty-five lines beyond the hawk-and-nightingale fable in *Works and Days*, Hesiod turns his attention to the kings and warns them of the consequences of "crooked judgments" – divine retribution (lines 248–55):

> For thrice ten thousand on the earth that nurtures all
> Are Zeus's deathless watchers of our mortal humankind;
> And they keep watch on judgments and on wicked works,
> Enwrapped in mist and roaming over all the earth.　255

Since at least the mid-nineteenth-century work of Rudolph Roth,[162] scholars have recognized the fundamental sameness of Zeus's mortal-watchers, on then one hand, and the spies dispatched by Iranian Mithra and by Indic Mitra and, especially, Varuṇa, on the other. In the *Avesta*, Mithra is said to have ten thousand spies (*Yašt* 10.24, 27, 60, 82, 141), stationed at every watch post, spying out those who are untrue to covenant, those who would harm the just (*Yašt* 10.44–6). The Vedas tell how Varuna similarly deploys thousand-eyed spies who scour the earth (*Atharva Veda* 4.16.4), spies whom he sends out to watch "well-fashioned" heaven and earth (*Rig Veda* 7.87.3); they roam about with eyes unblinking (*Rig Veda* 10.10.8). Mitra and Varuṇa send their spies into fields and homes – to all places – to watch without ceasing (*Rig Veda* 7.61.3).

The Greek poet returns to this imagery, in a slightly varied form, a few lines further along. After again warning the kings – given to "gift-gobbling" as they are – to judge rightly (lines 263–4), and punctuating the admonition with a proverbial couplet – the kind so familiar from the Near East – to drive home his point,

> The man who prepares evil for another prepares evil for
> 　himself,　265
> And an evil plan is the greatest evil to the one who plans it,

Hesiod declares that the eye of Zeus, all-seeing and all-knowing, also watches how justice is administered in the city (lines 267–9). The Indo-Iranian match is again exact. Returning to the *Mithra Yašt* (*Yašt* 10), we find frequent reference to Iranian Mithra's ten thousand eyes and thousand ears (*Yašt* 10.7, 82, 91, 141) and to all-knowing, all-seeing Mithra's thousandfold perception (*Yašt* 10.35, 82, 107). In *Yašt* 10.24, 60, 69, 82, 141, and 143, in conjunction with references to his ten thousand spies, Mithra is said to be all-knowing – as also in 10.27, where he is depicted as punishing the wayward country – and in 10.46, where all-knowing Mithra himself is said to be a spy. Likewise in India, Varuṇa is said to behold all things (*Atharva Veda* 4.16.5, following the reference to his spies) and to be all-knowing.[163] As West rightly observes, "We are dealing here with a piece of Indo-European heritage."[164]

Diametric opposition is a fundamental and well-known characteristic of Zarathuštra's Iranian religion. Writing more than 800 years after Hesiod, the Greek savant Plutarch explicates his view of Persian dualism: the Magus Zoroaster, he writes, recognized two gods, Oromazes and Areimanius, the first likened to light, the second – in contrast – likened to darkness and ignorance – two gods perpetually at war with one another. The opposition extends further: some plants are affiliated with the one god, some with the other; again, certain animals belong to the good Oromazes – such as dogs, birds, and hedgehogs – and others to the evil Areimanius – the single example provided being that of the water rat (*Isis and Osiris* 46–7).

Plutarch's Oromazes is Ahura Mazdāh (the Pahlavi Ohrmazd that we encountered above), the Iranian deity that the reformer Zarathuštra acknowledged as supreme god; Areimanius is Angra Mainyu, locus of the power of darkness. The two encapsulate the diametrically contrastive notions of *aša* 'order, truth' and *drug* 'lie'. At times the opposition is formulated as a contrast between Spənta Mainyu ('beneficent spirit') and Angra Mainyu, who are then described as twins – the former having chosen *aša*, the other *drug*. Among humankind, one who follows *aša* is an *ašavan*; one who does not is a *drəgvant*.[165]

The roots of Zoroastrian dualism clearly lie in an earlier period. With the Persian contrast of *aša* and *drug*, compare, for example, the Vedic distinction (with cognate terms[166]) of *ṛta* 'order, truth' versus *druh* 'harm; demonic spirit'. The Sanskrit term *ṛta* is eventually superceded by *dharma*; in the *Laws of Manu* 1.26, Brahma, in creating the universe, is said to have distinguished *dharma* from (its opposite) *adharma* and to have imposed on the creatures he brought forth oppositional pairs, such as happiness and unhappiness.

Cosmology and Cosmogony

The cosmological doctrine of cyclically recurring, progressively diminishing ages, each uniquely affiliated with a social caste, is complemented in Vedic lore by a well-known cosmogonic tradition. *Rig Veda* 10.90 (the *Puruṣa Sūkta*) records it. In the beginning there was a great cosmic giant, Puruṣa. The gods sacrificed this giant and with their victim's dismembered body fashioned the cosmos. Conspicuous attention is given to the creation of the *varṇas* (classes) of human society: from the giant's mouth they formed the *brāhmaṇa* class (priests), from his arms the *kṣatriyas* (warriors), and from his legs the *vaiśya* class (workers); his feet gave rise to the *śudra*, the non-Indo-Aryan slave caste.

The tradition is similarly rehearsed as a part of the creation discourse in the *Laws of Manu* (1.31). It is in this same discourse – subsequent to and dependent upon the cosmogonic Puruṣa-dismemberment tradition – that the account of cyclic cosmic ages, the four *yugas*, each affiliated with a particular *varṇa*, appears (1.68–74, 79–86). And again, immediately following the latter exposition of the *yugas* (1.79–86), the discourse turns back to the four classes, their creation out of the *dismembria* of Puruṣa and their consequent natural functions (1.87–93).

And so it is in the *Mahābhārata*. Sandwiched between his two descriptions of the fourth age, the *kaliyuga* (*Mahābhārata* 3.187), the Brahmin Mārkaṇḍeya tells Yudhiṣṭhira of how he had roamed a devastated, flooded earth at the culmination of a *kaliyuga* and encountered a god who identified himself as Nārāyaṇa (Viṣṇu) – creator and destroyer. In teaching the seer of his creative acts and his cosmic being, the god declares that the *brāhmaṇas* are his mouth and the *kṣatriyas* his arms, that the *vaiśyas* are at his thighs and the *śudras* at his feet. The god tells of how he creates himself when *dharma* begins to wane and of the four characteristic colors he takes on in the four successive *yugas*. When the time comes that *dharma* has diminished by three-fourths, it is Nārāyaṇa himself who destroys the cosmos. Cosmology and cosmogony are interlaced.

While the Vedic tradition of the sacrificed primeval giant has undergone culture-specific reworking to the extent that it has incorporated the indigenous (non-Indo-Aryan) *śudra* class, this creation account is widely acknowledged to be an Indo-European inheritance. Homologous traditions are broadly attested among Indo-European peoples – Irish, Slavic, Germanic, and others.[167] Especially close is the Norse cosmogony, preserved in the Eddic poem the *Grímnismál* (40–41) and by Snorri Sturluson in his *Prose Edda*, telling how the god Odin and his brothers dismembered the body of the primeval giant Ymir and from his body parts created the cosmos. An Old Russian version of the cosmogony survives in the poem entitled *Stič o golubinoj knig* ('Poem on the Dove King') and parallels the Vedic text in detailing the creation of the classes of society – in this instance the three canonical Indo-European elements only, that is, those of sovereignty, physical might, and goods production. In these and still other Indo-European traditions treating the genesis of human society, the priestly (sovereign) element arises from the head of the dismembered victim, the warrior from the arms and upper body (theirs is strength and heart), and the goods-producing stratum from the lower body.[168]

Especially relevant for our concerns are Iranian vestiges and permutations of this Indo-European cosmogony. For example, the Pahlavi *Škend Gumānīg Vizār* (1.20–24),[169] in the context of a creation account, compares body parts to the social classes of Iranian society, without reference to the sacrificed primeval giant. The head is likened to the priests, hands to the warriors, the belly to agriculturalists – that is, literally, to the 'pastoralist – herdsman' class[170] – and the feet to the *hūiti* class, a fourth element (a so-called artisan group[171]) appended to the three Indo-European classes, here structurally and functionally matching the position of the *śudra* in the Indic cosmogony of Puruṣa.[172] Interestingly, the comparison is made in conjunction with the symbol of a great tree, representing the religion created by Ohrmazd; on the tree are four twigs, each one symbolizing one of the four social classes.[173] Compare the cosmology of Zardušt's dream of a root of a tree with four branches – gold, silver, steel, and mixed iron – representing four successive ages. Again, cosmology and cosmogony intertwine.

Puruṣa, the Indo-European cosmic giant of *Rig Veda* 10.90, and homologous Indo-European traditions lead us back to the colossus of Nebuchadnezzar's dream in Daniel chapter two. The superficial similarity between the Biblical dream image and Indo-Iranian cosmology cum cosmogony is obvious. Given the proposed Iranian origin of the Biblical tradition, it would be but a small step to take to posit that the gigantic statue whose constituent metallic body parts represent successive political ages has its origin, in effect, in a mapping of the Indo-Iranian cosmology of world ages onto the Indo-Iranian (and Indo-European) cosmogony of the primeval giant (and indeed the Pahlavi text cited above comes very close to this). The subtlety of this fusion and its fidelity to the individual traditions involved is only reasonably contextualized within an "Iranian setting" (defined either more broadly or more narrowly) and gives the decidedly affirmative nod to the Biblical tradition having taken shape under Iranian influence.

TABLE 3.1. *Comparison of Indo-Iranian Traditions: Cosmogonic and Cosmologic*

Daniel Chapter Two		Iranian Cosmology	Indic Cosmology and Cosmology		Indo-Iranian Social Classes
Body parts of colossus	*Metal*	*Metal*	*Yuga colors*	*Body parts of Puruṣa*	*Affiliated with yugas and body parts*
Head	Gold	Gold	White	Mouth	Priests
Arms/breast	Silver	Silver	Red	Arms	Warriors
Belly/thighs	Bronze				(Goods producers)
Legs	Iron	Steel	Yellow	Legs	Goods producers
Feet	Clay/iron	Mixed iron	Black	Feet	Slaves/artisans

The similarities and connections are summarized in Table 3.1. In the rightmost column, the Indo-Aryan and Iranian social classes listed are those associated with the corresponding world ages (*yugas*) attested in Indic tradition and the corresponding body parts attested in both Indic and Iranian tradition. Notice that in the Biblical tradition, the Indo-Iranian stratum of the goods-producers has been effectively bifurcated by assigning "belly and thighs" and "legs" – both of which are body areas affiliated with the Indo-European goods-producing class – to separate eras, bronze and iron respectively. The Semitic prophetic adaptation is one in which the original Indo-European social symbolism has *no relevance*. While this lower body (i.e., goods-producing) division is reminiscent of the dichotomous opposition incorporated within Hesiod's iron age (age of goods-producers), the innovative bifurcation of Daniel is seemingly required simply to fill out the interpretative structure of the Biblical prophecy of successive political powers.

Conversely, unlike the Indic and (at least some) Iranian traditions, the Jewish prophecy makes only a partial distinction between the stratum of the feet and that of the legs: in Daniel's interpretation of the dream, the feet of iron mixed with clay provide additional interpretative information regarding the kingdom of iron (it will be divided); in

Indo-Iranian traditions, the feet symbolize a distinct fourth social class added to the Indo-European tripartite structure. This variation might be taken to suggest that Jews in Babylon adapted an Iranian (Median?) tradition that antedates the incorporation of a fourth class into Indic and Iranian cosmogony and cosmology. More likely, given the occurrence of a distinct "mixed-iron" stratum in the Pahlavi cosmologies, Daniel's departure from Iranian tradition again reflects the freedom of prophetic adaptation.

HESIOD'S MYTH OF THE "AGES": INDO-EUROPEAN PERSPECTIVES AND ADAPTATION

The evidence clearly leads us in this direction: the tradition of metallic ages underlying Nebuchadnezzar's dream vision as preserved in Daniel chapter two is of Iranian origin. That vision and its interpretation draw upon both a cosmology that is common Indo-Iranian and a cosmogony that is common Indo-European. That same cosmology is preserved no less in Hesiod's myth of the ages. And this shared cosmology is, in fact, only one of several motifs common to Hesiod and Indo-Iranian tradition. The ancestors of the Greeks and the Indo-Iranians, and of the Armenians as well, were once joined as members of a common culture, as the linguistic evidence unmistakably reveals. One can most reasonably conclude that the co-occurrence in Hesiod and Indo-Iranian tradition of an idiosyncratic set of features is the consequence of shared inheritance of a common ancestral tradition.

As one might expect, the Greek form of the inherited myth of world ages is not uniquely preserved in Hesiod's *Works and Days*. Other Greek instantiations of the tradition, attested directly or indirectly, show even closer agreement to the Indo-Iranian forms.[174] For example, Ovid's version of the myth in his *Metamorphoses* (1.89–162), which the Roman poet must have adapted from some Greek version other than that of *Works and Days*,[175] is particularly close to the Indo-Iranian accounts in its description of the ages. Aratus (*Phaenomena* 96–136), a Greek author of the third and fourth centuries, in his account of the goddess Dike ('Justice') and her flight from the earth to heaven, where she became the constellation Virgo (Greek Parthenos), describes the first three ages – golden, silver, and bronze (the age in which she fled)[176] – in terms, again, highly reminiscent of the Indo-Iranian traditions.[177]

And just a brief word regarding the metallic scheme for naming the ages in Iranian and Greek traditions: it is clear that there is full agreement in Persia and Greece in the first, second, and fourth age positions: those of gold, silver, and iron. The use of bronze for the third metallic age in Hesiod's *logos* equally finds a correspondence in Iran in Zardušt's dream of the seven branches and an exact positional match in the Iranian tradition underlying Nebuchadnezzar's dream in Daniel. The simplest (theoretically most economical) and, therefore, best hypothesis (other factors being equal) is that one which posits that the use of metals to designate the several ages in the descending order gold, silver, bronze, and iron is a feature of the ancestral Greek/Indo-Iranian tradition – an inherited feature preserved by Greeks and Iranians and not an independent, parallel innovation of each descendent people – a more cumbersome and a priori less likely hypothesis. The substitution of steel for bronze in Zardušt's four-branch dream is undoubtedly a specific Zoroastrian modification of the inherited Indo-Iranian tradition, as is the Indic replacement of the metal scheme by that one utilizing the colors affiliated with the several castes (*varṇas*, literally meaning 'colors'[178]). The common ancestral Indo-European community from which the historical Greek and Indo-Iranian (and Armenian) peoples descended must have existed as a cultural and linguistic entity the third millennium BC, a period that pre-dates the technology of iron production. One could of course argue that the insertion of iron – "mixed iron" – into the Greek and Iranian traditions is a secondary development occurring independently in Greece and Iran, but this is neither necessary nor desirable. Documentary sources attest to the knowledge and use of iron harvested from meteorites as early as the third millennium BC:

> Texts from Mari, Egypt, and Hittite archives refer to iron as black stone from heaven, and reflect elite, votive and ritual uses that correspond to archaeological finds in both Greece and Levantine contexts, in which iron is limited to ritual and burial contexts.[179]

Significant for the present study is the observation that iron-bearing meteorites in the vast majority of instances consist of a mixture of iron and other materials.[180] Iron from a stone fallen from heaven, typically "mixed iron," would seem a more than appropriate metal for symbolizing the age of cosmic dissolution and catastrophe.

Indo-Iranian Loss of Order and Erosion of Social Boundaries

What became conspicuously clear in the discussion of the preceding sections is that the Indo-Iranian myth of world ages is one in which each age is linked intrinsically to a social class. The structure is most transparent in India, where each age is marked by the color that is characteristic of the corresponding class, and the ages follow a hierarchical order, best to worst, that aligns itself with the hierarchy of social classes. *Dharma* progressively decreases by one-quarter as time runs down through the class-affiliated ages. It is, in fact, a breakdown in the proper relations and ordering of the classes – a loss of *dharma* – that is critically involved in the topsy-turvy unraveling of the cosmos in the final age. To recapitulate and elaborate the symptoms of that age from our earlier discussion of *Mahābhārata* 3: society becomes mixed – the three classes of Indo-European origin, the *brāhmaṇa*, *kṣatriya*, and *vaiśya*, intermarry; the *brāhmaṇa* forsake the Vedas and their sacred duties; judicious agricultural practices are abandoned; the *kṣatriyas* rape and steal and refuse to give protection; the three classes lose their distinctiveness – all blur as a single class; any person acts as a brahmin; the Indo-European classes are oppressed by the *śudras*; the *śudras* become the interpreters of the law, the brahmins their students. At the end, an apocalyptic destruction comes. But then, slowly, recovery begins – starting with the *brāhmaṇa* class – and a new *kṛtayuga* (the 'Winning Age') appears: the brahmins return to their rites; the *kṣatriyas* protect the earth; the *vaiśyas* look to their own tasks; the *śudras* serve the Indo-European classes. The cosmological process begins anew.

Prior to Zoroastrian reforms, the Iranian version of the myth of ages must surely have been one in which class hierarchy, and its decay and consequent disorder, figured prominently. This is strongly suggested when three factors are considered collectively. The first (and trivially obvious but necessary) consideration is the very survival and essential presence of the three ancestral classes (priests, warriors, cultivators) in Iran, as in India.

A second consideration is provided by that evidence adduced above for the Iranian survival of the Indo-Iranian (and Indo-European) cosmogony of the primeval giant – a cosmogony intimately affiliated with the creation of the three classes (a cosmogony even showing accommodation to a fourth class in Iran, just as in India). As in Indic tradition (evidenced by the *Laws of Manu*) the cosmogony is interlaced with the cosmological myth of ages by way of the three social classes, just so, in the Iranian-loan tradition of Daniel, the body-part-specific classes of the cosmogony are mapped onto the cosmological account of succeeding ages (see the homology of correspondences of Table 3.1). In other words, in Iranian tradition, as in Indic, each age is affiliated with a specific social class in the relative descending order of 1) priests, 2) warriors, and 3) goods producers.

Add to these a third consideration. The description of the fourth and final age, which sees the undoing of just religion and ordered society, is cast in terms of Zoroastrian historicized eschatology – it is a time of demonic rule. Even so, in spite of Mazdean reworking of inherited Indo-Iranian tradition, there remain specific references to elements of society functioning outside of their appropriate arena and to the blurring or inverting of social divisions, much as in *Mahābhārata* 3. Within the Zoroastrian litany of fourth-age lamentations, frequent reference is made to the degeneration of religious ritual (*Vahman Yašt* 2.36–7, 45–6) and of priests being treated with contempt (2.38–9) or forsaking their priestly responsibilities and devotions (2.40); commoners will marry the daughters of priests and noble persons (2.38); the unqualified will make legal and religious pronouncements (2.39); noble persons will beg and debase themselves (2.47); slaves will acquire sovereignty (2.49). To these similarities between the Indic and Iranian tradition could be added numerous shared symptoms of the final age that do not relate directly to social-class breakdown.

In both the *Vahman Yašt* (1.5 and 2.22) and the *Dēnkard* the final age of Zardušt's vision is described as one of "mixed iron."[181] In a completely parallel fashion, in the Iranian version of the tradition that is reflected in Daniel chapter two, the culmination of the fourth and final kingdom is presented in terms of "clay mixed with iron." For the Jewish prophet, the statue's feet of mixed iron serve to symbolize that the final foretold kingdom is one in which "they will mix with one another in marriage, but they will not hold together" (2:43). While the prophet has turned a foreign-born idea to a message of hope and promise for his own time and people – true to his role as a Biblical prophet – in origin, the notion of a "mixing in marriage that does not hold together" must have been engendered in an Iranian tradition of the social mixing of – the loss of distinction and proper ordering of – the Indo-Iranian classes, one that leads to the dissolution of society, a symptom of the diminution of order in the final age. As we have seen, there also occur in the Indic tradition explicit references to the intermarrying of *brāhmaṇa*, *kṣatriya*, and *vaiśya* classes in the last age, the *kaliyuga*, as there are references in the Zoroastrian text to perverse marriages between the lowly and the high-born in the final, "mixed" age. This cosmological doctrine of social mixing, of the mingling and confusion of the canonical Indo-European classes, and accompanying upheavals of the final age, must be at least Proto-Indo-Iranian in its inception.

Hesiod's Mixed Iron "Age"

And so we return to Hesiod. In the lines of the Greek poet, the notion of "mixed" receives a no less explicit expression in the description of the final age, the age of iron (*Works and Days* 174–84):

> But after that ... I wish I'd not have been among the men
> Of generation five, but that I'd died before, or else been
>   later born.   175
> For now indeed's a race of iron; and never will their toil
> And sorrow cease by day, nor exhaustion in the night;
> The gods shall give them grievous cares.
> **But even so for them will good be mixed with ill.**   179
> *And Zeus will end this race of mortal men as well,*   180
> *When'er at birth gray hair is on their temples seen.*   181
> A father his children will not resemble, nor children their father;
> And neither guest to host, nor comrade to comrade,
> Nor brother will be dear, as in the former time.

Line 184 is followed by a running list of yet more sorrowful symptoms marking the end of the time of the race of iron (symptoms to which we have already alluded): people – ruthless and ignorant of the wrath of the gods – will dishonor and bemean their parents; exercising power as they wish ("might makes right"), one man will sack the city of another; there will be no gratitude for oath-keepers and the just; the low-born man will defame the noble and oath-swear that his crooked words (*muthoi*) are truth; Zelos ('Envy' – the evil one) roams abroad; and Nemesis and Aidos flee the earth. After our exploration of the Indic and Iranian traditions, this is all familiar territory.

In his commentary on the *Works and Days*, West notes that lines 179–81 (those italicized above) "seem to interrupt the train of thought inopportunely: 182 ff. look more like a continuation from 178 than a series of portents parallel to grey-haired babies."[182] Leaving aside the matter of portents (lines 180–81) for the moment, one must agree that line 179 (bold and italicized) looks and feels decidedly out of place. This, however, is an artifact of translation.

Line 179 is of course the one that encodes the notion of 'mixed' or 'mingled' (*memeiksetai* [μεμείξεται]) – as we have seen, a fundamental characteristic of descriptions of iron-age society. The translation that I offered above – "But even so for them will good be mixed with ill" – is one typical of this line. What is being "mixed" is *esthla* (ἐσθλά) with *kakoisi* (κακοῖσι). In a typical reading of this line, these two neuter plural adjectives are interpreted as functioning (substantivally) as nouns: that is, 'good things' and 'evil things', respectively. As West notes,[183] Hesiod also invokes good and evil together in *Theogony* 609–10, where remarking on the man who has married a *good* wife, the poet declares, misogynistically, that his is a life in which evil (singular *kakon* [κακόν]) is constantly set against (*antipherizdei* [ἀντιφερίζει]) good (singular *esthlō* [ἐσθλῷ]); see Clay's remarks cited previously.

The idea that the human condition is characterized by the presence of both good and ill is one that is familiar to early Greek poets – as, undoubtedly, to the greater part of humanity, at all times, in all places. Homer knows it. In *Odyssey* 15.488–9, he places on the lips of Odysseus the phrase, addressed to the swineherd Eumaeus, "Zeus has surely given you good (*esthlon* [ἐσθλόν]) alongside ill (*kakō* [κακῷ])"; the utterance may very well be an adaptation of a common proverbial expression.[184] The concept recurs, embroidered with mythic details, in *Iliad* 24.525–33, as a mournful Achilles speaks to the grieving Trojan king, Priam, come to the Greek camp to collect the body of his son, Hector:[185]

> For thus the gods have spun the thread for wretched
>   mortalkind   525
> To live with grief – but they themselves are sorrow free.
> Two jars there are that sit in Zeus's floor – of gifts
> He gives – from one come ills, and blessings from the other.
> To him whom thunder-loving Zeus should grant a mix,
> He meets with ill at times, at other times with good;   530
> But whom he gives of only sorrows, him he makes the fool
> Of fortune – baneful hunger drives him on across the earth
>   divine,
> And here and there he wanders, honored not by gods nor
>   mortalkind.

The ancient Near Eastern wisdom tradition knew well this motif of the god who seemingly (from a human perspective) arbitrarily sends both good and ill to mortals: it is the problem of the so-called righteous sufferer. Thus, for example, in a Babylonian poetic text of the later second millennium BC – *Ludlul Bēl Nēmeqi* ('I Will Praise the Lord of Wisdom') – one Šubši-mešre-Šakkan rehearses how at the hands of his god Marduk he has fallen from prosperity into disease, ruin and rejection. The poem begins with a hymn to Marduk in which the deity's apparent capriciousness is rehearsed again and again, in lines such as (Tablet I, lines 13–14, 23–4):

> He it is, in the brunt of whose anger many graves are dug,
> At the same moment, he raises the fallen from annihilation.
> . . .
> He speaks and makes one incur many sins,
> On the day of his justice liability and guilt are dispelled.[186]

Forsaken by Marduk, other gods desert the sufferer, who wanders down-cast and defamed (Tablet I, 77–83):

> I, who walked proudly, learned slinking,
> I, so grand, became servile.
> To my vast family I became a loner,
> As I went through the streets, I was pointed at,   80
> I would enter the palace, eyes would squint at me,
> My city was glowering at me like an enemy,
> Belligerent and hostile would seem my land![187]

The ways of the gods are incomprehensible (Tablet 2, lines 43–5):

> (What the gods) intend for people changes in a twinkling:
> Starving, they become like corpses,
> Full, they would rival their gods.[188]   45

There is a flip side to the Greek view that Zeus doles out a mix of good and ill, or only ill, to a person. When Nausicaa, the Phaeacian princess, finds the destitute Odysseus washed up on the shores of her isle, she tells him that "Olympian Zeus himself dispenses happiness to humans – both to the good (*esthlois* [(ἐσθλοῖς)]) and to the bad (*kakoisi* [κακοῖσι]) – to each one as he wishes" (*Odyssey* 6.188–9).

Did such sentiments exert some measure of influence on "Hesiod's" own signification of the line 179 – shaped and reshaped throughout the oral performance history of *Works and Days*? Possibly so;

they have certainly influenced Hesiod's modern interpreters. The comparative evidence provided by Indic and Iranian parallels reveals, however, that the fundamental sense of the verse in its inception must certainly have been different from that conveyed in the above ("typical") translation (and, following from that, that lines 179–81 do not in fact "interrupt the train of thought," as will become clear). As in the homologous Indo-Iranian traditions, the entities being mingled in the final age are not "good things" and "bad things" – the good and bad experiences of life – but social classes. In other words, a more accurate translation of line 179 would be something like:

> But just the same, also among them the noble will be mingled
> with the low-born.

The verb is a future perfect (*memeiksetai* [μεμείξεται]), indicating that this intermingling will be an ongoing state of affairs characterizing the race of iron – precisely the picture painted in the Iranian and, especially, Indic descriptions of the final age. And why does Hesiod say "also"? To that we shall return.

GREEK EVIDENCE: HESIOD AND THEOGNIS Interwoven with the comparative evidence are at least two strands of Greek-internal evidence. First there is the remarkably apropos elegiac poem 183–92 of the archaic Greek poet Theognis. An aristocratic resident of the Greek city of Megara during the mid-sixth, or perhaps more likely, the second half of the seventh century BC, extending into the sixth,[189] Theognis laments the social changes taking place in his world, particularly the loss of class distinctions. People insist on having purebred livestock, he declares, but a noble man (*esthlos anēr* [ἐσθλὸς ἀνήρ]) has no qualms about marrying the low-born daughter of a low-born man (*kakēn kakou* [κακὴν κακοῦ]) if there is a profit in the deal (lines 185–6); and, vice versa, a woman is willing to become the wife of a low-born man (*kakou andros* [κακοῦ ἀνδρός]) if he has money (lines 187–8). In sum (lines 189–92):

> . . . Both the noble man marries the daughter of the lowly,
> And the lowly man the daughter of the noble; money has
>   mingled genes.   190
> So do not marvel, Polypaïdes,[190] that the citizens' genes
> Are being watered down: for the noble are being mingled with
>   the low-born.

The vocabulary throughout answers to that of Hesiod's lines: the "noble" (*esthlos* [ἐσθλός]); the "low-born" (*kakos* [κακός]); a "mingling" of the two (verb stem *mi(s)g-* [μι(σ)γ-]). Each with their common verb and neuter plural adjectives, Theognis' decrying of a present social upheaval in line 192 – "the noble are being mingled with the low-born" – recapitulates Hesiod's prophetic warning of a future state of affairs in *Works and Days* 179 – "the noble will be mingled with the low-born." In both Hesiod and Theognis we are surely dealing with the archaic (and inherited) stock-in-trade language of what was perceived to be the reprobate intermingling of the elements of society. While both poets' verses have a certain stand-alone proverbial ring, Theognis' line is nested within a fuller contextual framework; and from a similar greater formulaic context, Hesiod's must have been extracted. That context, in conjunction with the comparative evidence adduced above, suggests to us that for Hesiod (line 179), no less than for Theognis (line 192), the neuter adjectives *esthlon* and *kakon* (*esthla* and *kaka*) have lexically-specific referents, namely, the neuter noun *genos* (γένος), which Theognis uses in lines 190 and 191, prefacing the "mingling" phrase of 192.

This word – *genos* – is one that, in some of its uses, has no comfortable equivalent in present-day English.[191] In the translation of lines 190 and 191 above, I have rendered it by English 'genes' (and not only for the etymological connection). For their translations, Gerber and West both choose 'blood' and 'stock' (for lines 190 and 191, respectively);[192] Wender has 'blood' (190) and 'race' (191);[193] Fowler opts for 'breed' (190) and 'line' (191);[194] and Mulroy for 'lineage' (in 190 only – avoiding direct translation in 191).[195] It is a word of great antiquity, existing already in Proto-Indo-European *$\hat{g}enh_1$-os, leaving descendants not only in Greek, but in Latin (*genus* 'birth, origin, race, class') and Sanskrit (*janas-* 'race') as well. From its root *$\hat{g}enh_1$- ('to give birth, to beget') plus various appended suffixes, numerous words were formed in descendent Indo-European languages that were used to designate various units and levels of social structure: for example, Latin *gens* ('race, class', and a term for a family group); Old English *cynn* ('race, family'); Avestan *zantu-* ('tribe'); Sanskrit *jana-* ('race, tribe, people').[196]

Greek *genos* is of course the very term that Hesiod employs for conceptually framing his presentation of the myth of "ages." Rather than temporal ages or epochs of sovereignty, he talks of a "golden *genos* of mortal men" (line 109); which is followed in turn by a "silver *genos*, far inferior to the golden, like them neither in body nor mind" (lines 127–9); and then a "third *genos* of mortal men – one of bronze – not at all

TABLE 3.2. *Comparison of Greek and Indic Traditions*

Greek *Genos*	Indic *Yuga* and *Varṇa*
Golden	Kṛtayuga: Brāhmaṇa
Silver	Tretāyuga: Kṣatriya
Bronze	Dvāparayuga: Vaiśya
[Heroic]	
Iron (The period of mingled *genē*)	Kaliyuga: Śudra (The period of mingled *varṇas*)

the same as the silver" (lines 143–4). The poet's introductory description of the fourth *genos*, the heroes, is subtly different: they are said to be a godlike *genos*, demigods, lauded as simply "more just and nobler" – the implicit progressive degradation characterizing the previous three *genē* is here reversed. Less subtle is the very presence of the heroes in this *logos* of metallic ages – Hesiod's conspicuous addition. Finally comes the "*genos* that is iron," with all its attendant woes – the degradation is brought to fulfillment.

Once *genos* is identified as the referent of Hesiod's adjectives in line 179 ("the *noble* [*genos*] will be mingled with the *low-born* [*genos*]"), an unexpected, though fully transparent, parallelism reveals itself between the early Greek tradition upon which Hesiod is drawing and its Indic cognate. Consider Table 3.2.

Each age is affiliated with a particular *genos* or a particular *varṇa*; and, more idiosyncratically, the final age is not only affiliated with a particular *genos* / *varṇa*, but also with a mixing of *genē*/ *varṇas*. In India, the *kaliyuga*, identified with the social class (*varṇa*) of the non-Indo-European *śudras*,[197] is that period characterized by a disordered and degenerate jumbling of the social classes (*varṇas*) that are individually affiliated with the various ages (*yugas*) that precede – a mixing realized not only through intermarriage between distinct classes but through the topsy-turvy interchanging and confusion of the proper respective functions of those classes. The picture painted of the final age in Iranian tradition provides an exact match in this regard. The era of the final, iron *genos* in the early Greek tradition is precisely the same – the chaotic period in which the *genē* – equivalent to the Indic *varṇas* – are mingled, noble with base. In the Greek tradition, as in the Indic, this destructive "mingling" undoubtedly was not only construed as social but as functional – or dysfunctional – as in its Indo-Iranian counterpart – a result made clear in Hesiod's prophetic depiction of the inevitable future of his own time. Vernant's description (cited above) of that period – the "age of iron in its decline" – would apply equally well to its Indo-Iranian homologue: "essentially that of a revolt against order; an upside-down world where every hierarchy, rule, and value is inverted."

In the early Greek tradition that Hesiod is utilizing, in its full form and at some sufficiently ancient moment, the crucial social elements of each era, which Hesiod dubs *genē*, were undoubtedly explicitly invoked (as in India) in the narrative of iron-age decline. While there are reflexes of the more ancient arrangement preserved in *Works and Days*, as we shall see, Hesiod in his account of the final age makes no such explicit reference to the *genē* affiliated with the preceding periods – and could not, perhaps, do so, given the manner in which he has recast the tradition. In effect, what Hesiod has done is to take the inherited final-age tradition of the jumbled dissolution of the elements of (i) sovereignty, (ii) war and, (iii) goods-production and to project that topos subtly and cleverly back onto the preceding periods, in keeping with his programmatic contrast of *dikē* and *hubris*. Now it is the sphere of sovereignty that is degeneratively set *against itself* through the dichotomous opposition that Hesiod creates between the golden and the "far less noble" silver *genē*: in the end Zeus destroys the silver *genos*. It is the same with the warrior element: the bronze *genos* (*hubris*) that annihilating itself sinks nameless into Hades' realm dichotomously opposed to the heroic *genos* (*dikē*). And finally, Hesiod's own ambiguous iron *genos* knows a present in which *dikē* is possible, as opposed to a future in which *hubris* will run rampant and society will unravel completely – and Zeus will again bring destruction.

More than this, Hesiod retrojects yet other final-age traits on the earlier *genē*. The peculiar birthing and childhood phenomena characteristic of that final period in the several traditions show up in the silver *genos*, which Hesiod portrays as having an overlong childhood (100 years by mother's side) followed by a very short – and sorrowful – adult life. The Greek poet foretells that there will be a lack of intergenerational resemblance in the declining iron age – "A father his children will not resemble, nor children their father." Given the context in which the prophetic pronouncement occurs (line 182), this must certainly be construed as a consequence of the mingling of the noble and the low-born (line 179). Similarly, Hesiod declares that the silver *genos* was like the golden "neither in body nor mind" (line 129), and that the bronze was "not at all the same[198] as the silver" (line 144).

Bearing in mind the Greek poet's transference of traditional final-age social dissolution to earlier ages (instrumental in elaborating his system of dichotomies), we must revisit the (revised) translation of line 179 – the line with which we began this discussion:

> But just the same, *also* among them the noble will be mingled
> with the low-born.

The presence of "also" (Greek *kai* [καί]) in the line must be dictated by Hesiod's incorporation of the topos of a mixing of noble and base, of positive and negative, among the several *genē* that precede the iron age. And not only that – for the same motif of "mixed" is conspicuously evident in the age – that intrinsically hybrid age – that immediately precedes the age of iron: that of the heroes – demigods. As Clay has reminded us, the Neoplatonist philosopher Proclus writes, among his Hesiodic scholia, that "the demigods constitute . . . 'that which is a mixture from gods and men'" – a mixing of positive and negative of another sort, that of immortal and mortal.[199] The contrast of the hybrid iron age of cosmic dissolution with the preceding age of the hybrid heroes functionally parallels the contrast of the two hybrid categories of the *Theogony*: Clay's observation regarding those two groups (quoted above) would be equally applicable to the contrast of iron age with heroic: "Hesiod calls attention to the different kinds of μίξις [*mixis*], the one positive and controlled, the other destructive and disordered."[200]

GREEK EVIDENCE: HESIOD AND HOMER The claim that iron-age intermingling is to be understood as one that occurs between elements of society (rather than simply being a mixture of good and bad experiences) is further supported by the lines that immediately follow the prophecy of children and parents not resembling one another (lines 183–4):

> And neither guest to host, nor comrade to comrade,
> Nor brother will be dear, as in the former time.

Each clause involves the violation of a social relationship – guests and hosts, comrades, brothers – in the time of the iron *genos*. Hesiod has enumerated and distributed these three relationships not haphazardly, but in a way that conforms to the primitive Indo-European social structure that is crucial to the ancestral myth of the ages.

Xenos *and* Philos: *The Domain of Kings* In the dissolution of the final age, a guest – Greek *xenos* (ξένος) – will no longer be dear – *philos* (φίλος) – to his host – *xenodokos* (ξενοδόκος). The guest–host relationship, a type of institutionalized reciprocal friendship, was one of paramount importance in ancient Greece. The system provided a means whereby a stranger could be ensured lodging, personal care, and rights of protection when visiting a foreign place through the pledge of his host, who, in turn, would enjoy the same privileges whenever he might travel to the homeland of his guest. Such formalized guest–host relationships were hereditary, being extended for generations beyond the initial pledge. The practice was especially associated with kings – indeed, it was "the alternative to marriage in forging bonds between rulers"[201] – though was utilized by other aristocratic elements of archaic society as well. Mutually beneficial relationships between distant parties could thus be brokered: "In this respect a guest-friend was like a king; his worth was in direct proportion to his power."[202]

Hesiod's choice of words in these verses can be no accident. In his study of *philos* – the word translated nebulously in line 184 as 'dear' – and the related noun *philotēs* (φιλότης), Émile Benveniste points out there is a particular connection in Homer between *philos* and *xenos*, a connection that is so fundamental that it provides insight into the proper meaning of *philos*, a word of uncertain etymology:

> The notion of *philos* expresses the behavior required by a member of the community with regard to the *xenos*, the "guest" stranger
>
> . . .
>
> The pact concluded under the name *philotēs* makes the contractual parties *philoi*: they are thereby bound to a reciprocity of services that constitute "hospitality."[203]

The connection is further evidenced by the Homeric compound *philoxenos* (φιλόξενος), denoting a "hospitable" person – one "for whom the *xenos* is *philos*."[204] We encounter the word, for example, on the lips of shipwrecked Odysseus prior to his meeting with Nausicaa (*Odyssey* 6.120–21): awakened by the voices of the princess and other Phaeacian women, Odysseus frantically asks himself on whose shores he might have been washed up – are they a people of *hubris*, wild and without *dikē*? – or are they a people that show *philos* to a *xenos* (*philoxenoí*) and whose mind is set on "revering the gods" – *theoudēs* (θεουδής)? These formulaic lines will be repeated exactly at *Odyssey* 9.175–6, when Odysseus speaks of discovering what sort of beings the Cyclopes may be, and at 13.201–2, upon his unknowing return to his homeland, Ithaca. Homer also convenes a similar assemblage of traits, negative and positive, when

Alcinous the Phaeacian king, who has warmly welcomed Odysseus into his home, asks the wanderer to tell him of the many people he has encountered in his odyssey – of those who are harsh, wild, and without *dikē*, and of those who rightly receive a stranger (*philoxenoi*) and have a god-revering (*theoudēs*) mind (*Odyssey* 8.575–6).

That one who is *philoxenos* – showing *philos* to the guest stranger – should also be said to be *theoudēs* – revering the gods – comes as no surprise; this is no haphazard concatenation of adjectives on the poet's part. Zeus himself, sovereign deity, is at times called Zeus Xenios – "protector of suppliants and *xenoi* (guest strangers), the god who walks by the side of the esteemed *xenoi*" (*Odyssey* 9.270–71). Homer has the swineherd Eumaeus tell Odysseus – disguised as a beggar and received kindly into the herdsman's humble hovel – that "all *xenoi* and beggars are from Zeus; my gift [hospitality] is small but *philos*" (*Odyssey* 14.57–9) – again, formulaic phrasing, uttered similarly by Nausicaa upon finding Odysseus (*Odyssey* 6.207–8).

In contrast to the Phaeacians and Eumaeus, the savage Cyclops Polyphemus, who trapped Odysseus and his men within his cave, is by no means *philoxenos*. After Odysseus reminds Polyphemus of Zeus Xenios and the god's protection of the guest stranger, the Cyclops bellows (*Odyssey* 9.273–8):

> A fool you are, O *xenos*, or else you've come from far away,
> You who'd order me to fear the gods or skirt their path;
> For we Cyclopes pay no mind to aegis-bearing Zeus   275
> Nor any of the blessed gods, since better far are we than
>   they;
> Nor I'd spare your life – evading Zeus's wrath –
> Your comrades' either – not unless my heart should bid me to.

As Finley observes: "The giant was to pay for his *hubris* soon enough, tricked by the superior craftiness of god-fearing Odysseus."[205]

It is the gods, and Zeus most particularly, who set the standards for the treatment of the guest stranger – for the proper social response – one of *philos* toward the *xenos*.[206] And the social relationship of *xenos* (guest stranger) and *xenodokos* (host) is one that has particular affiliations with kings – and no less so with the king of gods. We find that Hesiod has gingerly and skillfully turned his audience back to his central theme; whether Homer assumes Hesiod (as Accius thought), or Hesiod Homer, or – almost certainly – both some common tradition,[207] the conjunction of *hubris* and *dikē* and the sphere of kings is here unmistakable.

Hesiod's prophetic message is one of the coming utter decay of right social relations within that realm – the ancient Indo-European realm of sovereignty.

Hetairos *and* Philos: *The Domain of Warriors* But it is not only the relationship of guest and host that will cease to be governed by *philos*; the right relating of comrade to comrade will likewise fall victim to social dissolution. The word translated "comrade" in line 183 is Greek *hetairos* (ἑταῖρος). Early Greek knows the term first and foremost as 'comrade-in-arms' – in the plural, 'a band of warrior followers,' such as the Myrmidons of Achilles.[208] To return to the Phaeacians – when the hospitable Alcinous spies Odysseus weeping as a bard sings of Greeks and their vanquishing of Troy, the king wishes to know the reason for his guest's tears: did some kinsman or friend fall before the city – or some cherished *hetairos* (*Odyssey* 8.581–5)?

At the heart of Homer's *Iliad* is the tale of Achilles and his ill-fated, cherished *hetairos*, Patroclus – most *philos* to Achilles of all *hetairoi* (*Iliad* 17.411). Angry with Agamemnon for taking away his slave-lover Briseis, Achilles has withdrawn from combat and from his *hetairoi*, but allows Patroclus to put on his own (Achilles') armor and enter the fray in his stead. Patroclus, the *philos hetairos*, is brutally slain (*Iliad* 18.80). While, as West notes, "*philos hetairos* is a common expression from Homer on,"[209] Nagy's 1999 study[210] makes clear the salient conjunctions of *hetairos* and *philos* that surround Homer's Achilles. It is the very death of Patroclus that turns Achilles back to a right relation with his *hetairoi*:[211]

> But it is really Patroclus who restores the *philotēs* 'state of being *philoi*' between Achilles and the Achaeans. As Sinos points out, Patroclus will have to sacrifice himself and die so that Achilles may recognize his social obligation to his *philoi*:[212]
>
> . . .
>
> "I did not become the Light for Patroclus or for the other *hetairoi*
> Who fell in great numbers at the hands of brilliant Hektor."
> (*Iliad* 18.102–3)

In Hesiod's waning iron age the *hetairos* will likewise fail to recognize "his social obligation to his *philoi*," but – unlike the case of Homer's Achilles – there will be no redemption for the warrior. The realm of the warrior, no less than that of the sovereign, will experience a complete degeneration of right social relations as the age draws to an end.

Brother and Philos: *Domain of the Goods-Producer* The pattern that we see emerging in lines 183–4 is clear. The poet is explicitly invoking the three canonical Indo-European social classes in his prophetic pronouncement of the apocalyptic demise of society – the same classes whose intermingling is both a symptom and cause of that dissolution – matching point for point the Indo-Iranian tradition, *mutatis mutandis*. Thus far it is the sovereign and warrior classes whose coming loss of *philos* has been proclaimed – now it is the turn of the goods-producers – or so we would expect.

What we find in the third position, however, is the poet's lamenting of the loss of familial *philos*: "Nor brother will be *philos*, as in the former time" (line 184). But *Works and Days* is, of course, at its core centrally concerned with the loss of a brother's *philos* – and that brother is Perses – the farmer – the goods-producer.

The loss of *philos* is directed precisely at the three ancestral Indo-European social classes. We see that this "Hesiod" has exercised a certain poetic license, while at the same time remaining unmistakably faithful to inherited Indo-European ideology. We perceive a light emanating from a distant Indo-European source, refracted through the prism of archaic Greece.

CYCLICITY

Hesiod reveals himself to be heir to a deeply archaic Indo-European cosmological tradition, one that, I have argued, has its beginnings at least as early as the period of communality of the ancestors of the Greeks and Indo-Iranians. In India the tradition is plainly a cyclic one – after the final, degenerate age is destroyed, *dharma* is renewed and a new "golden" age appears; and so the process begins again. Undoubtedly the cognate Iranian tradition was the same – cyclic – until Zarathuštra and his disciples transformed it into a tradition of apocalyptic progression culminating in Ahura Mazdāh's consummation of history. A fossil of an earlier Iranian cyclicity is likely to be found in the several distinct sequential millennial stages that make up the Zoroastrian tradition.

The tradition that Hesiod knows is unmistakably a cyclic one as well – the poet plainly tells us so: he wishes that he had died before the iron age, or else been born afterward. And though the poet predicts that the close of his iron age will see a definitive end of those mortals unfortunate enough to be members of that *genos*, he encodes within *Works and Days* a message of renewal and of the restoration of order – of the return of *dharma*. For what follows his *logos* of the ages constitutes, *grosso modo*, nothing less than a prescription for the restoration of order. After the ensuing injunctions to Perses and the kings, the remainder of the poem is a compendium of sage advice for living prosperously and in conformity with *dikē*. Though the genre generally and many of the poem's particular didactic elements find equivalents within the Near East, as demonstrated above, it is interesting that particular threads of advice have close parallels in Indic tradition. Thus, West and Nagy have pointed out that lines 727–32 and 757–9, in which Hesiod rehearses prohibitions against urinating while standing and facing the sun, while on the road, or into rivers and streams, are close to admonitions in the *Laws of Manu* 4.45–52 – a work, as we have seen, concerned with the preservation of *dharma* in a world given to unraveling.[213] Nagy offers an additional, highly a propos, insight:

> The legal traditions of the Indic peoples are clearly cog-nate with those of the Greeks, and in this connection it is especially interesting to observe the uses of *memnēménos* 'being mindful' at *Works and Days* 728, in the specific con-text of the injunctions now being considered, as well as else-where. . . . The root *men- / *mneh₂- of *memnēmenos* recurs in the Indic name *Mánu-*, meaning 'the mindful one': this ancestor of the human race gets his name (which is cognate with English *man*) by virtue of being mindful at a sacrifice. Manu is the prototypical sacrificer, whose sheer virtuosity in what Sylvain Lévi called "the delicate art of sacrifice" con-fers upon him an incontestable authority in matters of *ritual* [my emphasis]. Since sacrificial correctness is the founda-tion of Indic law, the entire Indic corpus of juridical/moral aphorisms is named after him.[214]

Hesiod's restorative prescription for *dikē* – for *dharma* – undoubtedly was no less a matter bound up with ritual – of the performance of his gnomic epic in ritual setting – a setting of ritual empowerment.

And what of the cosmogony? Does Hesiod preserve any vestige of that Indo-European cosmogony of the primeval giant whose body is divided for the creation of the cosmos – from whose body the three strata of Indo-European society were formed? Almost certainly.

In a somewhat enigmatically[215] worded verse (line 26) in the proem of the *Theogony*, the Muses, just prior to endowing Hesiod with poetic craft, speak to him a *muthos*, addressing him – Hesiod the shepherd – as a "belly" (*gastēr* [γαστήρ]):

Shepherds of the fields, lowly shameful things, mere bellies.

Shepherds are "lowly" – *kakos*, Theognis'– and Hesiod's – term for the low-born element of society. They are only "bellies" – having their origin in that lower portion of the cosmic giant's body, source of the goods-producing class, the Indo-European herders. Whatever synchronic use "Hesiod" has made of the phrasing,[216] we must see on the diachronic axis an endpoint lying in the Indo-European cosmogony – the cosmogony that we found in India, and Iran, to be tightly interwoven with the cosmology of ages.[217]

THE WARP AND WOOF OF *WORKS AND DAYS*

There is much more that could be said regarding Hesiod's use of inherited Indo-European mythic, religious, and ritual tradition.[218] This, however, will be enough, perhaps, to persuade the reader that Indo-European traditions do indeed survive in Greece. The playful, creative use to which Hesiod puts these inherited notions and conventions and the freedom that he displays in restructuring them on the surface, while preserving what we might term underlying structures, suggests to us that this "Hesiod" is fully conversant with traditions of his Indo-European ancestors. The ease with which he navigates the ancient Indo-European ideology of social tripartition and the confident skill with which he manipulates that ideology to his own ends reveal a comfortable familiarity with it. This is not the tired reworking of a tradition borrowed from some distant place and people but the playful juggling of an inherited tradition close at hand to the poet.

At the same moment, the poet exercises the freedom to frame these inherited Indo-European materials within a form acquired from the Near East – that of the didactic discourse. Here we see clearly the process of weaving together the disparate threads that must be common to the manufacture of the fabric of Greek mythic tradition. Perhaps the weave will prove to be so tight outside of Hesiod that the individual threads cannot often be so satisfyingly identified. Or perhaps with sufficient patience and scrutiny, we may be able more broadly to tease apart the warp and woof of Greek myth.

Suggested Reading

Lamberton (1988) provides a helpful overview of Hesiod's works for general readers. For the *Theogony* and *Works and Days*, West (1966) and (1978) are, respectively, standard commentaries, containing much valuable scholarly discussion, complemented by West (1997). Clay (2003) offers an integrated interpretation of the two poems. Hunter (2005) consists of thirteen recent articles treating various aspects of the *Catalog of Women*, within which can be found numerous references to earlier work on the topic. See, in the same volume, Richard Martin's chapter on Hesiod's *Shield*, with bibliography. For all of the preceding works, helpful scholarly treatments can be found in Janko (1982). Nagy (1990a) should be consulted for discussion of Hesiod and pan-Hellenism vis-à-vis Greek myth. For further treatment of many of the specific issues discussed above, the reader will find numerous bibliographic references within the notes.

Notes

1 Gellius (3.11.1–3) also tells us that the Greek historian Ephorus (fourth century BC) held a similar chronological view, while Philochorus (fourth/third century) and Xenophanes (sixth century) contend the opposite. See also n. 2 below.

2 "That Hesiod is earlier than Homer is no revolutionary view; but as the reverse is taken as axiomatic by most writers, it may be worth recalling that until the latter part of the fourth century BC, Hesiod's priority was widely accepted" – so West (1966) 46–7 reminds his readers. On the relative chronology of Hesiod and other early Greek poets and on chronological issues generally, see West (1966) 40–48; West (1978) 30–33.

3 On Hesiod's biographic statement as literary persona, see, *inter alia*, Stoddard (2004) 1–33, with references to scholarly work of each persuasion: for the literary persona view, see especially Nagy (1982, 1990b) and Griffith (1983); for recent advocates of the biographic position, see Stein (1990) and Nelson (1998). Edwards (2004) 19–25 argues that Hesiod the poet may have constructed a herder–farmer literary persona for himself, but that "if [he] does not really belong to this group, then he has successfully fashioned a persona for *Works and Days* able to voice their perspective on the world" (p. 25).

4 On the process by which a more localized Greek epic could undergo diffusion to become Panhellenic and the implications of such diffusion, see, *inter alia*, Nagy (1996a, 1996b, 2003).

5 Nagy (1990b) 79.

6 Cf. West (1966) 150. West notes that the title *Theogony* is first attested in the work of the third-century Stoic, Chrysippus. On Alexandrian scholars and their contributions to the traditions of Greek mythology, see chapter seven, "Hellenistic Mythographers."

7 For discussion with bibliography, see West (1966) 12–16.

8 Janko (2001) 1. For a translation of the papyrus, see Janko, pp. 18–33.

9 Burkert (2004) 89–98. On the Orphic texts in general, see West (1983).

10 The text of the *Theogony* used herein is that of West (1966); the text of *Works and Days* is that of West (1978).

11 On the significance of the distinction between the Heliconian and Olympian Muses, see, *inter alia*, Nagy (1990b) 57–61; Clay (2003) 54–7. For a *structural analysis* of the *Theogony* from the perspective of Panhellenic performance, see Nagy (1990b) 53–6.

12 West (1966) 276–7 observes: "It is a section of extreme interest for the student of Greek religion; for seldom elsewhere do we find a Greek setting out in so full a statement his personal beliefs concerning the nature of the powers of a god." It is something rather different, of course, for those who see in "Hesiod" a literary persona; see the discussion in Stoddard (2004) 7–15. For helpful discussion of the "Hymn to Hecate" with recent bibliography, see Clay (2003) 129–40.

13 The tale of Prometheus and Pandora is retold in *Works and Days* 47–105; on the variations between the two tellings, see Clay (2003) 100–128, with references to earlier work.

14 On the "authenticity" of the passage, as well as that of several lines at the end of the preceding section (by my division of the text), see West (1966) 356–8.

15 Gaea is predominantly supportive of Zeus, though Hesiod has just presented her as coupling with Tartarus to produce a creature that will overthrow Zeus, continuing the cycle of heavenly coups. Toward a resolution of this seemingly inconsistent behavior, see, *inter alia*, Clay (2003) 26–8; West (1966) 23–4.

16 See Burkert (2004) 35–7, (1992) 90, who emphasizes the similarity of the *Iliad* passage and the division of the cosmos into three parts found in the Mesopotamian *Atrahasis* (for translations of various versions, see Foster (2005) 227–80). Burkert (2004) 37 observes: "No other passage in Homer comes so close to being a translation of the Akkadian epic." Mondi (1990) 165 finds a Canaanite parallel in a Ugaritic tradition that presents the gods Baal, Yamm, and Mot as "manifested, respectively, in the cosmic realms of the atmosphere, the sea, and the lower world of the dead."

17 For a summary of the evidence for this position, see West (1966) 397–9.

18 West (1966) 398–9; Northrup (1983) – each with certain caveats.

19 Nagy (1990b) 80.

20 From a formal perspective, Nagy argues, the entire *Theogony* up to line 963 is "a hymn to the Muses, serving as a prelude to the catalogue of heroes and heroines that survives at verse 965–1020 [on which, see below].... Thus verses 1–963 of the *Theogony* are not a single, but rather a composite, hymn in comparison with most Homeric *Hymns*"; Nagy (1990b) 56.

21 On the *Catalog of Women*, see Hunter (2005); Clay (2003) 164–74.

22 For a balanced assessment of the causes of this *lapsus*, see Burkert (1992) 1–7, with further references.

23 For broad and reliable treatments of Near Eastern influences on early Greece, see especially Burkert (2004, 1992) and West (1997).

24 This is not to suggest that all Classicists have become ardent students of the Near East and its formative influences. West (1997) x captures it well: "The discovery in the thirties and forties of the Hurro-Hittite Kumarbi mythology, with its

undeniable anticipations of Hesiod's *Theogony*, finally forced Hellenists to accept the reality of Near Eastern influence on early Greek literature. Since then they have shown themselves increasingly tolerant of oriental comparisons, if not particularly active in investigating the oriental literatures for themselves. The outstanding exception is Walter Burkert, whose work will have opened many people's eyes." For an argument in favor of Hesiod's "kingship-in-heaven" tradition having an Indo-European antecedent, see Allen (2004).

25 For a summary account of the discovery and (ongoing) excavation of Boğazköy, see Güterbock (1997).

26 On the Hurrians and their non-Indo-European language, see Wilhelm (2004).

27 Three of the texts explicitly preserve the designation "song"; for others it is reasonably inferred. See Hoffner (1990) 38.

28 See Hoffner (1990) 38, with references to earlier work on the several texts.

29 The translation is that of Hoffner (1990) 41.

30 One *AMMATU* is probably 0.5 meters; thirty of these units make one IKU; see Hoffner (1990) 82.

31 Hoffner (1990) 54.

32 Hittite is written with a cuneiform script consisting chiefly of syllabic (phonetic) characters; but Sumerian logograms (transliterated with Roman capitals) and frozen Akkadian syllabic spellings (Akkadograms – transliterated with italic capitals) are employed as well. On the Hittite writing system and its transliteration, see Watkins (2004) 552–5.

33 On the reconstruction of the text of the Song of Silver, see Hoffner (1990) 45–8 and Hoffner (1988).

34 See Hoffner (1988) 164: "Classical mythology is full of examples of mortals sired by gods from mortal women. And we know of at least one good example of this in one version of the Hattian–Hittite myth of Illuyanka.... Silver might have been such an offspring of god and woman." On the dragon Illuyanka, see Hoffner (1990) 9–14; on Illuyanka vis-à-vis Typhoeus, see Watkins (1995) 448–59.

35 There is likely another feature that binds together these two gods. The Hurrian deity Kumarbi is a god of grain; see West (1997) 280, (1966) 204–5. What little evidence there is for identifying the nature of Cronus beyond his theogonic role – chiefly the celebration of his festival, the Cronia, following harvest – suggests he was an agrarian deity as well.

36 Mondi (1990) 155–6 notes Egyptian parallels to the swallowing of deities and, following Meltzer (1974), impregnation by blood that is shed from the genitals of a god. For parallels between the Orphic cosmogony and Egyptian traditions, see Burkert (2004) 93–98.

37 One of whom is named KA.ZAL 'shining face' and is born out of Kumarbi's head when some other deity cracks open the latter's skull. On the striking similarity of this account to the birth of "flashing-eyed" Athena out of Zeus's split skull (*Theogony* 924–5), see Hoffner (1975) 138, with further references. It is commonly Hephaestus who is credited with splitting Zeus' skull, as in Pindar, *Olympian Odes* 7.35–8.

38 At points, the Orphic theogony bears even closer resemblance to the Hittite tradition than does the Hesiodic; see Burkert (2004) 92–3.

39 Hoffner (1975) 138–9 discusses the alternating sequence of Hittite divine kings.

40 Hoffner (1990) 39. I have modified Hoffner's transliteration of some names to conform with the transliterations otherwise used herein.

41 As it is in Homer; see *Iliad* 5.749–52 and the remarks in Kirk (1990) 136.

42 The translation is adapted from Woodard, in press.

43 On Akkadian *titu* 'clay' as the possible source of Greek *Titēnes*, see Burkert (2004) 33–4; (1992) 38, 95.

44 West (1966) 201. On various Near Eastern traditions of gods imprisoned in the Netherworld, see Burkert (2004) 33; (1992) 94. West (1997) 298 compares the Titans, whom Hesiod also refers to as "former gods" (*Theogony* 424, 486) to "the Hittite 'Former Gods' (*karuilies siunes*). . . . " The first occurrence is found in the Hecate passage and is, specifically, a reference to Cronus' treatment of Hecate with regard to her proper share among the "former Titan gods." The second reference again entails Cronus, and editors disagree as to how "former" is to be construed – "former king of the gods" or "king of the former gods."

45 In his account of the event, the (AD) fifth-century Egyptian Greek writer, Nonnus (*Dionysiaca* 1.481–534), identifies the rescuer as the Phoenician Cadmus.

46 In certain other details Apollodorus' account of Typhon (Typhoeus) also shows particular similarity to the Hittite tradition. For example, he situates the creature's birth in Cilicia, a region of Anatolia (home of the Hittites), and his physical description of Typhon's gargantuan size – towering above mountains, his head reaching to the very stars – is particularly reminiscent of the depiction of the stone giant in the Song of Ullikummi.

47 There are, however, in regard to the intervening Hittite episodes, some enticing elements in the Hesiodic text. While considered in isolation they appear to have little comparative value, but when considered as features within manifestly parallel structures, they may take on greater significance.

What does intervene between the Titanomachy and the birth of Typhoeus? Hesiod's description of the Netherworld and attentiveness to its inhabitants (lines 736–819): Atlas, the giant who supports the heavens on his head and arms; Nyx and Hemera; Hypnos and Thanatos; three-headed Cerberus; the river Styx. Just so, Hittite LAMMA, Silver, and Ḫedammu (the focus of attention in the Hittite texts) are all denizens of the Netherworld. And while there is no Hittite description of that place, it is tantalizing – bearing in mind that these intervening texts are only fragmentarily preserved – that in the surviving bits of the Song of Ḫedammu, Kumarbi sends explicit direction to the Sea God to journey to him through the Netherworld, "below river and earth" – a trek that will follow such a course that the Sea God will come up exactly below the seat of Kumarbi. Not only is he to do so in order to avoid detection by the Sun and Moon Gods, but so that the gods of the "Dark Earth" will not see him as well. The notion of a subterranean journey clearly suggests a Netherworld geography and, more particularly, a (vertical?) complexity to the Netherworld such that the Sea God can travel there unseen by even the chthonic deities.

In his description (*Theogony* 758–66) of the children of Nyx 'Night' – Hypnos 'Sleep' and Thanatos 'Death' and their goings forth – Hesiod says that Helios, the sun, never looks on Sleep (gentle and kind) and pitiless Death (iron-hearted and bronze-hearted) as he arches from horizon to horizon (lines 759–61). It would seem a curious statement – do Sleep and Death only come upon mortals at night? (cf. the remarks of Caldwell (1987) 70, n. 756–66) – and more curious still in that Helios is frequently said to see all things. One must compare *Odyssey* 11:17–18, where Homer tells that the city of the Cimmerians, by the entrance to the Netherworld, blanketed in clouds and mist, is never seen by Helios, and allow that what Hesiod is claiming is, somewhat similarly, that the sun's rays never fall upon the Netherworld home of Sleep and Death (see West (1966) 368–9; Heubeck and Hoekstra (1989) 71–9). But one might also ponder an episode from one of the fragmenets of the Song of Silver, in which that Netherworld personification of metal pulls down the Sun and Moon from heaven, who then pay Silver homage and beg that he spare their lives, lest, with their lights extinguished, the lands that he governs be governed in darkness.

48 The tradition of the Gigantomachy is, however, far older than Apollodorus and his *Bibliotheca*. From the sixth century BC on, it is a common theme of Greek art; see Schefold (1992) 54–67.

49 Apollodorus 1.6.1; adapted from Woodard, in press.

50 For an English translation of the Enūma Eliš see, *inter alia*, Foster (2005) 436–86 and ANET (Speiser), pp. 60–72, from which latter source the quotations of the text appearing here have been drawn.

51 Burkert (2004) 30–32, (1992) 92–3 explores the possibility that Greek *Tēthys* [Τηθύς] 'Tethys', the name of the Titan consort of Oceanus and mother of rivers, is derived from Akkadian *Taw(a)tu*, 'sea', one form of the name *Tiamat* that occurs in the Enūma Eliš. On this etymological connection, see West (1997) 147–8, especially 147, n.200. In a cosmogonic passage in the *Iliad* (14.200–204), Burkert (2004) 30 notes, "Hera says that she is going to Oceanus, 'origin of the gods,' and Tethys the 'mother'; later on Oceanus is even called 'the origin of all'." This alternative theogony, in which Oceanus and Tethys are the primeval couple, appears to resurface in an Orphic verse rehearsed by Plato (*Cratylus* 402B); see Janko (1994) 181, with additional bibliography.

52 Foster (2005) 444, n. 1.

53 For a possible surfacing of this Babylonian motif in Homeric epic, see West (1997) 222.

54 For other discussions of Babylonian parallels to Hesiod's *Theogony*, again fundamentally sympathetic to the present treatment, see, *inter alia*, Littleton (1970) 109–15; Walcot (1966) 27–54; West (1997) 280–3, (1966) 22–4.

55 For the text of the myth, see, *inter alia*, Foster (2005) 489–91; ANET (Grayson), pp. 517–18; Lambert and Walcot (1965).

56 For further discussion of the Dunnu theogony, see Littleton (1970) 112–14; Lambert and Walcot (1965); Walcot (1966) 41–2.

57 The name appears to be actual Phoenician – Šakkūnyātōn, meaning 'the god Šakkun gave'; see West (1994) 294, n. 20, with additional references.

58 Philo's text is known chiefly through the work of Eusebius, bishop of Caesarea, the fourth-century Christian apologist and historian. The text used herein is that of Jacoby, *Fragmente der Griechischen Historiker* (FGrH), reprinted in Baumgarten (1981), in which work an English translation with commentary can also be found.

59 For discussion of these lines and their intended meaning, see, *inter alia*, Baumgarten (1981) 68–74, 77–82. Philo's reference may be to the script of the Ammonites, a Canaanite people closely related to the Hebrews and Phoenicians, and especially to the Edomites and Moabites.

60 For discussion of the term, see Baumgarten (1981) 183–5.

61 On the three, see, *inter alia*, Baumgarten (1981) 189–90, 202–3. El and Dagon are well-known deities among various West Semitic peoples (of whom the Phoenicians are one); Baitylos is otherwise attested through several sources, including a Phoenician treaty.

62 For a summary of the evidence, see Baumgarten (1981) 195–7.

63 On the reading "or Hadad" see Baumgarten (1981) 196, 215, 219.

64 For bibliography, see West (1994) 294.

65 See Baumgarten (1981) *passim*, but especially pp. 261–7.

66 For discussion of additional similarities, see West (1997) 285–6.

67 Other Indo-European cultures do know a form of the myth: notably, that version found in the Persian *Shāh-nāmeh* ('Book of Kings'), written by the poet Ferdowsī (Abū Ol-Qasem Manṣūr) in the tenth and eleventh centuries AD, and that of the *Prose Edda*, a work by the twelfth-century Icelander, Snorri Sturluson. Both are most likely borrowed. On the kingship-in-heaven tradition and its occurrence in Indo-European works, see Littleton (1970). See also Allen (2004) and comments in n. 24 above.

68 Prior to the acquisition of the Phoenician script, the Greeks had written with the syllabic script called Linear B during the mid- to late second millennium BC, and Cypriot Greeks continued to use a related syllabic writing system well into the alphabetic period; see Woodard (1997) *passim*.

69 See Woodard (1997) 133–62.

70 On which, see, *inter alia*, Karageorghis (2002); Walz (1997); Reyes (1994).

71 West (1994) argues that it is a Phoenician cosmogony that underlies not only variously reported Greek cosmogonic traditions but the cosmogonic doctrines of early Ionian philosophers as well.

72 West (1978) 151; Gagarin (1986) 107–9. For a recent examination of Hesiod's depiction of the kings with references to earlier work, see Edwards (2004) 64–73.

73 Gagarin (1986) 46–9; see also Nagy (1990b) 64.

74 "The problem is not only that the princes are arbitrary, arrogant, or careless.... Rather, Hesiod's charge of gift swallowing implies that they have deliberately chosen to deviate from known standards of fair and equitable judgment for one of two reasons: Either because of an illegitimate acceptance of gifts (*qua* bribes) from some interested party or because they accept the gifts traditionally offered to judges by disputants without rendering straight judgment in return"; Ober (2005) 399.

75 For further interpretative specifics, see Gagarin (1974), with references to earlier work. See also Clay (2003) 34–7.

76 The translation is adapted from Woodard, in press.

77 Hesiod devotes 17 lines to the gold race, 16 to the silver, 13 to the bronze, and 28 to the iron.

78 On which see West (1978) 203.

79 Nemesis is the deification of anger at things unjust; Aidos, respect for another.

80 Nagy (1990b) 66 makes it clear:

> The 'moral' of the fable about the hawk and the nightingale hereby becomes explicit: the hawk/king who threatens to devour the nightingale/poet as proof of his power is utterly disqualified as an exponent of *díkē* 'justice'. Moreover, since only those kings who are *phronéontes* 'aware' will understand the fable (202; cf. the idealized kings at *Theogony* 88, who are *eképhrones* 'aware'), the greedy kings are

implicitly disqualified even from understanding the 'moral,' in view of their general ignorance (see *Works and Days* 40–41). And if the kings cannot be exponents of *díkē*, they are utterly without authority and their raison d'être is annihilated. In fact, after verse 263, the kings are never heard of again in the *Works and Days*.

81 West (1997) 319–20, (1978) 204; Perry (1965) xxviii–xxxiv. For a general discussion of the Greek fable within a context of Near Eastern influence, see Burkert (1992) 120–124.

82 Perry (1965) xxxiii. Perry summarizes the Babylonian fable on pp. xxxii–xxxiii; for the Greek equivalent, which has substituted a bull for the elephant, see Perry p. 103.

83 Ebeling (1927) 50.

84 Walcot (1966) 90

85 ETCSL translation: t.6.1.08 (etcsl.orinst.ox.ac.uk/cgi-bin/etcsl.cgi?text=t.6.1.08).

86 The fable is itself akin to the Sumerian debate texts – texts pitting animals, plants, elements, and so forth against one another – such as the *The Debate between Bird and Fish*. See Black et al. (2004) 225–40 for discussion of the debate genre and the similarity between the heron-and-turtle fable and debate texts.

87 The translation is that of Black et al. (2004) 238.

88 West (1978) 3–22.

89 Chadwick and Chadwick (1986).

90 West (1978) 28.

91 The translation is that of Black et al. (2004) 285.

92 The proper placement and construal of this line is a matter of scholarly disagreement; see West (1978) 329–30.

93 Šamaš is the Akkadian sun-god.

94 The translation is that of Foster (2005) 412–13.

95 The translation of the Biblical text here and throughout this work is that of the *New English Bible*.

96 For a summary of the history of Egyptian wisdom literature, see Ray (1995).

97 On the *Instructions of Amen-em-Opet* and affiliations with Hesiod and the book of Proverbs, see Walcot (1966) 86–7; West (1997) 94; Eissfeldt (1965) 474–5. John A. Wilson (ANET, p. 421) observes: "Amem-em-Opet differs from earlier Egyptian books of wisdom in its humbler, more resigned, and less materialistic outlook." Some scholars have argued that Amem-em-Opet was itself influenced by the Hebrew proverbs, though this seems currently to be a view not widely held; see, however, the observations of Ray (1995) 24.

98 That is, a person who is mentally disabled.

99 That is, persons who would harm the one being addressed.

100 The translation is that appearing in ANET (Wilson), p. 424.

101 On the possible influence of Hesiod on *Ankhsheshonqy*, see Walcot 1966 (88) with reference to his earlier work on the problem. On other influential elements – Greek and Aramaic – see Ray (1995) 26.

102 On the *Wisdom of Ahiqar* see Harris et al. (1913); Lindenberger (1983); Greenfield (1995). Referring to the comparative study of Lichteim (1983), Greenfield (1995) 50 notes, "It is with the Syriac and Armenian versions that the important Demotic wisdom collection called 'The Instruction of Ankhsheshonqy' has definite ties."

103 West (1978) 28.

104 West (1978) 174.

105 West (1978) 174.

106 For an English translation of the Pahlavi texts discussed here, see West (1995) 1:191–235; 4:180–81.

107 The account of seven ages also survives in a Persian poem of the thirteenth century AD, the *Zardušt-nāmeh*. For the poem see Rosenberg 1904.

108 For discussion of variant forms of this millennial chronology, see West (1995) 1:xlvi–lv; Boyce (1996) 285–293.

109 Sanskrit *dharma*, which I choose to leave untranslated, is a semantically multifaceted notion, at the heart of which is 'order'. In the Introduction to their translation of the Sanskrit *Laws of Manu* (the *Manavadharmaśāstra*; on which, see below) – a work fundamentally concerned with the maintenance of *dharma* in a world in which chaos always threatens – Doniger and Smith (1991) xvii write of this text: "It is about *dharma*, which subsumes the English concepts of 'religion', 'duty', 'law', 'right', 'justice', 'practice', and 'principle'."

110 The graying of humans receives explicit mention in Mārkaṇḍeya's first list of the symptoms of the *kaliyuga* in 3.186; there boys are said to father offspring when 10 or 12, and girls conceive at 7 or 8. In 3.188 the corresponding ages are given as 7 or 8 and 5 or 6.

111 West (1997) 314; West (1978) 176, in which he writes: "The antediluvian kings reign for periods ranging from 10,800 to 72,000 years, and the great destruction of the Flood marks this off as a distinct historical age. The kings of the first dynasties after the Flood have much shorter reigns, but still of up to 1,200 years."

112 Koenen (1994) 14–18 seeks to show a similarity between Hesiod's prophetic language and certain Egyptian prophetic texts, as well as Mesopotamian, but points out that "in the early Near Eastern cultures, however, we have found no trace of four ages named after metals" (p. 24). He believes, however, that Egypt and the Near East provided both the Greeks and the Iranians with the idea of cyclic time, as well as an apocalyptic tradition, passed along to India (see especially pp. 12–14, 34). Koenen seems to stand alone in this imagined course of transmission, as he acknowledges (see p. 13, with nn. 26 and 28). No such influence needs to be posited; a primitive Indo-European concept of temporal cyclicity appears virtually certain, as revealed by comparative analysis of Celtic and Indo-Iranian traditions; see, in this regard, the comments of Lincoln (1986) 217, n. 24.

Some investigators, such as Koenen, have expressed concern over the "late" date of the Zoroastrian documents. The date is not a problem as far as the comparative value of the Iranian materials is concerned. The *comparative method*, in its application to both Indo-European linguistic and sociocultural data, is a powerful methodology, able to pierce deep into Indo-European antiquity from much shallower and variegated chronological levels (see my remarks in Woodard [2006] 32–5). The Sanskrit language, for example, though not attested in writing until c. mid-second century AD, shows many close linguistic similarities to Bronze-Age Greek and is a cornerstone in the reconstruction of the Proto-Indo-European language of the fifth millennium BC. As Dumézil (1995) 95–101, following Wikander (1947), demonstrated, certain primitive Indo-European elements find expression in the epic *Mahābhārata* that are not attested in the much-earlier-composed Vedas.

It may also be instructive to recall that the earliest extant manuscript of *Works and Days* is of medieval date (see West [1978] 75–86).

113 Dumézil (1987) 165.

114 Dumézil (1973) 37.

115 See especially Nagy (1990b) *passim*; Watkins (1995) *passim*.

116 Consider, for example, the Homeric traditions of the "Judgment of Paris" (see Dumézil [1995] 608–14) and the figure of Heracles as a "triple-sinning warrior" (see Dumézil [1983; 1970]). Several of Dumézil's later "100 essays" (published collectively as Dumézil [2003]) treat Greek topics – particularly several of the initial twenty-five that appeared in 1982 under the title *Apollon sonore*. Among the work of Dumézil's disciples, consider, *inter alia*, Yoshida's (1964) study of the shield of Heracles.

117 The work appears most recently in the 2006 republication of Vernant's *Myth and Thought among the Greeks* by Zone Books. Compare Vernant's further thoughts on a structural analysis of Hesiod in chapters two and three of that volume.

118 For discussion, see Woodard (2006) especially pages 14–20; there I write:

> ... as early as 1932, the French linguist Émile Benveniste had begun independently to explore and develop his own interpretation of Indo-European social classes. The most succinct expression of Benveniste's conclusions is to be found in his masterful work treating primitive Indo-European economy, society, law and religion, *Le vocabulaire des institutions indo-européennes* (1969); therein (as earlier) Benveniste argues for a similar hierarchically-ordered, three-part social structure. ... The structure is most readily perceived among the Indo-Iranian peoples, and indeed, in the research path followed by both Benveniste and Dumézil the reconstruction of an ancestral structure was first projected to Proto-Indo-Iranian society (see Benveniste 1932; Dumézil 1930).

119 On binary opposition generally in early Greek poetry, see the remarks of Nagy in Chapter 1 of the present volume.

120 See, *inter alia*, McKay (1963); cf. the remarks of West (1978) 236–7. At *Works and Days* 498–501 the poet suggests a contrast between an empty or bad hope (*elpis* [ἐλπίς]) and a more positive one.

121 Clay (2003) 123. And consider also Berg (1976) 19, who observes: "Similarly, the woman of the *Erga*-myth is called *Pandora*, 'All-giving', though Hesiod is quick to turn the etymology around and insist that it means 'Gifted by All (the Gods)' (81–2)."

122 See, *inter alia*, Marquardt (1982) 285–7; West (1978) 165–6.

123 Clay (2003) 121.

124 Clay (1993) 108. The tradition of the shared eye and tooth is first attested by Pherecydes (West [1966] 245), an historian of the fifth century BC whose work survives only in fragments; for his Graeae text, see Fowler (2000) 280, line 15 – 281, line 3.

125 Clay (1993) 116.

126 Clay (1993) 115.

127 Thus, see Berg (1976), especially 17–19.

128 Lines 124–5, in which the *daimones* are described, are identical to lines 254–5, lines that describe the actions of Zeus's invisible spies. Some scholars, such as West (1978) 183, propose that the earlier lines (124–5) were copied from the latter by

a post-Hesiodic hand. Vernant (1983a) 10–11 suggests that there is an intentional link between the golden age *daimones* and the spies of the divine sovereign Zeus.

129 Vernant (1983a) 11.

130 Vernant (1983a) 12. He also argues (p. 16) for extending the parallelism by comparing Hesiod's bronze age to the race of giants born from Gaea – whom Apollodorus describes as going to war against Olympus.

131 Vernant (1983a) 7.

132 Vernant (1983a) 12.

133 Vernant (1983a) 16.

134 Vernant (1983a) 16.

135 Vernant (1983a) 17.

136 See, for example, Dumézil (1992)176–7.

137 Vernant (1983a) 9.

138 Vernant (1983a) 19.

139 Vernant (1983a) 20.

140 Vernant (1983a) 23 concludes: "This is where Hesiod's profound originality lies and this is what makes him a true religious reformer, comparable in manner and inspiration to certain prophets of Judaism."

141 For discussion of the Babylonian Exile and its aftermath, see, *inter alia*, Mitchell (1991).

142 It is reminiscent of both the story of Nebuchadnezzar and Daniel in Chapter Two, in which Daniel interprets the dream of the giant with head of gold and feet of clay, and the story of Chapter Four, in which Daniel interprets yet another of Nebuchadnezzar's dreams (in which he saw a great tree), after which the king is driven into the wilderness and goes mad, but after seven years is healed as he calls upon the God of the Jews. See the discussions in Salvesen (1998) 149; Mitchell (1991) 417–18, 425–6; Ackroyd (1968) 36–8.

143 Oppenheim (1977) 150.

144 See ANET (Oppenheim), p. 562.

145 On Nabonidus, see Wiseman (1991) 243–51. On his relationship with Cyrus, his Persian deposer, see also Mallowan (1985) 408–15.

146 See ANET (Oppenheim), p. 562.

147 Mitchell (1991) 425–26.

148 Though Herodotus and Xenephon present the Persian takeover as involving greater bloodshed than do the Mesopotamian sources.

149 Mallowan (1985) 408–9.

150 Dandamaev (1991) 256, who continues, "It can be noted incidentally that a letter of the early sixth century BC mentions the arrest of several Babylonians whose father and brother had fled to Media. As can be seen from the same letter, several other Babylonians had fled to Media, and the king's order for them to return remained unanswered."

151 See Wiseman (1991) 248–9; see also Mallowan (1985) 411–12.

152 Mitchell (1991) 430, 436–7; Mallowan (1985) 409, 411–12.

153 On the various dialects and historical stages of Aramaic, see Creason (2004) 391–3.

154 Montgomery (1979) 20–22.

155 Mitchell (1991) 427; Kutscher (1970) 399–403.

156 Davies (1976) 399.

157 See Russell (1964) 19 and passim.

158 Montgomery (1979) 186.

159 The differences extend to at least the early twentieth century; see the discussion in Montgomery (1979) 188–9.

160 As in, for example, Hartman and Di Lella (1978) 146.

161 See, *inter alia*, Clackson (2004) 922; Burrow (1955) 15–16.

162 Republished in Heitsch (1966); see pp. 457–8.

163 Sanskrit *viśvavedas* ('all-knowing') is also used of Dyaus, the Indic deity cognate with Greek Zeus; see West (1978) 223–4 for the comparison and for a discussion of the Sun and its relationship to all-seeing Zeus in Greece and to Indic Mitra and Varuṇa, and to Iranian Ahura Mazdāh: "Hesiod's Zeus with his spies and his all-seeing Eye, and Homer's Sun ['who sees all things and hears all things'] (*Iliad* 3.277, invoked together with Zeus in swearing an oath...) are evidently fragmented survivals of this Indo-European system."

164 West (1978) 219. Added to this cluster of shared Greek and Indo-Iranian features appearing within this delimited portion of *Works and Days* is Hesiod's use of *ōkupetēs* (ὥκυπέτης) 'swiftly flying' to describe the hawk of his fable; Homer uses the adjective only of horses, "but the etymological equivalent *āśupátva* is applied to a hawk in *Rig Veda* 4.26.4...." (West [1978] 209). Also worth noting is what Herodotus (1.132) reports about Persian sacrificial practice: when a sacrificial victim has been dismembered and its flesh cooked, the various portions are placed on top of grass that has been scattered in the sacrificial space, whereupon a Magus approaches and chants a *theogony*.

165 On Zoroastrian dualism, see, *inter alia*, Boyce (1996) 192–3, 198–200.

166 By "cognate" I mean that Avestan *aša* : Sanskrit *r̥ta* and Avestan *drug* : Sanskrit *druh* each have a common origin in the parent Proto-Indo-Iranian language.

167 On the Indo-European cosmogony see, *inter alia*, Mallory and Adams (1997) 129–30; Lincoln (1986).

168 For further elaboration, see Lincoln (1986), especially chapters 1, 2, and 7.

169 For the Pahlavi text, see West (1995) 3:118–119.

170 Pahlavi *vastryōsīh*, from the Avestan compound *vāstryō fšuyant*.

171 Benveniste (1969) 1:279, 288.

172 On the *Škend Gumānīg Vizār* and other Iranian variants, see Lincoln (1986) 146–148. Of especial relevance are traditions concerning Iranian Yima (which cannot be discussed here), the first king, whose name is cognate with that of Norse Ymir; on Yima, see also Lincoln (1997).

173 For the text, see West (1995) 3:118.

174 See Fontenrose (1974) 3–5.

175 Fontenrose (1974) 4. West (1978) would disagree, stating that "Hesiod was the sole source for later Greek and Roman writers" (p. 177). But consequent to this position, he must append the claim that Hesiod's "attempt to historicize [the myth] by incorporating the Heroic Age was abandoned in favour of the strictly regular mythical scheme." If Hesiod were the only source for later Greek and Roman writers, how would they have known that his version was one that had been altered and historicized by the inserting of the age of heroes (and have universally deleted the same)? It is a cumbersome hypothesis – made much more so by the particular similarity of Ovid's account to the Indo-Iranian traditions – and one that this learned scholar seems to have moved away from in West (1997), where he writes, "We may note in passing certain features which appear here and there in

later Greek and Roman accounts of the Golden Age, though not in Hesiod, and which have Near Eastern parallels" (p. 314).

Ovid offers an account of the Gigantomachy, placing it immediately after his report of the iron age. Within the context of the myth of world ages, his description of the giants and the aftermath of their defeat seems teasingly familiar in light of the Indo-European cosmogony encountered above, with its cosmic giant whose dismembered body gave rise to the cosmos and the classes of human society. Ovid's giants have serpent feet and a hundred hands (*Metamorphoses* 1.183–4); when they are vanquished by Zeus, the primeval earth-goddess, Terra, creates from the bloody carnage a race of living beings of human form (156–62). Puruṣa, the butchered cosmic giant of Indic tradition, is described as having a thousand heads, a thousand eyes, and a thousand feet (*Rig Veda* 10.90.1). More overt in this connection is Ovid's unique account of how the giant Atlas was transformed into a mountain (*Metamorphoses* 4.655–62); see Lincoln (1986) 10.

176 For the text of Aratus' myth, see Kidd (1997) 78–83, with associated commentary.

177 Among other versions of the myth mentioned by Fontenrose (1974) are those of the Roman poets Horace (*Epodes* 16.41–66) and Juvenal (6.1–24). Horace makes oblique reference to the golden, bronze, and iron ages in verses extolling the glories of the Elysian Isles. Juvenal begins his sixth satire by rehearsing the nature of life in a bygone day, presumably the golden age, and concluding this passage with explicit, if brief, reference to the silver and iron ages. It was in the silver age, writes Juvenal (line 24), that adultery first appeared (all other sins appearing in the iron age; line 23). The remark is intriguing if the poet should prove to be preserving some more ancient tradition, given the Indo-Iranian affiliation of the second age with the second stratum of society, the warrior class. Dumézil identified a prominent Indo-European mythic figure that he called the triple-sinning warrior – the warrior who sins against each of the three canonical elements of Indo-European society. The warrior's sin in the realm of the goods-producers (Dumézil's third function) commonly entails an adulterous act; see, *inter alia*, Dumézil 1970 and 1983.

178 The Indic use of white, red, yellow, and black to identify the sequential *yugas* is not simply a matter of the ages being represented by "metallic colors," as some investigators have supposed (see, for example, Koenen [1994] 13). The use of color (*varṇa*) to symbolize the social classes is a Common Indo-Iranian phenomenon and one that has its roots in an earlier and more broadly attested Indo-European practice; see Dumézil (1992) 104–6, with references to earlier work.

179 Blakely (2007) 26, with extensive bibliography.

180 Blakely (2007) 27, n. 71 writes: "All meteors have some iron content, ranging from the siderites, which are 100% iron and nickel, to stony-iron siderolites, which are 50% iron and 50% silicate, and stony (aerolites), which are 10–15% iron and nickel, mixed with 85–90% silicates. Only one in ten meteors is a siderite. . . ."

181 As also in the *Zarduśt-nāmeh* (see n. 107 above). Boyce (1984) 71 interprets the phrase as a reference to iron still mixed with dross. She sees in the term an allusion to the mixture of good and evil in the fourth age – perhaps a necessary interpretation à la Hesiod, one could imagine, given her view that the Iranian world-ages tradition was acquired from the Greeks (pp. 70, 72). Boyce herself, however – inaccurately typifying the Greek final age as only "a fourth age of simple iron, which was in fact a prized and handsome metal" (p. 72) – views the "mixed" status from a Zoroastrian perspective: "for dualist Zoroastrians the concept of a mixture of good

and evil is an ever-present one, indeed the whole of this existence is characterized in their holy texts as the time of 'mixture' (*gumēzišn*), . . ." (p. 72). As we have already noted and will soon consider again, Hesiod also describes an iron age that is "mixed."

182 West (1978) 198. Though West does not advocate excising the lines from the text, as certain others before him had, but sagely advises: "We had better take the text as it stands, and try to understand how Hesiod came to write it so."

183 West (1978) 198: "It was a tenet of popular wisdom that human life is either a mixture of good and bad or wholly bad." See also West (1966) 334.

184 Heubeck and Hoekstra (1989) 262. Compare Helen's words at *Odyssey* 4.236–7: "But now to one and now to another, Zeus gives both good and ill."

185 "The language of the whole passage is untypical," writes Richardson (1993) 331.

186 The translation is that of Foster (2005) 395.

187 The translation is that of Foster (2005) 397.

188 The translation is that of Foster (2005) 399.

189 On the dating of Theogonis see West (1993) xiv and, especially, West (1974) 65–71. For additional points of agreement between Hesiod and Theognis see Nagy (1985).

190 Also called Cyrnus; this is a young male to whom many of Theognis' poems are addressed.

191 Fontenrose (1974) 1, n. 1 writes, for example:

> "Age" is, I grant, a not wholly satisfactory translation of *genos*, which means "stock" or "breed" in this text; but these words will hardly do for translation or discussion (can we talk about Hesiod's "golden stock"?); and "race" must be rejected altogether as both misleading and inaccurate. "Generation" is one meaning of *genos*, but is surely unsuitable for the myth, since each *genos* obviously consisted of several generations in the ususal sense of the term.

Similarly, Koenen (1994) 2, n. 3 observes:

> In the following pages I shall try to avoid the term "races" because of the restrictive sense in which the term is used in our vernacular. But "age," the word I shall use, is not precisely what Hesiod had in mind. He does not talk about the creation of periods of time, but about the human beings who lived in specific periods of their own.

192 Gerber (1999) 201; West (1993) 68.

193 Wender (1973) 103.

194 Fowler (1992) 95.

195 Mulroy (1992) 173.

196 On *genos* and its position within the structure of Indo-European society, see especially Benveniste (1969) 1:257–8, 314–16.

197 I have, of course, in the present treatment completely skirted the issue of a possible fourth Indo-European class, i.e., in Dumézilian terms, a "fourth function," on which see, *inter alia*, Allen (1996, 1987). Allen argues for a fourth function that is characterized by "two aspects, one positive or transcendent (F4 +), one negative and excluded (F4 -)" (Allen [2000] 279). Thus, in a certain sense, Allen's fourth function can be characterized as *mixed*, and in this regard his analysis may well have relevance to the fourth, mixed age of Indo-Iranian and Greek tradition. Particularly germane to the topic at hand is his treatment of an Iranian (pre-Islamic Afghan)

catastrophe tradition in Allen (2000), in which work he makes reference to the Hesiodic scheme of world ages, though his chief concern is with flood traditions.

198 The word here (line 144) translated 'same' is Greek *homoios* (ὁμοῖος). In line 182 – "A father his children will not resemble, nor children their father" – the word translated 'resemble' is *homoiios* (ὁμοίιος), which Hesiod uses for the former word, *homoios*. As West (1978) 199 notes, according to the ancient scholia on Hesiod, the particular sense of *homoiios* is "'at one with', or 'physically similar' in consequence of marital fidelity." The intended nuance in line 182 is undoubtedly the latter, in light of the comparative and Greek-internal evidence adduced above. West, however, inclines toward the former – though he knows no parallel for that sense – because the subject of the first clause is "father" and he would have expected wording more like that of line 235, in which (among those people who practice justice) women are said to bear children like their parents. Given the Indo-European antiquity of the forms and notions being expressed in Hesiod's prophetic description of iron-age social dissolution, the poet's wording is not problematic. Primitive Indo-European society was patriarchal and patrilineal, with the father enjoying significant familial authority; see, *inter alia*, Benveniste (1969) 205–76. The *Laws of Manu* (3.12–19) set out the unhappy consequences of a noble man marrying a low-born woman and fathering children by her. On the differences between Hesiod's generations being "a matter of genetic debasement," see Nagy (1985) §46; see also §43.

199 Clay (2003) 161.

200 Clay (1993) 116.

201 Finley (2002) 90.

202 Finley (2002) 93.

203 Benveniste (1969) 1:341.

204 Benveniste (1969) 1:342. Benveniste further notes that *philoxenos* is "the only compound with *philo-* [in Homer] that has a second term applying to a person."

205 Finley (2002) 92.

206 Benveniste (1969) 1:342; Finley (2002) 92.

207 With regard to which, see, *inter alia*, Nagy (1996a) 133–4 (with references to earlier work): "When we are dealing with the traditional poetry of the Homeric (and Hesiodic) compositions, it is not justifiable to claim that a passage in any text can refer to another passage in another text. Such a restriction of approaches in Homeric (and Hesiodic) criticism is one of the most important lessons to be learned from the findings of Milman Parry and Albert Lord on the nature of traditional 'oral' poetry. . . . There may theoretically be as many variations on a theme as there are compositions. Any theme is but a multiform (that is, a variant), and not one of the multiforms may be considered a functional 'Urform.'"

208 As in *Iliad* 1.179–80. On epic Greek *hetairos*, see, *inter alia*, Heubeck et al. (1988) 384–5.

209 West (1978) 200.

210 See especially pages 104–8.

211 Nagy (1999) 106.

212 Nagy references Sinos (1975) 74 = Sinos 1980.

213 West (1978) 334–5; Nagy (1990b) 70. Watkins (1995) 14 sees behind these passages "an apparent Indo-European tabu" concerning urinating while standing. For the

Manu passages, see the translations in Olivelle (2005) 126–7; Doniger and Smith (1991) 78–9.

214 Nagy (1990b) 70. The Sylvain Lévi quote is from Lévi (1966) 121. Nagy continues with observations concerning a "parallel thematic pattern in the *Precepts of Cheiron*," for which see his pp. 70–71.

215 "Enigmatic" to judge by some of its improbable interpretations.

216 On which, see Nagy (1990b) 45; see also Nagy (1999) 229–33. On the ugliness of the pot-bellied Aesop, see Compton (2006) 20–21, with references to earlier works; on Compton's theme of the ugliness of the poet, see his p. 20, n. 12, with references to the development of this theme throughout the work.

217 One is reminded of the Irish bard as a "third-function" figure within the first-function "learned class" (consisting of (1) druids, (2) *filid* [or *vates*], and (3) bards); see Rees and Rees (1989)140–41. On Cridenbél, the gluttonous poet of the Irish Tuatha Dé Danann, see Nagy (1999) 230–31.

218 There are, for example, also temporal and calendrical elements involved (aside from the actual agricultural "calendar" of *Works and Days*), which we do not have the luxury of exploring in the present work. I treat these and other issues (some of which were introduced above) in greater detail in a monograph now in preparation: *Hesiod: The Rupture of Time; The Restoration of Order.*

4: TRAGEDY AND GREEK MYTH

Richard Buxton

The theatre of Dionysus in fifth-century-BC Athens provided a unique context for myth-telling.[1] At the annual festival of the City Dionysia, myths were reembodied in performances by members of the citizen group. In these reembodiments, as heroes and divinities walked the stage, myths were not just narrated as past events: they were actualised as present happenings. Then and there, but also now and here; remote enough to allow room for pity, but close enough to inspire awe.[2]

In the present attempt to characterise tragic myths, I begin with a discussion (Section 1) of an apparently simple question: What happens in Greek tragedies? In order to suggest an answer, I contrast tragedy with the nontragic mythological tradition, examining in particular the kinds of actions and sufferings ascribed to heroes and heroines. In Section 2 I ask another seemingly straightforward question: Where are Greek tragedies imagined as taking place? My answer involves politics and psychology as well as topography and geography. Finally, in Section 3, I discuss ways in which tragedy represents the gods. Throughout the chapter, my aim is to ask how far it is possible to isolate features which are distinctively tragic.[3]

WHAT HAPPENS IN GREEK TRAGEDIES?

Across a wide range of Greek mythological narratives, in both texts and visual representations, the mighty heroes Heracles, Theseus, Agamemnon, and Oedipus are credited with formidable and triumphantly successful exploits. Heracles is the monster-slayer *par excellence*; Theseus, champion of idealised Athenian values, rids the world of unpleasant villains and puts an end to the Minotaur; Agamemnon leads the expedition which captures Troy, so justly avenging Paris' abduction of Helen; Oedipus destroys the oppressive power of the Sphinx. These same heroes appear, more specifically, in tragedies, including four which survive to the present day: Euripides' *The Madness of Heracles* and *Hippolytus*; Aeschylus' *Agamemnon*; Sophocles' *Oedipus Tyrannus*. What is noticeable about the way in which these heroes are represented in tragedy is the kind of *selection* of mythical material which tragedy practises. When in Euripides' play the peerless Heracles returns home after his culminating Labour (the seizing of the hell-hound Cerberus), he is struck by a frenzy sent upon him by Hera; while out of his senses he slaughters his wife and children and is only prevented from killing his father Amphitryon when Athena hurls a rock at him. In *Hippolytus*, Theseus witnesses the utter destruction of his family: when his son Hippolytus slights Aphrodite, the goddess's punishment leads to the suicide of Theseus' wife Phaedra and to the death of Hippolytus, intemperately cursed by his father in the false belief that the young man had raped Phaedra. In *Agamemnon*, Troy's conqueror is humiliatingly stabbed to death in his bath by his vengeful and unfaithful wife Clytemnestra. In *Oedipus Tyrannus*, the saviour of Thebes becomes an abhorred outcast, revealed as the killer of his father and as the husband to whom his own mother bore four children.

This pattern is typical. Greek tragedies do not narrate heroic exploits: instead, they explore the disruptions and dilemmas generated by such heroism, disruptions and dilemmas which almost invariably involve the catastrophic destruction of a household. Now of course tragedy is not the only genre to highlight the problematic aspects of heroism. We need only think of the *Iliad*, where heroic values are put under enormous strain by the conflict between Agamemnon and Achilles; where Achilles' clear-eyed awareness of the brevity of his glory contrasts with the all-too-human, indeed 'tragically' limited vision which characterizes Hector;[4] and where one of the poem's greatest affective climaxes, in which Priam ransoms from Achilles the body of his dead son Hector, precisely exemplifies the kind of emotional intensity later exploited in Attic tragedy.[5] Or we may think of the *Odyssey*, in which Odysseus' slaying of the suitors is by no means morally unambiguous (this is especially clear in Book 24, where the suitors' grieving families step forward to exact vengeance for their murdered brothers and sons). Nevertheless, it is above all in tragedy that the underside of heroism becomes pervasive, not simply as a 'theme,' but as the predominant perspective from which mythical events are selected and depicted. It will be useful to illustrate this in more detail, by examining one myth, that of Jason and Medea, in three different versions.

In *Pythian 4*, the praise-poet Pindar honours Arcesilas of Cyrene, victor in the chariot-race at Delphi in 462 BC. The poem includes what is, for Pindar, an unusually extended account of a myth, namely Jason's quest for the Golden Fleece. In spite of its length, this account is not a detailed narration, but rather a spotlighting of significant moments. Given that Pindar is celebrating the return of a victorious athlete after a competitive triumph, the choice of the myth of the Argonauts makes perfect sense as a paradigm of success in the world of heroic adventure: Jason left home in search of glory, and returned having won it.[6] The Pindaric Jason is formidable, handsome, and gentle of speech, even when he confronts Pelias, who has forcibly usurped sovereignty from Jason's 'rightfully ruling parents' (110). Thanks to his trust in the god (232) and to Medea's passionate assistance, Jason wins the Fleece, and is wreathed by his comrades like a victor in the Games (240). What of Medea? It is true that Aphrodite teaches Jason how to induce Medea to lose her shame for her parents and to desire a country – Hellas – which is not her own, so that she shall be burned and whirled by the lash of Persuasion (216–19). It is true, too, that her chaotic and disruptive emotions have been taken to exemplify her 'disturbing ambiguity.'[7] Nor can it be denied that at one point Medea is described as 'the murder(ess) of Pelias' (250), presumably an allusion to the later brutal episode in which she deceived Pelias' daughters into butchering and boiling him, in an attempt to effect his rejuvenation. Nevertheless, although this allusion has been cited as evidence of Medea's 'infamous duplicity,'[8] there is surely no implication that to be a murder(ess)-of-Pelias is necessarily a negative quality, since earlier in the poem Pelias has been portrayed as unlawfully and violently insolent (*athemin, biaios, hubrin* [ἄθεμιν, βιαίως, ὕβριν] 109–12). Moreover, about any possible future dissension between the Colchian princess and her Greek lover, Pindar is silent: Jason took her away secretly but *sun autai* (σὺν αὐτᾷ), 'with her acquiescence' (250). To put the matter in broad and direct terms: in *Pythian 4* the central function of the myth of the *Argo* is to shed lustre on the human victor Arcesilas by praising the mythical hero who stands as his exemplar.[9]

Argonautica, the great Hellenistic epic poem by Apollonius of Rhodes, narrates the tale of Jason and Medea in far richer detail than anything we find in Pindar; and in Apollonius it does indeed become imperative to recognise ambiguity. The portrayal of the two principals is subtle and complex: for the bright light of Pindaric heroism Apollonius substitutes something far more troubling. Jason can only achieve his goal by relying on others: even though, before yoking the fire-breathing Colchian bulls, he exults in the strength of his limbs like a proud warhorse (3.1259–62), he has by that stage already been sprinkled by Medea with potions which confer invulnerability. Not only is he far from self-reliant, but he also enters deeply worrying moral territory: his treacherous and religiously polluting murder of Medea's brother Apsyrtus overshadows the latter part of the epic, and partly determines the return course taken by the *Argo*, as Jason and Medea visit first Circe, and then Alcinous on Phaeacia, in a quest for purification.[10]

The differences between the Pindaric and the Apollonian Medeas are even greater than those between their Jasons. Compared to the near-evanescence of Medea in *Pythian 4*, the Medea of Apollonius is a strong and disturbing presence from the moment that she appears. When she abandons her home, she is torn apart by grief (4.34–40); she threatens Jason with the terrible consequences of his breaking of his oath to her, when it seems that he will negotiate with the pursuing Colchians (4.383–93). There is even a subtext which hints at the future rupture between Jason and Medea, since the myth of Ariadne, mentioned several times (3.997–1004, 1096–1108; 4.430–34), cannot but recall Theseus' abandoning of *his* foreign princess. Nevertheless, in spite of these darker characteristics of Jason and Medea, as the *Argo* sails into its home port of Pagasae at the end of the poem there is no mention of impending trouble. Indeed, about Medea's future career, we have learned explicitly only two things. First, according to Hera's plan, Medea will arrive in Iolcus as a *kakon* (κακόν), 'bane,' to Pelias (3.1134–6). Second – so Hera assures Thetis – Medea will ultimately marry Achilles in the Elysian Fields (4.810–16).[11] Whatever has gone before, the ending of the epic is serene, concluding as it does at the moment when the *Argo* itself bows out of the story:

> You sailed untroubled past the coast of Cecrops' land, past Aulis inside Euboea, past the towns of the Opuntian Locrians, and joyfully you stepped ashore at Pagasae.
>
> (4.1778–81)

Chronologically intermediate between the Pindaric and the Apollonian narratives is Euripides' tragedy. As might be expected from a story incorporating so many episodes of violent conflict, the myth of Medea was a favourite with the Greek tragedians;[12] but the only play on this theme to survive to the present day is the Euripidean masterpiece. Within the world of this play, the expedition of the *Argo* is just a memory; equally remote is the recollected love between Jason and Medea. From the perspective of the tragedy's Corinthian setting, Colchis and Iolcus lie in the past; Athens, Medea's eventual refuge, lies in the future. Concentrated into the transitional Corinthian present is an episode of horrifying cruelty, which encompasses the destruction of two families.

Jason has decided to put Medea aside in favour of a new bride, the daughter of the Corinthian king Creon. When Medea cunningly obtains from a nervous and reluctant Creon the permission to remain for just one more day before leaving Corinth, she seizes the opportunity to inflict a ghastly vengeance on her former lover and his prospective second family. As wedding presents to Jason's new bride, Medea sends a lovely gown and coronet, conveyed by her own little sons to make the gifts more persuasively welcome. But the gifts turn out to contain a fiery, flesh-eating poison, which causes the excruciating deaths of the girl and her father. A Newsbringer[13] recounts the final stages of the torment:

> Overcome by disaster, she fell to the ground;
> Except to her father, she was indeed hard to recognise;
> The form of her eyes was not clear, and her face was disfigured;
> Blood mingled with flame dripped down from her head; her
> flesh,
> Eaten away by the invisible jaws of poison, flowed away
> From the bones, like drops of pine resin –
> A terrible sight. Everyone was afraid to touch
> Her corpse. We had learned the lesson from what had happened.
> (*Med.* 1195–1203)

Going beyond even these horrors, Medea then kills her own two young sons – acting not as a monstrous psychopath, but as a mother torn apart by conflicting drives. At first she had found the thought of infanticide hideous beyond imagining:

> What am I to do? My courage has gone,
> Women, when I saw the bright eyes of my children,
> I could not do it. Farewell to the plans
> I had before. I'll take my children from this land.
> Why should I cause harm to my children in order to make
> Their father suffer, when I shall suffer twice as much myself?
> (1042–7)

But finally, overcome by the urge to punish the partner who has betrayed her, Medea convinces herself that she has no choice:

> Friends, the deed is decided: with all speed
> To kill the children and then leave Corinth;
> Not to delay, giving the children up to another
> More malevolent hand to murder them.
> At all events, they must die; and since they must,
> It is I who shall kill them, I who gave them birth.
> Arm yourself, my heart: why do I hesitate
> To perform wicked deeds that are terrible, yet inevitable?
>
> (1236–43)

With the boys lying dead, it might seem that any possibility for still greater cruelty has been exhausted. Yet as a final refinement Medea conveys her sons' corpses away from Corinth, in order to prevent Jason from embracing them in a last farewell. 'You are not yet mourning,' she chillingly informs Jason (1396): 'Wait until you are old.'

In exploring the catastrophic underside of heroism, Euripides' *Medea* exemplifies the inflection typically given by tragic playwrights to the mythical tradition. Tragedy is a world in which the tensions which ordinarily beset family life are unbearably intensified. In marriages, ancient and modern, husbands and wives quarrel and even fight: in tragedy, Clytemnestra goes further: she slaughters Agamemnon. In families, ancient and modern, children often face conflicts of loyalty towards their father and mother: in tragedy, Orestes goes further: he kills his mother because she killed his father. Tragedy is a crucible, a burning glass, an arena which displays events so terrible that one can hardly bear to contemplate them, yet so compelling that one cannot but watch to the end.

WHERE DO GREEK TRAGEDIES HAPPEN?

We turn now to the *location* of tragic myths. The action of Greek tragedies is, I shall suggest, imagined as unfolding 'in between.' The Euripidean Medea may once more serve as our initial guide.

Medea is in many senses an outsider. Not only is she a stranger to Corinth: this Colchian princess is a stranger to the Greek world altogether. At first she relies on Jason; later – for her escape plan – she relies on Aigeus. But throughout, her status is that of one who is 'citiless' (*apolis* [ἄπολις], 255, cf. 644).[14] This condition of exclusion applies, literally or metaphorically, to a large proportion of the protagonists in Greek tragedy. In Sophocles' *Philoctetes* the eponymous hero, abandoned on the island of Lemnos, lacks all the comforts which would have brought his life closer to that of a civilised human being; only his magically unerring bow raises him above the level of a brute. (The desolation and isolation attributed to Lemnos in this play constitute another example of tragic 'selection': inhabited since prehistoric times, the real Lemnos was by no means devoid of human population.) Another Sophoclean work, *Ajax*, depicts a hero whose position at the very edge of the beached Greek ships (*Aj.* 4) reflects his martial indomitability – the extremity of an army's lines is one of its points of maximum vulnerability – but also symbolises other aspects of his marginality, including his madness and his attainment, albeit briefly, of a sublime linguistic register unparalleled elsewhere in the play;[15] eventually he commits the ultimate act of self-exclusion by falling on his sword. In these and many other tragedies, explorations of the moral and emotional implications of exclusion and marginality illustrate the genre's predilection for 'testing to destruction' the concepts and categories of ordinary Greek life.[16] By dramatising the experiences of individuals driven out of their usual frameworks for living, tragedies depict actions which are simultaneously extreme and representative – just as the chorus of *Oedipus Tyrannus* can characterize the utterly extraordinary events surrounding Oedipus as a 'paradigm' of human existence (*OT* 1193).

There are various ways in which tragic actions may unfold in the gaps between states. Sometimes these states are *city*-states, as in Sophocles' *Oedipus at Colonus*, in which the plot concerns an outcast wandering in the no-man's-land between Thebes and Athens. Will hospitable Athens agree to admit a wanderer with a horrific past? Will Creon and Polynices, with their threats and persuasion, draw Oedipus back to Thebes? At the end Oedipus mysteriously crosses an even more dangerous, because sacred, boundary, that between life and death, eventually to occupy a post mortem position between the two poles – as a dead hero with the power to affect the living.

A similar sense of the precarious balance between states typically underlies works which turn on the acceptance or rejection of a ritual supplication. Central to Aeschylus' *Suppliant Maidens* is the dilemma faced by the Argive ruler Pelasgus, obliged to decide whether to accept a group of refugees in a crisis where such acceptance will entail the dangerous enmity of those angrily pursuing them. The asylum-seekers in question are the daughters of Danaus, desperate to avoid being forced

into marriage with their cousins, the sons of Aegyptus. To intensify
Pelasgus' dilemma still further, the Danaids threaten to commit suicide
upon the city's holy shrines. As Pelasgus expresses it to the chorus of
Danaid maidens:

> Yes, I see difficulties everywhere, hard to wrestle with;
> A surge of troubles overwhelms me like a river.
> I have entered upon a sea of ruin, bottomless and dangerous,
> With nowhere a harbour to escape from misfortune.
> If I do not fulfil this duty to help you,
> You threatened us with pollution unsurpassed;
> But if I stand against your cousins, Aegyptus' sons,
> Before our walls and fight the matter out,
> Is the cost not a bitter one, that men
> Should soak the earth in blood for women's sake?
> Yet I must fear the wrath of Zeus, the suppliants' god:
> For mortals that is the supreme fear.
>
> (*Supp.* 468–79)

The boundary between one community and another is a place of tension, and potentially a powerful generator of dramatic meaning.[17]

The gaps between states explored in Euripides' *Trojan Women* are at
once political and more than political. The action is suspended between
Troy and Greece, but also between past and present and, for the Trojan women themselves, between one male and another. The surviving
women of Troy find themselves in a city whose past already lies in
smouldering ruins, and whose future will consist of a slave existence
across the sea in Greece. Cassandra will be transferred from the service
of Apollo to the bed of Agamemnon; it is proposed that Hecuba and
Andromache shall serve Odysseus and Neoptolemus. The Trojan men,
it is true, died good deaths, achieving 'the most beautiful glory' by dying
for their country (*Tro.* 386–7). But dead they are: the only living Trojan
male to appear in the play is young Astyanax, a silent victim soon to be
hurled to his death from the city walls. In so far as a *polis* is defined by
the presence of its male citizens, Troy is a *polis* no longer; rather, it is an
empty space, abandoned even by Poseidon and Athena, who had ended
their prologue by walking away. The minimal scope for the expression
of personal preference which had momentarily opened up earlier on
('I would rather go to the famed and blessed land of Theseus' – i.e.,
Athens – the chorus had observed (207)) has given way by the end to
ineluctable trek toward the Greek ships.

Yet another boundary explored in tragedy is the problematic inter-face between 'Greek' and 'Barbarian.' *Medea* again provides a reference point. In the face of Medea's accusations about broken vows, Jason retorts that moving to Greece has introduced her to a society which respects justice and the rule of law (*Med.* 536–8). Yet, notwithstanding the 'barbaric' cruelty of Medea's revenge, Jason's breaking of his vows to her hardly allows such a dichotomy to stand unchallenged: there is heartlessness on either side of the division between Greek and non-Greek. An equivalent overlap between these two categories pervades Aeschylus' *Agamemnon*, whose subtitle might be 'A Tale of Two Cities.' The play evokes a series of characters who travel, or who once travelled, from Argos to Troy or vice versa, and one of the questions implicitly raised in the play is this: Will the generalisations which applied in Troy (for example: that the gods punish mortals who are impious) apply also in Argos? When Agamemnon is persuaded by Clytemnestra to perform the symbolically tremendous gesture of trampling on rich fabric as he reenters his palace, he admits that this is exactly what Priam would have done (*Ag.* 935–6) – another example of the characteristically tragic collapsing of boundaries.

In several other plays an analogous to-ing and fro-ing takes place; but in these cases the opposed locations are features of the landscape rather than different communities. More often than not, the *skene* (stage building), in front of which tragedies were played out, was designed to represent part of the built environment such as a house or palace, which in turn usually belonged within a *polis*.[18] Yet it often happens that significant action takes place in the off-stage space imagined to lie beyond the *skene* – typically in a mountain region adjacent to and contrasting with the world of human habitation. The reciprocal relationship between mountain and city constitutes yet one more permutation of the interstitial status of tragic action, since the action of many tragedies oscillates between an ostensibly civilised household/city and the sacred wildness of a mountain. The most obvious example is the role of Mount Cithaeron in myths based in the city of Thebes.[19] In both *Oedipus Tyrannus* and *Bacchae*, this mountain is where human beings come unusually and dangerously close to the sacred. For Oedipus, this proximity is strange and eerie: Cithaeron is where he was left to die and then miraculously saved. For the mortals swept up in the arrival of Dionysus in Greece, Cithaeron has a more sharply defined role: it is where the women go in search of Dionysus, abandoning their proper domestic role in a civilised community. By the end of the play, the mountain has become a place of nightmarish carnage, and yet the religious experiences which take place there are, at least when properly channelled through ritual, an integral part of the world of civilisation.

'Spaces between' are found not only in the physical world, but also in the mind. Several tragedies are shaped by the interplay of sanity and madness, though there are marked variations, from play to play, about what constitutes being out of one's 'right' mind, and what the causes and effects of such a condition might be. For Io in *Prometheus Bound* (attributed to Aeschylus), the distortion of her mind is provoked by the jealousy of Hera, whose agent is a fly which stings unremittingly. Being driven out of her senses is for Io analogous to other disastrous upheavals which she endures, namely metamorphosis from human to cow, and exile from her homeland as she wanders from continent to continent. Throughout all this, Io is a victim: she suffers but does not act. To some extent comparable is the madness of Cassandra in *Agamemnon*: she too has become a victim, having lost credibility as a prophetess after refusing to satisfy Apollo's lust. Io and Cassandra have in common the linguistic turmoil which the playwright lends to each: as they lurch in and out of frenzy, their utterances alternate between reasoned lucidity and tormented, wordless exclamation, whether it be the *otototoi popoi da* (ὀτοτοτοτοῖ πόποι δᾶ) of Cassandra (*Ag.* 1072) or Io's *io moi moi; he he* '(ἰώ μοί μοι· ἒ ἔ, *Prom.* 742).

For Heracles in *The Madness of Heracles* and Agave in *Bacchae*, the sufferings produced by madness are even more 'tragic' (if we take that word to signify, this time, a quality of experience, rather than 'that which is represented in a tragedy'). The agent of Heracles' delusion is once more the jealous Hera (acting now through Lyssa, goddess of Madness); the result is Heracles' commission of acts no less terrible for being unwitting. As for Agave, the god she offends is Dionysus, whose divinity she, like her sisters, denies. Her punishment is to be maddened, and in that state to dismember her still-living son Pentheus. Both of these explorations of madness involve the agonising return of the protagonists to their normal condition of mind, a process guided in each case by their father. Heracles' guide is Amphitryon:

> *Amph.* There: look at the bodies of these children, lying where they fell.
> *Her.* Ah! What is this that I see? Ah no!
> *Amph.* They were no enemies, these children you fought against, my son.
> *Her.* Fought? Who killed these children?

> *Amph.* You did, my son: your bow – and whichever god is
> responsible.
>
> (*Her.* 1131–5)

For Agave, it is Cadmus who gently steers her mind onto the path of horrified recognition:

> *Cadm.* Whose house did you go to when you were married?
> *Agave* You gave me to Echion, one of the Sown Men, so they
> said.
> *Cadm.* What son was born to your husband in your home?
> *Agave* Pentheus, the product of my union with his father.
> *Cadm.* Whose head are you holding in your arms?
> *Agave* A lion's head – at least, so said the women who hunted it.
> *Cadm.* Look directly at it: it is but a small labour to look upon it.
> *Agave* Ah! What am I looking at? What am I carrying in my
> hands?
> *Cadm.* Gaze at it; learn the truth more clearly.
> *Agave* I see the greatest pain. I am wretched.
>
> (*Ba.* 1273–82)

That Heracles was out of his 'right' mind when he slew his children is clear enough. But was Agave really deluded, while she was ecstatically worshipping Dionysus? How is 'true wisdom' to be defined? These are some of the many disturbing issues which *Bacchae* confronts.

In summary: tragedy does not occupy a comfortable space within accepted concepts and assumptions. The distinctive location of tragic myths is in the gaps between certainties. Tragedy is a place of edges and margins, an in-between territory where boundaries – literal and metaphorical – are ripe for exploration and contestation.

DIVINITIES AND MORTALS

I turn finally to a question fundamental to any attempt to clarify tragedy's distinctiveness within the mythical tradition: How are the gods portrayed?

The actions of divinities are highlighted in every narrative genre which retells Greek myths. In Homeric epic, and in all subsequent Greek epics down to Nonnus, the gods play a decisive part.[20] Hesiod's *Theogony* self-evidently centres on divinities, but the same poet's

Works and Days also accords a crucial role to the gods, for example, through the interrelated fates of Prometheus and Pandora – the gods' gift to humanity. Pindaric praise-poetry – composed for victors in the Games celebrated for Zeus, Apollo, and Poseidon – depends on constant reference to the gods' transcendent power, as a foil and a paradigm for the deeds of mortal heroes and the victors who strive to emulate them. Herodotus' *Histories* may focus on the glorious exploits of mortals in the Greco-Persian War, but the backdrop to these events is a structure of religious assumptions anchored in the mythical past.[21] As for comedy, Aristophanes' plays take the existence of the gods as read, even if the nature of the reading allows for outrageous mockery of the rulers of the universe; half a millennium later, in a quite different comic vein, the dialogues of Lucian still mine the deeds of the gods in order to extract humour. To all this textual evidence must be added countless visual images from every period of classical antiquity, including objects as disparate as temple friezes, statues, coins, vases, and gems, all of which embody or are adorned by representations of divinities involved in mythological episodes.[22] Each of these genres, indeed each individual poet or artist, works from a particular perspective; the same is true of tragedy and tragedians. What, then, can we identify as distinctive about the tragic portrayal of gods and goddesses?

First, a crucial preliminary. It must be stressed that the gods only very rarely form the centrepiece of a tragedy.[23] They are, rather, its framework, its backdrop, that which is beyond and behind the action – action which is carried forward by the mortal heroes and heroines, who choose, are deluded, come to grief, struggle courageously, in fear or madness or generosity or hatred. Nevertheless, those human actions always resonate against a more-than-human background, and it is this which we shall now investigate.

No single 'voice' dominates this portrayal. Tragedy was competitive: in the contest at the City Dionysia, each playwright staged his own version of the mythological past, striving to be adjudged superior to his rivals. Just as the music, choreography, and costuming of tragedies varied between play and play, so too did the representation of the gods. This variety is evident even in the tiny proportion of the total tragic output constituted by the surviving plays. To take one example: the dramatic device found in so many Euripidean works, whereby, during the prologue or epilogue, a divinity speaks authoritatively from the stage apparatus known as 'the machine,' is by contrast unusual in extant Sophocles, where we encounter a predominant sense of the *difficulty* of determining the gods' views and intentions.[24] Even within a single work we find changing emphases. In Aeschylus' *Oresteia*, the first play of the trilogy offers a picture of divine action which is at best enigmatic and at worst baffling;[25] only in the third play do the gods stride forth upon the stage, as Apollo, the Furies, and Athena argue their cases and defend their individual, explicitly stated perspectives on the action.

Making every allowance for such variations, however, we may still plausibly suggest a number of generalisations about the gods in tragedy. I shall mention four.

Tragedy Explores Conflicts among the Gods

Emphasis on conflict between divinities is far from being unique to tragedy. We need only think of the cosmic wars narrated in Hesiod's *Theogony*; of the battles between the gods in the *Iliad*; of the struggle between Athena and Poseidon in the *Odyssey* over the homecoming of Odysseus; of the squabble between Hermes and Apollo in the *Homeric Hymn to Hermes*, concerning the theft of his brother's cattle by the new-born trickster god. Nevertheless, tragedy does show a marked interest in such conflicts – another aspect of tragedy's location in 'the space between.' Sometimes these conflicts are about power and sovereignty; sometimes they are generated by boundary disputes over the various provinces of interest with which the gods are associated. In both kinds of conflict, human beings play the role of victims.

A classic struggle over sovereignty is dramatised in *Prometheus Bound*, in which Zeus, the new and (as depicted by his adversaries) tyrannical ruler of the universe, is pitted against the no less divine Prometheus. For having dared to champion humanity in the face of Zeus' intention to annihilate them, Prometheus is subjected to an interminable and horrible punishment: fixed to a rock in the Caucasus, he will have his endlessly self-regenerating liver torn to shreds daily by an eagle. However, the Titan, whose suffering is compounded by his knowledge of the full duration of his future torment (his name means 'Forethought'), refuses to defer to his tormentor, or to his tormentor's lackey:

> *Hermes* Bring yourself, rash fool, at last
> To think correctly in face of your present anguish.
> *Prom.* You exhort me in vain, as if you were talking to the waves.
> Never convince yourself that I, in fear
> Of Zeus' intent, will become feminised in my mind,

Begging my greatly hated enemy, with hands
Upturned in womanish supplication, to free me from these
     bonds.
No, never.

(Prom. 999–1006)

One aspect of the cosmic power-struggle dramatised in Prometheus Bound is the clash between two successive generations of gods. The same is true of the Oresteia, though here the climactic struggle is fought not over the fate of humanity as a whole, but over the fate of a single individual. Orestes' act of matricide is defended by the 'younger' god Apollo and attacked by the 'older' Furies, the goddesses whose primordial authority to punish kin-murderers long predates the coming to power of the Olympians. When Apollo's side of the argument is confirmed by the casting vote of his fellow Olympian Athena, the Furies' resentment is couched in terms of generational conflict:

You younger gods, you have ridden down
The ancient laws, and torn them from my hands.

(Eum. 778–9)

Seniority was not the only reason for a divinity to assert a claim to honour, or to resent the behaviour of a fellow god. Differences in spheres of operation between deities also held ample potential for clashes of interest. In Hippolytus, the conflict between Artemis and Aphrodite works itself out through the lives and deaths of the family of Theseus; the goddesses themselves merely frame the action by appearing in the prologue (Aphrodite) and in the finale (Artemis). When the young hunter Hippolytus prefers the chaste pursuits associated with the virginal Artemis to the world of sexuality presided over by Aphrodite, his agonising death at the hands of the goddess of love leads Artemis, at the end of the play, to locate the action firmly within the context of the eternal rivalry between the two goddesses. As she says to the dying Hippolytus:

Let be. For, even when you are under the dark of earth,
Aphrodite's zealous anger shall not fall upon you
Unavenged; your piety and noble spirit deserve requital.
I, by my own hand, with these unerring arrows
Shall wreak vengeance on the mortal she holds dearest.

(Hipp. 1417–22)

The time of gods is not the time of mortals. Human lives may come and go, but Artemis and Aphrodite will forever embody antithetical perceptions of sexuality.

In Tragedy the Gods' Use of Power Can Be Openly Criticised, yet at the Same Time That Power Must Be Acknowledged, because it is Omnipresent and Unavoidable

One feature of ancient Greek religion which can be particularly difficult to comprehend for a modern observer – especially one from a morally polarised monotheistic background – is its readiness to tolerate overt criticism of the gods' behaviour. In few works of Greek literature is the conduct of a god placed under more intense scrutiny than in Euripides' *Ion*. The plot narrates the consequences of the god's rape of Creusa, an event which she recollects in an aria of extraordinary bitterness:

> You came with hair flashing
> Gold, as I gathered
> Into my cloak flowers ablaze
> With their golden light.
> Clinging to my pale wrists
> As I cried for my mother's help
> You led me to a bed in a cave,
> A god and my lover,
> With no shame,
> Doing a favour to the Cyprian.
> In misery I bore you
> A son, whom in fear of my mother
> I placed in that bed
> Where you cruelly forced me.[26]

(Ion 887–901)

This is not, to be sure, the only view of Apollo which the play presents. In the opening scene a servant of the god's Delphic temple, a young man by the name of Ion – who (it will turn out) was born from Creusa's union with Apollo – associates this shrine and its patron deity with the qualities of brightness, healing, and, above all, purity – in a very literal sense (Ion reports that his duties include frightening away birds from the temple, and sweeping the floor of the shrine when it has been fouled). Moreover, after many twists and turns in the plot, mother and son will recognise each other, and Apollo's paternity will be cast in a positive light when Athena pronounces ex machina that 'Apollo then has managed all things well' (1595). However, such a view is expressed only after the goddess has excused Apollo's own attendance at the denouement in highly equivocal terms:

> I have come here in haste, sent by Apollo,
> Who did not think it right to come himself
> Into your sight, in case there should be blame
> For what has happened in the past. . . .
>
> (1556–8)

When Creusa does at last utter praises of Apollo, it is because he has restored her son to her, not because she feels any differently about the sexual mistreatment which she herself received at the god's hands (1609–10). The weight of the play leaves Apolline morality in at best an ambiguous light.[27]

Though the criticisms of Apollo in *Ion* are especially sustained and strident, in other tragedies too the conduct of various divinities is presented, at least by some of the characters, as worthy of censure. Sophocles' *Women of Trachis* highlights the ritual importance of Zeus, in relation to his oracle at Dodona and his altar at Cenaeum; Zeus is the addressee of numerous invocations, prayers and oaths; Zeus holds sway over Mount Oeta, the location of the funeral pyre to which Heracles will be conveyed. But as an agent within the drama the father of the gods is noticeable by his complete absence, even when his son Heracles cries out to him in anguish ('O Zeus, where in the world have I come?' – the hero's very first words, 983–4). Furthermore, although Heracles' expression 'Zeus in the stars' (1106) does not necessarily imply a tone of irony or resentment, the concluding reference by Heracles' son Hyllus to 'the great cruelty of the gods displayed in what is being done, gods who beget children and are called fathers but who can look upon such sufferings as these' (1266–9) can only be taken as a bitter accusation of a state of divinely ordered affairs which can tolerate such a waste of human life. And yet the seeds of a perception which counterbalances Hyllus' accusations are already present in the choral coda to the play:

> 'There is none of these things which is not Zeus.'
>
> (*Trach.* 1278)[28]

The gods are *there*, and they are powerful: mortals ignore them at their peril.

Two other Sophoclean plays bring home this realisation with particular force. In *Ajax*, long before the eponymous hero made his attempt on the lives of the Greek commanders, he had (so a Newsbringer reports) made a reckless boast about his lack of need of divine help: 'Father, together with the gods even one who is nothing could win mastery; but I trust that I shall grasp this glory even without them!' (767–9). When seen in the light of Athena's concluding words in the opening scene ('Look, then, at such things, and never yourself speak an arrogant word against the gods . . . For one day brings down all mortal things, and one day raises them up; the gods love those who think sensibly and hate the wicked' (127–33)), Ajax's arrogance shows a fatal misunderstanding of the proper relationship between mortals and gods. Equally heedless of the divine framework of human ethical behaviour is Creon in *Antigone*. Though Antigone herself might merely be using self-justifying rhetoric when she invokes 'the unwritten and unfailing laws of the gods' (454) to back her defiant burial of her traitorous brother Polynices, her position receives unequivocal support from the seer Tiresias, who describes how a horrific distortion of sacrificial practice has been precipitated by the exposing of Polynices' corpse (1016–22). Creon rescinds his decree forbidding burial, but too late; his refusal to comprehend how the world works culminates, not only in the death of Antigone, but also in the suicides of his own son and wife.

The Omnipresence of Divine Influence on Human Action in Tragedy Does Not Negate the Importance of Human Choice

Contrary to a common misperception of what Greek tragedy is like, tragic myths do not simply illustrate the inevitability of 'fate.' It is true that spectators and readers are often confronted with the subjecting of human beings to irresistible pressure from the gods: Heracles is sent mad by Hera, and Ajax by Athena; Phaedra does not choose to fall in love with her stepson – her passion is caused by Aphrodite; when Pentheus suddenly expresses a desire to see the maenads on Mount Cithaeron, it is because his mind has been invaded by Dionysus. But such cases must be set against those where the preponderant dramatic meaning is borne by actions which are squarely the consequence of human choice.

Two plays by Sophocles will exemplify this point. *Oedipus Tyrannus* has often been taken to be the paradigm of a work in which a human being is shown to be powerless against fortune. And yet the *plot* of the play – as opposed to the mythical events, and in particular the oracular predictions, which constitute its *antecedents* – concerns a man who, whatever the cost, is bent upon two interrelated courses of action: at first, doing everything necessary to free his city from the pollution which has engulfed it; then, finding out his own identity, from the moment when this has been called into question. These courses of action are, to put it crudely, what the play is about; and they are the product of Oedipus' own choosing. Even when the now blind king cries out to the chorus that 'It was Apollo, friends, Apollo who brought about these cruel, cruel sufferings of mine!' (1329–30), not only is it unclear in what sense Apollo can possibly be 'responsible' for what has occurred, but also Oedipus immediately goes on to maintain his own responsibility for the most shocking deed to have taken place within the time-frame of the play – his self-blinding ('And no other hand but mine struck my eyes, miserable that I am!' 1331–2). Whatever Apollo's oracle may have predicted, and whatever the putative relationship between such predictions and the eventual outcome, what is undeniable is that nothing in the play for a moment suggests that the truth was 'fated' to come out *in this way* – and it is the *manner* of the revelation of the truth which bears the weight of the work's dramatic significance.

Ajax offers another example of the overriding importance of human choice. The play begins with a demonstration of the cool, terrifying power of a divinity, Athena, first to drive a great hero mad, and then to mock and toy with him while he is in that condition: mighty Ajax ignominiously drips with the blood of sacrificial sheep, which he believes to be the blood of the Greek commanders whom he has, he thinks, put to death because (in his view) they had slighted him. But this state of helpless delusion, of powerless submission to the gods, soon gives way: initially to a consciousness of profound shame, and then to a decision to commit suicide. This decision is Ajax's alone: a decision taken with deliberation, like the deliberation with which he fixes in the earth the sword upon which he will fall (815–22). This is not the only crucial moment in the play for which the frame of reference is presented as completely within the hands of mortals. The rancorous debate about whether or not to allow burial to Ajax is driven exclusively by human emotions: anger, invective, loyalty, together with the ultimately decisive ingredient of self-interest added by Odysseus ('I too shall come to that need,' 1365). Athena's controlling presence left the stage long ago.

We have mentioned some cases where the gods evidently compel, and others where mortals unambiguously choose. But in still other cases tragic action occupies an intermediate ground between compulsion and choice. When, in *Agamemnon*, the chorus recalls the episode in which the Greek commander sacrificed his daughter Iphigenia in order to appease the anger of Artemis, the words they use are 'When he had put on the yoke-strap of necessity...' (218). The paradox could not be more stark. Agamemnon *put on* the yoke-strap: it was a freely chosen act. But the yoke-strap which he put on was that of *necessity*: he had no choice. In representing the involvement of the gods in human life, tragic myths dwell on crises in which precisely this kind of paradox comes into focus.

The Gods of Tragedy Are Partially Comprehensible, but Aspects of Them Remain Unfathomable, Incommensurable, and Unknowable

We have already met several instances in which the role and attitude of the gods is explicitly set out in the tragic action. Usually this is when the gods themselves appear on the scene and speak. Sometimes a divinity will set out the ground rules of the action only to depart for good (e.g., Athena in *Ajax*, Hermes in *Ion*, Athena and Poseidon in *The Trojan Women*); in other cases it will be left to a divinity at the end of a play to reintegrate the action into the audience's experience by referring to ritual (Artemis at the end of *Hippolytus*; Athena at the end of *Iphigenia in Tauris*) or by placing the events of the play in a wider mythical context (Castor in Euripides' *Electra*; Apollo in *Orestes*; Thetis in *Andromache*). Less often, divinities express their own point of view either throughout the action or at its midpoint, rather than at its beginning or end: Dionysus is on stage for much of *Bacchae*; Iris and Lyssa appear midway through *Heracles*; in *Eumenides* Apollo, the Furies, and Athena dominate the action in person.

But there are also cases in which that which receives emphasis is not the gods' visibility but their ultimate unpredictability and unfathomability. Of the three great Athenian tragedians, Euripides is the one who most insistently confronts spectators with what they seemingly could not have anticipated, so much so that a choral coda to this effect becomes a refrain in several of his works:

> Many are the shapes of the divinities;
> The gods bring many matters to surprising ends;
> The things we thought would happen do not happen;
> For the unexpected the god finds a way.
> Such was the conclusion of this story.[29]

Although it is usually impossible to determine precisely how far the spectators' background knowledge of mythology might have shaped their expectations, the manner in which Euripides introduces abrupt changes of dramatic direction suggests that even an audience acquainted with the general outlines of a myth might have reacted with astonishment: one example is the shocking arrival, in *Heracles*, of Lyssa goddess of madness; another – this time narrated as opposed to enacted – is the appearance of the monstrous bull from the sea as reported by the Newsbringer in *Hippolytus*. Such epiphanies sharpen an audience's sense of the gulf between mortal and divinity and dramatize the ultimate incommensurability of human with divine, even in a medium such as tragedy, in which god and mortal visibly tread the stage side by side.[30]

Fundamental though the unexpected may be to Euripidean dramaturgy, some of the most striking illustrations of the gods' unfathomability are to be found in works by the other two great tragedians. Near the beginning of *Agamemnon*, in the course of the chorus's monumental opening ode, the old men of Argos recall an episode from the outset of the Greek expedition against Troy. When the fleet was gathered at Aulis, two eagles were seen devouring a pregnant hare. The beginning of any military campaign was a sensitive and dangerous time, when – given a belief-system in which human and cosmic events were perceived to be mutually interconnected[31] – anything remotely unusual would be interpreted as ominous. The Greek seer Calchas duly read the strange occurrence as a sign: in this case, a sign of the displeasure of Artemis, who 'hates the eagles' feast' (138). But why Artemis should not only 'hate' this natural event, but also, if the Aeschylean text is taken to mean what it says,[32] take it as a justification for her subsequent injunction upon Agamemnon to sacrifice his own daughter – these matters are left opaque. At the origin of the action of the *Oresteia* is an enigma wrapped in a riddle; and at the centre of the enigma is the attitude of the gods towards humanity.

But it is neither Aeschylus nor Euripides who presents the purposes of the gods at their most inscrutable. The tragedian who does *this* is Sophocles; above all, in *Oedipus Tyrannus*. 'To the gods,' Oedipus maintains, just as the play is about to end (1519), 'I am most hateful.' If Oedipus *is* hated by the gods – as opposed to simply *feeling* that he is hated – then there must be a reason for it, since it would be out of keeping with everything we know of Greek religion if one or more divinities were to conceive an *unmotivated* hatred for a mortal. And the reason is not far to seek: the sending of the plague upon Thebes, an unambiguous indication of divine displeasure, follows inexorably upon the miasma generated by Oedipus' hideous transgressions. But that is far from being the end of the matter. For why should it have been precisely Oedipus, and not someone else, who has been put into the position, unwittingly, of incurring this displeasure? Did the gods will *that*? Nothing in the play entitles us to give an answer; indeed, nothing in the play raises the question at all. What the gods want for Oedipus remains as enigmatic at the end of the play as it was at the beginning.

Tragic myths offer a spectacle of a world in which mortals try to cope with events at the limits of or beyond their comprehension; even when these events *are* comprehended, they are comprehended too late. But Greek tragedy is not just a record of human inadequacy. The sense of limitation is offset by a whole range of positives: Oedipus' moral strength in his relentless quest for the truth; Neoptolemus' change of heart, when he decides to abandon his deception of Philoctetes and to take him home (even though the decision is eventually countermanded by Heracles); Theseus' generosity of spirit towards Heracles and Oedipus; the linguistic sublimity of Ajax and Cassandra when they gain insight into how the world is.[33] Most of the characteristics which I have described as 'distinctively tragic' can be paralleled in one or more other genres of myth-telling. But the combination of all of them in tragedy is what makes the genre unique. It is nothing less than an exploration, through the medium of traditional tales, of the place of humanity in the world, an exploration both popular and profound. Of all the ancient forms of myth-telling, only the Homeric poems can rival the tragedies in their continuing power to hold, enchant, shock, and unsettle.[34]

FURTHER READING

A variety of perspectives on the complex interrelation of myth, *muthos* and tragedy can be found in the studies by Vickers (1973), Vernant and Vidal-Naquet (1988), Burian (1997), Calame (2000a) and Buxton (2002). For commentary on specifically Aristotelian aspects of the *muthos*/tragedy relationship one should consult Jones (1962) and, especially regarding the history of scholarship on this problem, Lurje (2004).

For analysis of the representation of Medea in and out of tragedy, a good place to start is Clauss and Johnston (1997); see also Moreau (1994).

When it comes to investigations of the interplay between myth and tragedy in individual plays, literally hundreds of studies might be recommended; however, an excellent starting-point is the massive and reliable volume by Gantz (1993).

Discussion of the role of the gods in Greek tragedy is similarly extensive; a helpful article, with bibliography pointing towards the relevant scholarship, is Parker (1999). On this subject, as indeed on the whole topic of the present chapter, it would be impossible to read Gould (2001) without being obliged to reflect on the fundamental questions at issue.

NOTES

1 See Pickard-Cambridge (1968); Csapo and Slater (1994).

2 However exaggerated one may consider the reverence paid to Aristotle's *Poetics* over the centuries, the composite Aristotelian concept of pity-and-fear remains a pointer towards reconstructing the experience of Greek tragedy; cf. Buxton (2002). On the whole question of the role of the *Poetics* in the history of the interpretation of tragedy, see now Lurje (2004).

3 There are many ways of asking and answering this question: two examples, complementary both to my own approach and to each other, are the general account by Burian (1997) and the more specific one by Calame (2000a).

4 See Redfield (1975).

5 Plato (*Republic* 602b9–10) significantly takes 'tragic poetry' to be a quality of *both* epic *and* drama. Plato identifies a 'tragic' viewpoint which stresses humanity's subjection to indifferent or hostile divine forces – the opposite of his own metaphysical and ethical position, which locates happiness exclusively in the individual soul's capacity to choose between good and evil. On this, see the excellent discussion in Halliwell (2002).

6 For an insightful account of the motif of the return home in Pindaric poetry, see Crotty (1982), esp. 104–38.

7 O'Higgins (1997) 121.

8 O'Higgins (1997) 103.

9 On the whole I am sceptical of attempts, for example, by Segal (1986: 15–29), to emphasise at every turn the craftiness and duplicity of the Pindaric Jason-with-Medea; I prefer Burton's more straightforward reading (1962: 150–73). To find ambiguity *everywhere* is to risk bleaching out its impact when it does occur.

10 For a fascinating treatment of the Apsyrtus story, see Bremmer (1997).

11 According to the scholiast on this passage in Apollonius (Schol. Ap. Rhod. 4.814–15, p. 293 W), this intriguing detail was apparently also found in Ibycus and Simonides (*PMG* 291 Ibycus = *PMG* 558 Simonides); cf. Gantz (1993) 133.

12 See Moreau (1994) 174.

13 Modern critics usually refer to such characters as 'Messengers,' but as often as not there is no message: just news from elsewhere.

14 Compare also the Nurse's remarkable expression at 34–5, where she observes that Medea has realized what it means *not* to have been uprooted from one's native land.

15 I have explored the unique language of Ajax in Buxton (2006).

16 See Buxton (2002) 184.

17 This kind of 'boundary decision,' while typical of tragedy, is certainly not exclusive to it. A classic case from epic is that from Book 4 of Apollonius' *Argonautica*. The Phaeacian king Alcinous has to find a criterion by which to determine whether to return Medea to the pursuing Colchians, or to allow her to remain with Jason. His Solomon-like judgment is that, if Medea is still a virgin, she must go back to Colchis; but if she has already been united with Jason, she should not be forced to leave him (Ap. Rhod. 4.1106–9).

18 The imagined location of the building need not be Greece: cf. Euripides' *Helen* (set in Egypt) or Aeschylus' *Persians* (set in Persia); and there may be *equivalents* of a house, such as a more-or-less permanent warrior-tent (*Ajax*, set in the Greek camp at Troy). But there are exceptions: the scene of *Prometheus Bound* is the extreme wilderness of the Caucasus; that of Sophocles' *Philoctetes* is before a cave on the sea-shore of Lemnos.

19 N.b. also Mt. Oeta in Sophocles' *Women of Trachis*. On tragic mountains see Buxton (1992) 12–14.

20 On Homer see, for example, Griffin (1980) 144–204; Kraus (1984); Kullmann (1992); Kearns (2004). On post-Homeric epic, Feeney (1991) is fundamental.

21 For an incisive contribution to this much-discussed topic, see Gould (2001) 359–77.

22 The first place to turn for information about visual evidence for Greek mythology is the indispensable *Lexicon Iconographicum Mythologiae Classicae*.

23 Even in the case of *Prometheus Bound*, it could be argued that the central character is not simply a Titan, but also a kind of honorary hero, in virtue of his steadfast support for humankind.

24 The two appearances of divinities in the extant plays are those of Athena at the beginning of *Ajax* and the deified Heracles at the end of *Philoctetes*. For four other instances in the fragmentary plays, cf. the discussion in Parker (1999) 11–12.

25 On tragic 'bafflement,' see Buxton (1988).

26 Adapted from translation by R. F. Willetts (*The Complete Greek Tragedies*, Chicago, 1958). (The other translations from tragedy in the present chapter – which make no claim to literary merit – are my own.)

27 See chapter 3 of Zacharia (2003) for an exploration of the ambiguity of Apollo in this play.

28 In spite of the views of some scholars who assign this and the preceding three lines to Hyllus, I believe that the concluding voice of the play should be that of the chorus. For a justification of this view see Buxton (1988) 43–4.

29 This passage occurs at the end of *Alcestis* (1159–63), *Andromache* (1284–8), *Helen* (1688–92), and *Bacchae* (1388–92), and, with a variation in the first line (which now runs: 'Zeus on Olympus is dispenser of many things'), *Medea* (1415–19).

30 See Gould (2001) 203–34, on the incommensurability of the divine with the human.

31 A thought-provoking study of 'interconnectedness' is to be found in Oudemans and Lardinois (1987).

32 Compare Page (1957) xxv.

33 *Aj.* 669–77 and *Agam.* 1327–30.

34 Several friends and colleagues have helped me to think through the issues developed in this chapter. In particular, I must single out Michael Lurje, whose detailed and thoughtful comments enabled me to remove at least some of the shortcomings in my argument.

5: MYTH IN ARISTOPHANES[1]

Angus Bowie

One possible desideratum from the application of new tech-
nologies to the problem of reading the carbonised Hercula-
neum scrolls might be, for students of Greek Old Comedy
at any rate, a papyrus-roll of mythical comedies. When we look at the
scanty remains of Old Comedy, it appears that something like a third
of the extant titles could have come from comedies on mythological
topics:[2] and yet not one of them has survived in more than a tiny
number of fragments. Indeed, the only play that gives us any idea of
what they might have looked like is Plautus' *Amphitryon*, possibly based
on Philemon's New Comedy *The Long Night*. This treats the story of
Jupiter's lengthy dalliance with King Amphitryon's wife, and the king's
awkward return. It makes much play with the fact that the god has
disguised himself as the king, and pretends to have returned from the
war; his servant Mercury disguises himself as Amphitryon's slave Sosia.
Mercury has a long scene in which he punishes Sosia's presumption in
claiming to be Sosia, in order to delay him to give Jupiter time to escape.
Jupiter has the decency to step in to make up the quarrel that breaks
out between husband and wife as a result of the misunderstandings, and
makes an appearance at the end to sort everything out. As is generally
the case in later Greek comedy,[3] the gods are very much brought down
to the level of mortals in terms of character and concerns, and come
across as more rascally than the poor deluded mortals; their power to do
whatever they wish makes for a good deal of the comedy. How far this
later 'embourgeoisement' of the gods was a feature of Old Comedy is
not possible to tell.

Our best evidence for mythological Old Comedy lies in the survival on a papyrus of a substantial part of the ancient summary (*hypothesis*) of Cratinus' *Dionysalexandrus* (*Dionysus Plays Paris*), whose story

has similarities with the kind of escape-dramas that are associated with satyr-plays.[4]

> ...judgement, Hermes goes away and the chorus address a few words to the audience about the generation of children [?or poets] and when Dionysus appears they mock and ridicule him. When they [?the goddesses] come [?to him], he.... Hera offers unshakable tyranny, Athena courage in war and Aphrodite the chance to be the most beautiful and desirable of men; Dionysus decides that Aphrodite is the winner. After this, he sails to Sparta and brings Helen back to Mount Ida. In a while, he hears that the Achaeans are ravaging the land and looking for Alexander [Paris]. So, as quickly as he can, he hides Helen in a basket, and, changing himself into a ram, awaits developments. Alexander arrives, discovers them both and is about to give them to the Achaeans. When Helen cowers in fear, he pities her and keeps her to make her his wife; Dionysus he sends off to be handed over later, but the satyrs summon him and say they would never betray him. Pericles is mocked in the play very cleverly by implication (*di' emphaseos*), for having brought the war on the Athenians.

We can deduce a few points about mythological Old Comedy from this summary, though it would be dangerous to generalise too much. The myth of Troy is reworked so that Dionysus becomes as it were a failed actor in the role of Paris, which turns out to be too hot for him to handle. The humour of the play will also have consisted in the constant clash between the heroic tale of Troy and the buffoonery of the god. The god was mocked on his very first appearance, and this tallies with what we know of the treatment of Dionysus elsewhere in Old Comedy: it was a genre in which the gods were not spared mockery, even the god in whose honour the festival was being held. Indeed, Dionysus is the most frequent butt of humour in the comedies, as far as we can tell: the god features regularly in his own festival.[5] Also notable is the change in the story of the Judgement of Paris, whereby the vanity of Dionysus is marked by the way that Aphrodite offers not possession of the most beautiful woman in the world, as in the usual version, but the possibility of being himself the most beautiful of men. It may be that this element of sexual voraciousness accounts for the change into a ram, in what is also a parody of his change into animal forms, evident in his mythology and, for instance, in Euripides' *Bacchae*. Unfortunately, the summary does not specify how the play ended, but on the analogy of what we know of satyr-plays,[6] in which the god and satyrs are saved from whatever quandary they find themselves in, we may presume that the problems are finally resolved and the god celebrated; but how exactly this version of the Trojan story ended we cannot know. Aristotle has a salutary passage in which he says that 'in comedy, those who are the bitterest enemies in the story, such as Orestes and Aegisthus, become the best of friends by the end, and nobody is killed by anybody' (*Poet.* 1453a.36–9). It looks as though comedy could take considerable liberties with mythology if the relationships between two implacable enemies such as Orestes and Aegisthus could end, not in Orestes' murder of Aegisthus for the seduction of his mother and murder of his father, but in friendship. Finally, the similarity between the plot of this play and those of satyr-plays raises the question, which we are ill-placed to answer, of how such comedies differed from satyr-plays. A possibility is that there was a greater element of burlesque and excess in the comedies, but we do not know.

If we look elsewhere in the fragments of Old Comedy, we find, not surprisingly, that any potentially ludicrous aspects of the myths were seized on, as in this play. Metamorphosis of gods recurs in, for instance, Cratinus' *Nemesis*, which, in a manner reminiscent of the *Amphitryon*, dramatised the myth of how Zeus disguised himself as a swan to seduce Nemesis. He is to 'become a big bird' (fr. 114). The heroine Leda is given instructions: 'it's up to you: you must make an elegant attempt to make yourself as much like a hen as possible, sit on this egg, and hatch us some fine and amazing bird from it' (fr. 115). In this Attic version, Nemesis replaces Leda as the mother of Helen,[7] though she is appropriate for the story because she has herself the experience of seduction by Zeus in the form of a bird: he seduced her as a swan and she gave birth to Helen in an egg. Olympian deities were thus regularly put in ridiculous situations, but exactly how far they were sent up is, it must be admitted, not for the most part deducible from the fragments. On the other hand, Aristophanes' *Frogs*, though not strictly a mythological comedy, suggests that the humour against the gods was fairly hard-hitting: a comedian could go as far as to show on stage the god of the dramatic festival being incontinent with fear (479–91).

It was not, however, only deities whose stories featured in mythological comedy. Another striking play by Cratinus is his *Odysses* (*Odysseus and His Men*), which dealt at least in part with Odysseus' encounter with the Cyclops, as recounted in Homer's *Odyssey*. Some of the fragments look like reworkings of lines or part-lines of Homer's account, suggesting a relatively close reworking of the Homeric tale, with the humour coming from the clash between the Homeric situation and language and the comic treatment of it. One fact about it has been preserved by an ancient scholar: according to Platonius, 'it contains censure of no-one, but criticism of Homer's *Odyssey*,'[8] so in this it appears to differ from, for instance, the *Dionysalexandrus*, with its political flavour. We have here then a kind of mythological burlesque. The parody of Homer is quite learned, but the less learned would no doubt have picked up on the hexameter rhythms and Homeric diction, familiar from, say, the recitations of Homer at the Panathenaea.

The synopsis of *Dionysalexandrus* also tells us, tantalisingly, that the mythical story had a political purpose, that in some way Pericles' war-policy was mocked or criticised. It is always possible that this is a false deduction made by a later scholar, but the fact that Pericles was notoriously a sexually successful man would suit the depiction of Dionysus after Aphrodite has made him the most desirable of men, so that the play may have been more or less explicit in its reference to current history. The idea of Pericles involving Athens in war for sexual reasons is again used, by Aristophanes, in *Acharnians*, where the theft of some of his lover Aspasia's 'prostitutes' by drunken Megarian youths leads him to promulgate the Megarian Decrees, which restart the Peloponnesian War.

Furthermore, from what we can tell, politics was mixed into mythical comedy quite frequently.[9] Pericles was compared to Zeus,[10] and Aspasia to a number of goddesses and heroines, though these may, in some cases at least, have been simple comparisons, rather than allegorical representations as posited for *Dionysalexandrus* by the *hypothesis*.[11] Other plays seem actually to have introduced gods and heroes physically into fifth-century Athens. For instance, in Cratinus' *Pluti* the Titans came to earth from Tartarus to seek an unknown 'ancient relative' (possibly Plutus himself) and took part in the trial of Nicias' son, Hagnon, on a charge of unjust enrichment. Fr.171.22–3 has a political flavour: 'now that the reign of tyranny has been [?broken], and the people are in power. . . . ' The tyranny here is presumed to be Zeus' and so there might be another reference to Pericles, who was removed from power in 429. Similarly, Cratinus' *Runaways* somehow combined the mythical Theseus, who tells how 'I discovered Cercyon shitting at dawn among the vegetables and strangled him' (fr. 53), referring to a cruel figure to whom he put an end, and the historical Lampon, who was sent by Pericles to found a colony at Thurii.

The last-named play involved Theseus, but it is worth noting that in general Old Comedy, like tragedy, tends to use well-known, 'Panhellenic' myths; local Attic myths are seldom found, even at the Lenaea festival, where only Athenians were present. We have seen a rare exception to this in the *Nemesis*, where an Attic version of the birth of Helen is used. On the other hand, Theseus himself appears in the titles of only two plays, by Aristonymus and Theopompus, though he made an appearance not only in Cratinus' *Runaways* but also possibly in Philyllius' *Aegeus*.[12] Major Athenian mythical figures, such as Cecrops, Erechtheus and his daughters, Pandion, and Triptolemus, do not seem to have plays about them.[13] Local cults do sometimes furnish plots, but seldom. The best example is Aristophanes' *Anagyrus*, which dealt with the legend of an Attic farmer from that deme, who was punished for sacrilege by the loss of his wife and the mistaken banishment of his son, as a result of a false accusation by his mother-in-law; the farmer finally burned himself and his property, and his wife committed suicide. This was not, however, a case of a local legend simply staged for local people, since it also involved parody of Euripides' *Hippolytus*, to which the comedy's plot had obvious similarities. Indeed, one of the fragments contains a parody of lines of the tragedy, in which Phaedra's tragic expression of desire to engage in an ecstatic hunt becomes a comic desire to hunt and eat cicadas.[14] Telecleides' *Amphictyons* treated Amphictyon's introduction of Dionysus and his cult into Attica, a natural topic for a Dionysiac festival, and Pherecrates' *Ant Men* recounted the Aeginetan myth of the creation of men from ants.

The plays we have looked at so far, for which we have more evidence than for most, have given some idea, however threadbare, of what mythological comedy was like. We have needed to take this initial detour into the work of other comedians, because the amount of information we have about Aristophanes' own mythological comedies is unfortunately somewhat restricted. We can begin with a list of titles. The following may have belonged to mythical comedies: *Aeolosicon I and II, Daedalus, Daughters of Danaus, Dramata or the Centaur, Dramata or Niobos, Heroes, Cocalus, Lemnian Women, Polyidus,* and *Phoenician Women.* That is 10 titles out of the 43 we know, a little less than the crude average for the century. Even here, however, one has to be careful, since a title that suggests a play was mythological may be deceptive. For instance, the title *Amphiaraus* alone might suggest a play on the mythical seer who led the Seven against Thebes, but the fragments make it clear that the play was concerned with his prophetic shrine, which came into existence after his death at Thebes, and not with his myth.

The paucity of evidence is extremely frustrating. Sometimes the title tells us what the basic myth behind the play is, but then the fragments let us go no further, and we must always remember Aristotle's remark about the unexpected treatment of familiar myths by Old Comedy. The *Lemnian Women* will have told of the arrival of the Argonauts, after the Lemnian women had murdered their husbands for taking off with Thracian slave-girls, and of the marriage of Jason and Hypsipyle, but more than that we cannot say, though the same myth can be discerned structurally behind the extant *Lysistrata*.[15]

Two plays have intriguing titles, *Dramata* ('*Dramas*') or *The Centaur* and *Dramata or Niobos*, which may (but equally may not) point to a metatheatrical element. The former seems to have dealt with Heracles' entertainment by Pholus and with his fight with the Centaurs, thus introducing the hero who was the most popular hero in Old Comedy: not surprisingly, the few fragments talk of food and drink taken with enthusiasm. The second play is very opaque, but the masculine form 'Niobos' suggests that in some way a male figure took the role of Niobe, who was punished by Apollo and Artemis for boasting that she had borne more children than their mother Leto. An intriguing possibility, but quite obscure.

Sometimes, however, tentatively putting together what we do know allows us to discern some trends. On occasion, the fragments of other plays allow us glimpses into how Aristophanes may have treated the stories. Similarities to Cratinus' treatment of the *Nemesis* story can be discerned in the *Daedalus*. The story is of Zeus' seduction of Leto by taking the form of a swan, and the birth of Apollo and Artemis. Again, the comedy seeks the burlesque in the story. In Hesiod's account and in that of the *Homeric Hymn to Apollo*, the birth of the deities has nothing gynaecologically odd about it, but here Leto gives birth to 'a mighty egg' (fr. 193), about whose origins there is speculation (fr. 194). It has been suggested that the eponymous Daedalus was involved in creating a bird which Zeus used to approach Leto, much as he produced the cow which Pasiphaë used to seduce her favourite bull. Farce is thus brought into stories by the exploitation of their more bizarre elements, such as gods taking the form of birds.

The title of *Cocalus* points to the story of the murder of Minos at the hands of King Cocalus and his daughters when he came in search of Daedalus: before offering Minos the hospitality of his bath, Cocalus rigged up hot-water pipes so that he could scald Minos to death. This may seem a grim topic for a comedy, and how it was treated we do not know, but we may gain some insight into it from the *Proagon*, which dealt with an even grimmer tale. The 'Proagon' was a ceremony at which the playwrights displayed their choruses and revealed the plots of their plays; in some way, in the comedy this was combined with the treatment of the story of Thyestes, who was tricked into eating his own children by his brother Atreus, whose wife he had seduced. One of the characters says: 'I've tasted a sausage made of my children; how could I look at a roast snout?' (fr. 478), and it may be the same person who said: 'Ugh! What is causing my stomach to churn? Damn it! Where could I get a chamber-pot?' (fr. 477). Again, what in tragedy is grim and unpleasant becomes a source of amusement, and it is not impossible, indeed perhaps likely, that the children were not in fact eaten.

One not infrequent category of comedy is that which parodies earlier tragic performances of myths. The difficulty here is that it is not always clear whether Aristophanes is producing a parodic version of a myth or a parody of a particular tragic version of that myth. For instance, the *Daughters of Danaus* would have told the story of the arrival in Greece of the daughters of Danaus, fleeing from marriage to their cousins in Egypt, and of the marriage of Hypermestra, one of their number, to Lynceus, but whether it was a parody of, say, Aeschylus' trilogy on the subject cannot be known. Other cases are clearer. *Polyidus* was probably a parody specifically of Euripides' *Glaucus*, which had a complex plot involving the drowning of Glaucus, Minos' young son, in a vat of honey, a portent of a cow that changed colour three times a day, an owl that indicated to Polyidus where Glaucus was hidden, and snakes that were brought back to life by magical herbs and so showed how Glaucus could be revived. The comic potential in all this is obvious, but what Aristophanes did with it is obscure.

The *Phoenician Women* was more certainly, at least in part, a parody of Euripides' recent play of the same name, since two of the fragments are partial quotations from Euripides' play (frr. 570, 574). This example comes from the last decade of the fifth century, when there seems to have been a fashion for writing comedies that parodied recent tragedies (usually by Euripides), not just in part but so that the whole comedy was a takeoff of the tragedy. The fashion may possibly have been started by Aristophanes' own *Thesmophoriazusae*, which for much of its course is composed sequentially of parodies of Euripides' *Telephus*, *Palamedes*, *Helen*, and *Andromeda*. As we shall see below, *Thesmophoriazusae* engages closely with the nature of Euripidean tragedy, and this may have triggered the fashion for plays of this sort, though the other playwrights do not, as far as we can tell, have anything as complex as *Thesmophoriazusae*. Strattis seems to have been especially fond of this type of play.

Like Aristophanes, he also wrote a *Phoenician Women*, which again parodies lines of Euripides' play.[16] His *Anthroporestes* describes Euripides' *Orestes* as a 'very clever play' (fr. 1) and complains of Hegelochus' notorious mispronunciation of *Or.* 279, in which he pronounced a wrong accent and turned 'I see a calm coming from the sea' into 'I see a weasel coming from the sea.' Strattis also wrote a *Chrysippus*, as did Euripides around this time, and his *Philoctetes* may be a response to Sophocles' play of 409. The *Lemnomeda* may have imitated *Thesmophoriazusae*'s combination of plays by mixing Euripides' *Andromeda* (412) and his *Hypsipyle* (408 or 7).[17] There is one example of parody of a tragedian outside the 'big three': Strattis' *Zopyrus Ablaze* parodied Spintharus' *Heracles Ablaze*.

At the start of this chapter, and in the last paragraph, we came across titles of a double nature, such as *Dionysalexandrus*, *Lemnomeda*, and *Anthroporestes*. The point of the last title is obscure (there is also Pherecrates' *Anthropheracles*), but the point of the others is clear. There is one such title for Aristophanes, the *Aeolosicon*, which combines two names of people with very different status: Aeolus, the king who in the *Odyssey* controls the winds and presides over an unusual family where, unproblematically, six sons are married to six daughters in a palace of delightful luxury; and Sicon, a traditional name for a cook in Greek comedy. The play involved parody of Euripides' *Aeolus*. This told how Aeolus married his sons to his daughters and of the tragic consequences. Aeolus' son Macareus raped his sister Canace and, in the hope of regularising the union, persuaded his father to distribute the brides by lot. Unfortunately, in the ballot Canace and Macareus were not drawn together, and Aeolus eventually discovered the rape. He sent Canace a sword, with which she committed suicide, ironically just before Macareus persuaded his father to pardon her; Macareus then killed himself in grief. Unfortunately, quite how the cook Sicon fitted into this is unclear. The fragments mention food several times, and one of them seems to comment on the facilities in the palace: 'they have but one bedroom for them all and one bathtub serves them all' (fr. 6). On the basis of scenes with cooks in later comedy, one imagines that Sicon was an ill-tempered cook who has been engaged to provide the marriage-feast that is to celebrate the multiple marriages of sons and daughters, and who is unimpressed by the living arrangements of the house. In the comedy these are turned from Homer's richness to comic meanness: epic decorum becomes comic bathos. Again, on the basis of weddings at the end of extant plays, one imagines that Macareus and Canace were somehow happily united at the end of the play.

The haul from a reading of the fragments is not therefore very great, though some glimmers have been seen. As we might expect, comedy exaggerated the more unusual aspects of the myths it used, banalised the stories, and emphasised any eating and drinking that could be brought into the stories.

We have said that the extant plays are not mythological, but this does not mean that there is no mythology in them. Before looking at more structural uses of mythology, we will look at some of the ways in which mythology is used by characters in the plots. In tragedy, mythology is frequently used by choruses to give a perspective on the events of the play. This kind of use of myth is rare in Old Comedy. A passage which comes close to this is the exchange in *Lysistrata* 781–828, where the Old Men say they wish to tell the Old Women a 'story' (*muthos*), and recount the story of Melanion, who fled to the countryside because of his hatred of women. The Women then reply with the tale of Timon, who hated men but loved women. These stories continue the bantering rivalry between the two semi-choruses, but are odd in the way they seem to distort the stories. Melanion was famously the lover and conqueror of Atalanta; he did indeed stay in the countryside, but with Atalanta. Timon is not known to have had time for anyone, male or female, in the traditional versions. These distortions mirror the way in which Lysistrata will later distort history in her attempt to reconcile the two sides, recalling for instance Cimon's help in bringing four thousand Athenian hoplites to assist Sparta against the Messenians: she sees this as a reason for the Spartans to make peace, but the hoplites were unceremoniously sent home and Thucydides says that the split between the Athenians and Spartans became overt after this expedition (1.102.3). The point of these distortions in history and mythology would seem to be to indicate that peace between Athens and Sparta is, given past history, extremely difficult to achieve, and that the division between the sexes can only be maintained by falsely twisting traditional stories.

There are a number of occasions where mythology is used in more or less intellectual arguments, as a means of persuasion. The most notable example of this is Peisetaerus' great speech in which he persuades the birds to follow his advice and set up their own kingdom, and the Chorus' subsequent parody of Orphic cosmogony (*Birds* 471–703). Peisetaerus turns to Aesop for proof that the lark was the first of birds and existed before the earth and the gods: their kingdom was the original one therefore and can justifiably be regenerated. The Chorus similarly go back to the start of time and the production of an egg from Erebus before the world existed; from this egg Eros was born, whose union with Chaos produced the race of birds. These cosmic origins give a suitably legendary grandeur to the idea of the kingdom of the birds and foreshadow the frighteningly powerful nature of Nephelococcygia.

Otherwise, reference to mythology is not especially frequent in the mouths of comic characters, perhaps because it fits ill with the largely 'everyday' nature of comic life: it is suitable for the grand context in which Peisetaerus is speaking, but not otherwise. Perhaps it is for this reason that when, in *Acharnians*, Amphitheus gives the Assembly a convoluted mythological genealogy to justify his request for travelling expenses for a peace mission to Sparta, the Assembly is not in the least impressed and the officials immediately have him thrown out.

One place where mythology does figure in a substantial passage is *Clouds* 1047–70, where the Worse Argument uses it in his refutation of the Better. This is thus another special context, one of intellectual debate. Better complains that current philosophical discourse 'is filling the bath-houses and emptying the wrestling-schools' (1052–4). In the dispute, he says hot baths are bad for the character, but Worse points out that no cold baths of Heracles are known. Sitting about discussing philosophy is also condemned, but Worse points to that skilled debater, the admirable Nestor in Homer. When Better himself tries to give an example of a mythical hero who benefited from his possession of virtue, he chooses unwisely and selects Peleus, who, he claims, was given a knife as a reward. Worse scorns this and Better notes that Peleus was also rewarded with marriage to Thetis, but Worse is easily able to refute him by reminding him that Thetis left Peleus, according to him because Peleus was no good in bed. Knowledge of mythology is not enough: one needs to be able to employ it in a sophisticated manner, so that this is another example in the play of how a lack of sophistic rhetorical skill can leave a man exposed.

We can move now to discussion of comedy's engagement with mythology on a broader scale. The first topic to consider is its relationship with tragic myth. Two comedies make very different use of myth, and specifically tragic myth, in the context of a juxtaposition of the two genres. They are *Acharnians* and *Thesmophoriazusae*. In the former, the hero Dicaeopolis visits Euripides to find tragic garb sufficiently pathetic and affecting to enable him to defend before the hostile Chorus his decision to make a private peace with Sparta. He chooses that of Telephus, who was a king of Mysia and son-in-law of Priam, and whose land was invaded by mistake by the Greeks on their way to Troy. Telephus was wounded by Achilles' spear after he fell over a vine branch put in his way by Dionysus, whom he had angered. The wound did not heal and an oracle told him that 'the wounder will heal.' Telephus in disguise went to Argos to seek Achilles, and made a speech in defence of the Trojans and probably of himself, saying at one point that he would speak out even if threatened with an axe. Odysseus announced the presence of a spy and to avoid seizure, Telephus grabbed the infant Orestes and ran to an altar for sanctuary, threatening to kill the child if he were mistreated. Eventually, Telephus revealed the way to Troy, and was healed by the rust from the spear of Achilles, thus fulfilling the oracle.

In *Acharnians*, the Telephus myth has two functions. First, it is used to give 'the moral authority, literary prestige, and latitude that audiences have always given to more prestigious genres'[18] and to claim for comedy the kind of usefulness and advice-giving capability that was accorded to tragedy: 'comedy knows justice too'(500), says Dicaeopolis, using the word *trugodia*, from the word for 'wine-lees,' as a parallel term to *tragodia*. This prestige is then important, as Dicaeopolis tries to justify his making peace with Sparta in a speech to the Chorus of Acharnians, whose desire for war has been fired by the destruction of their crops. The adoption of a tragic garb for this scene should not, however, be interpreted simply as comedy's deference to its more prestigious elder sibling: the prestige nominally offered by adoption of a tragic figure was presumably not a little mitigated by the heterogeneous sight on stage of a comic character with his padded clothing and phallus topped by the further garments of the tragic Telephus. This compound figure thus represented king, beggar, Athenian, foreigner, and tragic and comic hero all in one, which enabled Aristophanes implicitly to pose 'the question how seriously, how comically, how literally to take (the) play.'[19] Comic political discourse adopts tragic myth's prestige, but at the same time undermines it by the bizarrely mixed figure on the stage.

But the Telephus story also has a much wider significance for the play as a whole, because its whole structure and plotline are imitated at various points by the comedy. The presence of Telephus is highlighted by the way he comes at the end of a list of Euripidean beggar-kings, but his tragedy has in fact been adumbrated before. When the Chorus of Acharnians will not listen to his justification of his private peace, Dicaeopolis says he will be willing to speak with his head on a butcher's block, so that he may be executed if he does not persuade. This picks up Telephus' lack of fear of any axe that might be used to silence him. In his great speech in response to the Chorus' attack on him for his peace, Dicaeopolis makes much of his awareness that a mere beggar addressing the Athenians is potentially problematic, drawing on the rhetoric the

Euripidean figure used. In the early part of the play, therefore, Telephus' main function is to increase the audience's sympathy for Dicaeopolis, whom they are made to think of in terms not just of a citizen with a grievance against the belligerent city, but also of ill-treated but noble tragic heroes. When he has persuaded half of the Chorus, the other half call out the belligerent Lamachus, whom Dicaeopolis discomforts with his cheeky and disrespectful attitude. We seem to have the 'little man,' garbed in tragic pathos, triumphing over the powerful and violent representatives of the state, which has appeared inhumane and inflexible through the first part of the play.

All of this changes in the second part of the play, however. Dicaeopolis gradually becomes a less sympathetic figure. That he will not give any of his treaty-wine, the symbol of his peace, to the slave of Lamachus is not perhaps surprising or disreputable, but the refusal to give it to a farmer who wants it to bathe his eyes that have become sore with weeping for the cattle he has lost in a Boeotian raid is more troubling. He then agrees to give some to anoint the cock of a Bride-groom so that he does not have to fight. This is all very amusing, but from the point of view of the defence of the city (i.e., what interests everyone but Dicaeopolis), it is not helpful. The Chorus eventually sum up Dicaeopolis' position thus: 'he's working on his own behalf... but it doesn't look as though he is going to share it with anyone' (1017, 1038f). The sympathy that was generated by the first part of the play for a man who was willing to stand up for his principles and for peace against the might of the *polis* gradually diminishes, as the selfishness of Dicaeopolis' actions become ever clearer.

This shift in sympathy is then clinched by return of motifs from the tragedy, when at the end the soldier Lamachus is brought in, wounded in driving off Boeotian invaders. Dicaeopolis, rather like Achilles in the tragedy, refuses to heal him with the treaty-wine, but unlike Achilles does not relent. Furthermore, it transpires that Lamachus has been 'wounded by a vine-prop as he leapt over a ditch' (1178) and 'struck down by an enemy's spear' (1194), that is, almost exactly as Telephus was wounded when the Greeks invaded his country. The most appro-priate cure for a wound from a vine-prop would be treaty-wine, but Dicaeopolis refuses. The sympathy-figure Telephus has thus migrated at the end of the play from Dicaeopolis to Lamachus, the unsympathetic figure of the end of the first half. This shift emphasises the way in which the audience are made to view Dicaeopolis in at least two ways: the rea-sonableness of his attitude to the city's devotion to war is displayed in the first part, the selfishness of his response in the second. The mythical character from tragedy is thus a floating signifier which migrates from one character to the other, allowing us to construct them in different ways.

The *Telephus* returns fourteen years later, in the *Thesmophoriazusae*, along, as we have seen, with parody of other Euripidean tragedies. Where in the *Acharnians* tragedy and comedy were contrasted and yet also complemented each other in the economy of the play, here they are much more opposed to each other. The literary context of this play of 411 is the recent composition by Euripides of plays which, though officially tragedies, contained a good deal of comedy or potentially comic features. The *Helen*, for instance, made great play of the confusion between a phantom Helen and the real thing and contained a highly amusing scene between the shipwrecked Menelaus and an Old Woman at the doors of the palace. Such door-knocking scenes are much more a feature of Greek comedy at all times, and Menelaus' concern at having to meet strangers in his ragged condition makes self-referential play with Euripides' supposed fondness for ragged kings, which we met in the discussion of *Acharnians* above. *Ion* contains a hymn by the boy Ion in which he laments the effects of bird-droppings in the sacred space, and *Andromeda* contained a scene with the figure of Echo. *Thesmophoriazusae* seems to be Aristophanes' reply to this move into comic territory, since he responds to Euripides' putting of comedy into tragedy by creating his comedy out of tragedies. After the prologue, we meet the tragedian Agathon, and the plot then develops through four plays of Euripides, as he tries to find ways, through imitation of his 'escape' plays, to free his relative, traditionally known as Mnesilochus, from the clutches of the women at the Thesmophoria festival. The informing idea throughout is comedy's superiority, in a variety of areas, to tragedy as a dramatic medium. Thus, in the Agathon scene, tragedy's fragility in the face of robust comic language is made clear. In revisiting the comic scene of Menelaus at the palace door, Aristophanes achieves the remarkably difficult feat of parodying an already comic scene, as if to say, 'if you want a truly funny scene, then it is to comedy you should turn, not tragedy.' In this scene, the Old Woman refuses to play her role as the Old Woman in Euripides' version of Menelaus' myth, so that Euripides' and Mnesilochus' attempts to act out the tragic version of the myth are constantly frustrated and ultimately collapse. The implication is that tragedy is a frail medium which cannot tolerate the refusal of spectators to suspend belief and accept that what they are seeing is a mythical drama and not real life: anything that gets in the way of this spoils it as drama. Comedy, however, can accommodate anything: as the tragedy collapses in the face of incredulity by the Old Woman, the comedy is succeeding famously.

All of this takes place in the context of the women's festival, the Thesmophoria. The myth of that festival was the rape by Hades of Demeter's daughter, Persephone, her mother's search for her, and the suspension of agricultural fertility in the world until Persephone was returned. The pattern of the festival replicated the myth. It began with the separation of husband and wife and the assumption by the women of roles in politics, religion, and sexuality normally held by men: the normal world was thus inverted. On the altar were placed the rotted remains of piglets, which had earlier been thrown into underground pits; these were to be mixed with the seed-corn to promote fertility in humans and crops. On the second day, the women then imitated the primitive existence led by the goddess when her daughter was lost and the goddess's search for her. On the final day, husband and wife were reunited and dined off roast pork, in contrast to the rotten pork of day one: the world was thus restored to normality.

The play makes use of this pattern of abnormality replaced by normality, found in the myth of the festival and in the festival itself. In the play, Euripides has introduced two abnormalities: his tragedies have come to concern themselves with the private lives of women in Athens, a private sphere that does not belong on the public stage; and they have strayed onto comic space, thus confusing the two genres. This abnormality is righted in two ways: at the end of the play, the price of the freedom of his relative Mnesilochus is that Euripides will no longer write plays which slander women; and by this time, the play has amply demonstrated comedy's superiority to Euripidean tragedy in the blending of tragic and comic. The comedy thus has (allegedly) the same benefit to the city as the Thesmophoria, in that it restores tragedy and comedy to their rightful places. It is comedy too which claims to offer a much clearer guide to the secret behaviour of women in the privacy of the *oikos* than tragedy with its myths.

This imitation of the patterns of myth and its related festivals is a frequent feature of Old Comedy, often in unexpected places. In *Lysistrata*, for instance, once the women have barricaded themselves into the Acropolis, the Chorus of Old Men attack the gates, bringing with them fire to burn the Women out. In a scene of burlesqued combat, the Women eventually douse the Men's flames with a 'nuptial bath.' Though the sight of two aged semi-choruses fighting it out might seem farcical and undignified, the scene is given a much greater seriousness and importance by the myths that underlie it, as Faraone has shown.[20] These are of two kinds. First, there are myths in which women are threatened with death by burning, as happened to Alcmene when she was discovered by her husband Amphitryon to be pregnant with Heracles, or to Heracles' own wife Megara at the start of Euripides' *Heracles*. In such stories, the women are victims of violent males, as are the women in *Lysistrata* when viewed through this schema. Second, there are stories where it is men who are threatened with such a death, but who are saved by women bringing water to quench the flames. This is the case for Dionysus, when his mother Semele is blasted by the sight of Zeus in all his glory. Aeschylus' and Sophocles' plays on this subject are both entitled *Hydrophoroi*, 'The Water-Carriers,' a reference to the women who doused the flames and saved the child Dionysus. Similarly, there are a number of depictions on vases of Heracles' death, in which there remains on the pyre the armour of the hero, but he himself is depicted taken up to heaven; at the side of this scene, women are depicted with jars, from which they are pouring water onto the pyre.

This apparently farcical scene therefore evokes two schemata which endue it with greater significance than its farcical nature might suggest. The first figures the women as victims, but the second suggests that it is they who are bringing salvation to the city. The dousing of the old men is comic, but also, through the evocation of the mythical stories, is much more important. It is indeed a 'nuptial bath,' in that in mythology a bath is often a new start, a purging of an old status and the adoption of a new, as we shall see in the next example.

In some cases, a whole play may be structured along the lines of a myth or myth-type. This is so with *Knights*, where the struggle of the Sausage-Seller to overthrow the Paphlagonian slave, the dominant force in Demos' household, is comically represented as a Gigantomachy, or Battle against a Giant: the allegedly violent and domineering politician Cleon is farcically figured as a monstrous being on a par with Typhoeus, the monster whom Zeus had to defeat to become master of the universe. The pattern of the play is generally that of Gigantomachies, but it is also very close to the Titanomachy in Hesiod's *Theogony*. The victories in each case come at the end of a 'succession-myth' in which, in Hesiod, the sequence is Uranus–Cronus–Zeus; in Aristophanes, hemp-seller–sheep-seller–leather-seller–sausage-seller. In each case, an oracle is crucial and the victor has helpers, the Hundred-Handers in Zeus' case, the Knights in the Sausage-Seller's. In Hesiod, the rivals fight on a cosmic scale, with lightning and thunder, and the imagery of the play is similarly shot through with such ideas. Furthermore, in the parabasis, when seeking approval for his work, Aristophanes evokes this Gigantomachy in his claim that he is worthy to ask for the audience's help because 'he goes out bravely against the whirlwind and the hurricane' (510–11). Once the victory is won, the losers are dispatched to disagreeable places, Typhoeus to Tartarus and the Paphlagonian to drink bath water in the Ceramicus among the lowlifes. The victory is then marked by figures allegorical of the newly created world: Zeus creates the Seasons, Peace, Good Government, and so on, and the Sausage-Seller introduces the Peace Treaties (*Spondai*) and symbolically boiles Demos to recreate him as he was in the great days of the past. Much of the comedy comes therefore from the gap between the squalid and squabbling slaves of the play and the grandeur of the victory of the king of the gods. Aristophanes also associates himself with his hero, through the image of the hurricane quoted above, so again the idea of the comic poet confronting the leading politician of his day is characterised hyperbolically as a Gigantomachy.

When Aristophanes wrote this play, he was barely more than twenty and, as in other plays, it is possible to find another pattern in *Knights*, in this case that of the young man undertaking various exploits that result in his attaining adult status, the myth of 'rite of passage,' as seen in the stories of Theseus or Jason. The nameless Sausage-Seller is young and at the very margins of society, selling cheap meats by the city gates in the insalubrious Ceramicus region, and finally takes his place as *prostates* of Demos, with the honorific name of Agoracritus. The importance of these patterns is then suggested by the way that, in a play such as *Wasps*, the pattern can be reversed, so that a mature male can become a young man again. Again, some of the humour for the original audience comes from seeing a familiar pattern reversed. The play concerns an old, poor, and nearly senile man who is obsessed with jury-service and dedicated to condemnation of the accused, and who is gradually weaned off this obsession and turned to the pleasures of the life of a rich young aristocrat. In the first part of the play, instead of gaining status as the young mythical hero does, Philocleon gradually loses it, starting as juror and being reduced to 'nothing.' This is done paradoxically by taking him through the pattern of a rite of passage. At the start of the play, he is associated with the imagery of marginality associated with the young hero in mythology: hunting-nets, night, animals, and the use of trickery. When he and his fellow-Wasps fight against his son and their slaves, the imagery become that of the hoplite, the mature male. Finally, he debates with his son on the true nature of his life as a juror, a profession which, in this play, is largely associated with old men. In each case, Philocleon is defeated in a contest and finally submits to his son's wish that he abandon the courts. His son then trains him in how to behave in a symposium, where his ultimate behaviour is no less chaotic and disruptive than it was in the courts.

The implication of this could thus be that the Attic spirit, whether manifest in law-court or symposium, is largely uncontrollable. The play in fact counterbalances the negative aspects of this spirit with more positive ones: these were the men who defeated the Persians and they are the ones who now (the concern for chronological precision is small) defend the city in its courts. The use of the reverse rite-of-passage myth can thus be seen to be not just an amusing move, but also an indication of the unnatural nature of what Bdelycleon is trying to achieve. In fact, matters are more complex. That the senile Philocleon should give up public life and settle down at home has a certain sense to it (and would have been required by Attic law), but then Philocleon is one of those complex Aristophanic characters[21] who manage to combine contradictory aspects in themselves. Again however, Philocleon is still possessed of a vigour that can defend the city, so that his removal from that sphere is questionable. Reversing the pattern of the myth is thus rendered problematic and even antidemocratic, as Philocleon himself claims.

We end with consideration of two plays in which we can discern an awareness of the way in which mythology functions and of its dangers. First, *Lysistrata*. The standard view of the sexes in Greek, and indeed other, mythology is that the woman is the source of danger, strife, and disruption in society, whereas the man is the opposite. What is striking about *Lysistrata* is that, in this myth of gynaecocracy (the rule of women) Aristophanes reverses the negative and positive signs normally attached to women and men. In other stories of women taking control, they often do so in the context of the murder of their husbands. For instance, on Lemnos, there was a festival that commemorated and imitated the story of how the women of the island were punished by Aphrodite for a misdemeanour: they smelled so much that their husbands sought solace elsewhere, and were murdered for it.[22] In the play, however, the occupation of the Acropolis is carried out by trickery, and the women otherwise for the most part sit quietly on Athena's rock. The men associate their actions with those of the Lemnians (296–301) and Amazons (676–9), but these evocations of traditionally violent mythical women are quite inappropriate to the behaviour of the women. By contrast, it is the men who offer violence to the women, by bringing Athena's own olive-wood against her doors, filling the market-place with frightening soldiers, and behaving violently when drunk (1216ff.);

it is men, after all, who have caused the war, and who in the play justify their actions by harping proudly on the violent events which surrounded the overthrow of Hippias' tyranny and on the 'myth' of the Persian Wars. Indeed, the men constantly refer to these violent historical events, whereas the women refer much more to their religious service to the city. By taking myth and reversing the signs it uses, Aristophanes produces 'reality,' thus deconstructing the ideology of myth which purveys an ideologically biased picture of society.

This unmasking of the constructed nature of mythology is also found in *Birds* and *Ecclesiazusae*. If Aristophanes' extant plays do not use mythology except in a structural fashion, their plots are in a way 'myths' themselves. This is especially true of plays such as these two, which tell of the creation of a fantasy city: 'Cloud-Cuckoo-Land' leads a list that includes 'Shangri-La,' 'Utopia,' and the 'Pays de Cocagne' as stereotypical of fantasy lands. In *Birds*, the origin of the bird-kingdom is found in the two Athenians' desire to find a land without 'problems' (*pragmata*). It has often been thought a problem in the play that this desire should turn into the decision to found an imperial city like Nephelo-coccygia, but this is the point the play makes: the only way to avoid *pragmata* is to be powerful enough to ward them off and impose them on others. It is precisely this lack of *pragmata*, this *apragmosune*, a word that means noninvolvement in affairs, which Peisetaerus blames for the birds' current servile condition (471): once they take the trouble, they become kings of the universe again. In other words, the play demonstrates the impossibility of achieving a peaceful existence by absenting oneself from affairs: the two Athenians at the start of the play are in an unknown place, a place detached from the real world, but even here they are shown paradoxically to be able to achieve anything approaching a trouble-free existence only by becoming great rulers. This is often said to be Aristophanes' most fantasy-filled play, but its myth in fact rejects any cosy notion that the fulfilment of such fantasies of ease is possible and hints that such fantasies are dangerous. It could be argued that the universe is a less pleasant place for all but the rulers by the end of the play than it was at the beginning, when the problems were the not very great ones of constant court-action and fines (39–41). At the same time, the story also provides a justification for imperial ambitions. Nephelococcygia is thus, like all myths, 'good to think with': it prompts reflection on fantasies of *apragmosune*, and at the same time on the kind of empire that Athens currently possessed.

The utopian agenda again comes under scrutiny in *Ecclesiazusae*, Aristophanes' penultimate extant play. Here, as in *Lysistrata*, the women set up a gynaecocracy, though this time it is one that is to endure, not be abolished when it has achieved its aim as in the earlier play. Not only do the women relieve the men of the need to trouble themselves with politics, but they turn the *polis* into a giant *oikos*, in which the men will be entertained for all time to sympotic pleasures. At first sight, this might seem a paradise, with signs of rejuvenation and much feasting, but on closer scrutiny the fantastic new laws, such as the one that says the beautiful must satisfy the old and ugly before the equally beautiful, turn out to produce horrors. The scene where a handsome young man is passed from one aged and disfavoured woman to another even less favoured one seems to justify the remark of one of the characters that there has been created 'a land of Oedipuses' (1040–2). The possible results of a retreat into mythical fantasies that societies can be simply improved are set out as a warning of such fantasies.

The absence of mythological comedy in the remains of Old Comedy is thus something to be regretted, but mythology's structures and meanings are still to be seen in our extant plays, as is an awareness of the dangers of too uncritical or simplistic an acceptance of what some myths may convey.

SUGGESTED WORKS FOR FURTHER READING

Bowie 1993: a structuralist reading of the comedies through their use of reference to, or the patterns of, myth and ritual.

Bowie 2000: a discussion of what can be gleaned about the use of myth and ritual in the fragments which survive of lost fifth-century comedies.

Faraone 1997: a discussion of the use of myths of salvation from burning in the interplay of genders in *Lysistrata*.

Lada-Richards, 1999: a full-scale literary, anthropological and cultural study of *Frogs*, with particular attention to how membership of fifth-century Athenian society would have shaped interpreation of the play.

Martin 1987: how the Lemnian festival of New Fire and its concomitant myth of the destruction and re-constitution of Lemnian society can illuminate meanings of the *Lysistrata*.

Nesselrath 1990: a historical account of the use of mythology in the fragmentary plays of fourth-century comedy.

Nesselrath 1995: on the parody of myth in comedy.

NOTES

1   For earlier work on this topic, cf. Moessner 1907; Cornford 1914; Hofmann 1976; Bowie 1993 (the reader is referred generally to this book on the extant plays of Aristophanes; reference on individual points or plays is not given in these notes), 1997, 2000; Nesselrath 1995; Carrière 1997: 413–42; Riu 1999.

2   The figure for Old Comedy is 125 plays that could fall into this category out of just under 400 known titles.

3   On which see Nesselrath 1990: 188–241.

4   On *Dionysalexandrus*, cf. most recently, Revermann 1997.

5   Cf. also Aristophanes' *Frogs* and *Dionysus Shipwrecked*; Eupolis' *Taxiarchs*, where he is taught military tactics, and the apparently similar Aristomenes' *Dionysus in Training*; the two plays entitled *Birth of Dionysus* by Demetrius and Polyzelus; Cratinus *Dionysus and his Companions* and so on.

6   For an account of satyr-plays, cf. Seaford 1984: 1–59.

7   Also in *Cypria*, fr. 9 Bernabé.

8   Platonius, *diff. com.* I.51-2, p. 5K; cf. K-A *Odysses* T i.

9   On the political content of Old Comedy, cf. Schwarze 1971.

10 Cf. Cratinus, frr. 73, 118, 258; Telecleides, fr. 18; Ar. *Ach.* 530.

11 Helen: Eupolis, *Prospaltioi* fr. 267; Hera: Cratinus, *Cheirons* fr. 259; Deianeira: fr. adesp. 704; Omphale: Plut. *Peric.* 24.9, Pl. *Menex.* 235E.

12 Apart from Theseus, Attic myths are not very common in tragedy, either: we find, for instance, the *Triptolemus* by Sophocles, the *Erechtheus* of Euripides, and a 'Pandion tetralogy' by Philocles (TrGF 24 T 6c, F 1); Cecrops, for instance, does not appear. Fragmentary plays about Medea may have concerned her time in Athens, but we cannot tell.

13 We find Erechtheus and Aegeus only once, summoned as witnesses, it seems, rather than as characters in the play (cf. Ar. *Banqueters*, fr. 217), Pericles as Buzyges (Eupolis, *Demes* fr. 103), and very sporadic mentions of other Athenian heroes, again not as characters.

14 Fr. 53; cf. *Hipp.* 219-22.

15 Cf. Martin 1987.

16 Fr. 47 = *Phoen.* 460-1; fr. 48-546.

17 A tantalising fragment, probably of Old Comedy, which discusses tragedy and may date from this time is studied by Bierl 1990.

18 Cf. Foley 1988; see in general 43-7.

19 Goldhill 1991: 201; see in general 167-201.

20 Cf. Faraone 1997.

21 Silk 2000: 207-55.

22 Cf. n.15 above, and Ephorus, FGrH 70 F 60a, for another example.

6: PLATO PHILOMYTHOS

Diskin Clay

The devotee of myth is in a way a philosopher, for myth is made up of things that cause wonder.

Aristotle, *Metaphysics* 1.982^b 18–19

THE MYTH OF *LOGOS* VS. *MYTHOS*

The luxuriant varieties of definitions of Greek "myth" are a symptom of the remoteness of our culture from the culture of ancient Greece. We have no real equivalent for the traditional stories and histories that circulated among the Greeks (and Romans) concerning their origins, the origins of their world, their gods and the progeny of their gods, the relation between humans and animals, and the fate awaiting mortals after death. The term myth now carries a pejorative sense in modern languages, as is evident from the use of the word in titles such as Wilhelm Nestle's *Vom Mythos zum Logos: Die Selbstentfaltung des griechischen Denkens* (1941) or Ernst Cassirer's *The Myth of the State* (1946), to name only two philosophical titles from the middle of the last century.[1] In Homer, *mythos* is a word that describes something said in the epic. But already in Herodotus the word *mythos* had come to describe an idle and unbelievable tale. The tradition concerning Oceanus and the Greek traditions concerning Heracles are cases in point; both are *mythoi* (*Histories* 2.23.1 and 2.45.1). Yet Herodotus' predecessor, Hecataeus of Miletus, can describe his own history as a *mythos* (FGrH 1 F 1 Jacoby) and, conversely, traditional but misleading historical accounts as *logoi*. In the age of Socrates, the philosopher Empedocles, who wrote in epic verse, could use the Homeric term *mythos* for his own philosophical arguments and religious teachings.[2] Thucydides rejected what he called the poets' "tendency to myth" (*to mythodes*, *The Peloponnesian War* 1.21), but, in his narrative of speeches made in assemblies and the facts on the ground, *logoi* were often the equivalent of myths. He constructs his history of the Peloponnesian War on the fatal contrast between what men say and the underlying reality of their situation.[3] Much later Strabo will distinguish between two radically different forms of writing: that presented "in guise of myth" and that presented "in guise of history."[4]

Plato, whose hostility toward poetry was notorious in antiquity, as it is now, would seem to be an enemy of myth, but his Socrates, who comes forward as the fiercest enemy of poetry in the Platonic dialogues, was captivated by Aesop and his myths. At the end of his life, in response to a recurring dream vision admonishing him to "become musical," Socrates took to setting Aesopian fables (usually called *ainoi*) into verse. Socrates calls them *mythoi* (*Phaedo* 60-C-D). How instructive it would be for humans, the possessors of *logos*, to speak with animals is evident in Plato's *Statesman* 272B, a scene beautifully illustrated by the red-figure kylix in the Vatican showing a fox instructing Aesop (Figure 1).

Plato bears a likeness to his Socrates. He would seem to qualify as the philosophical devotee of myth (the *philomythos* as *philosophos*) Aristotle describes in *Metaphysics* A. Or, perhaps, the order should be reversed to describe him as the philosopher devoted, not so much to traditional myths of his Greek culture, but to the creation of new myths to counter the charm of the old. Because of the deliberate ambiguity he has created in his dialogues as to what constitutes a *mythos* and what qualifies as a *logos*, Plato has contributed to our modern confusion over what can be described as a "myth." But, as he sometimes etches a sharp contrast between *mythos* and *logos*, he has also contributed to the common conception of Greek thought as evolving from the traditional, anonymous, and personified aetiologies of early Greek thinking to rational, logical, and "scientific" thought. In the *Gorgias*, for example, Plato has his Socrates give an account of the last judgment that awaits all humans in death, a possibility Socrates entertains briefly at the end of Plato's *Apology* (40C–1C). His interlocutor, the tough realist Callicles, will, Socrates thinks, regard his account as a fable (*mythos*); but what he will describe is in fact a noble and true account (*logos*) of reality (*Gorgias* 523A). The distinction does not hold. Elsewhere in Plato, what we would regard as his seriously meant truth is often treated as a *mythos*, and fictions, based on traditional accounts, are called *logoi*.

To approach the topic of Plato and myth, a fast definition of Greek "myth" is neither necessary nor possible. Our topic involves both the criticism of traditional Greek myths in the Platonic dialogues and the nontraditional "myths" that Plato created to replace what had become traditional. In many cases, his own language allows us to determine what he regarded as a *mythos*, but a shift in perspective can make a *mythos* of a *logos* and a *logos* of a *mythos*. As we approach what have long counted in the census of Platonic "myths,"[5] it should be noted that they are often based on a traditional story and that they correct this story by substituting a philosophical version of it. Thus, they tend to describe a supernatural reality or a reality that transcends our human experience but that our experience can give us some inkling of: that is, what lies hidden in the present, the remote past, and what awaits the human soul in the future. These Platonic myths are usually attributed to an anonymous oral source; they cannot be confirmed or falsified, except by someone who has had the experience of these realities, such as the fictional Er of the myth of Er in the *Republic* or the "heralds" responsible for our faint memory of the Golden Age, who lived on the "cusp" of the great periodic reversals of time in the myth of the *Statesman* (271A).

It has been said that myth died in Plato's youth.[6] It did not. Of all Greek philosophers, Plato is the most mythopoeic. For some of his myths he (meaning his Socrates) creates a philosophical counterpart to traditional poetic accounts of origins, as he does in the *Republic* (3.414B–415D), where he offers a myth of the metals to counter and supplant Hesiod's "myth of the metals" in *Works and Days* (109–201). In the "Great Myth" of the *Statesman*, Plato's visitor from Velia will connect and reconcile scattered and unrelated Greek oral traditions (268D–274E). His Socrates offers a striking version of the Underworld at the conclusion of the *Republic* (10.514A–517A). Plato designs it to supplant the Homeric book of the dead (*Nekuia*) in *Odyssey* 11. Myth, meaning the false or misleading traditions transmitted orally and anonymously in Greek culture, is often dismissed in the Platonic dialogues, but never simply as myth (*mythos*). Whether a narrative is called *mythos* or *logos* depends on the viewpoint of the teller of the tale (usually Socrates) and his audience. As Plato criticizes Greek myth and as he invents his own countermyths, his reader is confronted with constantly shifting perspectives. The old wives' tales (*mormolykeia*) of punishment in the afterlife are dismissed by Socrates as figments that instill fear in young children, who have no capacity for judging them. But in his own "myths of judgment" he has his own terrifying prediction of the fate that awaits the evil in death.[7]

A passage in the Platonic dialogues that reveals Plato's philosophical ambivalence toward myth comes at the opening of the *Phaedrus*, the dialogue that provides us with the best clue to the meaning of myth in Plato. Socrates and his companion, Phaedrus, have left the city of Athens for the Attic countryside in mid-August. As they ascend the stream of the Ilissus, Phaedrus asks Socrates if the place they had reached was not the site where Boreas, the god of the North Wind, had carried off the young Athenian princess, Oreithyia (*Phaedrus* 229B–230A). Socrates, who pretends that he is a tourist to the Attic countryside, has already noticed an altar to Boreas downstream. Phaedrus asks him if he believes in such traditional tales (*Phaedrus* 229A). Socrates remains noncommital. It is better, he says, to accept these tales than to take on the task of the intellectuals (*sophoi*) who give a laborious and rational explanation of such stories. That is: Boreas was not a god but the North Wind, and a gust of wind pushed Oreithyia off a cliff, either above the Ilissus or from the outcropping of the Areopagus. By this interpretation, the sophists remove the gods as active in human life; only the human actors remain. In the myths he tells in the Platonic dialogues Socrates never fails to invoke the gods.

Socrates adds a detail not recognized in Greek iconography: Boreas assaulted Oreithyia as she was playing with the nymph Pharmacea (the nymph of drugs and medicine). The subject of Boreas and Oreithyia appears on Greek vases,[8] but Pharmacea is Plato's invention. These legendary figures evoked by the divine powers present in the Attic countryside are deep down Plato's images of the conflict of Boreas (represented by the orator Lysias) and Socrates (as Pharmacea) for the soul of Phaedrus (cast as Oreithyia). This seemingly casual moment in the *Phaedrus* is symptomatic of Plato's simultaneous dismissal and use of Greek myth. His Socrates tells Phaedrus that he is not concerned with creatures such as centaurs, chimaeras, gorgons, and winged horses such as Pegasus (*Phaedrus* 229C); yet he invents a countermyth by inventing an image of the tripartite soul as a winged driver directing a chariot drawn by two winged horses (*Phaedrus* 246A–257A)[9] (an image reinterpreted in the frieze of the Medici villa at Poggio a Caiano and shown on the medallion in the bust of the young man attributed to Donatello now in the Bargello Museum of Florence; see Figure 2).[10] This long description of the life and progress of the soul in another world Socrates calls a *mythos*, but he also presents it as a *logos* (*Phaedrus* 253C).

Plato's real quarrel is not with Greek myth; it is with the poetry of the Greek *polis* and its false and debasing representations of reality. For this reason poets and myth are often associated in his dialogues, as is the case of the Hesiodic tradition of Uranus being castrated by his son Cronus, the first of the poetic lies condemned in the *Republic*.[11] Like Xenophanes of Colophon (c. 570–c. 478), the first philosopher to criticize Homer's portrayal of the gods, Plato rejected the mythological tales concerning the gods that Herodotus saw as being codified by Hesiod (first) and then Homer (*Histories* 2.53; cf. *Republic* 2.377D). Creatures such as the titans, giants, and centaurs, Xenophanes called the "fabrications of the ancients" (*plasmata ton proteron*, DK 21 B1.20–24).

But Plato is himself a fabricator, true to the etymology his name suggested to his Greek readers. Platon (in Greek) was rightly taken to suggest *platton*, the fabricator.[12] His Socrates, who was willing to accept Greek myths and was concerned to avoid becoming a raging giant like Typhon (*Phaedrus* 230A), offers Phaedrus at the end of the *Phaedrus* a "tradition of the ancients" (*akoen . . . ton proteron*, *Phaedrus* 274C–275B) in his strange tale of Theuth and Thamus. As Socrates confronts the poetic accounts of the gods in the *Republic*, he seizes on the tradition that the gods can disguise themselves in human or animal form. He sternly rejects any such possibility. The gods, who need nothing, have no need of movement or of becoming something other than what they are. They are content (2.380C–381E). Yet, the metamorphosis of the human into other forms of life after death is an essential theme of Platonic eschatology.[13]

Plato's myths offer countercharms to the traditions of Greek culture. The term "countercharm" is Plato's own. It describes arguments of the Platonic dialogues as the philosophical incantation that will free their hearers from the charm of traditional poetry (*Republic* 10.608A). They resemble Greek myths in that they all involve the marvelous (*to thaumaston*), the unknown, and the "transhuman" (to adapt Dante's word *trasumanar* in *Paradiso* 1.70). They connect humans with the divine and our world with a world that lies outside human ken. It is indifferent whether they are called *mythoi* or *logoi*. But their position and function within a Platonic dialogue has a bearing on their meaning. The placement of the so-called myths of judgment[14] at or near the end of the dialogue whose argument they seem to close – if not conclude – is symptomatic of the fact that the argument of the dialogue has reached an impasse. Socrates can bring his interlocutors no further by argument. This is true of the myths that come at the end of the arguments of the *Gorgias*, *Phaedo*, and *Republic*.

In the *Gorgias*, the bitter debate between Socrates and Callicles, who has taken the part of Gorgias, has ended in a stalemate. Callicles, who has maintained with great skill and energy the position that justice is by nature the interest of the more powerful, remains utterly unconvinced by Socrates' argument that it is better to be the victim of injustice than to commit injustice. At the end – but not conclusion of the dialogue – he is confronted with the prospect of the three judges of Hades, Minos,

Rhadamanthus, and Aeacus, who will judge him naked in death for any acts of injustice he has committed (*Gorgias* 522E–527E).

In the *Phaedo*, Socrates has concluded a series of three arguments for the immortality of the soul. The subject of the survival of the soul has a crucial bearing on the dialogue, since, after he has made his arguments, Socrates will be executed and his arguments tested. But his interlocutors, the Pythagoreans, Simmias and Cebes of Thebes, who should be sympathetic to the belief in the immortality of the soul, are not yet quite convinced by his arguments. Their persistent doubts shift the argument of the dialogue into Socrates' account of the "true earth" and the lower reaches of Tartarus where the souls of the wicked are punished after death (*Phaedo* 108C–115A). This is the single Platonic myth that reveals the "hidden present." Then follows Phaedo of Elis's description of Socrates' death (*Phaedo* 115B–118A). In the *Republic*, the Myth of Er comes as the unexpected sequel to the equally unexpected argument for the immortality of the soul in book 10 (614A–621D). The myth brings to an end a long day's conversation on the meaning of justice in the state and the individual soul that Socrates has taken the responsibility for directing, assisted by the usually obliging assent of Plato's two brothers, Glaucon and Adeimantus. The notion that the soul is immortal astounds Glaucon (*Republic* 10.608D), but he has nothing to say at the end of the dialogue.

These myths of judgment are "eschatological" in two senses. They give us a glimpse of a future that we must remain ignorant of in this life and they come at the end of a dialogue. They are, literally, "last things." The syntax of an argument for the immortality of the soul followed by a myth can be found at the middle of the *Phaedrus*, where Socrates' tight syllogistic argument for the soul's immortality is followed immediately by a "myth" of the discarnate experience of the soul, pictured as a winged charioteer directing a chariot driven by two winged horses (245C–246A, 246A–257A).

PARABLES OF THE PAST: PLATO'S "JUST SO" STORIES

The Platonic myths of the past are, like many Greek myths, "aetiological." That is, they explain the present state of things by the past. There are more of these in the Platonic dialogues than myths of the future. They occur in the *Protagoras*, the *Symposium*, *Phaedrus*, *Statesman*, and *Timaeus/Critias* (a single dialogue). They all have a philosophical moral, but they are quite unlike the "myths of judgment" in that they look back to the past not to subdue Plato's readers to virtue but to give them a sense of a history that had conditioned or could condition their lives. Five of these are told by characters in the dialogues other than Socrates: Protagoras (in the *Protagoras*); Aristophanes and Diotima (in the *Symposium*); the Eleatic Stranger (in the *Statesman*); and Critias (in the *Timaeus/Critias*). By contrast, all the myths of judgment are told by Socrates. Some of these myths of the prehistory of mankind have been taken with enormous seriousness. The myth of Protagoras has been seized on as evidence for this great thinker's lost treatment of "The Earliest Condition of Mankind," and Critias' recollection of an ancient Athenian tradition concerning the defeat of the island nation of Atlantis by prehistoric Athens has let a djinni escape from the bottle and produced the wisp of the lost continent of Atlantis.[15]

Protagoras (the Protagoras)

Let us begin with the myth of the *Protagoras* (320C–323D). It is directed to the young, like the myth of the *Statesman*, which is addressed to the young Socrates (268D). Like many of his contemporary sophists, Protagoras was interested in reshaping Greek traditions.[16] In response to the question the then young Socrates puts to him, Is virtue (*arete*) something that can be taught? Protagoras offers a story illustrating his contention that all humans possess some sense of civic virtue to suggest that it can. He offers a *mythos*, a term he contrasts with the argument he will then offer Socrates (the *logos* that follows in 323A–328D). Given his audience of young men gathered in the house of Callias, Socrates, the young Hippocrates, Alcibiades, and Phaedrus (among others), this older intellectual (*sophistes*) from Abdera in Thrace chooses to tell a story (320C). His Promethean myth of how mankind learned the "art" of justice and living amicably in civil society concludes in the argument he describes as a *logos* (328D). How are the two phases of his speech different? The simple answer is that his myth deals with Zeus, Prometheus, and Epimetheus and the creation of mankind; his argument concerns contemporary Athens and contemporary Athenians. Protagoras begins his story with the formula: "There was once a time when the gods existed, but the races of mortal creatures did not" (320D). Aristophanes will begin his speech in the *Symposium* in the same manner. Like many of the myths in the Platonic dialogues, the myth of the *Protagoras* has two distinguishing features: it is a "just so story" and at the same time a Platonic myth designed to counter and usurp the traditions familiar to his contemporaries. Here we encounter the myth of the creation of the human race by the gods that we find in Hesiod and other sources (and reflected in *Statesman* 274A) of how fire was fundamental to the development of human civilization. A short version of the story reads like this (*Protagoras* 320C–322D):

> There was once a time when the races of mortal creatures did not exist, only the gods. The gods created the human race out of fire and earth, but the new race remained within the earth. To Prometheus the gods assigned the task of providing animals and human kind with the capacities suited to them. But Prometheus' brother, Epimetheus, asked to take that role and leave his brother to judge the results. Unfortunately, Epimetheus began his distribution of the means of survival with animals and had nothing left for humans. On the day the new human race was to emerge into the light of day, Prometheus stole fire from heaven to assure the survival of vulnerable humans. Fire made burnt offerings to the gods possible, and only humans worship the gods. At first, they did not live in communities; they came to establish cities to protect themselves from wild animals. Yet they did not possess an art of civilized living until they learned the virtues of living in society. In his prudential fear of their extinction, Zeus sent Hermes down to them to convey from heaven a sense of justice (*dike*) and mutual respect (*aidos*). Hermes asked if he should distribute these divine gifts to all humans. Zeus replied "to all."

Protagoras' myth offers a solution to the difficult questions with which the young Socrates confronts him: Can virtue (*arete*) be taught? The decision of Zeus to distribute a sense of justice and mutual respect among all humans means that these virtues do not fall within the competence of only a few experts. Humans, however, need a training in virtue, and Protagoras, a renowned and well-paid professor (*sophistes*), claims that he is just the person to teach it (322D). In the part of his "Great Speech" he calls an argument (*logos*, 323A–328D), he does not invoke the distant past or the involvement of the gods in human life or the Athenian tradition of autochthony; he speaks rather of the educational practices of Athenian families and the Athenian democracy. When it comes to civic virtue, the Athenians believe that every citizen can be trained in it. The skill (*arete*) of a doctor is limited to a few gifted and well-trained individuals. The skills of political life are universal and democratic, in Athens at least, where no citizen is unskilled (an *idiotes*, 327A).

The myth of the *Protagoras* is unusual among Plato's myths in one respect. It is not assigned to Socrates (or one of his surrogates) and it conveys a point of view alien to Plato and his Socrates. By contrast, another intellectual (*sophistes*), the Athenian Critias, will be held responsible for the myth of Atlantis and its defeat by Athens, but the "strange, yet absolutely true" (*Timaeus* 20D) history of these two antagonistic civilizations conveys an elaborate philosophical invention that is Plato's and Plato's alone.

Socrates's Cicadas

The myth of the cicadas and the myth of Theuth (Egyptian Toth) and Thamus might well be Plato's inventions,[17] but they are not entirely original with Plato. Theuth, the inventor of writing, is the equivalent of the Greek Hermes and Thamus, the ruler of Egyptian Thebes, is the equivalent of the Egyptian god Ammon. Phaedrus is skeptical of Socrates' Egyptian tale of the interview between Theuth and King Thamus (*Phaedrus* 275B) and he has never heard of Socrates' story that the cicadas were once human poets and singers (*Phaedrus* 259D). The myths of the *Phaedrus* are told to the young Phaedrus by Socrates in the countryside of Athens in the heat of noon in high summer as cicadas "sing" (the Greek expression) on the trees overhead that grow along the Ilissus.

As for Socrates' cicadas, we recall that in the *Iliad* the old Trojans admiring Helen are compared to cicadas (3.145–53). This is significant because, after he has delivered his "palinode" to Eros, the dialogue returns to the question of rhetoric and the written speech of Lysias that has come into Phaedrus' possession. The Trojans at the Scaean Gate are too old for warfare, but "excellent speakers," like the cicadas that perch on the branches of trees and send forth their "soft, lily bright voice." Socrates' cicadas should not be strange to an Athenian: they recall the Athenian claim to autochthony, a claim that might be reflected in the archaic habit of wealthy Athenians of wearing gold cicadas in their hair.[18] The autochthonous mode of reproduction of cicadas is mentioned by Aristophanes in his parable of Eros (*Symposium* 191C).

According to Socrates, who is aware of this ancient tradition, the Muses were not the first poets (*Phaedrus* 258E–259D). These were men of long ago who were so devoted to poetry and music that they needed neither food nor drink, but sang, like La Fontaine's cigale, all their life. As they died, they were transformed into cicadas and vanished into the ground. In the present, the function of these insects is to "sing" at noon and to overhear conversations, such as that of the *Phaedrus*, and report them to the appropriate Muses. Terpsichore, Erato, Calliope, and Urania are the four Muses mentioned. Calliope and Urania are the Muses of philosophy. This reference to the Muses connects with the central myth of the *Phaedrus*, where Socrates, making his amends to Eros, explains the origins of earthy *eros* as deriving (literally deriving – or flowing from) from the soul's vision of the marvelous sights to be witnessed above the vault of heaven: justice, prudent self-control, knowledge, and true beauty (247B). This figures as one of the parables of Eros that we will turn to. The Muses take us back to the third type of divine madness defined in 249D (cf. 244B). Terpsichore takes us back to the eleven human "choruses" following the lead of eleven of the twelve gods (cf. 246E–247B, 252C). Erato defines the votary of the fourth type of divine madness of the lover (249D). Calliope and Urania preside over the followers of Zeus and the discourse of the philosopher (246E, 252D).

Socrates' Theuth and Thamus

The myth of Theuth and Thamus is not Greek, but it resembles the "Phoenician tale" of the *Republic* (3.414B–415D) in that it taps into Greek mythology. Socrates sets it plausibly in Egyptian Thebes and makes Theuth the inventor of many things, including writing. Many of his inventions are attributed to the Greek culture hero Palamedes, but Greeks were aware both of the Phoenician origin of their alphabet and of the great antiquity of Egyptian hieroglyphics.[19] Theuth advertises this invention to King Thamus as a drug that can promote wisdom and memory. Thamus replies: it is yours to invent, mine to judge the worth of your invention. The exchange between the two reminds us of the exchange between Epimetheus and Prometheus in the *Protagoras* (320D). Thamus cannot approve of Theuth's invention: "You have not discovered a drug to promote memory but rather a reminder."

This myth and Plato's discussion of the dangers of the written word have provoked a great deal of writing, in part because Thamus' judgment would seem to apply to Platonic writing.[20] This last myth of the *Phaedrus* certainly connects with the written speech in the form of a book roll that the young Phaedrus took out into the country to memorize and make his own (228A-B) and it would seem to connect with the central myth of the dialogue. The sight of a lovely boy and the reflection of the lover's image in the eyes of his beloved prompts a recollection that needs no written prompt of the visions both lovers had seen when winged and godlike in the presence of their gods.[21] Plato's deployment of the three myths that Socrates addresses to Phaedrus is also an illustration of the kind of philosophical discourse that is designed to attract the variegated soul of a reader like Phaedrus (271C–272B).

The Great Myth of the Statesman

The "Great Myth" of the *Statesman* (268D–274E) is the most revealing of Plato's myths for our understanding the intention and art of his philosophical mythopoeia. Not only is it described as a myth (thrice in 268D, 272D, and 274E), but also it describes "many amazing things" (270D) that lie beyond the ken of men in this recent order of the universe. It incorporates more Greek myths than does any other Platonic dialogue and it connects with many other dialogues: it looks back to the *Protagoras* and anticipates the myth of Atlantis in the *Timaeus/Critias*, and, most importantly, the "likely account" of the creation of the universe given by Timaeus in the *Timaeus* (30B). And, like the last Platonic "tetralogy" that includes the *Timaeus/Critias*, it figures in a "tetralogy": the *Theaetetus, Sophist, Statesman,* and the unwritten *Philosopher*. It is told to a young Athenian by the name of Socrates in the presence of an older Socrates who remains preternaturally silent. It is told by a visitor to Athens from Velia in southern Italy, who appears only in the *Sophist*, a dialogue in which the so-called Eleatic Stranger (from Velia south of Paestum in southwest Italy) speaks to the young Theaetetus (*Theaetetus* 143D–144C). Since Socrates is young, a myth seems in order (*Statesman* 268D-E). We are meant to recall the *Protagoras* and the myth Socrates addresses to the "boy" Phaedrus in the *Phaedrus* (256E). It is also meant for Plato's more mature readers.

In the case of the *Statesman*, the myth of the reversal of the movement of the heavens from east-to-west to west-to-east and, as a consequence, the reversal of human time is encased in a long and tedious attempt to define the statesman, as the sophist had been defined, by the method of division (*diairesis*) that Socrates announced in the *Phaedrus* (266D). The first "cut" is between theoretical and practical knowledge. This division leads to the conception of the ruler or statesman (*politikos*) as a shepherd directing a flock of terrestrial, feathered, solid-hoofed creatures. Now, at last, the Stranger introduces "play" and "the Great Myth" of the reversal of the course of the sun and heaven in order to push his inquiry on to a proper definition of the statesman (268D). So far, the bare notion of the shepherd ruler is nothing new. Homer had described Agamemnon as the "shepherd of his armies" (*Iliad* 2.243). The Stranger's myth is introduced by a portent or apparition (*phasma*) related to the feud between the sons of Pelops, Atreus and Thyestes (268E). Young Socrates misunderstands the meaning of the word "portent" and thinks of the golden lamb introduced into the flocks of Atreus (a myth recalled in Euripides, *Orestes* 986–1004, and expanded in the scholia). The Stranger has something else in mind – the reversal of the course of the sun is a natural revulsion to the crime of Atreus serving his brother the flesh of his children to avenge Thyestes' seduction of his wife, Aerope. The portent young Socrates remembered was the lamb with fleece of gold that Hermes had the shepherd Antiochus introduce into the flocks of Atreus to provoke a deadly quarrel between the brothers over the kingdom of Pelops. Antiochus at the very least connects with the theme of the ruler as shepherd.

Of more philosophical interest is the reversal of the course of the sun from east to west (Euripides, *Orestes* 1001–1004). This marvelous event introduces the Stranger's history of the periodic reversals in the movement of the heavens and the two states of mankind that obtain in each of the cycles. Under the reign of Cronus men are cared for like sheep by shepherding divinities (*daimones*); in the reign of Zeus, our present age, the world is released from control of the single god who directs the universe.

If the first part of the *Statesman* puts on display the method of division, the Great Myth suspends this mode of analysis, and Plato himself exhibits his method of "collection." His complex history of the alternation of two cosmic cycles incorporates more Greek myths than does any other Platonic myth. Hesiod's Uranus becomes the heavens; his account of the reigns of Cronus and Zeus (*Theogony* 154–84, 453–500) and the legends of the Age of Saturn are transformed into two opposing cycles of the heavens. The proud Athenian claim of autochthony that denies an origin of the inhabitants of Attica in sexual reproduction is justified in the myth that at the turn of the cycle from Zeus to Cronus humans grew younger, not older, and vanished into the earth from which they sprang up again (271A). The children born with grey hair in the Hesiodic Age of Iron (*Works and Days* 181) appear in the Stranger's myth (273E). In the Age of Saturn, all is reversed, and we are born old and grey. For the Age of Saturn and the destiny of some humans Plato engrosses the tradition of the Islands of the Blest (*Odyssey* 4.561–69; Hesiod, *Works and Days* 156–73). There are in fact four stages to this cycle: the two distinct ages of Cronus and Zeus and the two cataclysmic shifts from one cycle to the other when the human race is nearly destroyed.[22] As the Stranger says, the reports of the distant past that have come down to us have been extinguished with the passage of time or survive as they are scattered in incoherent bits and pieces (269B).

The myth of the *Statesman* reassembles fragments of Greek myth into a "philosophical" whole – philosophical because one of the functions of philosophy, poetry, and literature is to estrange us from the familiar. The myth also attaches this dialogue to other Platonic dialogues. It looks back to the history of primitive man told in the *Protagoras* and the doctrine of recollection in the *Meno*, *Phaedo*, and *Phaedrus*, which requires our forgetfulness, and, therefore, attests to the reality of what we have experienced in past lives. The elliptical becomes veridical. The description of the cosmic calamities that occur at the moment of the reversal of cosmic cycles prepares for the history of the destruction of Athens and Atlantis in the *Timaeus/Critias* (cf. *Statesman* 273A and *Timaeus* 25C). The god who lets go the rudder of the universe so well directed in the Age of Saturn (270C-D, 273 A) and the divinities who assist him in his work (274A) anticipate the Demiurge, the "god of the gods," of the *Timaeus* and the lesser gods who assist him in his work of creation (*Timaeus* 41A-D). It also prepares for Timaeus' exposition of the two motions of the heavens (*Timaeus* 36B-D). The Stranger goes on to describe the work of the statesman or ruler in the Age of Zeus (the only age in which there can be a human ruler) as that of a weaver combining the strands of the temperaments of his subjects into a whole (305E–311C). The paradigm describes Plato's art of weaving the strands of Greek myth into a fabric of his own design.

Critias: The War of the Worlds

The most notorious of Plato's myths is the myth of Atlantis (sometimes referred to as his *Atlantikos logos*). It is the most impressive philosophical fiction ever written and it bears all the hallmarks of a fiction: the earnest claim to truth; excessive documentation and correspondingly fussy detail; the authority both of Egypt and of the Athenian lawgiver Solon; an exact but impossible chronology; an epic never completed; an unreliable narrator; and a narrative that ends dramatically in a sentence fragment. The account of the defeat of the imperial island of Atlantis by early Athens is presented as a sequel to Socrates' description of an ideal state in the *Republic*. Critias, one of the thirty "tyrants" (of 404–403), is responsible for the narrative. His promised *logos* serves as a prologue to Timaeus of Locri's account of the creation of the world by the Demiurge in the *Timaeus* and continues in the dialogue that bears his name, the *Critias*. The *Timaeus* and *Critias* are in fact a single dialogue (the *Timaeus/Critias*), but Plato's larger project can be described inadequately as a tetralogy: the *Republic*, the *Timaeus*, the unfinished *Critias*, and the promised *Hermocrates*, the speech the general Hermocrates of Syracuse was to have given as the last of four speeches.[23] But he remains silent, since the *Critias* ends with these words of Zeus to the gods concerning the degenerate kings of Atlantis (121B-C):

> But as Zeus, god of the gods, reigning as king according to law, could clearly see this state of affairs, he observed this noble race lying in this abject state and resolved to punish them and to make them more careful and harmonious as a result of this chastisement. To this end he called all the gods to their most honored abode, which stands in the middle of the universe and looks down upon all that has a share in generation. And, when he had gathered them together, he said . . .

This assembly and the stern speech of Zeus echo not only the speech of Zeus in *Odyssey* 1.26–43 but more audibly the scene evoked by Aristophanes in the *Symposium* (190C-D).

What follows we learn from the *Timaeus* Prologue (24E–25C): imperial Atlantis launches an attack into the Mediterranean and is finally defeated by the early Athenians, whose virtues and manner of life correspond to those of the guardians of Socrates' ideal city. They defeat the aggressors from the Atlantic. An Egyptian priest relying on an Egyptian hieroglyphic history preserved in Sais recounts for Solon the end of the war of the worlds of Atlantis and Athens (25C-D):

> But, afterwards, earthquakes and floods of incredible violence struck, and in one terrible day and night, your entire warrior class disappeared as one body beneath the earth, and in this same calamity the island of Atlantis sank into the sea and disappeared. That explains why that distant sea cannot be navigated and resists exploration even now, since the mud produced as the island sank covers its surface to a great depth.

Here we have the account Solon gave of what he learned in Egypt. Like the *Critias*, Solon's poetic history was never finished. The civil strife he found in Athens on his return prevented him from completing it (*Timaeus* 21C). In his invention of the lost and unrecoverable, Plato discovered one essential element of the art of lying.

Plato's myth of Atlantis has prompted many of his incautious readers to explore the Sargossa Sea of his tale of Atlantis. If his *Timaeus/Critias* is a fiction, it is also a proper Platonic myth. It deals with an amazing past and gods in their relation to both the first Athenians and the descendants of Poseidon and the mortal Clito on Atlantis. It recognizes the Athenian traditions of autochthony and the struggle of Athena and Poseidon for control of Attica; it also recognizes the Greek tradition of the deluge. In creating this fiction, Plato relied on the authority of Greek myths. But in creating the island nation of Atlantis he created a distant mirror in which the image of the imperial Athens of his youth could be seen.[24]

THREE PARABLES OF EROS

Aristophanes (Symposium)

We come now to Eros and Thanatos, to origins and ends. Eros, the god of passionate desire, and *eros*, the passion of desire itself, are the subject of three Platonic parables. Two of these are told in the *Symposium*, a third in the *Phaedrus*. The first is the myth of Aristophanes in the *Symposium* (which Aristophanes calls a *logos*); the second is Diotima's speech, recalled by Socrates in the *Symposium* (which has no description); and the third Socrates' speech in the *Phaedrus*, his "palinode" to appease the god Eros (which he calls a *mythos*). All these parables involve the divine inasmuch as human passion and desire are taken to have their origin in the god Eros. Aristophanes is the "author" of the first of these. His is the fourth speech of the seven speeches of the *Symposium* (229B–238A). When his turn comes, Socrates will give the sixth; it is not his own, but a speech he attributes to Diotima of Mantinea (189B–193D). All of the first six speeches of the *Symposium* are intended as praise of the neglected god, Eros. The drunken Alcibiades will conclude by speaking seventh in praise of Socrates, a Socrates who uncannily fits Diotima's description of Eros.

The speeches are delivered as part of the after-dinner entertainment at a banquet celebrating the victory of the tragic poet Agathon at the dramatic competitions of 416. Phaedrus, who suggests the topic, begins by celebrating Eros as the oldest of the gods and for this reason a god who has no parents (178A). He cites the poets Hesiod and Parmenides as his authorities. Aristophanes' myth is something that he is the only source for; he will instruct Agathon's guests and they in turn will instruct others (*Symposium* 189B–193D):

> Originally, human beings were different from what they are today. In the distant past, they had powerful round bodies surmounted by two heads which, like their genitals, faced in opposite directions. They had four arms and four legs that propelled them in circular motion, like tumblers. At that time there were not two sexes, male and female, but three. A hermaphrodite (*androgynon*) existed then as a composite of male and female. These three sexes owed their natures to three rotund gods: the compound of male and male to Helios, the Sun; the compound of female and female to Ge, the Earth; and the compound of male and female to Selene, the Moon. Impelled by their power and lack of any restraint, they made an assault of Olympus, as did once the giants Otus and Ephialtes.
>
> Zeus was alarmed by this threat, but decided not to destroy this human race. Rather he cut these round creatures in half (and thus he doubled the number of humans offering sacrifices). He instructed Apollo to draw the skin over the exposed halves of these creatures as a leather worker draws a purse together by a string. The small opening is what we now call the "navel." Now desire (*pothos*) arises. These severed halves immediately sought their other halves: male and male, female and female, and male and female. This desire for our missing halves and our instinctive need to be reunited with our lost halves is *eros*, or Eros – the philanthropic god who can heal us and make us whole. If the blacksmith Hephaestus were to stand over us as a reunited couple clasped in an embrace and offer to fuse us and unite us into our original self, who could refuse the offer?

There are many comic details in Aristophanes' myth,[25] but Plato is not mainly concerned with making him a comic figure. Aristophanes' speech does not begin to ascend to the heights of Diotima's as she describes our ascent in the objects of our desire from an individual to the idea of Beauty itself. Yet, Aristophanes' conception of love has one thing in common with that of Socrates and Diotima. Eros, not now the god, but the god demoted to human desire (*eros*), is fundamentally a desire for something that the lover lacks, whether the object of his desire is another person or something as remote as wisdom (*sophia*). The objects of human desire are, ultimately, unattainable, and such is the human condition. No god can reunite us with our other halves, either in this life or in death. Like the inhabitants of Dante's Limbo, we live in desire but without hope (*Inferno* 4.42). With Diotima's speech the desire of the philosopher for wisdom (a desire implicit in the word *philosophia*) enters into the dialogue of the seven speeches of the *Symposium*. This connection surfaces in a dramatic detail. When Socrates has finished speaking, Aristophanes is the only guest who does not praise his speech. He says rather that it reminds him of something that he had said (212C).

Diotima (Symposium)

Socrates learns from Diotima that Eros is not a god, but a great *daimon* intermediary between and mediating the human and the divine. Socrates asks about his parents. Diotima answers (203A–204A):

> He is the son of Poros (Resourceful) and Penia (Poverty). Since Penia managed to seduce the drunken (and then resourceless) Poros at a feast of the gods celebrating the birth of Aphrodite, he takes after both of his parents and Aphrodite as well. On his mother's side he is poor, tough, and wiry, with no fixed home or bed. He sleeps in doorways and on the streets. Taking after his father he is clever at entrapping the fair and virtuous, and brave, impetuous, and intense. He craves understanding and is resourceful and desires wisdom throughout his entire life.

Socrates' "Palinode" (Phaedrus)

The longest of all of Socrates' accounts of Eros is given in the *Phaedrus*, a dialogue devoted to the twin themes of rhetoric and *eros* and to the overarching and unstated theme of erotic and philosophical rhetoric. It comes in the middle of the dialogue after Phaedrus has read Lysias' speech that features the absurdity of a "nonlover" attempting to convince a boy to grant him his "favors" and after Socrates has improvised a speech in favor of Lysias' "nonlover." But Socrates realizes at high noon that he has offended the powerful god Eros and makes amends by offering a "palinode" giving a cosmic account of Eros and the power of love. Some of this speech will be presented as we turn finally to Plato's "myths of judgment." In the *Phaedrus*, there is no myth of Eros as a god, although the recantation is addressed to "dear Eros" (257A). The closest Plato comes to acknowledging and transforming the representations of Eros in Greek art is to offer an image of the powerful god as winged. An image of the divine is all that is possible in human discourse (246A). Unlike the winged Eros of vase painting, this Eros does not swoop down upon the soul but lifts it upward.

As in Diotima's speech in the *Symposium*, Eros has a greater empire over human life than passionate desire (lust) for another human being. In the cosmic setting Socrates introduces, the *eros* that unites two human males is their vision of transcendent realities in a winged state above the "back" of heaven. This vision is reawakened on earth as the lover looks into the eyes of his beloved and, like Narcissus, sees his own image there. But unlike Narcissus, both lovers are reminded of another form of existence. Plato is at great pains to connect the word *eros* with the Greek word to flow (*rhein*); he also connects the word *himeros* (a longing) with the expression for sending off parts of oneself (255C-D and 251C). In his concluding prayer to Eros Socrates apologizes for his "poetic language" (257A). He has resorted to poetry (and myth) to appeal to Phaedrus. But throughout a dialogue that begins with an address to "dear Phaedrus," continues with a prayer to "dear Eros," and strangely concludes with Socrates' prayer to "dear Pan," Plato exposes his reader to the divine presence of divinities of the Attic countryside – Boreas, Oreithyia, Pan – at noon in midsummer, far from the walls of Athens and its sophists.

THANATOS: THREE MYTHS OF JUDGMENT

Socrates: *The* Phaedo

Myths of the past are by far the most common in the Platonic dialogues. In Greek mythology there is no such thing as a myth of the future save in prophecies concerning the fate of heroes such as Menelaus in the afterlife and the cult of heroes predicted at the end of some Euripidean tragedies such as the *Hippolytus*. And there is no such thing as myth of the "hidden present." But in one of Plato's so-called myths of judgment we confront Socrates' description of the "true earth" given to a small group of his friends in the last moments of his life on earth. This is in the *Phaedo*, a dialogue dated after the *Gorgias*. I will address it first, since it addresses a radically new cosmology in which Tartarus is described as one of the three divisions of the universe. At the end of three arguments Socrates has made to convince Simmias and Cebes of Thebes that the soul is immortal and immediately after the autobiographical description he gives of what we would call the "Presocratic" science of causes (96A–99D), he speaks of what he believes the "true earth" to be (108C–115A). It is here that we discover the sole Platonic myth of the hidden present in Socrates' complex description of the true earth and its regions, including its interior. In what he calls a "myth" (110B), Socrates describes what the *true* earth looks like when seen from a prospect not of earth but of heaven. He enters into a description of reward or punishment in the afterlife as he describes the great subterranean cavities that receive the waters of the lower earth and the souls of those who are destined for happiness or punishment in the afterlife (110B–115A).

This is an odd myth and significantly different from the myths of judgment that conclude the *Gorgias* and *Republic*. Socrates, of course, has been judged himself and has just spoken of the judgment against him (98C-E). But in this account of the Underworld there are no judges. Nor is there any narrative. The gods are mentioned only once. Socrates gives rather a long, static, and complex description of a universe more vast in both its heights and depths than humans can easily conceive of, especially in the confines of a prison in Athens. Yet this strange and fascinating digression reveals more than do the other myths of judgment the transcendental genius of Plato's myths.

In the first stage of this description, Socrates creates a three-tiered proportional scheme that will reappear in the image of the cave in the *Republic* (7.515A–517A).[26] What we think of as our earth is in fact only a tiny part of the universe and our conception of it is as dull and limited as the perspective of frogs or ants at the edge of a pond. We actually live in a small hollow filled with water and mist in a realm of decay and deformed and eroded shapes. In our own terms, we are like men who live at the bottom of the sea and look up to the light and air above us as if it was heaven. This is our bogus earth. The "true earth" is located above our atmosphere in the *aither*, or the pure and brilliant light of the heavens. The scheme can be set out in the following terms: the depths of the sea are to the air and light of the earth as our dull, dark earth is to the purity and light of the "true earth." But the picture is more difficult and complex in that it has a basement beneath our earth. Our earth extends down into great chasms that receive rivers that flow into them. These descend down to the center of this spherical earth located in the center of the universe and are then repelled and forced upward in an alternating rhythm. The deepest of these is the pit of Tartarus, which pierces our world.

Socrates' mythical account begins as he describes the universe, including our world at its center, as a *sphaira*, or ball, made up of twelve strips of variegated colors[27] more intense than anything found in this lower world. And, just as we discover the souls of the dead in the hollows below us, we discover in the *aither* of the true earth perfect plants, fruits, and men; here are sacred groves of the gods and sanctuaries in which the gods are truly inhabitants (111B). Evidently, Plato is already announcing his conception of celestial deities, the planets and the stars, that we will find in the *Timaeus* and *Laws*.

Tartarus lies below, perhaps as far below the earth as the true earth is from the surface of our earth. It is only at this infernal stage of Socrates' description that he recalls for Simmias the Greek myths concerning the Underworld and the punishments that await the evil there. He has already invoked the Islands of the Blest (111A). Now he quotes a line from Homer's *Iliad* (8.14) not only to recall a poetic or "mythic" conception of the Underworld but to suggest a proportional scheme to be discovered two lines later (8.16). For Homer (as for Hesiod, *Theogony* 720–25), Tartarus is as far from earth as earth is from heaven. Oceanus, the four rivers of the Underworld, and the vast Lake of Acheron suggest a topography of crime and punishment more complicated than we will find in either the *Gorgias* or the *Republic*.

Socrates: *The* Gorgias

Plato taps into Greek heroic myth in the *Gorgias*, a dialogue for which Plato has erected as a dramatic background (*skene*) the debate of the twin brothers Zethus and Amphion of Thebes and their irreconcilable dispute over which of their two lives is the better. He knew this best from Euripides' *Antiope*, a play that dramatizes their dispute over which of their lives (*bioi*) is superior, that of the man engaged in political life or that of the poet and musician. This is the Theban myth that prepares for the final myth of the afterlife. Socrates casts Callicles in the role of Zethus and himself in the role of Amphion. Euripides' play has a happy ending that is made possible only by the appearance of the god Hermes, who resolves the quarrel. In the *Gorgias*, Plato rejects the artificial solution of Euripides and by rejecting it reveals his understanding of how deliberately artificial it is in Euripides.[28]

At the end of the *Gorgias*, Callicles has nothing more to say to Socrates. He remains utterly unpersuaded by Socrates' argument that it is better to be the victim of injustice than to commit injustice and that the truest form of rhetoric is not the deceptive persuasiveness of a sophist like Gorgias or his understudy Polus but that of the knowing philosopher (513C). With rude reluctance Callicles allows Socrates to conclude his argument by extending it to the afterlife (522E). As is often the case, Socrates' *logos* comes from an anonymous source, but the account itself is confirmed in part by Homer and the tradition that the sons of Cronus, Zeus, Poseidon, and Hades (here Pluto), divided their domains into the heavens, sea, and Underworld. (The earth is common to all three, *Iliad* 15.187–92.) Like the myth of the *Protagoras*, this narrative has two stages; it features Zeus speaking, and involves Prometheus. At first, under the rule of Cronus, men were judged when still alive on the day of their death. Then the just were sent to the Islands of the Blest, the unjust to the prison of Tartarus. But Zeus comes to recognize that there is a problem in judging the living who are still "clothed" in their imposing bodies, reputations, and living witnesses to speak on their behalf. He commands Prometheus to put an end to such superficial judgments (a tradition reflected in Aeschylus, *Prometheus Bound* 248). In the improved system, judgment will come unexpectedly after death, and judged and judges will stand "naked," that is, as souls freed from their bodies (523D), a condition that seems to reflect the conception of *Odyssey* 11.218–22.

Three new judges are appointed. They are sons of Zeus. Rhadamanthys is judge of the souls that come from Asia; Aeacus of the souls that come from Europe. In case of dispute, the "Asian" Minos will arbitrate. These judges will have no knowledge of a soul's identity. Their task is to discriminate between the souls of the just and unjust. Among the unjust Plato introduces two categories (as he will in the *Republic*): those who can be cured and whose punishment will serve as a deterrent to the living and those beyond curing. Archelaus of Thessaly is a living example of the second criminal type, as are Tantalus, Sisyphus, and Tityus of Homer's *Nekuia* (or book of the dead). These are the criminals sighted by Odysseus in the Underworld.[29] Two "seals" distinguish the just from the unjust (as they will in the Myth of Er in the *Republic*). Socrates speaks of the philosopher and names Aristides, "the just," as an example of the soul that will be rewarded in the afterlife. In a dialogue in which the trial and conviction of Socrates cast a shadow over the conversation, the fate of Socrates will surely come to the mind of Plato's reader. Socrates ends by saying that he has been persuaded by this account, but perhaps Callicles will regard it as a tale (*mythos*) told by an old woman (527A). Callicles remains unpersuaded.

Socrates' Myth of Er (Republic)

In these three "myths of judgment," there is a strict connection between rational and earthbound arguments for the immortality of the soul that, in the language of the *Phaedo* (108D), take us from "here to there" (*enthende ekeise*). Plato recognized, as did Dante after him, that human experience and human rationality cannot reach to that world beyond. There is nothing in this life to falsify a claim about the afterlife. All that the human mind here on this earth can offer as a conception of that other world must be an approximation or an image drawn from our limited experience on earth. Dante understood these limits and he used the example of Glaucus of Anthedon on Euboea to intimate that his transformation from a fisherman to a god of the sea serves as an example of how the human can go beyond the human, as had Plato (in *Phaedo* 108D). For this transcendence Dante invents the word *trasumanar* (*Paradiso* 1.70). In commenting on this passage in his *Letter to Can Grande*, he cites Plato's technique of using "metaphors" to move us from here to there. That is, after all, the function of metaphor.[30]

In Plato, there is finally no last judgment. His souls migrate from one form of life to another. The words of Christ in Matthew 24 and 25 are not appropriate to his conception of the punishments and rewards that await the soul after "death," although Christian writers found confirmation of their own belief of a Last Judgment in the *Gorgias* and the *Republic*. Socrates' final myth of judgment is the most complex and fascinating of all. It is the myth of Er with which the long conversation of the *Republic* concludes (10.614A–621D). The *Republic* is concerned with the conception of justice and injustice, both within the individual human soul and in the state. Socrates' last words are addressed to Glaucon, Plato's brother, whom he addresses repeatedly by name, as if recalling him to himself. (He did the same with Callicles in the *Gorgias*.) After reading the last words of the *Republic*, we can well believe that Glaucon might have been persuaded. It could well be that there is something in all of us that, if trained by argument, responds to myth rather than argument.

Interlude – Socrates: The Phaedrus

This is not, as we have seen, the last time that Socrates will speak of the fate of the soul in the afterlife. He returns to this possibility in his speech of recantation to appease the god Eros for what he had said in praise of the sober restraint of the "nonlover." In this dialogue, his account of the judgment that awaits the souls of the just and unjust is expressed in the image of the tripartite soul he offers as a winged charioteer controlling two winged horses. Here the "decree of Adrastia" gives Socrates' final version of the judgment that distinguishes between the souls of the just and unjust (248C–249D). In Plato's myths of judgment there is a great variety in visualizing this judgment, but the larger context in which it fits remains the same.

In the *Phaedrus*, we confront a place above the vault of heaven from which the winged human soul in the company of the gods can contemplate something of reality. Adrastia (the equivalent of Atropus in the myth of Er) makes her decisions guided by a single consideration: has the soul witnessed the highest reality and "justice itself" (247D). Thus, the soul's glimpse of truth and therefore its justice will determine the lives of the soul after the termination of one particular life. Eros enters into this image in that the soul of the philosopher and the soul of the proper lover of young men will regain their wings and be judged in a place below Dike (Justice) and the vault of heaven. The unjust and ignorant (and, the worst of these, the tyrants) are dispatched to the courts established under the earth. As in the *Meno*, the knowledge or vision of the winged soul that has returned to earth comes from the "recollection" of what it has seen above (*anamnesis*, *Meno* 80E–81D).

The central "myth" of the *Phaedrus* might not conform neatly to our provisional definition of what constitutes a myth in Plato. Let us attempt to refine this definition. Platonic myths do, indeed, connect the human and the divine, and the divine is an object of wonder, even as it is recalled on earth (*Phaedrus* 254D). The myth has its obvious attachment to Greek myth and its iconography: it recalls the image of Eros as winged. Socrates even cites (and Plato invents) two verses from the "descendants of Homer" that give the divine name for Eros as *Pterotos* (Winged Love, 252B). The myth of the *Phaedrus* is designed to serve as a counter to the charm of Greek poetry and myth; it is meant to take wing above them.

Back to Er

The myth of Er is explicitly introduced as a counter to the tale (*apologos*) of the Underworld that Odysseus told Alcinous on Phaeacia (*Republic* 10.614A). It is a narrative and it is dramatic, in that it reproduces speech directly. As judges it features not Minos, Rhadamanthys, and Aeacus, but now the Fates (Moerae): Lachesis, Clotho, and Atropus. What Er saw in his out-of-body experience needs an acute visual imagination to register. In his near-death experience he saw a divine place with chasms opening right and left. To the left of those to be judged is the pit of Tartarus; to the right is the passage up into the heavens. This is not unfamiliar. We find the parting of the ways in Orphic texts. But the "spindle of Necessity" is Plato's invention. It is his philosophical image of the tradition of the Fates (Moerae), who are represented as women working at a loom. One, Lachesis, measures out the wool (the length of a life); another, Clotho, weaves the wool; and the last, Atropus (the Inevitable), cuts the thread of life. In Plato's version of the myth, Lachesis judges the past, Clotho the present, and Atropus the future (10.621A). In the Myth of Er we discover other familiar figures from Greek myth. Eight Sirens are perched on the spindle of Necessity; we find the infernal River Lethe flowing through a sweltering plain.

The myth is also a narrative. Socrates gives an account of Er, the son of Armenius of Pamphylia in Asia Minor, and his miraculous experience of death and revival and the judgment that awaits the soul in a "divine place," a meadow where souls are judged and swept up into a chasm in the sky to the right or plunged down beneath the earth to the left. His experience of the judgment, from which he is exempt, makes him a messenger (*angelos*) to the living. Without giving any other authority, Socrates tells Glaucon what Er reported. Er is Plato's invention. After he revives twelve days after he had fallen in battle and his body was placed on a funeral pyre, he returns as a living witness to the rewards for justice and punishments for injustice in the afterlife.

In reinforcing the myths of rewards and punishment in the afterlife, Plato also enlists Orphic beliefs in the rewards of the pious in the afterlife. And he adds a striking feature to both traditions. After the dead have completed 1,000 years of reward or punishment, they are called by a prophet who proclaims: "Souls, who live but for a day: This is the beginning of another cycle of living for you as a mortal and death prone race" (10.617B). He offers the souls assembled before him a choice of life. Ajax chooses the life of a lion; Agamemnon that of an eagle. Remarkably, Odysseus makes the last choice – the life of a private person who minds his own business. Thunder rolls overhead and a terrible tremor shakes the earth. Socrates ends the tale by urging Glaucon to keep to the upward path for another 1,000-year cycle. When Plato's reader leaves the conversation of the *Republic*, he does not leave a medieval

Italian church and look up to a terrifying scene of The Last Judgment. He leaves a strange Greek temple to face still other judgments and still other lives.

FURTHER READING

The fullest bibliographical guide to the myths in Plato is that of Luc Brisson (1994, English translation 1998); Gerard Naddaf's Introduction to the English translation is an excellent point of orientation ([1998] vii–liii). The three most important and comprehensive studies of Platonic mythopoeia are those of Stewart (1905), Frutiger (1930), and Reinhardt (1960). Any interpreter of a Platonic myth is obliged to place the myth in its context, both within the domain of Greek myth in general and within the dialogue in which it appears. I have noted what I consider the most important contributions to an understanding of a particular Platonic myth in the notes. Plato's reader also has the expert direction of the more general studies of Graf (1993) and Morgan (2000), which place him in the context of the wider philosophical appraisal of Greek myth. Valuable too is the short general assessment of myth in Plato by Edelstein (1949).

NOTES

1 This fictive antithesis is well addressed by Morgan (2000) 30–37. It is only in later rhetorical theory that *mythos* is distinguished from *historia* (history) and *plasma* (a plausible fiction) as "an account of things that never happened and are false," Sextus Empiricus, *Against the Professors* 263–5; anticipated in the source of *ad Herennium* 1.8.13.

2 *Mythos* is the preferred word: DK 31 B17.14–15; 23.11; 24.2; 62.3 (in *Purifications* B114.1), and *logos* is used only in *Purifications* B 131.4. By contrast, *logos* is the only term Heraclitus uses for the principle of rationality in his book and his own argument, as in DK B1, 2, and 51. Plato can describe the utopian projects of the *Republic* or *Laws* as existing only in theory (*logoi*), *Republic* 9.952A. In justifying his involvement with the tyrants of Syracuse, he could say that he did not want to be all theory (*logos*), *Epistle* 7.328C.

3 He dismissed this poetic tendency, but in his history of the Peloponnesian War the common formula *logoi men . . . ergoi de* ("this was what was said" . . . "but in reality") is a sign of his deep distrust of what men say, of his actors' delusions (*elpis*) and their ability to ascertain the real situation on the ground (*akribeia*). The contrast is common; 2.65.9 and 3.38.4–6 are good examples.

4 *Geography* 1.2.35 and 11.6.3.

5 Most of these were isolated and translated in Stewart (1905). They are treated as a group by Frutiger (1930) and Reinhardt (1960), but none of these scholars arrives

at exactly the same census of Platonic myths. What is often called "the myth of the cave" in the *Republic* (7.514A–517A) does not count as a Platonic myth: it is meant as an image (*eikon*) illustrating the levels of reality plotted on the divided line of *Republic* 6.509D–511D. Although this vivid comparison addresses a marvelous reality in the world outside the cave, it is not attributed to any anonymous oral source, it contains no narrative of the past, it involves no divinities, and it takes no Greek myth in its sights. For recent and pertinent reflections of what constitutes a myth in the Platonic dialogues there is Charles' Kahn's "The Myth of the Statesman" (2007).

6   By Reinhardt (1960) 220.

7   *Mormolykeia*, *Gorgias* 473D, *Phaedo* 77E; old wives' tales, *Republic* 1.350E, 2.378D, and 9.571B.

8   The iconography of Boreas, who gained in importance for the Athenians after the gales (Norwesters) that destroyed the Persian fleet on Cape Artemisium (Herodotus, *Histories* 7.189), and Oreithyia is treated by Erika Simon in LIMC VIII 1.64–68.

9   Whose tale is told by Glaucus in *Iliad* 6.154–202.

10 The charioteer of this frieze controls three horses, not two.

11 In Socrates' long discussion of the traditional poetry the young guardians should not be exposed to, 2.377E–378A.

12 Plato deliberately puns on his name in *Republic* 3.415A, when he speaks of the "plastic god" (*ho theos platton*) who fashioned human beings in the depths of the earth. The philosopher and satirist Timon of Phlious understood this well, as we can tell from his epigram on Plato, DL 3.26.

13 *Republic* 10.620A–B, *Timaeus* 90E–92C.

14 As they are termed by Annas (1982).

15 Thus, *Protagoras* 320C–322D is reproduced as an "imitation" of Protagoras' treatise in DK 80C1. The description of the Platonic invention of the myth of Atlantis is that of Cherniss (1947) 254.

16 The role of the sophists in the interpretation of Greek myth is well presented in Morgan (2000). An elegant characterization of the sophistic and philosophical treatment of myth can be found in Graf (1993), chapter 8.

17 Frutiger took them to be the only Platonic myths that were his pure invention, (1930) 233.

18 Thucydides, 1.6; Aristophanes, *Knights* 1321–34, *Clouds* 984–6.

19 *Timaeus* 23A; the passage attributed to Manetho by Syncellus, *Manetho*, ed. W. G. Waddell (Cambridge, MA and London 1940) p. 208, gives Plato's version of Thoth's invention of writing.

20 The best-known written response is that of Jacques Derrida (1972).

21 Lebeck (1972) reveals still more connections.

22 There is great disagreement in the reading of this myth. To assess its difficulties and ambiguities the reader should turn first to Vidal-Naquet (1986) 285–301, and then to Kahn (2007).

23 There is a presentation of the *Timaeus/Critias* and the unwritten *Hermocrates* and their relation to the *Republic* in Clay and Purvis (1999) 36–40 and 53–97.

24 The tradition of the struggle of Athena and Poseidon for possession of Attica (displayed on the west pediment of the Parthenon) is reflected in *Critias* 108B; the Athenian pride in autochthony in *Critias* 113D (and *Menexenus* 238D–E); the

deluge in the tradition of Deucalion in *Critias* 112A. It was Vidal Nacquet (1986) who most clearly discerned the reflection of imperial Athens in Plato's description of Atlantis.

25 Indeed, the comparison of the severed halves to soles (*psettai*) derives directly from Aristophanes' *Lysistrata* 515–6. The comic cobbler's task assigned to Apollo, the god of healing, might well have inspired the cobbled repair of the severed halves of the crusader on Italo Calvino's *Il Visconte Dimezzato* (1966).

26 The Greek for "proportion" (*ana logon*) occurs in 110D. The best introduction to these three-tiered proportions in the Platonic dialogues is Hermann Frankel's (1938).

27 Perhaps the geometry of pentagons stitched together as in a soccer ball or, just possibly, the twelve sections of Martin Waldseemüller's "gores" of his world map of 1507.

28 This background of the dialogue is well brought out in the revealing study of Nightingale (1992).

29 Tityus in *Odyssey* 11.576–81; Tantalus in 11.582–92; and Sisyphus in 11.593–600. Plato parodies this scene in *Protagoras* 315B-C, as he has Socrates recognize the great sophists gathered in the light of early morning in the house of Callias.

30 Dante's citation of the myth of Glaucus (Ovid, *Metamorphoses* 13.904–68) comes in *Paradiso* 1 70–72. I argue that Plato refers to this Glaucus as his inspiration for Socrates' description of "the true earth" in the *Phaedo* (1985). Dante's reference to Plato's metaphors comes in his Letter to Can Grande, *Dantis Epistulae* X 21 Toynbee.

7: HELLENISTIC MYTHOGRAPHERS

Carolyn Higbie

From sometime in the fourth century BC on, Greeks developed an interest in collecting, documenting, and interpreting the important literary works of their past. The central texts to which they devoted much of their energies were the Homeric epics, the *Iliad* and *Odyssey*, but these were not the only ones. They also acquired the works of the lyric poets, tragedians, comedians, orators, historians, and philosophers. The centers for these projects became the great libraries of antiquity, most notably in Alexandria and Pergamum, but there were others, including some that focused on philosophical texts.[1] Scholars who worked in these libraries faced a monumental task of organizing the texts, before they could begin real study of them. As part of their initial work, they had to create a catalog of the collection, which may be the reason for one of two lists that Callimachus, an Alexandrian scholar and librarian of the third century BC, was said to have composed, in addition to his learned poetry: *Tables of Illustrious Persons in Every Branch of Learning Together with a List of their Works.*[2] This seems to have been some sort of catalog to the holdings of the Alexandria Library, though the fragments are so brief and so few that it is difficult to be certain.

Once these preliminaries were complete, though additions to the libraries, particularly that in Alexandria, continued for centuries, scholars could turn their attention to studying the works themselves. The texts reflected an often double transmission, since many had probably survived through both oral transmission and then as written documents that had been copied and recopied in different cities, by different scribes with varying abilities, and for many purposes. Generations of oral transmission of poems meant they had been reworked and adapted each time they were performed, depending on the abilities of the performer, the setting of the performance, and the response of the audience. Mistakes that inevitably accompany the copying and recopying of written texts, especially those that contain unusual dialect forms and archaisms or difficult metrical patterns, meant that the Alexandrian scholars would have been confronted by texts that not only were difficult to read but also were filled with a bewildering array of versions of the most popular authors and works. These might also contain versions of myths peculiar to a location, which might either contradict another or might simply be otherwise unknown. In the Homeric *Odyssey*, for example, a central theme is Penelope's twenty years of faithfulness to her husband and her clever trick with the burial shroud for Laertes, which enables her to put off the suitors. The second-century-AD traveler Pausanias, however, reports that the Mantineans in the Peloponnese preserve a very different account of life on Ithaca during Odysseus' absence: Penelope was unfaithful to Odysseus with many suitors. When Odysseus returned home and discovered this, he threw Penelope out of the house, and she returned to the home of her father in Sparta and then died in Mantinea (Paus. 8.12.6–7). Another tradition, also perhaps from Arcadia, said that Penelope had had an affair with either Hermes or Apollo or all the suitors and had given birth to Pan (Herodotus 2.145.4; Apollodorus, *Epitome* 2.7.38; Duris of Samos *Die Fragmente der griechischen Historiker* 76 F 21; Pindar fr. 100).

MYTHOGRAPHY AND PARADOXOGRAPHY

Some Hellenistic scholars devoted themselves to attempting to restore what they believed to be the original version of a work. Their focus on the text then led them to produce commentaries and essays. Others saw in texts mines of material to be extracted for any number of uses. From this double opportunity – the need for texts to be explicated and the wealth of material contained within them – developed at least two genres, mythography[3] and paradoxography, which flourished for some four centuries, from the mid-third century BC into the second century AD. Students of literature scanned texts and extracted from them material grouped around a theme or focus, such as stories of the weird or unusual (paradoxography) and stories about the gods and heroes (mythography).

In addition to his list of the library holdings, in fact, Callimachus was also credited with a second catalog, *A Collection of Wonders from the Entire Earth Arranged by Locality*.[4] This seems to be an early, if not the first, example of paradoxography. Unfortunately, Callimachus' work does not survive complete, but the third-century BC writer Antigonus of Carystus includes forty-four selections from Callimachus in his own *Historiae mirabiles* 129–73 (= fr. 407 Pfeiffer).

The fate of Callimachus' collection of oddities was not unique. Many other paradoxographies and mythographies survive only in fragments, as excerpts in the work of later authors. More than twenty Greek paradoxographers, of whom only seven survive, compiled collections of the bizarre from the time of Callimachus until the third century AD.[5] Of the many mythographies written during the same period, very few survive even in fragmentary or abridged form. We know the mythographical work *Diegesis* of Conon, for example, only from a summary made by Photius in the ninth century AD, supplemented by a few lines from a papyrus fragment (FGrH 26).[6] Such collections, in straightforward and generally plain prose, without any attempt to achieve literary effects and usually lacking documented sources, seem to have been regarded not so much as the work of a single author to be preserved in its original form but rather as material available to subsequent generations of readers for their own purposes. These later writers might be thought of more as compilers rather than authors, more interested in presenting the stories briefly and clearly than in achieving some sort of literary effect (there are no speeches, similes, or metaphors, for example) or elucidating the presentation of the myth in an earlier text of a poem or play. In compiling their own collections, they seem not to have returned to the early literary sources used by their predecessors in the field, but simply to have drawn on the collections of their predecessors. The original and complete versions of these texts thus disappeared, since the digests satisfied readers' needs. It is difficult, therefore, always to attribute to any one author a particular collection or to be confident about the purpose he had in collecting, especially if the author is early in the history of writing in these genres, unless there is a specific statement about sources, goals, and authorship.

A story from Phlegon of Tralles' *De mirabilium libellus* (*Book of Marvels*), compiled in the second century AD, illustrates the kind of lurid tales and the prosaic style typical of paradoxography, as well as its links with mythography (chapter):[7]

> In Messene not many years ago, as Apollonius says, it happened that a big jar [*pithos*] was broken up by the force of a storm when a lot of water came pouring down. From it there fell out a triple head of human form. It had two rows

of teeth. When they tried to find out whose head it was, an inscription revealed it: for "Idas" had been inscribed. The Messenians prepared another jar [*pithos*] at public expense and put the head in it. They attended to the hero more carefully, since they understood that this was the one about whom Homer says [*Il.* 9.558–60]:

> And of Idas, who of men on earth at that time
> Was the strongest. He drew his bow against lord
>   Phoebus
> Apollo for the sake of his lovely-ankled bride.

In this anecdote, there are many clichés or elements of folktale – the storm that reveals an ancient artifact, a monstrous relic, an inscription, the identification of a Homeric hero's remains, and the creation of a hero shrine. Whereas the Messenians draw on their own sense of the past, supported by their knowledge of the Homeric poems, to gain status in their world through mythology,[8] Phlegon of Tralles, loosely citing Apollonius, an earlier paradoxographer, as a source, tells the story as an example of the oddities in the world. Other tales in his collection concern the discovery of immense bones and coffins, the birth of deformed babies and animals to women, the birth of children to men, and the existence of living centaurs. He offers no comment on any aspect of the stories that are in his collection, nothing about their believability, the evidence for them, or any context into which they might fit.

When we read of Idas in the most famous book of mythography to survive from the ancient world, that identified as the work of Apollodorus, we first meet him in the narrative of important families in Calydon, preparatory to the story of the Calydonian boar hunt (1.7.8–9):

> Evenus fathered a daughter, Marpessa, whom Apollo sought, but Idas, the son of Aphareus, took her away in a winged chariot from Poseidon. When Evenus pursued him in a chariot, he came to the Lycormas river, but he could not overtake him, and so he killed his horses and threw himself into the river. And the river is called Evenus after him. Idas came to Messene and when Apollo came across him, he took away the girl. When they fought over marriage to the girl, Zeus separated them and allowed the girl to choose which one

she wished to live with. Since she was afraid that Apollo would abandon her when she grew old, she chose Idas as her husband.

In Apollodorus' narrative, the story of Idas is introduced by a long string of genealogical links (not translated here) and includes an etymologizing explanation for the name of a river before the tale of how Idas finally won his bride is told. Unlike Phlegon of Tralles, who seeks to highlight the grotesque element in stories, Apollodorus concentrates on genealogies, etymologies, and the deeds of heroes. The authors share a similar tone and style and compile their materials from already published works, but they have different interests.

THE ROOTS OF MYTHOGRAPHY AND PARADOXOGRAPHY: MYTHOLOGY AND CHRONOGRAPHY

Mythography and paradoxography both developed in the late fourth century BC, although the roots of each can be traced further back in Greek thought. The immediate impetus for the development of mythography lies in the awareness of their literary past and the desire to preserve it that Greeks felt by the end of the fourth century BC, but other genres, mythology and chronography, together with genealogy and local history, also lay behind mythography. In some respects, mythology itself can be seen as a counterpart to chronography in early Greece, especially in the hexameter catalogs that recorded the names, families, and deeds of the gods and heroes. Organized roughly by generations of families, such poems were a chronological guide of sorts to the Greek mythological past and enabled Greeks of historical times to link their families with gods and heroes. Catalog poetry also provided both material and a structuring principle to later prose works.[9] No version could be claimed as Panhellenic and definitive, but the poems did impose a structure on the stories. Two excerpts from the Hesiodic *Catalog of Women* illustrate the kind of information that such poems offered and how they might survive into later times (frr. 1, 53):

That Deucalion was the son of Prometheus and Pronoea Hesiod says in the first *Catalogue*, and also that Hellen was the son of Deucalion and Pyrrha.

About the Myrmidons Hesiod says thus:

> She became pregnant and bore Aeacus, delighting in
>   horses.
> But when he came to the boundary of lovely youth,
> he was distressed at being alone. The father of both
>   men and gods made whatever ants there were
>   on the beautiful island
> into men and deep-girdled women.
> These were the first to yoke rolling ships
> and the first to use sails, the wings of a sea-crossing
>   ship.

These two fragments from the catalog, the first a paraphrase and the second a direct quotation, survive only because they became part of the scholia – marginal notes – to other poems: the genealogy of Deucalion and his son Hellen appears in a scholion to Apollonius of Rhodes' *Argonautica* 3.1086 and the origins of the Myrmidons are in a scholion to Pindar's *Nemean* 3.21. Scholia such as these are an important source of obscure mythological stories for modern readers, since the texts from which they were taken do not often survive.

Myths certainly appeared in prose texts before the Hellenistic world, but they lack, so far as one can tell from the fragmentary remains, the flavor of a compilation, of time spent in libraries gathering stories from different sources. Instead they often are part of a work that covers a wider chronological range than the era of gods and heroes, and that is not simply a catalog of mythological stories.[10] Mythological figures play an often major role in narratives of early prose writers such as Hecataeus (FGrH 1), Acusilaus (FGrH 2), Pherecydes (FGrH 3), Hellanicus (FGrH 4 and 323a), and Herodotus. Later authors remark that Hellanicus and Acusilaus disagree about genealogies and that Acusilaus often corrects Hesiod, or they claim that Acusilaus merely reworked Hesiod in prose and then published the work as his (FGrH 2 T 5–6).

Mythological figures turn up in these early prose works often because of the importance that the past played for Greeks in debates over contemporary matters. The political allegiance of the island of Salamis, for example, depended in part on where Trojan War figures, such as Ajax, were said to have been born, lived, or died. In his history of the Persian Wars, Herodotus crosses the divide between mythological and human time:[11] he opens his account with a look at the kidnapping of women such as Io, Europa, and Helen and ends with the second invasion of Greece by Persians in 480–479 BC, perhaps about the time that he was born. Even as he spans these two kinds of time, he recognizes that they are in some way different, as he shows in his comment about "the human generation" in his discussion of Polycrates (3.122.2). Pherecydes was said in his ten books of *Histories* or *Genealogies* to have traced the family of Thucydides the historian back through Miltiades to Philaeus, son of Ajax, and thus to Zeus (FGrH 3 F 2).[12]

The second genre that influences mythography is chronography. By the end of the fifth century BC, some Greek thinkers developed a view of the past as a time different from their own, one that could be studied through documents. Hellanicus of Lesbos produced lists of priestesses at the Argive Heraion (FGrH 4 F74–84) and of victors at the musical competitions of the Carnea (F85–86), Hippias of Elis gathered names of Olympic victors in the *stadion* (FGrH 6 F 2), and someone compiled a list of the archons in Athens and inscribed it on stone at the end of the fifth century-BC.[13] Aristotle, an innovator in the study of literary texts, was also innovative in his use of inscriptions to answer historical questions: he seems to have read through inscriptions at Delphi in order to compile a list of victors at the Pythian games, for example, and he, together with his adherents, gathered information from inscriptions in his project on the constitutions of Greek city states. Craterus of Macedon, perhaps part of Aristotle's circle, even assembled and placed in chronological order public inscriptions from fifth-century-BC Athens, though no historian following him seems to have made much use of his sourcebook.[14]

THE *BIBLIOTHECA* OF APOLLODORUS

The most famous and influential, in modern times, of these mythological compendia is the *Bibliotheca* – "Library."[15] Although the *Bibliotheca* has been attributed to the famous second-century BC researcher Apollodorus of Athens, who did write on mythology, it is probably not his work, and no other author has been identified. Nevertheless, the author is still referred to as Apollodorus. Photius, who read and excerpted Conon's *Diegesis*, also knew of this work and said of it (*Bibliotheca* 186):[16]

> It encompassed the antiquities of the Greeks, whatsoever time had brought them to believe about both gods and heroes, as well as the naming of rivers and lands and peoples

and cities as to their origins, and whatever else runs back into the past. It comes down to the Trojan War and it runs through both the battles with one another of certain men and their deeds, and their wanderings from Troy, especially of Odysseus with whom the account of the far past [*archaeologia*] stops. Most of the book is a summary account and not unhelpful to those seeking to understand the distant past.

Photius neatly summarizes both the chronological range of Apollodorus' work and its subject matter. The *Bibliotheca*, having devoted perhaps one-half of its narrative to the Trojan War, ends with Odysseus, whose final journey and death are the last story in the work. It agrees with other texts in seeing a division at this point in the Greek past. Along the way, the *Bibliotheca* offers explanations, often based either on folk etymology or on an event in a hero's life, for names of rivers, towns, and regions.

Apollodorus organizes his text by family and generations, as he makes clear in the opening to book 2, for example, (2.1.1): "Since we have worked our way through the family of Deucalion, we next speak of that of Inachus." This chronographical element can be traced to works such as Hesiod's *Theogony* or *Catalog of Women*, the works of Hecataeus and Acusilaus of Argos entitled *Genealogies*, and the attempts to place a chronological structure on the past. One consequence of this approach is the appearance of many long lists of names in the text – names of daughters and sons, names of heroes on expeditions (in the Trojan horse, for example), names of rivers, and names of hunting dogs.

Unlike other mythographers, so far as we can tell, Apollodorus devotes a certain amount of space to citing sources. The references are brief and generally unspecific, as these sentences from his discussion of the family of Io reveal (2.1.3):

> Iasus was the son of Argos and Ismene, daughter of Asopus, and he [Iasus] was said to be the father of Io. But Castor, who wrote the *Chronologies*, and many of the tragedians say that Io was the daughter of Inachus. But Hesiod and Acusilaus say that she was the daughter of Peiren.... Pherecydes says [Argos] was the son of Arestor, but Asclepiades says of Inachus, and Cercops a son of Argos and Ismene, the daughter of Asopus. But Acusilaus says that he was born of the earth.

This section of the text may contain rather more references than is usual in the *Bibliotheca*, but is otherwise very typical of the work. Apollodorus cites a wide range of sources, including hexameter poets (Hesiod, Homer, Eumelus, Panyassis, and Apollonius of Rhodes), lyric poets (Pindar and Simonides), tragedians (Euripides), and prose authors, (Acusilaus of Argos and Pherecydes, in particular.) He also cites authors such as Asclepiades of the late fourth century BC who gathered mythological stories from the tragedians (FGrH12). Most often, such references are to provide additional or conflicting versions of a story, frequently, as here, about the identification of a figure's parents; Apollodorus does not argue for one version or another, but simply includes the different sources. His aim in citation may be completeness in source material, just as he is complete in his chronological range of stories.

The *Bibliotheca* is difficult to date, though many scholars place it roughly in the first century AD. The author gives no explanation for its composition in a preface or anywhere else; modern writers refer to it as a "handbook," which reflects modern attitudes toward it, but may not accurately convey its role when it was compiled. Finally, the work has not survived whole: we have a full text for most of the first three books that breaks off in the story of Theseus, but we have only epitomes – summaries – of the other seven books.[17] Nevertheless, because of its existence in a more complete form than any other mythography and because of the wide scope of the stories included, it is the best known and most used of such collections today.

OTHER MYTHOGRAPHIC WORKS

Unlike the all-inclusive Apollodorus, other mythographers gathered together stories focused on a theme. Eratosthenes retold myths about stars in a work known as *Catasterisms*. Eratosthenes' collection survives not in its original form, but only because it was helpful in understanding Aratus' astronomical poem, *Phaenomena*, and so it appears in the scholia to that work and in an epitome of star myths, as well as a couple of Latin texts. A manuscript, probably of the ninth century AD, preserves a wide range of texts, including the only surviving version of two mythographers: Parthenius of Nicaea of the first century BC, who collected myths of love, and Antoninus Liberalis, probably of the second century AD, who collected myths culminating in metamorphosis.

Parthenius

The Greek literary man Parthenius of Nicaea, who was brought to Rome after being taken captive during the Third Mithridatic War, composed a mythographic work known as the *Erotica Pathemata*. It is important not only as an example of mythography but of Greek prose from the middle of the first century BC.[18] As Parthenius says in his dedicatory epistle to Cornelius Gallus, the *Erotica Pathemata* were thirty-six tales of love taken from Greek works, perhaps to be used by the Roman as a source for his poetry:

> Because, Cornelius Gallus, I thought that the collection of sufferings in love suited you very much, I have selected them and sent them to you in as abbreviated form as possible. For those among the present collection that occur in certain poets where they are not narrated in their own right, you will find out for the most part from what follows.[19] The ones which are most agreeable can be put by you into hexameters and elegiacs. Do not look down on them because there is not present that elegance which you seek. For I have collected them in the style of a little notebook, and they will serve you in a similar manner, perhaps.

Parthenius emphasizes the fact that he has collected these tales from different authors and that he presents them to Gallus as source material, which the latter might versify.[20] The prose, Parthenius asserts, is straightforward and lacks any elegance or style, but this is of no consequence, since he expects that the stories will be reworked. The stories themselves often involve incest, homosexuality, and disasters associated with ill-fated love. Some are not set in the mythological world, but in the generations some time after, but those that take place in historical times seem as distant as those from the mythological era.

Parthenius' proposal to Gallus reflects two different, but parallel traditions. In first-century-BC Rome, prominent Romans might present a client, especially one with a reputation for literary or historical work, with notes for him to work up into a text that would enhance their joint reputations. Among others, Cicero sent notes on his year as consul to the historian Lucceius, in hopes of seeing them transformed into a history glorifying his deeds of 63 BC (Cicero, *Ad familiares* 5.12.10). The second tradition goes back to the work done in the Library at Alexandria and perhaps even to Peripatetic monographs, in which notes were abstracted either from lectures or books and then organized by topic. Such notes could then be put to use in any of several different genres, including mythography, paradoxography, ethnography, and even poetry. We might speculate both about the sources of Callimachus' poetry, for example, and the purposes to which he intended to put his *Collection of Wonders*.[21]

One, rather brief, tale from the *Erotica Pathemata* may serve as an example of the collection. Parthenius reports what happens to Odysseus after he returns to Ithaca and kills the suitors (III):[22]

> Odysseus did wrong not only to Aeolus [see tale II], but even after his wanderings, when he killed the suitors, he came to Epirus because of some oracles. There he seduced the daughter of Tyrimmas, Evippe; he had been very hospitable to him and had been his host with every kindness. The child born to Odysseus from this girl was Euryalus. His mother, when he came of age, sent him to Ithaca, having given him some tokens hidden in a wax tablet. As it happened, Odysseus was not there then and Penelope discovered all these things, since she had already known of Odysseus' love affair with Evippe. She persuaded Odysseus, when he came back, before he knew anything of these goings on, to kill Euryalus because he was plotting against him. And Odysseus, because he lacked strength of character and he was not otherwise reasonable, killed his son himself. And not much time after he did this, wounded by the prickle of a stingray, he died at the hands of his own offspring.

Like Phlegon of Tralles' story of Idas, Parthenius' tale is full of folktale motifs. The tokens in a wax tablet remind us of the sandals and sword that served as tokens to identify the young Theseus, while Penelope's actions recall those of Medea, who attempted to kill her stepson Theseus when he turned up in Athens, or Phaedra, whose false accusations against her stepson Hippolytus caused Theseus to bring about his death. Parthenius draws no moral, but presumably any poet who used this narrative could.

The sources for Parthenius' stories are not often identified by the author. Only in three instances does he briefly name them: in his story of Byblis, Parthenius states, "Nicaenetus says ... " (XI); in that of Antheus, he prefaces some verses that he quotes with the name of Alexander the Aetolian (XIV); similarly, in the story of Corythus, he prefaces a quotation of verses with the name of Nicander (XXXIV).

An oddity of the single manuscript that preserves the *Erotica Pathemata* is the presence of marginal notes, in the same hand as that of the main text, that name authors and works that also tell the story.[23] Thus, for the tale of Odysseus quoted above, the marginal note remarks, "Sophocles tells the story [*historeî*] in his *Euryalus*." Where these attributions can be checked, they seem to be accurate, but this does not necessarily mean that Parthenius drew either on that text or a summary of it; an earlier author can tell the same story as a later one without being the source for it. Notably, the three names mentioned by Parthenius in XI, XIV, and XXXIV do not appear in the marginal notes for those stories.

Antoninus Liberalis

Antoninus Liberalis' collection of forty-one stories all culminate in metamorphosis, which is visited by the gods on a human either as a punishment for outrageous behavior or as a release from some sort of disaster. Some of his tales explain the establishment of a cult, and his language can be repetitive. Typical is this story about the war between the pygmies and cranes with its concluding remark that provides the link to a story familiar to his readers (XVI):[24]

> Among the people known as pygmies there was a girl named Oenoe, who was not without beauty, but who was unpleasant in character and arrogant. She had no thought for either Artemis or Hera. After she was married to Nicodamas, a reasonable and upright citizen, she gave birth to a son, Mopsus. And to her all the pygmies because of their good nature took very many presents for the birth of her son. But Hera, who was angered at Oenoe, because she did not honor her, made her into a crane, lengthened her neck, and created a lofty-flying bird. And she brought on a war between Oenoe and the pygmies. Oenoe, on account of her love for her son Mopsus, kept on flying around their houses and did not cease. The pygmies armed themselves and pursued her. And from then until now there has been war between the pygmies and the cranes.

Antoninus Liberalis seems to have drawn on two sources almost exclusively. From Boios' *Ornithogonia* (FGrH 328 F 214), he took tales involving birds, and from Nicander's *Metamorphoses* came stories not only about birds, but also animals, trees, and stones.[25] Like Parthenius, Antoninus Liberalis' sources – or authors who told the same tales – were also identified in marginal notes.

Conon

About other collections it is impossible to say what their purpose or focus was. Conon's *Diegesis* is a good example of such a miscellany.[26] Alive during the reign of Augustus, Conon assembled some fifty stories that lack any thematic link or any other discernable organizational principle, at least as far as can be determined from the later summary of it by Photius. The dedication of the work to King Archilaus of Cappadocia offers no hint of its structure or purpose (FGrH 26 T1). There are myths that explain the foundation of cities and establishment of cults, stories of love, and stories that explain proverbs or place names, and even three examples of paradoxography.[27] Perhaps of most interest are the three stories preserved in no other source: the foundation of Olynthus, the establishment at Ephesus of the cult of Apollo Gypaieus, and how the oracle of Apollo at Didyma was transferred from Branchus to the Evangelidae. Conon gives the myth behind Olynthus (FGrH 26 F 1 [IV]):

> The fourth book of the *Diegesis* reports on the affairs concerning the city of Olynthus and Strymon, king of the Thracians, from whom the ancient Eioneus River took its name. And that there were three sons of his, Brangas and Rhesus and Olynthus. And Rhesus, who fought at Troy for Priam was killed at the hands of Diomedes. Olynthus, who fought with a lion unintentionally, died on a hunt. And Brangas, his brother, after he lamented greatly his misfortune, buried Olynthus on the spot where he died. When he came into Sithonia, he founded a prosperous and great city, which he called Olynthus after the boy.

The details of the story are not unique and could be paralleled from many other such tales, but no other source gives this foundation myth for Olynthus. Unfortunately for modern scholars interested in such matters, Conon seems not to have identified his sources. Completely absent from Conon's text is any story in which a god is a major character.

HOMERIC MYTH AND SCHOLARSHIP

The Homeric poems received the greatest attention from scholars over the centuries, attention that was directed both to explicating the language and meter of the epics and to elucidating some of the more obscure figures. It is difficult to say in exactly what form these studies were originally published, whether texts of the poems were accompanied by commentaries or whether texts were prepared separately from commentaries and essays on various subjects. Nothing has come down to us in its original form, and we are often dependent either on compilations and abridgements of works or on hostile remarks about someone's scholarship as we try to reconstruct this scholarship. Nor is it always certain for whom these treatises were written: although some texts were clearly directed to other scholars and some to students just learning to read the poems,[28] many surviving fragments of Homeric scholarship are not obviously designed for a particular audience. Part of the problem may be yet again the endless working and reworking of previous material, recasting, for example, comments that were originally designed for scholars so that they might be useful to students. Nonetheless, mythographers clearly found much to interest them in the Homeric poems; their work is preserved for us today in the scholia, particularly the so-called D scholia, the scholia minora, and in independent texts such as the Mythographus Homericus.[29]

The Mythographus Homericus is an example of Hellenistic scholarship on the mythological stories in the Homeric epics. Although it existed for the first five centuries of our era as a text in its own right, it has not been published as such in our time.[30] Study of it is complicated by the wide variety of forms in which fragments have survived: the manuscript tradition must be supplemented with fragments in papyri and on ostraca. But the basic structure and purpose of the collection are clear: to elucidate the Homeric epics by giving brief versions of myths wherever relevant. The stories are introduced by a word or phrase from the poem, followed by the comment or mythological tale, and the entry concludes most often with a subscription in which an authority is cited. Within the *Iliadic* D scholia, in which the Mythographus Homericus has become embedded, there are approximately 200 of these *historiae*, as they are known; there are many fewer for the *Odyssey*.

Preserved in the D scholia and probably from the Mythographus Homericus is, for example, a different version of the story told in the *Iliad* about the rebellion of the gods against Zeus.[31] In the *Iliad*, Hera, Poseidon, and Athena are identified as the gods who sought to overthrow Zeus (1.399–400). In a long narrative of this rebellion, a D scholion names the ringleaders: "Poseidon and Hera and Apollo and Athena plotted to bind him and then subdue him." The scholion describes punishment taken by Zeus against only three of the gods; Athena seems to escape their fate. At the end of the entry comes this statement about the source of the story: "Didymus tells the story [*historeî*]." This scholion does not discuss the significance of the participation of the various gods, as other scholia on the lines do, and seems to conflate versions without regard for the differences. But it does cite a learned source for the variant, the Homeric commentator Didymus of the first century BC, and it uses the verb *historeî*, which we have already seen in the marginal notes to the mythographies of Parthenius and Antoninus Liberalis.

Modern scholars have identified a number of writers of the Hellenistic era as mythographers, writers who collected stories of gods and heroes from a variety of sources and presented them in unadorned prose narratives. Almost none of these mythographers survives intact; for most, we have either fragments cited in later authors, often in scholia, or only a name with or without a book title. This means that we must depend on reconstruction and analogy in our studies of these authors, but they form an interesting and neglected part of the Hellenistic literary culture.

Mythographies seem to have been compiled for a wide range of purposes. They could serve a scholarly function, providing readers of archaic and classical poetry with explanations of myths and rituals, and offering explanations for place names. In this regard, they were the scholarly counterpart of essays on grammar and language in the early poets. Some of the material from these mythographies seems to have been abstracted and reworked for students just beginning to read poets like Homer. Such students needed more basic help than scholars, so were given stories of the gods as well as explanations of verb forms and glossaries for obscure and difficult words. Mythographies might also have provided reading material which was interesting, but not taxing to the reader. In this guise, it could be seen as a parallel to paradoxography, in which oddities from the natural world were compiled for reading pleasure.

The rich and complex Hellenistic world fostered the rise of literary scholarship and the development of new genres. Readers became aware of new texts and authors, as well as different versions of works already well known. They drew from these texts, once they were accessible, material that could be organized and juxtaposed in new ways. Thus, compilers of paradoxographies showed their readers bizarre phenomena and compilers of mythographies enabled readers either to explore the whole of the mythological past or to read stories focused on a theme.

Modern readers of mythographies are able to discover the variety and obscurity of Greek myth. These collections can illuminate otherwise mysterious references in poets and preserve local traditions which might vary greatly from a Panhellenic version. These texts enable us to have a greater understanding of the Hellenistic literary world, which we can get in no other way.

FURTHER READING

To learn more about Hellenistic mythography, the best place to begin is Albert Henrichs, "Three Approaches to Greek Mythography," in Jan Bremmer, ed., *Interpretations of Greek Mythology* (London: Croom Helm, 1987) 242–77. For accessible translations of some of the most important texts, see Michael Simpson, trans., *Gods and Heroes of the Greeks: The Library of Apollodorus* (Amherst, MA: University of Massachusetts Press, 1976); William Hansen, ed. and trans., *Anthology of Ancient Greek Popular Literature* (Bloomington, IN: Indiana University Press, 1998); William Hansen, *Phlegon of Tralles' Book of Marvels* (Exeter: University of Exeter Press, 1996).

NOTES

1   See, for example, Strabo 13.1.54 (= C608), Plutarch, *Life of Sulla* 26.1–2, and Athenaeus 5.214d–e for different versions of the fate of Aristotle's books.

2   This title is not that given to the work by Callimachus, but a descriptive title given to it by a later author. We do not know what Callimachus called his catalog, which also had the much shorter title *Pinakes*. On Callimachus as a bibliographer, see Rudolf Blum, trans. by Hans H. Wellisch, *Kallimachos: The Alexandrian Library and the Origins of Bibliography* (Madison, WI: University of Wisconsin Press, 1991) 124–60, esp. 150–60.

3   See Albert Henrichs, "Three Approaches to Greek Mythography," in Jan Bremmer, ed., *Interpretations of Greek Mythology* (London: Croom Helm, 1987): 242–77, for an invaluable introduction to the topic. His definition of mythography is worth quoting (243): "Once a myth became fixed in the literary tradition, it would either survive indefinitely along with the poem, play or other work of literature in which it was recorded, or it would eventually perish together with that record, unless some interested scholar saved it for posterity by including it in a collection of various myths. Such collectors of myths, who wrote down the mythical

stories in plain prose, are called mythographers, and their collective product is mythography, a handmaiden of mythology."

4   See Blum, *Kallimachos*, 134.

5   See Alexander Giannini, *Paradoxographorum Graecorum Reliquiae* (Milan: Instituto Editoriale Italiano, 1965).

6   Henrichs, "Three Approaches to Greek Mythography," 244–7, has a very useful introduction to Conon.

7   See William Hansen, ed., *Anthology of Ancient Greek Popular Literature* (Blooming-ton, IN: Indiana University Press, 1998): 249–58. For a complete translation of Phlegon of Tralles' work, see William Hansen, *Phlegon of Tralles' Book of Marvels* (Exeter: University of Exeter Press, 1996).

8   See Carolyn Higbie, *The Lindian Chronicle and the Greek Creation of Their Past* (Oxford: Oxford University Press, 2003); also "Ancient Greek Archaeology?", forthcoming in the Acta of the 16th International Congress of Classical Archae-ology.

9   See M. L. West, *The Hesiodic Catalogue of Women: Its Nature, Structure, and Origins* (Oxford: Oxford University Press, 1985); Henrichs, "Three Approaches to Greek Mythography," 248–9.

10 As Robert L. Fowler states, "'mythography' is not a fifth-century genre" (*Early Greek Mythography*, vol. 1 [Oxford: Oxford University Press, 2000]: xxvii). Fowler includes 29 authors in his edition of Greek mythographers up to the early fourth century BC; see his discussion of his choices in the Introduction to his text, xxvii–xxxviii. He excludes any text that records events after the Ionian migration and the return of the Heraclidae (xxx).

11 See Fowler, *Early Greek Mythography*, xxx–xxxi.

12 See Carolyn Higbie, "The Bones of a Hero, the Ashes of a Politician: Athens, Salamis, and the Usable Past," *Classical Antiquity* 16 (1997): 279–308; Rosalind Thomas, *Oral Tradition and Written Record in Classical Athens* (Cambridge, UK: Cambridge University Press, 1989): 161–95.

13 Russell Meiggs and David Lewis, eds., *A Selection of Greek Historical Inscriptions to the End of the Fifth Century BC* (Oxford: Oxford University Press, 1969): no. 6. For a translation, see Charles W. Fornara, ed. and trans., *Archaic Times to the End of the Peloponnesian War* (Cambridge, UK: Cambridge University Press, 1977): no. 23.

14 See Carolyn Higbie, "Craterus and the Use of Inscriptions in Ancient Scholarship," *TAPA* 129 (1999): 43–83.

15 See Aubrey Diller, "The Text History of the Bibliotheca of Pseudo-Apollodorus," *TAPA* 66 (1935): 296–313; M. H. A. L. H. Van der Valk, "On Apollodori Bib-liotheca," *REG* 71 (1958): 100–168; Marc Huys, "125 Years of Scholarship on Apollodoros the Mythographer: a Bibliographical Survey," *L'Antiquité Classique* 66 (1997): 319–51.

16 See René Henry, *Photius, Bibliothèque*, 3 vols. (Paris: Budé, 1962).

17 Epitomes became an important part of literary life from the time of the Hellenistic world. There were even epitomes of epitomes, as in the case of the *Historia animal-ium*, epitomized by Aristophanes of Byzantium, which in its turn was epitomized by Sopater.

18 See J. L. Lightfoot, *Parthenius of Nicaea* (Oxford: Oxford University Press, 1999).

19 I have taken the translation of this difficult and corrupt sentence from Lightfoot, *Parthenius*; see her discussion in the commentary ad loc.

20   See Lightfoot, *Parthenius*, 74, 217–24, on the significance of this dedication and epistolary preface.

21   See Lightfoot, *Parthenius*, 217–20.

22   See Lightfoot's discussion of this story in her commentary ad loc.

23   These notes also survive for the mythography of Antoninus Liberalis. See Lightfoot, *Parthenius*, 246–56 and 303–5.

24   See Manolis Papathomopoulos, *Antoninus Liberalis, Les Métamorphoses* (Paris: Budé, 1968).

25   On Nicander, see A. S. F. Gow and A. F. Scholfield, *Nicander: The Poems and Poetical Fragments* (Cambridge, UK: Cambridge University Press, 1953): 205–8. On Boios, Nicander, and Antoninus Liberalis, see P. M. C. Forbes Irving, *Metamorphosis in Greek Myths* (Oxford: Oxford University Press, 1990): 20–36.

26   See Henrichs, "Three Approaches to Greek Mythography," 244–7.

27   See Henrichs, "Three Approaches to Greek Mythography," 268–9.

28   On the sort of help that a student beginning to read Homer was given in the Hellenistic and Roman worlds, see Teresa Morgan, *Literate Education in the Hellenistic and Roman Worlds* (Cambridge, UK: Cambridge University Press, 1998): 166; also Raffaella Cribiore, *Gymnastics of the Mind: Greek Education in Hellenistic and Roman Egypt* (Princeton: Princeton University Press, 2001): 140–42, 204–5.

29   See Cribiore, *Gymnastics of the Mind*, 207–8, for a brief introduction. More information is to be found in Franco Montanari, "The Mythographus Homericus," in eds. J. G. J. Abbenes, S. R. Slings, and I. Sluiter, *Greek Literary Theory after Aristotle* (Amsterdam: VU University Press, 1995): 135–72.

30   See Henrichs, "Three Approaches to Greek Mythography," 243 and fn. 5.

31   See Montanari, "The Mythographus Homericus," 158–61.

PART TWO

RESPONSE, INTEGRATION, REPRESENTATION

'Alas! My son,' quoth King Ægeus, heaving a long sigh, 'here is a very lamentable matter in hand! This is the woefullest anniversary in the whole year. It is the day when we annually draw lots to see which of the youths and maidens of Athens shall go to be devoured by the horrible Minotaur!'

'The Minotaur!' exclaimed Prince Theseus; and like a brave young prince as he was, he put his hand to the hilt of his sword. 'What kind of a monster may that be? Is it not possible, at the risk of one's life, to slay him?'

But King Ægeus shook his venerable head, and to convince Theseus that it was quite a hopeless case, he gave him an explanation of the whole affair. . . .

But when Theseus heard the story, he straightened himself up, so that he seemed taller than ever before; and as for his face, it was indignant, despiteful, bold, tender, and compassionate, all in one look.

'Let the people of Athens, this year, draw lots for only six young men, instead of seven,' said he. 'I will myself be the seventh; and let the Minotaur devour me, if he can!' . . .

Just as Prince Theseus was going on board, his father bethought himself of one last word to say.

'My beloved son,' said he, grasping the prince's hand, 'you observe that the sails of this vessel are black; as indeed they ought to be, since it goes upon a voyage of sorrow and despair. Now, being weighed down with infirmities, I know not whether I can survive till the vessel shall return. But, as long as I do live, I shall creep daily to the top of yonder cliff, to watch if there be a sail upon the sea. And, dearest Theseus, if by some happy chance you should escape the jaws of the Minotaur, then tear down those dismal sails, and hoist others that shall be bright as the sunshine. Beholding them on the horizon, myself and all the people will know that you are coming back victorious, and will welcome you with such a festal uproar as Athens never heard before.'

Theseus promised he would do so. Then, going on board, the mariners trimmed the vessel's black sails to the wind, which blew faintly off the shore, being pretty much made up of the sighs that everybody kept pouring forth on this melancholy occasion. . . .

No sooner had they entered the harbour than a party of the guards of King Minos came down to the waterside, and took charge of the fourteen young men and damsels. Surrounded by these armed warriors, Prince Theseus and his companions were led to the king's palace, and ushered into his presence. . . .

'Young man,' asked he, with his stern voice, 'are you not appalled at the certainty of being devoured by this terrible Minotaur?'

'I have offered my life in a good cause,' answered Theseus, 'and therefore I give it freely and gladly. . . . Sitting there on thy golden throne, and in thy robes of majesty, I tell thee to thy face, King Minos, thou art a more hideous monster than the Minotaur himself!'

'Aha! Do you think me so?' cried the king, laughing in his cruel way. 'Tomorrow, at breakfast-time, you shall have an opportunity of judging which is the greater monster, the Minotaur or the king! Take them away, guards; and let this free-spoken youth be the Minotaur's first morsel! . . .

Without more words on either side, there ensued the most awful fight between Theseus and the Minotaur that ever happened beneath the sun or moon. . . . At last, the Minotaur made a run at Theseus, grazed his left side with his horn, and flung him down; and, thinking that he had stabbed him to the heart, he cut a great caper in the air, opened his bull mouth from ear to ear, and prepared to snap his head off. But Theseus by this time had leaped up, and caught the monster off his guard. Fetching a sword-stroke at him with all his force, he hit him fair upon the neck, and made his bull head skip six yards from his human body, which fell down flat upon the ground. . . .

On the homeward voyage the fourteen youths and damsels were in excellent spirits, as you will easily suppose. They spent most of their time in dancing, unless the sidelong breeze made the deck slope too much. In due season they came within sight of the coast of Attica, which was their native country. But here, I am grieved to tell you, happened a sad misfortune.

You will remember (what Theseus unfortunately forgot) that his father, King Ægeus, had enjoined it upon him to hoist sunshiny sails, instead of black ones, in case he should overcome the Minotaur, and return victorious. In the joy of their success, however, and amidst the sports, dancing, and other merriment, with which these young folks wore away the time, they never once thought whether their sails were black, white, or rainbow-coloured, and indeed, left it entirely to the mariners whether they had any sails at all. Thus the vessel returned, like a raven, with the same sable wings that had wafted her away. But poor King Ægeus, day after day, infirm as he was, had climbed to the summit of a cliff that overhung the sea, and there sat watching for Prince Theseus, homeward bound; and no sooner did he behold the fatal blackness of the sails, than he concluded that his dear son, whom he loved so much and felt so proud of, had been eaten by the Minotaur. He could not bear the thought of living any longer; so, first flinging his crown and sceptre into the sea (useless baubles that they were to him now!), King Ægeus merely stooped forward, and fell headlong over the cliff, and was drowned, poor soul, in the waves that foamed at its base.

Nathaniel Hawthorne; from "The Minotaur," *Tanglewood Tales* (1853)

---

[7]Theseus was included in the third tribute sent to the Minotaur, or, as some say, he offered himself as a volunteer. Since the ship had a black sail, Aegeus commanded his son, if he should return alive, to rig the ship with white sails.

[8]When Theseus arrived in Crete, Ariadne, the daughter of Minos, being romantically inclined toward him, promised to help him if he would agree to take her away to Athens and then make her his wife. With Theseus affirming upon an oath that he would do that, Ariadne begged Daedalus to disclose the way out of the Labyrinth.

[9]Following his advice, she gave Theseus some thread as he entered the maze; this he attached to the door and then went in, trailing the thread behind him. Coming upon the Minotaur in the last part of the Labyrinth, Theseus killed him, pounding him with his fists, and then made his way out, drawing up the thread again. During the night he arrived at Naxos with Ariadne and the Athenian youths. There Dionysus

fell in love with Ariadne and took her away; carrying her to Lemnos, he had intercourse with her and fathered Thoas, Staphylus, Oenopion, and Peparethus.

[10]Grieving over Ariadne, Theseus forgot to rig the ship with white sails as he made for the harbor. From the Acropolis, Aegeus saw that the ship carried a black sail and imagining that Theseus had been killed, he threw himself off and so passed from this life.

[11]Theseus succeeded to the kingship of Athens and killed the sons of Pallas – numbering fifty. In the same way, any who wanted to rebel were killed by him, and he alone held all power.

Apollodorus, *Bibliotheca* Epit. 1.7–11

8: GREEK MYTH AND GREEK RELIGION

Claude Calame

N either "myth" nor "religion" constitutes a category native to Greek thought. Neither myth nor religion were conceived of as such by the Greeks – neither myth as a corpus of (fabulous) tales of gods and heroes dependent on a frame of comprehensive thought, nor religion as a set of beliefs and practices relative to a divine configuration (not even in the Roman sense of regulated cult observance).[1] But, in the case of the former, we have a series of narratives with argumentative and pragmatic value that describe, in poetic form, the heroic past of Greek cities or of the "Greek" community (experienced as *tò Hellēnikón* only from Herodotus on), narratives that, recited or sung as *palaiá* or *arkhaîa*, make reference to the ancient history of Greece and correspond to *mûthoi*. In the case of the latter, we can think in terms of divine and heroic figures, in terms of civic spaces reserved for them, and in terms of the numerous ritual practices that sought, through offerings of various types, to influence divine intervention in the present: *tà hierá* ('offerings, victims'), *tà nómima* ('what is prescribed'; hence 'customs, rites') to cite only terms related to sacrificial offerings and to the implicit rules animating cult practices, and to underscore that these practices are always integrated into the calendar that gives rhythm to the religious and political life of each city, in conjunction with the particular assemblage of gods and heroes who are honored there.[2]

No mythology, then – neither as an established narrative consciousness, nor as a framework of thought, unless considered in the form of manuals of mythography, such as the one in the *Library* attributed to Apollodorus. Such a collection of heroic intrigues, organized according to their protagonists' genealogical relationships, a systematic catalog of proper names evoking a bygone epic past, was evidently destined for a reading public of erudite poets or inquisitive minds in large Greek cities where political institutions and civic relationships had weakened and the heroic past of classical Greece provided reference points in a quest for renewed identity.[3] In particular, as *mûthoi*, the narrative actions of Greek gods and heroes are not simply demonstrated and modeled by different poetic and historiographic forms, but they exist in these forms alone; such concrete manifestations, by virtue of their pragmatic dimension, guarantee that these narrative actions retain the flexibility to fulfill their social, religious, and ideological function and efficacy.

Whether it be the *Homeric Hymns*, preludes addressed to a god in order to introduce the rhapsodic recitation of Homeric poems into his cult, or Sappho's *Epithalamia*, designed to punctuate the different ritual moments of the marriage ceremony by commemorating the misfortunes of the hero Hymenaeus, or Bacchylides' profoundly narrative, if not outright dramatic, *Dithyrambs* for singing an episode of the heroic biography of hero-founders in local cult, or the often anonymous cult hymns that, as at Delphi or Epidaurus, formed an integral part of the celebration of a titular god by singing his divine biography, or Pindar's *Epinicia*, which insert into the observance of a local cult the choral celebration of a victory at the Panhellenic games by allusions to the great deeds of the heroes of epic cycles, not to mention the hymnic prayers or paeans composed by many melic poets – there exists no story of gods or heroes that does not come to the public in a ritualized discursive form. Full of self-referential gestures by which the poet or the choral group allude to the singing activity in which they are engaged – *hic et nunc* ('here and now') – the poems belonging in particular to the major genre of *mélos* present themselves as cult acts, inscribed in religious practices celebrating the gods and heroes of the city. By the intermediary of hymnic proems that present epic recitation as an offering to a divinity in a particular cult, this is also the case of rhapsodic recitation of Homeric poems – the *Iliad* or the *Odyssey*. And the great heroic plots that are dramatized on the Attic stage in the classical tragedies do not escape this aspect of the religious act, since the performances of tragedies, as well as the civic performance of dithyrambs, are presented as offerings: in the shadow of the Acropolis, at the sanctuary of Dionysus Eleuthereus, they were mimed, sung, and danced on the occasion of one of the greatest celebrations of the festal Athenian calendar.[4] The works of the logographers and historiographers contemporary with the great tragedies of classical Athens, even if they abandoned the rhythmic and ritualized forms of poetry, remain inscribed in constant efforts to reformulate a heroic past and adapt it to the exigencies of a social and political present strongly marked by the influence of the gods and by ritual and discursive acts used to communicate with them.[5]

Notably, under the influence of the cult celebrations imparting rhythm to the annual calendar, the social life of the various groups forming the civic community carries, in its relationships with its heroic past, the imprint of practices that seem, at least to us, to be "religious" in nature and of discursive forms to which correspond certain ritual acts. In effect, the retelling of episodes of the great epic cycles, as well as the self-referential means and performative indices of such poetic forms, are inscribed in the rules of the genre. Divided between verbal regularities, such as the forms for invoking a divinity, and ritual rules related to the musical "performance" of a poem, these rules assure the pragmatic link that transforms the narrative song of the "myth" into a ritual act inserted into a particular cult. Thus it is impossible to distinguish, as scholars often do in the wake of the idealistic "evolutionism" of Ernst Cassirer, between myth and language:[6] what our modern anthropological frame of mind has identified as myth exists only in the forms of discourse that connect pragmatic function and religious practice.

In a manner undoubtedly paradoxical, this holds true particularly for Attic tragedy, a seemingly inexhaustible source of the stories that we have amassed as Greek "mythology." Even if it is performed ritually within the frame of the aforementioned great cult and music festival dedicated to Dionysus (or probably because it is dedicated to this god), tragedy frequently offers in the mimetic representation of a heroic action a *mise en question* of epic values, if not of the powers of the gods themselves, by a dramatic mirroring of the social rules and political institutions of the present. The religious dimension of classical tragedy not only appears in the rituality proper of the musical competition of the Great Dionysia and in the ritual forms, both in the orchestra and on the stage, which, in turn, become integrated into the heroic action, but also manifests itself in the frequently aetiological conclusions of the individual plays.

Such is the case of Euripides' *Hippolytus*, performed during the initial years of the Peloponnesian War. This tragedy is only the reworking of an earlier drama dedicated to the same plot – one that Aristophanes seems to have criticized for its having shown Phaedra in an unflattering

light. Notwithstanding the literary conceit of using a written message
to attenuate Phaedra's accusation of Hippolytus and salvage her honor,
the deleterious love that Aphrodite inspired in the heart of a mature
wife for her stepson opens the way for Artemis to offer redress for the
misfortunes that the young man had endured. His disappearance would
soon come to constitute the occasion of the highest cult honors in the
city of Troezen, and in a heroizing process common in classical Greece,
each year young girls entering into marriage would commemorate, with
songs and offerings, the drama of his death due to a love offered too
exclusively to Artemis, the virgin.[7] Pausanias, in fact, tells us that the
city of Troezen celebrated the memory of Hippolytus with various rituals, performed in the sanctuary and before the temple, consecrated to
the deified young hero. Thus the epic intrigue staged by Euripides gave
birth to a cult, instituted by Artemis herself, that corresponds to a ritual
practice contemporary with the staging of the drama. This strong relationship between religious observance and the dramatic performance
of a heroic story is especially marked at the beginning of the tragedy
when Hippolytus assumes the role of *khorēgós* ('leader of the chorus')
among his companions, and the group performs a processional song and
ritual to accompany the offering of a garland of pure flowers to Artemis.
Moreover, near the end of its participation in the ceremony, the chorus
of the women of Troezen evokes the ritual functions assumed by the
young man in his ambiguous devotion to the virgin goddess.[8] The process of explication and aetiological legitimization occurs through poetic
expression; this poetic expression follows the rules of genre, respecting
the conventions of a performative melic form and of a dramatization that
itself is a ritual. Indeed, it is the pragmatic dimension of the tragic form
that allows a traditional story – one that sets on stage the heroes Hippolytus, Phaedra, and Theseus in the clutches of Artemis, Aphrodite,
and Poseidon – to become the foundation-legend of a religious practice
alive both in Troezen, the place of the unfolding heroic drama, and in
Athens, the city where spectators celebrate Dionysus Eleuthereus at his
theater-sanctuary.

This is the relationship between "Greek myth" and "Greek religion" that I would like to explore here through a series of five cases.
In each case, we can see how an individual heroic tale is called upon
to legitimate a particular cult practice through an intermediary poetic
form that influences both the narrative and semantic characteristics of
the account and the religious and political conception underlying the
ritual concerned.[9]

THE HYMN OF THE ABDUCTION OF
PERSEPHONE AND THE FOUNDING OF A CULT:
THE MYSTERIES OF ELEUSIS

Seduced by the mysterious charm of the narcissus while gathering flowers in a green pasture with her companions, Persephone, daughter of Zeus and Demeter, is kidnapped by Aidoneus (the god Hades), lord of the Underworld, and dragged into the gloom of Hades (the place). Heartbroken, Demeter sets out at once to search for her daughter and is finally informed by Hecate and then by the Sun of the fate reserved for the young virgin – by the will of Zeus. As she leaves Olympus in a fit of anger and grief, taking the form of an old woman, the goddess encounters at Eleusis the daughters of Celeus, king of that place. Manifest through a quasi-epiphany, she becomes the nurse of the family's youngest son, Demophon, whom she secretly attempts to render immortal by anointing him with ambrosia and hiding him within fire. Surprised by Metaneira, the child's mother, Demeter is forced to reveal her divine nature and insists that a sanctuary be built in her honor. Celeus and his people set out to construct a temple, where the goddess of agriculture will shut herself in, leaving the fields infertile and men devoid of the fruits of the earth. Fearful of being deprived of the honors owed to him by mortals, Zeus intervenes, ordering Hermes to bring Persephone back from the land of the dead. Hades consents only after having made the young woman ingest the pomegranate seed of memory. From that time on, Persephone will spend two-thirds of the year on Olympus in the company of her mother and return for the remaining one-third to Hades. When Zeus thus acquiesced to Demeter, the earth flowered again at last and produced the most beautiful grains:

> Straightaway, Demeter made the tilled and fecund earth bear
>   fruit;
> The entirety of the vast earth became heavy with plants and
>   flowers.
> She went to teach – to the kings who administer justice,
> To Triptolemus and to Diocles, the able horseman,
> To the powerful Eumolpus and to Celeus the leader of the
>   people –
> The celebration of the sacred rites;
> She revealed to them the beautiful mysteries . . . ,
> The august acts that it is impossible to transgress, to uncover,

To divulge. Because great is the respect that the gods inspire,
   rendering us mute.
Happy is he who, among the men on earth, has seen these things;
But he who is not initiated into the sacred rites, he who has no
   part in them
Does not share the same destiny, even when departed into the
   gloomy darkness.[10]

From *drēsmosúne* ('service, celebration') to *hierá* ('sacred rites') and from *órgia* ('ritual actions, mysteries') to *atelés* ('not initiated'), all the terms used to designate the acts taught by Demeter in gratitude for the return of her daughter and the concomitant renewal of the fertile fields are technical terms. They allude to the institution of the different ritual acts composing a cult, and more precisely a mystery cult.[11] It falls to Demeter to inaugurate, under her own aegis and that of her daughter Persephone, the famous Mysteries of Eleusis, representing one of the preeminent moments in the cult calendar of classical Athens. From the perspective of an epic and rhapsodic narrative that unfolds in a four-hundred-line *Homeric Hymn*, the institution of the cult of the Mysteries of Eleusis by Demeter herself forms the coda of the action. According to the narrative logic that gives the account of this divine act its coherence, to the moment of rupture at the beginning – which the abduction of Persephone and the anger of Demeter that interrupts the cycle of agricultural production represent – there corresponds, at the end, the reestablishment of the fecundity of the fields and the institution of a cult in recognition of the assistance that the kings of Eleusis have provided for the goddess.

Yet the "sanctioning" part of the narrative would be incomplete if the poem did not move from the past tense of the divine act to the present tense of enunciation. In effect, the ritual acts that Persephone's mother initiated at Eleusis would have no comprehensible meaning if the end of the story, recounted in the aorist (past) tense of Greek, did not lead, via the expression "happy is he who...," to an initial *makarismós* ('blessing') in the present tense: thanks to the completion of the rites inaugurated by the goddess in the narrative past tense, mortals can henceforth enjoy, as much on earth as in Hades, a more favorable destiny. That is to say, the present moment of the ritual is integrated into the logic of the narrative and divine action in the past: not only has Demeter reestablished communication between the terrestrial sphere and Olympus, but initiation into the mysteries uses ritual to reestablish the relationship between life on earth and the underworld, a relationship that had been disturbed by the violent kidnapping of the young Persephone. The life that Persephone shares between Olympus, in the company of the gods, and Hades, in the midst of the dead, evokes the condition of mortal men who can communicate with the gods and share in their privileges, yet remain destined for an inevitable sojourn in Hades, on the misty obscurity of which initiation into the mysteries can shed some light.

In the transition from "myth" to "rite," the role of aetiology renders the ritual and initiation rites taught by the deity herself more than a simple mimetic dramatization of the rape of Persephone. By the performance of specific acts dedicated to the two divine protagonists of the narrative action, the ritual becomes a symbolic expression of human mortality and of possibilities for mankind to attain a condition more like that of the gods, both on earth and beyond. It is also a codified expression of religious devotion to the extent that the realization of the hope expressed depends on the action of the divinity. By inscribing the heroic or divine action in the present, by inscribing the logic of narrative action into the expression addressed to all mortals "happy is he who . . . ," the role of the *aítion* ('cause') is not limited to simply explicating the "rite" by the "myth" – it is not uniquely a question of origin. The logical succession of events that leads from the abduction of Persephone to the institution of the cult of the Mysteries of Eleusis is only achieved, in effect, in the performance of ritual practices taught and instituted by the divinity.

This progression of narrative logic that leads to practice itself is confirmed by the concluding verses of the *Homeric Hymn*. After the first *makarismós*, the poem briefly returns to the narrative tense to describe Demeter's ascension from Eleusis to Olympus, where she henceforth remains, in the present, at her daughter's side. Yet another, more general, *makarismós* – "Exceedingly happy is he whom the august goddesses love among men living on earth" – confirms the relationship between the actions of mother and daughter and the earthly happiness of men; this relationship is affirmed in the present but made possible through ritual acts instituted in the past. "Straightaway," the bard concludes, "they send to this [blessed] man in his vast dwelling, Ploutos ('Wealth') who, installed by the hearth, bestows prosperity on mortal men."[12] Through this second ritualized utterance of the *makarismós*, the tense of the narration again leads to the present of religious practice; it has an immediate effect on the life of the mortal who worships the two goddesses.

But there is more. In effect, this epic composition, telling the story of a young girl's abduction and the sorrow of a mother, conforms to a tripartite structure common to the majority of the *Homeric Hymns*: (i) a brief formula of *evocatio* to the divinity concerned; (ii) a narrative, more or less developed, of the god's biography and description of one or another of his functions, called the *epica pars*; and (iii) a rapid conclusion where a request (*preces*) is addressed directly to the divinity concerned. The long *Homeric Hymn to Demeter* concludes thus by a direct address to the two goddesses of Eleusis. The performer of the hymn implores the two goddesses – in a final discursive movement that brings together the tripartite structure of every sung hymn with that of a prayer – that he too be included in the prosperity that they are capable of bestowing. To support his request, the performer verbally engages in the ritual of reciprocity – *do ut des* ('I give in order that you might give') – that in classical Greece as well as in many other cultures marks each offering to a hero or a god: in exchange for the favor that he asks of the god, the bard or rhapsode offers his own song (*aoidé*, verse 494). We not only perceive that the "now" of the beneficent action of the two goddesses corresponds in fact to the *hic et nunc* ('here and now') of the enunciation of the poem, but also we equally understand that the singing of the hymnic poem itself, its psalmodic recital, corresponds to a cult act. In its supposed efficacy, this cult act is not unlike the ritual acts that Demeter instituted at Eleusis.[13]

Attested in several of the poetic texts probably related to the Mysteries of Eleusis, the formula of *makarismós* promising the initiated a happier destiny in the underworld at Persephone's side undoubtedly formed part of the *legómena* ritually pronounced during worship under the vow of secrecy, along with the acts performed (the *drõmena*) and the objects displayed (the *deiknúmena*). Its dual presence in the *Homeric Hymn* thus allows for the insertion of the poem itself, as a sung performance, into the service of the cult. Given the absence of any reference to Athens in this *Homeric Hymn*, it is most probable that it was composed and performed before the integration of Eleusis and its sanctuary into the territory controlled by the great city.[14]

At this point, it is essential to remember that, using a designation already employed by Thucydides, the *Homeric Hymns* are defined as "proems." As shown by the transition formula that concludes certain of these hymnic compositions, sung by bards or rhapsodes, the *Homeric Hymn* as a proem assumes the double function of introducing a particular epic song in a bardic or rhapsodic competition and of consecrating this song for the cult of a specific deity. The hymnic proem thus renders Homeric recitation as a whole an offering to a deity, and, consequently, a ritual act in the framework of competitions of Homeric recitation that marked the great festivals of numerous cities or classical cult sites. Such is the case of the Panathenaic festival or, as we shall see, of the Delia at Delos.[15]

The aetiological relationship between the divine story and the cult practices instituted by Demeter is thus established by essentially poetic and discursive means. More than the allusion to the components of the rites of Eleusis that the use of torches to seek Persephone, the fasting of Demeter, the double epiphany of the goddess, or the attempt to immortalize Demophon all represent, it is above all the recitation of the poem itself as a cult act that confers upon this relationship its pragmatic, even performative, function. Even more than the example of Euripides' *Hippolytus*, where it also falls to the goddess herself to institute cult practices for the hero, the words sung in the *Hymn to Demeter* guarantee the religious significance of the "myth" through ritual observance. Whether the divine or heroic story is told in dactylic hexameter or dramatized in iambic trimeter, the form it takes is invariably poetic.

DITHYRAMB AND THE LEGEND OF THESEUS TO LEGITIMIZE ATHENIAN "IMPERIALISM": THE DELIA AT DELOS

The story, sung in Bacchylides' *Dithyramb* 17 in the years following the end of the Persian Wars and painted in the same period by Micon in the new sanctuary devoted to the national hero of Athens, is well known. Before addressing the context of the enunciation of this cult song, we will first consider the poetic account that Bacchylides of Ceos gives of an episode inserted into the saga of Theseus. Based on the figure of the young Athenian citizen, Theseus came to replace Heracles as the hero who brings civilization and a founding personality for Athens; he would go on to be, six centuries later, the subject of one of Plutarch's *Lives*, in the company of Solon, Themistocles, and Pericles.

In the first part of the story, which divides the poem into two aspects, Minos takes the lead. Sailing through the Cretan Sea, that king of Cnossus is escorting seven young men and seven young women intended as tribute for his monstrous son the Minotaur. While the young Athenians are accompanied by the hero Theseus, himself protected by Athena, it is Aphrodite who inspires in the Cretan general an unseemly act committed against one of the beautiful young Athenian women, whose beauty has seduced him. Invoking the authority of his divine father Poseidon, Theseus condemns the *húbris* of the Cretan hero, who, in turn, claims the authority of his own divine father, Zeus, to challenge his accuser to a duel. Minos is able to summon a thunderbolt of Zeus and dares Theseus to bring back from the watery depths, home of his father Poseidon, the ring that Minos threw there. Moera (Fate) intervenes to create a twist in the unfolding of the plot. Theseus, henceforth the narrative subject, is led by dolphins into the underwater dwelling of his father, where he is welcomed by the dances and choral songs of the daughters of Nereus. Then, he receives from his father's wife, Amphitrite, a purple cloak and the crown that she had been given for her nuptials. In the light that emanates from these erotic and matrimonial gifts of the young woman, Theseus miraculously springs up onto the deck of the boat carrying the young men and women from Athens to Crete. With the splendor of a god in his epiphany, he reappears like a betrothed woman, displaying traits that, at the very least, are ambiguous in terms of "gender." The hero's return from the depths of the Cretan Sea is celebrated by the paean performed by the seven young Athenian men, while the seven young women accompany the victory song with the traditional ritual cry. *Paiánixan* and *ōlóluxan*: the terms used by Bacchylides to describe this song embedded in the narrative refer us to the performance of a cult paean.

It is only by the means of the narrative performance of this paean that we come to the end of the story and pass, quite briefly, to the time and place of the enunciation of the dithyramb itself, with an implicit reference to the *hic et nunc* of its ritual and historical execution (verses 122–32).

> He springs from the depths of the sea without being wet,
> To the astonishment of all;
> On his limbs shone the gifts of the gods.
> The young girls in luminous garments
> Shouted ritual cries with a new joy.
> The sea echoed them.
> Next to them, the young men sang the paean
> In a lusty voice.
> God of Delos, after having delighted in your heart
> At the choral dances of the Ceans,
> Bestow upon the worthy the good fortune sent by the gods.

The god of Delos is, of course, Apollo, worshipped each year at the place of his birth and in his island sanctuary during the great festival of the Delia. The *Homeric Hymn to Apollo* sings of athletic and musical contests that Greek men from Ionia, accompanied by their wives and children, organized. The climax of the festival was marked by the choral performance of the young Deliads (Delian maidens), who sang, under the aegis of a Homeric bard, the glories of Apollo and Artemis and of heroes and heroines. When recounting the history of the sanctuary, Thucydides tells of the progressive taking of control of the pan-Ionian festival by the Athenians, who would annually send an important choral delegation. Assuming each year the form of a *theōría* (an official mission), this naval procession was the source, as Phaedo describes in the eponymous Platonic dialogue, of the delay in the execution of Socrates after his trial. It was led by that very boat on which Theseus was said to have sailed with the seven young men and seven young women of Athens – who were in the end saved from the Labyrinth of Crete. Displaying the finest aetiological logic, Phaedo attributes this naval procession to a sacred vow that the Athenians made to Apollo, promising to send an annual and ritual fleet of ships to Delos in exchange for protection of the Athenian youths. It is thus through this lead ship, appropriately crowned by the priest of Apollo, that the people of Athens perpetuate and celebrate, "regularly and still now" (*aeì kaì nûn éti*) in ritual reiteration, the memory of one of the founding moments of Athenian citizenship.[16]

According to such logic, the episode in which Theseus plunges into the Cretan Sea and his subsequent reemergence for the benefit of the seven young men and seven young women he accompanies appear to be the *aítion* of the song that itself contains the account of the event. Added to the identification of the ship bearing the legendary tribute of Athenian youths to Crete with the ship that conveys the cult procession to Delos and back, there are significant musical echoes. The ritual performance of Bacchylides' dithyramb, composed for a choral group and intended as an offering to Apollo at Delos, is foreshadowed in the poetic narrative by the Nereids' choral dances in Amphitrite's underwater home, which will become the Aegean Sea, as well as by the paean performed on the deck of the ship by the young men and women. It is an aetiological paradox that a dithyramb penned by Bacchylides of Ceos intended for choral groups is announced by the narrative performance of a paean: probably prevalent here are the rules of genre, which impose the dithyrambic form upon a story with substantial narrative sophistication, frequently detached from the context of the cult of Dionysus and, moreover, attested at Delos itself.[17]

However, the aetiological relationship between a narrative episode in the "mythical" biography of Theseus and the great cult gathering at Delos with its musical competitions in honor of Delian Apollo is not realized uniquely on the religious level. In effect, in the opening of his history of the war between the Athenians and the Peloponnesians, Thucydides presents Minos, the king of Cnossus, as the ancestor of the thalassocracy – in other words, as the hero who first liberated the Cretan Sea from barbarian pirates and maintained political and economic control over its waters. He chased away the Carians and Phoenicians from the Cyclades and established, by placing his sons there, a colonial power from which he drew considerable revenue. Minos thus becomes, as a civilizing hero, the founding hero of the politics of expansion that Athens undertook at the end of the Persian Wars – played out on a sea that from the time of Theseus' return from the Labyrinth of Crete and by reason of the suicide of his father, Aegeus, in the wake of the misunderstanding over the black sail, bore the name of the king of Athens. Under the pen of Thucydides, the heroic legend thus becomes history, and the very name of the Aegean Sea carries within it the aetiological relationship between the colonial and economic power of Minos over the islands of which the center is Delos and the enthroning of Theseus in Athens as a democratic king following his father's suicide. Foreshadowed in an early era by Minos' civilizing activities in the former Cretan Sea, the taking of political and economic control by Athens in the Aegean Sea would be consecrated by the creation of the Delian League just after the Persian Wars, with Delian Apollo's sanctuary serving as its cultic and administrative center, precisely in the period when Bacchylides composed his *Dithyramb* 17.[18]

Through poetic creation and musical performance, the heroic story of Theseus' dive into the depths of the Cretan Sea to join his father Poseidon, tutelary god of Athens, lends legitimacy to both the Athenian choral dances during the cult celebration of Apollo at Delos and the expansionist politics of the city in the Aegean basin. In the ritual performance of *Dithyramb* 17 of the poet of Ceos, it is a patriotic and colonial policy that symbolically mimes the young Athenian men and women singing the heroic exploit of Theseus and offering their song to Delian Apollo.

EPINICIA AND THE ABDUCTION OF THE NYMPH CYRENE: THE COLONIAL CELEBRATION OF THE SPARTAN CARNEIA AT CYRENE

The Greeks of the classical period understood in terms of colonial and civilizing activity not only the progressive settling of the territory of

Hellas itself with civic communities but also their efforts at external domination around the rim of the Mediterranean basin. Thus, in the mimetic hymn that he dedicated to Apollo, the Alexandrian poet Callimachus recounts how the seat of the Carneian god was consecutively moved from the city of Sparta to the island of Thera, and then from Santorini to Cyrene on the coast of Libya, first by Theras, a descendant of Oedipus and heroic founder of Thera, and then by Battus, the historical founder of Cyrene. In the great Alexandrian tradition that Callimachus himself inaugurated, that strange form of mythography cloaked in epic diction takes on an aetiological function. This summary foundation-tale of Cyrene and its antecedents serves in effect to explain the construction of the temple and the annual offering of a sacrifice in honor of Apollo Carneius in this Greek city of Libya.[19] Fed by a constantly tended flame, these sacrificial offerings were accompanied during the celebration of the Carneia by a choral dance of armed men, in keeping with a tradition that stretches back to the institution of the Cyrenean cult of Apollo. A new aetiological cord in Callimachus' hymnic account traces its origin to the dance that the Dorian migrants performed at the springs of Cyre: the god himself had led the Greek colonists there, and he rejoiced, in the company of a young nymph, at the sight of their progress; the nymph, Cyrene, had given her name to the place, having been abducted by the god from her native Thessaly. This choral dance and the memory of the abduction of a young huntress-heroine explain, again in an aetiological mode, both the benefactions that Apollo henceforth constantly accorded to the city of Cyrene and, via the reciprocal relationship of *do ut des*, the reverence accorded him by the descendants of the heroic founder Battus.[20] In its double invocation of the Carneian god, one reminiscent of the form of cult hymns, this hymnic narrative is aetiological on a third level, for it is accompanied by another enigmatic aetiology that refers the god of the Carneia to the poet and narrator and, in so doing, to the *hic et nunc* of the singing performance. The various enunciative processes of this erudite hymnic poem designate the *hic et nunc* as mimetic, without reference to a specific instance of an actual performance.

Be that as it may, the pattern that structures the hymnic narrative of the founding of the sanctuary of Apollo at the springs of Cyre in Libya and the itinerant locales of the Spartan festival of the Carneia brings to mind the close of the narrative passages of the *Homeric Hymn to Demeter*. In the case of the latter, it is the goddess herself who, as we have seen, institutes the cult honors that will be regularly consecrated to her; as for the former, the god participates, on the narrative and enunciative levels, in the founding of rites whose performance delights him, at first in the time of the Dorian heroes, and then in the seasonal cycle leading up to the moment of the poem's enunciation where Apollo is invoked directly. However, if the location of the institution of the cult coincides in principle with the place where the poem is recited, the sheer number of foundation acts that Callimachus rehearses in the aetiological narration of his mimetic hymn renders such an identification impossible: from Thessaly to Delphi, on a route that leads through Delos and Cyrene before the story reaches its end in a place that can only, according to a poetic itinerary set under the aegis of the god of music, correspond to a space of a purely poetic enunciation.[21]

It was quite a different matter two centuries earlier, when Pindar chose to recount the "historical" version of the founding of Cyrene on the occasion of a ritual celebration of the chariot victory at the Pythian Games of the king of Cyrene, Arcesilas IV. Independent of the divine version of the story in the ninth *Pythian Ode*, which traces the foundation of the Greek city in Libya to the abduction of the eponymous nymph Cyrene by the young Apollo, and independent also of the heroic version in the fourth *Pythian Ode*, which associates the founding of Cyrene by the people of Thera with the legend of the Argonauts, the story that Pindar tells in the fifth *Pythian Ode* underscores the special relationship between Apollo, whose oracular voice at Delphi ordained the foundation of a colony, and the heroic founder Battus, who, with his prodigious voice, was able to scare away the lions that prowled around the savage land that was to be colonized and civilized. The double invoking of the oracular voice that names the land to be colonized and the civilizing voice that removes savagery leads the narrator to sing of the triple powers of Apollo as a god of healing, god of musical inspiration and god of prophecy who guides the foundation of Hellenic cities. Then, in a move that blends genealogical narrative and enunciative intervention, the heroic antecedents of the foundation of Cyrene by Battus of Thera are praised:

> It is my role to sing an admirable glory,
> Come from Sparta.
> Natives of this city, the heroic Aegids, my forefathers,
> Came to Thera, not without the aid of the gods;
> Destiny guided them.
> Having inherited from there the tradition of the communal
>   banquet
> Accompanied by numerous sacrifices,

We celebrate during the feasts in your honor, Apollo Carneius,
The resplendent city of Cyrene.
The foreign warriors occupy it, Trojans, sons of Antenor;
They arrived there with Helen,
After they had seen their homeland
Razed by the fire of Ares.[22]

From Sparta through Thera to Cyrene, the itinerary that Pindar's poetic tale describes is identical to the one offered in the mythographical summary of Callimachus' poem, save the subtle nuance that the first-person narrator introduces, by alluding to the descendants of Aegeus as "my fathers," to include his own city of origin, Thebes. It is indeed this itinerary from Sparta that seems to have been customarily followed in celebrating Apollo Carneius at his festival of the same name. In the same way, in Callimachus' poem, the intervention of the "I" of the narrator in the heroic tale allows the establishment of a relationship between this legendary past and the history and origins of his own family. On the other hand, the tense shift from the past to the present that the direct address to Apollo Carneius provokes in Callimachus' poem corresponds to a shift from "I" to "we" in Pindar's epinicion. It is no longer the "I" of the poet who, like the Aegids, hails from Thebes, but the collective "we" who honor the city of Cyrene with a ritual banquet devoted to the god of the Carneia. Moreover, in a manipulation of narrative time that Pindar masters so artfully, the flight of the Antenorids from the devastated city of Troy to Cyrene is invoked at this juncture and, in yet another shift from the heroic past tense to the ritual present, the Trojan heroes are summoned to receive the sacrificial offerings presented at the Carneia by the heroic founder's companions and their descendants.[23]

When combined with the strong presence of the first-person utterances of the "I" of the poet and the choral "we," these successive temporal shifts from a heroic time to the present of the religious ceremony honoring Apollo Carneius indicate that the very performance of the fifth *Pythian Ode* coincides with the celebration of the Carneia in Cyrene – and this is all the more likely in that the beginning of the poem designates in a deictic and self-referential manner the choral procession that, in the guise of a *kômos* (a group of merrymakers), sings of the victory of Arcesilas IV in the present. The choral performance entertains Apollo in a garden of Aphrodite; this place could correspond to a cult site in the great sanctuary of the tutelary god of Cyrene, but could equally be a metaphorical allusion to the region of the Greek colony of Libya captured in the splendor of its legendary fertility.[24]

Thus, on the one hand, the poetic allusion to the legend of the founding of Cyrene by Battus, two lengthy versions of which Herodotus inserted into his *Histories*, is twice linked by Pindar with the age of the heroes: first, by the reference to the Aegids who came from Thebes, passing through Sparta and Thera, whose founder was Theras, the grandfather of Aegeus; then, by rehearsing the founding of Cyrene itself by heroes descended from Antenor, fleeing the destruction of Troy.[25] On the other hand, through a subtle enunciative technique that Pindar frequently employs in his choral poems, the poet lends his authorial voice to a choral group, which then performs the poem in dance and song: by this act of "choral delegation," the poet singing the chariot victory of the king of Cyrene at the Pythian Games in honor of Apollo becomes the group of choral singers who perform his song in Cyrene during the Carneia celebrating the same god[26] – the god who, with his oracular voice, ordered Battus to found a colonial city in Libya is also the "horned" god (the leading ram of the flock) who leads colonial expeditions and who controls the acts of foundation. In an aetiological relationship of an essentially ritual nature, the time of the heroic founders of the Aegid family and the time of the Trojan war and of those other founders who would become the Antenorids augment the profound import of the time of the arrival of Battos, the founder of Cyrene; these three temporal threads of the "myth" converge in the celebration of the Carneia and of the king of the colonial city of Cyrene honored in the fifth *Pythian Ode*.

The poetic relationship established between the different temporal moments of foundation and the ritual song of the poem has the effect of reinforcing the heroizing of Battus himself; his actions in founding the city fill up the verses that follow and that lead to the conclusion of the epinician song. Exactly at the end of a wide road, used for cult processions, that the founder had paved all the way to the agora lay the tomb of Battus, the heroic founder, whose lineage Pindar traces down to Arcesilas IV in a final return to the present moment of the enunciation of the poem, under the protection of sovereign Zeus. Thus temporal and spatial continuity is established in an aetiological manner between the "mythic" ancestors of the founders, the founder who is himself heroicized, and the present royal power celebrated on the occasion of a Pythic victory performatively recounted in the fully Apollonian frame of the Carneia. The ritual celebration of a god who is a founder of cities and himself a bearer of civilization through the introduction of nymphs that incarnate the passage from savagery to Hellenic culture confirms, between his continental oracular center and the peripheral colonies, the heroization of the founders, between legend and history.

CULT SONG AND THE INSTALLATION OF DIONYSUS AT DELPHI: THE APOLLONIAN FESTIVAL OF THE THEOXENIA

In 340–339 BCE, a citizen of Locrian Scarphea – one Philodamus – dedicated in Delphi, near the sanctuary of Delphic Apollo, then under-going renovation, the text of a paean.[27] This dedication on a marble stele commemorated various favors accorded Philodamus and his fam-ily by the clergy or the Amphictyons of Delphi; among such privileges were *proxenía* (an agreement of reciprocal friendship and hospitality) and *promanteía* (the right to consult an oracle).

Set out in twelve strophes in Aeolian melic rhythm, this anony-mous cult song has the tripartite structure typical of cult hymns that one also finds, with some variation, in those proems to epic recitations that are the *Homeric Hymns* (as discussed above): invocation – narrative – prayer. Explicitly designated as a paean in the dedicatory inscription, the poem begins in an overtly ritual fashion with an invocation to Diony-sus. As tradition requires, the presence of the god is invoked with a sequence of asyndetic epicleses: "Lord, Dithyrambus, Bacchus, Euius, Bull with ivy tresses, Bromius." From the first strophe, also according to the tradition of cult song, a "hymnic" relative pronoun, whose gram-matical antecedent is the invoked god, introduces a lengthy narrative passage, no longer in the present tense, which would correspond to that of the enunciation, but in the aorist (past) tense. This narrative, which is not heroic but divine, retraces the path of Dionysus from the place of his birth as far as Pieria near Olympus: Bacchic Thebes, where the birth of a beautiful boy to Zeus and Thyone (Semele) is celebrated by choral dances among immortals and by revelry among mortals; then Orchomenus and Euboea, caught up in Bacchic delirium like the city of Cadmus; Delphi, sacred and blessed land that dances for Dionysus, making the crevices of Parnassus alive with young Delphian women; Eleusis, where the young god arrives with a torch in hand, under the name of Iacchus, breathing divine possession into the celebration of the mysteries by locals and by initiates from across Greece; finally, after one or two stops that lacunae in the text prevent us from identifying, Pieria and Olympus, where Dionysus is sung by the Muses and crowned with ivy – their circling choral dances are led by Apollo, who is himself *khorēgós*.[28]

It turns out that the first section of the narrative portion of the paean, denoted as "of Philodamus," does not correspond exactly and formally to a "myth." In effect, the young Dionysus, the principal protagonist of the narrative action in his trek of spreading Bacchic possession from Thebes to Olympus, remains continually connected, through the use of the second person, to the invocatory element at the beginning of the poem. This blending of the level of story or narrative (*histoire/récit*) and that of discourse (*discours*) is reinforced in the second section of the narrative part, constituting the predominant portion of the poem (from the second half of strophe I to the end of strophe XI).[29] Despite the large lacuna that robs us of the text of strophes VI, VII, and VIII, we can see that it is Apollo, presented as *khorēgós* of the Muses celebrating Dionysus at the end of stanza V, who is henceforth the subject of the narrative action – in the third person, of course, but in the present tense! After a probable allusion to the oracle he controls at Delphi, the god becomes the protagonist of a series of acts of inauguration. In stanza IX:

> The god commands the Amphictyons
> To perform the rite quickly
> So that he who strikes from far
> Holds back his wrath.
> *Euoi ô io Bacchus ô ie Paean*
> He orders them to display this hymn here,
> At the time of the annual *xenia*,
> For his brother, the sacred scion of the gods,
> And organize a shining sacrifice
> Punctuated by communal supplications
> To all of Hellas, the most fortunate.
> *Ie Paean*, come as a savior,
> Protect, good guardian, this city here,
> By granting happiness and prosperity.

In a turn analogous to the one that closes the narrative in the *Homeric Hymn to Demeter*, it falls to the god to inaugurate the ritual honors that are bestowed upon him. But the act of institution pertains not to the rites of the Theoxenia as a whole, which are well attested at Delphi, but to a sacrifice with Panhellenic import and to the performance of the present song, which, while praising the god of the oracle, is destined for Dionysus. Owing to the intervention of the god in the story, the narrative component of the poetic composition leads to the performance of the hymn itself that sings the life of Dionysus and the benefactions of Apollo.

The third section of the paean, particularly well developed, begins with a direct address to those fortunate mortal men who are in the process of reconstructing and adorning the temple of Apollo. Instead of the prayer expected at the end of the poem, a *makarismós* appears; it proclaims the joy of those men who have the privilege of contributing to the restoration of the splendor of the sanctuary that hosts – the following strophe adds – the quadrennial Pythian Games. Apollo had already brought in Dionysus by instituting for him a sacrifice and cyclical chorus competitions (in other words, dithyrambs) and by erecting in a grotto set aside for the god a statue of Bacchus on a sun-chariot pulled by golden lions. To the introduction of Dionysus into the present celebration of the Theoxenia corresponds his cultic association, in the past, with the festival of the Pythia – always by the will of the god who is lord of Delphi. Henceforth, for the prayer to a god who had already several times sought ritual inauguration on behalf of his half-brother Dionysus can be substituted a prayer addressed to a plural "you" that surely designates not only the members of the chorus singing the paean, but also the Amphictyons who organized the performance: a petition to welcome and invoke Dionysus in ivy-crowned choruses and by choral dances evoking the musical performance of this strange paean shared by Apollo and Dionysus, for the prosperity of all Greece.

These different relationships established between acts of the gods in the past and religious actions performed by humans in the present make of the very performance of the paean of Philodamus a particular ritual integrated into the Theoxenia at Delphi, a festival that henceforth welcomes Dionysus.[30] The pronounced ritual character of the hymn that glorifies Dionysus and Apollo is accentuated by the repetition at the end of each strophe of a long refrain, but also by the insertion in each strophe of an intermediate refrain. The latter, which is an *epíphthegma* punctuated by two minor Ionic meters, speaks to the cult complementarity between the two gods: Dionysus and Apollo are both invoked by a ritual cry inscribed in cult tradition and designed to call forth the presence of either the god Bacchus or the god Paean. The divine epiphany will be conjoined, underscored by the phonic echo of the double invocation: *Euoi ô io Bacchos, ô ie Paean.*[31]

The more developed *ephúmnion* that closes each strophe, in a combination of minor Ionic meters and Aeolic metric rhythm, is introduced by a single ritual call to Paean. It takes the place of a properly spoken prayer, since it corresponds to a request addressed directly to this savior deity: that he afford protection and prosperity to a city – a city that, by the deixis implicit in the demonstrative pronoun *hóde*, can only be Delphi, the place of the performance of the song. It is undoubtedly no accident that the unfortunately damaged lines of the poem's final strophe close with the mention of a lord of health. This designation leads, in a final reiteration of the refrain, to the last ritual call addressed to Paean and, consequently, to a renewed prayer for prosperity for Delphi. It is thus Apollo who is designated in this final phrase, the actor of the second section of the narrative component of the poem, and not a Dionysus metamorphosed into a paean god, as has been too often affirmed. The paean repeats in order to reestablish the cult collaboration of Apollo Paean with Dionysus Bacchus, under the control of the former, in a relationship of asymmetric complementarity that inverts the terms of that one imagined by Nietzsche in his famous essay on the origins of tragedy and of the Dionysian arts.[32]

In a hymnic cult song, such as the paean of Philodamus, the aetiological relationship established between the acts of gods in the past and the present ritual circumstances is realized through the performance of the poem itself. This performative act, both musical and religious, is not merely reflected in choral executions that traverse the entirety of the composition – the choral dances of the immortals to welcome Dionysus at his birth; the territory of Cadmus roused by Bacchic exuberance and the blessed land of Delphi animated by choral dance; the choir of Muses, under Apollo's direction, singing Dionysus at his arrival in Pieria and on Olympus; the performance of the paean at the Theoxenia; the choral competition at the Pythian Games, the actual welcoming of Dionysus by ivy-crowned choral groups. The song must encourage the reconstruction of Apollo's oracular temple by the people of Delphi and the Amphictyons, with the aid of all the Greeks, and probably under the control of Athens. Despite substantial lacunae, the penultimate strophe seems to contain an allusion to a golden statue of Dionysus surrounded by goddesses; according to evidence from Pausanias, who identifies these dancers with the Thyiades (devotees of Bacchus), this statue formed part of the group of sculptures that adorned the western pediment of the sixth Delphic temple of Apollo.[33] The aetiological relationship between divine actions and the introduction of Dionysus into the Theoxenia by the very singing of the paean is thus enriched by a referential relationship with this other type of religious practice and offering, the execution and consecration of grand-scale iconographic projects in classical Greece. If only by the means of its financing, this religious practice resorting to the plastic arts takes on — even as with the consecration of the paean — sung first, then monumentalized — an eminently political dimension.

IN CONCLUSION, THE TRAGEDY AND GENEALOGY OF ION: ATHENIAN POLITICS AT THE GREAT DIONYSIA

From the point of view of the aetiological relationship, in its several manifestations, that establishes a link between a divine or heroic past and a ritual or religious practice, the tragedies of Euripides are of particular interest, insofar as the dramatic unfolding of narrative intrigue sets before the audience acts of cult practice. Like *Hippolytus*, invoked above in the guise of a prelude, the Euripidean tragedy dramatizing the story of Ion, son of the Athenian queen Creusa and of Apollo, the god of Delphi, concludes with an aetiological explication of the events dramatized on the stage. As with Artemis at the end of *Hippolytus*, it falls to Athena to confer upon the young man, at last recognized by his divine father and mortal mother, the function of young heroic founder. Leaving behind his lowly role as a servant in the sanctuary of the oracle of Apollo at Delphi, he will gain that form of immortalization that will make him worthy of the glory of being successor to his maternal grandfather Erechtheus on the throne of Athens.

For the establishment of a cult recalling the memory of a young-man-become-hero, there is substituted, for young Ion, an inscription, bearing the names of his descendants, of the organization of the inhabitants of Athens into four tribes: the Geleontes (farmers), the Aegicores (shepherds), the Hopletes (soldiers), and the Argades (craftsmen) — that Plutarch describes in the *Life of Solon*, substituting for the names of the four sons of Ion etymologies related to the social functions of these four Athenian tribes, undoubtedly Ionian in origin.[34] In a foreshadowing of Athenian domination of the Aegean, also aetiologically evoked in Bacchylides' *Dithyramb* 17, their descendants would be called to inhabit the Cyclades and the two shores of the sea separating Asia from Europe; corresponding to the bipartition of the civilized world as Herodotus conceives it in his investigation of the Persian Wars, the territorial representation evoked by Athena on the stage at the Great Dionysia of the penultimate decade of the fifth century is profoundly marked by the ideology of Athenian foreign policy after the victory over Xerxes — as far as the maternal lineage of Ion is concerned, the son of Creusa, herself the daughter of the king of Athens, Erechtheus.

As for Ion's stepfather Xuthus, this "foreign" son of Aeolus, Achaean by birth, he will become, by Creusa, the father of Dorus, the heroic founder of the Dorian region, and of Achaeus, the eponymous hero of the Achaeans: a remodeling of the transmitted tradition that accorded a prominent role to Aeolians and Dorians, this genealogical lineage serves, at the time of the Peloponnesian War, to subordinate the Peloponnesians to the Ionians; as the son of a god, Ion holds a privileged status over Dorus and Achaeus.[35] Thus, at the end of the tragedy, by means of an eponymic and etymologizing aetiology, the installing of Ion, son of Apollo and Creusa, successor of Erechtheus, on the throne of the city under Athena's protection takes the place of the usual worship rendered to the hero: Euripides' drama is there to perpetuate ritually, together with the Athenian audience gathered in the theater and sanctuary of Dionysus Eleuthereus for the tragic competition, the memory of the young heroized king.

Now, at the beginning of the tragedy, the god Hermes, who pronounces the *párodos* ('entrance song'), had already made recourse to the aetiological technique – at first for setting out the genealogy of the future king of Athens: Erichthonius, the autochthonous ancestor of the king Erechtheus (father of Creusa), the babe born from the soil of Attica, left in a basket and entrusted by his virginal "mother" Athena to the care of the virgin daughters of Aglaurus and two serpents – hence the custom of Erechtheus' descendants wearing those golden serpents that Creusa had herself worn as a young girl and placed in the basket with her newborn son whom she abandoned deep in a grotto of the Acropolis. As renewed by Euripides, the legend thus makes of Ion a second Erichthonius: if Ion does not have the same autochthonous birth as the child who grew from the sperm of Hephaestus that fell to the ground as he pursued the fleeing Athena, he nonetheless is also born of a virgin; he is placed in a basket guarded by the serpents of the Erechtheids, in the very grotto where the little Erichthonius was placed in the care of the three daughters of Aglaurus and Cecrops, the first king born from the soil of Attica.[36] Raised by his father Apollo and finally recognized by his mother, Ion ('he who goes') is proclaimed by Hermes to be the future hero-colonizer of the "land of Asia," by the will of Apollo, god of civilization and of the founding of cities: the aetiological relationship with the Hellenization of the Ionian coast of the Aegean Sea, which itself anticipates the Athenian policy of expansion during the classical period, is assured anew by etymologizing word-play.[37] Thus, at the end of the tragedy, Athena, the patron goddess of Athens, can affirm in her concluding epiphany:

> The descendants (of the four sons of Ion), when the time will
>   come,
> Marked by destiny,
> Will occupy the island cities of the Cyclades,
> And the coasts of the sea, giving strength to my land.
> Then they will inhabit the plains of the two facing continents,
> Europe and Asia, and be called Ionians after the name of this
>   very Ion,
> And will enjoy glory without end.[38]

By manipulating Ion's genealogy in order to associate the young hero with the Athenian autochthon and make him the pivot of a hierarchized ethnic identity, Euripides keeps pace with his historiographic colleagues Acusilaus of Argos or, above all, Pherecydes of Athens. This course of an aetiological genealogy of an ethnic and political order is all the more surprising because Ion seems not to have been the object of an important hero cult in Athens.[39] All unfolds as if it were, in the end, the tragedy itself, in its ritual performance at the Great Dionysia in the city, that takes the place of a heroizing celebration for the son of the god of Delphi. The tragedy makes a statement by inserting the young hero, via both maternal bloodline and the law of the *epíklēros* ('heiress'), into the lineage of the legendary kings and founders of Athens – an insertion that seems to be tied to a particular political situation and that appears not to have been retained by the official historiography of the city, if, for example, the chronicle of the *Marmor Parium* is to be believed. Creusa is a *parthénos* ('virgin') like Athena – this is certain – and above all Ion is a young man like Apollo: Athena herself, at the end of the tragedy, confirms the veneration that the son-turned-king of Athens holds for his divine father in respect of the divine order.

Considered as religious practices, the stories that we identify and place under the rubric of "myth" thus reveal themselves to exist only in particular poetic forms. It is the rules of genre that, divided between institutional ritualities and regularities of discursive order, contrive to make "myths" socially and ideologically active. Supported by poetic genre, this or that episode of the divine and heroic past of the Greek communities is inserted in both a specific cult institution and in a form of ritual poetry, most often choral. These poetic forms make from narratives, appearing to us as mythic, an active history, inscribed in a collective memory realized through ritual.[40] Far from forming a system of thought, far from being inscribed in some structure of the human unconscious, far from constituting a particular language, the ensemble of the myths of the Hellenic tradition is characterized by a certain plasticity that allows the poetic creation of versions constantly readapted for cult and for religious and ideological paradigms offered by a polytheism that varies within the multifarious civic space and time of the cities of Greece. It corresponds to a polymorphous cultural memory, at the same time ritually creative and reactive, and to a religious memory that, given the ritual dimension of the poetic forms that the legend assumes, is fulfilled in a performative manner by the acts inscribed in the cult calendars of the cities and of the great cult centers of Greece – here, Athens and Sparta, Delos and Delphi, but Troezen or Cyrene as well.

FURTHER READING

On Greek mythology, there are two good recent introductions: R. Buxton, *Imaginary Greece. The Contexts of Mythology*, Cambridge 1994 and F. Graf, *Greek Mythology. An Introduction*, Baltimore and London 1993; see also S. Saïd, *Approches de la mythologie grecque*, Paris 1993, C. Calame, *Poétique des mythes dans la Grèce antique*, Paris 2000b, and the very useful book by Ch. Delattre, *Manuel de mythologie grecque*, Paris 2005; on Greek religion, besides the indispensable *Greek Religion* by W. Burkert (Oxford 1985), see the very well-balanced *Greek Religion*, by J. N. Bremmer (Oxford 1999, 2nd ed.), and P. Schmitt-Pantel and L. Bruit-Zaidman, *Religion in the Ancient Greek City* (Cambridge 1992).

NOTES

1   The question of definitions assigned to the concept of religion beginning with Cicero has been notably dealt with by Bremmer (1998) 9–14; for a treatment of the problems that modern concepts of myth and mythology pose and their lack of pertinence for Greek antiquity, see Detienne (1981) 9–49 and Calame (2003a) 3–27.

2   Regarding the native designations of the different cult practices offered to gods and heroes, see the numerous individual studies cited in Calame (1991) 196–303; see also Bremmer (1999) 2–6. For the civic framework of Greek religious practices, see, for example, Sourvinou-Inwood (1990).

3   See, for example, Pellizer (1993) 289–99.

4   For the celebration of the Dionysia, see Easterling (1997) 37–44 as well as the recent work of Sourvinou-Inwood (2002) 67–119 and the contribution of R. A. Buxton on "Tragedy and Greek Myth," chapter 4 in this volume.

5 See Thomas (1989)108–54 and Bowie (2001) 47–62. For a definition of the first Greek historiographers as "historiopoietai," see Calame (2006) 42–64.

6 There is nothing more misleading than the distinction that E. Cassirer makes in his *The Philosophy of Symbolic Forms* (1923–29; English translation 1953–96) and later summarizes (1946) between "mythical concepts," "linguistic concepts," and "intellectual concepts," leading him to tautologies such as: "L'enracinement premier de la conscience linguistique dans la conscience mythico-religieuse s'exprime avant tout dans le fait que toutes les figures linguistiques apparaissent en même temps comme des figures mythiques ..." (p. 62).

7 Euripides, *Hippolytus* 1423–30; cf. Segal (1996)159–62, who gives other examples of tragedies whose action contains an aetiological conclusion.

8 Pausanias 2.32.1–4, with the references to the heroic cult devoted to Apollo at Troezen as well as at Athens (the hero had a *mnêma* there) that I gave in Calame (2000b) 221–4. Also see Euripides, *Hippolytus* 58–87 and 1135–41.

9 Many examples of the aetiological relationship between "myth" and "ritual" are given by Graf (1993) 101–20; cf. also Bremmer (1999) 55–64. For the complex symbolic relationships between these two orders of the demonstration and practice of religion, see Calame (1996) 15–52.

10 *Homeric Hymn to Demeter* 471–82; the Greek text of this passage probably comes from the coincidence of two different rhapsodic versions: cf. Richardson (1974) 304.

11 For the meaning of these different technical terms related to the mystery cults, see Burkert (1987) 7–11, and, of course, the excellent remarks by Richardson (1974) 251 and 302–8.

12 *Homeric Hymn to Demeter* 483–9; for a comparative analysis of these two *macarismoí*, whose form is attested in other cults of an initiatory nature, see the ample commentary of Richardson (1974) 310–14. The *bíos*, understood as material abundance stemming from agricultural labor in relation to the mortality of man and his efforts to come closer to the gods, dictates the action of Hesiod's poem *Works and Days*; cf. Calame (2005) 48–51.

13 I have described this discursive transition divided between enounced and enunciation and leading to the *hic et nunc* of the poem's performance in Calame (1997) 118–33; for the tripartite structure of the hymnic forms in relation to that of prayers, see the numerous references given in Calame (2005) 21–32.

14 On this historical question, see Richardson (1974) 12–30 and Calame (1997) 132–3.

15 Thucydides 3.104.4, who cites under this designation two passages of the *Homeric Hymn to Apollo* (146–50 and 165–72), sung at the time of the musical competitions of the great Panhellenic festival in honor of the god of Delos, Apollo; for other attestations of this and for bibliographical orientation, cf. Calame (2005) 19–22; as for the musical competition at the Panathenian festival, see, for example, Shapiro (1992) and the remarks of Nagy (1996b) 42–3 and 99–112 regarding the Pisistratid version of the Homeric poems, perhaps established at this occasion.

16 We can add, to the references on the Delia given in note 13, Plato, *Phaedo* 58ab. The issue of the reference of the final verses of the poem to the historical circumstances of its delivery is well treated by Maehler (1997) 167–70. Other references and commentary can be found in Calame (2003a), a study developed in Calame (2006) 143–94.

17 As for the circumstances of the performance of the dithyramb and issues of form, see Ieranò (1997) 233–303.

18 Thucydides 1.4 and 8.1–3; see also Herodotus 3.122.2, who nevertheless attributes the first true thalassocracy to the tyrant Polycrates of Samos, making Minos merely a precursor of sorts. For the historicity of the maritime colonial power of Minos and its relationship to the external policy of Athens in the fifth century, see the bibliographical references given by Hornblower (1991) 18–23, as well as Calame (1996) 420–32.

19 The role of Apollo *Archēgétēs* (the 'Founder') in colonial expeditions and as the architect of new foundation-sites is explored by Detienne (1998) 88–133; for the colonizing functions of Apollo Carneius, the horned ram (i.e., leader of the flock), in relation to the diffusion and the celebration of the Carneia, see Malkin (1994) 143–58.

20 Callimachus, *Hymn to Apollo* 69–96, whose mythographical and aetiological allusions can be deciphered with the aid of the indispensable commentary by Williams (1978) 66–82; for the question of possible bibliographical references to the utterances of the intervening narrator and poet, see Calame (2005) 76–8, along with the secondary bibliography on the issue.

21 On the question of the mimetic character of Callimachus' hymn and a poetic program that is the object of much controversy, see Calame (2005) 84–7.

22 Pindar, *Pythian Ode* 5.72–85, with the commentary offered by Gentili et al. (1995) 531–4, as well as Calame (2003b) 79–86.

23 See, on this question in particular, Krummen (1990) 108–41.

24 Reconstructed from indicators given by the poet himself; the context of the presentation of the fifth *Pythian Ode* is treated in the commentary of Gentili et al. (1995) 159–63 and 516–18.

25 The two versions, Theran and Cyrenean, of a colonization largely directed and guided by oracles of Apollo at Delphi are recounted by Herotodus 4.145–57; cf. Calame (2003b) 86–108; for the foundation of Thera, see also Malkin (1994) 98–111.

26 On the question of the monodic or choral nature of Pindar's "I," see, in particular, D'Alessio (1994) 120–4, who makes reference to terms of an animated controversy; cf. also Calame (2005) 5–7.

27 The issue of the date of the consecration of the stele containing the text of the paean in relation to the renovation of the temple of Apollo is addressed by Vamvouri Ruffy (2004) 187–92.

28 *Paean* 39 Käppel; these different stopping points are the subject of the commentary by Furley and Bremer (2001) 58–84. For the complex structure of the poem, see the exhaustive analysis by Käppel (1992) 222–73; for the structure of the different Greek hymnic forms, see Calame (2005) 21–32.

29 On this operative distinction between "history/story" and "discourse" and on the numerous occasions for interference between these two levels of any utterance, see the references in Calame (2005) 1–7.

30 On the indices of enunciation that are inserted into the performance of the paean of Philodamus during the Theoxenia, and on this important holiday in the Delphic calendar, see Vamvouri Ruffy (2004) 189–96.

31 The use of this double ritual invocation, widely attested in various cult circumstances, is illustrated in the exhaustive remarks of Käppel (1992) 65–70 and 225.

32 The renovation of the sanctuary at Delphi during the second half of the fourth century was undoubtedly an occasion, notably under Athenian pressure, for reaffirming the cult links between Apollo and Dionysus; cf. Vamvouri Ruffy (2004) 196–205.

33 See the hypotheses and detailed commentary offered by Käppel (1992) 252–70 and by Furley and Bremer (2001) 82–3.

34 Euripides, *Ion* 1571–94; for the four tribes presented by Solon, see Plutarch, *Life of Solon* 23.4–5 and already in Herodotus 5.66.2 as well as Aristotle, *Constitution of Athens* 41.2, who attributes this division of the Attic people into four tribes to Ion himself.

35 The manipulation of the genealogy is evident here – indeed contradictory – since in the tradition attested as early as Hesiod (fr. 9 Merkelbach-West), Xuthus' father was Hellen and his brothers were Dorus and Aeolus, and he himself was the father of Ion: thus it is the Ionians who, from an eponymous standpoint, held the subordinate position to the Aeolians and the Dorians: cf. also Herodotus 7.94 and 8.44.2, as well as the study by Hall (1997) 51–6. On the genealogy and the status of Xuthus from the Athenian perspective, see Euripides, *Ion* 290–3, 673–5, 808–16, and 1058–73.

36 Euripides, *Ion* 8–36; see also 260–82 and 492–506. In the structuralist perspective adopted by Loraux (1981) 207–9, the birth of Ion would replicate, inverted, that of the "*autochtone primordial*," Erichthonius. For the different versions of the birth of Erichthonius and of his *kourotróphia* (the 'raising of a boy') by the daughters of Cecrops, see the study of Parker (1987) 193–203.

37 Euripides, *Ion* 69–81; see also 661–3, where Xuthus appropriates the same pun. On *Ion* as a "tragedy of empire," see the references offered by Loraux (1981) 213–15.

38 Euripides, *Ion* 1582–8.

39 Cf. Parker (1996) 142–6, 313, and 325. Only Pausanias 1.31.3 (cf. also 8.1.5) mentions the *mnễma* ('monument') consecrated in the deme of Potami to Ion, whose father Xuthus, having moved to Athens, assumed the leadership of the Athenian army against Eleusis; see also Strabo 8.7.1, who takes up the genealogy proposed by Hesiod (cf. supra n. 35), but who indicates that after the victory of Ion against the Thracian army of Eumolpus, the Athenians entrusted their city to Ion. On Ion as the son of Apollo, see Plato, *Euthydemus* 302cd (yet another isolated testimony).

40 Concerning the "culture of choral song" that Greek culture is, see the references cited by Kowalzig (2004) 42–65; for ritual memory, see Calame (2006) *passim*.

9: MYTH AND GREEK ART: CREATING A VISUAL LANGUAGE

Jenifer Neils

In perusing any book devoted to Greek art, one is struck by the ancient Greeks' obsession with their gods, heroes, and mythological creatures. From the earliest extant work of figurative art produced in the so-called Dark Ages, the terracotta centaur from Lefkandi (ca. 950–900 BC), to that icon of late Hellenistic group sculpture, the marble Laocoon (ca. 30–20 BC), Greek artists and their patrons were drawn to mythological subjects not only for their intrinsic interest but also for the important roles they played in explaining the cosmos and shedding light on human nature. Although Greek artists shared this interest in mythological narrative with poets, they did not illustrate written texts; rather, they were guided by that oral culture or *Volksvorstellung* that was an essential part of every Greek's upbringing.[1] They, like all artists, were heavily influenced by the work of their predecessors, the demands of the marketplace, and the restrictions imposed by their medium. That said, Greek narrative art displays an amazing degree of imagination, ingenuity, and originality that continues to fascinate today, as it must have engaged viewers in antiquity.

Numerous books, not to mention multivolume lexica, have been devoted to the subject of myth in Greek art.[2] It would be foolhardy to attempt to encompass the entirety of this intriguing and vast topic in a single essay. Therefore, this chapter will examine two specific concerns of Greek painters and sculptors when faced with the challenge of narrating in visual, as opposed to literary, terms a specific story involving gods, heroes, or fantastic creatures. First, what devices did the artist employ for depicting a myth and how did this visual language come about? Second, how did the artist make his chosen theme relevant to a particular audience at a specific point in time? In order for a work of art to succeed in narrating a myth, it must employ a grammar understood by its viewers and relate in some fashion to the *Zeitgeist* of contemporary society. As much as possible, I will let the art speak for itself and examine it independent of any literary tradition.[3] This essay will also concentrate on the art of ancient Athens not only because of the quantity of extant material, especially painted vases, but also because we know more about the cultural and political history of this city than that of any other Greek *polis*. Before analyzing the origins of the visual language devised in the Greek pictorial tradition, we will begin with a highly developed example of mythical narration.

AN EXEMPLUM

At about the time that the Parthenon was nearing completion, an Athenian vase painter (whom we call the Codrus Painter) decorated a wine cup, inside and out, with seven deeds of the local hero Theseus (Figure 3). In the central tondo the hero is shown in his most readily recognizable exploit, the slaying of the Minotaur. Encircling the tondo (beginning at 12 o'clock and moving clockwise) and repeated on the exterior of the cup are six additional deeds of Theseus: he contends with the wrestler Cercyon, fells Procrustes with an axe, topples Sciron off his cliff, drives the Marathonian bull to Athens, binds Sinis to his pine tree, and slays the sow in spite of the protests of its aged mistress Crommyo. This painted vase is the result of a long tradition of heroic imagery in Greek art, and as such represents a fully evolved, sophisticated visual language – imagery that cannot be taken literally, but must be carefully "read" to be understood. So, for instance, the male figures are all "heroically" nude, although as a traveler Theseus might be expected to wear a tunic, cloak, and traveling cap. His human opponents are portrayed as distinctly "other" or unheroic: heavily bearded, balding, older. They are shown in compromised poses (falling, legs splayed) and gesturing frantically for a reprieve.[4] Theseus' sword accompanies him in every episode, although it is distinctly out of place in the wrestling match; however, as one of the *gnorismata* (tokens) of the hero it is his most significant identifying attribute. There are few elements of setting, only those necessitated by the scene: Sciron's rock, the pine tree of Sinis, and perhaps the old woman as a local personification of Crommyon.

But there is more here than meets the eye. Ancient viewers would have noticed that some of Theseus' deeds resembled those of the great Panhellenic hero Heracles who captured a boar and a bull and wrestled an ogre named Antaeus, but that other deeds demonstrated greater mental than physical prowess by turning the tables, so to speak, on his human opponents. Theseus also bears a club, the traditional weapon of Heracles, as he drives the bull to Athens. (Later texts claim he obtained it in defeating the club-man Periphetes, but this episode is not represented on cups such as these.) A more subtle reference to Heracles can be found in the tondo where, instead of slaying the Minotaur as in earlier images, Theseus is shown dragging the monster from a Doric porch-like structure; the meander pattern to the right alerts the viewer to the concept of the labyrinth. This rare composition deliberately recalls earlier vase paintings of Heracles leading Cerberus from the entrance to Hades and so may represent an attempt on the part of the Athenian mythmakers to suggest that their hero too overcame death itself and so attained immortality.[5]

There was nothing radically new in the depiction of these deeds, which had been part of the vase painters' repertoire since ca. 510 BC, nor in the vehicle for their display, the so-called cycle cup – although both were quite novel at the end of the previous century.[6] What would have impressed viewers of this vase is the startling visual device where the figures appear in exactly the same location inside and out, as if one were seeing through the walls of the cup. Only in the Sciron and sow episodes is Theseus' pose reversed from back (interior) to front (exterior) so that he can maintain the weapon in his right hand. Why would the artist go to such pains to echo the pose, placement, and action of the hero inside and out? Is it simply an artistic conceit or does it convey a specific message to the viewer? It has long been recognized by scholars that Theseus here takes on the poses of the famous sculptural group set up in the Agora in 477-6 BC, namely the Tyrannicides by the sculptors Kritios and Nesiotes (Figure 4). With his cloak draped over his extended left arm Theseus not only is defending himself from the tusks of the sow, but also is mimicking the older tyrant-slayer Aristogeiton; and with Sciron's foot basin raised overhead he takes on the undefended pose of the younger Harmodios. Ironically (to us) the future king of Athens is portrayed as a freedom fighter, a hero of the early democracy.

Further political references could be seen in the episodes placed directly above (Cercyon) and below (bull) the Minotaur-slaying. The former took place at Eleusis, the latter at Marathon. In Herodotus' account of the Persian Wars (8.64), an omen in the form of a dust cloud arose at Eleusis and drifted to Salamis, foretelling the naval victory over the Persians. At the earlier battle of Marathon Theseus was said to have arisen from the ground to aid his fellow Athenians. The deeds are not depicted in chronological order, since Theseus captured the bull after his arrival in Athens. So it seems the artist has given these two deeds special prominence in the axis perpendicular to the handles because they reference locations in Attica closely associated with the defeat of the Persians. With its emphasis on the poses of Harmodios and Aristogeiton and its subtle references to Salamis and Marathon, this cycle cup does much more than recount some of the deeds of the hero Theseus; it rewrites history by associating Athens' glorious Bronze-Age hero with its glorious present. For the Athenians their myths were their history, and they saw no problem in embellishing them for the greater glory of the *polis*.

If we think of this wine cup in its original context of the Greek symposium, it could have served as an exemplum to young Athenian males. They too should perform heroic deeds for the good of their city as well-trained athletes, skilled hunters, and brave warriors. The calculated poses of Theseus may have recalled to the symposiasts the general Miltiades' exhortation before the great encounter at Marathon to the polemarch Callimachus to fight to make Athens free, as the Tyrannicides had done before him (Herodotus 6.109). Given the date of this vase, its depiction of the hero Theseus served as a role model for Athenian youth at the beginning of a new military challenge to the democratic polis, that of the recently begun Peloponnesian Wars. Thus the Codrus Painter not only invented a new referential form of imagery for the myth of Theseus, but also devised a compositional format that placed the hero in a position to serve as an example for contemporary viewers in late fifth-century Athens.

When did this sophisticated visual language of myth begin and how did it evolve? When did artists incorporate allusions to recent events in mythological narratives to reinforce their message? What roles did the depictions of Greek myth in media ranging from minutely carved gems to vast temple pediments play in society? Because of the great losses from antiquity, such as most monumental paintings, these questions are not easy to answer. But by starting at the beginning we can perhaps trace a likely scenario for how a work of art as multivalent as the Theseus cup came about.

HORSE, BIRD, AND MAN: THE ARTIST'S TOOLKIT

In the first two centuries of Greek art (900–700 BC), the figurative repertoire of artists consisted of simple geometricized forms: humans, quadrupeds, and birds. With this basic toolkit the artist could create super- or subhuman creatures of myth by devising imaginative combinations. Thus, for instance, attaching a horse's hindquarters to a human resulted in a creature that combined the powers of human intelligence and equine strength – making it an equal opponent (Nessus) as well as a tutor and friend (Chiron, Pholus) of gods and heroes. In precanonical Greek art this hybrid, commonly known as the centaur, was also used to depict other monsters such as Medusa (by the addition of a skirt) or the Minotaur. A male figure with only an equine tail and ears became the subhuman satyr, while a horse protome (forequarters) attached to a rooster's body produced the somewhat ridiculous *Mischwesen* known as the hippalektryon. To create a daemon of subhuman intelligence the artist would surmount a human body with an animal's head, as in the case of the canonical Minotaur (see Figure 3). Wings were added to horses, enabling them to fly (Pegasus) and power the chariots of heavenly divinities. A female with wings could be either a goddess (*potnia theron*, Iris, Nike) or a monster, if given an ugly or leering frontal face (Harpy, Fury, Medusa). Fish tails added to human torsos resulted in fantastic marine creatures such as Triton or Skylla. Finally, perhaps only the Greeks would invent a semidivine being that was both male and female, Hermaphroditus.

Another method available to the creative artist for fabricating a mythological daemon was simply to multiply its form. Dual- and triple-bodied humans, such as the Molione/Actorione and Geryon, are formidable opponents of heroes, as are multiheaded dogs (Cerberus, Orthus), snakes (Hydra), and hybrids (Chimera). Many mythological figures take the form of male twins (Dioscuri, Cercopes, Boreads) or female triads (Gorgons, Fates, Graiae). Hecate could be depicted either as a normal woman or as a triple-bodied divinity. Most of the canonical hybrids were either invented or adapted from Near Eastern or Egyptian prototypes (e.g., sphinx, siren) by the mid-seventh century and continued relatively unchanged throughout classical art and well beyond.[7]

Other conventions that generally operate in Greek figurative art are *horror vacui*, the horizontal ground line, isocephalism, avoidance of the frontal face, and size as an indicator of status. Until specific attributes or inscribed names are included in narrative scenes, we cannot always be sure that myths are intended, as for example in late-eighth century BC scenes of a man hunting a deer (Heracles and the hind?), two males confronting a tripod (boxers or Apollo and Heracles?), or a man and woman boarding a ship (Figure 5: Theseus and Ariadne? Paris and Helen? Jason and Medea?).[8] Items of dress, such as belts or special headgear, in archaic Greek sculpture and painting may indicate heroic or divine status, but are too generic to be decisive for identification. Old-fashioned conveyances such as the chariot or types of armor such as the Dipylon shield (as in the hold of the ship in Figure 5) presumably were not used in battle in historic times, but whether they allude to the Homeric past is an issue that has not been satisfactorily resolved.[9] In later Greek art, the figure moving to the right or auspicious side is usually the victor, although when this principle was adopted is not easy to determine. It is clear enough in two similar Trojan War compositions that are popular on Attic black-figure vases of the mid-sixth century: Ajax carrying the corpse of Achilles usually moves to the left, while Aeneas rescuing his father Anchises moves to the right.[10]

In painting and relief sculpture, elements of setting such as landscape are minimal,[11] and temporal indicators are almost nonexistent. Archaic and earlier works of art tend to illustrate the high point of the action, for example, the slaying of the monster or the heat of battle, rather than episodes taking place before or after the main event. In order to represent two events in any particular narrative, an artist might conflate two scenes such as King Priam being killed at the altar and his grandson Astyanax being hurled from the walls of Troy (Figure 6). In the powerful and shocking formula adopted by Attic vase painters, the slayer Neoptolemos uses the child as a weapon to cudgel the old man to death. Thus, in one blow, two generations and the future of Troy are extinguished. This same schema was adapted to a more comic context in which Heracles likewise slays a king (Busiris) at an altar, holding another Egyptian upside down by the ankle.[12]

That these basic principles persisted throughout Greek art can be illustrated by a large red-figure skyphos painted about the same time as the Theseus cup, ca. 430 BC (Figure 7).[13] The subject is the Return of Hephaestus at the point at which the smith god rides his mule into the presence of his mother Hera, trapped on a magic throne. The figures move to the right on a horizontal ground line and fill the space from top to bottom, a principle that results in making Hephaestus much shorter than Dionysus. The music-making satyr is also smaller, either because he is an attendant, like the girl fanning Hera, or on account of his younger age (which, however, is not consistent with his balding head). Each figure lugs along his distinctive attributes (tongs and hammer for Hephaestus, kantharos [high-handled cup] and thyrsus [ivy-bedecked wand] for Dionysus), although they are hardly necessary for the action at hand; in lieu of inscriptions they serve to identify the protagonists. There is no reference to the past (Hephaestus does not appear to be drunk – although he wears an ivy wreath – or even lame) or the future (no sign of the prize-bride Aphrodite), nor is there any indication of setting. Dionysus is the key player here and he is appropriately placed in the center of the composition on a large wine vessel.

A depiction of this same myth on a vase painted a mere ten years later demonstrates how radically these basic conventions could be altered under the influence of monumental wall painting. The body of a volute-crater by Polion (Figure 8) depicts the same scene, but with the figures scattered over the surface, and with hints of landscape in the form of rocks and trees.[14] The action moves to the left as a satyr helps the drunken Hephaestus up from the couch of Dionysus. Hera is relegated to the upper left corner, seated frontally to indicate her helplessness, and her fan-waving attendant is now a siren with arms. Much of the surface is taken up with extraneous satyrs and maenads conversing in pairs. Reflecting the composition and style of major painting, this vase shows how artists could combine the temporal and spatial aspects of a specific episode within a larger format. It also demonstrates how a vase-painter could transpose the setting of an age-old myth: instead of an equestrian procession it has become a symposium with cushions, music, and Dionysus featured in the role of the symposiarch. Such a scene is particularly appropriate to the shape of the vase, a wine crater, which served as the centerpiece of the symposium. The running figure of a satyr who holds the smith god's tongs and lights his way with a torch may have suggested to the painter the ritual torch-race held at the Hephaisteia in Athens, for he has represented this event on the neck of the vase. Hence this mythological narrative on a symposium vessel (like Theseus on the cycle cup, Figure 3) can reference aspects of the real life of its users, their drinking parties and their festivals.[15]

Naturally, format and medium play major roles in determining how mythological scenes are depicted. So, for instance, a vase painter portrays the birth of Athena as a tiny doll-like goddess emerging from the head of a large enthroned god flanked by as many standing attendants as fill the available space. For a sculptor decorating a temple pediment, the small goddess would be invisible from below. Thus, on the Parthenon's east pediment, Athena is depicted full-sized standing beside her father, flanked by Olympians in various poses to fit the raking angles of the pediment. In the small corners are Helios rising and Selene descending, who together symbolize both the setting (the heavens) and the time (dawn). Round fields such as those of gems, coins, and cup interiors usually restrict the protagonists to one or two figures, while square fields, such as painted or carved metopes (square plaques in the Doric frieze), admit two or three. Long friezes are the most suitable formats for multifigured narratives such as the divine procession to the wedding reception of Peleus and Thetis painted on several early sixth-century Attic vases, or the gigantomachy that is carved in low relief on the Treasury of the Siphnians at Delphi (ca. 525 BC) and in high relief on the altar of Zeus at Pergamon (mid-second century BC). In both of these multifigured reliefs, the gods and giants are labeled for the sake of the viewer, who might otherwise have trouble distinguishing individual combatants.

By examining what myths Greek artists avoided or clearly had difficulty depicting, we can come closer to understanding the relationship of myth to art and life. Although a favorite *topos* of Greek myth, the act of metamorphosis is especially challenging for any artist.[16] Dionysus' transformation of the Tyrrhenian pirates into dolphins is not essayed in Greek art until the later fourth century on the sculpted frieze of the Lysicrates monument in Athens, and Actaeon's conversion into a stag is simply a matter of attaching horns to his head, enough to impel his hunting dogs to attack him. Artists succeed better at the metamorphosis of Odysseus' companions into swine by the magician Circe, for they can revert to the time-honored tradition of tacking animal heads onto human bodies to create figures of subhuman intelligence.[17] The multiple transformations of Thetis in her wrestling match with her suitor Peleus can be symbolized by a lion atop her shoulder, a simple but legible solution to the problem of representing corporeal change. Differentiating between different states of consciousness such as sleep and death was also a challenge, and so winged male personifications could represent these altered states. Hypnos is much more common and is often depicted in miniature, like the lion of Thetis, crouching on the body of the sleeping giant Alcyoneus.[18] This marked tendency in Greek art to personify abstract concepts even carries over into inanimate objects that could easily be represented concretely. A case in point is the elixir of immortality that is offered by Athena to one of the Seven who marched against Thebes, Tydeus. While in Etruscan art it is depicted as a jug held by Athena, the Attic vase painter invents a personification labeled Athanasia, a young girl whom the goddess leads by the hand to the mortally wounded warrior.[19]

No doubt some myths were too repellant to the ancient Greeks to be depicted in art. While fairly common in Greek myth, portrayals of human sacrifice are a rarity. As in depictions of animal sacrifice, the few images of the sacrifice of Iphigeneia show her being led to the altar, not the cutting of her throat. The one rather bloody Attic vase painting of the sacrifice of Polyxena was almost certainly intended for an Etruscan audience, since most amphorae of this type (Tyrrhenian) have been found in central Italy. Likewise, the dismemberment of Pentheus by his mother and her bacchic companions was not a common subject. When it came to depicting physical deformities, the Greek artist was clearly at a loss or unwilling to render the human body in a less than ideal form. The one-eyed giant Polyphemus is often larger than Odysseus and his men, but given the predilection for profile views, his single eye is not evident in the numerous seventh- and sixth-century painted depictions of his blinding. The multieyed monster Argos who guarded the cow Io was endowed either with two Janus-like faces, or more often multiple eyes covering his body. The lame Hephaestus is seldom depicted with a deformed foot; only his riding of the mule alludes to his disability (see Figure 7). One of the only mythological figures represented as severely deformed is Geras, the personification of old age; his pathetic emaciated body sometimes bears the brunt of Heracles' club.[20] Clearly the preferred figure of Greek artists was the perfect male specimen, namely, the hero.

HERACLES: FROM HERO TO GOD

As the Panhellenic hero *par excellence*, Heracles is represented in all periods of Greek art and in nearly all regions of Greece. He appears struggling with Apollo for the tripod in the earliest narrative art of the Late Geometric period (ca. 750–700 BC) and can be found in a Roman copy of a late Hellenistic painting transformed into a weary family man with Arcadia and his son Telephos. The iconography of Heracles changes over time, as does his meaning for a Greek audience, but his popularity never seems to wane. He is especially prevalent in Attic vase painting from the sixth to the fourth centuries, and it is in this medium that one can best plot the changes that occur in his imagery.

Not surprisingly, in sixth-century Athenian vase painting, myths highlighting military, athletic, and hunting prowess predominate, as these represent the primary values of elite male society at that time. Scenes of the Trojan War, funeral games in honor of kings (Pelias) and heroes (Patroclus), and group expeditions in search of major prey (Calydonian boar hunt) are popular themes. Because he exemplifies all of these talents, Heracles is the sixth-century hero *par excellence*: he fights formidable opponents (Kyknos, Amazons, Geryon), competes in athletic contests (wrestling Antaeus, archery competition with Eurytos'

sons), and single-handedly conquers wild beasts (Nemean lion, Cerynitan hind, Erymanthian boar, Stymphalian birds). By contrast, other
heroes such as Theseus, Perseus, and Bellerophon have only one claim
to fame in the art of this period – the conquest of a monster (Minotaur,
Medusa, Chimera). The labors, deeds, and *parerga* of the hero fit a variety of formats (vases, pediments, metopes, gems) and had a universal
appeal throughout Greek lands.

It is enlightening to compare the number of Attic vases with representations of Heracles with those of other heroes. According to the
Beazley Database there are 3,751 vase paintings of Heracles, compared
to 786 of Theseus, 114 of Perseus, 27 of Bellerophon, and only 10 of
Jason. Predictably, Heracles is also the most popular mythical hero in
Laconian vase-painting, which is limited to the sixth century, and it is
interesting to note that he is sometimes dressed as a warrior, a feature
calculated to appeal to the Spartans.[21] On Corinthian vases, Heracles
is also a common motif, but the choice of deeds is rather different
from that in the Attic corpus. While the Nemean lion is by far the
most popular deed on Athenian black-figure vases, that of the Lernaean
hydra predominates on Corinthian vases, perhaps because the labor was
performed not far from Corinth.[22] Naturally, Theseus is more popular
in Athens than elsewhere, but his sixth-century repertoire is limited
almost exclusively to the Cretan adventure. On the archaic Acropolis,
Heracles is far more prevalent, being featured on at least four pediments. This sampling of regional variations demonstrates how local
taste affected not only the choice of myths but also their manner of
representation.

Looking at Attic vase representations of Heracles diachronically is
also revelatory. While the Nemean lion constitutes twenty-five percent
of all black-figure scenes of Heracles, in red-figure before 450 BC the
percentage drops to a mere four. After 450 a significant shift occurs from
depictions of his Labors and other adventures to the hero's apotheosis
and his appearance in the company of the Olympian gods. In the fourth
century, the favorite themes are the apples of the Hesperides and his
initiation into the Eleusinian Mysteries. These more metaphysical scenes
can be related to the humanizing process that takes place in literary and
philosophical circles. Likewise, his appearance as an infant strangling
the snakes sent by the jealous Hera on early fourth-century silver coins
from Byzantion to Croton demonstrates a more human side to the
brawny hero.[23] The fact that Alexander the Great minted coins with
the head of Heracles in his own likeness attests to the universality of the
hero as an emblem of "Greekness" in the early Hellenistic period. This

ubiquitous and long-lived hero even survived pagan antiquity, emerging as the figure of Fortitude in Christian art.

ICONOGRAPHIC INNOVATORS

Some especially gifted artists could rise above the restrictions of their particular medium and artistic conventions to produce new perspectives on traditional themes. Within the standard repertoire of sixth-century mythological vase paintings, one Attic painter, Exekias, stands out for his individual treatment of traditional themes and his invention of new motifs. In contrast with the work of his contemporaries, Trojan War scenes predominate in his repertoire. He takes the suicide of Ajax, normally crudely shown as a nude, bleeding warrior on hands and knees impaled on his sword, and makes it a psychological drama in which Ajax is methodically planting his sword into the ground (see Figure 18). Even the palm tree behind the hero is said to be "weeping" in sympathy with the hero, an unusual instance of the pathetic fallacy.[24] Exekias can also be credited with the new motif of Achilles and Ajax gaming, first seen on the amphora now in the Vatican, but not attested in any extant literary account of the Trojan War. Again, this scene succeeds in portraying the personalities of the heroes with a detail as small as the heel of Ajax lifted slightly off the ground, which suggests his impetuous nature.[25] Even the artist's portrayal of Achilles slaying the Amazon Penthesilea (the menacing face of the hero encapsulated in his black helmet contrasting with the unprotected white face of his victim) projects in its simplicity more of the drama of the encounter than other depictions of this duel. By limiting his mythological scenes to one or two figures where lesser artists jammed them with subsidiary figures to fill the space, Exekias achieved a dramatic intensity not found elsewhere in archaic Greek art.[26]

The same kind of innovative iconography can be found in the Early Classical sculptural program of the Temple of Zeus at Olympia (ca. 465–457 BC), which also displays an interest in the temporal progression of a narrative and the psychologically potent moment. The labors of Heracles, son of Zeus, were appropriately chosen for the twelve metope slots of the porches; this hero was credited with establishing the sanctuary of Zeus as well as its games. The fact that Heracles is shown without one of his distinctive attributes, his bow, has been interpreted as a calculated response to the Persian War, which was viewed as a contest of spearmen (Greeks) versus archers (Persians).[27] The pediments display a quiet, localized scene on the east, with Zeus in the center, and a turbulent battle in the west, presided over by Apollo.

Because these metopes represent the first known *dodecathlon* of the hero in Greek art, the format may have dictated the number twelve, which subsequently became the canonical number of Heracles' labors. The anonymous master designer at Olympia not only varied the temporal aspects of these labors by showing some already completed (Nemean lion, Figure 9, Stymphalian birds), but also portrayed the hero physically aging as he progressed from his first labor (lion), where he is beardless, to his attainment of immortality. In a prescient way, the Nemean lion metope with its exhausted hero heralds the famous image of the "Weary Heracles" devised by the sculptor Lysippus at the end of the fourth century. The last and least represented of Heracles' labors, cleaning the stable of Augias, is one that took place near Olympia and so perhaps was invented for this locale.

Locale is almost certainly responsible for the subject of the temple's east pediment, the chariot race of Pelops and King Oinomaus – a scene that clearly references the most prestigious contest of the ancient Games. What the viewer beheld was not the race itself, which resulted in the death of the king, but a group of figures flanking the central deity Zeus, rather like a Renaissance *sacra conversazione*. As in the suicide of Ajax by Exekias, the viewer is presented with the psychologically tense moment before the inevitable bloodshed; only the face of the seer registers the tragic events to come. The artist has managed to convey the personalities of the protagonists with the subtle language of stance (haughty Oinomaus with arm akimbo), gesture (his brooding wife with her hand to her chin), and facial expression (furrowed brow of the seer) so that it is easy to identify them even if the story is not well known. While the east pediment represents the prelude to a wedding, the west shows the outcome of a wedding where chaos has erupted because of the drunkenness of the centaurs. In many ways, the west pediment is more traditional, with its big on-going battle (centauromachy), a subject readily adaptable to the challenging triangular spaces of temple facades and one much favored by Archaic and Classical artists.[28]

THE BIG BATTLES

Although battle imagery had been part of the Athenian painted repertoire since at least the end of the Middle Geometric period (ca. 770 BC) and had remained a popular theme, it came into its own in the wake of the Persian Wars. The most commonly depicted multifigured battles were the centauromachy and the Amazonomachy, which became ubiquitous in architectural sculpture and wall painting during the Classical period, especially in Athens, where the themes were reprised on large red-figure vases. Perhaps this is not surprising, since the beloved heroes Theseus and Heracles took part in both. These battles make their appearance in monumental wall painting in the Theseum in Athens, in friezes within the Temple of Apollo at Bassae, and not once, but twice on the Parthenon (west and south metopes, and statue of Athena Parthenos). We have already noted the centauromachy of Theseus in the west pediment at Olympia, and it was engraved on the shield of the colossal Bronze Athena by the Athenian sculptor Phidias on the Acropolis. The battle of Theseus and the Amazons was depicted in the Stoa Poikile by the mural painter Mikon and by Phidias on the footstool of the chryselephantine statue of Zeus at Olympia, while that of Heracles was carved on the bar of the throne. The trend continues in the fourth century outside Athens, with the Amazonomachy and centauromachy on the metopes of the Tholos at Delphi and the battle with the Amazons in the west pediment of the temple of Asclepius at Epidaurus and on one of the friezes of the Mausoleum at Halicarnassus. And even in the Hellenistic period these themes are reprised in the architectural sculpture of numerous monuments, particularly heroa (mausoleum at Belevi, Ptolemaion at Limyra).[29]

Scholars have detected a slight but important change in these popular battles in the early fifth century BC. The battle with the centaurs moves indoors to the wedding feast, so that women are present, including the important bride Hippodameia. The Amazonomachy, at least in Attic depictions, is the female warriors' expedition to Athens to rescue their queen Antiope and takes place on the slopes of the Acropolis itself, recalling the Persians' violation of Athena's sanctuary in 480 BC. Tellingly, Mikon's painting of Theseus fighting the Amazons was juxtaposed with the famous painting of the Battle of Marathon in the Stoa Poikile in Athens, and it is generally believed that these "big battle" scenes allude to the Greeks' victories over the Persians. These instances demonstrate the malleability of myth in art, which can be adapted to new political circumstances as needed. However, the appearance of the Amazonomachy on the tomb of a Persian satrap in Caria would indicate that they had become stock themes by the mid-fourth century BC, and the political allusions were either different or irrelevant. The Amazon theme was revived ca. 200 BC, when Attalus I dedicated the two-thirds life-size bronze figures of dead barbarians (giant, Amazon, Persian, Galatian) on the Athenian Acropolis, in commemoration of his own victories over the Gauls.[30]

MYTH AND POLITICS

This symbiosis between mythical representations and contemporary politics is most evident in Athens because of the large number of extant vases and sculptures, as well as texts describing lost works of art. It has been documented that the cycle cups devoted to the youthful deeds of Theseus began to appear just as Cleisthenes was reforming the political system from tyranny to democracy, ca. 510–500 BC. Needing something grander than a mere Minotaur-slayer to reflect their new status, the Athenians embellished the life of their local hero by giving him a series of youthful deeds akin to those of the renowned hero Heracles. The cycle cup (and later the metopes of the Treasury of the Athenians at Delphi and those of the Hephaesteum) was the vehicle invented to publicize these new exploits, which by combination with the Minotaur made clear to the viewer that Theseus was being depicted. While many scholars have posited an epic poem of the life of Theseus as the source for these representations, the cycle cups almost never show the deeds in chronological order; rather, we have here a scenario where Athenian artists faced the challenge of grafting new exploits onto the persona of a well-known local hero, and so devised an until-now novel, cyclical mode of narration for the dissemination of the hero's early life.

Similarly, in the mid to late fifth century, when the Athenians wished to highlight their myth of autochthony, they commissioned artists to depict the birth of Erichthonius, the offspring of Hephaestus' unsuccessful attempt on Athena that resulted in the impregnation of the earth. The baby is usually shown in the arms of Ge, who rises out of the ground to hand him over to his surrogate mother Athena, while male figures such as Cecrops, Zeus, or Hephaestus look on with approval.[31] However, on one of the latest versions (Figure 10) produced during the Peloponnesian Wars, the earth goddess is shown seated on the ground in a luxurious garden filled with lovely women; Athena dashes forward with a receiving blanket while baby Erichthonius reaches toward her. Because the three girls looking down from above must be the daughters of Cecrops on the Acropolis, Ge is here identified as Attica, both earth in general and a place personification. This vase by the Meidias Painter is a squat lekythos, or perfume flask used by women, and its function may account for the unique feminization of this founding myth of Athens.[32]

In the past, scholars argued for a close correlation of myth depictions and contemporary political events. The classic example is Boardman's argument that the mid-sixth-century black-figure hydriae (water jugs) with scenes of Athena driving Heracles to Olympus in a chariot were prompted by the tyrant Peisistratus' stratagem for retaking the Acropolis, namely driving into Athens with a tall girl dressed up as Athena (Herodotus 1.60). Peisistratus' personal identification with Heracles would then be the impetus for all the Archaic pediments on the Acropolis that depict the hero, and much else in sixth-century Athenian art.[33] More recently doubts have been cast on this approach, especially, as we have seen above, because Heracles was such a universal hero and one of great popularity at all times in Greek art. In his apotheosis, he represents the aspirations of Everyman to become immortal.

GODS

Immortal, ageless, and omnipotent, the Olympian gods were objects of intense veneration; consequently their most significant form of representation in Greek art was the cult statue, few of which survive. Although these statues per se had little or no narrative content, they often bore subsidiary decoration of a mythological nature, as we have already noted in the case of the *Athena Parthenos* (centauromachy on sandals, Amazonomachy and gigantomachy on shield). Likewise, the throne of Zeus at Olympia and the painted fence surrounding it carried a number of disparate themes, but some clearly related to his role as the god of justice (the slaughter of the Niobids, the rape of Cassandra, Prometheus). Cult statue bases, in particular, seem to have been loci for myths relating to the famous progeny of the gods in the Classical period; so, for instance, the bedecking of Pandora in the Parthenon, the birth of Erichthonius in the Hephaesteum, the *anados* (rising from the ground) of Aphrodite at Olympia, and the presentation of Helen on the Nemesis base at Rhamnus. These contexts, like the east pediment of the Parthenon with the birth of Athena, allowed for the inclusion of all or most of the Olympian gods, as well as other lesser deities such as Helios and Selene.[34] While the collectivity of the canonical twelve gods is represented for the first time on the Parthenon frieze in the mid-fifth century, they were certainly referenced in earlier imagery where groups of them are shown seated together (e.g., east frieze of the Siphnian Treasury at Delphi, ca. 530–525 BC).

The one narrative episode in which a large number of gods participate is the gigantomachy, a theme that first occurs in the early sixth century on large Attic vases dedicated on the Acropolis and continues until the Hellenistic period in relief sculpture. Its most famous manifestation may have been in textiles, for the subject was woven into the *peplos* or woolen robe presented to Athena Polias at her major Athenian festival, the Panathenaia. The central figures in most of the fuller versions of this battle are Zeus, Athena, Heracles, and Ge, but even deities from an earlier generation, such as Themis, can take part, as on the north frieze of the Siphnian Treasury. Thereafter, and on smaller fields such as amphorae and metopes, individual duels are depicted, the most popular being Athena versus Enceladus. That this theme could also allude to the Persian Wars is perhaps indicated by the red-figure lekythos in Cleveland of ca. 480 BC (Figure 11), where the giant's shield device is a centaur brandishing a tree.

Another popular theme involving the gods is amorous pursuit, particularly of mortals. Young Trojan princes appear to be the most attractive victims; Zeus pursues Ganymede, who is given a hoop to indicate his youth, while Eos carries off Tithonus with his usual attribute, a lyre. She also snatches up the young hunter Cephalus, son of the Athenian princess Herse by Hermes. Taking after their mother Eos, the winged wind gods are also notorious pursuers in Attic art; Zephyrus was attracted to the beautiful boy Hyacinthus, while his brother Boreas chased the Athenian princess Oreithyia.[35] Perhaps not surprisingly, given its consequences for mankind, the myth of Hades' rape of Persephone is largely ignored in Greek art, except in ritual (terracotta plaques from Locri) or funerary contexts (Vergina tomb).[36]

One of the most common manifestations of the individual gods in Greek art is what one might call their epiphanies. Whether descending from the sky, as in the case of Nikes alighting on the roofs of temples in the form of marble acroteria (roof sculptures), or emerging from the earth, as in the various *anadoi* of goddesses like Persephone and Aphrodite, divinities who magically appear in human or heroic contexts are especially favored. Athena, for instance, is regularly depicted at the side of heroes (Heracles, Theseus, Perseus, Jason), not actively involved (see Figure 9), but simply standing in a bouleutic capacity as their patron deity. Apollo and Artemis are often depicted as a pair at weddings, providing music as the bridal couple depart in their chariot. Most common of all is Eros, who flutters around mortal brides on wedding vases, ensuring the appropriate romantic ambience. On a somewhat darker note, divine mothers (Thetis, Eos) look on as their sons (Achilles, Memnon) fight duels in the Trojan War. Often, on Classical vases and votive reliefs, deities are shown pouring libations onto altars, either singly or in groups, such as the Delian triad (Apollo, Artemis, and their mother Leto). As Himmelmann has shown, the pouring of a libation by the gods is not a rite performed for the benefit of someone else, but is an act in which the gods reveal their own sanctity.[37]

CONCLUSION

As we have seen in the discussion above, mythical representations are hardly static, and they changed considerably over the many centuries of Greek art. Some common trends are the "youthening" of gods and heroes, the decline in monstrosity, along with increasing naturalism, and the tendency for narrative subjects to become purely decorative. Thus Dionysus and Hermes lose their beards in the change from black- to red-figure vase painting, and Apollo can be portrayed as a young boy playfully killing a lizard (*Apollo Sauroktonos*) in the mid-fourth century. Medusa becomes a beautiful woman (albeit with snaky locks), and Athena no longer pops out of Zeus' head as a doll-like creature, but stands regally beside him. Sirens become conventional mourners on late Classical grave stelae, battles with Amazons and centaurs are stock themes in post-Classical architectural sculpture, and Dionysus and his retinue are ubiquitous on painted pottery of the fourth century. Nike, who once bore tokens of victory to mortals, becomes a purely symbolic figure, as does Eros.

In this discussion, readers may have missed some of their favorite subjects, such as the Trojan Horse, faithful Penelope, the birth of Helen from the egg, or the voyage of the Argo, themes that are strangely nearly absent from Greek art. Why Greek artists or their patrons preferred certain subjects over others is still a matter of speculation since we have no testimonials to guide us. Future excavation, especially of areas beyond the Greek mainland, may bring to light new and different mythical representations to add to our vast store of images. This artistic legacy remains one of the richest sources for our understanding of Greek myth and its role in Greek life.

BIBLIOGRAPHIC NOTE

Rather than provide a footnote for every image mentioned in this essay, I recommend that readers pursue their own interests by consulting the appropriate entries in the comprehensive *Lexicon Iconographicum Mythologiae Classicae* (Zurich 1981–1997). Those without access to this resource can consult the handbook of Carpenter (1991), a compendium of over 300 images arranged typologically. Books devoted to Greek art and myth abound; some of the more recent include Shapiro (1994), Woodford (2003), and Small (2003). For textual sources on works of art no longer extant, see Pollitt (1990).

NOTES

1   For the argument that Greek artists do not illustrate texts, see Snodgrass (1998) and Small (2003).
2   See Steuben (1968); Gantz (1993); Carpenter (1991). The most useful source for illustrations of Greek myth is LIMC.
3   For this reason, I will not consider the vase-painting of South Italy, which directly references theatrical performances. For representations of Greek tragedy, see O. Taplin's essay in Easterling (1997): 69–90.
4   For behavior and gestures that characterize the Other in Athenian vase painting, see McNiven (2000).
5   On Heracles in the Underworld, see Wünsche (2003)
6   For these youthful deeds of Theseus, see Neils (1987) and LIMC 7 (1994) s.v. Theseus (J. Neils).
7   On the origins and development of Greek *Mischwesen* see Padgett (2003). Medusa is an exception to the rule, as she eventually loses her monstrous appearance and paralyzes men with her beauty. Mayor (2000) proposes that some mythological creatures owe their invention to the Greeks' discovery of fossils. For illustrations of some of these precanonical hybrids, see Schefold 1966.
8   For such problems of identification in early Greek myth scenes, see Fittschen (1969) and Ahlberg-Cornell (1992).
9   For the problems surrounding the Dipylon shield, see Hurwit (1985) and the convenient summary by M. Moore in CVA New York 5 (USA 37, 2004): 8.
10   See Woodford and Loudon (1980).
11   See Chapter 11 by Cohen in this volume.
12   I owe this observation to Ian McPhee. On Heracles and Busiris, see M. C. Miller (2000).
13   Toledo Museum of Art 1982.88. See CVA Toledo 2 (USA 20, 1984): pls. 84–7 (C. Boulter and K. Luckner).
14   Ferrara, Museo Archeologico 3033. See *Archeologica classica* 5: pls. 62–5.
15   For the relation of this vase to the Hephaisteia, see Froning (1971): 78–81.
16   See Davies (1986).
17   It should be noted that the men are given a variety of heads, not just swine as in the *Odyssey*. See Giuliani (2004).

18 For these and other personifications, see Shapiro (1993). On Hypnos ibid. 148–58.
19 See Neils (1994).
20 On mythical figures with physical deformities, see Garland (1995).
21 For Heracles in Laconian vase painting, see Pipili (1987): 1–13, 111–12.
22 For Heracles in Corinthian vase painting, see Amyx (1988) 2: 628–32.
23 On Heracles in the Classical period, see Vollkommer (1988).
24 On weeping palms see Hurwit (1982) and the responses in *CJ* 78 (1983): 199–201.
25 On this point, see Moore (1980).
26 Boardman (1978) demonstrates Exekias' special interest in Trojan War scenes and credits him with the invention of nine previously unrepresented scenes.
27 For the suppression of Heracles' bow, quiver, and arrows on the Olympia metopes, see Cohen (1994).
28 For the sculptures of the Temple of Zeus at Olympia, see Ashmole (1972): 1–89.
29 For Amazons in Greek art until the end of the fifth century, see Bothmer 1957. For examples in Hellenistic architectural sculpture, see Webb (1996).
30 For the Attalid dedication, see Stewart (2004): 181–236.
31 On representations of the birth of Erichthonius and their relation to Athenian autochthony, see Shapiro (1998).
32 Cleveland Museum of Art 82.142. Attic red-figure lekythos attributed to the Meidias Painter, ca. 420–410 B.C. See Neils (1993).
33 See Boardman (1972).
34 On sculpted cult statue bases, see Kosmopoulou (2002): 111–44.
35 On these scenes in Attic art, see Kaempf-Dimitriadou (1979) and Lefkowitz (2002).
36 On the tomb painting at Vergina, see Andronikos (1994): esp. 100–114.
37 Himmelmann (1959).

FIGURE 1. A fox telling Aesop fables. Red-figure kylix of the Bologna Painter from Vulci, fifth century BC. (Museo Nazionale di Villa Giulia, Rome. Photo: Alinari/Art Resource, New York.)

FIGURE 2. The Charioteer of the Phaedrus, Andrea Sansovino, the Medicean Villa of Poggio a Caiano. (Photo: Scala/Art Resource, New York.)

FIGURE 3. Deeds of Theseus. Attic red-figure cup attributed to the Codrus Painter from Vulci, ca. 430 BC. London, British Museum E 84. (Photo: Courtesy of the Trustees of the British Museum.)

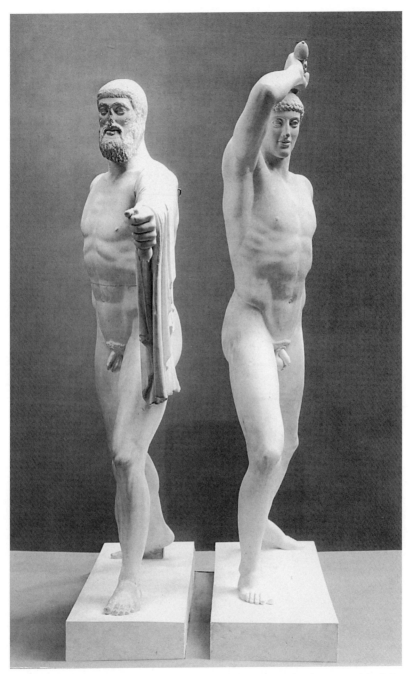

FIGURE 4. Tyrannicides. Casts of Roman marble copies after bronze originals by
Kritios and Nesiotes, ca. 477–476 BC. (Photo: Metropolitan Museum of Art
94510.)

FIGURE 5. Departure of a Hero. Attic Late Geometric spouted crater from Thebes, ca. 730–720 BC. London, British Museum 1899.2–19.1. (Photo: Courtesy of the Trustees of the British Museum.)

FIGURE 6. Death of Priam. Attic black-figure amphora by Lydos from Vulci, ca. 550 BC. Berlin, Antikensammlungen 1685. (Drawing after Gerhard 1843.)

FIGURE 7. Return of Hephaestus. Attic red-figure skyphos attributed to the Curti Painter, ca. 420 BC. Toledo Museum of Art 1982.88. Purchased with funds from the Libbey Endowment, Gift of Edward Drummond Libbey, 1982. (Photo: Photo Inc., Toledo, Ohio.)

FIGURE 8. Return of Hephaestus. Attic red-figure volute-crater by Polion from Spina, ca. 420 BC. Ferrara, Museo Nazionale di Spina 3033. (Drawing after Aurigemma 1935.)

FIGURE 9. Heracles and the Nemean Lion. Metope from the Temple of Zeus at Olympia, ca. 465–457 BC. (Photo: American School of Classical Studies at Athens, Alison Frantz Photographic Collection, PE 199.)

FIGURE 10. Birth of Erichthonius. Attic red-figure squat lekythos attributed to the Meidias Painter, ca. 420–410 BC. Cleveland Museum of Art 1982.142. Purchase, Leonard C. Hanna Jr. Bequest, 1982. (Photo: Cleveland Museum of Art.)

FIGURE 11. Battle of Athena and a Giant. Attic red-figure lekythos attributed to Douris, ca. 490 BC. Cleveland Museum of Art 1978.59. Purchase from the J. H. Wade Fund, 1978. (Photo: Cleveland Museum of Art.)

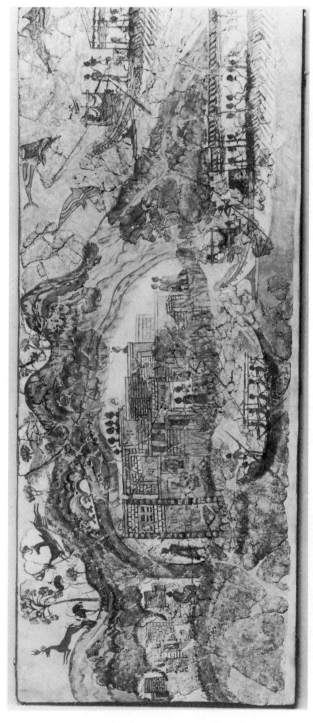

FIGURE 12. Naval Fresco from Akrotiri, Thera. Detail. Museum of Prehistoric Thera, Phira. Ca. 1650–1600 BCE. (Photograph courtesy of the National Archaeological Museum, Athens.)

FIGURE 13. Nymphs and Pan. Marble votive relief from Sparta or Megalopolis. Athens, National Archaeological Museum, 1449. Ca. 330–320 BCE. (Photograph courtesy of the National Archaeological Museum, Athens.)

FIGURE 14. The Blinding of Polyphemus. Fragment from a vase. Argos Museum, C149. Ca. 650 BCE. (Photograph: École Française d'Athènes, E. Serafis.)

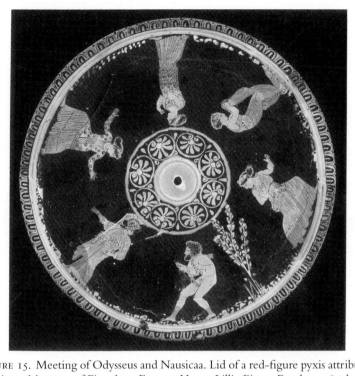

FIGURE 15. Meeting of Odysseus and Nausicaa. Lid of a red-figure pyxis attributed to Aison. Museum of Fine Arts, Boston, Henry Lillie Pierce Fund, 04.18a–b. Ca. 420 BCE. (Photograph © 2008 Museum of Fine Arts, Boston.)

FIGURE 16. Abduction of the Leucippides by the Dioscuri and Garden of the Hesperides. Attic red-figure hydria by the Meidias Painter. London, British Museum, London, E 224. Ca. 410 BCE. (Photograph after A. Furtwängler and K. Reichhold, *Griechische Vasenmalerei* I (Munich 1904) pl. 8.)

FIGURE 17. Odysseus' Descent to the Underworld. Drawing of Attic red-figure pelike attributed to the Lykaon Painter. Museum of Fine Arts, Boston, William Amory Gardner Fund, 34.79. Ca. 440 BCE. (Photograph © 2008 Museum of Fine Arts, Boston.)

FIGURE 18. The Suicide of Ajax. Black-figure amphora by Exekias (drawing). Boulogne, Château-Musée, 558. Ca. 530 BCE. (Photograph after E. Pfuhl, *Malerei und Zeichnung der Griechen*. III. Band (Munich 1923) fig. 234.)

Oh that my wayes were Directed
to keepe thy Statutes. Ps. 119. 5.
W. Simpson Sculp:

FIGURE 19. Book 2, Emblem 2, in Frances Quarles, *Emblemes*, Cambridge, 1643 (courtesy of Beineke Library, Yale University).

FIGURE 20. "*Venus*," from *The Copenhagen Planet Book* (Statens Museum for Kunst, Copenhagen). See Filedt Kok (1985) for a similar blockbook, by the Master of the Amsterdam Cabinet.

FIGURE 21. *Clash of the Titans.* Zeus and the "Arena of Life." (Metro-Goldwyn-Mayer.)

FIGURE 22. *Jason and the Argonauts.* Hera (back to camera) observing Jason and Medea on the Olympian screen. (Columbia Pictures.)

FIGURE 23. *Jason and the Argonauts.* Talos towering above the Argonauts. (Columbia Pictures.)

FIGURE 24. *Hercules*. Our hero at the climax of the film that made him immortal on the screen. (Courtesy of the William Knight Zewadski Collection.)

FIGURE 25. *Hercules Conquers Atlantis*. Hercules, descended from his twelve-horse chariot, discovers massacre victims at the palace of Atlantis. Note the panther reliefs on the wall. (SpA Cinematografica/Studio Canal.)

10: MYTHIC LANDSCAPES
OF GREECE

Ada Cohen

The survival of a substantial body of ancient Greek literary production – together with roughly two centuries of modern scholarship – has left no doubt that the ancient Greeks had a very rich mythic imagination, constantly preoccupied with the deeds of gods and heroes. Especially influential was the cluster of tales narrated in Homeric poetry, which over the centuries consistently served as the basis for Greek education. Myth was so pervasive in Greek life and thought that in the fourth century BCE Plato sought to control its telling. In the second book of the *Republic*, Plato's Socrates severely criticized the fictitious stories told by Homer, Hesiod, and other poets (even though Plato himself employed myth in his philosophical dialogues). Socrates argued that the majority of myths should be left out of the ideal state and its curriculum for the young, unless they communicated noble ideas (*Republic* 376C–377E). Real Greek cities, however, tolerated and celebrated a variety of mythical traditions, including those whose messages were less than uplifting, making it clear that Greece was fundamentally a culture of myth. But did the Greeks care to envisage the highly varied landscape configurations that hosted their myths? Was Greece a culture of landscape in addition to being a culture of myth?

Archaeology has recently done much to reconstruct aspects of ancient Greece's physical environment, both in its natural and in its cultivated states, and to clarify the relation of city to countryside, as well as the patterns of exploitation of the latter by the people who lived in it. Landscape, however, is not only a form of physical environment but also an artistic genre. Less self-evidently, it has been defined as an attitude, a particular way of looking at the world. Because they are conceptual, the two interrelated issues of landscape as a genre and as an attitude are controversial. The question of whether ancient Greek culture and art had a concept of landscape, and by extension an appreciation for it, goes back to the nineteenth century and continues to be debated in the present day.

More often than not, the answer to this question has been negative. Histories of landscape in the western world typically ignore ancient Greek manifestations and consider the art of landscape an invention of modernity, a belief that goes back to the middle of the nineteenth century, if not before. Literary scholars have noted the lack of a precise ancient Greek word for landscape, the term *topia* dating to the Roman period, though Socrates does speak periphrastically of "places and trees" – "*khôria kai dendra*" (χωρία καὶ δένδρα). They have also noted that ancient Greek literature demonstrates greater concern for human actions and feelings than for descriptions of natural scenery; when it does describe nature, literature may use it metaphorically in order ultimately to assign human values to it.[1] Furthermore, it is typical for geographical and landscape features to be conflated with eponymous deities resident in them and imagined in human form.

A similar anthropocentrism is evident in the visual arts, which focus on human narratives and human situations more than on their setting. Already in the Archaic period, there was the occasional vase painting or relief sculpture that attempted to convey a sense of environment, usually via trees, bushes, shoots of grass, rocks, or caves, as well as human-made items such as doors, fountain houses, columns, or temple-like structures. On very rare occasions, the waves of the sea appeared. The Classical period did not go much beyond the Archaic and continued with a restrained repertoire and a symbolic employment of landscape.[2]

When viewed against other ancient visual cultures such as Egypt, the Near East, or Rome, where landscape views abound, Archaic and Classical art's use of landscape seems quite modest, manifesting a distinct preference for single elements and close-ups rather than panoramic views. This was still the case in the Hellenistic period, when the impulse to render spacious environments quickened, both in literature and, less emphatically, in art. In literature, the third-century-BCE poet Theocritus has been considered the inventor of the genre of pastoral, which gave Hellenistic urban elites, via its imagistic language, opportunities to dream about nature.[3] In the visual arts, the city of Alexandria and the artists who worked there have been credited with an equivalent orientation. Even then, however, the human figure continued to be the main carrier of meaning. Despite an observable intensification of Hellenistic artists' willingness to incorporate aspects of landscape in their work – similar to contemporary poets' interest in bucolic themes – they continued to offer condensed visions of physical space and to render landscape as a relatively discontinuous conglomeration of individual elements.

THE QUESTION OF ORIGINS

Given this complex state of affairs, scholars of Greek antiquity have discerned the "origins" of the landscape form variously in the Archaic, Classical, and Hellenistic periods, while scholars of landscape art have largely ignored Greece, considering it an example of a "pre-landscape" culture. In recent years, however, prehistoric Aegean wall painting has started cautiously to appear in some histories of the landscape genre in the West. A premier example is the "miniature" fresco with a naval scene from the so-called West House at the prehistoric settlement at Akrotiri on the island of Thera. This and other wall paintings – some figural, others omitting the human body entirely, and still others, such as the *Naval Fresco*, combining the two – were miraculously preserved after a volcanic eruption, which has most recently been dated around 1650–1600 BCE. The *Naval Fresco* decorated the upper section of the south wall of a second-story room. It was accompanied by a scene of warfare on the opposite wall, along with a "Nilotic" landscape with animal chases on an adjacent wall, as well as other scenes that no longer survive. It seems to have been part of a program featuring at least five towns distributed on four walls, and at least partly associated with warfare.

Best preserved are the two towns of the *Naval Fresco* with a stretch of sea between them, on which a fleet of festively decorated ships with warrior passengers travels in the company of dolphins. In the Aegean this is the earliest visual manifestation, rather than simple insinuation, of the idea of travel within a landscape. The town on the left, built near a river and mountains, is smaller and lacks a harbor (Figure 12). The larger town on the right (not illustrated) is built on a rocky promontory with two small harbors. Both towns are seen from a distance and feature storied buildings of varying size, stacked in depth. The buildings are placed in encompassing landscapes, populated by animals and male and female figures, who watch the departure (or passage) of the fleet in the town on the left and welcome the fleet on the right. The variety of cartographic perspectives utilized – plan, elevation, oblique views – aids the interpretation of this scene as an early form of topographical map, aiming to portray specific locations, although, given the generic appearance of the towns, there is little agreement on which ones.[4] In a general sense these towns conform to what we know about Aegean island landscape and architecture at large.

The question to ask here is the reverse of the one posed above in connection with Greek culture of the historical period. In this case we can easily agree that the prehistoric Aegean was indeed a landscape culture, with an interest in visually expressing expansive views. But was it a culture of myth? More specifically, had it begun to formulate the foundations of the mythic imagination of the historical Greeks centuries later? Recent scholarship has entertained the possibility that the marine iconography of the Theran miniature fresco enacts an epic/heroic scene with poetic connections, rather than history or daily life.[5] The fresco has thus been taken as evidence for the existence of an early genre of epic poetry contemporary to it. People and places are not identifiable, at least from our distant vantage point, but they speak of a mythical worldview, populated by heroes and communicated via a set of pictorial conventions. Accordingly, all walls of the Theran room could have participated in interlinked narratives enacting an adventurous voyage in the eastern Mediterranean, much like the later *Odyssey Landscapes*, a famous Roman fresco from a house on the Esquiline Hill in Rome.[6] Dated in the first century BCE and inspired by Homer's *Odyssey*, this selectively depicts Odysseus' adventures on his long return trip home to Ithaca after the fall of Troy. The setting clearly dominates over the figures. The atmospheric vistas are quite different from the crisp linear style of the *Naval Fresco*, but the underlying narrative impetus may be similar. A new interpretation of the *Naval Fresco* disassociates it from the epic genre but maintains the mythical connection, this time in light of the cluster of myths associated with the Hyperboreans, a fantasy group living at the far reaches of the earth.[7]

ART AND LITERATURE

Whether we include or exclude the prehistoric Aegean from consideration, it seems that the story of Greek landscape is discontinuous, its employment governed more by the particulars of given situations than by subscription to period-wide totalizing worldviews. Of course the search for the origins of genres should have a place in intellectual history, but it would be wrong to elevate Greek emphases and preferences to a consistently held viewpoint and to conclude that the culture lacked a concept of landscape. Both literature and the visual arts invoke landscape strategically. In real life, a pilgrim may pay attention only to the sacred elements in a landscape: a choice of emphasis, not a conceptual or perceptual limitation. When invoking single trees and groves as noteworthy spatial markers in the second century CE, the travel writer Pausanias, to whom we owe much of our knowledge of ancient sites and now-lost monuments, did not linger on their greenery or on the flowers and fruits they produced, but on their cultic associations, as well as associations with important events of the classical past. He described buildings and other monuments of the cityscape for similar reasons.

Pausanias' literary vision was selective because of the circumstances and aims of his work, but this does not mean he did not see or appreciate more than he recorded. In trying to communicate, he pointed out what he considered communicable: memorable features of historical, mythological, and religious importance, landmarks of communal value. The beauty of nature may be apprehended privately and need not be shared with others. A statement about the audiences of tragedy preserved by Athenaeus, a writer of the end of the second century CE, and attributed to the comedian Antiphanes suggests that prior knowledge completes what genre leaves unsaid: "Let me but mention Oedipus, and they know all the rest: his father was Laius, his mother Iocasta; they know who his daughters are, his sons, what he will suffer, what he has done. If, again, one speaks of Alcmeon, straightway he has mentioned all his children, and has told that he killed his mother in a fit of madness" (6.222B, trans. C. B. Gulick). In the case of landscape, both knowledge and imagination may be put to work at the prompting of a visual or literary clue.

In contrast to their predecessors in the nineteenth and earlier twentieth centuries, art theorists and art historians today embrace a view of landscape as a system of notional signs rather than as a record of perception; as a medium of cultural expression rather than as a genre. Recent landscape theory has done much to draw attention to the prescriptive and rhetorical ambitions of landscape and has blurred the boundaries between the ideal and the real. Even the interpretation of extremely naturalistic landscapes of the seventeenth through the nineteenth centuries in Europe, periods traditionally believed to have developed a concept and genre of "pure" landscape, has been moving away from reality in order to highlight the symbolic and the political dimensions. This interpretive shift has implications for antiquity: it enables us more than ever before to explore ancient landscape in light of its roles and functions in particular situations, rather than as an all-embracing mentality. If all landscape art is a system of signs and a body of

representations more than an empirical fact, Greek art's insistent but discontinuous use of landscape elements as signs is nothing extraordinary
or unusual. Furthermore, in our own era we have become especially
aware of the evocative aura of the close-up, particularly in photography.
If a tree photographed by Ansel Adams constitutes landscape, why not
one painted by the "Kleophrades Painter"?

The selectivity of the Greek imagination – with its emphases as
well as its exclusions – is one of its most interesting aspects, and it is relevant to the study of both mythological narrative and landscape description. What follows is an exploration of this intersection of narrative
and description in light of common as well as rarely depicted myths in
painting and sculpture. In the context of the visual arts, scholars have
repeatedly stressed that landscape served primarily narrative functions
by localizing events. It has recently been argued that landscape elements
in vase painting may have even served to link events and scenes that
were temporally and spatially separated. For example, the presence of a
palm tree may have forged narrative links between depictions of Ajax'
suicide and his game of dice with Achilles at an earlier time.[8] Given
the dominance of mythological narrative in Greek art and culture, the
intersection of myth, as known to us via various textual sources, and
landscape emerges as a key issue for understanding the range of the
Greek mythical imagination.

Greek anthropocentrism is clearly expressed by Socrates in Plato's
Phaedrus (230C–D), where the philosopher states that he learns from the
people in the cities, not the trees in the country. Nevertheless, evocative
descriptions of trees and other landscape elements do occur in Greek
texts, articulated not least by Socrates himself when he describes, in the
very same work, the beauties of the banks of the Ilissus River, where he
has gone with his companions. This is a pleasant, breezy, fragrant spot
with a shady plane tree, a spring, and soft grass under the summer noise
of the cicadas (Plato, *Phaedrus* 230B–C).

Literary descriptions refer equally to the human landscape, the
Olympian realm, and the landscape of the Underworld. The mythical
landscape is a combination of all three realms, which are united by the
occasional hero but primarily by the gods, who move freely back and
forth. Homer has passages on the Greek landscape, as is occasionally the
case with Hesiod's *Works and Days*. The contexts in Greek tragedy are
varied and flexible, however briefly referred to in the text or summarily
indicated on stage by scenic props and painted backdrops. In Sophocles'
Oedipus at Colonus, Antigone describes the grove of the Semnai Theai,

full of trees and plants. The play also includes a beautiful hymn to Attica, addressed by the chorus to an arriving stranger and populating the physical landscape with deities:

> In this country of fine horses, stranger, you have come to the choicest rural dwellings, to white Colonus, where the melodious nightingale most likes to stay and sing her song beneath the green glades, living amid the wine-dark ivy and the inviolable leafage of the goddess, rich in fruit, never vexed by the sun or by the wind of many winters, where the reveller Dionysus ever treads the ground, in company with his divine nurses.
>
> And there flourishes ever day by day, fed by dew from heaven, the narcissus with its lovely clusters, the ancient crown of the two great goddesses, and the crocus that gleams with gold; nor are the sleepless streams that flow from the waters of Cephisus diminished, but ever each day the river, quick to bring crops to birth, flows over the plains of the broad-breasted earth with moisture free from stain. Nor is this place rejected by the choruses of the Muses, nor by Aphrodite of the golden reins.
>
> (668–93, trans. H. Lloyd-Jones)

The chorus in *Antigone* transports the audience to the city and its natural setting in a very economical but effective way:

> Sun's beam, fairest of all
> that ever till now shone
> on seven-gated Thebes;
> O golden eye of day, you shone
> coming over Dirce's stream.
>   (100–105, trans. D. Grene)

Philostratus the Elder's *Imagines* in the second/third century CE (1.12–13) contains a lengthy ekphrastic description of the landscape of Bosphorus. Homer (e.g., *Odyssey* 10.505–15; 10.528–9; 11.573; 24.10–14; 24.204; *Iliad* 23.71–4), Hesiod (*Theogony* 726–813), Pindar (*Olympian* 2.56–80; fragments 129–30), and Lucian, much later (*Verae Historiae* 2.5–12), describe the landscape of the Underworld, which they had obviously never seen.

Odysseus is the hero most persistently associated with changing landscapes, and it is not surprising that clusters of descriptions of localities, blending reality with fantasy, occur in the *Odyssey*, which is devoted to Odysseus' adventurous journey back home. Here Homer masterfully describes notable landscapes: coasts, caves, groves, and gardens. He provides sufficient clarity to conjure up specific places (mostly around the Mediterranean) and sufficient fantastic detail to thwart the pursuit of identification. (In the Hellenistic period Apollonius of Rhodes' *Argonautica* similarly resorted into geographical blends.) The scholarly interest in the Homeric geography of Odysseus' adventures is long-standing and much contested. No one, however, can reasonably doubt the reality of Odysseus' homeland of Ithaca.

CAVES

In Book 13 of the *Odyssey* Odysseus arrives home by ship with the help of the Phaeacians. The harbor, with its two protective promontories, has an olive tree at its head and a shaded well-watered cave nearby, sacred to the nymphs (13.96–112). Visited by both humans and deities from separate entrances, this is a cave where myth and reality converge. Actually, one of the *Odyssey*'s most unusual contexts is associated not with Odysseus but Menelaus, who also, though less famously, met difficulties on his way back home to Sparta after the end of the Trojan War. One of Menelaus' adventures was the encounter with Proteus, a creature capable of transforming himself into animals and elements, who held information on how to return home (*Odyssey* 4.384 ff.) The land where Proteus lived exudes a familiar Mediterranean aura and is described in evocative detail: the rocky shore with its caves, the flow of the sea, the sun shining from above on a group of seals, whom Proteus joined in one of his spectacular transformations.

Some of the *Odyssey*'s landscapes are idyllic and luxurious; some are threatening; and some are both. Nymph Calypso's remote island of Ogygia, in which Odysseus was imprisoned, was simultaneously lovely and dangerous. Homer describes it on the occasion of Hermes' arrival with the request that Calypso release Odysseus. Surrounded by beautiful blue waters, Calypso lived in a cave nested within a lush wood teaming with animal creatures of all sorts. This cave, its entrance covered with vine, was made into a comfortable home, complete with fragrant fire in the hearth, evocatively described (*Odyssey* 5.55–74). The landscape was invested with an emotional dimension, a sadness that insightfully contradicted the natural beauty. Odysseus could not experience the beauty when trapped against his will.

For some reason Greek art did not give visual form to Calypso's cave, but several votive reliefs of the late Classical period take the form of shallow caves, inhabited by unidentified nymphs and other deities. The nymphs were female water and landscape deities, and they inhabited a variety of landscapes, such as springs, groves, and meadows (*Iliad* 20.8–9; *Odyssey* 6.123–24). Mountains and caves were especially important backdrops for their activities. In real life, caves were conceived of as possible sites of prophesy and healing, and many, both in Attica and in other locations, became loci of worship of the nymphs, their companion Pan, and other deities, especially in the Classical period. Visitors left offerings of pottery, terracotta figurines, clay plaques, marble reliefs, as well as various metal objects, decorative or utilitarian.

Pan, a hybrid god of woods and caves from Arcadia, part goat part human, was worshipped in a cave on the north slope of the Athenian Acropolis, a site where nature and civilization coexisted in close proximity. Pan's was one of several caves on the north slope.[9] (In Euripides' tragedy *Ion*,15–19, 936–9, 955–9, the eponymous baby was born and abandoned by his mother Creusa in Apollo's grotto, whose precise relation to that of Pan on the same slope is ambiguous.) Pan's caves also dotted the Greek countryside. The Attic cave of Vari on Mt. Hymettus, used from the fifth century BCE to the middle of the second century CE and into late antiquity, is especially noteworthy. In the late fifth century BCE, Archedemus of Thera, whose name was inscribed six times in this cave and who was also depicted life-sized in crude relief, labored hard to create a garden for the pleasure of the nymphs, among other embellishments.[10] The cave was very complex, with both conventionally beautiful areas and other less hospitable and more mysterious.

There was also the Thessalian cave near Pharsalus – sanctuary to the nymphs, Pan, Hermes but also Apollo, Heracles, Cheiron, Asclepius, and Hygeia – whose remote locale was landscaped in the early fifth century BCE (or in the fourth) by Pantalces for easier access and also became a place of pilgrimage. Indeed, an inscription by the entrance informed visitors about this man's actions and the rewards that the honored deities offered him in return. It also exhorted passers-by to pay homage to the gods, make sacrifices, pray, and enjoy themselves, "for forgetfulness of all cares is here and your share of good things, and victory in strife."[11]

Vases of the Archaic and Classical period as well as late Classical votive reliefs pare complexity down and present us with highly stylized and flat visions of caves, shaped like irregular partial or complete arches, dominated by their mythical inhabitants.[12] Usually nymphs are shown walking or dancing in the company of Pan, Hermes, or Apollo. In Figure 13, a votive relief of ca. 330–320 BCE from the Peloponnese, three nymphs in voluminous mantles (other plural divinities such as the Horae have been invoked) dance in the direction of the goat-legged Pan, who sits on a rock and plays the pipes.[13] This is a landscape made strange by the fact that the women's heads almost reach the ceiling of the shallow cave in typical expression of the figural prejudices of Greek art. On occasion, mortals, distinguished by their smaller size, intrude in Attic nymph reliefs, even holding hands and dancing with the nymphs, but generally it seems as if the mysterious nature of the cave made it suitable predominantly for supernatural beings. Dionysus, for instance, was reared by the nymphs of Mt. Nysa in a cave. Even though they offered worship there, the ancient Greeks thought of caves as fantastic, transgressive, and implausible surroundings for ordinary human life.

Caves were not only mysterious but at times also uncivilized. In the *Odyssey*, the monstrous man-eating Cyclopes, on whose island Odysseus unhappily landed, lived individually in mountain caves:

> These people have no institutions, no meetings for counsels;
> rather they make their habitations in caverns hollowed
> among the peaks of the high mountains, and each one is the law
> for his own wives and children, and cares nothing about the
>   others.

> (*Odyssey* 9.112–15, trans. R. Lattimore;
> cited in Plato's *Laws* 3.680C)

Although set in an idyllic land where nature bloomed effortlessly, Polyphemus' cave was the site of the brutal killings of Odysseus' companions, whom the Cyclops ate. Odysseus eventually escaped from this trap because of his cunning. Both the cunning and a version of the cave are captured on a fragment from a bowl dated ca. 650 BCE in the Argos Museum (Figure 14).[14] Odysseus and a companion drive a spear into the giant's single eye. The rocky bed on which he lies localizes the story in a highly condensed and symbolic manner. As was typical of this early period and this medium, the style is sketchy and linear and eschews atmospheric effects. Yet the roughness and polychromy of the rock are communicated clearly.

COUNTRYSIDE AND GENDER

By contrast to Polyphemus' world, the landscape of Phaeacia on the island of Scheria was both civilized and thoroughly pleasant. Shipwrecked, naked, and exhausted, Odysseus washed up on its shores early in book six of the *Odyssey*. There he met Nausicaa, beautiful daughter of Alcinous and Arete, king and queen of the Phaeacians. She and her companions had gone to the river to wash clothes. As the clothes dried, they played ball (6.96–100) and awakened the sleeping Odysseus, who descended upon them "like a lion" and begged for food and shelter. Pausanias saw a panel painting depicting this encounter in the Pinakotheke (Picture Gallery) of the Propylaea on the Athenian Acropolis (1.22.6). Painted by Polygnotus, a fifth-century artist famous for his innovations in the depiction of space, it does not survive, but a couple of vases give us a glimpse into that world.

One example is the lid of a red-figure pyxis in the Museum of Fine Arts, Boston (Figure 15).[15] Predictably, this is a world structured by the bodies that inhabit it, but a restrained and refined use of landscape creates a sense of environment. A bearded Odysseus, bent in a crouching pose, tries to hide his naked state – which in this case communicates vulnerability rather than heroic status – with a now indistinct branch. Nausicaa is shown calm, collected, and upright, placed diagonally across from Odysseus. Their bodies mark one of the imaginary diameters of the scene and are thus visually interlinked. Two companions of the girl flee expressively in fear, while a third, unaware of Odysseus' appearance, continues to wring out clothes. All the girls are named. Diagonally across from the unsuspecting girl is the helmeted goddess Athena, whose imaginary presence guides Odysseus' actions. Athena frames Odysseus on one side, while a skinny tree frames him on the other. At first sight, this leafy tree, whose existence simultaneously conjures up landscape and ornament, seems to be the only sign of locale. However, the addition of a pebbly ground line, highlighting the circumference of the lid with subtle naturalistic irregularities, articulates economically but clearly the river bank. It is carefully rendered in relief with the addition of bits of clay.

Scholars have rightly discerned an aura of eroticism in the Homeric encounter between the beautiful young maiden Nausicaa and the suppliant visitor, despite his ultimate ineligibility for marriage. Homer filled his narrative with hints that participate in the broader gendering of Greece's mythical landscape. Unlike this one, mythical encounters between men and women tend to be violent. They usually occur in nature, away from the protected urban environment that sheltered women both in reality and in the mythic imagination. In literature, misty meadows with fresh grass and fragrant flowers are frequently the context in which erotic pursuits and rapes take place. Typically, beautiful and innocent maidens (heroines but sometimes even goddesses) gather flowers (whose patron was female, the goddess Chloris) and enjoy the glories of nature, when they are unexpectedly attacked by a male god or hero lusting after them. For instance, Boreas, the north wind, raped the maiden Oreithyia when she was dancing on the banks of the Ilissus River (Plato, *Phaedrus* 229B; Apollonius, *Argonautica* 1.211–18). Apollo seized Creusa in a flowery meadow and raped her in a cave (Euripides, *Ion* 887–96). Poseidon raped Medusa (Hesiod, *Theogony* 278–9), and Zeus, in bovine form, abducted Europa (Moschus 63–71) in similarly beautiful landscapes. Pluto abducted Persephone while she was picking flowers in a dewy meadow, violently thrusting her into both sexuality and the landscape of the Underworld. The *Homeric Hymn to Demeter* mentions roses, crocuses, violets, hyacinths, narcissus, irises, and lilies (6–8; 425–8), but art was uninterested in the profusion of species. The message overall seems to be that, despite the enticing attractions that nature holds for girls, danger lurks around the corner.

A fragment from an Attic red-figure column-krater of ca. 470–460 BCE in Boston is difficult to situate within a broader narrative framework but excellently conveys a sense of carefree and idyllic integration of girls in nature.[16] It shows two young women on a seesaw, consisting of a plank resting on a boulder. One girl (on the left) has her weight on the plank, while the other (whose head is lost) is shown jumping in midair, about to land on the plank. A wonderfully drawn fruit tree in the background suggests the countryside. We do not know who these girls are, though the frieze of winged horses near the hem of the one on the left suggests they are special. We also do not know whether they belong to the realm of myth, although the sharp division we now tend to draw between genre and mythology may not have been so stark in antiquity. These girls help us recall the romanticism of passages in lyric poetry as well as tragedy, where love, femininity, and nature are drawn together. In their suggestively fragmentary state they also help us recall the world of the goddess of love and beauty, Aphrodite, who in the visual arts is often surrounded by landscape elements and sits close to the ground.

Nature and nature's gardens were symbols of virginity and erotic meeting places, but they could also be places of agrarian productivity. After meeting Nausicaa and receiving clues that Phaeacia was indeed a hospitable place, Odysseus proceeded to Alcinous' palace. Prior to entering, he stopped to admire its orchard, vineyard, and vegetable garden, all productive, in bloom, carefully taken care of, and lovingly described (*Odyssey* 7.112–31). Art did not engage with such expansive vistas, but the mythical Garden of the Hesperides did receive visual attention. It was there, near the Atlas mountains, that the goddess Hera had planted the tree of immortality, which bore golden apples. Hesiod tells us that other species of fruit-bearing trees also grew in this magical garden, and they were all guarded by the Hesperides (Hesiod, *Theogony* 215–16). The place was so lovely that Zeus and Hera made love for the first time there, as Euripides (*Hippolytus* 748–51) implies.

The Garden of the Hesperides is shown on the lower register of a well-known red-figure hydria by the Meidias Painter in the British Museum, dated to the end of the fifth century BCE (Figure 16).[17] The apple tree is shown roughly in the middle of the composition with a guardian serpent wrapped around it. It is surrounded by a group of very elegant Hesperides, all labeled. Two Hesperides are shown to the left of the sacred tree. One of them, labeled Chrysothemis, reaches for one of the apples. The other, Asterope, is behind Chrysothemis and leans forward on her shoulder. On the other side of the tree, the Hesperis Lipara looks toward Heracles. Heracles, for whom fetching the apples was one of his twelve labors, is easily identifiable by the lion skin on which he sits and the club he holds with his right hand. He is accompanied by his henchman Iolaus, who stands behind him holding two spears. Clytius and Hygeia are shown on the far left; she sits, while he stands, leaning forward on rocky ground. Two other trees punctuate this landscape, one behind Clytius and one between Lipara and Heracles. Additional figures, including one more Hesperis, are revealed as one turns the vase, without contributing any additional dimensions to the garden aspect.

The main scene lacks a sense of narrative and danger, with Heracles avoiding any exertion and waiting for the Hesperides to give him the apples. This lack of action heightens the pictorial significance of the garden, and the idyllic nature of the setting is made palpable despite its restrained visual expression. This particular painter and his circle loved to set their figures in gardens, marked by trees, shrubs, flowers, and rocks. Put together, the extremely elegant Meidian figures and their meadowy paradisiacal environments paint a carefree and luxurious world inhabited by gods and heroes. Even the scene of the abduction of the Leucippides from a sanctuary punctuated by a stiffly posed female statue, which is the main scene on this hydria, has an idyllic aura conferred on it by the occasional delicate tree, flowery tendril, and wavy ground line. The goddess Aphrodite, associated with gardens and flowery meadows, sits gracefully next to an altar in the frieze below the abduction scene.

THE UNDERWORLD

The Greek imagination located the Garden of the Hesperides on the edge of the earth. Another edge, albeit much less pleasant, was the Underworld, to which the Greeks devoted compelling attention. Homer's Underworld was lush in vegetation but also dark and foggy, a dreary place for all its inhabitants, however excellent and heroic. In book 11 of the *Odyssey*, Odysseus, following the directions of Circe, traveled by ship and then on foot to that dark, gloomy, and watery spot, marked by a grove of poplars and willows, at the junction of two rivers (see *Odyssey* 10.508–15). There he sought information from the soul of the soothsayer Tiresias about how to return home. Although there is nothing specifically otherworldly about these landscape elements, the *Odyssey* describes them in such a way as to arouse fear and dread. The discussion of the dead, who cannot communicate with Odysseus unless they drink sacrificial blood, contributes in no small measure to this effect.

Dated ca. 440 BCE, a pelike in Boston by the Lykaon Painter depicts the visit to the land of the dead (Figure 17).[18] The bearded figure of Odysseus, equipped with boots and with traveling hat on his back, sits on a rock in the middle of the composition, his right hand brought to his chin in a mournful, somber pose suitable to the context. He holds a sword with the other hand and seems to have performed a sacrifice of the two bloody sheep that are placed by his feet. The story demanded that he perform such a sacrifice in order to draw out the souls of the dead and enable them to speak to him. On the right stands Hermes, with winged hat and shoes, holding his herald's staff in his left hand. On the left, facing the other two figures, emerges one of the dead, Elpenor, a nude and youthful beardless man. His legs are partly obscured by the hilly environment, and his arms convey the effort he makes as he climbs up from the underground. Elpenor, one of Odysseus' companions, died in an accident on Circe's island and his body was left unattended by his comrades in their hasty departure. Here he appears to Odysseus to ask for cremation, a proper burial, and a tomb marker.

This is a rocky landscape, as suggested by its painted wavy lines indicative of different layers of space. It is also a marshy spot, marked by the reeds of a riverine environment. The use of multiple ground lines,

the distribution of figures at various levels on the pictorial surface, and
their partial concealment behind landscape elements, such as the hill that
partially hides Elpenor here, participate in a mode of depicting space
that scholars call "Polygnotan." Its invention has been attributed to the
painter Polygnotus of Thasos, who famously employed it in his now-lost
wall paintings of ca. 470–460 BCE at the Treasury of the Cnidians at
Delphi. His painting of the Underworld was described in minute detail
by Pausanias in the second century CE (10.25.1–31.12), and it included
Odysseus as well as the marshy environment of the River Acheron
with Charon's boat. Figures placed on a higher elevation were meant to
occupy some space in the distance; those at lower levels were meant to
be progressively closer to the viewer.[19] Polygnotus' painting contained
many more figures (roughly seventy human and animal figures) and
activities than a vase painting can possibly include, but Figure 17 may
be used to conjure up something about that lost work, at least its spatial
tendencies and somber effect.

Light and misty darkness are two environments that Greek vase
painting – with its emphasis on crisp outlines, its restrained colors, and
their dense application – cannot readily depict. The Lykaon Painter goes
farther than usual in providing visual clues for the Underworld's environment. Even so, the illusion of space in the vase painting is counteracted
by the palmette motifs that frame the scene and ultimately proclaim this
to be a decorative surface. Furthermore, Elpenor, Odysseus, and Hermes inhabit different levels of reality. Odysseus is a mortal hero whose
mythological status allows journeys impossible for ordinary humans
(here to the Underworld and back); Hermes occupies an imaginary
divine landscape; Elpenor, despite his substantive corporeality and the
naturalistic fusion with his environment, is meant to be an eidolon, a
ghost or apparition, and thus he exists less in a real than in a notional
space.

It is unclear whether Polygnotus' painting went farther in the
depiction of the Underworld's misty atmosphere. Certainly his medium
would have allowed him to do so, but the study of Greek landscape
underscores the unpredictability of artistic expression. Certainly both
the large-scale painting, as transmitted to us by Pausanias, and the Boston
pelike seem to have been inspired by the Homeric description of the
Underworld. Other conceptions of the world of the dead and the journey by which that place was reached also existed, not least because
no perfect agreement is possible when the subject is beyond empirical
knowledge. Constant references occur in Greek tragedy, while Aristophanes' *Frogs*, the texts of the so-called Orphic gold tablets, which

accompanied a few burials from the fifth century BCE to the third century CE, and to some extent Plato's *Phaedo* present their own conceptions and rearrange standard landscape features such as springs, lakes, and trees that mark the route. Hesiod knew the Underworld as a dreary place for the masses, but he also imagined another much more pleasant locale, the Islands of the Blessed, exclusive to heroes, where they lived by the Ocean in eternal heavenly comfort in an ever-productive environment (*Works and Days* 170–73). Pindar made that place accessible to the average dead, if good, just, and noble (e.g., *Olympian*, 2.63–80; fragment 129).[20] The breezy landscape of the Islands of the Blessed (or Elysian Fields) was characterized by sunshine, flowery meadows, verdant woods, and flowing waters. Lucian imagined the Elysian Fields as an idyllic sunny place in full bloom, full of aromas and gentle breezes, a fabulous city in perpetual spring (*Verae Historiae* 2.6–13). The Garden of the Hesperides discussed above (Figure 16) helps us visualize the Islands of the Blessed (to which the Garden was conceptually related).

One of the most unusual visual renderings of the realm of the dead occurs on the interior of an Athenian white-ground cup in the British Museum attributed to the Sotades Painter. The cup dates to ca. 470–460 BCE and was reportedly one of nine white-ground vases found in the same woman's tomb in Athens.[21] It does not give an expansive view of the Underworld but rather zooms into the interior of a single tomb. The story is rare and concerns the encounter of the Athenian seer Polyidus with Glaucus in the latter's tomb (Apollodorus, *Library* 3.3.1; Hyginus, *Fabulae* 136). Glaucus, son of Minos, had drowned in a pot of honey, and Minos locked Polyidus up in the tomb and charged him with the task of reviving the boy. Polyidus succeeded after seeing a snake that he had killed be revived by its mate. This is a quiet and contemplative rendering of boy and seer, both of whom are named. Glaucus is shown in a crouching position on the right, all covered up in his dark clothing, as if alive. Polyidus is shown half-nude in a kneeling position, holding a stick, apparently a weapon against the snakes. Both figures are fully absorbed in the seer's activity. The tomb has a beehive shape, whose outline is faintly preserved and is shown in section. Above it stands a tripod, while the ground of the tomb is marked by naturalistically textured pebbles, tiny spots of clay that support the main figures. The two snakes, which signal the method by which Glaucus was revived, are placed below this pebbly layer near the rim of the cup.

This combination of a natural and a human-made funereal environment is quite extraordinary for Greek art, as is the spaciousness of

the tomb's interior. Its manner of enclosing the figures is wonderfully
encompassing and atmospheric, despite the fact that there is no consistency of perspective and the spatial relation of snakes and humans
is unclear. The beauty of drawing and the delicate visual effects that
characterize this scene are shared by this vase's companion pieces, especially another white-ground cup, also from the workshop of the Sotades
Painter, which shows a young woman stretching on tiptoe to reach the
highest fruit on a slender apple tree. Another woman, poorly preserved
and labeled Melissa, crouches by the tree, perhaps picking up fallen
apples.[22] The identity of the story represented is unclear, but scholars
conjecture that the women are nymphs in the Garden of the Hesperides,
which, as we saw, forced artists to think about nature, however imaginary and fabulous, as a context of mythic action.

M OUNTAINS , T REES , AND B ODIES OF W ATER

Collectively, the incomplete and scattered bits of evidence we possess
might be taken to suggest that the effort to imagine other worlds –
the worlds in which gods, heroes and the mythical dead existed and
moved – produced an attendant effort to give visual form to the landscapes in which those movements occurred. The landscapes seem to
have abstractly fused experiences of Greece's real environments with
mental images. Sometimes the result of this process seems self-evident;
other times it seems surprising in both its inclusions and its exclusions. Mountains, for example, although they were the location of
important mythical events, were not represented often. This is surprising, for mountains can easily be shaped into image. In myth they
were mysterious and dangerous places, often inhabited by outsiders to
civilization.[23] There hunters pursued wild animals; maenads roamed,
and frenzied Theban women, turned into maenads, tore Pentheus apart;
infants were exposed, but also found and reared by strangers. Laius gave
infant Oedipus for exposure in a meadow of Hera on Mt. Cithaeron
(Euripides, *Phoenissae* 24). Occasionally mountains were idyllic, such as
Mt. Ida in Mysia, where the Trojan prince Paris herded and where he
delivered his famous Judgment. The most famous, Mt. Olympus, was
a serene and blissful environment with perfect weather, home of the
gods (*Odyssey* 6.41–5). For real Greeks, mountains were places where
one could worship the gods and might even "meet" them. But artists
opted for caves, which go together with mountains, or simply for rocky
terrain.

Depictions of landscape tend to cluster around mythical stories more than the "genre" scenes of everyday life. It is possible, however, for the real and the mythological to inhabit the same spaces. Some Athenian white-ground lekythoi of the fifth century BCE show Charon, ferryman of the dead, leading a figure to the Underworld across the River Acheron. White-ground lekythoi, like white-ground cups, formed a circumscribed group explicitly associated with death. In the so-called Charon scenes the references to the Underworld are explicit. The expressive means are calm but infused with sadness. The child on a lekythos of ca. 430 BCE in the National Archaeological Museum in Athens must be an ordinary mortal boy. Charon has placed him in his boat in a swampy landscape by a rocky shore, communicated with striking naturalism because of the medium's polychromous effects. The boy turns to look at his mournful parents, who stay behind and must relinquish their child to the company of the otherworldly figure of Charon.[24] When Charon accompanies an adult, it is not always possible to know whether the figure is "real" or a mythological character, a generic woman or Alcestis dying for the sake of her husband.

Sometimes determining the status of entire scenes is problematical. Take, for example, a black-figure panel amphora of ca. 515–500 BCE by the Priam Painter in the Villa Giulia in Rome. One side shows an extremely unusual atmospheric scene with strong depth of field, where seven nude women bathe and swim in a rocky grotto. The scene is framed by two multibranched trees, from which clothing and equipment hang. Even the slightly wavy and glistening water is depicted, and one swimmer's body is partly covered by it in unexpected illusionism. The painter has rendered her in perspectival diminution to suggest that she is farther away from the foreground plane than others. Roughly in the middle of the composition there is a structure, apparently a diving platform. Are these "real" women or are they nymphs? One cannot be sure, but the latter seems more likely. It is reasonable to assume some correspondence in level of reality with the vase's other side, which is firmly set in the world of myth. Here the majestic figure of Dionysus sits in profile on a diphros (a stool), with cup in hand.[25] He is surrounded by luxuriant vines, heavy with grapes, on which seven satyrs climb energetically in order to pick them. Large baskets on the ground receive the fruit. This side is flatter in effect than the grotto on the other, but it too offers an encompassing landscape view. Still, the bodies carry the scene, as the body does even in a famous diving scene often invoked in association with this amphora. That scene is depicted on the lid of the early classical *Tomb of the Diver* in the Greek city of Paestum in southern Italy (500–480 BCE). An agile nude man jumps off from a masonry platform into a shallow body of water below, in a landscape also punctuated by two spindly trees.[26]

A tree might indicate a generic outdoor setting, but in the past it may have pointed to something more specific. In art there are a variety of tree shapes, whose species is sometimes identifiable.[27] Among the easiest to identify is – not surprising for the Mediterranean – the olive tree, which had both economic and symbolic value, given its association with Athena, patron goddess of Athens. In all periods, despite the recognizability, there is a strong degree of stylization and little effort put in the transmission of precise botanical facts. The frequency of the depictions of the god Dionysus entails an attendant profusion of vine motifs in vase painting.

Although it is not a typical Greek plant (Theophrastus, *Historia Plantarum* 3.3.5), the palm tree occurs in Greek art more often than one would expect, in intriguing combinations of naturalism and abstraction. Sometimes its presence makes good sense as a sign of location, as in the case of Troy. In that case palms might serve to underscore a distant exotic place. On other occasions, as in the struggle between Heracles and Apollo over the Delphic tripod, such explanations are difficult to carry through. But the majestic palm tree was persistently associated with Apollo, whose mother Leto clung to such a tree on Delos while giving birth to him in a soft meadow (*Homeric Hymn to Apollo* 116–17), and with his twin sister Artemis. Palms appear in scenes showing Achilles and Ajax playing dice, a prominent example being a late sixth-century-BCE black-figure calyx krater by the Rycroft Painter in the Toledo Museum of Art, where each hero has a palm tree behind him in a symmetrical arrangement.[28] Scholars have proposed that the number of branches assigned to each tree may have been used symbolically to signal which side would win.

Archaic painters paired Ajax with the palm also in depictions of his suicide. The hero resorted to suicide in a frenzy of anger after his comrades voted to award Achilles' armor to Odysseus rather than to him. In Sophocles' play by that name, which seems unusually to have depicted the suicide on stage, Ajax took his life in an isolated spot by the beach. His last words address the landscape of Troy directly: "Springs, rivers, and the wide plain of Troy – you have all sustained me. Farewell! Aias calls out his last word to you" (*Ajax* 862–4, trans. H. Golder and R. Pevear). The Archaic vase painter Exekias reduced all landscape to a single palm tree on a famous black-figure amphora dated ca. 540 BCE and today in Boulogne (Figure 18). The silhouette of the tree, with its memorably drooping branches, frames Ajax' nude body from one side. On the other side we see his armor: shield with apotropaic Medusa, spear, and helmet (unless these are symbolic of the cause behind his imminent suicide, and thus allude to Achilles' armor). The palm has been considered by some scholars a sign of foreign setting but has been read by others symbolically, as an emotional participant in the hero's death or as a means of suggesting his elevated status.[29] In all interpretations the tree serves to enhance aspects of the pictorial narrative. A well-known red-figure hydria by the Kleophrades painter in Naples, dated ca. 490–480 BCE, features a similarly expressive palm tree.[30] The context is the fall of Troy, and a distraught woman pulling her hair sits by the tree, whose leafy branches curve towards her. On the tree's other side sits the hapless Trojan king Priam, victim – together with his dead grandson – of Neoptolemus' brutal attack. This tree too, bent and mournful, sympathetically participates in the human suffering as an example of the so-called pathetic fallacy,[31] whereby nature reflects human emotions, but it has also been interpreted neutrally as a simple signal of location.

FIGURE AND LANDSCAPE – FIGURE AS LANDSCAPE

In Figure 18, the stark geometry in the juxtaposition of Ajax' body and the tree, which echoes the curvature of his body, suggests a fundamental correspondence between the human figure and landscape elements. So far we have set the depiction of landscape and Greek culture's fundamental anthropomorphism in some sort of opposition. But it is also striking that the visual arts treat bodies and landscape features in similar ways. In all periods there is an emphasis on clear contour, a preference for complete views without too much overlapping of forms, and an aura of self-sufficient poise. Even when rendered in flat style, both human and landscape forms exude a sculptural effect. (White-ground vases of the classical period and monumental wall painting, which is largely lost, allowed more atmospheric renderings.) It turns out that Greek literature is punctuated by references implying the correspondence between human and landscape bodies. When Odysseus encountered Nausicaa in the scene discussed above, he compared her enthralling beauty to a young palm tree (phoenix), the specific one that he had once seen beside Apollo's altar on the island of Delos (Odyssey 6.162–3). Set up in this juxtaposition, girl and tree become analogous bodies. Centuries later the Hellenistic poet Theocritus compared Helen's radiant beauty to a magnificent cypress tree (*Idylls*, 18.29–30). She adorned her homeland Sparta just as the tree adorns a garden or field. Much less pleasantly but equally significantly, the *Iliad* compares young Euphorbus, fallen in battle, to an olive tree fallen in a storm (17.53–9). Aristophanes compared the tough old woodsmen of the chorus in *Acharnians* to maple and prickly oak (178–85). And in the *Odyssey* the monstrous solitary Cyclops is compared to "a wooded peak of the high mountains seen standing away from the others" (9.190–92, trans. R. Lattimore). Landscape has personality. If tree and person can be analogous, the whole humankind may be envisaged in terms of vegetation as part of a philosophically inclined conceptual leap:

> As is the generation of leaves, so is that of humanity.
> The wind scatters the leaves on the ground, but the live timber
> burgeons with leaves again in the season of spring returning
> So one generation of men will grow while another dies.
>   (*Iliad* 6.146–9, trans. R. Lattimore)

The employment of such metaphorical values in literature suggests a keen awareness of the symbiosis between humans and the landscape that frames their actions, and this is evident also in Greek philosophy. In the fourth century BCE, the relation between place (topos) and the bodies that inhabit it attracted Aristotle's attention in the fourth book of his *Physics*. His search for a definition of place resulted in a highly complex and somewhat contradictory analysis, which has taxed scholarship. It is clear, however, that Aristotle believed in the intimate interdependence of place and the bodies that inhabit it; one begins where the contours of the other end. Furthermore, he regarded place as something finite.

LANDSCAPE AS FIGURE

We may discern a concern with the finite in the employment of personification to suggest landscape. Book 21 of the *Iliad* is a wonderful exploration of thought process and mental imaging. It shuttles back and forth between the watery landscape properties of the River Xanthus/ Scamander and a humanized/deified conception that allows the river to confront Achilles and express his outrage at the heap of Trojan bodies that the Greek hero dumps into his waters. In book 20 Scamander stands against the god Hephaestus in the battle ranks (20.73–4; 21.365–84). Many centuries after Homer, Philostratus' ekphrasis on *Scamander*, making explicit reference to the *Iliad*, described a painting that included the personified Trojan river fighting against Hephaestus (*Imagines* 1.1.1). The Hellenistic poet Callimachus in his *Hymn to Delos* described the island as if it were a female swimmer.

> There is an island on the water, shining,
> slender, roaming the waves. Her feet have yet
> to touch the ground. She floats
> on the current like a stem of asphodel, winds
> from south and winds from east
> blowing her hither and thither, and the sea
> sweeps her where he wishes.
>
> (191–4, trans. F. Nisetich)

Among landscape elements, it was rivers and springs that most often became mythological characters, even deities. Rivers were typically gendered male and springs female. The great River Achelous in Acarnania in western Greece, who wrestled with Heracles for the hand of Deianeira (Sophocles, *Trachiniae* 507–30), was animated in various animal and human guises in literature and was usually rendered as a bull with a human face in art. His bearded human face emerges abruptly in profile from the chiseled ground of a votive relief from the richly outfitted cave at Vari previously mentioned.[32] Today in the Archaeological Museum in Athens and dated ca. 320 BCE, the relief is shaped in the form of a cave's entrance, similar to that of Figure 13. One female figure sits against the left wall of the cave, and Achelous' bearded head emerges in profile next to her rocky seat. Above her head the god Pan is shown in low relief. Another seated figure delineates the cave's right wall, with a hunter and dog rendered in relief above. A third woman stands in the middle, facing the viewer and resting with one hand against the cave's ceiling. Socrates knew Achelous to be the father of the nymphs (Plato, *Phaedrus* 263D; cf. *Iliad* 24.616), though others cited a different parentage, and it is most likely that the three women are nymphs. Achelous' head is the only one still preserved in this composition.

The River Cephissus was shown as a bearded man with bull's horns leading three nymphs on one of the two sides of a late fifth-century BCE Attic relief in the Archaeological Museum in Athens,[33] while the figure on the north corner of the Parthenon's west pediment is often identified as Cephissus or Ilissus in human form. Alpheius and Cladeus reclined on the east pediment of the early Classical temple of Zeus at Olympia, where Pausanias identified them (5.10.7), though not to every scholar's satisfaction.

CONCLUDING REMARKS

Personification brings us full circle back to ancient Greek art's most prominent characteristic in all periods, its anthropocentrism. It is difficult to overestimate the importance of the human body as primary carrier of identity and narrative meaning. The Greek mythological landscape was fundamentally a bodyscape. Whether conveyed naturalistically or metaphorically, the motifs of nature served primarily to frame human actions and movements, as recent research has reaffirmed. This aspect of the mythical tradition seems to have been resistant to social and historical change over time, even though the engagement with nature intensified in the course of the Classical and, especially, in the Hellenistic period. Dated to the middle of the second century BCE and today in Berlin, the Hellenistic Telephus frieze from the Altar of Zeus at Pergamon, which narrated this hero's life story, depicts numerous geographical notations. It includes recognizable species of trees such as plane and oak, but its focus remains the narrative that the figures enact.[34] Landscape is not rendered as an expansive luxurious whole but as a stark collection of individual features in close-up.

Generally, in Greek art, there is little by way of blue skies and green vegetation, lofty distant mountains, expansive lakes and seas, or meandering rivers. But so much more was accessible through the imagination. The crisply demarcated and stylized forms of bodies and landscape elements do not speak of dreamy romanticism, but solitary forms could act as signals for the imagination to roam in dreamy places. This surely amounts to a rich and viable conception of landscape. Vision and imagination, real life and mythology worked in synergy, as in the conversation between Phaedrus and Socrates on the banks of the Ilissus mentioned above. Their search for a beautiful spot in which to read occasioned an unexpectedly detailed and experiential description of place, as well as the impression that this real place was marked forever by the presence of the mythical Boreas and Oreithyia. In typical philosophically rational mode, Phaedrus and Socrates questioned the reality of this myth, but in the end they were unwilling to dispense with customary belief. When, centuries later, Pausanias, who was much less philosophically inclined,

327

combed the Greek landscape, he too was able to experience myth and reality simultaneously, tangible landscape elements together with imaginary deities resident within them, even though he often questioned the veracity of his sources. Both the longevity of mythical traditions and the fact that Greece's physical landscape changed rather slowly over time allowed Pausanias to experience and record a sense of continuity with the past as he traced the location of springs, caves, mountains, and also cities and sanctuaries.

The literary aesthetic and the visual aesthetic of Greece were highly eclectic, and landscape was a flickering phenomenon that can be traced discontinuously through the course of antiquity. Not surprisingly, art and literature did not select the same features to engage with and describe. At the same time that they subscribed to broad cultural ideals, individual artists manipulated the mythical landscapes for expressive purposes and took their viewers to new territories. When they felt the need, such individuals could locate their culture's anthropomorphism and the narrative requirements at hand within expansive spatial frameworks. Their works coexist with countless others – from the Geometric to the Hellenistic period – that insist on completely blank, undifferentiated backgrounds. In all cases artists took for granted their audiences' deep familiarity with the Greek landscape and asked the imagination to fill the voids. This situation is in the end not so different from that of mythical discourse itself, whose multiple versions were the result of traditions colliding with individual tellers' points of view and emphases.

FURTHER READING

As the present volume makes abundantly clear, the bibliography on ancient Greek myth is immense. Among works on myth, Buxton 1994 and 2004 are especially sensitive to matters of Greece's landscape. Osborne 1987 and Rackham 1990 highlight Greece's physical landscape and the uses in which it was put, while Luce 1998 explores the physical aspects of key Homeric locations. Cole 2004 engages with the intersection of gender, landscape, and ritual space from the perspective of textual and physical evidence. The essays in Alcock et al. 2001 discuss Pausanias, who in the second century CE selectively recorded aspects of the mythical and sacred landscape of Greece. Given the discontinuous nature of its evidence, the visual representation of landscape is a problematical topic, quite difficult to synthesize. The relevant scholarship is dispersed and carried out in various languages. Especially helpful among English publications are Hurwit 1991, which surveys the depiction of natural features and charts intersections with early Greek literature, and Hedreen 2001, which pays special attention to the narrative roles of landscape elements in images of the Trojan War. Both are concerned with the Archaic and early Classical periods and focus on the contribution of vase painting. Hurwit 1982 (with Madden 1983) raises the question of the emotive implications of landscape elements. Carroll-Spillecke 1985 surveys the evidence from relief sculpture, while Cohen 2001 studies aspects of myth and landscape in the Hellenistic period. It was once customary to study landscape in Greek art in light of the much more profusely documented genre of Roman mythological landscape painting. The hypothesis that the latter copied or variously echoed Hellenistic Greek precedents is no longer favored by scholars. Earlier scholarship, however, such as Schefold 1960 and von Blanckenhagen 1963 (together with Dawson 1944, which studies landscape as a distinctly Roman invention), is still valuable to the student of ancient Greek mythological landscapes. Clark 1947, Mitchell 1984, Hirsch and O'Hanlon 1995, and Roskill 1997 explore theoretical issues that the landscape genre raises.

NOTES

1   Plato, *Phaedrus* 230D; Parry 1957, 3; Pattichis 2001; Roger 2001.
2   For discussion of various aspects of the landscape genre, see Gardner 1988; Pochat 1973, 17–39; Elliger 1975; Borchhardt 1980; Carroll-Spillecke 1985; Wegener 1985; Siebert 1996, 7–10; Rouveret 1989, 318–36; Hurwit 1991; Schnapp 1994–95; Roger 1995; Halm-Tisserant 1999; Hedreen 2001; Venit 2002, 85–90, 101–18; Rühfel 2003; Rouveret 2004; Cohen 2005; Doukellis 2005. See Andronikos 1984, 102–19 on a nonmythological wall painting from the second half of the fourth century BCE whose depiction of landscape is unusually expansive.
3   Halperin 1983 distinguishes bucolic from pastoral poetry and considers Theocritus the originator of only the former; see Phinney 1967 and Williams 1991 on Apollonius Rhodius; Nishimura-Jensen 2000 on Apollonius and Callimachus; Parry 1957, 15 on Plato as the originator of a pastoral attitude to be elaborated in the Hellenistic period. Thesleff 1981 discusses early occurrences of the *locus amoenus* ("lovely place") in Greek poetry, going back to Homer.
4   Morgan 1988, 121–42; Doumas 1992, pls. 35–48; Televantou 1994, esp. 95–9, 114–15, 264–74, 295–307, 309–38.
5   Warren 1979; Morris 1989; critique in Farnoux 1996, 28–30.
6   von Blanckenhagen 1963; Biering 1995.
7   Ferrari forthcoming.
8   See Hedreen 2001 in connection with narratives of the Trojan War (91–119 on Ajax).

9   See Siebert 1990, 153 for others. On Pan's attributes and natural domain, see the
    Homeric Hymn to Pan; Borgeaud 1988.

10 Weller et al. 1903; Connor 1988; Borgeaud 1995; Larson 2001, 14–19, 242–5, fig.
    5.9; Schörner and Goette 2004, 16–30, pl. 11.

11 Connor 1988, 163.

12 See Siebert 1990 for representative examples on vases. He notes that Archaic vases
    tend to show caves in profile views, while Classical vases usually opt for frontality;
    see Carroll-Spillecke 1985, 56–61 on reliefs.

13 Athens, National Archaeological Museum, 1449; Kaltsas 2002, 219 (Cat. No. 454).

14 Argos Museum, C149; Hurwit 1991, 43, 45, fig. 10.

15 Boston, Museum of Fine Arts, 04.18; attributed to Aison; Shapiro 1995, 158–79,
    fig. 27.

16 Boston, Museum of Fine Arts, 10.191a-b; attributed to the Leningrad Painter.
    See Neils and Oakley 2003, 274 (Cat. No. 82) with bibliography. On the literary
    theme of girls in nature, see Bremer 1975.

17 London, British Museum, E224; Burn 1987, 15–25.

18 Boston, Museum of Fine Arts, 34.79; Giesecke 1999; Rühfel 2003, 106, fig. 65.

19 See Stansbury-O'Donnell 1990 for a reconstruction.

20 On literary visions of the Underworld, see Cole 2003; Edmonds 2004.

21 London, British Museum, D5; Burn 1985, 93, 94, 101–5, figs. 23.1, 24.2; Hoff-
    mann 1997, 120–126, figs. 66–9.

22 London, British Museum, D6, ca. 460–450 BCE; Burn 1985, 94–5, fig. 23.2;
    Rühfel 2003, 100–102, fig. 61.

23 On mountains in Greek literature, see Hyde 1915–16; Buxton 1992 and 1994,
    81–96.

24 Athens, National Archaeological Museum, 16463. See Oakley 2004, 123, fig. 86;
    113–25 generally on Charon scenes.

25 Rome, Museo Nazionale Etrusco di Villa Giulia, 2609; Borchhardt 1980, 259–
    60, pl. 55.1; Moon 1983, 110–13, fig. 7.19a–c (scene with nymphs), fig. 7.18a–c
    (Dionysus); Moon 1985, 63, fig. 18a–b; Hurwit 1991, 40–42, fig. 5; Rühfel 2003,
    66–7, fig. 39.

26 Borchhardt 1980, 260–61, fig. 1; Hurwit 1991, 36, 39, 40, fig. 3.

27 Rühfel 2003 for extended discussion. On the significance of trees, see also Davies
    1988 and Birge 1994.

28 Toledo Museum of Art, 63.26; Moon 1985, 47, 61–2, fig. 11a; Hurwit 1991, 42–3,
    fig. 8.

29 Boulogne, Château-Musée, 558; Hurwit 1991, 51, 52, fig. 23; Hedreen 2001, 102,
    112, 117–19, fig. 27; Rühfel 2003, 80–82, fig. 48.

30 Naples, Museo Archeologico Nazionale, H 2422 (81669); Hurwit 1991, 51, 52,
    fig. 24; Hedreen 2001, 64–8, 77, fig. 3a–b.

31 Hurwit 1982; Fowler 1989, 104–9.

32 Athens, National Archaeological Museum, 2012; Kaltsas 2002, 218 (Cat. No. 452);
    Schörner and Goette 2004, 71–4, pl. 42.1. Generally on rivers and river iconog-
    raphy, see Gais 1978; Klementa 1993; Brewster 1997. On springs, see Hill 1964;
    on personification, Webster 1954.

33 Athens, National Archaeological Museum, 1783; Kaltsas 2002, 134 (Cat. No. 258).

34 Cohen 2001, 98–100.

11: POLITICS AND GREEK MYTH

Jonathan M. Hall

ausanias has long been essential reading for archaeology students and those interested in reconstructing the topography of ancient *poleis*. Yet – as anybody who has been frustrated by such infuriatingly vague directions as 'not far from' or 'a little further on' can testify – Pausanias is not overwhelmingly interested in offering his readers a detailed guided tour of sites to see. Rather, the monuments that are described are the repositories of local narratives, both factual and fictional, that constitute an important part of the cultural heritage of a Greece now enslaved to Rome.[1] In the description of the Argive *agora*, for example, the reader is introduced in short order to the tomb where Danaus' daughter Hypermnestra and her husband Lynceus are buried (2.21.2), the tumulus where Perseus interred Medusa's head (21.5) and the underground bronze chamber in which Acrisius incarcerated Danae (23.7). Each *polis* that Pausanias visits grounds its unique identity in the specific matrix of myths and memories that are conveyed through such visible monuments.[2]

Myth was not, however, confined to affairs *within* the *polis*. From at least the fifth century, diplomatic relationships between *poleis* had been articulated through the vocabulary of kinship (*syngeneia*), often explained in terms of mythical connections between the two communities. Thus, at about the time when Pausanias was writing (probably in the 160s and 170s CE), an inscription was set up in the Argive *agora* celebrating the kinship between Argos and Cilician Aegeae and noting that it dated back to the time when Perseus, son of Danae, travelled to Cilicia in his hunt for the Gorgons.[3]

Yet, for all that, the kinship that is publicized in inscriptions of the Late Hellenistic and Roman periods seems ever more artificial, and the mythological routes by which it is justified often seem so contrived and contorted that it is difficult to believe in the sincerity of its signatories.[4] Similarly, spend a lot of time with Pausanias and the novelty begins to jade, with the various myths that are dutifully recounted taking on something of an ossified aspect. The incessant accumulation of such narratives may invoke a potent cultural legacy, but the myths themselves, which are variously derived from local lore, epic poetry, the written accounts of Hellenistic scholars, and rational deduction, lack any internal organizing structure or function. The fact is that myth meant something entirely different to Greeks of Pausanias' generation than it had to their ancestors. Originally, the term *mythoi* connoted authoritative utterances that sought to advance powerful truth claims. Born in a predominantly oral environment, their potency relied in large part on their capacity to respond, adapt to, and seemingly explain new and changing circumstances. By contrast, Pausanias and his intellectual contemporaries belonged to a milieu that was decidedly bookish and in which the learned literary allusion was the guarantee of the educated man. Confined within the written word, *mythoi* not only were divorced from their original performative contexts but also were deprived of their fluid and adaptive faculty. Tellingly, when the Romans referred to Greek *mythoi*, they called them *fabulae* (mere 'tales' or 'stories').[5]

One of the more significant contributions to modern scholarship on myth was the notion – advanced by Georges Dumézil and, more especially, Claude Lévi-Strauss – that myth is taxonomy in narrative form.[6] That is to say, myth classifies, demarcates, and seeks to establish the relationship between categories. But, as the historian of religions Bruce Lincoln has pointed out, 'taxonomy is hardly a neutral process, since the order established among all that is classified . . . is hierarchic as well as categoric.' Furthermore, the timeless, authoritative quality of myth serves to naturalize and legitimate the hierarchic categorization that it conveys. For this reason, Lincoln argues that myth may be defined as 'ideology in narrative form.'[7] To view myth as ideology introduces the issue of agency – something that was lacking in the theory of Lévi-Strauss, for whom myths think themselves through humans. Through the dynamic dialectic between narrator and audience, traditional materials could be reconfigured and modulated to stake claims about the natural order and to advance partisan interests, and it is precisely myth's ideological character that made it so effective in the practice of ancient Greek politics.

There is also, however, another feature of Greek myth that made it particularly apt for the politically fragmented landscape of the Greek world. Individual myths may have sought to express ideological messages in narrative form, but they derived their authority and legitimacy from the fact that they drew on a relatively stable repertoire of symbolic resources. This was particularly important in the context of relationships between Greek city-states, since, as Arjun Appadurai has pointed out, 'any past must be interdependent with other "pasts" to ensure minimal credibility.'[8] Put another way, Greek Myth (with a capital 'M') constituted what structural linguists call a *langue* ('language') or universally comprehensible system of symbols, from which a particular conjunction of symbols – a *parole* or 'speech' – could be assembled, deconstructed, and reassembled to achieve a particular ideological aim. The credibility and intelligibility of the *parole* was directly dependent upon the familiarity with, and recognition of, the *langue*, and for this reason myth was most effective not when it was invented *ex nihilo* but when it represented itself as a modulation of a preexisting theme. In the remainder of this chapter, I will consider three case studies that demonstrate myth's capacity to charter and justify changing political circumstances.

CASE STUDY 1: THE BONES OF ORESTES AND SPARTA'S 'PHILACHAEAN POLICY'

The Atreids at Sparta

Around the middle of the sixth century, according to Herodotus (1.67–8), the Spartans exhumed what they claimed were the bones of Agamemnon's son Orestes at the city of Tegea in Arcadia and transported them with much solemnity back to Sparta.[9] As a result, Herodotus says, the Spartans began to enjoy military success against the Tegeans, despite an earlier crushing defeat, and quickly subjugated most of the Peloponnese. According to rumours, a high-ranking Spartan agent named Liches, on the instigation of the Delphic oracle, located the superhuman cadaver in the courtyard of a blacksmith's forge. Whatever was really inside the coffin that the Spartans transported to Sparta, it is clear that the procession was viewed as a return home. Pindar (*Pyth.* 11.16, 32) describes Orestes as Laconian and narrates how his father, Agamemnon, met his pitiful end at 'famous Amyclae,' the village that lies 8 km to the south of Sparta.[10] This was no Pindaric invention, designed to flatter an aristocratic patron: already in the sixth century, the poet Stesichorus is said to have located Agamemnon's palace at Sparta.[11] During his visit to Amyclae, Pausanias was shown a sanctuary and a statue of Alexandra – locally identified with the Trojan princess Cassandra – together with a statue of Clytaemnestra and 'what is considered to be the tomb of Agamemnon' (3.19.6). Clement of Alexandria (Protr. 32) and the Scholiast to Lycophron (1123, 1369) added that Agamemnon was also worshipped in the sanctuary under the title Zeus Agamemnon. Archaeological exploration of the sanctuary, located at Ayia Paraskevi, testifies to cultic activity since the late eighth century but, interestingly, it is only from ca. 525 BCE that inscribed dedications to both Agamemnon and Alexandra begin to make their appearance.[12]

The priority that Pausanias gives to Alexandra might suggest that she was the original recipient of cultic honours at Amyclae and that her association with Cassandra and the installation of a funerary cult to Agamemnon were innovations of the sixth century. That certainly seems to be the case at another sanctuary, conventionally but perhaps erroneously known as the Menelaion, situated near a Mycenaean 'mansion' at Therapne, on the eastern banks of the Eurotas river.[13] Here, too, offerings are attested from the later eighth century and the earliest inscribed dedications – a seventh-century bronze *aryballos* and a sixth-century *harpax* – are to Helen. Helen seems to have occupied a particularly important place within Spartan cult: Herodotus (6.61.3) explicitly describes her as a goddess (she was, after all, the daughter of Zeus and sister of the Dioscuri). Menelaus was, however, to find a place in the sanctuary: the seventh-century *aryballos* mentions him (though only in terms of his spousal connection to Helen), but it is once more the sixth century that finds him the recipient of a dedicated bronze *phiale*. Finally, Pausanias (7.1.8) records that the Spartans also brought to Sparta the bones of Orestes' son Tisamenus, who had been buried at Helice in Achaea after falling in a battle against the Ionians.[14] No date is offered for this episode, but it is difficult to avoid the suspicion that it should be grouped with all the other attempts to 'repatriate' the members of the Atreid family in the sixth century.

A Spartan Agamemnon? Homer had, of course, located Atreus' son at Mycenae, and it is presumably Pausanias' supposed autopsy of Agamemnon's grave at Mycenae (2.16.5) that causes him to question the Amyclaean claim. Yet Mycenae was singularly ill equipped to accommodate Agamemnon's sovereignty. In the *Iliad* (2.108), he is described as ruling over 'the whole of Argos' (where 'Argos' probably signifies the Peloponnese generally rather than the Argive plain specifically), and yet only a few hundred lines later, in the *Catalogue of Ships* (2.559–80), the Argive plain is under the joint sway of Diomedes, Sthenelus, and Euryalus, the inheritors of the original Argive triarchy established by Anaxagoras, Melampus, and Bias.[15] To rehabilitate his otherwise slighted status, Agamemnon is assigned, in addition to Mycenae, a large part of

Corinthia, but this results in Bellerophon (whom the Corinthians of
the historical period considered to be a civic hero) being consigned to
the obscure village of Ephyre (6.152).[16]

In fact, Homer was almost certainly aware of a tradition that associated Agamemnon with Sparta. In the *Odyssey* (4.514–20), Agamemnon
is described as running into a storm off Cape Malea in the southern
Peloponnese on his way home from Troy, and it is difficult to understand what he was doing so far south if his intention was to return
to Mycenae.[17] Similarly, his attempts in the *Iliad* (9.149–53) to appease
Achilles' wrath by offering him seven cities between Laconia and Messenia would be an empty act of magnanimity were they not his to offer in
the first place.[18] A long-standing tradition that placed Agamemnon on
the throne of Sparta rather than Mycenae might at least explain why,
in the list of Helen's suitors in the pseudo-Hesiodic *Catalogue of Women*
(fr. 197 Merkelbach-West), it is Agamemnon who seeks Helen's hand
'on behalf of Menelaus.' We might conjecture that the compiler was
attempting to reconcile Spartan tradition with Homeric narrative. The
Spartans in the sixth century, then, were resurrecting – rather than fabricating – a mythical tradition that associated Agamemnon with Sparta.
But why?

Spartan Foreign Relations

The traditional explanation sees Sparta's new 'philachaean policy' in
terms of a desire to secure the goodwill, not only of the Tegeans but
also of various other non-Dorian cities in the Peloponnese, by empha-
sizing Sparta's pre-Dorian 'Achaean' heritage. For many, this marks an
abrupt change from an earlier policy of aggressive annexation – as took
place in Messenia from the eighth century, for example, and as seems
to have been the Spartans' original intention towards Tegea – to the
adoption of more pacific relations that sowed the seeds for the system of bilateral alliances that modern scholars term the Peloponnesian
League.[19] The problem with this theory is that the Spartans never denied
the fact that they believed themselves to be Dorian immigrants from
further north who had expelled the former Achaean population from
its home.[20] Indeed, their claims to Laconia were based precisely on the
rights of conquest, and a cynical appeal to an Achaean heritage can
hardly have carried many hopes of success. Another theory suggests
that the 'philachaean policy' was designed to legitimate the authority
of the two Spartan kings who, at least since the time of Tyrtaeus in
the seventh century, did regard themselves as Achaean.[21] Indeed, the

early fifth-century king Cleomenes, when barred from trying to sacrifice on the Athenian acropolis because he was a Dorian, is supposed to have responded that he was an Achaean, not a Dorian.[22] But this theory too is not without difficulties, because the Spartan kings traced their lineage back to Heracles through his son, Hyllus, and not to the Atreid dynasty, which had only very loose connections to the Heraclids (Heracles' great-uncle, Sthenelus, married a sister of Atreus).

Deborah Boedeker, pointing to the problems with the traditional explanations, has argued that the Spartans' promotion of the Atreid dynasty was designed to restore unity among a citizen body that had become increasingly riven by political, social, and economic differences.[23] This is certainly plausible, but Herodotus explicitly connects the transferral of Orestes' bones both with Sparta's relationship with Tegea and with her position in the Peloponnese. I should like to suggest that, while the 'ethnic' Achaean dimension has been overstated, the attention given to the Atreid dynasty was indeed designed to offer a mythological precedent for the hegemonic alliance that the Spartans were constructing in the Peloponnese (perhaps originating in the orbit of her own neighbouring perioecic cities) and that it was a direct response to the mythological claims that were being staked by Argos, a city whose longstanding hostility towards Sparta had, according to Herodotus (1.82), reached a particularly critical juncture around the middle of the sixth century.

The Argive Response

We might perhaps have expected the Argives to co-opt Homeric authority and claim Agamemnon for themselves. That they did not is probably due to two factors. First, Homer located Agamemnon at Mycenae, not Argos, and although Mycenae was, in the sixth century, a relative backwater compared with its more powerful neighbour, it does seem to have retained its political (and cultural) independence.[24] (It was Aeschylus who transferred Agamemnon to Argos in the *Agamemnon* of 458 BCE, following the Argive destruction of Mycenae a decade earlier, while in the Atreid tragedies of Sophocles and Euripides, the two toponyms are used interchangeably.) Second, the inhabitants of Mycenae never seem to have warmed to the hero that Homer foisted on them. In later times, Agamemnon was honoured in a small sanctuary, 1 km from the citadel of Mycenae, but since all of the inscribed dedications to him date to its Hellenistic refurbishment, some scholars have suggested that in its earlier phase (from the late eighth century down to the fifth-century destruction of Mycenae), the sanctuary was a roadside shrine of Hera.[25] Instead, a far more important mythical personage was Perseus, and even as late as the Roman period, long after Argos had annexed the territories of Tiryns and Mycenae and expropriated their epichoric heroes, it was 'the honours of Heracles and Perseus' that were awarded to notable worthies, not 'the honours of Agamemnon.'[26]

A chance archaeological discovery in 1986 gives us a fairly good idea of the mythical discourse the Argives were employing in the sixth century. In the northern sector of the ancient *agora*, built into a fourth-century CE enclosure, was a reused pillar that had evidently served as part of a much earlier enclosure. On it, in letter forms dating to the mid-sixth century, was the inscription EPOON TON EN ΘEBAIΣ (probably to be translated as 'The Heroon of those in Thebes').[27] We do not know where the original enclosure stood, but the reused pillar was found in a part of the *agora* where Pausanias (2.19.7, 20.4) reports seeing a statue group of the seven Peloponnesian heroes who marched on Thebes in support of Polynices' claim to Oedipus' throne, as well as the altar of Zeus Hyetius, on which the heroes are supposed to have sworn an oath to capture Thebes or else die in the attempt. Pausanias describes a number of monuments associated with the myth, including the house of Adrastus and the sanctuary of Amphiaraus, but this archaeological finding at least demonstrates that the myth already possessed a functional significance in the mid-sixth century.

The heroon was not a tomb. Although the Athenians claimed that Theseus had buried the heroes at Eleusis,[28] the inscription seems to imply that the Argives believed their remains were interred at Thebes itself. Nor were the Argives claiming that the heroes were all local sons: Parthenopaeus was said to be Arcadian, while Tydeus, the father of Diomedes, hailed from Aetolia. But it was under an Argive leader, Adrastus, that the seven marched against Thebes, it was from Argos that they set out after swearing their fateful oath, and it was as Argives that their Theban opponents were to know them. As in the epic poem, the *Thebais*, where the city of Argos is invoked in the very first word, the establishment of the heroon was presumably intended to express the Argives' claims to centrality and primacy within the Peloponnese by appealing to their leadership of a legendary Peloponnesian alliance against the most powerful Bronze Age city north of the Corinthian isthmus.

If this reconstruction is correct, both Sparta and Argos employed mythical prototypes of alliances to justify their own claims to Peloponnesian hegemony in the mid-sixth century. It was the Spartans, however, who played the trump card, because Agamemnon's 'coalition of the willing' was far more expansive and inclusive than that of the Seven and, unlike the disastrous Theban expedition, it was collectively (if not individually) successful. If Herodotus (7.159) can be believed, the mythological precedent of Agamemnon's hegemonic alliance had lost little of its symbolic potency even as late as the 480s BCE. When the Syracusan tyrant Gelon demanded the leadership of the Greek army in return for his aid against the invading Persians, the Spartan ambassador is said to have exclaimed 'The Pelopid, Agamemnon, would wail greatly if he learned that the Spartans had been robbed of hegemony by Gelon and the Syracusans.'

CASE STUDY 2: THESEUS, PISISTRATUS, AND THE CLEISTHENIC DEMOCRACY

Theseus and Heracles

Somewhere around 500 BCE (though the date is disputed), the Athenians dedicated a small marble Doric treasury on the Sacred Way at Delphi.[29] On the long northern side of the building, nine carved metopes depicted the Labours of Heracles (the tenth Labour, the battle with the triple-bodied Geryon, was represented on the west frieze). On the more visible southern side was shown a parallel cycle of adventures involving Theseus, including combats against the Minotaur, the Bull of Marathon, the Sow of Crommyon, an Amazon, and the brigands Sinis, Cercyon, Procrustes, and Sciron. It has long been recognized that the decorative scheme of the building reflects a sea-change in Athenian iconography, whereby the exploits of the Athenian hero Theseus were championed at the expense of those of the more Panhellenic Heracles. The metopes of the Athenian treasury are compared with part of a statue group, found on the Athenian acropolis and conventionally dated between 510 and 500, that may represent Theseus' combat with Procrustes, as well as with scenes that appear in the same decade on Attic red-figure pottery and that portray Theseus' exploits on the road from Troezen to Athens. The normal explanation offered for the sudden interest in Theseus in the final decade of the sixth century is that he was promoted as the emblematic hero of the new Athenian democracy, established by Cleisthenes shortly after 508 BCE, with the explicit intention of neutralizing and eclipsing the iconographic importance of Heracles, a hero championed by the former Pisistratid regime.[30]

From around the middle of the sixth century, Heracles receives a prominence in Athenian art that he had not known before and that even outweighs artistic representations of the hero in his native Peloponnese. Scholars are generally agreed that the guiding hand behind this phenomenon was probably the Athenian tyrant Pisistratus, who is supposed to have ruled Athens continuously from ca. 546 to ca. 528 BCE after a couple of shorter-lived coups.[31] Particular interest has focused on scenes on Attic black-figure pottery that seem to begin in the 550s BCE and that portray Heracles being conveyed in a chariot to Mount Olympus alongside the goddess Athena because, according to Herodotus (1.60), after his first period of exile, Pisistratus processed to the Athenian acropolis in a chariot, accompanied by an extraordinarily tall woman named Phye, whom he dressed as Athena. It has also been noted that Pausanias (1.15.3) claims that the first people to recognize Heracles as a god, rather than a hero, were the people of Marathon – an area where the Pisistratid family seems to have commanded particularly strong support and to which Pisistratus' son Hippias was to guide the Persian army in 490 BCE.[32] But, even if we accept that Pisistratus was responsible for cultivating Heracles' popularity in Attica, is it really so inevitable that he would have reserved his loyalty for this hero alone? Or is it possible that it was he or his sons, rather than the nascent democracy of ca. 500 BCE, that first began to promote the claims of Theseus?[33]

Pisistratus or Cleisthenes?

There has been something of a concerted campaign in recent decades to credit the Pisistratid tyrants with absolutely nothing. A notice, purportedly attributed to Aristotle, that connects Pisistratus with a reorganization of the Panathenaia festival is normally dismissed in favour of Eusebius' statement that an athletic contest was established in 566/5 – a date considered by many to be too early for Pisistratid involvement.[34] Yet, quite apart from the fact that the chronology for the earlier phases of Pisistratus' tyranny actually rests on extremely precarious evidence,[35] little effort has been expended in explaining how Eusebius, writing in the early fourth century CE, arrived at his date or in asking whether the introduction of games in the 560s (which does roughly correspond with the first production of the Panathenaic amphorae that were awarded as prizes) necessarily excludes later Pisistratid involvement. Religious building projects such as the Archaic temple to Artemis at Brauron, the sanctuary of Artemis Brauronia on the Athenian acropolis, the second Telesterion (Initiation Hall) at Eleusis, or the City Eleusinion, once unproblematically dated to the reign of Pisistratus or his sons, have gradually been downdated so that their construction falls within the final decade of the sixth century, after the expulsion of Pisistratus' son Hippias in 510 BCE.[36] A case in point is the so-called *Archaios Neos*, dedicated to Athena Polias on the Athenian acropolis. Originally dated to the last quarter of the sixth century and generally attributed to Hippias and his brother, Hipparchus, the argument has recently been advanced that it dates more precisely to the period 510–500 and hence cannot be associated with the tyranny.[37]

Is it pure chance that many of these revisionist chronologies were published around the year 1993 (the year widely acclaimed as marking the 2,500th anniversary of Cleisthenes' reforms and the invention of democracy) or that many of them should have been written by scholars from America – the modern inheritor of the form of governance that the Athenians supposedly invented? Is it possible, in other words, that a particular ideology is being advanced in narrative form, thus revealing – as Lincoln reluctantly admits – scholarship to be itself a form of myth?[38] There are actually very few signs that the Pisistratid tyranny was execrated immediately after Hippias' expulsion. In fact, a member of the family held the archonship or chief magistracy in 496 BCE and it may not have been until the 480s BCE, after the Battle of Marathon, that the regime suffered a *damnatio memoriae* and statues of the 'tyrannicides' who had assassinated Hipparchus in 514 BCE were set up in the Athenian *agora*.[39]

One thing that needs to be pointed out is that, despite undeniable advances in method in recent decades, chronological assignments that are based on stylistic considerations such as floor plans, measurement ratios, or the evolving profile of Doric capitals are not nearly as precise as they might initially appear. Not only are they predicated on the probably erroneous fallacy that stylistic evolution is unilineal, uniform, and universal, but also they are anchored to an absolute chronology by dates that are very often little more than hazarded guesses. The events by which the Pisistratid tyranny ended in 510 BCE involved a siege of the Acropolis by the Spartan king Cleomenes that lasted only a few days. Archaeological chronologies based on purely stylistic considerations are simply incapable of determining which side of that brief event a monument or an artefact should fall.

Furthermore, attempts to assign a precise, or relatively circumscribed, date to a building fail to give due attention to issues concerning planning and execution. Both the Temple of Zeus at Olympia and the Parthenon seem to have taken about fifteen years to build. Not all buildings would have taken as long, but even if we could be confident that the sculptures on the pediments of the *Archaios Neos* seem more advanced than – and therefore postdate – those on the pediments of the Temple of Apollo at Delphi, or that the treatment of Athena's drapery belongs more properly in the final decade of the sixth century,[40] it is by no means impossible that the temple was conceived and commissioned prior to the fall of the Pisistratids – especially since the architectural sculpture would have been the last part of the temple to be executed. A further complication is that it is difficult to gauge the amount of time that it would have taken Athenian artists to adopt and adapt new mythological themes. Even if it were the case that *not a single scene* portraying Theseus' exploits on the road from Troezen pre-dates 510 BCE (and since we do not know how representative our extant sample is, absolute certainty is impossible), we still cannot rule out the possibility that tales concerning the hero's deeds were circulating in written or oral form at an earlier date, with the active encouragement of the Pisistratid family.

In fact, the reassignment of late sixth-century monuments away from the Pisistratids to the Cleisthenic democracy presents two fundamental historical problems. The first is that it compresses far too much into far too narrow a chronological window. The immediate years subsequent to Hippias' expulsion were tumultuous; Cleisthenes did not enact his reforms until 508 BCE, at the very earliest, and they probably took some time to effect, so in essence it is unlikely that major monuments were commissioned before ca. 506 or thereabouts. Some have suggested that the *Archaios Neos* was built as a thanks offering after the Athenian defeat of the Boeotians and Chalcidians in 506, but that is something that we might have expected Herodotus to mention, especially since he discusses the erection on the Acropolis of a bronze four-horse chariot group as a commemoration of the victory.[41] The second is that one is left wondering exactly what it was that the Pisistratids did during their almost fifty-year reign.[42] Despite the overwhelmingly negative tone of narrative traditions about tyrants in general,[43] the Pisistratids were remembered as patrons of the art and it would be odd if this had not extended beyond the merely literary sphere to include public works.[44] It is, for example, generally accepted that Hippias and Hipparchus began construction of a new temple to Olympian Zeus in the Ilissus valley.

When, shortly after the middle of the fifth century, the Athenian democracy embarked on its ambitious building project on the Athenian acropolis, detractors are said to have compared it not with a programme executed half a century earlier by the fledgling democracy but with the acts of a tyrant.[45] The Periclean works were largely financed with the proceeds of the Athenian Empire, but where would the first democracy have found its funds? It is inconceivable that the spoils won from the Boeotians and the Chalcidians would have been sufficient. The fact is that it was tyrants who were particularly well placed to mobilize manpower and resources and it is for this reason that the literary sources consistently credit them with building projects. Furthermore, even under a democracy, such an undertaking required resolute planning and firm direction. The names of Pericles and Phidias are forever associated with the fifth-century refurbishment of the Acropolis; nobody – least of all Cleisthenes, who vanishes completely from the historical record after his tribal reforms – is associated with a project at the end of the sixth century. Such deliberate anonymity might, in fact, suggest that its initiator was the tyrant or his sons.

Pisistratus and Theseus

Let us return to Theseus. If representations of Theseus and in particular his exploits on the road from Troezen multiply in the last decade of the sixth century, it remains the case that he is not invisible in Athenian art prior to this date (it should be noted that one can have a little more confidence in the relative chronology of painted pottery as opposed to architecture, though this should not be exaggerated). Just a little earlier than the Troezen scenes, Theseus is portrayed battling against the Crommyonian Sow on a red-figure cup found at Cerveteri, while his abduction of the Amazon Antiope is represented on a red-figure cup ascribed to Euphronius, thought to be active from ca. 520 BCE. A little earlier still, probably around 530 BCE, a black-figure amphora now in Paris may depict the episode with the Marathonian Bull. From the middle of the sixth century, he is commonly depicted fighting the Minotaur and on the famous Attic volute krater known as the François Vase, found at Chiusi and dated to ca. 570 BCE or a little later, he is portrayed battling the centaurs and instituting a victory dance (the *geranos* or 'crane dance') on the island of Delos.[46] If Theseus enjoyed an upsurge in popularity under the Cleisthenic democracy, he was certainly not an invention of that regime.

There are, in fact, a number of reasons that Pisistratus might have found the figure of Theseus appealing. Theseus' ordeals on the road to Athens could have been thought to prefigure Pisistratus' own difficult efforts to seize power, while the hero's birth in Argolic Troezen offered a precedent for Pisistratus' marriage to the Argive Timonassa and, with it, an alliance that yielded dividends during his final, successful attempt at the tyranny, when he enlisted the support of 1,000 Argive mercenaries.[47] Similarly, Theseus' celebrated friendship with Pirithous, king of the Thessalian Lapiths, could serve as a charter for Pisistratus' ties to powerful Thessalian families – he named one of his sons Thessalos and, against a first unsuccessful Spartan invasion under Anchimolus, Hippias was able to count on the assistance of 1,000 cavalry under the Thessalian Cineas.[48] According to one, possibly Troezenian tradition, Theseus was the son of Poseidon, as was Neleus, the Pylian king from whom Pisistratus claimed descent. A homonymous descendant of Neleus was credited with the foundation of Miletus, the most important of the Ionian cities of Asia Minor that regularly celebrated their ethnic communion in Poseidon's sanctuary at Mycale.[49] The religious centre for the western Ionians, however, was the sanctuary of Apollo, Artemis, and Leto on the sacred island of Delos. Delos had a particular connection with Theseus because it was here that he is supposed to have conveyed the Athenian youths he rescued from the Minotaur's labyrinth and instituted the dance known as the *geranos*.[50] But it also boasted a connection with Pisistratus, who is said to have purified the island and reorganized the festival of the Deleia.[51] One scholar has even hypothesized that the Athenian *theoria* or sacred embassy that was dispatched to the island in anticipation of the festival passed through Brauron – the area of eastern Attica where the original home of the Pisistratids was said to be located.[52]

As we have seen, the Pisistratids were also associated with the area around Marathon, where Theseus is said to have battled a ferocious bull.[53] Across the Euripos straits from Marathon, on the island of Euboea, lay the city of Eretria, which served as the base for Pisistratid operations immediately before the final, successful attempt at the tyranny.[54] Indeed, another of Pisistratus' wives was said to be an aristocratic woman from Eretria named Coesyra.[55] In the centre of the city was the sanctuary of Apollo Daphnephoros, where cult stretches back to at least the eighth century, if not earlier. Towards the end of the sixth century, the Eretrians constructed a limestone temple with marble decoration, including a group that stood in one of the pediments and depicted Theseus' rape of Antiope. The date of the group, once confidently given as ca. 510 BCE, has surreptitiously slipped down in more recent scholarship, and one explanation given for the theme is that 'democratic' Eretria 'borrowed' the fresh hero of the Athenian democracy to celebrate its close alliance with Athens – especially on the occasion of the aid the two *poleis* offered to the rebellious cities of Ionia in 498 BCE.[56] But there really is no compelling evidence to suggest that the 'horsemen who controlled the government of Eretria'[57] and who had supported Pisistratus had lost control of the city before its destruction by the Persians in 490, and it is more likely that the sculptural decoration of the temple commemorates Eretria's close ties with one of the more prominent (albeit tyrannical) families of Attica than with the incipient democracy of Cleisthenes.

The Unification of Attica

It was, however, for the *synoikismos* or unification of Attica that Theseus was most remembered. According to Thucydides (2.15.2), Theseus dissolved the councils and offices of the other communities of Attica and compelled them to use a single *bouleuterion* (council chamber) and *prytaneion* (town hall) in Athens. The legendary event was commemorated in an annual festival named the Synoikia. It is easy to see why this might suggest a parallel with the legislation of Cleisthenes. The centrepiece of his reforms was to distribute the around 140 rural communities and urban wards among ten newly created 'tribes' to ensure that each tribe included communities from various parts of Attica, be it the interior, the coastal communities, or the city of Athens itself. Yet it is also becoming clear that the reforms were not a brand-new invention, designed to replace loyalties to particular lineage groups with ties based on locality, but rather a reorganization or reconfiguration – possibly for partisan political purposes – of a preexisting system in which various local units known as *naukrariai* had been distributed among the original four tribes of Attica.[58] Furthermore, undue emphasis on the Cleisthenic reforms underestimates the measures that Pisistratus and his sons seem to have taken to promote Attic unification.

Pisistratus is said to have introduced circuit judges who would go out into the countryside of Attica, dispensing the same standard of justice to all,[59] while Hipparchus is credited with setting up herms (ithyphallic pillars supporting the bust of the god Hermes) on the principal thoroughfares of Attica – one has been discovered at Koropi in southern Attica – on which were inscribed distances from the Altar of the Twelve Gods, dedicated in the centre of the Athenian *agora* by Pisistratus' homonymous grandson, probably in 521 BCE.[60] With the recent attempts to downdate the construction projects at Athens, Brauron, and Eleusis, definitive conclusions as to whether the Pisistratids sought to integrate these rural cults into an Athenian cultic system, marked by regular processions to the major sanctuaries from their urban counterparts, must remain *sub judice*.[61] Nevertheless, a late source does explicitly associate Pisistratus with the temple of Artemis at Brauron, and the cult at Eleusis can only really have become truly Athenian once Athens had been victorious in its war against neighbouring Megara – a victory that is said to have been secured under the generalship of Pisistratus. It is surely not insignificant that, way back in the past, Theseus is said to have captured Eleusis from the Megarians.[62]

As with the case of the Spartans and Agamemnon, Pisistratus could claim no direct lineal relationship with Theseus. Neleus' son Melanthus was an outsider from Pylos – a mythical antecedent that evidently proved useful to Pisistratus initially – and he assumed the royal power that had formerly been exercised by Thymoetes, the last descendant of Theseus.[63] But, as too in the Spartan example, Theseus offered an attractive prototype of the strong, wise, and just leader and, according to the myth, the transfer of power from the Theseids to the Neleids had been by the common consent of the people: in a certain sense, Melanthus promised a renewal of those qualities that Theseus had once demonstrated and from which his descendants had departed.

The author of the fourth-century Aristotelian *Constitution of the Athenians* (15.4–5) evidently believed there was a strong association between Pisistratus and Theseus. In describing the ruse by which the tyrant disarmed the population, he notes that Pisistratus gathered the people at the sanctuary of Theseus and addressed them *sotto voce*, compelling them to come closer while his henchmen gathered up their arms and deposited them in the shrine. The evidence considered here also supports the argument that it was Pisistratus, and not the Cleisthenic democracy, who first elevated the figure of Theseus to Panathenaic status. And this, I would venture, is why the eventual democratic cooption of Theseus was so successful. Rather than introducing a completely new component into the mythological vocabulary of Athenian art and culture, the democracy usurped a preexisting figure and endowed him with a different signification. The clearest example of this democratic usurpation is presented by Theseus' appearance on the friezes above the *pronaos* and *opisthodomos* of the Temple of Hephaestus, overlooking the Athenian *agora* and dating to the mid-fifth century. The friezes depict early events from Athenian history (including Theseus' defence of Athens against the Amazons, which appears above the *opisthodomos*), but what is truly remarkable is the stance in which Theseus is depicted on the two friezes, echoing precisely the two statues of the 'tyrannicides' that Critius and Nesiotes produced ca. 475 (the same motif appears on red-figured vases of the 460s and 450s; see Figures 3 and 4).[64] Theseus – at root, an autocrat like Pisistratus – had been recast as one of the tyrant-killers that popular Athenian belief, however incorrectly, regarded as the founding fathers of democracy.

CASE STUDY 3: BETWEEN DARDANIANS AND PHRYGIANS: REPRESENTATIONS OF THE TROJANS IN GREEK MYTH

The Trojans in Archaic Literature

One of the most enduring mythological themes in classical antiquity was the Achaean expedition against Troy. Constituting the backdrop not only for the *Iliad* and the *Odyssey*, but also for Rome's national epic, the *Aeneid*, the ten-year war that pitted Achaeans against Trojans came to stand as the epitome of an eternal and implacable hostility between east and west and one of the foundation stones for an 'orientalist' mentality that has, as Edward Saïd so powerfully demonstrated, pervaded western culture down to the present day.[65]

It had not always been so. In the *Iliad*, the Trojan protagonists bear Greek names, worship the same gods as the Greeks, have the same civic organization as the Greeks – indeed, in many respects, Troy is an archetypal Greek *polis* – and are portrayed by the poet no less (and perhaps even more) sympathetically than the Greeks. Greeks and Trojans might find themselves contracted to long-standing institutionalized guest-friendships, as in the famous case of Diomedes and Glaucon.[66] This is not to say that there are no differences between Greeks and Trojans. The Trojans – and Paris especially – are represented as being fond of luxury and good living, as well as a little excitable and disordered compared with their Greek counterparts. Furthermore, the language of the Achaeans tends to be more aggressive, externally directed, public, and political, while that of the Trojans is more reflective, introspective, private, and poetic. But there is nothing to suggest that this is a result of anything more than the dictates of characterization or that there is any ethnic significance to the distinctions.[67] Priam's son Hector received funerary cult in the Boeotian city of Thebes and Cassandra was, as we have seen, the recipient of cult at Amyclae and perhaps also at the Laconian sites of Leuctra and Thalamae, prompting some to suspect that the *Iliad*'s story originally recounted a war between two Greek cities that was later transposed to the Troad.[68]

The Homeric epics do not seem to be exceptional in their representation of the Trojans. One of Sappho's poems (fr. 44 Lobel-Page) celebrates the wedding of Hector to Andromache. In it, the poetess describes the adornments that accompanied the bridal party – golden bracelets, purple robes, ornate trinkets, countless silver drinking-cups, and ivory. There is no hint here of disdain for such luxuries: indeed, Sappho elsewhere extols items of Lydian dress and says that she is 'in love with *habrosyne*' (luxurious delicacy).[69] Ever since the tenth century, when objects of predominantly North Syrian origin begin to be deposited in graves in Attica, Euboea, Crete, and the Dodecanese, the elite had demarcated their status through the consumption and display of orientalia, whose prestige value was guaranteed by the difficulty of their acquisition.[70] By the time of Sappho in the late seventh century, the elites of the East Greek world looked to Lydian fashions and accessories to communicate social distinction; by the last third of the sixth century, the vogue had reached Athens, witnessed by the luxuriant and sumptuous garments sported by the *korai* dedicated on the acropolis. Not everybody was seduced: Xenophanes of Colophon (fr. 3 West) criticized his fellow citizens for learning 'useless luxuries' from the Lydians, but this is more of a social critique than an ethnic aspersion. On Attic vases of the second half of the sixth century, the Trojans – the Lydians' mythical prototype – are not distinguished by any pronounced ethnic characteristics (unlike, for example, the Scythians and the Thracians). Indeed, on the east frieze of the Treasury of the Siphnians at Delphi, constructed ca. 525 BCE, both Greeks and Trojans alike are depicted as hoplites – the heavily armed infantrymen who were later considered to be the embodiment of everything that made the Greeks unique.[71]

The Trojans also feature prominently in the *ktiseis* or foundation-narratives of overseas settlements – a genre that appears to become popular in the course of the sixth century. Trojan women are said to have accompanied their Achaean captors and settled in the territory of Croton in South Italy; further up the coast, the city of Siris had, according to one tradition, been founded by Trojans, while Thucydides (6.2.3) and Hellanicus (4 FGrH 31) both record the Trojan origins of the Elymians of western Sicily.[72] The most famous Trojan foundation in the west was, of course, Rome. Best known to us from Vergil, the story of the city's Trojan origins had already been accommodated – alongside the traditions concerning Romulus and Remus and the Arcadian Evander – within the official account of Roman *origines* by the third century BCE, though it is possible that Aeneas had already been associated with the West in the works of Stesichorus.[73] It was once believed that the identification of indigenous Italian populations with the Trojans was a device by which their 'otherness' might be articulated. This picture is complicated, however, by a tradition – possibly attested first in Hellanicus (4 FGrH 84) – that Aeneas had founded Rome together with Odysseus. Conversely, the Greek city of Aenea in the Thracian Chalcidice seems to have displayed no qualms about attributing its foundation to the Trojan prince Aeneas: silver tetradrachms of the sixth century portray Aeneas with his aged father, Anchises, on his shoulders and his wife and son at his side.[74] This has prompted the suggestion that the attribution of Trojan ancestry may have been designed to bridge, rather than emphasize, the divide between the Greek and non-Greek worlds.[75]

The Orientalization of the Trojans

In the fifth century, however, the Trojans were 'orientalized,' becoming assimilated with the generic antitypical figure of the barbarian and, more especially, with the Phrygians, for whom a distinctive iconographic stereotype simultaneously emerged in Attic vase painting.[76] The Trojans' penchant for luxurious living was now recast in unremittingly negative terms but, in addition to this, they were regarded as wily, effeminate, and cowardly. In Euripides' *Andromache*, probably performed in the 420s BCE, Hermione castigates the play's Trojan protagonist for bearing children by those who murdered her kin: 'That's how the whole barbarian race is: father sleeps with daughter, son with mother and sister with brother' (173–5).[77]

It has long been recognized that the development of a barbarian stereotype was a consequence of the Persian War of 480–479 BCE. Attested only very infrequently before this date, the term *barbaros* now becomes far more common in Greek literature and Attic drama in particular. By embodying every characteristic that was thought to be the negation of Greek qualities, the invention of the barbarian invited speculation on what it was that Greeks had in common and was therefore crucial for conceiving of Hellenic identity more widely.[78] But the historical circumstances in which the figure developed meant that the archetypal barbarian was the Persian and that all other non-Greeks – especially easterners – were, in a certain sense, proxies for the historical foe that the Greeks had repulsed. This was no less true for the Trojans. Pindar's fifth *Isthmian Ode*, written in the 470s BCE, explicitly compares the Battle of Salamis, in which the Greeks scored a crushing victory over the Persian fleet, to the Battle of Troy. The ode was written for a victor from Aegina, and it is interesting that the Aeginetans, whose valour at Salamis was commented upon by Herodotus (8.93.1), chose to adorn the pediments of the Temple of Aphaea with scenes depicting Agamemnon's expedition against Troy and the earlier assault on the city by Heracles.[79] On the Parthenon, the juxtaposition of carved metopes depicting the Greek sack of Troy with those portraying combats between Gods and Giants, Lapiths and Centaurs, and Athenians and Amazons was almost certainly designed to evoke the more recent historical conflict with the Persians. Any subtle allusions were discarded in the Stoa Poikile in the Athenian *agora*, where a painting of the Greeks at Troy was hung alongside one recording the Athenian victory over the Persians at Marathon.[80]

Athens, in whose art and literature the barbarian figures most prominently, had much to gain by perpetuating this symbolic stereotype, since the league over which the Athenians presided and from which much of their wealth was derived was maintained by the threat of a permanent hostility with the east. There was, however, more to it than that. The term *demokratia*, which seems to have emerged as a political slogan in the 460s BCE, certainly carried connotations of equality but literally signified the power of the *demos* – a word that had been used, in Archaic poetry, to describe the general populace as opposed to the elite. Put another way, the political victory of the Athenian people – and, of course, it was this section of Athenian society that had crewed the ships at Salamis – was achieved at the expense of the elite. But, as we have seen, one of the ways in which the elite communicated its distinctiveness in the Archaic period was in the consumption and display of eastern artefacts and practices. By fostering the sense of an eternal and implacable enmity between west and east, the Athenian populace was effectively proscribing elite practices and seeking to dissolve visible cultural distinctions between classes.[81]

The assimilation of the Trojans to the Persians was to exercise a powerful effect on politics in the fourth century. Before setting out on his disastrous expedition against the Persian empire in 396 BCE, Agesilaus II of Sparta attempted to offer sacrifice at Boeotian Aulis – from where Agamemnon's fleet had supposedly sailed out – until the rituals were disrupted by the Boeotian cavalry.[82] This was a period in which conflict between Greek cities was endemic. The solution proposed by the Athenian orator Isocrates was to launch a Panhellenic campaign of vengeance against the Persian Empire – purportedly in the name of retribution for the Persian invasion more than a century earlier, but with the principal intention of persuading the Greek city-states to submerge their differences in a common undertaking. In the *Panathenaicus*, completed in 339 BCE, Isocrates embarked on a eulogy of Agamemnon, 'the only man deemed worthy of being the general of the whole of Hellas' (76), before asking who of his contemporaries might be worthy of serving as a second Agamemnon. The Spartans, he argues, are ruled out because of their injustices against cities in the Peloponnese (74). The Athenians, by contrast, have offered ample demonstration of their goodwill to other cities (96). Isocrates was not, however, convinced that Athens had leaders of the right calibre. In time, albeit reluctantly, he came to believe that the only person worthy of assuming Agamemnon's mantle was Philip II of Macedon.

Philip never led the Panhellenic campaign against Persia. He was assassinated in 336 BCE, days before he planned to set out for the east, and the task fell to his son, Alexander the Great. Alexander was acutely conscious of how mythical discourse might be exploited for political ends. In reality, Greeks constituted less than one-sixth of his infantry forces, yet Alexander was keen to promote the campaign as a Panhellenic venture, especially in his appeal to Homeric authority. Shortly after crossing the Hellespont, following a route that largely replicated in reverse that taken by Xerxes more than a century and a half earlier, Alexander insisted on visiting Troy, where he offered sacrifices at what he was told was the tomb of Achilles – supposedly an ancestor on the side of his mother, Olympias.[83] The symbolism was not, however, to outlive either Alexander's ambitions or the vicissitudes that beset his army and, within just a decade, the great Panhellenic avenger had himself been recast in the role of the oriental despot.

A Tourkokratic Epilogue

I have suggested throughout that the efficacy of myth for political ends in the Greek world resided in the fact that it constituted a familiar communicative system in which modulations on a theme commanded greater acceptance and acquiescence than would have been the case with wholesale invention. Myth derived its dynamic vitality and capacity to provide symbolic resources for ideological narratives precisely because it was constantly being refreshed and rejuvenated in oral performative contexts. Once it was divorced from those original contexts, frozen or fossilized in learned literary tomes, it largely lost its former potency though it continued, of course, to exercise the imagination of later writers and artists who followed in the western tradition.

In his memoirs, the Comte de Marcellus describes a literary evening held in the Bosphoran mansion of a Phanariot Greek in the winter of 1820/1821, just months before the outbreak of the Greek War of Independence. A young man, who was later to lose his life in that struggle, proceeded to give a reading of Aeschylus' *Persians*, interspersed with a recitation of the *Thourios*, a war hymn written by Rigas Pheraios, whose appeals for liberation from the Ottoman Turks resulted in his execution in Belgrade in 1798.[84] Just as the Trojans had served as mythical antecedents for the Persians, so now the Persians were reemployed as the prototypes for a new eastern power, intent on subjugation and the suppression of liberty. There was nothing mythical about the Persians, but their literary redeployment on that winter evening created a new narrative with an ideological purpose and, even in the afterglow of the Enlightenment, a new myth was born.

FURTHER READING

Graf (1993) offers an excellent introduction to Greek myth and how it has been studied in recent centuries. Though now rather dated, Nilsson (1951) is still an important introduction to how myth functioned within politics in the ancient Greek world. Some valuable insights can also be gleaned from Burkert (1979) and Dowden (1992), while Calame (2003b) explores the complex interplay between myth, history, and politics in relation to the foundation accounts for the Greek colony of Cyrene in Libya. For the view of myth as ideology in narrative form, I am indebted to Lincoln (1999), who tests the hypothesis not only against Greek, Old Irish, Norse, Iranian, and Hindu myths but also against the scholarship on myth from the Renaissance through to the present day.

Malkin (1994) presents a fascinating general account of how the Spartans 'thought themselves' through myth. The specific cases concerning the Spartan promotion of Agamemnon and the Argive promotion of the Seven against Thebes are treated in more detail, with full references, in Hall (1999) and Philips (2003). Anderson (2003) provides a lively account of Athenian politics of the sixth century and how they were reflected in art, myth, and cult, although he may underestimate the role that Pisistratus played; the most recent consideration of Pisistratus, and especially his earlier career, is that of Lavelle (2005). Shapiro (1989) is still a useful overview of art and cult under the tyranny. For the changing representation of the Trojans in Greek thought and lit-erature, Erskine (2001) is essential. An early, but thorough, account of Greek perceptions of non-Greeks is that of Jüthner (1923); for a more recent treatment see Hall (2002) 172–228 and, with particular reference to Greek tragedy, Hall (1989).

NOTES

1   See, for example, Bingen and Reverdin (1996); Alcock et al. (2001).
2   For the interaction between memory and the landscape, see Alcock (2002).
3   *SEG* 26 426. See Curty (1995) esp. 13–15 and Jones (1999).
4   Musti (1963).
5   See, for example, Vernant (1983b), Detienne (1986), Veyne (1988), Buxton (1994), and Bietenholz (1994).
6   See the discussion in Lincoln (1999) 146–7.
7   Lincoln (1999) 147.
8   Appadurai (1981) 203.
9   Cf. Pausanias 3.3.7.
10 Cf. *Nem.* 11.34.
11 In the Scholiast to Euripides, *Or.* 46.
12 Preliminary reports of the excavation appear (in Greek) in the *Praktika* of the Greek Archaeological Society for 1956, 1960, and 1961. For a general account, see Hooker (1980) 60–62. The dating of the inscriptions is argued by Johnston in Jeffery (1990) 447.
13 Catling and Cavanagh (1976); Catling (1986); Tomlinson (1992); Whitley (1994) 221; Antonaccio (1995) 155–66; Hall (1995) 602.
14 Leahy (1955).
15 Pausanias 2.18.4.
16 For Bellerophon's associations with Corinth, see Nilsson (1972) 51.
17 Podlecki (1971) 315; Malkin (1994) 31.
18 Malkin (1994) 125.
19 For example, Cartledge (1979) 139; cf. McCauley (1999).
20 Tyrtaeus fr. 2 Diehl; Herodotus 8.73.1; Pausanias 7.1.5–7.
21 Nafissi (1991) 140–44.
22 Herodotus 5.72.3.
23 Boedeker (1993).
24 Hall (1995) 587–92.
25 For the excavation of the shrine, see Cook (1953). For doubts about an early identification with Agamemnon: Marinatos (1953) 87–8; Morgan and Whitelaw (1991) 89 n. 50; Hall (1995) 602–3.
26 *IG* IV 493. See Jameson (1990) 222.
27 Pariente (1992).
28 Plutarch, *Thes.* 29.4–5; Pausanias 1.39.2.
29 For a discussion of the dating: Bommelaer and Laroche (1991) 133–5.
30 Among the more recent advocates of this view are Brommer (1982), Neils (1987), Kearns (1989), Calame (1990), and Anderson (2003).
31 See, especially, Boardman (1972, 1975, 1989).

32 Herodotus (1.62.1) seems to imply that the Pisistratids had political supporters in the area of Marathon.

33 As suggested by, among others, Connor (1970) 145–50; Shapiro (1989) 147–9; Tyrrell and Brown (1991) 161–5.

34 Aristotle fr. 637 Rose; Scholiast to Aelius Aristides, *Panath.* 189.

35 Sancisi-Weerdenburg (2000).

36 For the association of many of these projects with the Pisistratids, see Boersma (1970). For revised datings: Shapiro (1989) 66; Stewart (1990) 124–5; Hayashi (1992) 19–29; Miles (1998).

37 Childs (1994).

38 Lincoln (1999) 207.

39 For the *damnatio memoriae*, Lycurgus, *Leocr.* 117. See, generally, Lavelle (1993).

40 For example, Stewart (1990) 129–30.

41 Herodotus 5.77. The inscription commemorating the victory was found on the Athenian Acropolis (Meiggs-Lewis no. 15).

42 The length of time, with interruptions, given by the Aristotelian *AthPol* 19.6.

43 See McGlew (1993).

44 For Pisistratid cultivation of the arts, see *AthPol* 18.1.

45 Plutarch, *Per.* 12.

46 Cerveteri cup: *ARV* 83.14. Euphronius cup: *ARV* 58.51. Paris amphora: *ABV* 315.2. See, generally, Anderson (2003) 254.

47 Herodotus 1.61.4; *AthPol* 17.4.

48 *AthPol* 17.3, 19.5.

49 Herodotus 9.97; cf. 1.145; Hellanicus 4 FGrH 125.

50 Plutarch, *Thes.* 21.

51 Herodotus 1.64.2; Thucydides 3.104.1.

52 Peppas-Delmousou (1988). For the location of the Pisistratid home at Philaidai, near Brauron: [Plato], *Hipparch.* 228b; cf. Plutarch, *Sol.* 10.3.

53 Plutarch, *Thes.* 14.1.

54 Herodotus 1.61.2.

55 Scholiast to Aristophanes, *Nub.* 48.

56 Stewart (1990) 137.

57 *AthPol* 15.2.

58 *AthPol* 21.5; Pollux, *Onom.* 8.108.

59 *AthPol* 16.5.

60 [Plato], *Hipparch.* 228b–229d; cf. Thucydides 6.54.6.

61 The model is that of Polignac (1995).

62 Pisistratus and Brauron: Photius s.v. Brauronia. Pisistratus' command in the Megarian war: Herodotus 1.59.4. Theseus' capture of Eleusis: Plutarch, *Thes.* 10.3.

63 Hellanicus 323 *FGrH* 23; Strabo 9.1.7. For Pisistratus' exploitation of his Neleid ancestry, Lavelle (2005) 18–29.

64 Taylor (1991).

65 Saïd (1978).

66 *Il.* 6.120–236. See Erskine (2001) 53.

67 Mackie (1996).

68 Hector: Pausanias 9.18.5. Leuctra: Pausanias 3.26.5. Thalamae: Plutarch, *Agis* 9. See Erskine (2001) 113, 124. The suggestion of an originally Greek location appears in Hall (1989) 22–3.

69 Sappho fr. 58 Lobel-Page; cf. frs. 39, 92, 98. See Kurke (1992).

70 See, for example, Morris (1992) 101–49.

71 Erskine (2001) 58. Herodotus (7.9ß.2) recounts the Persian general Mardonius' surprise at the 'ill-advised way' in which 'the Hellenes are accustomed to wage war.'

72 For Croton and Siris, see Strabo 6.1.12, 14.

73 The *Tabula Iliaca Capitolina* (849 FGrH 6b), which associates Aeneas with the foundation of Troy, purports to illustrate Stesichorus' narrative, though some suspect it of being a creation of Augustan propaganda. See Malkin (1998) 172 and Erskine (2001) 149.

74 See Erskine (2001) 94.

75 Erskine (2001) 137.

76 DeVries (2000) 348–50.

77 For the representation of non-Greeks in the tragedies of Euripides, see Saïd (2002). For barbarians in tragedy generally, see Hall (1989).

78 See, generally, Hall (2002) 172–89.

79 Erskine (2001) 62–6. The pediments may date to shortly after 480 BCE, though this is controversial.

80 See Castriota (1992) 33–58, 76–89.

81 Hall (2002) 199–202.

82 Xenophon, *Hell.* 3.4.3–4.

83 Arrian, *Anab.* 1.11.7–8.

84 See Clogg (2003) 41–2.

12: OVID AND GREEK MYTH

A. J. Boyle

The reason for the continuous mutation of myth . . . is its cultural relevance.

F. Graf, Greek Mythology: An Introduction

The social, cultural, and religious milieu in which the poet Ovid moved and wrote was complex, if not chaotic. Myth was a central ingredient of that complexity and chaos. The foundational myths of Aeneas and Romulus were probably current in Rome in the sixth century BCE,[1] and other foundational myths involving the Arcadian king Evander and the Greek hero Hercules followed. But it is from the third century BCE onwards, after the 'invention' of Roman literature, that we witness the start of the complex, multifarious use of Greek myth that was to define the Ovidian treatment. Early Roman epic and drama and late republican poetry, architecture, sculpture, and wall-painting turned to Greek myth as a grammar of Roman experience. They used it for social, exegetic, validatory, discursive, exemplary, referential, and (increasingly) overtly political purposes. Livius Andronicus' *Odusia*, for example, seems to respond to a mid-third-century need for transcultural validation. Naevius, who introduced the historical drama, the *fabula praetexta*, seems almost self-consciously political, highlighting aspects of Rome's religious policy in *Lucurgus*, for example, and aetiologising and possibly galvanising political sentiment in *Danae*. He and Ennius underscored national pride (and that of the Julian and Aemilian families) in *Bellum Poenicum* and *Annales* through their epics' affirmation of the city's descent from Venus. The second-century tragedian Accius dramatised the Atreus myth, perhaps to attack the 'tyranny' of Tiberius Gracchus; Catullus' epyllion, *Peleus and Thetis* (poem 64), used a concatenation of myths to examine the social and moral turmoil following the civil wars of the early first century BCE.[2]

Signally, the civil wars of the late republic elicited several mythic responses. Virgil expressed fervid and fragile optimism in his Golden Age pastoral (*Eclogue* 4); Horace advocated flight to the Isles of the Blessed (*Epode* 16) or moralised with a gigantomachy (*Odes* 3.4); Varius presented *Thyestes* as an indictment of Mark Antony. Some mythic responses were architectural and sculptural. Most famously, the Temple of Apollo on the Palatine, dedicated in 28 BCE, used its Portico of the Danaids to transform a civil war into a triumphant conquest of Egypt. It was a more subtle continuation of the politicisation of myth already evident in Julius Caesar's Temple of Venus Genetrix (dedicated 46 BCE), which housed a statue of both Caesar and Caesar's mistress, Cleopatra, and in Octavian's Temple of Divine Julius (dedicated 29 BCE), which housed a painting of Caesar's and Rome's divine ancestress, Venus. The Augustan Forum (completed 2 BCE), with its imbrication of Mars, Venus, Aeneas, Romulus, the Divine Julius, and Augustus himself, proved a decisive moment in both politicised myth and Ovid's life. The iconic fusion of Augustus and Jupiter on cameos and gems (notably on the Gemma Augustea) made explicit what Augustan politicised myth had implied.[3]

Much of this discursive and political use of Greek myth was made possible by its separation from Roman ritual, its function in Roman intellectual life as an instrument of thinking. By Roman intellectuals Greek myth was generally regarded as *fabulae*, a collection of fictions. Cicero proclaimed myth to be neither true nor plausible (*De Inventione* 1.27), as did the anonymous author of the *Rhetorica ad Herennium* (1.13); Lucretius condemned the fictions of myth but used those fictions in his poetic argument (see, for example, *De Rerum Natura* 1.82–101); Varro objected to myth's unworthy portrayal of the gods (Cardauns fragments 6–11). More in line with myth's appeal to Roman poets was the definition of myth by Aelius Theon (first century CE) in *Progymnasmata* 3 as 'a fictitious story which illustrates the truth.' The definition, of course, recalled Plato's *eikos muthos* ('myth resembling (the truth),' *Timaeus* 29d) and gave precise formulation to a view embedded in Roman poetry's prolific use of Greek myth as a prime instrument of discourse. For Ovid myth was both good to think and to write with.

MYTH AND INTERTEXTS

It has been observed that Ovid's 'range of mythological interest is vast.'[4]
So too is Ovid's range of use. The poet is fully aware of the contemporary categorisation of myth as fiction. He refers to it as *men-
dacium* (*Amores* 3.6.16, *Fasti* 6.253) and *licentia* (*Am.* 3.12.41); he uses
fabula (with its connotations of unreliability) of 'mythic' narrative (*Ars
Amatoria* 3.326, *Fas.* 3.738) and acknowledges the unbelievability of his
own metamorphoses (*Tristia* 2.63–4). His interest in myth is neither
religious nor ritualistic, but poetic. And one of his primary poetic uses
is referential. Take, for example, *Heroides*, an early work of Ovid and a
self-proclaimed revolutionary one (*Ars* 3.346), in which a whole collection of poems focusses on the female voice, female memory, and
female desire,[5] expressed through the area of writing most readily open
to elite Roman women, the letter. Mythical heroines, such as Penelope, Briseis, Phaedra, Hypsipyle, and Dido (to cite the 'writers' of five
of the first seven epistles), are allowed to give their own 'psychological' version of legendary events. What results referentially is a dynamic,
ludic interplay between Ovid's poems and several canonical texts of the
Greco-Roman tradition: Homer's *Odyssey* and *Iliad*, Euripides' *Phaedra*,
Apollonius' *Argonautica*, Virgil's *Aeneid*. The referentiality itself achieves
several effects. It locates Ovid within the Greco-Roman literary system. It critiques the values of the canonical texts. It underscores the gap
between the realities implied by those texts and Ovid's contemporary
world. It problematises myth itself by exposing its arbitrary construction
by canonical texts. And it does all these things with seriocomic wit.

Consider that Homeric paradigm of wifely beauty and virtue,
Penelope, whose undeliverable epistle to the absent Ulysses begins
Ovid's collection of letters. Penelope focusses on events from both the
Iliad and the *Odyssey* in her catalogue of anxieties, loneliness, and depri-
vations. But in her letter she puts to the fore her devotion to Ulysses –

> haec tua Penelope lento tibi mittit, Vlixe
> > *Heroides* 1.1

> Your Penelope sends you this, slow Ulysses

– and the maintenance of that devotion in the midst of great difficulties
and pressure (83ff.); at the same time she brings herself to articulate a
fear that Ulysses may not be showing such devotion (71–80). As the

reader 'knows' from Homer, Penelope's anxiety that Ulysses' 'delay' in returning home may have erotic causes, that behind the *mora* may lie *amor* (74–6), is not as foolish as she proclaims. This gap in 'knowledge' between the Ovidian reader and the fictive writer makes irony the dominant mode of *Heroides* 1 (as it is of the whole *Heroides*) and is central to its questioning of the canonical mythic narrative, especially of Ulysses' brand of heroism and its cost. The reader is invited to view that cost in terms not only of Penelope's pain but of the un-Homeric and unhumorous reality of the wasting of a life. Throughout the letter Penelope plays the role of an elegiac *puella* or 'girl,' pining for her man, only to display that what Ulysses' absence has done is transform a girl into a crone. The final lines of *Heroides* 1 hit home – ironised by the reader's 'knowledge' that Ulysses' return is imminent:

> certe ego, quae fueram te discedente puella,
>   protinus ut uenias, facta uidebor anus.
> *Heroides* 1.115–16.

> What's certain is that I, whom you left a girl,
>   Though you come now, will seem a crone.

The other heroines of these elegiac epistles play similar roles in rewriting their inherited myths. Dido, for example, in *Heroides* 7, subverts aspects of the *Aeneid*'s myth, making the latter seem a prejudicial construction.[6] Penelope will later become an instrument of self-referentiality. In *Tristia* 1.6 (21–34), Ovid uses a comparison between her and his wife to allude to *Heroides* itself, which he asks to be able to rewrite with his wife placed first.[7]

Complex, often multifunctional referentiality pervades Ovid's use of Greek myth throughout his *oeuvre*. No more so than in *Metamorphoses*, in which the poem's sustained reference to, and utilisation of, central works of the mythographic tradition (Homer's *Iliad* and *Odyssey*, Hesiod's *Theogony* and *Works and Days*, the 'Hesiodic' *Catalogue of Women*, Nicander's *Heteroioumena*, Eratosthenes' *Katasterismoi*, Boios' *Ornithogonia*, Parthenius' *Erotica Pathemata* – and, of course, Callimachus' *Aitia*) – together with the poem's demonstrable use of more routine mythographic handbooks[8] – ensures that the reader sees the poem as in some sense or senses mythographic epic. What those 'senses' are is perpetually in negotiation throughout Ovid's innovative masterwork, in which one of the prime metamorphoses is of myth itself,[9] as the poet rewrites the master narratives not only of the Greeks (as in the Erysichthon and Iphis and Dryope myths in Books 8 and 9 with their significant deviations from Callimachus and Nicander, or Achilles' fight with Cygnus in Book 12, which expands on Homer,[10] or the downplaying of genealogy throughout) but of their Roman successors. Virgil's colloquy between Venus and Jupiter in *Aeneid* 1 (227–96) is rewritten at the end of Ovid's epic and this time as a colloquy over Aeneas' descendant (*Aeneaden, Met.* 15.804), Julius Caesar, and Augustus (*Met.* 15.761–842). Even more substantial is Ovid's rewriting of Virgil's own rewriting (*Georgic* 4. 453–527) of the Greek Orpheus myth in *Metamorphoses* 10 and 11, where Ovid's playful, self-consciously irreverent treatment transforms the fabled singer into a pompous narcissist and turns the song that moved hell into a rhetorician's prosaic and verbose set-piece with a bizarre effect upon its audience. Virgil does not give us Orpheus' song; Ovid does and it is intentionally bathetic. The Greek mythic prototype of all poets begins with language filled with qualification, exegesis, and banality, and decidedly not of the kind to make the Virgilian dead weep. Ominously, the Ovidian Orpheus, though he plucks his lyre in accompaniment to his 'song,' does not 'sing' as in Virgil (*Geo.* 4.466), but 'says.'

> pulsisque ad carmina neruis
> sic ait: 'o positi sub terra numina mundi,
> in quem reccidimus, quicquid mortale creamur,
> si licet et falsi positis ambagibus oris
> uera loqui sinitis, non huc, ut opaca uiderem
> Tartara, descendi, nec uti uillosa colubris
> terna Medusaei uincirem guttura monstri:
> causa uiae est coniunx, in quam calcata uenenum
> uipera diffudit crescentesque abstulit annos.
> posse pati uolui nec me temptasse negabo:
> uicit Amor. supera deus hic bene notus in ora est;
> an sit et hic, dubito: sed et hic tamen auguror esse,
> famaque si ueteris non est mentita rapinae,
> uos quoque iunxit Amor.'
>
> *Metamorphoses* 10.17–26

> And striking his chords for the song
> He says this: 'O powers of the subterranean world,
> Where we fall back, all of us created mortal things,
> If it is allowed and you let me lay aside the labyrinth
> Of false speech and speak the truth, I came down here

Neither to view dark Tartarus nor to enchain
The Medusan monster's triple snake-haired necks:
The journey's cause is my wife, in whom a trodden viper
Spread its poison and removed her growing years.
I wanted the strength to endure, I'll not deny I tried;
Love conquered. This god is famed in the upper world;
Whether he is here, I don't know; but I guess he is even here,
And, if the story of that ancient rape is not a lie,
Love also joined you two.'

Above is the first half of Orpheus' song of deliverance. Ovid's
dead do weep; Tantalus pulls back from the disappearing water, Ixion's
wheel stops, vultures cease from eating Tityus' liver, the Danaids rest
from filling their unfillable urns, and Sisyphus sits on his stone in a
profusion of sibilants (*Met.* 10.44). It is a Monty Pythonesque scene. The
consuming passion of Virgil's Orpheus, the *dementia* and *furor* ('madness')
which make him fatefully look back, are replaced by fear of failure and
an eagerness to view his wife (*Met.* 10.56). It is fitting that the effect
of this wordy poetaster on Eury*dice* is to reduce her speaking ability
(*dicere*) to a single word. The plangent five lines of Virgil, filled with
bewilderment, pain, and loss (*Geo.* 4. 494–8), become a single and
barely audible 'farewell' (*uale, Met.* 10.62). That is all 'she said': *dixit*
(*Met.* 10.63). When Orpheus finally betakes himself to love of young
boys, enjoying the 'brief spring' (*breue uer*) and 'first flowers' (*primos
flores*) of their youth (*Met.* 10.83–85), it fails to surprise. We have to
wait for the opening of the next book before the Ciconian women
dismember the poet. Again Ovid jettisons Virgilian restraint, this time
turning his predecessor's three-line description (*Geo.* 4. 520–22) into
an extended narrative of violence and death (*Met.* 11.1–43). The reader
sheds no tears.

MYTH AS PARADIGM

Few cultures, if any, have been so committed to the exemplary function
of the past as that of Rome. The appeal to precedent was a major form
of argumentation.[11] Inevitably, one of the most frequent functions of
Greek myth in Roman poetry was as moral or behavioural paradigm.
Such paradigms could be apparently positive, as in Propertius' list of
unadorned legendary beauties at 1.2.15–24 and Horace's citation of
Homeric heroes in love with slave-girls at *Odes* 2.4.1–8. They could

also be ambivalent, as in Catullus' use of the Peleus and Thetis saga in poem 64, or negative, as in the use of the Iphigenia sacrifice at Lucretius 1.82–101. Ovid's employment of Greek myth as paradigm is as varied and complex as that of his poetic predecessors. Positive *exempla* of love's 'martial' spirit are provided by Achilles, Hector, Agamemnon, and Mars himself at *Amores* 1.9.33–40; at *Amores* 2.14.13–18 Thetis, Ilia, and Venus support an argument against abortion. A catalogue of negative mythical paradigms is featured at *Remedia Amoris* 55–66, where Phyllis, Dido, Tereus, Pasiphae, Phaedra, Paris, and Scylla index behaviour to be avoided and illustrate the consequences of not following the poet's healing precepts. Both these positive and negative *exempla* function in the rhetoric of their poems – like those of Propertius and Lucretius noted above – as instruments of persuasion.

Ovid's elegiac poems, erotic and exilic, are filled with mythical *exempla* designed to persuade.[12] Sometimes such persuasion is less than persuasive, as in the use of the myths of Io, Leda, and Europa at *Amores* 1.3.19–26 to argue for sexual/poetic capitulation, or in the failed attempts at self-justification using Ajax, Orestes, Atalanta, Ariadne, and Cassandra in *Amores* 1.7 (7–18)[13] and the myth of Althaea and the Meleager-brand in *Tristia* 1.7 (15–20) – the latter an attempt to justify Ovid's alleged burning of his *Metamorphoses*. At other times the use of mythical *exempla* is itself questioned (*Am.* 2.1.29–32). Notoriously, in the second half of the exilic curse poem, *Ibis* (251–638), an unprecedented, excessive (almost 400-line) catalogue of mythical (and historical) paradigms suggests the speaker's fury, even 'deranged *persona*,'[14] not his conviction. Occasionally, too – and here the debt to Catullus and Propertius is clear – mythical paradigms combine to suggest an ideal world (of female beauty and availability, for example: *Am.* 1.10.1–8), against which sordid reality is to be judged. In some *exempla*, the reality being evaluated is political:

> sed mora tuta breuis: lentescunt tempore curae,
> uanescitque absens et nouus intrat amor.
> dum Menelaus abest, Helene, ne sola iaceret,
> hospitis est tepido nocte recepta sinu.
> quis stupor hic, Menelae, fuit? tu solus abibas,
> isdem sub tectis hospes et uxor erant.
> accipitri timidas credis, furiose, columbas?
> plenum montano credis ouile lupo?
> nil Helene peccat, nihil hic committit adulter:
> quod tu, quod faceret quilibet, ille facit.

cogis adulterium dando tempusque locumque;
    quid nisi consilio est usa puella tuo?
quid faciat? uir abest, et adest non rusticus hospes,
    et timet in uacuo sola cubare toro.
uiderit Atrides: Helenen ego crimine soluo:
    usa est humani commoditate uiri.

Ars Amatoria 2.357–72

A short absence is safe: passion wanes with time,
    The absent love vanishes, the new enters.
With Menelaus absent, lest Helen lie alone,
    Her guest's warm breast welcomed her at night.
What folly, Menelaus, was this? You went away alone,
    Guest and wife were under the same roof.
Do you trust timid doves, madman, to a hawk?
    Trust a full sheep pen to a mountain wolf?
Helen does no wrong, this adulterer commits no crime.
    He does what you, what anyone would do.
You force adultery by providing time and place;
    What did the girl use except your advice?
What could she do? The husband's not there, a charming guest is,
    And she fears to lie alone in an empty bed.
Let Atrides see to himself; I absolve Helen of blame;
    She used her kindly husband's complaisance.

The politics of this passage need addressing.[15] Released about 1 BCE, and certainly after the completion in 2 BCE of Augustus' prime ideological monument, the Augustan Forum, the *Ars Amatoria* inevitably challenged the prescribed *mores* of Augustan Rome. Its treatment here of adultery is remarkable. The social and moral legislation of 18 BCE, the *lex Iulia de maritandis ordinibus* and the *lex Iulia de adulteriis coercendis*, radically departed from the norms of Roman law by taking that law into the bedroom. The transformation of adultery and other forms of transgressive fornication (*stuprum*) into crimes with severe penalties imposed by a special permanent court (*quaestio perpetua*) suddenly made sexual morality and practice subject to political control.[16] Prior to the *leges Iuliae* adultery was essentially left to the respective families to deal with; it was a form of social behaviour from which Roman law kept a respectful distance. The effect of the Augustan legislation was 'revolutionary,'[17] and signalled a shift in regulatory power from the family to the state. In 2 BCE after the opening of his great forum Augustus had to banish his own daughter, Julia, to the island of Pandateria for her conspicuous and multiple adulteries.[18] Four of her illustrious adulterers – and several less illustrious ones – met similar fates; the most prominent adulterer a worse one.[19] The scale of the scandal and its attendant embarrassment are reflected in Velleius' description some thirty years later: *foeda dictu memoriaque horrenda in ipsius domo tempestas* ('a storm foul to mention and dreadful to remember fell on his house,' Vell. Pat. 2.100.2). Certainly from 2 BCE onwards, at the head of Rome was a frustrated and frustrating autocrat, as much a victim of his own ideology as its proponent, and one not given to tolerance of that ideology's breach.[20] Earlier, in *Ars Amatoria* (1.89–134), Ovid had 'humorously' used the Roman myth of the Sabine Rape as precedent and thus justification for erotic pursuits in the theatre.[21] In the passage quoted above, the poet develops his subversion of Augustan sexual codes by turning to Greek myth – to the famous mythical adulteress Helen, who is chosen to exemplify the dangers of male absence. That in or around 1 BCE Ovid should have 'published' this passage not as a denunciation of adulterers but rather as a text for pontificating on the excusability, even innocence, of certain kinds of adultery, astonishes.

nil Helene peccat, nihil hic committit adulter.
Ars Amatoria 2.365

Helen does no wrong, this adulterer commits no crime.

Myth's paradigmatic function dissolves into political and social critique.

MYTH AND HUMANITAS

Ovid's *Metamorphoses* is rightly seen as (to a substantial degree) a mythic study of the human condition, a grammar of *humanitas*.[22] From the Greek rationalist myth of creation in the opening book to the Augustan political settlement of its close, the fifteen-book epic structures its narrative to present the Roman reader/listener with an image of his/her world's evolution from natural chaos to political order. Within this evolution, myth regularly functions as an aetiological, explanatory force, making of the human environment (it appears) a knowable, comprehensible world. Natural and cultural phenomena alike are amenable to aetiological exegesis. Dew, thunder, earthquakes, springs, mountains, islands, trees, the foundation of cities, the source of their names, the inauguration of religious games, the origin of religious cults at Rome – have their precise mythical explanations.[23] One prime aetiology is that of the human species itself, in which the Ovidian narrator promotes an ontological hierarchy and locates the human 'animal' between the divine and the rest of 'animal' creation, even attributing to it elements of divinity:

> sanctius his animal mentisque capacius altae
> deerat adhuc et quod dominari in cetera posset.
> natus homo est, siue hunc diuino semine fecit
> ille opifex rerum, mundi melioris origo,
> siue recens tellus seductaque nuper ab alto
> aethere cognati retinebat semina caeli.
> quam satus Iapeto mixtam pluuialibus undis
> finxit in effigiem moderantum cuncta deorum,
> pronaque cum spectent animalia cetera terram,
> os homini sublime dedit caelumque uidere
> iussit et erectos ad sidera tollere uultus.
> sic, modo quae fuerat rudis et sine imagine, tellus
> induit ignotas hominum conuersa figuras.
>
> *Metamorphoses* 1.76–88

A holier animal than these and more receptive to lofty thought
Still was lacking which would have dominion over the rest.
Humankind was born: either the universe's craftsman
Made it from divine seed, designing a better world,
Or the fresh earth, recently parted from the high
Aether, retained the seeds of its kindred sky,
And mixed by Iapetus' son with rain water
Was moulded to an image of all-controlling gods.
And, whereas other animals gaze down upon the ground,
He gave humankind an upright face and bade it
View the sky and lift its soaring gaze to the stars.
So earth, which just now was crude and formless,
Changed, and put on unfamiliar human shapes.

This extraordinary proclamation of man's perfection builds upon the post-Hesiodic tradition of Prometheus' creation of man and inserts into it the Stoic theory familiar from Cleanthes' *Hymn to Zeus* of humanity's divine origins and imaging of god. It is followed immediately by an account of man's fall, in which Hesiod's myth of deteriorating races is modified into a myth of deteriorating ages, in which humankind degenerates from a golden to an iron age. The major crime of this iron age, Lycaon's attempt to deceive Jupiter with human sacrifice (*Met.* 1.226–31), is signally a gross breach of the alimentary codes separating divine, human, and animal. Appropriately, Lycaon's metamorphosis into a wolf not only (as with several metamorphoses)[24] reveals his essential nature but also itself dissolves the boundaries Lycaon had transgressed. A massive flood follows to cleanse the world of wickedness and the human race is replenished by the two survivors, Deucalion and Pyrrha, and a new world order begins.

This post-Deucalion world – divinely remade, explained, known – is the one inhabited by the reader. It is no moral paradise. Ovid conjoins in almost seamless continuity a narrative constructed from a myriad of Greek myths illustrating various aspects of human appetite, ambition, folly, greed, jealousy, bloodlust, treachery, anger, desire, fear, vengeance, vanity, hybris, inventiveness, piety, courage, love, nobility, moderation, wisdom, hope, and disaster. The narrative's psychological focus and the abundance of self-presentational monologues expand the techniques and insight of the earlier *Heroides* to create a *pinacoteca* of the human mind. Medea begins the sixty-one line soliloquy, in which she wrestles with her passion for Jason and her *pudor* (modesty) and *pietas* (filial duty) towards her father, thus:

> 'frustra, Medea, repugnas;
> nescio quis deus obstat,' ait, 'mirumque nisi hoc est
> aut aliquid certe simile huic, quod amare uocatur.
> nam cur iussa patris nimium mihi dura uidentur?
> sunt quoque dura nimis. cur, quem modo denique uidi,
> ne pereat, timeo? quae tanti causa timoris?
> excute uirgineo conceptas pectore flammas,
> si potes, infelix. si possem, sanior essem.
> sed trahit inuitam noua uis aliudque cupido,
> mens aliud suadet. uideo meliora proboque,
> deteriora sequor.'
>
> *Metamorphoses* 7.11–21

> 'You struggle, Medea, in vain;
> Some god thwarts you,' she says; 'I wonder if this isn't –
> Or something like this at least – what is called love.
> Else why do father's instructions seem to me too harsh?
> They are indeed too harsh. Why do I fear for a man's life

Whom I've just seen? What is the cause of such great fear?
Strike from your virgin breast the fires you have lit,
If you can, poor thing. If I could, I'd be back to health.
A strange force draws me against my will. Desire points one way,
Reason another. I see and approve the better course,
I follow the worse one.'

Seneca learnt much from Ovidian monologues,[25] as he is presumed to have done from Ovid's lost and admired tragedy, *Medea*. And, as in the later tragedian, there is a profoundly moral dimension to the preoccupation with human psychology. This extends, of course, to *Metamorphoses'* narrative preoccupations and emphases. The Ovidian myths of (*inter alios*) Phaethon, Battus, Aglauros, Cadmus, Actaeon, Tiresias, Narcissus, Pentheus, Pyramus, Perseus, Triptolemus, Marsyas, Pelops, Tereus, Medea, Theseus, Minos, Daedalus, Meleager, Philemon, Erysichthon, Hercules, Midas, Peleus, and the Trojan War seem designed to confirm the moral and existential boundaries of human aspiration and life by illustrating the disastrous consequences of their transgression and (more rarely) the rewards of their maintenance. Myths of human savagery, such as those of Tereus and Medea, set up models of the Roman Other and provide negative *exempla* of the conventions defining civilized humankind. Similarly antithetical to Roman ideals are myths exemplifying the failure to reach adulthood or adult male sexuality (Phaethon, Narcissus, Pentheus) – and the sexual perversion myths of Iphis, Biblis, and Myrrha, which reinforce the incest and homosexual taboos of Romankind.

Many problems, however, surround the narrative's implicit condemnation of human excess, prime among which is the conspicuous absence of any metaphysical framework for such condemnation in *Metamorphoses* itself. The work focusses, especially in its first third, on the arbitrary power and erotic predilections of the gods. The narrative's concern with *amor* develops, of course, the pun embedded in the poems' title and may be indebted to the pseudo-Hesiodic *Catalogue of Women* with its attention to the amours of the gods and the resultant genealogies. The Ovidian 'catalogues,' however, seem very different. The attention given by Ovid to the amalgam of divine power and divine injustice makes of these amatory exploits a destabilising force that negates the narrative movement of the epic from chaos to order and ensures that, despite such a surface movement and its aetiological underpinnings, the poem supplies no laws for man's orientation. Aetiology seems to function ironically in suggesting the knowability and controllability of a world in which the paradigmatic human status seems that of victim. The emphasis of the early books on the gods' anger, power, injustice, and rape,[26] beginning with Jupiter's destruction of the whole of mankind for the crime of an individual, through Apollo's attempted rape of Daphne and Jupiter's rapes of Io, Callisto, Europa, and Semele, Diana's killing of Actaeon, and Juno's blinding of Tiresias, to Pluto's rape of Proserpina, overwhelms. Resistance to divine rape is emphasised:

> 'ne fuge me!' fugiebat enim. iam pascua Lernae
> consitaque arboribus Lyrcea reliquerat arua,
> cum deus inducta latas caligine terras
> occuluit tenuitque fugam rapuitque pudorem.
> *Metamorphoses* 1.597–600

> 'Don't flee from me!' For she was fleeing and had left
> Lerna's meadows and Lyrcean fields and thickets,
> When the god concealed the wide earth in a veil
> Of darkness, stopped her flight and raped her modesty.

Such resistance prevents neither rape nor ensuing punishment. Despite the narrator's moral indictment of Jupiter – 'raped her modesty,' *rapuit pudorem*, is tonally unambiguous – it is the victim of rape against whom Juno rails. When at the beginning of Book 6 Minerva weaves a tapestry illustrating the power, justice, and 'August/Augustan majesty' (*augusta grauitas, Met.* 6.73) of the gods, while Arachne weaves one detailing the 'crimes of heaven' (*caelestia crimina, Met.* 6. 131), the former's separation from and the latter's connection with *Metamorphoses*' earlier narrative are patent. The hint in Arachne's tapestry of the divine rapists' vainly rebellious progeny serves to underscore the gap between justice and power. Minerva's destruction of both tapestry and weaver leaves little doubt about the moral nature of the poem's universe. What Ovid presents in *Metamorphoses* is a world of unaccountable otherness,[27] in which the controllers of that world and the putative guardians of its morality exemplify the vices they condemn. Ramifications of this mythic world for that of contemporary Rome and its controllers and moral protectors are patent.

MYTH AND ROMANITAS

Right from the start of *Metamorphoses* myth and political reality conjoin. Jupiter's first appearance in the poem is on a Romanised Olympus, equipped with its own Palatine, where the powerful and 'noble' gods dwell apart from the Olympian *plebs* (*Met.* 1.163–76), and the meeting with the gods at which he complains of the sin of Lycaon resembles nothing so much as a convocation of the Roman senate,[28] which, as we know from Suetonius (*Augustus Diuus* 29.3), Augustus sometimes held in the Palatine library by his own house. The analogy between Jupiter and Augustus is explicitly stated (*Met.* 1. 204–06); the response of the gods mirrors that of the senate to Augustus:

> dicta Iouis pars uoce probant stimulosque frementi
> adiciunt, alii partes adsensibus inplent.
>
> *Metamorphoses* 1.244–5

> Some shout approval at Jove's words and add fuel
> To his roar, others fulfil their role through assent.

A consequence of the poem's early establishment of the analogy between Jupiter and Augustus is that the reader is encouraged to view the presentation of Jupiter in the epic's narrative as reflecting, however obscurely, the realities of Augustan Rome. When the reader reaches the end of the poem the analogy is restated almost heavy-handedly:

> Iuppiter arces
> temperat aetherias et mundi regna triformis,
> terra sub Augusto est: pater est et rector uterque.
>
> *Metamorphoses* 15.858–60

> Jupiter controls
> Heaven's towers and the realm of the triformed world,
> Earth is subject to Augustus: each is father and ruler.

When Ovid proclaims the invulnerability of his poem to the wrath of Jupiter (*Met.* 15.871), its political translation requires no effort.

A rather more subtle political use of Greek myth is evident in the poem's treatment of metamorphosis itself. Several of *Metamorphoses*' mythographic intertexts were mentioned above. It is well known that Ovid plundered catalogues of Greek mythic metamorphoses from Nicander's *Heteroioumena* and elsewhere. But what needs to be observed is that these metamorphoses are often made by Ovid to serve discursive purposes and to elicit political judgments. The Apollo–Daphne myth of *Metamorphoses* 1 (452–567), for example, is used to generate an aetiology of the laurel tree, into which Daphne is transformed. This aetiology, however, grounded in Apollo's failure to rape, does anything but cast an admirable glow on the Roman triumphs and Augustus' house which (the poem emphasises: *Met.* 1.560–63) laurel is used to adorn. Notably, too, Ovid's 'plundered' catalogue of Greek metamorphoses climaxes in metamorphoses that are Roman, political, radical, and religious: the metamorphosis of Caesar and prospective metamorphosis of Augustus into gods. Nor is this metamorphosis of Roman religion restricted to Augustus and his adoptive father. The great public divinities, Vesta and Apollo, are revealed by the poem to have been transformed into members of Augustus' household and inhabitants of his *domus* on the Palatine.[29] The great goddess of the public hearth of Rome, Vesta Publica, on whose eternally burning flame the survival of Rome depended and whose sacrosanct place was at the heart of Rome itself (see Livy 5.52.7, 14), is now one of Augustus' *penates*:

Vestaque Caesareos inter sacrata penates,
et cum Caesarea tu, Phoebe domestice, Vesta.
Metamorphoses 15.864–5

And Vesta, hallowed among Caesarean *penates*,
And household Phoebus beside Caesarean Vesta.

Here recent Roman religious realities (the creation of a shrine for Vesta in Augustus' house,[30] which was itself connected to the Palatine Temple of Apollo, and the resulting appropriation of these two deities) are presented as a blatantly political metamorphosis of inherited traditions and as much a transformation of *romanitas* as the Greek mythic metamorphoses were a transformation of human bodies. Not that the transformation of human bodies could not also be political. In his first poem from exile (*Tr.* 1.1.117–22), Ovid asks that his own translation from Rome to Tomis be added to his epic's collection of transformed bodies (*mutata corpora*).

Clearly the metamorphosis that had the most potent ramifications for Roman politics and religion was apotheosis. Introduced in the first book of *Metamorphoses* in connection with Io (who became Isis: *Met.* 1.748), it becomes a structuring motif in the second half of the poem, in which the reader witnesses the apotheosis of Hercules (*Met.* 9.134–272) leading into those of Aeneas, Romulus, Caesar, and (prospectively) Augustus. The evolution of differences in grounds for apotheosis merits comment. In the cases of Hercules, Aeneas, and Romulus, apotheosis is merited through a combination of great deeds and divine paternity/

maternity. Hercules' accomplishments are rehearsed (*Met.* 9.183–98), his status as 'earth's protector,' *uindex terrae,* affirmed (*Met.* 9.241), and his immediate descent from Jupiter underscored at the moment of deification (*Met.* 9.265). Divine blood and worthiness are similarly emphasised in the cases of Aeneas and Romulus (*Met.* 14. 588–9, 594–5, 805–15). In the case of Julius Caesar, though great deeds are his (*Met.* 15. 746–58), and the proclaimed ancestress of the Julian line is Venus, neither provides the stated grounds for the apotheosis. Political power and political expediency deify Caesar:

> ne foret hic igitur mortali semine cretus
> ille deus faciendus erat.
> > *Metamorphoses* 15.760–61

> Therefore, lest the one [Augustus] be born of mortal seed,
> The other [Julius Caesar] had to be made a god.

The contemporary institution of divine metamorphosis is exposed as a self-serving political fiction in part through contrast with Greek mythic apotheoses. There is a double fiction here, since, as every contemporary reader of this text knew, Augustus was not born of the seed of Julius Caesar, mortal or otherwise. *Metamorphoses* began with a nongenealogical creation myth in which the universe was formed by 'a god and nobler nature' (*deus et melior natura, Met.* 1.21). It ends with a politically motivated and blatantly false genealogy creating a god. The emperor's biological father is as tellingly absent here as any reference to the actual political processes – the triumviral acts, senatorial decree, and vote of the comitia – that in 42 BCE made Caesar into a god.[31]

The political use of myth dominates Ovid's late masterpiece, *Fasti.* Reworked during Ovid's exile and concurrent with the first crisis of the principate (the translation of power from Augustus to Tiberius), *Fasti* contains Ovid's most mature thinking on the imperial system and on Rome. As in *Metamorphoses,* the association of Augustus with Jupiter is emphasised, but the negative implications of that association are made more explicit through striking juxtapositions. In the entry on the Nones of February, for example, Augustus is praised as a Jupiter on earth (*Fas.* 2.131–2) only to have that praise juxtaposed with allusion to Ganymede (145–6), the Trojan youth raped and abducted by Jupiter, and a detailed account of the latter's rape of Callisto (153–92), in which even the narrator intervenes to proclaim her innocence (178). *Fasti* contains a great deal of rape, much of it by Jupiter, and this mythic rape frames the focus on mythohistorical 'foundational' rapes, such as those of Silvia, the Sabine Women, and Lucretia, all of which take place at moments of crucial political change. The one rape that is not stated in *Fasti* but that is implied by both the mythic and the mythohistorical 'foundational' rapes is the one accompanying the most momentous political change of all: that of *romanitas* by Augustus during the 'refoundation of Rome.'

Indeed, Ovid's *Fasti* seeks to undermine the political mythmaking of the Augustan regime. The myths of Augustus' descent from Venus and of his status as a second Romulus, recurring constituents of Augustan political imagery, are undermined in *Fasti* through the poem's exposure of the fictive nature of the former and the ideological inconcinnity of the latter. This deconstruction of Augustan mythmaking had occurred earlier in Ovid's poetry. *Amores* 1.2, for example, casts an irreverent eye over Augustus' Venusian ancestry by making him Cupid's relative; *Ars Amatoria* 1 (101–30), as noted above, contains a titillating account of the Romulean mass rape of Sabine women in a theatre vainly segregated along Augustan gender lines.[32] In *Fasti*, the undermining of Augustan imagery permeates and structures the whole six books. Against imperial mythmaking Ovid sets a parade of myths associated with cultural figures (Evander, Hercules, Sabine Women, Anna Perenna, Remus) and institutions (Carmentalia, Lupercalia, Megalensia, Parilia, Floralia, Vestalia) that the Augustan 'restitution' had transformed, rewritten, or marginalised and that represented a different kind of Roman cultural inheritance.

Several of these seem Ovid's invention and self-consciously fictive. The authority of myth seems deliberately deconstructed in *Fasti* and its collapse is reflected in the self-induced collapse of the authority of the narrator. The narrator's own myth-making is accorded as much and as little authority as that of the *princeps* himself. Better to hand authority to the reader:

> hic quoque mensis habet dubias in nomine causas:
> > quae placeat positis omnibus ipse leges.
> > > *Fasti* 6.1–2

> This month, too, has dubious causes for its name.
> > All will be listed. Pick the one you like.

Even as the Roman political system was removing popular suffrage from its operation, Ovid began the final book of *Fasti* by moving authority to the individual reader. It was a courageous act of political anachronism. Though he was later to proclaim that poetry makes gods (*Epistulae ex Ponto* 4.8.55), he knew only too well that the gods that mattered were made elsewhere.

MYTH AND POETICS

Amores 3.12 is a central text of Ovidian poetics. It is entirely devoted to the issue of poetic authority and truth, both of which are disavowed. What the poem focusses upon is the power of poets to make fiction, a major paradigm of which is that of myth.

> Nec tamen ut testes mos est audire poetas;
> > malueram uerbis pondus abesse meis.
> per nos Scylla patri caros furata capillos
> > pube premit rabidos inguinibusque canes;
> nos pedibus pinnas dedimus, nos crinibus angues;
> > uictor Abantiades alite fertur equo.
> idem per spatium Tityon porreximus ingens,
> > et tria uipereo fecimus ora cani;
> fecimus Enceladon iaculantem mille lacertis,
> > ambiguae captos uirginis ore uiros.
> Aeolios Ithacis inclusimus utribus Euros;
> > proditor in medio Tantalus amne sitit.
> de Niobe silicem, de uirgine fecimus ursam.
> > concinit Odrysium Cecropis ales Ityn;
> Iuppiter aut in aues aut se transformat in aurum
> > aut secat inposita uirgine taurus aquas.
> Protea quid referam Thebanaque semina, dentes;
> > qui uomerent flammas ore, fuisse boues;
> flere genis electra tuas, Auriga, sorores;
> > quaeque rates fuerint, nunc maris esse deas;
> auersumque diem mensis furialibus Atrei,
> > duraque percussam saxa secuta lyram?
> exit in inmensum fecunda licentia uatum,
> > obligat historica nec sua uerba fide.
> > > *Amores* 3.12.19–42

Yet no one listens to poets as if they're in court;
> I wanted my verses to lack authority.

We made Scylla steal her father's precious hair
    And crush rabid dogs in her groin and womb.
We have given wings to feet, snakes to hair,
    Made Abas' son victorious on winged horse.
We also stretched Tityos over a huge terrain,
    And created three mouths for the snake dog.
We made Enceladus throw with a thousand arms
    And snared men with the doubtful virgin's voice.
We enclosed Aeolus' Easterlies in Ithacan skins,
    Made traitor Tantalus thirst in mid-stream.
We made a rock of Niobe, a bear of a maid;
    Cecrops' bird sings Odrysian Itys because of us,
And Jupiter changes to a bird or gold or bull,
    Cleaving ocean with a maid on his back.
Why mention Proteus or the teeth which sowed Thebes,
    Or the existence of flame-spewing oxen,
Or your amber-weeping sisters, Charioteer,
    Or ships which are now sea-goddesses,
Or the day averted from Atreus' mad feast,
    Or the hard rocks following the lyre's note?
Fertile poetic licence extends to infinity
    And binds none of its words with history's truth.

The disavowal is more complex than it seems. For even as Ovid advertises his own products as fictive the reader is drawn into creating the very poetic realities (Perseus and Pegasus, Tantalus' thirst, Jupiter's abduction of Europa, etc.) denoted as false. This is precisely the ontological game played throughout *Metamorphoses* in Ovid's narrative of myth.[33]

Right from the start of this most mediated and ludic of epics, in which the reader needs to be continually alert to narrative strategies and stratagems, Ovid uses his mythic subject matter to play several poetic games. The defeat of Apollo by Cupid in *Metamorphoses* 1 (452–73), for example, is simultaneously the triumph of elegy over epic, and replays the same god's victory over the would-be epicist, Ovid, in *Amores* 1.1. But perhaps more importantly, in this opening book, Ovid continues the ontological game of *Amores* 3.12, playing slyly but overtly with the reader's suspension of disbelief. After drawing the reader into his narrative of the great flood and its survivors, Deucalion and Pyrrha, who are to regenerate the human race, the poet pauses at the crucial

moment – the creation of humankind out of stones – to make the
reader recognise the fictive nature of the world to which he/she has
given credence:

> saxa – quis hoc credat nisi sit pro teste uetustas? –
> ponere duritiem coepere suumque rigorem,
> mollirique mora mollitaque ducere formam.
>
> *Metamorphoses* 1.400–402

The stones – who'd believe it without antiquity
For witness? – began to lose their hardness and stiffness
And slowly soften and softened take on form.

Similar interventions occur elsewhere in *Metamorphoses* (see, e.g., *Met.*
10. 301–3, 13. 733–4), ensuring that the reader brings to bear on the
narrative a fusion of literary sophistication and a willingness to commit to the poetic fiction. Sometimes the characters themselves question the truth of the mythic subject matter (*Met.* 8.614–15, 9.203–4);
sometimes the ontological game is played out through the manner of
the narrative itself, as anthropomorphic features of divinities of natural
phenomena are inappropriately emphasised (Tmolus sits on the mountain which is himself and shakes his ears free of his trees, *Met.* 11.157–8),
mythic figures are given too contemporary a flavour (Jupiter on the Palatine, Phaethon at the circus), or the myth explodes through narrative
inconcinnity (the Furies combing serpents from their hair at *Met.* 4.454)
or excess (the catalogue of trees at *Met.* 10.90–105, the similes at *Met.*
13.789–807).

At other times the ontological game takes a decidedly more serious
twist, where Ovid asks the question: what would happen if there were
no distinction between the artist's fictions and reality itself? Pygmalion
(*Met.* 10.243–97) is the paradigm case. His artefact, the statue of a beautiful woman, becomes flesh and blood; the consequence (*Met.* 10.298–
502) is the birth of a son (Cinyras) who will be desired by, and have
sex with, his own daughter (Myrrha). The dissolution of ontological
boudaries between image and reality begets the dissolution of moral
boundaries between father and daughter.

At important moments, too, in *Metamorphoses'* self-reflective use
of myth the poetic and the political fuse. The end of Book 5 and the
beginning of Book 6 are two such moments, where myth is used to
address the issue of the relationship between art and political power. The

Musomachia of Book 5 features the description of a contest between the Olympian Muses and the Emathides, daughters of Pierus, that is, the Pierides. The Emathides, whose song is summarised (apart from a brief quotation) rather than related in full, had offered a politically subversive song praising the victory of the giants over the gods. The song of the Muses is given in full, and in it the tale of the rape of Persephone is told as part of a hymn glorifying Ceres. The Muses are declared victorious and the Emathides/Pierides are punished by being transformed into magpies. But, even so, their speech cannot be silenced, as the Muse-narrator acknowledges in her prejudicial, but revealing final image of her rivals:

> nunc quoque in alitibus facundia prisca remansit
> raucaque garrulitas studiumque immane loquendi.
> *Metamorphoses* 5.677–8

Even now as birds their verbal facility remains,
Their grating garrulity and boundless passion for speech.

If the reader remembers Ovid's first definition of himself as one of the 'poets of the Pierides' (*uates Pieridum, Am.* 1.1.6), this failure to silence subversive speech has ramifications for Ovid and *Metamorphoses* itself, as the following book immediately confirms. In the plebeian Arachne's competition with the Olympian Minerva (noticeable is Ovid's 'Roman' focus on Arachne's low social place: *Met.* 6.10–11) the former's tapestry exposes the 'crimes of the gods' (*caelestia crimina, Met.* 6.131) ignored in Minerva's ideological representation of the Olympians seated in 'august/Augustan majesty' (*augusta grauitate, Met.* 6.73). And the tapestry exposes these crimes by focussing on two recurring features of divine behaviour already underscored in *Metamorphoses* 1–5: deception and rape. The neoteric, asymmetrical style of Arachne's tapestry similarly mirrors Ovid's epic.[34] Arachne's aristocracy, like that of Ovid, is located in art, not birth. When, inevitably, she is punished by Minerva, she is allowed to live on (*uiue, Met.* 6.136), and as a spider continues to practise her art. Like the Pierides, her art is not destroyed, just her body; the art transcends death.

As Ovid proclaims that his art will, too, in *Metamorphoses'* allusive epilogue.[35] There he not only asserts the eternity of his poem and thus its *ueritas* (its poetic reality and its not simply 'poetic' truth), but claims, too, the identity of *uates* and work, of self and poem, and the undying 'life' of both:

> iamque opus exegi, quod nec Iouis ira nec ignis
> nec poterit ferrum nec edax abolere uetustas.
> cum uolet, illa dies, quae nil nisi corporis huius
> ius habet, incerti spatium mihi finiat aeui.
> parte tamen meliore mei super alta perennis
> astra ferar nomenque erit indelebile nostrum,
> quaque patet domitis Romana potentia terris,
> ore legar populi perque omnia saecula fama,
> siquid habent ueri uatum praesagia, uiuam.
>
> *Metamorphoses* 15.871–9

Now my work is done, which no wrath of Jove, no fire,
No steel, no corrosion of the ages can destroy.
When it will, let that day, whose jurisdiction is
But this body, end my span of uncertain time.
I'll be borne, the finer part of me, perennial
Above the high stars, my name beyond erasure;
And where Roman might extends over mastered lands,
I'll be read with the people's voice, and through all time
In fame, if bards' prophecies are true, I shall live.

The poet had made the *uiuam* boast as early as the final line of *Amores* I (*Am.* 1.15.42), where he presented himself as the inheritor of the Greco-Roman poetic tradition from Homer, Hesiod, and Callimachus through to Virgil, Tibullus, and Gallus; and that claim, too, was made in the context of contemporary hostility. But there Ovid's 'enemies' were reduced to the vague figure of 'Corrosive Envy,' *Liuor edax*,[36] and the criticisms of him made specific (adoption of an un-Roman, idle life-style and rejection of the vigorous Roman pursuits of the military, law, and politics). Here the criticisms of him are unmentioned and the opposition is embodied in a transparent mythic metaphor that makes clear the inimical relationship between the poem and the world of power. As the lines preceding this passage imply and *Tristia* I will clearly state, the *ira Iouis* is in part a metaphor for the wrath of his earthly counterpart on the Palatine. Ovid develops the earlier position and gives it political edge. It is neither Jupiter nor the *princeps* who guarantees immortality: it is poetry, or more specifically, the reader of poetry, who will ensure the truth value of *Metamorphoses'* final claim. The *lector* alone has power over Ovid's life; and he has power to make that life transcend the 'stars' to which deified generals aspire and to ensure that life's survival of the empire that they ruled.

MYTH AND EXILE

In 8 CE Ovid was Rome's most distinguished living poet.[37] Virgil and Horace were long dead and Ovid's poetic achievement extensive, brilliant, and lauded. In the same year he was banished. In an act virtually unprecedented in Roman history the empire's major poet was removed by its political leader – and removed, in part, for his verse. Ovid was expelled to a half-Greek city called Tomis (modern Constanza), situated on the Black Sea in what today is Rumania at the extreme edge of the Roman empire. The effect on the fifty-year-old poet was devastating. Tomis was the inverse of the Rome he loved: barbarous, insecure, intemperate of climate, and spiritually and culturally barren. Its inhabitants spoke Getic, Sarmatian, hybrid Greek, and no Latin. For a man such as Ovid, separation from friends, society, the literary world, and even his own native tongue constituted a death sentence.

Ovid reached Tomis in 9 CE and immediately sent back to Rome a volume of eleven short poems composed on the outward journey, the first book of *Tristia* ('Sorrows'). It is an innovative, experimental, polyvalent book of verse, the first of a collection of five books (each composed as a separate entity), in which the poet articulates the pain and deprivations of exile and petitions for imperial clemency (for at least amelioration of the place of exile, if not return to Rome itself). In a sense *Tristia* begins a new genre. Ovid's readers were devouring the recently disseminated (allegedly unrevised) narrative epic *Metamorphoses* and awaiting completion of the narrative *Fasti*. They would have been surprised – but not disappointed. Ovid's search for the kind of poetry that would reflect his traumatic situation had led him to break with the present, to return to the past, and to rewrite both. What he did was complex and has been widely discussed. What merits attention here is Ovid's use of myth. For evaluative and ironic purposes Ovid mythologises his own situation – through analogies with his earlier epistolary heroines such as the 'stolen/raped Briseis,' *rapta Briseis* (cf. *Tr.* 1.1.13f. and *Her.* 3.3), whose tears at her abandonment become those of the banished poet; through analogies, too, with such epic figures as Ulysses, whose travails, the poet protests, pale to insignificance in comparison with his own (*Tr.* 1.5.53–84). One reason for Ovid's greater suffering is that he suffers the wrath of a greater god:

> me deus oppressit, nullo mala nostra leuante;
> > bellatrix illi diua ferebat opem.
> cumque minor Ioue sit tumidis qui regnat in undis,
> > illum Neptuni, me Iouis ira premit.
> adde quod illius pars maxima ficta laborum,
> > ponitur in nostris fabula nulla malis.
> > > *Tristia* 1.5.75–80

> A god persecuted me, no one soothing my pain;
> > The warrior goddess helped Ulysses.
> Though Jove is greater than swelling ocean's king,
> > He's harassed by Neptune's wrath, I by Jove's.
> Add that the greatest part of his toils are fiction,
> > But my sufferings contain no myth.

The greater god, 'Jove,' of course, is Augustus, whose identification with the storm-god Jupiter is secured early in *Tristia* 1 (1.1.69ff.) and sustained throughout (3.11ff., 4.26, 5.3, 5.75ff., 9.21); 'the wrath of Jove,' *Iouis ira* (*Tr.* 1.5.78), is the anger of the *princeps*. But, even as Ovid mythologises his own situation and uses the mythic metonym of *Metamorphoses* to achieve this, the poet plays it both ways by insisting on the nonmythological nature of his pain. And, if Ovid out-Ulysseses Ulysses, so in the next poem his wife is superior to all Homer's women, to Andromache, Laodamia, and even Penelope herself (*Tr.* 1.6.19–22).

There is also another mythic analogy – with Aeneas. It is brilliantly and subtly achieved, and its semiotics are potent. Ovid's movement into exile is a movement from Rome, but Ovid mythologises and Romanises that movement to invert its surface meaning by portraying himself as a latter day Aeneas and his putative descendant in Rome as a latter day god of *furor*. *Tristia* 1.1 focusses on Ovid persecuted by the anger of a deity; 1.2 presents Ovid buffeted by a storm; 1.3 describes Ovid's departure from a city (Rome), which is compared to fallen Troy:

> si licet exemplis in paruis grandibus uti,
> > haec facies Troiae cum caperetur erat.
> > > *Tristia* 1.3.25–6.

> If one may use mighty examples in humble cases,
> > This was the face of Troy as she was captured.

Most readers of these three poems would have discerned Ovid's mirroring of the narrative sequence of the first two books of Virgil's *Aeneid*: Aeneas' persecution by the anger of a deity; the storm sent against the Trojan fleet; Aeneas' account of his departure from Troy. Within the context of his banishment for 'un-Roman activities,' Ovid mythologises himself as the epic paradigm of Rome.

This mythologisation of personal experience, the reality of which is insisted upon, generates a densely textured fusion in *Tristia* 1 of the literary, the mythological, and the biographical. It is a fusion that is typical of and even defines the exilic works, in which Ovid's extensive allusion to and rewriting of other poetry,[38] including his own, not only create an image of himself as poet, but signal the fusion for Ovid of literature and life. By showing how his own exile is a construct of experience and of myth and literature recycled and remade (the storm in *Tr.* 1.2 is both a real and a mythic/literary storm made into a new mythic/literary storm), he both indexes this fusion and injects it with compelling irony: the storm that Homer controlled at *Odyssey* 5.291ff., that Virgil controlled at *Aeneid* I.81ff., and that he himself controlled at *Metamorphoses* 11.474ff., now controls him.

Ovid's *Tristia* are and are not personal poetry. The *persona* of the poet in the work is a manufactured one, and the work is that most public form of writing, a petition – its addressees are Augustus and the Roman people. But the poetry is grounded in history and Ovid's life in a way that had not occurred before, and its conjunction of myth, literature, and experience exemplifies that life. Appropriately for Rome's greatest mythographer, literary and mythic constructs generated by Ovid's own metamorphosis image poet and man.

FURTHER READING

Recent analyses of Ovid's poetry abound, many of which may be found in the bibliography at the end of this book. Galinsky (1975) and Solodow (1988) remain useful introductions to the *Metamorphoses*, the poetics of which are treated perceptively by Hardie (2002b); Cameron (2004), Feeney (1991), and Graf (2002) provide a gateway into Ovid and myth. Development and ramifications of the arguments of this chapter may be found in Boyle (2003). Recommended English translations of Ovid's erotic poetry and the *Metamorphoses* are Melville (1998) and Melville (1999) and of the *Fasti* Boyle and Woodard (2000).

NOTES

1 See Cornell (1995), 60–68.
2 On Livius, Naevius, Ennius, and Accius, see Boyle (2006), ch. 2–4.
3 On Varius, see Leigh (1996) and Boyle (2006), 161–2; on Caesarian and Augustan monuments and the Gemma Augustea, see Zanker (1988) and Boyle (2003).
4 Feeney (1991), 189.
5 Even if we include the epistles by 'heroes' to 'heroines' (*Her.* 16, 18, 20), which are commonly regarded as non-Ovidian, the main focus in the collection is still on the female voice/memory. For a Lacanian analysis of female desire in *Heroides*, see Lindheim (2003).
6 'An unjustified appropriation,' Kennedy (2002), 226.
7 See Hinds (1985), 27–8.
8 On this, see esp. Cameron (2004), 261–303, who notes the clear use of such handbooks in Ovidian lists (e.g., Actaeon's hounds at *Met.* 3.206–25, Jupiter's and Neptune's rapes at *Met.* 6.103–22, Calydonian boar hunters at *Met.* 8.300–17).
9 See Galinsky (1975), 4–5, who cites the Ovidian Ulysses' frequent reformulation of the Trojan saga at *Ars* 2.128: *ille referre aliter saepe solebat idem* ('He would often retell the same tale differently').
10 See Graf (2002), 119.
11 See Nisbet and Hubbard (1978), 69–70.
12 See Graf (2002), 111–15.
13 On *Am.* 1.7, see Barsby (1973), *ad loc.*
14 Williams (1996), 126. For detailed discussion of this catalogue, see Williams, 81–111.
15 See the discussion of Davis (1995), 184–5.
16 For details of the adultery law and its penalties see Cantarella (1991), 229–34; on the *leges Iuliae* see Treggiari (1996), 886–93, who offers a more generous view of Augustus' motivation than that presented here.
17 See Cohen (1991), 110.
18 For Julia's adulteries and *impudicitia*: Velleius Paterculus 2.100.2–5; Tacitus *Annales* 1.10, 1.53, 3.24, 4.44; Suetonius *Augustus Diuus* 65.1–5, 101.3, *Tiberius* 11.4.
19 This was Iullus Antonius, 'lover' of Julia, the son of Mark Antony and the closest of Julia's adulterers to the imperial household – he was married to Augustus' niece. He either committed suicide (Vell. Pat. 2.100.2–5) or was executed (Tac. *Ann*.1.10.4; Dio 55.10.15).
20 As his grandson and adopted son, Agrippa Postumus, and his granddaughter Julia were to demonstrate in 7 and 8 CE, respectively. For, whatever the conspiratorial realities underlying the feuding of Augustus' household, the charges on which his grandchildren were banished were moral: loose *mores* in the case of Agrippa Postumus, adultery in the case of the younger Julia (Vell. Pat. 2.112.7; Tac. *Ann.* 1.3.4, 3.24.2, 4.71.4; Suet. *Aug.* 65.1–5; Dio 55.32.1–2)
21 See Boyle (2003), 22, 260–61.
22 Feeney (1991), 205, sees the Ovidian gods as 'extremely powerful and economical strategies for communicating his vision of human experience.' Contrast Galinsky (1975), 16–19, 62–3, who restricts Ovid's interest in myth in *Metamorphoses* to its 'narrative and entertaining function.'
23 See Myers (1994), viii–ix.

24 For example, the metamorphosis of Arachne into a spider (6.139–45) and of the Propoetides into stone (10.238–42). Solodow (1988), 157, defines Ovidian metamorphosis as 'a process through which the characteristics of men are only rendered visible and manifest.' But, even if one allows 'men' to mean 'men and women.' this only applies to some metamorphoses.

25 With the final two lines of this soliloquy, compare Phaedra's remarks: *quae memoras scio/ uera esse, nutrix, sed furor cogit sequi/ peiora*, 'What you say I know/ To be true, nurse, but passion compels/The worse' (*Phaedra* 177–9).

26 On the Ovidian treatment of rape, see Richlin (1992b).

27 Cf. Feeney (1991), 204.

28 Well discussed by Solodow (1988), 84–5.

29 See Feeney (1991), 214–17; Boyle (2003), 49–51, 184–5, 225.

30 On April 28 12 BCE, by decree of the senate, a statue and altar of Vesta were erected by Augustus in his house on the Palatine. See *Fasti Praenestini* and *Caeretani*: Degrassi (1963), 13.2: 66, 132f., 452.

31 Dessau *ILS* 72 (Aesernia); Cic. *Philippic* 1.13, 2.110; Dio 47.18.3–19.3; Weinstock (1971), 390.

32 See Hollis (1973), 105, who cites Suet. *Aug.* 44. See also Boyle (2003), 260–61.

33 In the discussion of myth and fiction, I draw on the excellent treatment of Feeney (1991), 224–49.

34 On Arachne's style, see Feeney (1991), 191–2, who calls her tapestry 'a neoteric masterpiece.'

35 On the allusivity and texture of this epilogue, see Boyle (2003), 9–11.

36 A figure that did not disappear from Ovid's poetry: see also *Rem.* 369, 389, *Met.* 6.129, *Tr.* 4.10.123, *Pont.* 4.16.47

37 This section rewrites material from Boyle and Sullivan (1991), 1–5, with kind permission of Penguin Books.

38 Especially of Catullus (cf. esp. Catullus I.1ff. and IV with *Tr.* I.1.5ff. and I.10), Horace (cf. esp. *Epistle* I.20 with *Tr.* I.1), and Virgil.

PART THREE

RECEPTION

Long, long ago, when this old world was in its tender infancy, there was a child, named Epimetheus, who never had either father or mother; and, that he might not be lonely, another child, fatherless and motherless like himself, was sent from a far country, to live with him, and be his playfellow and helpmate. Her name was Pandora.

The first thing that Pandora saw, when she entered the cottage where Epimetheus dwelt, was a great box. And almost the first question which she put to him, after crossing the threshold, was this, – "Epimetheus, what have you in that box?" "My dear little Pandora," answered Epimetheus, "that is a secret, and you must be kind enough not to ask any questions about it. The box was left here to be kept safely, and I do not myself know what it contains." . . .

But Epimetheus himself, although he said very little about it, had his own share of curiosity to know what was inside. . . . Thus, after all his sage speeches to Pandora about restraining her curiosity, Epimetheus turned out to be quite as foolish, and nearly as much in fault, as she. So, whenever we blame Pandora for what happened, we must not forget to shake our heads at Epimetheus likewise.

As Pandora raised the lid, the cottage grew very dark and dismal; for the black cloud had now swept quite over the sun, and seemed to have buried it alive. . . . It seemed as if a sudden swarm of winged creatures brushed past her, taking flight out of the box, while, at the same instant, she heard the voice of Epimetheus, with a lamentable tone, as if he were in pain.

"Oh, I am stung!" cried he. "I am stung! Naughty Pandora! Why have you opened this wicked box?" . . .

Now, if you wish to know what these ugly things might be, which had made their escape out of the box, I must tell you that they were the whole family of earthly Troubles. There were evil Passions; there were a great many species of Cares; there were more than a hundred and fifty Sorrows; there were Diseases, in a vast number of miserable and painful shapes; there were more kinds of Naughtiness than it would be of any use to talk about. In short, everything that has since afflicted the souls and bodies of mankind had been shut up in the mysterious box, and given to Epimetheus and Pandora to be kept safely, in order that the happy children of the world might never be molested by them. Had they been faithful to their trust, all would have gone well. No grown person would ever have been sad, nor any child have had cause to shed a single tear, from that hour until this moment. . . .

Suddenly there was a gentle little tap on the inside of the lid. . . .

So, with one consent, the two children again lifted the lid. Out flew a sunny and smiling little personage, and hovered around the room, throwing a light wherever she went. . . .

"Pray, who are you, beautiful creature?" inquired Pandora.

"I am to be called Hope!" answered the sunshiny figure. "And because I am such a cheery little body, I was packed into the box, to make amends to the human race for that swarm of ugly Troubles, which was destined to be let loose among them. Never fear! We shall do pretty well in spite of them all." . . .

"We do trust you!" cried Epimetheus and Pandora, both in one breath.

And so they did; and not only they, but so has everybody trusted Hope, that has since been alive. . . . No doubt – no doubt – the Troubles are still flying about the world, and have increased in multitude, rather than lessened, and are a very ugly set of imps, and carry most venomous stings in their tails. I have felt them already, and expect to feel them more, as I grow older. But then that lovely and lightsome little figure of Hope! What in the world could we do without her? Hope spiritualizes the earth; Hope makes it always new; and, even in the earth's best and brightest aspect, Hope shows it to be only the shadow of an infinite bliss hereafter!

Nathaniel Hawthorne; from "The Paradise of Children," *A Wonder Book* (1851)

So thus he spoke, and they obeyed the son of Cronus, Zeus,
    the lord.
Straightway the famous god of two lame legs from earth   70
Did mold a gentle virgin-form, by Cronus' son's own will;
And gleaming-eyed Athena, goddess, dressed and primped
Her, while the Charities divine and lady Peitho decked
Her flesh with golden chains, and Horae, with
Their lovely tresses, wreathed spring flowers round her
    head;   75
And every decoration Pallas fit upon her frame.
Within her breast the messenger, the Argos-slayer, wrought
Both lies and wheedling words, a cheating habit too –
Loud thund'ring Zeus's will it was. And speech
The herald of gods instilled in her; he gave the name   80
Pandora to this woman, since Olympus-dwellers all
Did give her as a gift – a bane to men sustained by grain.
Then when the utterly relentless lure he'd made complete,
The father sent to Epimetheus the Argos-slayer of renown,
The gods' swift messenger, to bear the gift; and
    Epimetheus   85
Ignored the thing Prometheus had said to him – "Don't
    ever take
A gift from Zeus Olympian, but send it back instead;
It might turn out to be some ill for mortal men." But take
The gift he did; and when the ill was his, he understood too
    late.
They used to live upon the earth, the human tribes before
    this time,   90
Apart from woes, apart from grueling work,
And painful sicknesses that bring on death to men;
"For quickly men grow old in misery."
But now the woman with her hands the jar's great lid
    removed,
Its contents scattered wide, and baneful troubles wrought on
    humankind.   95
But Hope alone remained inside an everlasting home,
Within the jar beneath its rim, and did not fly away,
Because she'd put the jar's great lid back on,
By Aegis-bearing Zeus's will, cloud-gatherer.
But miseries uncounted roam among the human race,   100

For earth is filled with woes, as is the sea;
And sickness visits humans in the day, as in the night,
For no apparent cause, and brings to mortals silent doom,
Since Zeus all-wise removed from them their voice.
You see, there is no way to flee the will of Zeus.   105

Hesiod, *Works and Days* 69–105

13: WOMEN AND GREEK MYTH

Vanda Zajko

What I want is a mythology so huge
That settling on its grassy bank
(Which may at first seem ordinary)
You catch sight of the frog, the stone,
The dead minnow jewelled with flies,
And remember all at once
The things you had forgotten to imagine.

Rebecca Elson

The question of how to characterise the relation of women and myth is primarily one of definition. For just as myth is widely acknowledged to be a problematic category that signifies quite differently at various historical moments, so too the designation of woman has no clear definition outside of specific cultural formations. There is an aspect of the combination of women *and* myth that complicates the issue still further: are we concerned here with myths in which women are regarded as the main protagonists or myths that have been creatively interpreted by or for women? Although both have continuously provided a resource with which writers and artists have explored the relations between the sexes, either within the landscape of myth itself, or in relation to the particular social and historical contexts of its various instantiations, the latter category has become particularly associated with the feminist interpretation of myth and thus with its explicit positioning as either liberating or oppressive for women. This essay will explore some of the tensions surrounding the description of stories about women as being either 'pro' or 'anti' women and the ideological entailments of such descriptions. It will also argue that the way the category of myth itself is conceptualised has a direct bearing on what it is perceived to be able to say 'about women.' There is a sense in which the categories 'myth' and 'women' ought both to be regarded as imaginative constructs.[1]

Myth has generally been negatively defined against other forms of discourse, against history, philosophy, theology, or science, and it has been claimed that it was the Greeks themselves who invented this kind of taxonomy. Marcel Detienne uses as an example the genealogy of criticism of the oldest Homeric stories and argues in *The Creation of Mythology* that the single most important reason that an individual or a group stood outside the corpus of myth and commented upon it was that it had been scandalised. When practitioners of philosophy and theology felt themselves under attack, they reinterpreted myth using strategies such as allegory and euhemerism, rather than rejecting the offending stories outright. The debate concerning whether the resulting interpretations constitute new versions of the original scandalising myth or interpretations of it continued and continues to participate in the process of defining myth negatively against what it is not, although these days it tends to be resolved by a recourse to pragmatism. A scholarly consensus may highlight the provisionality of any definition of myth in the diversity of narrative contexts that existed in ancient Greece,[2] yet a graded nomenclature indicates the scale of value used to differentiate between different kinds of stories: a narrative in Apollodorus is likely to be designated a 'version' of a Greek myth; Ovid and Servius may also offer us 'versions' but may alternatively be involved in 'interpretation'; Frazer and Lévi-Strauss without doubt 'interpret,' whereas Hélène Cixous and Donna Haraway are more likely to 'appropriate' (where the term appropriate signifies an account of a myth that overtly displays its ideological commitments).

Even within the time-frame accepted as 'the ancient world' it is a far from simple procedure to identify which narratives should be regarded as constituting a particular myth and which should be excluded for not being sufficiently or primarily 'mythological.' If we take as an example the myth of Atalanta, there are traces of her story across the whole tradition, from the earliest literate sources onwards, and yet some of these traces are from sections of fragmentary texts, such as Hesiod's *Catalogue of Women*, that have been reconstructed from papyri or from citations in considerably later works. How are we to contextualise these fragments, particularly when the preliterate Greece where such a myth has its notional origin is unavailable to us, and other accounts that may have been hugely influential in the shaping of the tradition are now lost to us too? Even explicitly mythographical sources, namely those self-consciously concerned with the collation of mythic narratives, can hardly be considered neutral: of the more complete collections, Apollodorus is at pains to show the variety of versions available to him, Ovid is regarded as giving traditional stories a subversive Roman twist, and Hyginus is undatable and judged to be a poor narrator. The medieval collection of earlier sources known as the 'Vatican Mythographer,' which includes material from Servius as well as commentaries on Pindar, Theocritus, Statius, and Apollonius, is also undatable and, in the fashion of its time, not attributable to any one particular author.

Given the complexity of the tradition, the pragmatism of the critics can be seen as an appropriate response to an intractable problem, but it may also be motivated by a desire to preserve a space for myth that is untouched by criticism or interpretation. And when schematised as above, the pragmatic distinctions between the various terms for myth may seem simply arbitrary. The word "mythology" combines both 'muthos' and 'logos' and so can be seen to encode the struggle for mastery between the story and the explanation. I have argued elsewhere that if those working with Greek myth want to use it as a source for religious and social practice or as a guidebook to understanding something about the way the Greeks conceptualised their world, then it is convenient to emphasise the historical particularity of their material and to downplay the inconveniences of its sometimes fragmentary form and muddled genealogy. But if the myths are being examined as part of a study of the history of Western thought, or as a construction of symbols in whose repetition psychological truths emerge, what will be highlighted is not what the stories may have meant to the Greeks but the use that has been made of them by succeeding generations or the extent to which they might contribute to an understanding of mental life.[3] In the latter case the category of 'myth' is much more capacious than in the former, and both examples demonstrate how the categories of myth and interpretation fluctuate, depending on the work that myth is being required to do.[4]

We have examined so far the 'myth' part of the equation. What, then, about the role of the 'women'? First, there are the ancient Greek women whose lives must be reconstructed from disconnected evidence and whose 'mentalité' belongs primarily to the realm of the imagination. These women are less visible in the historical and archaeological record than women from later periods, and there are only a few textual fragments that we can confidently assert were produced by a woman's hand. There are significant effects of this absence: despite the exhaustive collation of the sources relating to women, which span a wide time frame and a variety of genres, the impression still dominates of women being the absent presence of the ancient world, and a frustrating sense of lack often seems to characterise the endeavours of those wanting to form a connection with them. As a result of this, myth becomes a haven of plenitude, a place where women thrive and behave in provocative and interesting ways; myth helps fulfil the fantasies of those who are unwilling to face the prospect of a past inhabited by cowed and sequestered women and allows the possibility that women then, in their imaginations at least, participated in more contemporary kinds of defiance. Alternatively, an excavation of the 'mythic imagination'[5] has been seen as providing a way of exposing the deep roots of the misogyny that continues to contribute to the inequity of the world; once exposed, there is the opportunity for regrowth and change.

One area where there is a clear desire for there to have been dynamic women is the area of storytelling itself. Although there is very little explicit indication from ancient Greece that women told stories to each other in a domestic setting,[6] material obtained from anthropological studies has been used to argue that women in preliterate communities are inevitably involved in creating, retelling, and passing down myths, often with a different emphasis and in a subversive way. Indeed, it has become something of a commonplace that women are 'natural' storytellers, and within many different spheres of feminist theory and praxis, storytelling has become a model for both the construction and the dissemination of knowledge. The following passage comes from Judith Plaskow's essay on 'The Coming of Lilith' in the feminist theological collection *Womanspirit Rising*, and it typifies the use of this kind of model: Lilith, Adam's first wife, who left the garden of Eden because she disliked being ordered around, is visited by Eve, who has come to feel excluded by the closeness that has developed between God and Adam and climbs over the garden wall to find her:

> She did not wander long on the other side before she met the one she had come to find, for Lilith was waiting. At first sight of her, Eve remembered the tales of Adam and was frightened, but Lilith understood and greeted her kindly. "Who are you?" they asked each other, "What is your story?" And they sat and spoke together, of the past and then of the future. They talked for many hours, not once, but many times. They taught each other many things, and told each other stories, and laughed together, and cried, over and over, till the bond of sisterhood grew between them.

Meanwhile, back in the garden, Adam was puzzled by Eve's comings and goings, and disturbed by what he sensed to be her new attitude toward him. He talked to God about it, and God, having his own problems with Adam and a somewhat broader perspective, was able to help out a little – but he was confused, too. Something had failed to go according to plan. As in the days of Abraham, he needed counsel from his children. "I am who I am," thought God, "but I must become who I will become."

And God and Adam were expectant and afraid the day Eve and Lilith returned to the garden, bursting with possibilities, ready to rebuild it together.[7]

Here Plaskow 'retells' a story from the Jewish tradition in order to interrogate its authority, and storytelling itself forms the basis of, and makes possible, the epistemological shift that is described. The idea that women tell stories to each other more readily than men can, of course, be questioned from a variety of perspectives, but the point here is that a tradition has developed of associating women with potent and transgressive storytelling and this association is often retrojected to include women in ancient Greece.

A recent example from within Classics draws on an anthropological model of preliterate societies to discuss and demonstrate the feasibility of recovering possible traces of women's storytelling from the canons of literate Greece. Discussing the Hesiodic *Catalogue of Women*, Lillian Doherty argues that 'before there was feminist thought, there were women's traditions and women's genres, forms of expression practiced by specific groups of women within larger cultural formations.'[8] She goes on to maintain that the effacement of these traditions by the written text of the *Catalogue* is replicated by the reluctance of modern scholarship to acknowledge that myths about women constitute its subject matter. In emphasising the importance of myth to the work of a 'feminist classicist,'[9] she articulates a sense of myth as plenitude as outlined above:

Myth is important to feminism because it is one element of literate culture that has the potential to incorporate women's traditions and perspectives. By this I do not mean simply that at some time in the distant past men's poetry incorporated a women's tradition once and for all – for example, by reflecting vestiges of matriarchal social or political organization.

Rather, because myths are stories that combine an imaginative fluidity with an authoritative force, and because they are told in a variety of contexts even when they are also written down, they provide a point of entry for women's perspectives and concerns in the discourse shared by women and men.[10]

For Doherty, myth is a place where the influence of women's creativity may legitimately be felt.

Another context in which the active participation of women is presupposed is that of ritual, and when it comes to interpreting myth, the use of a ritual framework clearly exemplifies the methodological point that the way the category of myth is conceptualised to some extent determines what it can say 'about' women. The whole question of the relation of myth to ritual is something that has been repeatedly discussed over the years, and there is a complex range of opinions as to how that relation should be expressed. On a large scale, it is possible to describe myth and ritual as complementary forms of expression, the former conveying in actions what the latter articulates in words;[11] alternatively, it is possible to describe them as contrasting forms of expression that operate in different ways, myth 'tending to make explicit and absolute' that which ritual leaves 'implicit and temporary.'[12] One of the benefits of discussing myth in the context of ritual is that it makes plausible the speculation about the meaning of myth within wide social groupings: while the claim that an audience would have a collective response to any particular myth is impossible to verify, the very existence of a 'myth and ritual complex'[13] testifies to some investment in the concerns of that ritual by a community or part-community. Ritual is above all a collective phenomenon and so it renders the category of 'women' visible.[14]

When it comes to piecing together the constituent details of particular rituals, deciding who took part in them, and speculating as to what meanings they had for the communities they involved, the problems are as great as those entailed in reconstructing the details surrounding the transmission of a myth. The sources for a ritual practice are generally taken from a similar variety of literary and archaeological texts, and only the argument that it is a feature of ritual to remain unchanged over a long period of time makes their synthesis respectable.[15] And in relation to certain rituals, such as that of 'the Bears of Brauron,' relatively late and obscure sources such as the scholiast to Aristophanes have surprisingly taken on something of a canonical status. This ritual, connected with the shrine of Artemis at Brauron, involved young Athenian women 'playing the bear' in order to be tamed for marriage.

It has become a *locus classicus* for discussing the conceptual importance of liminality in the ancient Greek world and has contributed significantly to the emergence of the picture painted by ritual whereby the process of moving between different stages of sexual life is central to the definition of women.[16] Since ritual is broadly conceived as functioning to ease societal anxieties, 'particularly those involving killing, sexuality, transitions, or death,'[17] the myths associated with rituals are regarded as expressing similar anxieties and as playing a part in alleviating them. Women within such narratives may temporarily escape restrictive conceptual categories, but the narrative is judged to be concluded when the categories are reaffirmed.[18]

Despite the obscurity shrouding the details of what they entailed, the idea that there were cults specifically designed for women, in which men played little or no part, has proved tantalising for those looking for contexts in the ancient world in which to imagine self-determining women. Even if only temporary, the stage of segregation such rituals required provides an uninterrupted period in which to envisage women engaging in 'women-identified' behaviour and telling subversive tales. An eroticised context that is particularly potent in this respect is that associated with the poet Sappho on the island of Lesbos at the end of the seventh and the beginning of the sixth century BCE. Not only does this provide another so-called liminal space where young women may have spent time separated from men, but it also offers the unique and mouth-watering prospect of reconstructing the experience from textual fragments written by a woman. Margaret Reynolds has recently argued that, far from discouraging attempts at reconstruction, the lack of conclusive evidence for any aspect of Sappho's life has contributed compellingly to the Sappho myth:

> ... we know very little about her poetry, hardly anything about her life, not much more about her society, nothing to speak of about her character and nothing whatsoever about her personal appearance. But this lack of facts has not stopped people – virtually from that day to this – making up stories about her. Quite the contrary ... 'Sappho' is not a name, much less a person. It is, rather, a space. A space for filling in the gaps, joining up the dots, making something out of nothing.[19]

In her unknowability, Sappho functions as a metaphor for all the women of antiquity whose absence inspires both a sense of familiarity and an overwhelming longing: 'Sappho seems known to us, familiar, capable of being translated into our everyday lives. Yet still she remains utterly remote – if anything, all the more insinuating and full of meaning because she is, and always will be, absent.'[20]

In an essay that is generally pessimistic about the capacity of Greek myth to say anything much about women ('the subject of women in mythology offers better value to the student of mythology than to the student of women'[21]), Ken Dowden suggests that it is the indiscriminate classification of 'Greek myth' as 'Greek myth' that encourages its use as the basis for large-scale generalised statements about the attitudes of 'Greek society':

> Any material which looks so non-historical misleads us into thinking that it is somehow unaffected by exact historical circumstance, that it is supra-historical . . . It is possible therefore to see in Greek mythology certain recurrent and characteristic social views. For instance, the categories of women visible in myth undergo a certain ideological distortion: females may be parthenoi (maidens) or gynaikes (matrons), but not unmarried women. Widows, too, barely register, except maybe for the Graiai who confront Perseus – marginal, disabled, disgusting. So, elementary social data of broad application, the constants of Greek society, are embedded in myth – even if a study of the orators might deliver this information more reliably.[22]

Dowden's argument is that if the different versions of a myth are amalgamated and treated as one account, as 'the myth of' x or y, which is very common practice both inside and outside the academy, the precise contexts of the myth will not form part of its analysis. From this standpoint, myth is not historically reliable enough to function as a source of information about women per se, but it can be envisioned as a complex narrative system that has the potential to supplement the information derived from less ambivalent sources, such as the surviving speeches of the professional orators. For Dowden, one task of the interpretation of myth is to measure the extent of its 'ideological distortion.' But this task is complicated by the way in which the representations of women in a wide variety of texts, some of which themselves might be described as mythical, have in the past been used to build up a picture of what women's lives were like, so that the two categories of women being assessed are not so obviously distinct. There is a tension between the particularity of individual realisations of a myth and the wider system, which encodes broad ideological commitments: the former constructs a more historical woman, the latter a woman who inhabits the generalised Greek mind.

The tendency to think of myth as ahistorical has led, over the past 50 years or so, to its frequent association with structuralism, a mode of analysis that operates, for the most part, synchronically. For those engaged in structuralist analysis, we can see once again that the myths exemplify the principles of their own analyses, so that they become, in this case, stories 'about' binary oppositions and mediations.[23] Within such analyses, the male/female polarity operates as the primary model of binarism for the ancient Greek cultural system, and the female becomes an allegory for one side of all sorts of other oppositions which, on the face of it, have little to do with women. A particularly ingenious example of such an analysis is Jean-Pierre Vernant's treatment of the myth of Pandora in *Myth and Society in Ancient Greece* (1980), where marriage, sacrifice, and agriculture are 'shown' to be intimately linked in myth, ritual, and institutional practice. Mapped onto broader cultural territory, this myth about the creation of woman comes to signify the need for regulation of women's sexuality. Commenting on this essay, Eric Csapo wryly points out the cost of the analysis:

> Not only is the place of women in society determined through the vast network of meaning that makes up the cultural system as a whole, it is rigidly overdetermined. Every place in the conceptual system is ultimately cross-referenced by every other, indeed ultimately determined by every other. Structuralism's model of ideology is a totalising system, from which there is no escape, and no position from which one can opt out or even criticize the system. It is a steel trap gripping the minds of men and women, without their knowledge, but naturally with full consent, since even prostitutes joyfully celebrate their uselessness and social inferiority.[24]

The woman who emerges here is a long way away from the subversive storyteller, the inheritor of women's traditions. She has been effaced in favour of a figure defined by her sexual behaviour, whose moderate compliance with the dominant social mores functions to reinforce the potency of the family. Even when she appears to choose her own destiny, the semblance of freedom is illusory: her only role in myth is to show a male-dominated society the apocalyptic consequences of allowing her a choice:

> Marriage is violated in the myths by both sexes, but with very different consequences. Violations by men, though harmful to women, do not in themselves cause the collapse of order. But their actions prompt women in the myths to act, and when that happens, the female is released and marriage is undone as a structure of order. There ensues the downfall of the household, and, if the man is a king or leader, his city plummets into chaos.[25]

In querying the inevitability of the conclusions of this kind of study, feminist interpreters of myth are more likely to work with mythic amalgams than with particular variants, although there have been significant exceptions amongst those working within classics, the discipline that might be argued to 'own' Greek myth. Feminists have been inclined to turn to myth because they regard it as a potent discourse in the conceptualisation of women within the cultures of the West. The special relationship women have with myth because of this potency goes some way towards explaining why the editor of a collection such as *The Cambridge Companion* has commissioned an essay on women and myth but not an equivalent one pertaining to men. Feminist engagements with myth have taken many forms – optimistic liberationist readings are certainly not the only possible readings of myth that can be labelled feminist – and they have been shaped by developments in thinking about sex and gender across a wide cultural spectrum. Nor is there necessarily a consensus about what constitutes liberation: it could be argued, for example, that structuralism's exposure of the double bind, the 'steel trap' of patriarchy, is itself potentially liberating. But invariably at the heart of these engagements is the idea that classical myth possesses huge cultural authority and has operated, for the most part, to perpetuate the oppression of women:

> For feminists, the rewriting of myths denotes participation in these historical processes and the struggle to alter gender asymmetries agreed upon for centuries by myth's disseminators. When feminists envisage that struggle, they often think of the rewriting or reinterpretation of individual stories: for example, by changing the focus of the narrative from a male character to a female character, or by shifting the terms of

the myth so that what was a 'negative' female role-model becomes a positive one.[26]

The rewriting of the myth of Lilith and Eve we looked at previously is an excellent example of such a shift in terms and shows that it is not only classical myth that provokes these responses. It also demonstrates the tensions inherent in the 're-' of rewriting: if the new 'version' of a myth changes its emphasis sufficiently radically, it may become difficult to associate it with the tradition, so that it becomes read instead as a story 'about' contemporary feminist experience. The editors of the collection from which the essay comes commented as follows:

> "The Coming of Lilith" retells a story from the biblical–rabbinic tradition. While this might mark the essay as reformist, the retelling threatens to move beyond the tradition from which it stems. Not only does it reverse the traditional image of Lilith as the archetypal evil woman, seeing her instead as the archetype of female freedom, but it also leaves open the question of whether Eve and Lilith will "reconstruct the garden or create it anew.[27]

Those with an investment in a particular configuration of a mythic tradition may police its boundaries with considerable vigour and authorise themselves as arbiters of what it can include. But tradition can be seen as a less static concept that is, and always has been, reshaped and reenergised by continual retellings. Doherty's statement that 'the modern rewriting of myths is a continuation of ancient practice'[28] subscribes to this kind of notion and emphasises that ancient poets and artists freely imported the issues of their own times into their treatments of myth. Feminist retellings can thus be positioned on a continuum with, say, Euripides' *Medea* or the *Heroides* of Ovid, in that all of these texts change the focus of traditional narratives to serve their own ideological ends.

Such rewritings of myth have not been restricted to the academy; there is an enormous amount of writing, both poetry and fiction, which has utilised the strategies outlined above to revivify myth for contemporary audiences. Indeed, feminist mythopoiesis can be seen as one of the areas where the distinction between the scholarly and the imaginative has been successfully deconstructed. The preponderance of the female characters who populate Greek myth has often been a source of comment, as has the discrepancy between the potency of women in myth and literature and the lack of autonomy of their more historical counterparts. Virginia Woolf famously summarised the position as follows:

> Imaginatively, she is of the highest importance; practically she is completely insignificant. She pervades poetry from cover to cover; she is all but absent from history. She dominates the lives of kings and conquerors in fiction; in fact she was the slave of any boy whose parents forced a ring upon her finger. Some of the most inspired words, some of the most profound thoughts in literature fall from her lips; in real life she could hardly spell, and was the property of her husband.[29]

The abundance and influence of women in the literary contexts of myth is something of a solace to commentators such as Woolf: even if women cannot be named as the indisputable creators of popular stories, they can at least inhabit a different status and achieve recognition as the driving forces of narrative:

> Mythical stories are fabulations of women, probably not created by women. In those narratives, as in other dominant discourses, they are used as metaphors. Still, contrary to official history, women have been important motors of mythical (his)stories. History comes from discord, and discord comes from women. Helen, Medea, Europa, Arianna, Io, Pasifae and Phaedra were objects of rape, kidnapping, abandonment and betrayal; but they were also subjects of pleasure, of movement, of revenge.[30]

Their centrality to mythic stories goes some way towards correcting the gender imbalance of our picture of the ancient world. But mythological women also take on a life of their own and provide modern women with personae with whom they can identify. Harnessing the power of a mythical name might be a means of legitimising an otherwise disreputable project, or invoking a genealogy for an innovative claim. Myth-making for feminism has continuously functioned as a utopian activity and 'brings the imaginative possibilities of what is not into the concrete realm of what could be'.[31] But successive generations of feminist writers and critics have adopted different strategies of mythmaking in part determined by their commitment to particular models of sex and gender.

The grand narrative of the theorisation of woman is often troped in such a way that the most recent mode of analysis becomes the most sophisticated. And yet the idea that each generation has access to, learns from, and enhances an ever-expanding archive of thought and interpretation in a consensually minded fashion is easily challenged. Within the specialised field of classics, it is possible to give a similarly progressivist account of scholars' engagement with issues relating to women, but, again, it is undemanding to point to ways in which such an account does not represent the diversity of opinion or methodology that is current at any one time. There can be substantial value in gaining a sense of how particular accounts of the subject relate to particular discursive contexts, but all too often such accounts are emplotted within a broader narrative under the sign of progress and are marked by a tendency to take the earliest less seriously. This kind of teleology is paradoxically at odds with a subject matter which more often than not privileges the earliest telling of a story over versions from later in the tradition. In an explicitly self-reflective analysis of her own previous essay on the Vestal Virgins, Mary Beard shows how contemporary mythologies of women and gender constantly evolve:

> The mythology of the Vestal Virgins is on the move. *Our* mythology. The spinster dons of ancient Rome (Balsdon's vision of a Julio-Claudian Oxbridge) have had their day. So too have the pagan nuns of the Roman forum – Christian holiness and self-denial *avant la lettre*. *Our* Vestals are much stranger than that: they are touched with a primitive, anthropological 'weirdness'; key players in a game of sexual ambiguity (interstitiality, marginality, anomaly, paradox and mediation) that in Balsdon's time would have seemed – if anything – the concern of ethnography rather than Classics. But not now. We have decided to take the Vestals seriously – at the cost of turning them into a model of primitive strangeness, forever lodged at the heart of sophisticated Rome.[32]

In rejecting her earlier contribution to the formation of the myth, Beard could be seen as colluding with the kind of teleological narrative outlined above. But this second essay takes great pains to emphasise the open-endedness of the process of interpretation and to show how arguments about one specific cultural institution in ancient Rome are inevitably bound up with wider issues concerned with conceptualising women's studies more generally. It argues that the limitations of the old myth of Vestal ambiguity are partly 'the limitations of a history of "women" conceived without reference to a history of "gender"; or rather the limitations of a history of "gender" conceived as an objective category, without reference to its debated and contested construction within the wider cultural matrix.'[33] But lest we begin to feel complacent, the essay ends with a rhetorical display that evades an easy sense of closure:

> Fifteen years ago it was very hard to rethink the Vestals: hard to identify the problem, hard to find the analogies, hard to deploy the anthropology of ambiguity. Yet at the same time, it was so easy to convince: so easy to feel that the effort had worked; so easy to show that the problem had been cracked; so easy to back a new orthodoxy. Yes, 'there *was* something queer about the Virgines Vestales'. The 'queerness' was the answer. If that is now changing, if what was easy now seems too easy, then it is, of course, because our story of Rome, and of gender within Roman culture, has moved on. Beard 1980 (and the work that followed from it) is in a sense a final flourish of a dead subject: 'the history of women'. Rewritten as 'the history of gender' the simplicities and certainties of ambiguity ('the Vestals were not either virgins or matrons; they were both, and ... they were also men') could not and should not convince. Not, then, 'women in Roman history', but 'Roman history writes "woman"'; reading is always preliminary, before you ...[34]

If the replacement of the history of women by the history of gender can be figured within descriptions such as Beard's as a sign of 'moving on,' there are other accounts of feminist-inspired thought that are much less sanguine about its onwards-and-upwards trajectory. The debate surrounding the status and value of so-called postfeminism' is a case in point. There are those who perceive this movement as nothing more than a media-inspired con trick that betrays the history of feminist struggle and rejects its considerable achievements. For others, it represents a more sophisticated continuation of that struggle, involving the replacement of 'dualism with diversity' and 'consensus with variety,' thus establishing 'a dynamic and vigorous area of intellectual debate, shaping the issues and intellectual climate that has characterised the move from modernity to postmodernity in the contemporary world.'[35]

If Beard's revisiting of the Vestal Virgins shows how the interpretation of a particular myth has been influenced by changing configurations of sex and gender in the wider cultural sphere, the reverse process is also demonstrable: classical myth has made a substantial contribution to the development of feminist thought in areas so diverse as politics, philosophy, and the history and theory of science, as well as in the highly influential psychoanalytically informed sphere.

In a whole range of projects undertaken by contemporary women, the reworking of myth exemplifies the enduring power of the past. Different strategies are used for a variety of purposes, although this diversity is not always recognised by those who are inclined to homogenise feminism. The classic statement of what has become known as 'revisionist myth-making' comes from Adrienne Rich's essay 'When We Dead Awaken: Writing as Re-Vision.' Here, Rich argues that the myths of the past continue to structure the experience and identity of women in the present and that their power must urgently be broken:

> Re-vision – the act of looking back, of seeing with fresh eyes, of entertaining an old text from a new critical direction – is for women more than a chapter of cultural history: it is an act of survival. Until we can understand the assumptions in which we are drenched we cannot know ourselves. And this drive to self-knowledge for women, is more than a search of identity: it is part of our refusal of the self-destructiveness of male-dominated society. A radical critique of literature, feminist in it impulse, would take the work first of all as a clue to how we live, how we have been living, how we have been led to imagine ourselves, how our language has trapped as well as liberated us, how the very act of naming has been till now a male prerogative, and how we can begin to see and name – and therefore live – afresh.[36]

Rich emphasises the continuity between representations of women in the past and those of the contemporary moment because of the shared assumptions that underlie them. The process of excavating these assumptions is the process of revision, which can thus be said to describe many mythographic enterprises. For example, we might think of Luce Irigaray's deconstruction of the allegory of the cave from Plato's *Republic*, which works to dismantle the symbolic structure in its own terms, from within. Or we could consider Carol Gilligan's repositioning of the Psyche and Cupid myth as 'a feminist tale' by tracing its lineage from classical mythology to its description as a narrative about the losses that constrain both men and women's capacity to love.[37] There is an optimism motivating the production of these texts that resides in the belief that the quarrying of myths can have an effect in the world. 'Entertaining an old text from a new critical direction' can either place the emphasis on the perspective of the reader, or it can take the form of revivifying the characters of the myth itself so that they become significant in newly imagined and sometimes surprising ways.

Hélène Cixous' laughing Medusa is probably the best known example of such a revivification. But empowering a formerly denigrated figure is not the only means of transforming her significance. Sometimes a notable female is domesticated in order to challenge prevailing cultural and literary hegemonies. So, for example, Dorothy Parker's neighbourly Penelope explicitly questions the idea that bravery consists in travelling the world[38] and, in one of her manifestations, Jenny Joseph's Persephone is removed from her mother by the decision of a family court.[39] Some readings of Sappho regard her as having participated in similar kinds of domestication. She is often described as being unconcerned with external affairs and continually rejecting the values of the male-dominated world in favour of the considerations of herself and her friends and lovers. She uses the language and imagery of war but redeploys it in articulations of female amatory activity and marriage. In fragment 1, for example, she speaks as a thwarted lover calling on Aphrodite for help in winning over the girl she desires. Concerned with erotic encounters past and present, the poem is like the prayers of epic heroes to their patron gods, which occur frequently in Homer and belong predominantly to the scenes of military encounters. The transference of theme, style, and phraseology from the 'elevated' genre of epic into a poem concerned with a love affair can be argued to have the effect of ennobling Sappho's passion for the girl while poking fun at the exclusivity of the heroic male stance.

It is interesting that the way of reading Sappho outlined above is not restricted to a feminist position that would regard her subversion of heroic values as an obviously good thing.[40] The identification of women with the domestic sphere has, after all, been controversial and something that some feminists themselves have resisted. Whether we are dealing with excavatory mythography or creative mythopoeia, there is no straightforward consensus as to the merits of any individual case, and mythmaking continues to be a contentious activity that divides opinion even as it supplies a means for the articulation of common aims. One of the things that myth has made available to feminists has been the sense of a space prior or external to patriarchy where alternative models of societal organisation can exist. This has sometimes taken the form of historical claims about matriarchal or matrilineal societies that once were but have disappeared from view, and sometimes of a metaphor for resistance to dominant symbolic structures. Angela Carter, who herself engaged extensively in mythopoiesis, has contended eloquently that such escapist formulations function to dissuade women from actually intervening in the world:

> If women allow themselves to be consoled for their culturally determined lack of access to the modes of intellectual debate by the invocation of hypothetical great goddesses, they are simply flattering themselves into submission (a technique often used on them by men). All the mythic versions of women, from the redeeming purity of the virgin to that of the healing reconciling mother, are consolatory nonsense; and consolatory nonsense seems to me a fair definition of myth, anyway. Mother goddesses are just as silly a notion as father gods. If a revival of the myths of these cults give women emotional satisfaction, it does so at the price of obscuring the real conditions of life. This is why they were invented in the first place.[41]

Carter's position demonstrates how women's involvement with myth has been deeply problematic to some strains of feminism. It also suggests that feminist thought and practice may come at times to constitute yet another category against which myth is negatively defined. What emerges clearly from these debates is that the task of examining the topic of women and Greek myth is in no way a marginal or limited activity, but rather involves the scrutiny of the definition, operation, and potential of myth in its most capacious sense.

FURTHER READING

Representative of the 'second wave' collections on women in antiquity are Cameron, A. and Kuhrt, A. (eds.) *Images of Women in Antiquity*, (London, 1983), Peradotto, J. and Sullivan, J. P. (eds.) *Women in the Ancient World: the Arethusa Papers* (Albany, NY, 1987) and Skinner, M. (ed.) *Rescuing Creusa: New Methodological Approaches to Women in Antiquity* (*Helios* special edition 13.2, 1987). The classic statement of a revisionist approach to myth is Rich, A. 'When We Dead Awaken: Writing as Re-Vision' in *On Lies, Secrets and Silence: Selected Prose, 1966–78* (NY, 1979). Zeitlin, F. *Playing the Other* (Chicago, 1996) is a stimulating collection of essays that focus on the representations of gender in a variety of ancient Greek texts. Of more recent work, Doherty, L. *Gender and the Interpretation of Classical Myth* (London, 2001) gives an overview of the mutability of myth within ancient and modern settings and Zajko, V. and Leonard, M. (eds.) *Laughing with Medusa: Classical Myth and Feminist Thought* (Oxford, 2006b) explores the multifarious ways in which myth has inspired feminist thinking in a wide range of disciplines. Recent fictional 'retellings' include Cook, E. *Achilles* (London, 2001) and Atwood, M. *The Penelopiad* (Edinburgh, 2005).

NOTES

1. Two very real women have helped me with this piece: I would like to thank Miriam Leonard and Genevieve Liveley for their customary acuity and munificence.

2. The following extract from Buxton (1994) 14 typifies this kind of pragmatic rhetoric: 'Quite apart from this, it is convenient for us as observers to have a designation for a group of stories which are of outstanding interest because of their symbolic richness, their centrality to Greek culture, and the authority which they commanded. I propose, then, to retain "myth" to do what seems to me to be a respectable heuristic job. But I stress two reservations: (1) no automatic equation can be made between Greek myths and apparently similar stories found in other cultures; (2) mythology is not being regarded as constituting an autonomous, hermetically-sealed territory.'

3. Another possibility is that myth provides a language for the dramatisation of issues too painful for the ordinary world. So Hélène Cixous in Prenowitz (2004) 18, talking about her choice of Aeschylus' *Eumenides* as a vehicle for her play about blood contaminated by AIDS: 'This is where the Eumenides came to my aid. I immediately saw the transposition by way of *The Eumenides*. I thought: This can only take place in a mythic universe where there will be Aeschylus, the Eumenides. Something that is poeticised in such a strong way that the suffering will find expression in extremely poetic words.'

4. For an extended exploration of these ideas, see Zajko (1998).

5. See, for example, Froma Zeitlin's essay 'Signifying Difference: The Case of Hesiod's Pandora' in Zeitlin (1995) 53–86.

6. Some scattered exceptions are Euripides *Melanippe* Fr. 488, where a young woman hears the creation myth from her mother, Euripides *Ion*, and Plutarch *Life of Theseus* 23.3, where it is said that tales are told at the festival of the Oschophoria because mothers, for the sake of comforting and encouraging their children, spun out tales for them. Nurses are represented as telling stories to the children in their charge at Plato *Laws* 887d and *Republic* 378c and Philostratus *Imagines* 1.15. An example highly pertinent to this essay is the tale of Cupid and Psyche in Apuleius *Metamorphoses*, which is intended to be told by an old woman to a young girl. Part of the long-standing debate about this myth is how to reconcile its framing

with its potential meaning and so whether to define it as myth (which is typically gendered feminine) or philosophy (typically gendered masculine). It is interesting therefore that Carol Gilligan's 2002 reworking of the myth sites it very firmly 'in the province of both women and men.'

7   Plaskow, J. (1979) 207.

8   Doherty, L. (2006) 421.

9   Doherty (2006) 422.

10 Doherty (2006) 423.

11 See, for example, Jane Harrison (1927) 16: 'Ritual is the utterance of an emotion, a thing felt in action, myth in words or thoughts.'

12 Buxton (1987) 74.

13 Versnel (1990) 27 comments thus: 'It may not seem adventurous to say that the concept of myth *and* ritual was engendered by the tension that sprang from having to choose: myth *or* ritual.'

14 There are those who would want to argue that for a myth to be classified as a myth it must be a narrative with some collective significance (see, e.g., most recently, Csapo (2005) 134). The point here is that ritual actualises that significance.

15 At the start of one such synthesising account of a wedding ritual, James Redfield (1982) 182 put the case as follows: 'Historically this will be in soft focus; I shall be mentioning items from various places and periods as if they were all part of the same ceremony, with the assumption that even features not in general use would have been generally intelligible to the Greeks. Of course from other points of view the differences might make all the difference.'

16 See Dowden (1989) 25–32.

17 Csapo (2005) 180.

18 For the imposition of limits on what constitutes any myth, the demarcation of where it begins and where it ends, is itself determined by the interpretative position being adopted.

19 Reynolds (2000) 2. This volume contains a comprehensive bibliography of the secondary material, which attempts to reconstruct aspects of Sappho's lifestyle on the basis of her poetry.

20 Reynolds (2000) 6–7.

21 Dowden in (1995) 56.

22 Dowden in (1995) 46.

23 There are those, of course, who would argue that there is a natural congruency between the binarisms embedded in the structures of ancient Greek thought and the binarisms beloved of structuralist analysis. See, for example, Paul Cartledge's *The Greeks* (1993) passim. Some myths may then seem to lend themselves to this kind of interpretation: 'Like Pandora, the mythic figure of the Amazon fits the structuralist approach hand and glove.' Doherty (2001) 137.

24 Csapo (2005) 276.

25 Blake Tyrrell (1984) xvi.

26 Larrington (ed.) (1992) 441–2.

27 Christ, C. and Plaskow, J. (1979) (eds) 194.

28 Doherty (2001) 10.

29 Woolf (1929) 43

30 Curti (1998) viii–ix.

31 Bartkowski (1989) 10

32 Beard (1995) 166.

33 Beard (1995) 167.

34 Beard (1995) 174–5.

35 Gamble (2001) 50.

36 Charlesworth Gelpi and Gelpi (1993) 167.

37 Gilligan (2002) 46–7.

38 In the pathway of the sun,
     In the footsteps of the breeze,
Where the world and sky are one,
     He shall ride the silver seas,
     He shall cut the glittering wave.
I shall sit at home, and rock;
Rise to hear a neighbour's knock;
Brew my tea, and snip my thread;
Bleach the linen for my bed.
     They will call him brave.

39 Joseph (1986) 41.

40 See, for example, Page (1955) 110: 'We discern in both old and new the same
    narrow limitation of interests, the same simplicity of thought, the same delicacy in
    expression, the same talent for self-detachment and self-criticism.' See also Podlecki
    (1984) 82: 'Sappho's poetry is as empty of overt political allusions as Alcaeus' is full
    of them.'

41 Carter (1979) 5.

14: Let Us Make Gods in Our Image: Greek Myth in Medieval and Renaissance Literature

H. David Brumble

E arly in the book of John a Pharisee, Nicodemus, "came to Jesus by night." Jesus said to Nicodemus, "Very truly, I tell you, no one can see the kingdom of God without being born from above." Nicodemus was quite puzzled: "How can anyone be born after having grown old? Can one enter a second time into his mother's womb and be born?" (John 3:1–4). John wants us to understand, of course, that Nicodemus is puzzled because he is not illuminated. Nicodemus cannot *see* with the eye of the spirit; he cannot understand allegory. He is spiritually blind, limited to a merely literal understanding. This notion of seeing things with the eye of the spirit, seeing things allegorically, was widely applied during the Middle Ages and Renaissance. Consider this passage from Erasmus, where he explains how a good Christian should look not just at art, but at the *world*:

> it behooves us never to be idle, but by means of some appro-
> priate analogy, to refer whatever assaults our senses either to
> the spiritual world or – a more serviceable procedure – to
> ethical values and that part of man which corresponds to the
> spiritual world. . . . So it will come about that anything pre-
> senting itself to the senses at any time will become for you
> an occasion of righteousness. When this visible sun daily
> refreshes your physical eyes as it bathes the earth with new
> light, think immediately of . . . that joy of a pure mind illu-
> minated by the radiance of God. . . . Recollect . . . places in
> the Holy Scriptures where here and there the grace of the
> Holy Spirit is compared to light. If night seems dark and

foreboding to you, imagine a soul deprived of divine radiance and darkened by sin. . . . If physical beauty is pleasing to
the eye, think how splendid is beauty of soul. If an ugly face
seems disagreeable, remember how odious is a mind steeped
in vice.

(*Enchiridion*: 101–3)

Erasmus, the most popular writer of his day, is encouraging his readers
to make a habit of looking at *everything* allegorically. The Bible was to
be understood allegorically; the Book of Nature was to be understood
allegorically. And the great works of the pagans were also to be understood allegorically. Augustine, for example, wrote that when the pagans
write things that can be read by the light of Christ, these pagans "should
not be feared";

> rather, what they have said should be taken from them as
> from unjust possessors and converted to our use. Just as the
> Egyptians . . . had vases and ornaments of gold and silver and
> clothing which the Israelites took with them secretly when
> they fled, as if to put them to a better use. They did not do this
> on their own authority but at God's commandment. . . . The
> teachings of the pagans contain not only . . . superstitious
> imaginings . . . , but also liberal disciplines . . . and some most
> useful precepts concerning morals.
>
> (*On Christian Doctrine*: 2.40,
> referring to Exodus 3:22, 11:2, 12:35)[1]

Poets, preachers, painters, cosmologists, mythographers, theologians –
they all took Augustine at his word; they all took what they could from
the pagans. To cite a single example, Chaucer used some 282 personal
names derived from the Greek and Roman classics, everything from
Achilles and Ariadne to Venus and Zephyr.[2] Chaucer took not a third
so many from the Bible, just 84 names. Shakespeare did not use as many
Biblical and mythological names – but his balance is tilted even more
heavily toward the mythological.

We can understand some of Chaucer's, Christine de Pizan's, and
Milton's mythic figures simply by referring to a classical dictionary.
Priam, for example, was well known to Medieval and Renaissance writ-
ers, but Priam did not acquire allegorical habiliments, as did Helen and
Paris. As we read Petrarch or Spenser, what we need to know about
Priam is the *stories* in which he appears. For another example, Arion

was a singer upon a lyre; he was on a ship when the sailors decided to throw him overboard to get his gold. Arion begged leave to sing one last song, and then threw himself into the sea, trusting to Apollo, the god of singers. A dolphin came and bore Arion on his back to Corinth. This is the sort of thing that one can find today in any dictionary of classical mythology; and this is enough to make sense, for example, of these lines from *Twelfth Night*. The good captain tells Viola of the wreck at sea:

> I saw your brother,
> Most provident in peril, bind himself,
> Courage and hope both teaching him the practice,
> To a strong mast that lived upon the sea;
> Where, like Arion on the dolphin's back,
> I saw him hold acquaintance with the waves
> So long as I could see.
>
> (1.2.11–17)

Some in Shakespeare's audience, however, would have known more than the mere story of Arion; some would have remembered Arion and his spell-binding music as an allegorical figure for the ordering principle of the universe, the divinely instituted harmony.[3] They might have remembered this as they watched Orsino, Olivia, Toby Belch, Viola, and the rest tumbling into their little temporary slice of chaos. Allegory works this way. And in most cases, when Medieval and Renaissance writers make references to classical mythology, they do have allegory in mind. Early in Spenser's *The Faerie Queene*, for example, the Red Cross Knight loses his way in the Wood of Error. Spenser calls this wood a "labyrinth" (1.1.11) – an apt word for the kind of thick, dark forest in which one could be lost. But most of Spenser's readers would have been aware of the thousand-year-old tradition in which the labyrinth was an allegorical figure for the world in the theological sense, that place of temptations and dark turnings where Christians could so easily lose their way (Figure 19).

MEDIEVAL AND RENAISSANCE ALLEGORY

George Puttenham, writing in 1589, defined allegory as that form of expression in which "we speake one thing and thinke another, and that our wordes and our meanings meete not" (*Arte of English Poesie*). Puttenham's example is Plato's *Republic*, which "speakes" of a cave, and a fire, and people looking at shadows cast upon the wall of the cave – but these are, Puttenham says, merely the "wordes," the literal surface. Plato's "meanings" have to do with human reluctance to turn from what merely *seems* to be real (the shadows) to what is really real (the fire).

It is difficult to say just when allegory entered into Western thought. Homer is probably thinking allegorically as he describes the role of Terror, Fear, and Hate in the gathering battle:

> And Terror drove them, and Fear, and Hate whose wrath is
>   relentless,
> she the sister and companion of murderous Ares,
> she who is only a little thing at the first, but thereafter
> grows until she strides on the earth with her head striking
>   heaven.
>
> (*Iliad*: 4.440–43 trans. R. Lattimore)

There are a few other passages, too, that Homer might have intended allegorically. But whatever Homer's intentions may have been, allegorical interpretation of Homer predominated from Heraclitus in the first century AD down to the seventeenth century. Virgil, Ovid, Statius, and other ancient writers were also interpreted allegorically. Servius (c. 400), Fulgentius (sixth century), Bernardus Silvestris (twelfth century), and Cristoforo Landino (fifteenth century) were among the most important allegorizing interpreters of Virgil's *Aeneid*. Allegorical interpreters of Ovid's *Metamorphoses* were legion: Lactantius Placidus (sixth century), Arnolphe of Orléans (eleventh century), the *Ovide Moralisé* (fourteenth century), Berchorius (fourteenth century), George Sandys (1632), and Thomas Hall's *Wisdoms Conquest. or, An explanation and . . . Translation of the thirteenth Book of Ovids Metamorphoses* (1651) – to mention just a few. (For these and many other allegorizing mythographers, see "Further Reading," below; for a still longer listing, see Brumble 1998.)

Spenser read Medieval and Renaissance mythographers closely, closely enough sometimes to derive whole episodes from such as Boccaccio's *Genealogia Deorum Gentillium* or from Natale Conti's *Mythologiae*. To read Chaucer, Lydgate, Gower, Shakespeare, Milton, and de Meun, or to look at the paintings of Botticelli, Titian, and Cranach, without a sense of the meanings the myths accumulated is like reading *The Divine Comedy* or *Paradise Lost* without knowing what Christian tradition had added to the meaning of such words as *cross, fall, faith, dark,* and *light*.

What of Chaucer's 282 classical names? According to my count, close to half of them would not be adequately glossed by a good dictionary of classical antiquities. Theseus appears in "The Knight's Tale." A good classical dictionary would not tell us that Chaucer's readers might have interpreted Theseus as a wisdom figure; as an example of perfect friendship, of the ideal ruler, of the unfaithful lover; as a type for God or Christ; as an allegorical figure for the balance of the active and contemplative lives.

Chaucer's Theseus marries Hippolyta, an Amazon. A classical dictionary will not tell us that Theseus' conquest of the Amazons and his marriage to Hippolyta could be understood as a reestablishment of the proper natural order – an idea that goes back at least to Ovid's *Art of Love*, where the poet tells us that his purpose is to teach men how to subdue Amazons (2.743–4). According to Giovanni del Virgilio's early fourteenth-century commentary, a man conquers Amazons "*a virtuoso*" – Latin *vir*, man – by his *virtue* (*Espositore della Metamorfosi*: 85). A classical dictionary will not tell us that the Minotaur, the monster whose image we see on Theseus' standard ("Knight's Tale": 978–80), was interpreted as a figure for human bestiality; nor would a classical dictionary tell us that Medieval Christians could understand Theseus' killing of the Minotaur as a victory over the flesh or the devil.

Chaucer's Palamon and Arcite are Thebans. A classical dictionary would tell us about the fratricidal strife between Theban Eteocles and Polynices, but we would need to consult the allegorizing mythographers to discover why Chaucer would have thought of Thebes, in contrast with Athens, as a place that exemplifies the disastrous consequences of misordered love.[4] Most of Chaucer's readers would have known some of these traditions; the better read would have known them all.[5]

THE VARIETIES OF MYTH ALLEGORY

If we, like most Medieval and Renaissance writers, think of this old, old word in its most inclusive sense,[6] there were many kinds of allegory.

In moral allegory mythic figures personify virtues, vices, states of mind, desires, and inclinations. Venus, for example, might serve as a figure for libidinous desire, Diana for chastity. Medieval Neo-Platonist cosmographers, for example, called the locus of the Platonic Forms *Noys*. Minerva served as an allegorical figure for *Noys*; this, for Bernardus, was the "true Minerva" (*Cosmographia*: 1:1).

Often mythic and legendary figures were used as examples (*exempla*)[7] of one or another virtue or moral failing. Abraham Fraunce, for example, writes that Arachne was "worthily plagued" because of "her excessive pride and contempt of God" (*Countesse of Pembrokes Yvychurch*: 14). Shakespeare could assume that his educated audience would know that Pyramus and Thisbe were traditional *de casibus* examples of the dangers of unbridled passion. And so, as Elizabethan theatergoers watched the rude mechanicals' play of Pyramus and Thisbe, their laughter could have been complicated by their awareness of the moralizing tradition.

There was also physical allegory, or nature, or cosmic allegory: beginning with the Stoic philosophers, the gods were interpreted as representing elements of the natural universe.[8] Jupiter, for example, could be a figure for the fiery ether, Apollo the sun, or Venus the (morally neutral) generative impulse. We see this kind of allegory, for example, in the complex interactions of Venus, Cupid, Genius, and Dame Nature in Bernardus's *Cosmographia*, Alanus's *Complaint of Nature*, De Meun's *Romance of the Rose*, Gower's *Confessio Amantis*, and Spenser's *Faerie Queene* (2.12.47–9).[9]

Venus, Mars, Jupiter, and others also figured importantly in astrology.[10] Astrology, then, could be used by the poets to explain or describe personality traits. These ideas were widely made use of. In Medieval blockbooks, for example, we find Venus depicted at the top of the page, above behaviors typical of those she was thought to influence (Figure 20) – note in particular the love in a bathhouse. And Chaucer's Wife of Bath explains her own concupiscence in astrological terms: she is, she says, "al Venerian / In feelyne, and myn herte is Marcien" ("Wife of Bath's Tale": 609–10). Mercury was the god of eloquence and of deception; and so Shakespeare's Autolycus – a thief and gambler – was "litter'd under Mercury" (*Winter's Tale*: 4.3.23–31).

Properly speaking, a Renaissance "emblem" should combine a picture, a motto, and a poem, to invite profound meditations on a single subject. Quarles's *Emblemes* does not do all of this, but a page from the book (Figure 19) – depicting this world as a Labyrinth – does convey a sense of the genre.[11] The emblem books are thickly inhabited by the gods.

The gods were also interpreted typologically – just as Medieval and Renaissance Christians understood the Old Testament. The sacrifice of innocent Isaac was understood to be a "type" of the sacrifice of Christ; Jonah going into the mouth of the whale was a type of Jesus going into the tomb, and Jonah coming out of the mouth of the whale a type of Christ's resurrection. The sacrificial lamb was a type of Christ. According to the same assumptions, mythic figures, then, were sometimes understood to be types of Biblical figures; Deucalion and his wife survived a universal flood, and so Deucalion was a type of Noah. Because Hippolytus was once falsely accused by a seductress, he could be a type of Joseph, who had fled the adulterous advances of Potiphar's wife (Genesis 39). Alanus refers to this tradition (*Anticlaudian*: 7.2), as does Sandys (*Ovid*: 710). Later this same Hippolytus died and was brought back to life by Aesculapius (Virgil, *Aeneid*: 7.761–82; Ovid, *Metamorphoses*: 15.497–546). Hippolytus was thus irresistible as a type of Christian spiritual renewal (e.g., Dante, *Paradiso*: 17.46–8). Hippolytus, Theseus, Hercules, Orpheus, and many others served as types of Christ.

In historical (or topical) allegory a mythic figure would personify a real person, usually a contemporary. Botticelli's mythic paintings sometimes refer (at one level of allegory) to members of the Medici family (Wind 1968: 112). From 1578 to 1582, for another example, the Duc d'Alençon courted Queen Elizabeth – a courtship that Lyly's "Sapho and Phao" treats allegorically: we are supposed to recognize Alençon in Phaon and Elizabeth in Sappho. Endymion, in Lyly's *Endimion*, seems to have been the Earl of Leicester, hopelessly in love with chaste Cynthia (Elizabeth). Spenser's *Shepheardes Calender* is full of intricate historical allegory (McLane 1968).

Following the Greek mythographer Euhemerus (c. 300 BC), Medieval and Renaissance mythographers frequently explained the gods in terms of supposed human origins.[12] In the "Euhemeristic" tradition, then, Atlas, for example, was explained as having been originally a man named Atlas; this man was the discoverer of astrology; and so he came to be considered a god, specifically the god who holds the earth upon his shoulders. Saturn could be explained as a famous early king who reigned during the Golden Age, who then came to be remembered as a god. But it seems obvious to me that the poets and artists were a good deal less interested in Euhemerism than were the mythographers.

MULTIPLE INTERPRETATION

I have suggested that Spenser's reference to the Labyrinth assumes a familiarity with certain traditions of interpretation. But we should not imagine that Medieval and Renaissance writers were much confined by such traditions. It is certain that the mythographers were not. Consider Berchorius, for example.

In the introduction to his book of moral-allegorical commentary on Ovid's *Metamorphoses*, Berchorius lists the authorities he has consulted – Fulgentius, Rabanus (*De Universo*), and Petrarch, among others – and then he assures us that he "separated the chaff from the wheat," that he "gathered the wheat into the storehouse for the praise and glory of the true God" (*Ovidius Moralizatus*: 36). This separation of the chaff from the wheat was not an easy matter. For Berchorius, the main criterion had to do with how well a certain allegorization might teach lessons of Christian morality and theology. And because moral instruction was paramount for him, Berchorius can allow himself allegorical flights that are quite idiosyncratic, as in his comment on the story of Io, the beautiful maid whom Jupiter changed into a heifer to hide her from jealous Juno. According to Ovid, Io was eventually changed from a heifer back into a woman. Berchorius paraphrases Ovid:

> The rough hair falls away from her body, her horns disappear, her great round eyes grow smaller. . . . Though she has gained back her form she did not dare speak lest she moo like a heifer, and she was timid in trying her abandoned speech again.

And then he provides the following interpretation: "It is useful for those who are newly converted to be silent lest they speak as heifers – that is carnal and indiscreet people" (147).

Now, the idea that Io's metamorphosis into a heifer suggested something about the carnality of her desires was quite common, quite traditional. But the notion that in not mooing, the de-metamorphosed Io represents bashful Christian converts – this is pure Berchorius. Berchorius invents such allegories with gusto. And Berchorius was not unusual: Medieval and Renaissance Christians did not always feel themselves limited by interpretive traditions, however well such interpretations were known.

This hearty embrace of idiosyncratic interpretation went hand in hand with Medieval and Renaissance interpreters' tendency to concentrate on detail. Berchorius's disquisition on Io's failure to moo may be idiosyncratic as an interpretation, but it is typical in its willingness to dwell upon the significance of what a modern reader might be forgiven for considering an insignificant detail. And this is a concentration on detail that can cheerfully disregard Ovid's *Metamorphoses* as a whole, the story of Io as a whole – even others of Berchorius's own comments on the story.

I do not mean to suggest that Medieval and Renaissance interpreters were fashionably anticipating postmodern ideas about "the indeterminacy of the text." I mean that Medieval and Renaissance interpreters felt free to concentrate on details, without regard for the meaning of the whole. The mention of Io might call forth a little nonallegorical disquisition on cows. Io, we read, ended up in Egypt – and this might be the commentator's occasion for a geography lesson. Medieval and Renaissance commentators often provided alternative interpretations both of details and of whole stories.

And the gods were understood in sometimes contradictory ways. Fulgentius (*Mythologies*: 1.2), for example, first explains Saturn euhemeristically, as a tyrant king of ancient Italy; then he explains Saturn in terms of nature allegory: Saturn "is reported as having devoured his own sons because every season devours what it produces." Then Fulgentius tells us that Saturn is a figure for "the divine intelligence as it creates all things." Then more nature allegory: Saturn, father of four sons, is "the father of the four elements" – all of this within some three hundred words! Elsewhere Fulgentius interprets Saturn as a planet (*Mythologies*: 1.18) and as a figure for time (2.1).

Bernardus provided a rationale for this kind of reading early in his commentary on Virgil's *Aeneid*:

> One must remember in this book as well as in other allegorical works that there are equivocations and multiple significations, and therefore one must interpret poetic fictions in diverse ways. For example, in Martianus's book one should interpret Jove sometimes as the superior fire, sometimes as a star, and even sometimes as the Creator himself. . . . Hence, one must pay attention to the diverse aspects of the poetic fictions and the multiple interpretations in all allegorical matters if in fact the truth cannot be established by a single interpretation.
>
> (*Commentary*: on book 1)

It is interesting to consider the method of fourfold allegory in this connection. Dante's formulation in his Letter to Can Grande is well known;[13] it may be summarized as follows:

First, there is the literal, or historical, level of understanding.
Second, the typological level, where we search for typological connections between what we read and the events of the New Testament; Dante calls this the level of allegory.

Third, the moral, or tropological level, where we search for moral analogies as we read.

Fourth, the anagogical level, where we search for analogies between
what we read and final things – the final things according to the
Christian conception of the last days.

Fourfold allegory exercised the ingenuity of poets and commentators
alike. Sometimes poets worked at two levels, sometimes one, sometimes,
in a *tour de force*, all four. But of course, it was easier for commentators
to discover three or four levels than it was for poets to produce them. As
late as 1591, Harington structured his commentary on Ariosto's *Orlando
Furioso* with a version of fourfold allegory in mind: at the end of each
canto we find commentary under the following four headings: *Moral,
Historie, Allegorie,* and *Allusion.* Much more could be said about fourfold
allegory.[14] But here it is worthwhile simply to point out that whatever
else it might be, fourfold allegory is just one expression of the Medieval
and Renaissance inclination to multiple interpretation.

This inclination seems to have been pervasive, especially from the
late Middle Ages to 1650. It is as much a guiding principle for the *Ovidé
Moralisé* and Berchorius in the fourteenth century as it is for Sandys's
commentary on Ovid and Ross's *Mystagogus Poeticus* in the seventeenth
century. In his commentary on Arachne, Alexander Ross provides a
nice example of the wandering-eclectic reader:

> 1. The cause of Arachnes overthrow was the rejecting of
> the old womans counsel, into whose shape Pallas had trans-
> formed her self: Then are young people ready for ruine,
> when they follow their own heads; and despise the counsel
> of the aged, whose experience and gravity, should temper
> their temerity.... 2. This Arachne did learn of the spider
> to spin and weave, for the Beasts are in many things our
> Schoolmasters. 3. It is not good to be proud and insolent of
> any art or knowledge. 4. Subtil and trifling Sophisters... are
> no better then Spiders, whose captious fallacies are no less
> hateful to the Wise, than Arachnes web was to Minerva. 5.
> Partial Judges use their laws, as Spiders do their webs, to
> catch little flies and let the great ones pass through. 6. Cov-
> etous men are like Spiders... Envy and slandering tongue
> is like a Spider.... 8. We should be Spiders in Providence;

they hang their nets in windows, where they know flies most
resort ... and like Mice, they fortel the ruin of a house, by
falling and running away, as Pliny sheweth. (29–30)

There is no concern for consistency here, let alone for anything like
Coleridge's "organic unity." Peacham wrote that a metaphor is "like a
starre in respect of beautie, brightnesse and direction" – while allegory
is like a "signe compounded of many stars, ... a constellation" (*Garden
of Eloquence*: 27).

Now, I am not suggesting that Medieval and Renaissance readers
were incapable of understanding works as a whole. Three major interpretive commentaries on Virgil's *Aeneid* – Fulgentius *(On the Content of
Virgil)* in the sixth century, Bernardus (*On Virgil's Aeneid*) in the twelfth,
and Landino (*Disputationes Camuldenses*) in the fifteenth – largely agree
as to the meaning of the poem in general and the meaning of Aeneas
in particular. According to these commentators, Aeneas matures over
the course of the poem, moving from heedlessness and sin to spiritual
insight and grace. For all three commentators the journey to the underworld in Book 6 is central: this journey provides Aeneas with the key
elements of his understanding. Dante's brief commentary on the *Aeneid*
in the *Convivio* (4.26.8–9) is in this same tradition.[15]

Fulgentius may be taken as typical: "'This is a tale of arms and man'
[*Aeneid*: 1.1], indicating manliness [L. *virtutem*: *virtue* or manliness] by
'arms' and wisdom by 'man,' for all perfection depends on manliness of
body and wisdom of mind" (*On the Content of Virgil*: 6). For Fulgentius,
Aeneas' shipwreck is "an allegory of the dangers of birth" (12); the death
of Aeneas' father shows that "youth as it grows up casts off the burden of
parental control" (15); and so the dalliance with Dido suggests "the spirit
of adolescence, on holiday from paternal control." Thus it is that Aeneas
"is inflamed by passion and, driven on by storm and cloud, that is, by
confusion of mind, commits adultery. ... Mercury is introduced as the
god of the intellect; it is by the urgings of the intellect that youth quits
the straits of passion" (16). Influenced by Mercury/intellect, Aeneas will
now investigate "the secrets of knowledge." This is why "Aeneas goes
down into the lower world and there, looking on as an eyewitness, he
sees both the punishments for the evil, the rewards for the good, and
the sad wanderings of those given over to passion. Then piloted by
Charon he crosses the Acheron" (22). Finally, Aeneas enters Elysium,
"where, the labor of learning now over, he celebrates the perfecting
of memory." When eventually Aeneas comes to Italy, his marriage

to Lavinia is (rather unflatteringly) the good and proper "road of toil" (24).

Many other commentators provided variations on this basic theme. John of Salisbury, for example:

> Under the cloak of poetic imagination in his Eneid [Virgil] subtly represents the six periods of life by the division of the work into six [sic] books. In these, in imitation of the Odyssey, he appears to have represented the origin and progress of a man. The character he sets forth and develops he leads on and conducts down into the nether world. For Eneas who therein represents the soul, is so named for the reason it is a dweller in the body, for *ennos*, according to the Greeks, is "dweller," and *demas* "body." The name Eneas is formed of these two elements to signify life dwelling, as it were, in a hut of flesh.
>
> (*Policraticus*: 8.24)

Such interpretations-of-the-whole there certainly were, then. And Sidney, Spenser, and others were aware of the Aristotelian unities. Still, it seems clear that careful Medieval and Renaissance readers were much more likely to interpret, comment upon, and delight in individual lines and details out of context than careful modern readers are likely to do. For we are Coleridge's children: we do, even the Deconstructionists among us, tend to assume organic unity in the things we read.

But if we want to understand Medieval and Renaissance texts historically, if we want to try to imagine ourselves into the minds of Medieval and Renaissance readers, then we probably ought to devote more attention to multiple meanings, less to organic unity. And we certainly should pay very close attention to individual lines, passages, and details.

Finally, let us return to John. John assumed that Nicodemus failed to understand allegory because he was not spiritually illuminated. Because he could not see with the eye of the spirit, Nicodemus was limited to a merely literal understanding of "born from above." Spiritual illumination, however, seems not to have sufficed for Medieval and Renaissance Christians. Then as now, few would recognize Hippolytus as a typological reference to Joseph or Minerva as an allegorical figure for Bernardus's *Noys* without some merely earthly assistance – without what was sometimes thought of as a key. And thus it is that the title page of Alexander Ross's *Mystagogus Poeticus: Or the Muses Interpreter* has a woodcut of Ross, standing all robed in scholar's sober black, holding a great key – while Apollo and the Muses make music in the background. Apollo, we are to understand, is the fountainhead of all music and poetry. The mythographer, Ross himself, stands with his key, ready to unlock the secret allegories of the poetry that Apollo and the Muses inspire.

But the notion of a key is a bit misleading; it suggests that there is one key that will unlock the meaning of *Apollo* or *Pan* or *Procne*. When we read Lydgate, Chaucer, Spenser, and Shakespeare, we might better think of mythic figures, simply, as Medieval and Renaissance vocabulary items. Like other vocabulary items, their meanings are largely, but not entirely, determined by previous usage. And like other vocabulary items, their meanings have changed over time.

FURTHER READING

For allegorizing commentary on Ovid, see Berchorius (d. 1362), *Ovidius Moralizatus*; this book, with its predilection for Biblical typology, was one of the most influential interpretions of Ovid. This book was also known by its French title, *Ovide Moralisé*, not to be confused with the earlier, anonymous, metrical *Ovide Moralisé*. See also Giovanni del Virgilio (fl. c. 1330), *Espositore*; Thomas Hall (1610–65), *Wisdoms Conquest. or, An explanation and . . . Translation of the thirteenth Book of Ovids Metamorphoses*; Lactantius Placidus (6th century), *Narrationes Fabularum . . . in . . . XV Metamorphoseon*. Lavinius (fl. 1st half of 16th century), *Metamorphoses*, was an influential commentary on the first book of Ovid's *Metamorphoses*. Carel van Mander (1548–1606), *Wtlegginghe op den Metamorphosis* and *Uytbeeldinghe der Figuren*, are actually sections of a large work called *Het Schilderboeck* – a book which has long been recognized as important especially for historians of Dutch art. Thomas Waleys (fl. 1320–40), *Metamorophsis Ovidiana moraliter explanata*, is another allegorical commentary. Georg Wickram (fl. 1545), *Ovidii Nasonis des aller sinnreichten Poeten Metamorphoses*, is a German allegorical commentary on Ovid.

For translations of Ovid that include allegorizing commentary, see Agostini, *Di Ovidio Le Metamorphosi*; William Caxton (1422–91), *Metamorphoses of Ovid*; Lodovico Dolce (1508–68), *Le Transformationi*. The *Ovide Moralisé* (probably between 1316 and 1328) is a huge poem that retells the stories in Ovid's *Metamorphoses*, providing allegorical commentary along the way. It is perhaps the main wellspring of typological connections between the Bible and Greek mythology. (This book should not be confused with Berchorius's *Ovide Moralisé*.)

Nicolas Renouard (fl. early 17th century), *Les Metamorphoses d'Ovide*, is a French translation, with commentary. George Sandys (1578–1644), *Ovid's Metamorphosis, Englished, Mythologized, and Represented in Figures*, is for moderns one of the best introductions to Medieval and Renaissance ideas about classical mythology. Sandys provides in many instances what may be taken as a summary statement of 1500 years of allegorical interpretation of classical myth and legend. (Sandys was, by the way, resident treasurer of the Jamestown colony from 1621 to 1625.) Isaak Verburg (fl. 1732), *De Gedaant-wisselingen*, is a Dutch translation and allegorical commentary. Sanchez de Viana (fl. 1589), *Las transformaciones*, is a Spanish translation of Ovid with allegorical commentary. Internet sites come and go, but *http://etext.virginia.edu/latin/ovid/* is, at least as of this writing, a fine source for Ovid mythographic commentaries. Judicious Googling will doubtless discover others.

For myth allegory having mainly to do with Nature, the gods of love and generation, see Alanus de Insulis, *The Complaint of Nature*; Francis Bacon, *On Principles and Origins, According to the Fables of Cupid and Coelum*; and Bernardus Silvestris (fl. 1136), *Cosmographia*. Marsilio Ficino (1433–99), *Commentary on Plato's Symposium*, is an explanation of the whole cosmos, by the most influential of the Renaissance Neo-Platonists.

For general allegorizing guides to classical mythology, see Albricus of London, *Allegoriae Poeticae* (still widely read in the Renaissance); Thomas Munckerus, *Mythographi Latini* (includes an abridgement of Albricus's *Allegoriae Poetica* entitled *De Deorum Imaginibus Libellus* (1681); Boccaccio (1313–75), *Genealogie Deorum Gentilium Libri*. Vincenzo Cartari (b. c. 1500), *Imagini de i Dei de Gli Antichi*, was particularly important to artists, since it included detailed iconographies and many illustrations (see Lynche for an early English translation). Natale Conti (1520?–80?), *Mythologie*, one of the most important Renaissance mythographies, went through many editions. Abraham Fraunce (fl. 1582–1633), *Third Part of the Countesse of Pembrokes Yvychurch*, is a delight; this is, to my mind, the best introduction to Medieval and Renaissance myth allegory. Fulgentius (fl. early 6th century), *Mythologies*, was an important Medieval authority. Hyginus (fl. before 207 AD), *Fabulae* and *Poetica Astronomica*, were unknown from about the 6th century until his work was published in Basle in 1535; thereafter Hyginus was frequently consulted. Richard Lynche (fl. 1600), *Fountaine of Ancient Fiction*, is a truncated translation of Cartari's *Le imagini*. Georgius Pictorius

(c. 1500–1569), *Theologia Mythologica*, was the first large-scale treatment of the gods after Boccaccio's *Genealogie*. Pictorius's *Apotheoseos* is a revised, expanded edition of *Theologia Mythologica*, including illustrations of the gods. Cesare Ripa (fl. 1600), *Iconologie*, was, with Cartari's *Imagini*, the most important Renaissance source for the iconography of the gods.

Alexander Ross (1590–1654), *Mystagogus Poeticus*, is a late and large compendium of allegorizing mythography. Sallustius (fl. 2nd half of 4th century), *Concerning the Gods*, is a fervent, Neoplatonist, allegorizing defense of mythology. Antonio Tritonio (16th century), *Mythologia*, is an attempt to make mythic allegory easily accessible; Tritonio proceeds mainly by compiling categorized lists of gods and mythic figures. Some gods are listed, then, under "The Libidinous," others under "The Wrathful," and so forth. Vatican Mythographers I (8th or 9th century), II (9th or 10th century), and III (12th century), are to be found in *Scriptores Rerum Mythicarum Latini Tres*, an edition of three early, important allegorical mythographies.

For commentaries, encyclopedias, and other works that include important allegorical mythography, see Pietro Alighieri (fl. first half 14th century) *Commentarium* (Dante's son's commentary on the *Divine Comedy*). Bartholomaeus Anglicus (fl. 1320–40), *On the Properties of Things*, is arguably the greatest of the Medieval encyclopedias. For a 1582 English translation, see Stephan Batman, *Batman uppon Bartholomae*. Batman also wrote *The Golden Booke of the Leaden Gods* (largely based on Pictorius's *Apotheoseos*). Bernardus Silvestris (fl. 1136), *Commentary on the First Six Books of Virgil's Aeneid*, and *Commentary on Martianus Capella's De Nuptiis Philologiae et Mercurii*, and *The Cosmographia*. Robert Burton (1577–1639), *Anatomy of Melancholy*, includes a good deal of myth allegory. Jacob Cats (1577–1660), *Proteus, ofte Minne-beelden Verandert in Sinne-beelden*, was popular in the Netherlands. Fulgentius (fl. early 6th century) wrote an influential commentary on Virgil and another on Statius' *Thebaid*.

The Chess of Love is a long commentary (1295 pp. in Jones's translation) on the anonymous, late-fourteenth-century *Les Echecs Amoureuse*, which was itself written in imitation of de Meun's *Romance of the Rose*. This translation deserves to be more widely known. Thomas Cooper (1517–94), *Dictionarium Historicum & Poeticum*, which included mythological lore, was widely used by the Elizabethan poets. Donatus (fl. mid. 4th century), *Interpretationes Vergilianae*, was published, imitated, and expanded upon down through the Renaissance. Gawain Douglas (1474?–1522), "Preface" to Virgil, *xii Bukes of Eneados*, interprets *The*

Aeneid allegorically. Eustathius (d. c. 1194), *Commentarii ad Homeri*, was still consulted in the Renaissance. Guillaume de Conches (c. 1080–c. 1150) wrote a commentary on Macrobius that is rich in Platonic myth interpretation. Guillaume's commentary on Boethius' *Consolation* has a good deal to say about astrological interpretation of mythological figures. John Harington (1561–1612) wrote *An Apologie of Poetrie* as a preface to his translation of, and commentary upon, Ariosto's *Orlando Furioso*. Since Harington was the godson of Queen Elizabeth, and since his translation of Ariosto was undertaken at her command, one might say that Harrington's allegorical commentary was the reigning interpretation of Ariosto.

Heraclitus (sometimes Heraclides, probably 1st century AD), *Allégories d'Homère*, is the earliest surviving allegorical commentary on Homer. Isidore of Seville (c. 560–636), *Etymologiarum*, is the quintessential expression of the conviction that one can discover the nature of things by studying the names of things – including the classical gods. This belief was general all the way from antiquity down to the Renaissance. John the Scot (815?–77?), *Annotationes in Marcianum*, is an early example of the Medieval encyclopedia. Lactantius Placidus (6th century), *Commentarium in Statii Thebaida*, was important not least because it was a conduit of the Pythagorean method to the Middle Ages. (The attribution to Lactantius is not certain; it seems that some of the commentary was written as early as the fourth century – and this commentary continued to enjoy accretions during the Middle Ages.)

Macrobius (fl. c. 430), *Saturnalia*, is full of antiquarian lore about the gods and their festivals. Books 3 and 4 are devoted to a commentary on Virgil. Martianus Capella (fl. probably first quarter of 5th century), *Marriage of Philology and Mercury*, is a description of the liberal arts that was considered authoritative throughout the Middle Ages. The book also established a number of allegorical and iconographic traditions that continued down to the 17th century. Alexander Neckam (c. 1157–1217), *De Naturis Rerum*, is one of the great Medieval encyclopedias. Henry Reynolds (fl. 1627–33), *Mythomystes*, is the most important English Neoplatonist account of poetics. Reynolds provides some allegorizing commentary on the gods along the way. John Ridewall (mid 14th century), *Fulgentius metaforalis*, purports to be a renewal of Fulgentius, but in fact its sources are quite various. Coluccio Salutati (1331–1406), *De Laboribus Herculis*, was an important source of humanist/allegorical Hercules lore. Servius (fl. c. 400), *In Virgilii Aeneidos*, is the earliest allegorical commentary on the *Aeneid*. Charles Stephanus (d. 1559), *Dictionarium*, includes articles on the gods and goddesses, with an occasional allegorical gloss. This dictionary was widely used, not least by most of the English poets, as it went through 20 editions between 1553 and 1693.

Theodulph of Orléans (c. 760–821), *Ecloga*, was a particularly influential book, since it was one of six elementary Latin texts in the widely used Medieval schoolbook *Liber Catonianus*. The *Ecloga* is a "debate" between the truth of Christianity and pagan falsity. But since Theodulph proceeded by juxtaposing (false) mythic figures with corresponding (true) Biblical figures, the *Ecloga* was often read as a guide to classical/Biblical typology (see Clogan 1968: 2–3).

For myth in relation to the emblem tradition, see Andrea Alciati (1492–1550), *Latin Emblems*; Francis Bonomii (1626–1705), *Chiron Achillis*; and Francis Quarles (1592–1644), *Emblemes*. Geffrey Whitney (1548–1603), *A Choice Book of Emblemes*, is the first emblem book in English.

NOTES

1 Augustine borrowed this figure from Origen's "Letter to Gregory." For a book-length treatment of the Medieval and Renaissance uses of Greek mythology, see Brumble (1998).

2 This book is devoted to Greek mythology, but Medieval and Renaissance writers usually made use of Roman rather than Greek names. In what follows, then, the names for gods, goddesses, and the rest usually follow Medieval and Renaissance practice: Venus rather than Aphrodite, Juno rather than Hera, etc.

3 See, for example, the last chapter of Martianus Capella, *The Marriage of Philology and Mercury*; and Gower, *The Confessio Amantis* (907–1075); for more explanation and further references, see Brumble (1998, under *Arion*).

4 Statius' *Thebaid* was the principal authority on Thebes down through the Middle Ages; Fulgentius' *On the Thebaid* was the most important allegorical commentary, but see also, for example, Lactantius Placidus' commentary on the *Thebaid*. See also Anderson (1986).

5 For each of these allegorical traditions, see Brumble (1998).

6 For a history of *allegory*, see, for example, Whitman (1987: 263–8).

7 For treatments of the tradition of the literary *exemplum*, see, for example, Welter (1927) and Bath and Russell (1995).

8 See Buffiere (1956: 136–54).

9 For more on Genius and nature allegory, see Brumble (1998, under *Genius* and *Nature*) and Chance (1975).

10 For Medieval astrological allegory see, for example, Kay (1994) and Wood (1970); for Renaissance astrology see, for example, Richardson (1989).

11 For examples of the genre, see Alciati, Bonomii, Quarles, and Whitney in "Further Reading." For a book-length bibliography of emblem-book editions and scholarship, see Daly and Silcox (1990).

12 For Euhemerus and euhemerism, see Chance (1994: 25–6).

13   The actual attribution to Dante is, however, uncertain; see Minnis and Scott (1988: 440–1) for a brief summary of the related scholarship. Fourfold allegory was first written about in relation to the Bible; see Lubac (1959).

14   See Hollander (1969: 15–56) for a wide-ranging discussion of fourfold allegory, particularly in relation to Dante's statements in the Letter to Can Grande and in the *Convivio*.

15   For Dante's interpretation of Aeneas, see Chance (1985: 56–64).

15: 'HAIL, MUSE! *ET CETERA*': GREEK MYTH IN ENGLISH AND AMERICAN LITERATURE[1]

Sarah Annes Brown

I n Keats's 'Ode on a Grecian Urn' we are invited to view the urn from conflicting perspectives. From one angle it seems sterile and artificial, a 'cold pastoral' (45) depicting 'marble men and maidens overwrought' (42), but it can also be seen as a site of primitivism and passion, of 'wild ecstasy' (10). The narrator seems as unsure of his own feelings about the urn as he is about its nature, being in turn repulsed and frustrated by its chilly reticence – 'Thou silent form, dost tease us out of thought' (44) – and attracted to its ancient beauty. The ambiguities inhere even within individual words and phrases. Are the 'overwrought' maidens panic-stricken (and thus real) or merely engraved? And do the famous last lines offer an answer to the poem's problems or are they, as T. S. Eliot thought, 'meaningless'?[2]

The Ode's uncertainties mirror similar tensions and shifts, though on a larger scale, in the post-Renaissance reception of Greek myth more generally. It is possible to identify times when Greek myth has been a potent literary influence and others when it has been largely ignored by most major writers. But to characterise this period in terms of a stark debate between classicism and anticlassicism would not be accurate. Equally important have been the debates *between* classicists, between different versions or constructions of Greek myth. Many of the most interesting responses to Greek myth register its polyvalency and display a corresponding ambivalence towards their sources, a combination of reverence and antagonism. It has been thought to signal sterility or fertile invention, tradition-bound conformity or rebellious subversion. It has been co-opted by Christians and pagans alike, perceived both as occidental and oriental, and identified with wholesome vigour as easily as with decadent sexual (particularly homosexual) practices.

Mythology is central to the works of Pope, Keats, Pound, Toni Morrison, and Carol Ann Duffy, *inter alia*, but each of these writers figures his or her relationship with the classical past in a distinctive way. Whereas some writers appear to seek an unmediated correspondence with an 'authentic' and pristine past, wherever possible sloughing off intervening layers of adaptation and reception, for others Greek myth represents a continuous tradition whose origins may certainly be traced back to Homer, Hesiod, Euripides et al., but which owes at least as crucial a debt to such mediating forces as Chaucer, Shakespeare, and Milton. Keats seems to articulate and in a sense bridge this divide when he addresses the urn as 'Thou foster-child of silence and slow time' (2). Greek myth is simultaneously ancient and childlike, younger and older than its modern offshoots. It is paradoxically true of cultures, as of individuals, that 'the child is father of the man.'[3] These competing versions of classicism may be compared with rather similar schisms within the Christian tradition. Whereas Catholicism is the product of centuries of accrued tradition, including non-Biblical texts, and depends on the mediating authority of the priest, Protestantism rejects this intervening process and places great emphasis on an unmediated and personal reading of the Bible. Protestantism is in a sense the newer religion, but its adherents would claim that it is actually older, representing a return to the primitive church. (And in fact the impetus for Protestantism was partly derived from Erasmus' rejection of the Vulgate (Latin) translation of the Greek New Testament on the grounds that it misrepresented the original.)

SEVENTEENTH- AND EIGHTEENTH-CENTURY LITERATURE

As the seventeenth century drew to a close, Dryden emerged as a central figure in Greek myth's transmission, although, like most of his contemporaries, he engaged with the mythic tradition via Rome. His translations of selected tales from Ovid's *Metamorphoses* and of the complete works of Virgil were particularly influential. Outside translation, the classical tradition during this period was most clearly manifest in lyric pastoral. After Milton, Marvell is the most important exponent of the genre, and perhaps his most striking example of classical pastoral is the elusive and much interpreted poem, 'On the Nymph Complaining for the Death of her Fawn.' The 'nymph' of the title seems to hover between a remote Arcadian or Latian world and the realities of Marvell's own age. On the one hand, she plans to place a vial containing the fawn's tears in 'Diana's shrine' (104) and imagines her pet has gone to 'Elysium' (107), yet she tells us that the animal was shot by 'wanton troopers' (1) and she sees it die 'as calmly as a saint' (94), details which suggest a setting that is not just Christian but specifically Cromwellian. Other successful exponents of the same genre include Rochester and Aphra Behn. Their witty and erotic pastorals are less 'mythical' than Marvell's, and owe to Greece little more than their protagonists' names (such as Cloris and Lysander) and a climate suited to al fresco dalliance. These works are significant as explorations of sexual desire and of gender politics, but their contribution to the traditions of Greek myth is negligible

The comparative failure of Behn and Rochester to engage with myth heralds a general decline in the status of neoclassical pastoral. Samuel Johnson's cutting dismissal of the genre in an account of Milton's 'Lycidas' typifies this shift in taste:

> Its form is that of a pastoral, easy, vulgar, and therefore disgusting: whatever images it can supply are long ago exhausted; and its inherent improbability always forces dissatisfaction on the mind.[4]

In the eighteenth century, the 'pristine' rather than the more layered and mediated mythological model became increasingly significant. This is reflected in (and reflects) a fast-growing enthusiasm for Greek culture and literature at this time. The reception of Greek myth now relied far less heavily – at least on the surface – on a mediating Latinate culture than had been the case in previous centuries. During the Middle Ages and Renaissance Latin writers were the supreme literary models, and Greek language and literature comparatively little known. But gradually, over the course of the eighteenth and nineteenth centuries, interest in Greek antiquities, literature, and society intensified, and a movement away from Roman culture towards Greek can be identified, although the shift was not stark or absolute.[5] This drive towards a more 'authentic' engagement with Greece was accompanied by a move away from the traditional classicizing reflex which Joseph Addison criticises in the Spectator.

> At other times when I have searched for the Actions of a Great Man, who gave a subject to the Writer, I have been

entertained with the Exploits of a River-God, or have been forced to attend a Fury in her mischievous Progress, from one end of the Poem to the other. When we are at school it is necessary for us to be acquainted with the system of pagan theology, and may be allowed to enliven a theme or point an epigram with an heathen god; but when we would write a manly panegyric that should carry in it all the colours of truth, nothing can be more ridiculous than to have recourse to our Jupiters and Junos.[6]

On balance, it would seem that the major writers of this period agreed with Addison. Whereas Renaissance literature is full of fresh and inventive mythological writing, such as Shakespeare's *Venus and Adonis* or Marlowe's *Hero and Leander*, in the eighteenth century the mythological tradition slumped, being largely confined to the works of comparatively conventional writers – Sir Samuel Garth's 'Claremont' (1715), a reworking of the story of Narcissus, is a typical example. Outside translation and such influential reference works as Tooke's *Pantheon* (1698) and Spence's *Polymetis* (1747), myth's most memorable manifestations in this period can be found in comic and satirical works, where a disjuncture between classical antiquity and banal modernity is exploited to amusing effect. There are many examples of this neoclassical bathos in the *Dunciad* – the account of Smedley, rising from the mud, is typical:

> First he relates, how sinking to the chin,
> Smit with his mien, the Mud-nymphs suck'd him in:
> How young Lutetia, softer than the down,
> Nigrina black, and Merdamante brown,
> Vy'd for his love in jetty bow'rs below;
> As Hylas fair was ravish'd long ago.[7]

But although in his original poetry classicism was generally confined to burlesque, Pope's decision to translate the *Iliad* reflects the growing status of Greek language and literature. By virtue of being a translation, a direct engagement with a Greek original, this work might seem to be a representative of the 'pristine' or Protestant model of classicism. Up to a point this is true, yet this is not of course to say that Pope's Homer represents an unmediated engagement with his original – indeed it would be difficult to claim that any translation can ever be completely unmediated. Echoes of other writers – Dryden and Milton for example – colour the translation, and Homer's gods are refracted through the lens of Roman epic, in particular the works of Ovid and Virgil. Robert Wood, a Greek antiquarian, criticised Pope's translation for being over-refined and thus unhomeric in *An Essay on the Original Genius and Writings of Homer* (1769).[8] In 1791 Cowper put forward his own translation of Homer as a more 'primitive' and therefore more authentic version than Pope's.[9] One might argue as to which version is more truly 'Homeric,' but it can be stated with some certainty that the differences between the two translations are accurate indicators of the changes in taste which took place over the course of the eighteenth century. This later eighteenth-century preference for the 'primitive' was also reflected in the popularity of James Macpherson's 'Ossian' poems of the 1760s. Macpherson set up his own brand of native, Celtic epic in explicit rivalry with Homeric epic. Goethe's Werther, another proto-Romantic creation, tellingly declares his preference for Ossian over Homer. But this Celtic (and Teutonic) repudiation of Greek myth was neither complete nor unequivocal. Hugh Blair, even while celebrating Ossian as an example of Celtic genius, cannot find a more effective way of praising his ancestors than by implicitly aligning them with the Greeks:

> There flourished among them the study of the most laud-able arts, introduced by the bards, whose office it was to sing in heroic verse the gallant actions of heroic men; and by the druids, who lived together in colleges, or societies, after the Pythagorean manner, and philolosophizing upon the highest subjects, asserted the immortality of the human soul.[10]

And representations of Ossian or other bardic figures betray a similar impulse by drawing on images of Homer. Bearded, robed, often depicted as blind, and carrying an instrument which resembles a Greek lyre more than a Celtic harp, painters of the period, like critics such as Blair, found it difficult to devise a completely fresh idiom with which to depict literary genius.

ROMANTICISM

The most inventive eighteenth-century poets shunned pat neoclassicism, but certainly did not reject all aspects of the classical tradition. The first generation of Romantic poets moved far more decidedly away from almost all manifestations of neoclassicism. In poems such as the *Lyrical Ballads* in which Wordsworth and Coleridge turned to 'incidents and situations from real life' presented using 'the real language of men,' there was little room for nymphs or satyrs. Although undoubtedly Wordsworth's familiarity with classical writings left traces on his writing (on *The Excursion* and *Laodamia* for example), his least mythological works have proved most influential. In poems such as *Christabel* Coleridge demonstrated a greater readiness to depart from 'real life,' but he drew on native European traditions of faerie rather than the classical pantheon.

The next generation of Romantic poets, notably Byron, Shelley, and Keats, turned round the fortunes of Greek myth in English literature. In this context, Byron was the least influential of the three. He was more interested in modern than in ancient Greece, and his most striking mythic creation has perhaps proved to be himself. Keats's classicism is strongly mediated through the works of his English predecessors. Offered a limited formal education and unable to read Greek or Latin in the original – he famously needed Chapman's translation of Homer to access the 'pure serene' of Greece[11] – his sources were mythological dictionaries and the works of earlier English poets. His sensuous and edgy poem *Lamia*, for example, is very much in the lush tradition of the Elizabeth epyllion, perfected by Marlowe and Shakespeare. This mediation is explicit as well as implicit in Keats' works. In his sonnet 'How many bards gild the lapses of time' he describes how earlier poets penetrate and inform his own works:

> And often, when I sit me down to rhyme,
> These will in throngs before my mind intrude:
> But no confusion, no disturbance rude
> Do they occasion; 'tis a pleasing chime. (5–8)

Shelley, by contrast, was educated at Eton and was an accomplished classicist. Yet he viewed the classics with some ambivalence, recognizing that they might offer a liberating escape from orthodoxy, while complaining that classical learning was a tool of the establishment, even of despotism.[12] This attitude is reflected in his response to Aeschylus' *Prometheus Bound*, which he reverses in *Prometheus Unbound*, allowing the rebellious Prometheus to emerge triumphant.[13] At the end of the play, because Prometheus (contrary to myth) fails to reveal that Thetis' son will be greater than his father, Zeus is destroyed by his son

Demogorgon. This championing of Prometheus implies a link between Shelley's powerful precursors, the Greek tragedians, and the Olympian gods. Shelley, like Prometheus, wants to throw off the shackles of the tyrannous past. Yet various factors complicated this apparent identification. As a Titan, Prometheus belonged to the race which had predated the Olympians and been dethroned by them, and it is thus Jove, in a sense, who represents rebellious youth. Also, as Shelley himself acknowledged in his Preface to the play, in altering Aeschylus so radically he was only following the example of Greek writers themselves, who freely adapted their own sources.[14] And in any case, Aeschylus' treatment of Prometheus is already enmeshed in a dialectic too complex to be simply reversed. Even if the Titan does seem obstinate and vengeful by the end of the original play, Aeschylus was surely, to some degree, himself of Prometheus' party.

If Shelley rebels against his source it is always in a sense on Aeschylus' own terms. Inverting the title of Aeschylus' surviving play (Aeschylus' own *Prometheus Unbound* only exists in fragments and was predicated on Prometheus' warning Zeus to avoid marrying Thetis) is a deidentifying move, but one which proclaims Shelley's own dependence upon a model. An interesting contrast is provided by another Romantic response to the legend of Prometheus. In *Frankenstein, or the Modern Prometheus*, Mary Shelley engages with the same debates as her husband – Dr. Frankenstein is simultaneously a sympathetic and creative victim and a hubristic overreacher. Both writers use Milton's *Paradise Lost* as a powerful vector of the Prometheus myth and display a Romantic partiality for Satanic rebels. But in other respects their projects are very different. Although in some ways antagonistic to Aeschylus, Shelley engages very directly with his source, maintaining the structure and conventions of Greek tragedy, just as Prometheus, in articulating resistance to Jupiter, adopts Jupiter's language in order to express his hostility.[15] The form and setting of *Frankenstein*, by contrast, are contemporary and, although it is in many respects a flawed work, *Frankenstein* is 'unbound' from its source in a way Shelley's play never quite manages to be. As the Greek gods defeated the earlier Titans, so Frankenstein today has become a far more resonant name than Prometheus. Mary Shelley's novel may be less Greek than her husband's play, but it is also a good deal more mythical.

Her reinvention of modernity as a new site of mythmaking chimes with the Romantic preoccupation with the figure of the Last Man and with the idea of a future England in ruins. Images of modern buildings in a state of eventual decay, such as Joseph Gandy's paintings of the ruined Bank of England, disorient the viewer and collapse the apparent gulf between antiquity and modernity, reminding us of the relativity of both terms.[16] Similarly, Horace Smith's companion poem to Shelley's 'Ozymandias,' 'On a Stupendous Leg of Granite,' envisages a chillingly primitive Englishman of the future who stops to gaze at the ruins of London just as the narrator of the Anglo-Saxon poem 'The Wanderer' reflects on ruined Roman remains:

> When through the wilderness
> Where London stood, holding the wolf in chase,
> He meets some fragment huge, and stops to guess
> What wonderful, but unrecorded, race
> Once dwelt in that annihilated place. (10–14)

Through these imaginative projections of their own decay this later generation of Romantics demonstrates an odd blend of humility and complacency, an awareness of their civilisation's mortality combined with a sense that their culture might one day be as resonant as that of Greece or Rome.

VICTORIAN BRITAIN AND NINETEENTH-CENTURY AMERICA

The precedence of Greek over Latin in public school teaching was firmly established early in the nineteenth century. Greek culture became internalised, even naturalised – Thomas Arnold claimed that 'they are virtually our own country men,'[17] and for nineteenth-century students and educators the classical languages forged a bond between successive generations of the English gentry rather than between ancients and moderns. Defending the study of classics, Vicesimus Knox, headmaster of Tonbridge School, asked 'who would chuse to be a stranger to that, in which almost every gentleman has been in some degree initiated.'[18] Social exclusivity, to use Keats's image again, was very much a 'foster child' of the classics of course, for in fifth-century Athens everyone would have spoken fluently the language that would later signal membership of an elite minority.

Given Britain's capacity to appropriate the ancient Greeks as honorary Englishmen – a proprietorial fondness reflected in its unwillingness to give up the Elgin marbles – it is perhaps not surprising that America viewed Greek myth with some hostility during the eighteenth and nineteenth centuries. Thomas Paine, for example, saw the study of Latin and Greek as a diversionary tactic and declared 'I have no notion of yielding the palm of the United States to any Grecians or Romans that were ever born.'[19] But, as so often, Greek myth, and the classical tradition more generally, demonstrated its capacity to adapt and survive. In the Southern states slave owners frequently gave their slaves classical names (such as Homer or Caesar) and, more positively, many Americans looked to Greece and Rome as important republican role models.[20] Within American literature, attitudes towards Greek myth are similarly complex and contradictory. In his useful study of classical mythology in English literature, Geoffrey Miles positions Walt Whitman as an American 'anticlassicist,' offering as evidence the poet's 'Song of the Exposition,' written in 1876:

> Come Muse migrate from Greece and Ionia,
> Cross out please those immensely overpaid accounts,
> That matter of Troy and Achilles' wrath, and Æneas', Odysseus'
>   wanderings,
> Placard 'REMOVED' and 'TO LET' on the rocks of your
>   snowy Parnassus,
> Repeat at Jerusalem, place the notice high on Jaffa's gate and on
>   Mount Moriah,
> The same on the walls of your German, French and Spanish
>   castles, and Italian collections,
> For know a better, fresher, busier sphere, a wide, untried domain
>   awaits, demands you. (15–21)[21]

But Whitman's ostensibly antagonistic response to Greek myth cannot be interpreted as unequivocal rejection. He implies that old stories, such as those of Aeneas and Odysseus, are played out, yet signals a continuing reliance on the Muse, herself a figure from Greek myth. Whitman's reliance on classical culture does not stop there. His apparently radical plan to import the Muses to America had long been anticipated. Nearly two thousand years earlier, Virgil made the same bold claim at the beginning of his third Georgic.

> I first, if life but remain, will return to my country, bringing the Muses with me in triumph from the Aonian peak; first I will bring back to thee, Mantua, the palms of Idumaea.... (10–12)[22]

The Muses' travels were naturally extended by later poets. Pope, in *An Essay on Criticism*, brings them North from Italy:

> But soon by Impious Arms from Latium chas'd,
> Their ancient Bounds the banish'd Muses past;
> Thence Arts o'er all the Northern World advance;
> But Critic Learning flourish'd most in France. (709–12)[23]

Whitman's own intervention represents less a radical break with tradition than just another stop on the Muses' long journey westward. It is a sign of Greek myth's power and complexity that Whitman's attempt to engage directly with Greece rather than tap into its myths via the intervening generations only serves to inscribe him within a continuous classicizing tradition.

The difficulties faced by American artists trying to extricate themselves from a tradition as slippery and polyvalent as Greek myth are also suggested in Nathaniel Hawthorne's short story, 'Drowne's Wooden Image.'[24] Drowne the wood carver is given a special commission by the captain of the *Cynosure*; he must create a figurehead modelled on the captain's Portuguese mistress. The task brings out a genius in Drowne, previously only a competent sculptor, and the lifelike beauty of the female figure astonishes his friends. The painter Copley exclaims, 'Who would have looked for a modern Pygmalion in the person of a Yankee mechanic!'[25] Like Whitman, Hawthorne seems to want to suggest the possibility of a fresh new idiom for American artists:

> To you ye reverent sane sisters,
> I raise a voice for far superber themes for poets and for art,
> To exalt the present and the real,
> To teach the average man the glory of his daily walk and trade,
> To sing in songs how exercise and chemical life are never to be
>   baffled,
> To manual work for each and all, to plough, hoe, dig,
> To plant and tend the tree, the berry, vegetables, flowers,
> For every man to see to it that he really do something, for every
>   woman too . . . (137–44)[26]

Drowne similarly articulates rebellion against a Greek aesthetic, protesting against the taste that elevates white marble above painted wood:

'I know nothing of marble statuary, and nothing of a sculptor's rules of art . . . Let others do what they may with marble, and adopt what rules they choose. If I can produce my desired effect by painted wood, those rules are not for me, and I have a right to disregard them.'[27]

But Drowne's apparent rebellion is, ironically, a return to the past, for those famously white Greek statues were themselves of course once garishly polychrome. The wood carver has rejected one version of classicism – the mediated version, which can be seen as bleached, sterile, and elitist – but he has unwittingly embraced a more 'pristine' version of Greek myth, a young, original, and primitive reincarnation of classicism more suited to a raw young nation. The tensions in this story are typical of many later responses both to 'Greek myth' as a cultural site and to specific individual tales. In many cases, including that of Drowne, apparent rebellion against Greek myth in general (or one tale in particular) becomes an act of homage in spite of itself – Greek myth proves itself too protean to be captured or defeated.

Back in Britain, the status of Greek continued to rise over the course of the nineteenth century; from the cultured Victorian perspective both the glamour and the *kudos* of antiquity were located in Athens rather than Rome.[28] Picturesque mythic females, such as Pygmalion's statue and Andromeda, were particularly favoured by artists as well as writers.[29] Yet Greek myth, and Greek culture more generally, was not universally embraced. In the field of architecture, for example, the Greek influence was countered by the Gothic revival, theorised by Ruskin and put into practice by Pugin.[30] Ruskin's irritation is less with the original buildings of Greece than with the debased vulgarity of the Greek Revival.

The most familiar position of Greek mouldings is in these days on shop fronts. There is not a tradesman's sign . . . which has not upon it ornaments which were invented to adorn temples and beautify kings' palaces.[31]

His position thus resembles that of Addison or Johnson; he attacks the hackneyed overuse of Greek motifs rather than the original works.

Victorian literary culture found its most striking and successful expression in the novel. The broadly realist tradition in which Dickens, the Brontës, Eliot, and Hardy worked might seem antipathetic to a serious engagement with Greek myth. Yet in their desire (comparable with Whitman's) to validate literature focused on humble people and everyday situations, these novelists made strategic use of the more familiar and elevated Classical tradition. Elizabeth Barrett Browning articulates their implicit argument in *Aurora Leigh*: Aurora asserts that the glamour cast by time on its foster child, Classical antiquity, should not overshadow the mythical and heroic potential of the nineteenth century.

> The critics say that epics have died out
> With Agamemnon and the goat-nursed gods;
> I'll not believe it . . .
> All actual heroes are essential men,
> And all men possible heroes: every age,
> Heroic in proportions, double-faced,
> Looks backwards and before. . . . [32]

Hardy offers us several reminders of his own art's affinities with classical literature. In his account of the farm workers' Bacchic celebrations in *Tess*, he suggests how little separates his characters from those of myth:

> Of the rushing couples there could barely be discerned more than the high lights – the indistinctness shaping them to satyrs clasping nymphs – a multiplicity of Pans whirling a multiplicity of Syrinxes; Lotis attempting to elude Priapus, and always failing. [33]

But Greek tragedy rather than Ovidian pastoral is Hardy's natural mode. At the novel's climax we are told that 'the President of the Immortals, in Aeschylean phrase, had ended his sport with Tess' (420), and in *Jude the Obscure* Sue Bridehead, who buys two plaster casts of Venus and Apollo which she has to conceal from her landlady, helpfully draws both Jude's and the reader's attention to the similarities between the houses of Fawley and Atreus. [34] George Eliot also alludes to Greek tragedy, but in her novels the allusions are characteristically more subtle and more complex. Richard Jenkyns (117) argues that Hetty Sorrel, the seduced country girl in *Adam Bede*, is tacitly aligned with both of Jason's wives, the wronged and vengeful Medea and the naïve and thoughtless Glauce. The mythic resonances of Euripides' *Medea* are thus imported into the novel and further complicated by the elision of its two heroines. It is painful enough that a passionate and wilful woman should kill her children but perhaps still more disturbing when the child murderess is a pretty, flimsy butterfly like Hetty. More covert but perhaps still more striking is Emily Brontë's debt to Greek tragedy. The intense close-knit family relations of *Wuthering Heights*, the themes of sibling love and rivalry, and their power to affect subsequent generations, the importance of exile and revenge, the combination of a strongly patterned dialectic with wild disorder, and the use of Nelly and Lockwood as choric mediators, align the novel with Aeschylean tragedy. By recontextualising Greek myth within a new genre, the novel, Emily Brontë, George Eliot, and Hardy succeeded in reanimating its traditions by grafting them on to the fates of 'ordinary' characters such as Jude, Heathcliff, and Maggie Tulliver.

At the opposite extreme from the comparatively embedded and diffused presence of Greek myth in the Victorian novel, we can trace a more scholarly and antiquarian engagement with Greek language and literature during this period, most clearly manifest in translations and imitations of Greek texts, in particular Greek drama. Paradoxically, in looking for a real and authentic Greece, these scholarly Victorian writers often only succeeded in making Greek myth seem more artificial and remote. This effect can be seen in the reformed spelling of Greek words which many adopted at this time, changing Alcibiades into Alkibiades and Circe into Kirke. The familiar forms were thus made strange.[35] Jenkyns writes that 'we see Greek mythology hazily, through the veils successively laid over it by the Romans, the Renaissance and the classicism of the eighteenth century.'[36] This may be true, but we have grown so accustomed to the 'haze' that its removal seems a jarring innovation rather than a restoration. In a similarly paradoxical way, performances using original instruments strike older listeners as 'modern' because they are accustomed to the tones of nineteenth- and early twentieth-century orchestras. Of course, such defamiliarising moves can be pleasing and stimulating. As Emily Dickinson rather cryptically observes in 'In a Library':

> A precious – mouldering pleasure – 'tis –
> To meet an Antique Book –
> In just the Dress his Century wore –
> A privilege – I think – (1–4)[37]

Arnold and Swinburne were two of the best known of such consciously classicizing writers. In his preface to *Merope* Arnold explained that he 'decided to try, therefore, how much of the effectiveness of the Greek poetical forms I could retain in an English poem constructed under the conditions of these forms.'[38] Swinburne's *Atalanta in Calydon* is a similar imitation of Greek tragedy, best known now for its effective and much anthologised chorus 'When the hounds of the spring are on winter's traces.' Although both writers' projects are impressive, they are somehow static, fossilizing the traditions of Greek myth rather than reinvigorating them. We miss the tension created when classical source and derived text are in some way at odds or at least in dialogue, for it is this dialectic that maintains the dynamism and energy of the mythic tradition. Although these poets' plays were originals, they sometimes exhibit a strain more typical of translated works. Quite different is Browning's *Agamemnon* (the 'Browning Version' of Rattigan's play), a strikingly bizarre exercise in literal translation, retaining as far as possible the word order and collocations of ancient Greek:

> Agamemnon: Ah me! I am struck – a right-aimed stroke within me!
> Chorus: Silence! Who is it shouts 'stroke' – 'right-aimedly' a wounded one?
> Agamemnon: Ah me! Indeed again – a second, struck by![39]

Browning's dislocatingly strange solutions, his apparent determination to emphasise the alien in *Agamemnon* – in fact, everyone in the play sounds like a character from another mythic trilogy set in the distant past, Yoda from *Star Wars* – are in marked contrast with Arnold's vision of the perfect union between translator and original which 'takes place when the mist that stands between them – the mist of alien modes of thinking, speaking, and feeling on the translator's part . . . disappears.'[40]

As the nineteenth century drew to its close, a significant apparent fissure in the image of ancient Greece developed. For the Victorians ancient Greek culture was associated with wholesome and manly vigour but also with proscribed homoerotic feelings. Eve Kosofsky Sedgwick's account of homosexual panic, whereby male bonding operates confusingly as a sign both of hetero- and homosexuality, helps to resolve this apparent contradiction within attitudes towards a society in which the role played by women was so strikingly circumscribed.[41] Pater's description of Sparta as a wholesomely tough regime can be read as a homoeroticised fantasy:

> Lacedaemon was in truth before all things an organised place of discipline, an organised opportunity also, for youth, for the sort of youth that knew how to command by serving – a

constant exhibition of youthful courage, youthful self-respect, yet above all of true youthful docility; youth thus committing itself absolutely, soul and body, to a corporate sentiment in its very sports . . . Whips and rods used in a kind of monitorial system by themselves had a great part in the education of these young aristocrats, and, as pain surely must do, pain not of bodily disease or wretched accidents, but as it were by dignified rules of art, seem to have refined them . . .

The capacity of Greek male bonding to slide into supposed corruption is suggested by Henry James. The *fin-de-siècle* writer portrayed in his short story 'The Author of "Beltraffio"' is tainted by suspicions which are never quite articulated. A clue as to their nature is provided when the writer tells the narrator why his wife limits his access to their son: 'She thinks me, at any rate, no better than an ancient Greek.'[42] Another, less equivocal, example of this identification between ancient Greece and homosexuality can be found in E. M. Forster's *Maurice*. Maurice's awareness of his sexual identity is triggered when, during a translation class: 'Mr Cornwallis observed in a flat toneless voice: "Omit: a reference to the unspeakable vice of the Greeks."'[43] When, during the twentieth century, homosexuality became increasingly accepted, the importance of the link between Greece and homosexuality, sometimes employed almost as a secret code to sound out potential sexual partners, declined.

Although Forster felt unable to write openly about his sexuality (*Maurice* was published posthumously), his short stories also hint at a link between Greece and homosexuality. Myth is presented as anarchic, sensual, countercultural – 'queer' in the broadest sense. 'The Other Kingdom,' for example, presents a metamorphosis straight out of Greek myth as a fantasy alternative to conventional wedlock, perhaps concealing another, more achievable, 'Greek' way of avoiding marriage. The story also offers the reader a rematch of the debate between 'mediated' and 'pristine' classicism, earlier staged in the works of Keats, Hawthorne, and Whitman. Evelyn Beaumont, a naïve Irish girl engaged to a conventional English gentleman, Harcourt Worters, seems distracted and frivolous when she studies Latin with her fiancé's ward. The Classics, in so far as they signify social status and the veneer of learning, are antipathetic to her nature: 'Mr Harcourt had picked her out of "Ireland" and had brought her home, without money, without connexions, almost without antecedents, to be his bride.'[44] But this very rawness, in particular this lack of 'antecedents,' gives her a great affinity with Greek myth if we see it, not as something very old, but as something as young and crude as Evelyn herself. The tale reaches its climax when Evelyn demonstrates her own unconventional classical credentials by following the example of Daphne and turning into a tree as a refuge from the patronising control of Worters.

Although he wrote at the beginning of the twentieth century, Forster's brand of Hellenism, his strong sense of the historical and geographical realities of Greece, and the association he forges between its culture and his own desires align him more with late Victorian writers such as Wilde and Pater. By contrast with the earlier period of Greek myth's reception, the nineteenth century engaged directly with Greek writers, the Greek language, its landscape, and its ruins. This (comparatively) unmediated engagement with Greece had now enabled the emergence of a tradition of ornamental and languid Hellenism as hackneyed as the rather different brand of conventional classicism condemned by Johnson and Addison. Wilde's 'Ravenna' is typical:

> O Hellas! Hellas! in thine hour of pride,
> Thy day of might, remember him who died
> To wrest from off thy limbs the trammelling chain:
> O Salamis! O lone Plataean plain!
> O tossing waves of wild Euboean sea!
> O wind-swept heights of lone Thermopylae!
> He loved you well – ay, not alone in word,
> Who freely gave to thee his lyre and sword
> Like Aeschylus at well-fought Marathon . . . [45]

Whereas the mythical pastoral of post-Renaissance literature was a Latinised and indeed anglicised tradition, the decadents' mythical idiom was exotic and oriental. In *Mythology and the Romantic Tradition in English Poetry* Douglas Bush thus suggests its limitations: 'The wine of nineteenth-century Hellenism has lost all its body, and only a stale bouquet remains.'[46] The next important shift in the reception of Greek myth would reinvigorate it by reincorporating the earlier poetic traditions and by putting back some of the layers which most nineteenth-century writers had aimed to peel away.

THE TWENTIETH CENTURY

Over the past hundred years, Greek myth has been appropriated in many different ways and for many different purposes. The story of

Greek myth's reception in the twentieth century, still more than in the earlier periods, is characterised by its collagist fragmentation rather than by a straightforward or continuous narrative. The most important early development in the century was the rise of Modernism, a movement (like Romanticism) associated with many different and even contradictory impulses, one of which was the reinvigoration of the classical tradition.

The tendency of Modernist classicism was to emphasise the place of Greek myth within a wider cultural perspective. Through the study of anthropology, the singularity of Greek myth was in a sense diluted by research which linked its core narratives to those of other cultures and existing primitive traditions, aligning Adonis with Christ for example – a move which unexpectedly takes us back to the Medieval mythographers discussed in the previous chapter. Freud and Jung, although they explained the precise significance of myth in different ways, both foregrounded the primal power of stories such as Oedipus, seeing them as archetypes which determined the urges and desires of successive generations rather than as the productions of a unique cultural moment. In *Ulysses*, for example, James Joyce mapped the quasi-paternal relationship of Bloom to Stephen Daedalus onto two powerful precursors, the stories of Odysseus and Hamlet. Joyce achieves an effect of bathos similar to Pope's in the *Dunciad* by restaging Homeric epic in modern Dublin, metamorphosing Nausicaa, for example, into Gerty MacDowell, immersed in cheap scent and cheap fiction as she fuels the sexual fantasies of Bloom/Odysseus. (Although his antiepic heroes and heroines have of course themselves become part of twentieth-century mythology.)

This positioning of Greek myths within a kind of cultural vortex of literary reenactment is particularly apparent in the works of Pound and Eliot. In the fourth Canto Pound combines the troubadour tradition with Greek myth (via Ovid) when he merges Pierre Vidal with Actaeon and Cabestan with Itys.[47] Similarly, in *The Waste Land*, Greek myth is filtered through the works of other writers. A reference to the tale of Philomela – 'Above the antique mantel was displayed/ As though a window gave upon the sylvan scene/ The change of Philomel' (97–9)[48] – is bracketed between allusions to two Shakespearean moments (from *Cymbeline* and *Titus Andronicus*) which reference this myth. Metamorphosis, like conflict between the generations, has the power to generate a kind of reflexive charge when imitated. 'The change of Philomel' alluded to by Eliot suggests both her bodily and her literary metamorphosis. Greek myth has become the starting point of a palimpsest which accrues different layers of significance but whose original form and meaning can still be deciphered, just as the victims of Ovidian metamorphosis typically retain some vestige of their former nature.

The use of Greek myths by Modernists such as Eliot has been characterised as elitist. Whereas Hardy and George Eliot used mythic tradition to give characters such as Michael Henchard and Adam Bede a tragic or heroic gravitas, Eliot, some have claimed, seems to view ordinary people and the modern world with fastidious distaste.

> While the Elizabethans wrote of courtly love or of Cleopatra's golden barge, modern living offers only the crowds streaming over London Bridge and the polluted Thames flowing underneath . . . The poem berates popular culture throughout its five sections, as Eliot compares his observations of contemporary life with his knowledge of the past, viewed almost exclusively through poetry.[49]

But this account does not do justice to the complexity of Eliot's poetry. The crowds are Dantesque as well as modern and pollution is in fact an absent presence:

> The river's tent is broken; the last fingers of leaf
> Clutch and sink into the wet bank. The wind
> Crosses the brown land, unheard. The nymphs are departed.
> Sweet Thames, run softly, till I end my song.
> The river bears no empty bottles, sandwich papers,
> Silk handkerchiefs, cardboard boxes, cigarette ends
> Or other testimony of summer nights. The nymphs are departed.
> And their friends, the loitering heirs of City directors;
> Departed, have left no addresses. (173–81)

The sense of desolation here seems at first to support Childs' reading. 'The nymphs are departed' suggests perhaps the loss of a beautiful resonant mythology, an impression which may in turn encourage the reader to misread the lines which follow and ignore the word 'no,' creating a mental picture of a river cluttered with rubbish. The rubbish thus seems to symbolise the bleak modern world, which is being contrasted with a plangent and picturesque classical past. But this divide between ancient and modern is destabilised by the poem. This river has *no* rubbish in it – just as it has no nymphs by it. And the nymphs are not after all so classical – if their friends are 'the loitering heirs of city directors' they would appear to be simply modern girls. What is actually being described is less a twentieth-century cityscape than a posthuman wilderness from whose perspective all human culture and life have the potential to seem valuable and picturesque. Here we return to the relativism of Elizabeth Barrett Browning and of Horace Smith, a perspective which acknowledges the mythmaking potential of modernity.

Although both Pound and Eliot were American, they spent most of their working lives in Europe. A more characteristically American take on Greek myth can be found in Eugene O'Neill's trilogy *Mourning Becomes Electra*, an updated *Oresteia*, set during the American Civil War. Aeschylus' drama about love and hatred between parents and children acquires fresh significance when it is thus adapted. Like Shelley, O'Neill seems a participant in his drama, not simply the translator, for he enters into a tacit rivalry with an older text which already has intergenerational conflict at its heart. The Mannons seem doubly fated, by the deeds of the earlier generation within the fiction of O'Neill's drama and by the works of O'Neill's own literary 'parent,' Aeschylus. This confusion between real life and story seeps into *Mourning Becomes Electra*. Christine Mannon seems to represent not simply Clytemnestra, but Aeschylus himself. She is 'furrin lookin' and queer.'[50] Her daughter Lavinia, by extension, can be seen as an avatar of O'Neill, and thus of the American tradition more generally. She strongly resembles her mother, 'But it is evident Lavinia does all in her power to emphasise the dissimilarity rather than the resemblance to her parent' (897). While her mother looks younger than her age, Lavinia looks older, a further reflection of the contradictory relationship between the Greek and the American traditions, the difficulty of characterizing one as 'older' than the other.

Like *Frankenstein*, *Mourning Becomes Electra* simultaneously proclaims its debts to antiquity and its alignment with a new mythology, the American Gothic. The fall of the incestuous, enervated, and self-destructive house of Mannon seems as indebted to Poe as to the *Oresteia*. And with its atmosphere of melodrama and its focus on two powerfully calculating women, *Mourning* looks forward to the American Gothic's best-known productions, created for the new medium America made its own, the female-dominated films of the 1940s such as *Now, Voyager* and *The Little Foxes*. Yet (as earlier with Whitman) American myth is rather an offshoot of Greek myth than a completely new tradition. O'Neill implies a misfit between his native culture and Greek source in *Mourning Becomes Electra* when he describes the Mannons' house as having a 'pagan temple front struck like a mask on Puritan gray ugliness' (904). But the trilogy suggests – or perhaps creates – an unexpected affinity between the native American Gothic mode and Aeschylean tragedy, just as white-columned porticoes now seem as much American as Greek. (More recently Donna Tartt, in *The Secret History*, has created a Euripidean New England of similar Gothic intensity.)

Myth is a more muted but no less powerful presence in the works of the next generation of American dramatists. Through the choric figure of the lawyer Alfieri, Arthur Miller's *A View from the Bridge* reminds us how passion and violence link the present to the past:

> . . . in some Caesar's year, in Calabria perhaps or on the cliff at Syracuse, another lawyer, quite differently dressed, heard the same complaint and sat there as powerless as I, and watched it run its bloody course.[51]

The ambiguous Rodolpho, an immigrant distrusted by his kinsman Eddie yet petted by the play's women, motivates the action. His blond androgyny and destructive charm recall Euripides' Dionysus, but the play cannot be pinned down to a single mythic source. Tennessee Williams's *A Streetcar Named Desire* has similar mythic resonances; the tensions between a man and two sisters, one his wife, one his raped victim, represent yet another 'change of Philomel.' Like the great Victorian novelists, these playwrights use Greek myth tactfully, perhaps unconsciously, to season their own modern myths based on the experiences of blue-collar America.

In Britain, as in the United States, there was a movement towards a more gritty style of writing, and British literature of the 1950s saw the publication of works such as John Braine's *Room at the Top* and John Osborne's *Look Back in Anger*, both groundbreaking depictions of lower-middle-class life. This movement was, or seemed to be, difficult to reconcile with Greek myth, and it was in the same decade that the poet Philip Larkin notoriously voiced an active disapproval of the earlier modernists' reliance on a 'myth kitty,' echoing earlier related attacks on a supposedly played-out classical tradition by Addison, Johnson, Ruskin, and, of course, Wordsworth.

> As a guiding principle I believe that every poem must be its own sole freshly created universe and therefore have no belief in 'tradition' or a common myth-kitty or casual allusions in poems to other poems or poets, which last I find unpleasantly like the talk of literary understrappers letting you see they know the right people.[52]

But Greek myth, rather like a virus mutating in the face of new antibiotics, continued to find fresh ways of combating such disaffection. The famous lines from Louis Macneice's *Autumn Journal* – 'It was all so unimaginably different/ and all so long ago'[53] – are often quoted by classicists pointing out the apparent gulf which separates us from the Greeks. This more modern historical awareness of disparity, as opposed to romantic identification with Greece, might seem calculated to encourage writers to conform to Larkin's wishes and reject the irrelevant classical tradition. But the sense of Greece as something mysterious, primitive, and alien might in fact be said to accommodate Greek myth into a modernist or postmodernist aesthetic, which is itself characterised by alienation and fragmentation, by a recognition of the primitivism within modernity and of civilization's inability to perfect mankind. And read in context, Macneice's lines are pointedly ironic, implying the parallels between a flawed, savage, and unjust past and Europe under the shadow of the Third Reich.

> And when I should remember the paragons of Hellas
> I think instead
> Of the crooks, the adventurers, the opportunists,
> The careless athletes and the fancy boys,
> The hair-splitters, the pedants, the hard-boiled sceptics
> And the Agora and the noise
> Of the demagogues and the quacks; and the women pouring
> Libations over graves
> And the trimmers at Delphi and the dummies at Sparta and
>   lastly
> I think of the slaves.
> And how one can imagine oneself among them
> I do not know;
> It was all so unimaginably different
> And all so long ago.

In fact, the prominence of working-class voices (both as writers and as characters) in later twentieth-century literature, perhaps counterintuitively, served to give the mythic tradition yet another new lease of life. Writers such as Tony Harrison, Steven Berkoff, and Tom Paulin have all in their different ways made Greek myth compatible with a more proletarian and more politicised idiom. They embrace the original myths or plays but generally reject the intervening classical tradition, by contrast with Pound and Eliot. But their practice may be differentiated from the similar avoidance of mediation in many nineteenth-century writers. Rather than trying to return to the classical past, carefully recreating or imitating Greek forms in the manner of Swinburne, these modern writers drag Greek myths into the present, forcing them to inhabit modern forms. The defamiliarising authenticity of spelling reform which made Creon into Kreon can be contrasted with the familiarizing irreverence with which Berkoff rechristens Oedipus Eddy.[54] But, as we saw with Whitman, it is difficult to devise entirely new ways of responding to Greek myth. In *A Common Chorus*, his adaptation of Aristophanes' *Lysistrata* set in 1980s Britain during the Greenham Common protests, Tony Harrison echoes Romantic projections of a ruined England to equal Athens or Rome, envisaging a waste land as empty as Eliot's. A third world war would collapse all distinctions between present and past as memories of both would be totally annihilated:

> So Greece is Greenham, Greenham Greece,
> Poseidon is Poseidon, not just for this piece . . .
> In the Third World War we'll destroy
> Not only modern cities but the memory of Troy . . . [55]

But this presentist privileging of the twentieth century is not universal. One significant twentieth-century writer who didn't choose to update Greek myth is Mary Renault. Her novels about heroes such as Theseus and Alexander, scholarly, romantic, and often homoerotic, in some ways represent a return to Victorian constructions of Greece.

The same impulse which led to the co-option of Greek myth as a medium with which to express the concerns of working-class culture encouraged later twentieth-century writers to use myth to highlight the situation of other oppressed groups. In Toni Morrison's *Beloved*, whose subject is the dreadful dilemma faced by slave mothers, driven to kill their children, the reader is invited to import the horrific action of Medea, another racial outsider, into the novel. Morrison's work is not without precedent. Two centuries earlier the reader was invited to make the opposite move, reading the horrific experiences of slaves into an ostensibly academic translation of Ovid's tale of Niobe whose children were all killed by the gods:

> One only daughter lives, and she the least;
> The queen close clasp'd the daughter to her breast:
> 'Ye heav'nly pow'rs, ah spare me one,' she cry'd,
> 'Ah! spare me one,' the vocal hills reply'd:

In vain she begs, the Fates her suit deny,
In her embrace she sees her daughter die. (207–12)[56]

Only if we know that the author, Phillis Wheatley, was herself a
Gambian slave does the rather conventional translation acquire this contemporary edge. Phillis Wheatley is invoked by another late twentieth-
century African American poet, Norman Loftis, in *Black Anima*. His
narrator journeys through a strange dreamscape in which he glimpses
many shades, most of them fellow African Americans such as Wheatley.
Whereas Wheatley, and later Morrison, were happy to use Greek myth
to express or imply their own experiences, Loftis seeks to destabilise
the cultural hegemony of Greek myth, replacing it with an alternative, African, myth kitty. *Black Anima* is, among other things, a parodic
response to *The Waste Land*. Section Four of *The Waste Land*, 'Death by
Water,' for example, is relocated to New York:

> Phlebas the Phoenician, a fortnight dead,
> Forgot the cry of gulls, and the deep sea swell
> And the profit and loss.
> A current under sea
> Picked his bones in whisper. As he rose and fell
> He passed the stages of his youth and age
> Entering the whirlpool.[57]
> A naked figure flowed
> along the Harlem River
> turning, turning in sunlight . . .
> it fell under sea
> but at Wall Street was free
> fish nipping in the Bay
> picked its fingers clean.[58]

The body in the Harlem river is changing, picked clean just like Phlebas,
and so is Eliot's poem. The corpse becomes the corpus, which must
be transformed and not simply revived. In one of *Black Anima*'s prose
sections, Loftis returns to the image of a bone picked clean of flesh to
describe his journey back into a cultural past in which echoes of Eliot
and other western myths such as that of Pygmalion are combined with
images of African and African-American history:

> Images from your past rushed on you, and you sucked them
> clean as a bone. The dead king searching the shore of the

Nile for the perfect ebony figure. The hanged man drenched
with gasoline and set aflame down in Mississippi. And the
grass that year grew green as fire, the cotton heaped high
as the Alps and an old man covered with wheat rose out of
the river wet with water and ambergris. All this filed past
you sorting itself out in your feeling, already frayed from the
journey.[59]

The replacement of ivory with ebony in this apparent allusion to the
Pygmalion story typifies Loftis' combative engagement with Greek
myth. Yet there is clearly an attraction here too – his dissection of
Eliot and of the western mythical tradition is loving as well as forensic.
It is difficult to parody *The Waste Land* (itself already so parodic), just as
it is difficult completely to rewrite a tradition as labile as Greek myth.
Returning to the distinction I made earlier between pristine and mediated responses to myth, *Black Anima* might seem to be a thoroughly
mediated response, mediated not by Anglo-Saxon culture, Greek culture's most obvious heir, but by a quite different, alien, African tradition.
But from another point of view *Black Anima* could be seen as a return to
the pristine roots of Greek myth, roots which (according to Afrocentrist
scholars, such as Martin Bernal, the author of *Black Athena*) are African,
via Egypt. Like Drowne, Loftis seems to add inauthentic colour to the
classics but may only be removing the whitewash. Such theories are
much contested but, like the nineteenth-century German enthusiasm
for tracing the society of Sparta to Teutonic invaders, have at the very
least a mythic energy.[60]

A similarly ambiguous stance distinguishes many women writers'
responses to Greek myth. Carol Ann Duffy's *The World's Wife* is a collection of monologues by the wives of famous men, many of them characters from Greek myth. Witty and lively, they emerge from the strong
late twentieth-century reawakening of interest in classical myth, in part
a response to Ted Hughes' much praised *Tales from Ovid*. (We seemed to
have returned to the Renaissance preference for Latinised mythology.)
Like most of these neo-Ovidian writings, Carol Ann Duffy's poetry is
colloquial and racy, often self-consciously anachronistic – very much
like Ovid himself in fact. The monologue spoken by Pygmalion's statue
implies irritation with the original story's creation of a pliable fantasy
wife:

So I changed tack,
grew warm, like candle wax,

kissed back,
was soft, was pliable,
began to moan,
got hot, got wild,
arched, coiled, writhed,
begged for his child,
and at the climax
screamed my head off –
All an act. (39–49)[61]

But her poetry suggests Duffy isn't faking her response to Ovid. The half pun of 'tack,' suggesting 'tacky' because it (nearly) rhymes with sticky wax, and the slightly disconcerting idiom – 'screamed my head off' – somehow too easy to visualise when the speaker is a fragile statue, are very Ovidian moves. Indeed Duffy's entire project in *The World's Wife* was anticipated by Ovid in his *Heroides*, letters written by mythical women, such as Dido and Ariadne, complaining about their ill treatment at the hands of men. We can push this tradition of quasi-feminist rewriting back even further than Ovid to the sixth-century Greek poet Stesichorus, whose *Palinode* rehabilitates Helen from the supposed slanders of Homer. (In his version of the story, later followed by Euripides' *Helen*, the real Helen spent the war blamelessly in Egypt while a phantom took her place in Troy.) The feminism – or effect of feminism – created by so many classical writers – Ovid, Stesichorus, and perhaps particularly Euripides – means that works by modern women writers almost inevitably function as *hommages* as well as palinodes.

Thus, the afterlife of Greek myth can be likened to the Lernean hydra or to Antaeus – attacks only seem to result in a new lease of life. But the influence does not just work one way. Greek myth may have its coils tightly wrapped around modern literature, but modern literature has also permeated Greek myth. Shakespeare is a particularly potent force in this counterattack, and his unique status ensures that the classics which most influenced him are now almost invariably encountered by readers who already know Shakespeare, and thus seem to owe a debt to him. This is reflected in many later translations of the Classics which, either deliberately or instinctively, lend a Shakespearean colour to writers such as Ovid, Sophocles, and Homer. In Browning's *Balaustion's Adventure* (1871), it is Euripides who is Shakespeareanised. The inset retelling of *Alcestis* presents us with an Admetus who is both more clearly faulty and more decidedly redeemed than Euripides' equivocal hero, a reinflection which implies that Browning has been influenced by *The*

Winter's Tale, another play about a faithful wife who cheats death. Similarly, in his translations from the *Metamorphoses*, Ted Hughes presents us with a Shakespeareanised Ovid. In *Venus and Adonis*, Shakespeare offers us an alarmingly physical and massive Venus whose oppressive passion for the infantilised Adonis is spurned by the youth with alarmed distaste. Hughes' Venus is nearer Shakespeare's than Ovid's, a galumphing giantess:

> Now goes bounding over the stark ridges,
> Skirts tucked high like the huntress, or she plunges
> Down through brambly goyles, bawling at hounds . . . [62]

Shakespeare's version of Venus and Adonis was influenced by another Ovidian tale, that of Salmacis and Hermaphroditus. The son of Hermes and Aphrodite, Hermaphroditus shunned the advances of Salmacis, but the forward nymph accosted him in a pool, refusing to loosen her grip. She prays to the gods that they may be forever united; her prayer is answered and they merge to form one androgynous being. The tale's dynamic, its focus on attraction, repulsion, and eventual union, provides a useful emblem for the reception of Greek myth over the past three centuries, characterised as it is by the Hegelian triad of thesis, antithesis, and synthesis. But whereas the feminised Hermaphroditus cursed the pool's waters with an enervating power, the similarly synthesised tradition of Greek myth has been blessed with a unique *energeia*, retaining its traditional hold on literary culture and exerting influence on new genres and media – westerns, science fiction, film, animation, and computer games are all in its debt.

FURTHER READING

Douglas Bush's *Mythology and the Romantic Tradition in English Poetry* (first published in 1937 and reissued with a new preface in 1969) offers a lively overview of the topic and traces the mythological tradition up to the beginning of the twentieth century. Many monographs focus on a particular period or strand of Greek myth's reception. Jennifer Wallace's *Shelley and Greece: Rethinking Romantic Hellenism* (1996) is an excellent scholarly study, and the next phase of Greek myth's reception is well served by Richard Jenkyns's readable and entertaining *The Victorians and Ancient Greece* (1980). Particularly useful for undergraduates is Geoffrey Miles's *Classical Mythology in English Literature* (1999), which includes a substantial anthology of mythological writings as well a beginners' guide to myth and its reception. Although their focus is not exclusively literary, Oliver Taplin's *Greek Fire* (1989) and Simon Goldhill's *Love Sex and Tragedy* (2004) offer stimulating accounts of the interface between Greek and modern culture. Many 'Greek' myths can be found in Ovid's *Metamorphoses*, and the second half of my own *The Metamorphosis of Ovid: From Chaucer to Ted Hughes* (1999) analyses the poem's reception in post-Renaissance literature.

NOTES

1 'Hail, Muse! *et cetera*.' The opening words of Canto III of Byron's *Don Juan*.
2 Eliot (1932, repr. 1972) 270.
3 William Wordsworth, 'My heart leaps up when I behold,' line 7.
4 Johnson (1984) 699.
5 A good recent account of this shift can be found in Wallace (1996) 8–9.
6 Addison (1963) Vol. 4, 149.
7 Alexander Pope (1963) *Dunciad Variorum* II 307–12.
8 Wood (1769) 72–92.
9 The two translations are compared by Richard Jenkyns (1980) 8.
10 Blair (1763, repr. 1765) 22.
11 'On First Looking into Chapman's Homer' 7.
12 Wallace (1996) 32–3.
13 Byron treats Prometheus with comparable admiration in his poem 'Prometheus' (1816).
14 Shelley (1977) 132.
15 Wallace (1996) 166.
16 An account of the phenomenon is given in Stafford (1996).
17 Thomas Arnold (1834) 240.
18 Knox (1781) 9.
19 Reinhold (1984) 126.
20 For a detailed account of the impact of Classical culture on the United States, see Reinhold (1984).
21 Whitman (1855).
22 Fairclough (1978).
23 Pope (1963).
24 Hawthorne (1982). Hawthorne's most important contribution to Greek myth was his *Tanglewood Tales* (1853), retellings aimed at children.
25 Hawthorne (1982) 936–7.
26 Whitman (1855).
27 Hawthorne (1982) 938.
28 For a very detailed account of the impact of Greece on Victorian Britain, see Turner (1981).
29 Munich (1989) and Joshua (2001).
30 The competing influences of Medievalism and Hellenism are easily identifiable in the poetry of Tennyson, who used Arthurian legend as the basis for

Idylls of the King, but frequently turned to Classical sources, most notably in 'Ulysses.'

31   Ruskin (1903–12) Vol. 8, 157.
32   Barrett Browning (1993) V 139–41, 151–4.
33   Hardy (1891, repr. 1974) 91.
34   Hardy (1895, repr. 1978) 224.
35   Miles (1999) 14.
36   Jenkyns (1980) 160.
37   Dickinson (1970) 176.
38   Arnold (1858) ix.
39   Browning (1877) 116–7.
40   Arnold (1861, repr. 1896).
41   Kosofsky Sedgwick (1985) 2–5.
42   James (1899) 892.
43   Forster (1971) 50.
44   Forster (2002) 67.
45   Wilde (1990) 861.
46   Bush (1937, reissued 1969) 422.
47   Pound (1975) 13–14.
48   Eliot (1971).
49   Childs (1999) 80.
50   O'Neill (1988) 895.
51   Arthur Miller (2000) 12.
52   Herbert and Hollis (2000) 151.
53   Macneice (1939) 39.
54   Berkoff (1980).
55   Harrison (1992) 49.
56   Wheatley (1973) 112.
57   Eliot (1971) 312–18.
58   Loftis (1973) 7.
59   Loftis (1973) 86.
60   Goldhill (2004) 287.
61   Duffy (1999).
62   Hughes (1997) 130.

16: GREEK MYTH ON THE SCREEN

Martin M. Winkler

S ince Georges Méliès made *Pygmalion et Galathée* (*Pygmalion and Galatea*) in 1898, Greek mythology has afforded filmmakers endless opportunities to display their medium to great public success, if at varying levels of artistic achievement. From short films such as those of Méliès at the dawn of cinema to gigantic widescreen and color epics, films set in ancient Greece and Rome have proven most durable for their sheer appeal as spectacles. Critics and historians have come to call them peplums or pepla after *peplum*, the Latin equivalent of the Greek word *peplos* ("mantle, cloak"). But Germans and Italians tend to use an expression that characterizes most of these films even better: *Kolossalfilm* or *il kolossal*. Colossal visual pleasures unfolding in splendid if fake-classical architecture and involving invincible heroes, scheming villains, pretty damsels, wily seductresses, and menacing monsters had not been this easily available before. Cinema and its offspring, television, have proven the most fertile ground for reimagining and reinventing antiquity, not least by means of increasing technological wizardry such as computer-generated images. Long-running television series such as *Hercules: The Legendary Journeys* and its spin-off, *Xena: Warrior Princess*, animated Disney films such as John Musker and Ron Clements's *Hercules* (1997) and its sequels, and big-screen extravaganzas such as Wolfgang Petersen's *Troy* (2004) all attest to our continuing fascination with ancient myth.

To provide a comprehensive overview of films of Greek myth in this chapter is impossible. It is also unnecessary, for several surveys already exist.[1] Instead, I will turn to representative examples of mythological films to illustrate some of their major aspects. A few of the films are works of art; others are sophisticated or revealing in surprising ways. But they all require viewers to go along with changes, simplifications, inventions, and contradictions of original sources. If we are willing to accept the films for what they are and what they want to be, their study is worth our while. Pedants and churls may tear their hair, but they are not the audience for which these films or this chapter are intended.

THE NATURE OF MYTHOLOGICAL CINEMA

Filmic representations of antiquity are adaptations of classical sources, invented stories, or a combination of both. Most are fanciful and partly or completely contradict ancient factual or textual evidence. This has always been the case in the cinema, but it is more significant today because films are now the most influential way in which we tell stories. As a scholar of Homer recently put it: "At the beginning of literature, when heroic poetry reached society as a whole...society *listened*; in the twentieth century society *views*....the modern heroic medium is film, and not necessarily the productions that are held in highest critical regard."[2] A cinema scholar sees the most important aspect of historical film in "the use of historical understanding in the life of a society" – that is, of the society that makes such films.[3] The same goes for adaptations of literature, including myth: modern uses of ancient texts say something about ourselves. So demands for authenticity in historical films or for fidelity in literary adaptations are beside the point. They fail to take into account the nature of film as a narrative medium that needs creative freedom to tell its stories effectively. Factual or textual correctness is neither a necessary nor a sufficient condition to ensure the quality of the result.

The tradition of imagining alternatives to well-attested and even canonical versions of myth goes back to antiquity itself. Our surviving texts reveal different or mutually exclusive variants of certain parts of or individual moments in a myth, and we have visual evidence of myths or versions of myths unattested in any text. It is therefore difficult to maintain that certain accounts of a myth are correct and that others are false or wrong. In antiquity, alternate versions spread far and wide throughout literature and the visual arts, as the texts of playwrights, mythographers, and epic and lyric poets and the works of sculptors and painters attest. A case in point is the variety of ancient portrayals of Odysseus, from hero of the *Odyssey* to villain on the Athenian stage.[4] This tradition has never ceased. Today, even complex myths can be told or retold entirely in images. Italian director Vittorio Cottafavi, who made several films about ancient history and myth, aptly described this phenomenon as "neo-mythologism."[5]

Genre fiction, whether in texts or images, has to rely on certain stereotypes, standard ingredients of plot and style that audiences have come to expect. Mythological cinema provides us with numerous examples of such formulas. Duccio Tessari, one of the most prolific contributors of stories and screenplays to a number of the best-known Italian mythic-historical epics from the late 1950s to the mid-1960s and later a writer and director of adventure and action films in several genres, once devised "a kind of handbook collecting the basic points that 'make' a historical film."[6] Tessari's Fifteen Commandments, as we might call them, apply equally to historical and mythological films because the one kind is just as fictionalized as the other and combines ancient source material with a freewheeling invention of characters, settings, and plots. Tessari's points are instructive:

1. Always begin with a scene of violence: a slave killed by guardsmen, the rebels' assault on the palace, the destruction of a bridge.
2. The love story should never be limited to only two people. Better to present one woman loved by two men than two women in love with the same man.
3. The colors of costumes should be well distinguished: white or yellow for the good characters, black or red for the bad. The public must recognize at once the characters whose sides they take.
4. Many supporting characters surround the protagonist. For these roles hire stage actors. There are [several] good ones . . . they cost little, do not waste time, learn their lines, and dub themselves [in postproduction].
5. Don't give the public time to ask why something has happened. After a crash have a lion leaping onto the scene, then a duel, finally a fire.
6. Wild animals are very useful: jaguars, lions, elephants. Horses have fallen a little out of favor: they almost don't appear any more in battle scenes but only as means of transportation.
7. The classic *coup de théatre* in a scene – a bad character revealed as good and vice versa – is to be reserved for the second half of the film, the battle or the fire invariably for the end.
8. Of female characters there should be at least two: one elderly and a bitch, one young and innocent and a whiner.

At the end the bad woman redeems herself by dying in order to save the young one.

9. Always use a lot of smoke and a lot of fire: a brazier, burning cloths, a red-hot spear are worth more than any kind of dialogue.

10. The main character must be strong like Superman, clever like a detective in Mickey Spillane, intelligent like a rocket scientist, ironic and cultured like Voltaire, irresistible like Rudolph Valentino, loyal almost like a boy scout.

11. A river or a mountain range is always pleasing. The river is better: it's long, goes well with CinemaScope, and enriches the color.

12. Two comic characters as a pair are obligatory: they quarrel frequently with each other but at the end one dies to save the other. A child, a foundling, is [also] useful.

13. Take care that the make-up people retrieve the blood from scenes of violence: it costs 6,000 *lire* a liter and can be used at least one more time.

14. Female extras must be extremely pretty. It's better if under their tunics they don't wear a bra. But pay attention that chest and legs are always well covered, at least by a thick veil. The censors' tolerance only goes a little above the knee.

15. Save dangerous scenes for the last days of shooting: if actors get hurt, the insurance company pays, and now the film is finished.[7]

Tessari delivers sound advice in a humorous way, revealing both the constraints inherent in the making of historical-mythological films and their appeal to creators and audiences. With the peplum as with all genre fiction, familiarity does not breed contempt but a comfortable sense of feeling at home in an otherwise alien world. But what about the gods, whom Tessari does not mention?

GODS: PRESENCES AND ABSENCES

The portrayal of gods is more problematic to filmmakers and viewers than any other aspect of mythological cinema. The Greeks famously created their gods in their – that is, the Greeks' – own image, and the gods are described in human terms and usually appear in human shape. So there is nothing wrong with actors playing them in films. Still, gods can be distracting or may look ridiculous to audiences who do not believe in them, have a hazy understanding of their functions or characters, and immediately recognize familiar actors. Even an actor of such high reputation as Laurence Olivier, who plays Zeus in Desmond Davis's *Clash of the Titans* (1981), runs the risk of coming across as little more than a human with delusions of grandeur. Wearing swirling robes and a false beard, he turns into a Big Daddy on Olympus, if with some nifty superpowers up his long sleeve. So the process of humanizing gods on film tends to fall short of doing justice to their complexity. The Olympian family too easily turns into a more or less functional and occasionally dysfunctional modern family: a henpecked husband (Zeus), a nagging wife (Hera), and a bunch of unruly children. Most of them do not even make it onto the screen in any one film; only those gods tend to appear who are indispensable for the plot. All others are likely to vanish or provide mere background color in an occasional scene. (In *Clash of the Titans*, several of them stand around on Olympus and have little to do or say.) Wolfgang Petersen, director of *Troy*, a loose adaptation of the *Iliad*, has summarized the dilemma filmmakers face in this regard:

> Do you remember how Laurence Olivier as Zeus descended from the clouds in *Clash of the Titans*? At [seeing] this, the sixteen-year-old filmgoers today would giggle or yawn. They want to see how Brad Pitt as Achilles takes his destiny in his own hand; they want Orlando Bloom [as Paris] to fight and then run away because he is a coward – and not because the gods command him to.
>
> I think that, if we could consult with him up there, Homer would be the first today to advise: "Get rid of the gods." He knew exactly how stories were to be told in his time. The gods are permanently present [in *Troy*], in the dialogue. But the audience today can no longer deal with gods jumping out of the clouds and interfering in the duel between Hector and Achilles.
>
> I imagine Homer sitting up there on Olympus, looking down on our project, smiling, and saying: Hmmm, not bad. He wrote down his story only a few hundred years after it all happened, and you can see clearly that he did everything to make his story gripping for the audience of his time. We tried to do the exact same thing. In this sense he could under-stand us.[8]

457

The god most prominent in the dialogue of Petersen's film is Apollo, although he is never seen on screen except as a large gilded statue that suffers the neo-mythological indignity of decapitation by Achilles' sword. Achilles' mother Thetis is the one goddess who makes it onto the screen, if only in a single brief scene.

Yet the rule of gods over humans may find telling representations along the lines of modern life. In Don Chaffey's *Jason and the Argonauts* (1963), Zeus and Hera, a bickering couple, engage in a power play by means of a kind of cosmic game of chess. They move figures of Jason and other humans and of the Argo around a large board with a map of the Mediterranean world. Ray Harryhausen, the animation expert and chief creative artist for the film, has explained the rationale behind this set-up:

> We wanted to have a physical means by which the gods are seen to play with the fates of mankind. We accomplished this with a chess-like board game played by Hera and Zeus . . . which reflected the events on Earth. . . . It was important to the story that the human characters feared the gods but also saw them as vulnerable and fickle by treating the mortals as chess pieces . . . the chessboard . . . communicated to the audience that a deadly game was being played by the gods for the hearts and lives of the Greeks.[9]

Years later Harryhausen invented another revealing metaphor for divine power over human fate in *Clash of the Titans*, the earlier film's companion piece: "I came up with the idea of using a miniature arena. Behind this 'arena of life' were niches containing hundreds of other characters reflecting all the Greek legends. Zeus would put the figures in the arena, where the gods would control their destinies"[10] (Figure 21). Zeus even crushes one figurine in his hand, thereby killing the man it represents.

Jason and the Argonauts gives its viewers another clever modern analogy. In Book 8 of the *Iliad*, Zeus comfortably settles on Mt. Ida outside Troy and surveys the battle between Trojans and Greeks, "looking out over the city of Troy and the ships of the Achaians."[11] Homer's Zeus here resembles the viewer of a peplum, taking delight in watching the heroic exploits on the battlefield purely for the sake of spectacle. His position affords him a panoramic overview of the Trojan War that corresponds to that of the filmgoer looking at a long shot composed for the CinemaScope screen. But the Zeus of *Jason and the Argonauts* need not leave Mt. Olympus, for he and Hera have a decorative indoor pool in their "living room," whose rectangular surface yields bird's-eye views of the mortals over whose story and fate these gods contend (Figure 22). In other words, they have a kind of home theater. The aspect ratio of its "screen" is virtually identical to that of the film in which they appear. Alternatively, we may think of a television set, which Zeus and Hera turn on and off. (They move their outstretched hand laterally across the pool's surface.) This ingenious invention, patterned on technology appropriate for a visual medium, is retroactively incorporated into a pretechnological world. In *Clash of the Titans*, Harryhausen uses a related idea to visualize the gods' power over humans, because the building he calls the "arena of life" is really a theater.

By contrast, the absence of gods from films reveals modern sensibilities concerning divine influences on human characters and their deeds, as Petersen has already told us. Most of the religious differences between antiquity and today derive from the replacement of polytheism by more rigid monotheistic belief systems. Neither Greeks nor Romans had any sacred scriptures that prescribed rules of behavior or contained absolute dogma. And today we believe in the concept of a free will that leaves decisions, especially those about good and evil, largely to ourselves. The Greeks and Romans had a different view: divine will, even if it is called destiny or fate, is decisive. It may be incomprehensible or senseless, but gods are not accountable. ("The gods of Olympus are mysterious, and their motives are erratic," a character explains in *Clash of the Titans*.) The myth of Oedipus is the most familiar example. By contrast, a modern God must be wholly good and just. It is not in his essence to punish or destroy someone decent, and so, unlike ancient gods, he may not be capricious or vindictive. God is not morally questionable. As a result, what we would regard as indefensible or unfair behavior of ancient gods is not likely to make it onto the screen.

Closely related to any modern omission of gods is the removal of double motivation or overdetermination, a famous feature of Homeric storytelling in which a certain act or decision is attributed both to human and to divine agency.[12] An example are the dying words of Patroclus, who identifies destiny and Apollo but also two mortals, chiefly Hector, as his killers.[13] Modern rationalism is likely to find this puzzling or self-contradictory. So we need not be surprised if, for instance, in *Helen of Troy*, the 1956 film directed by Robert Wise and the 2003 television film directed by John Kent Harrison, and in Petersen's *Troy* Helen elopes with Paris because the two fall in love, not because the goddess Aphrodite forces this to happen. (The Judgment of Paris is omitted from the big-screen versions.) As a result, Helen's husband Menelaus has to be shown as unsuitable for her: he is too old, does not love or understand her, is liable to have casual affairs (despite being married to the most beautiful woman in the world), or all of the above. The films' perspective on their marriage is modern, as if Helen were the precursor of an upper-middle-class housewife living an unhappy life in suburbia.

Similarly, the cinematic death scenes of Hector and Achilles occur without divine interference. In Book 22 of the *Iliad*, the goddess Athena provides Achilles with decisive aid in his duel with Hector, the greatest of the Trojan heroes. Hector notices this and is dismayed. No god helps him, and he knows that he has no chance to survive. The one-sided participation of a divine power makes this duel an utterly unfair business. The omission of Athena seems to redistribute the odds against Hector somewhat, satisfying our demands for poetic justice. In the case of Achilles' death, of which we know from non-Homeric sources, Apollo enables Paris to kill Achilles. But Apollo's absence from this moment, an important action point for any film about the Trojan War, makes it more difficult for an audience to suspend its disbelief. For one thing, Achilles is a far superior fighter. For another, it is virtually impossible to accept that someone will die from an arrow to his heel. Incorporating Apollo at this time in a believable fashion would have balanced the scales between Achilles and Paris and would have lent the heel wound at least a measure of that credibility that we are willing to grant tales involving the supernatural. The depiction of Achilles' death in *Troy* without Apollo is therefore telling. For the sake of realism, Paris shoots several arrows into Achilles' body, including the expected one. Achilles does not die from the wound in his foot but from his other wounds. The fact that we see him pull out all of Paris' arrows except the one sticking in his heel is crucial: it shows us how the death of a practically invincible hero may have come about realistically and how it could have given rise to a famous myth about this death. So a story that is incredible if we remove the gods has been made credible without any recourse to them. Such manipulation of the myth concerning Achilles' death is nothing new. A simpler variant had occurred in Giorgio Ferroni's *La guerra di Troia* (*The Trojan War* or *The Trojan Horse*, 1961), in which a line of dialogue informs viewers that Paris' arrow was poisoned.[14]

MONSTERS

Like mythology, the cinema is fundamentally a purveyor of action stories. Archetypes about heroes and their deeds appear in many film genres. As Tessari's points and Cottafavi's expression "neo-mythologism" show, filmmakers follow their own rules when they make mythological films and do not consider themselves bound by their sources. In the process, they become adaptors of stories comparable to the ancient poets themselves, who took the materials for their epics or dramas from older versions of myth, including orally transmitted ones. A filmmaker can even become a godlike creator – that is, a "poet" in the word's literal sense of "maker" – when he gives life to heroes, monsters, or even gods in a process aptly named "animation" (from Latin *anima*, "soul" or "life force"). Harryhausen has described this creative process, contrasting his art of stop-motion animation with later computer-generated effects:

> To bring a creation to life is a rare gift, indeed a miracle that the very gods of Olympus would have been envious of. I was blessed with wanting to do just that and, even more incredibly, being able to. . . . for all the wonderful achievements of the computer, the process creates creatures that are too realistic and for me that makes them unreal because they have lost one vital element – a dream quality. Fantasy, for me, is realizing strange beings . . . removed from the 21st century . . . [and] creatures from the mind. . . . Stop-motion supplies the perfect breath of life for them, offering a look of pure fantasy because their movements are beyond anything we know. . . . The way the creatures moved encouraged a sense that one was watching a miracle, but when the miraculous becomes commonplace, the concept of miracles ceases to be miraculous.[15]

Harryhausen's mention of Olympus is echoed by Petersen's reference to Homer on Olympus – as if the ancient poet and the modern filmmaker were both godlike creators. They are. Harryhausen has even said about himself: "I call it [his work] the Zeus Complex because the ancient Greeks used to think the gods manipulated their life down on earth and the gods were just big people . . . looking down on earth and saying, 'You go there, and you go there, and this is your destiny,' so perhaps I have a Zeus Complex."[16] Harryhausen naturally turned to Greek myth for his projects. (Among his earliest works was a short retelling of the story of King Midas.) "Greek and Roman mythology," he has said, "contained a vivid world of adventure with wonderful heroes, villains and, most importantly, lots of fantastic creatures. . . . Because myths are usually very episodic and lack strong continuity, such stories need some degree of manipulation" if they are to succeed with audiences.[17] But these myths "contained characters and fantastic creatures that were ideal for cinematic adventures."[18]

Harryhausen is the creator of a number of monsters inspired by Greek myth: the Hydra, several Cyclopes, the Harpies, Medusa, and Cerberus (with the neo-mythologist name Dioskilos, that is, "Double-Headed"). But the one accomplishment that best shows Harryhausen's understanding of the epic nature of ancient myth is his recreation of the bronze giant Talos in *Jason and the Argonauts*. The film's source is the *Argonautica* by Apollonius of Rhodes, a Hellenistic scholar and epic poet. Jason, Medea, and the Argonauts encounter Talos on Crete, from which he attempts to keep all seafarers by throwing rocks at their ships.[19] In Apollonius, Talos is the last menace to the Argonauts, but the episode is only an interlude of 51 lines, as if Apollonius had become tired of his own epic. Since he tells a famous story to learned readers closely familiar with its details, Apollonius could not simply leave this episode out. (Nick Willing's 2000 television version of *Jason and the Argonauts* omits it, presumably either because his audience never heard of Talos or because Harryhausen's Talos was too daunting a precursor.) But Apollonius' heart is clearly not in the telling. His Talos is a one-dimensional figure, a standard monster of myth. This part of the *Argonautica* leaves modern readers cold. (It probably did not do much for ancient readers, either.) Apollonius focuses not on Jason, his main hero, or on Talos, but on Medea, who makes Talos fall victim to her sorcery from a distance. She casts a spell on Talos while being well out of danger. Talos hits his ankle against a sharp rock, his life blood (*ichor*) drains away, and he collapses and dies. In an epic, the unheroic manner of his death is anticlimactic.

Harryhausen, however, rises to the occasion. Talos is the Argonauts' first challenge on their journey into supernatural dangers and shows Harryhausen's animation to spectacular effect.[20] In the adventure on the Isle of Bronze, which substitutes for Apollonius' Crete, Talos becomes an almost tragic hero in his own epic-within-an-epic because Harryhausen manages to give the bronze giant a full-fledged personality. Disturbed by Hercules and Hylas, who trespass into and steal from a treasury of the gods which Talos guards – this is the filmmakers' invention that sets the scene – the statue of Talos comes to life to do what any epic hero would consider his duty: punish the intruders for their crime and hubris. Talos is not just an ogre but an instrument of divine retribution with a sense of justice, out to right a wrong. When Hercules and Hylas run away, Talos follows them and comes upon the rest of the

Argonauts. Harryhausen now conveys to his viewers another side of Talos' character. He is not only menacing but also smart. When he sees the Argonauts trying to row out of the bay into which they have sailed, he heads them off at its opening to the sea and lifts the Argo out of the water. Brawn and brains together make Talos appear invincible. So far, he has been a highly effective threat to the Argonauts, whom Harryhausen has put at great risk through close proximity to Talos (Figure 23). But now comes the turning point. Having received vital information about Talos' vulnerable heel from Hera, Jason devises an attack. The Argonauts taunt Talos, who was ready to leave them alone, and provoke him into coming after them. They want to distract him so that Jason can approach him unnoticed and drain the *ichor* from Talos' heel. In this they succeed, and Talos is doomed. Harryhausen shows us the bronze giant desperately struggling for breath. He appears to be suffocating, throwing both hands up to his throat as if to loosen a noose around his neck. But in vain. Cracks appear along his body. Talos crumbles into pieces and falls to the ground. Crushing Hylas, he succeeds in getting even with one of his tormentors.

Talos' drawn-out agony affects an audience differently from his quicker death in Apollonius. The two die in like manner: each "for a while [swayed] from side to side on his unwearying feet, but then collapsed strengthless with a thunderous crash," to quote Apollonius.[21] But while readers are unlikely to be moved, viewers respond emotionally. Talos, grasping his throat and then cracking apart, turns into a figure of pity. We are meant to feel sympathy for the helpless giant and regret that he has been taken in unfairly. The effect is the more astonishing in that Harryhausen cannot give different facial expressions to a bronze figure; Talos' features remain rigid throughout his ordeal.[22] The episode is a convincing demonstration that a modern visual retelling of an ancient story can surpass the original.

HEROES: EPIC AND TRAGEDY

Standard film adaptations of ancient hero myths tend to be much less sophisticated. Most of them provide visual and narrative pleasures that are simpler if more risqué than those in Harryhausen's kind of cinema. Sex and titillation have always been effective at the box office, especially in Catholic Italy and Puritan America. In mythological films, musclemen and curvaceous ladies are on prominent display and afford greater spectacles than action, sets, or special effects. Ladies sport low-cut dresses. Stars and starlets of both sexes appear in miniskirts, with the men's generally tinier than the women's. The casting of male body-builders and buxom actresses is a requirement for such films. Perhaps the most revealing instance is Carlo Ludovici Bragaglia's *Gli amori di Ercole* (*The Loves of Hercules*, 1960), in which American bodybuilder Mickey Hargitay, a former Mr. Universe, plays Hercules and his wife Jayne Mansfield plays his true love but also an evil seductress. She is equally pneumatic as either. It seems that Tessari was too timid in his Point 14. Censors could wield powerful scissors, but they had to retreat as hemlines advanced, necklines descended, and men's miniskirts turned into micro-minis.

The myths of Heracles or Hercules, the most popular of ancient heroes in the cinema, provide ample material for studies of ancient Greek masculinity and femininity.[23] So they do on the screen. Since the feminist revolution, however, women have made heroic strides in overcoming bastions of male power. They have done the same on our big and small screens. Women now fight alongside men on an equal level and can often show them a thing or two about courage, endurance, smartness, and sheer mastery of assorted weaponry. Hercules and all the other heroes have their counterparts in Amazons and warrior princesses.

Herculean epics go back to Giovanni Pastrone's *Cabiria* (1914), in which Maciste, a fictional strongman so named after Hercules by Gabriele D'Annunzio, made his first appearance.[24] But after World War II, ancient spectacles fell out of favor. Fascist Italy had claimed antiquity as its own justification, making it questionable to many. Later, Neo-realist cinema had made ancient heroes outdated. If antiquity was to have a rebirth on Italian screens, something firmly established and unlikely to be manipulated politically was called for. In 1954 veteran director Mario Camerini made *Ulisse* (*Ulysses*) with Italian and American stars. Among the screenwriters was Ennio De Concini, who did not take the epic subject as seriously as his director wished and who made fun of Greek myth in his contributions to the script. Camerini fired him. But De Concini got his revenge, as it were, by turning to the figure of Hercules, in whom another director, Pietro Francisci, had been interested as well. Both had already collaborated on historical spectacles. In 1958, they made film history with *Le fatiche di Ercole* (*Hercules*; literally, "The Labors of Hercules"), which became an immense success. Their sequel, *Ercole e la regina di Lidia* (*Hercules and the Queen of Lydia* or, more dramatically, *Hercules Unchained*), followed the next year. Both films starred American bodybuilder Steve Reeves, whose photograph Francisci had seen on the cover of a bodybuilding magazine with the heading: "The body of Hercules and the face of an angel." Reeves, a former Mr. America, Mr. World, and Mr. Universe, is still the quintessential celluloid Hercules to most aficionados (Figure 24). When savvy producer Joseph E. Levine exported the two films to the American market – "Mighty Saga of the World's Mightiest Man" proclaimed giant billboards for the first – the genre of muscleman epics swept theaters for years.[25] With their various and interchangeable heroes – Hercules, Maciste, Samson, Ursus, Goliath, and others – these films even stayed within the tradition of classical art. The famous Farnese Hercules, for example, a Roman marble copy of a fourth-century-BC bronze statue by Lysippus called "Heracles Resting," shows us the father of all modern bodybuilders: a massive physique with bulging muscles but with a disproportionately small head – all brawn, little brain.

The appeal of Herculean heroes rests largely on their being a combination of Robin Hood, Buffalo Bill, Tarzan, Superman, James Bond, and their band of brothers from innumerable genre stories, novels, and films. An Italian film scholar wittily but accurately summarizes the connections between Francisci's Hercules and his ancient model:

> Hercules is a unique personality: a man tall, big, muscular, endowed with terrible strength, irascible and vindictive but with a calf's heart, a lover of quiet just like a civil servant, who is forced, a little by fate, a little by bad luck, to lead a dog's life. Troubles happen to him one after another, he has to kill himself with labors, and on top of that he runs into every kind of rascal.
>
> He is not very smart, and it is easy to deceive him. He carries out the heaviest labors and does not get paid; he gets robbed, his lovers betray him, and his wife, in an attack of jealousy, kills him. . . .
>
> According to legend, Hercules carried out twelve tremendous labors, but perhaps his most stupendous feat is the thirteenth . . . : brought to the screen in 'scope and color, the mythical hero has again raised up, at a single stroke, our already crisis-shattered film industry by throwing wide open the gates of the American market.[26]

Muscleman epics have received large amounts of derision from film critics and historians and from the few classical scholars who have deigned to watch one.[27] But we should be hesitant to dismiss all these films. The better ones manage at least in part to avoid the naïve plots, clichéd dialogue, and silly ogres of the worst. A few are even labors of love. Their limitations, such as small budgets and short shooting schedules, called forth their makers' creative impulses. One of them represents the best in mythological epic. "The masterpiece of the Italian spectacular," as it has been called, is *Ercole alla conquista di Atlantide* (*Hercules Conquers Atlantis*, 1961), directed and cowritten by Vittorio Cottafavi, "the poet of the spectacular."[28] Its director enjoys cult status among the cognoscenti.[29]

In this film Hercules and Androclus, king of Thebes, set out on a journey to deal with a powerful threat to the very survival of Greece. They eventually reach Atlantis, a hidden island of rocks, caves, and desert. Its rulers, led by the evil queen Antinea, practice human sacrifice to placate Proteus, a shape-shifting god whom Hercules kills.[30] But more important is the cult of Uranus, a god of cosmic terror, who also demands human lives. This god is behind the menace to humanity, as Hercules learns when he begins to come into conflict with Antinea and her henchmen and is told what lies in store for mankind:

> Do you think that you can fight Atlantis with the puny strength of your human muscles? . . . You will perish in a sea of blood, which will cleanse the earth. . . . And the heavens will be on fire. . . . A new god will arise from the chaos: Uranus. He will . . . rule the skies.

Soon Hercules finds out that a living rock is the source of all danger. It is a congealed drop of Uranus' blood that had fallen on Atlantis when Uranus, one of the Titans who ruled before the Olympian gods, was overthrown. A priest describes it as "the source of all good and all evil," containing "all the glories of heaven and all the horrors of evil." It is master of life and light but also of death. Hercules overcomes its power, and in the process Atlantis is consumed by a fiery apocalypse.

Cottafavi's film is a prime example of neo-mythologism, but it is more. It exemplifies a society's understanding of the past in modern terms. The Atlantis from whose sinister threat Hercules saves the world reflects the twentieth century in two major aspects. In 1961, at the height of the Cold War, Uranus was very topical. The one power that quite literally could cause the end of the world was nuclear power, and for the film the name Uranus was chosen, as Cottafavi said, in analogy to uranium, an element crucial for the building of atomic bombs.[31] Our ability to split the atom is indeed the source of good and evil, expressing all glories and horrors. The atomic flash, brighter than a thousand suns, even has a film analogy in the light emanating from the stone of blood. It kills one character on the spot: "When the light touched him, he dissolved into nothing and vanished," says Hercules. The destruction of Atlantis represents a contemporary warning: those who think they can tame and use apocalyptic powers that really remain beyond their control will find themselves on the brink of annihilation. Antinea's megalomania, in which she wants to involve Hercules as her lover by sharing with him unlimited power, is the ultimate case of hubris: "One day we will rule over all men and all gods."

The filmmakers' atomic perspective on Atlantis is enough justification for recasting an ancient myth for modern audiences. But talk about the earth being cleansed in a sea of blood alerts us to another side of modern history. Such cleansing had come about in two closely related totalitarian ideologies, Nazism and, to a lesser degree, Fascism. New kinds of men with almost godlike powers had arisen in Italy and Germany out of the bloody chaos of World War I and proposed eventually to rule the world after exterminating all opposition. The rulers of Atlantis are "breeding a new race" for the postapocalypse that is "invulnerable, invincible." This will be, in Antinea's words to Hercules, "the chosen race, born from the blood of Uranus," which will then rule the world. This master-race ideology effectively complements the film's nuclear theme. Antinea commands an army of soldiers who resemble a specific master race that many in the audience will have seen in action not that long ago: blond, tall, wearing black helmets and dark uniforms. They look robotic and are indistinguishable from each other, a force of super-warriors. Two other scenes reinforce this historical analogy. A large number of the population are kept in a primitive outdoor prison; they have become disfigured after being used for medical experiments to bring about the new race. Later the queen's troopers slaughter them in large numbers. The images of them lying dead on the ground evoke comparable images of concentration-camp victims, although they are not as harrowing. (They cannot be in this kind of film.) At a later point Hercules and his son Hyllus find themselves imprisoned in a subterranean dungeon, into which a dangerous vapor is creeping at ground level. To us, this looks like a gas chamber. Cottafavi carefully prepared us for these modern overtones in an earlier scene when he showed the effect that something like chemicals can have on the human body. Antinea condemns an incompetent officer to submersion in a kind of acid bath that instantly turns him into a skeleton.

Despite these serious aspects, Cottafavi's film is anything but a moralizing tract. The participation of Tessari in the screenplay alone would have prevented that. Rather, the film fully delivers as epic spectacle. Viewers receive an early hint during the credits when a Miss Glamor is named among the cast. And the film can boast the most stupendous chariot ever driven on the screen, once at top speed: it is drawn by no fewer than twelve white or dappled stallions. Cottafavi also turned the film into one of the most enjoyable comic romps about a mythic hero. He and Tessari give us an adroit mixture of comedy, action, thrills, and romance. Hercules' teenage son Hyllus, for instance, provides the romance; a braggart midget adds comic relief. The film opens with a lengthy tavern brawl that need not shun comparison with its obvious model, the saloon fights of Western films. On the soundtrack, sensuous instrumental and choral music accompanying the tavern dancers sets an exotic and erotic atmosphere that the film will sustain throughout. Electronic music will later convey the presence of supernatural danger and mystery. An attractive color design, fanciful costumes, and a magnificent set for the palace of Atlantis also stand out. The palace décor, for instance, features stylish, if free, renditions of the Lions' Gate at Mycenae and the downward-tapering columns of Minoan Knossos. Most unusual are wall reliefs of panthers, whose body posture and facial features are taken directly from the panthers found on ancient Corinthian black-figure vases. Here they appear hundreds of times larger than their originals, and the effect is equally eerie and elegant. All this serves a thematic purpose as well, for the splendor is only a façade that covers moral emptiness (Figure 25). The barrenness of nature reveals the true lifelessness of society on Atlantis.

Cottafavi sticks to the archetype of the reluctant hero, but with a comic twist. His Hercules is chiefly interested in domesticity (he wants to stay in Thebes with his family instead of going on another dangerous trip), eating (the humor of the opening brawl derives in part from the fact that Hercules does not participate but only wants to eat his meal in the midst of the ongoing melee), and sleeping. But he could not be a mythic or cinematic hero if he were successful in this. Once embarked on his journey, he rises to all challenges. Cottafavi's view of Hercules indicates that both ancient and modern sensibilities are required for successful neo-mythologism:

> The message of Hercules is: be brave, and be children of god, and it will go well with you. Christianity, too, declares us to

be children of God, if less in a physical than in a spiritual sense. But as far as strength and power are concerned, Hercules lived at a time in which strength was everything. There was no machinery, only arms and hands. In fact, in my films Hercules also takes on agricultural labors, those of the animals working a farm. He was a domestic god.[32]

Scholars may not entirely agree with this assessment, but it works well for popular culture. Moreover, Cottafavi was aware of the comic side in the ancient myths of Heracles:

You know, making fun of something is one of the elements of loving it. If you don't love something you don't have the desire to make fun of it. That Hercules today seems a bit ridiculous is a fact, but you don't think he was ridiculous at the time of the Greeks and Romans. Look at the legends: he was the son of a god, very strong, who was forced to clean the shit from the stables of Augias . . . Well, that's a bit ridiculous, isn't it? So I think that we, too, could amuse ourselves a bit with him. . . . Hercules is a man half serious, half a joker, but a joker in a good sense. . . . I have the feeling that Hercules is someone whom we know intimately. He's a friend.[33]

It is difficult to imagine a more concise summary of the timeless appeal of classical heroes. And if Cottafavi was aware of the importance of ancient legends and myths for us, he was equally aware of a filmmaker's responsibilities in retelling them: "We must not make political or ethical speeches, we must *be* political and ethical, then people will understand us more directly than through words."[34]

Hercules films may strike some viewers as insufficiently serious to do justice to the greatness of Greek literature or myth. They may prefer films of tragedy, a literary genre that takes most of its subject matter from myth. Screen adaptations of tragedy range over various styles and approaches from filmed, videotaped, or now digitized records of stage productions to fully cinematic reimaginings of their source texts.[35] They deserve a more extended discussion than is possible here, so I limit myself to a brief appreciation of one film, based on the most famous of all classical tragedies, Sophocles' *Oedipus the King* (or *Oedipus Rex*). This film, *Edipo re* (*Oedipus Rex*, 1967), was written and directed by Pier

Paolo Pasolini, essayist, novelist, dramatist, poet, and filmmaker. It is a personal work imbued with parallels to Pasolini's own life.[36] He shows us an archetypal story that is also a modern comment on the human condition. The film's prologue is set at the time of Pasolini's birth and infancy. Laius and Jocasta are patterned on Pasolini's parents: "The baby in the prologue is I, his father is my father, an infantry officer, and the mother, a schoolmistress, is my mother."[37] Pasolini also shows us his version of the origin of the Oedipus Complex when Laius, jealous of his son in whom he sees a rival for his wife's affections, pulls baby Oedipus by the ankles.

With Oedipus' exposure, Pasolini moves from modern Italy to a prehistoric society, in which he sets Oedipus' life until Oedipus has blinded himself. Non-Western music and a desert landscape tell us that we are now in a time of myth, not of reality. Pasolini's Oedipus is both an archaic figure and an Everyman, as the scene of Oedipus at Delphi illustrates. The oracle is not the magnificent sanctuary it was in antiquity but a tiny desert oasis. Apollo's priestess, the Pythia, wears a disconcerting double mask. For inspiration, she stuffs some strange substance into her mouth. When she has told Oedipus his fate, she laughs uproariously and with such great contempt that viewers instantly feel pity for Oedipus.

Michael Cacoyannis, the writer-director of three films based on tragedies by Euripides, has observed: "Pasolini did not make Greek tragedy. He made very striking films about the myths on which tragedy is based."[38] So Pasolini's Oedipus is not Sophocles' tragic hero but "an impetuous, unthinking, and violent hunter-warrior, product of a pre-literate society riddled with superstition, subject to forces beyond his understanding and control."[39] The film's long sequence at the cross-roads, in which Oedipus in a fit of rage kills his father Laius and all his attendants except one, best illustrates Pasolini's conception of Oedipus and the elemental nature of his environment and society. Remarkably, however, Pasolini adheres to Sophocles' conception of the tragic hero, for anger and a short temper characterize the protagonists of Sophocles' plays.[40]

In the film's epilogue, Oedipus, now blind but still wearing his ancient clothes, wanders through a modern city, then returns to the meadow where we had first seen him as an infant with his mother. This ending is indebted to Sophocles' *Oedipus at Colonus*, a play in which Oedipus is reconciled with the gods at the end of his life. *Edipo re* effectively illustrates Pasolini's concept of "the cinema of poetry" and is the most profound rendition of the Oedipus myth on film.[41]

UNDERWORLD AND AFTERLIFE

Ancient beliefs concerning what happens to humans after death provided little comfort. The Isles of the Blessed were not easily accessible to average mortals, and the Elysian Fields were largely reserved for epic heroes. Tartarus or Hades was a gloomy and forbidding place, best known for the extreme measures of punishment meted out to evildoers. Today, the myths of Tantalus, Sisyphus, and Ixion strike us as choice examples of pure sadism for the very futility that these sinners have to undergo. Eerie creatures such as Charon who ferried the dead across Styx, the River of Hate, the three-headed dog Cerberus, and assorted other monsters make it clear that this was a hellish place.

But its gloominess has long attracted visual representations, sometimes filtered through the eyes of Christianity. Michelangelo's *Last Judgment*, for example, includes Charon and Minos, one of the underworld judges. Gustave Doré's illustrations of Dante's *Inferno* exerted great influence on the cinema and exemplify how much filmmakers have relied on painting or drawing for their imagination. (Harryhausen, for instance, has acknowledged his debt to Doré.) With advancing technology came a veritable unleashing of harrowing horrors. In *Clash of the Titans*, for instance, Charon is a hooded skeleton, and Perseus defeats the screen's scariest Medusa in her lair in Hades. Much earlier, Guido Brignone's *Maciste all'inferno* (*Maciste in Hell*, 1925) fused Christianity (with a plot indebted to Dante) and antiquity (in the person of its titular hero) and showed devils and dragons galore. When Maciste returned to the underworld in Riccardo Freda's 1962 film of the same title, he encountered characters from classical myth (Sisyphus and Prometheus) among more generic infernal monsters. That is because this time Maciste descended from seventeenth-century Scotland, at that time ravaged by witchcraft; hence the film's alternate English title *The Witch's Curse*. For true peplum heroes, time or space travel is not a problem.

A hero's descent to the realm of the dead – *katabasis* or *nekyia* in Greek – is an archetypal theme in all mythology. The first instance in Greek literature occurs in Book 11 of the *Odyssey*. It is difficult to do justice to its moving and atmospheric quality on the screen, but one example stands out. This is *L'Odissea* (1968), an epic television film chiefly directed by Franco Rossi, the most accomplished adaptation of the *Odyssey* ever put on screen. It succeeds better than more famous films in its rendition of Book 11, abbreviated and free as it must be. Appropriately for its supernatural aspects, the whole sequence shows its own artifice. We are meant to realize that it was shot indoors in a studio, in contrast to the magnificent outdoor scenery filmed on Mediterranean locations. Rossi communicates to his viewers a sense of sorrow and loss in Odysseus' encounters with some of his closest friends and with his mother Anticleia. Rossi creates his supernatural atmosphere with a subdued visual style. The dominant colors are black, grey, and a washed-out blue. The actors who play the deceased deliver their lines without any emotion, a manner suitable to the dead. Nevertheless, Rossi does not neglect the horrifying side of Odysseus' *katabasis*. At its beginning we see the body of a black lamb, slaughtered to call up the spirits of the dead, and the pool of its blood. In a medium close-up, Tiresias' mouth is smeared with this blood after he has drunk from it. The chief technical effect to which Rossi resorts is double exposure. The dead have no bodies but are only shades, and the rocky background of Hades is visible through their silhouettes. This technique leads to a moving climax when Odysseus encounters his mother. Differently from the *Odyssey*, she appears as an image of quiet domesticity. Sitting in a simple chair and engaged in woolworking, she reminds us of Penelope. (Rossi is tasteful enough not to have Anticleia drink any blood.) During their conversation Odysseus kneels before her and begs to embrace her, but she explains that this is impossible for the dead. Homer's Odysseus remembers:

> So she spoke, but I, pondering in my heart, yet wished
> to take the soul of my dead mother in my arms. Three times
> I started toward her, and my heart was urgent to hold her,
> and three times she fluttered out of my hands like a shadow
> or a dream, and the sorrow sharpened at the heart within
> me. . . .[42]

In his adaptation of these lines Rossi shows what Homer tells. Odysseus appears briefly to be stroking his mother's knees and then putting his head on her lap, but since she is insubstantial his head sinks lower and lower until it touches the ground. Over complete silence Rossi now gives us a close-up of Anticleia looking down on her son. She, too, longs to embrace him but cannot, and the image of her shade fades from the screen. The moment achieves a high level of emotion without being in the least sentimental.

The best-known cinematic instance of *katabasis* in mythological adventure cinema is cult favorite Mario Bava's *Ercole al centro della terra* (1961).[43] The plot is standard fare. To save his sweetheart,

Hercules journeys to the underworld with Theseus and Odysseus' son Telemachus. They encounter Persephone and various monstrosities, return safe and sound against all odds, and finally defeat the evil king whose sinister machinations had caused all the trouble. But the film is remarkable for its immense visual flair. Bava had been a cinematographer famous for his extraordinary style, which he brought to the horror films and thrillers he later directed. On his Hercules film, Bava was his own cameraman and created just the right atmosphere, imaginatively overcoming budget limitations and plot clichés. He told his neo-mythologist tale in the style of a horror film. Christopher Lee, famous in film history as Dracula, is the archvillain, aptly named Lykos ("Wolf"). He wears a cape and approaches his victims with arms outstretched. Other vampire-like creatures can also be seen rising from their graves. Small wonder that Bava was hired to direct the Polyphemus episode of Rossi's *Odissea*. The animated Disney *Hercules* continues Bava's tradition with its portrayal of the underworld and of the villainous god Hades.

The examples selected so far show various approaches to the afterlife in ancient or pseudo-ancient settings. Modern ones occur as well. A unique achievement is *Orphée* (*Orpheus*, 1949), written and directed by poet, dramatist, and painter Jean Cocteau.[44] This film is a profound meditation on love, life, death, and the love of death. It brings aspects of modern culture and history to Greek myth and illustrates, literally through its filmed images and figuratively through its meaning, the original story's timeless validity. Cocteau's Orphée encounters the Princess, a mysterious woman, and her chauffeur Heurtebise. Both are emissaries of the underworld. Orphée and the Princess fall in love, just as Heurtebise falls in love with Orphée's wife Eurydice. In doing so, they knowingly transgress the laws of the underworld and are severely punished. To save him from death, the Princess renounces Orphée and reunites him with Eurydice; both stay alive but remember nothing. "The actions of the Princess, which actuate the drama," said Cocteau, "are taken by her of her own accord and represent free will. . . . The entire mystery of free will resides in this, that it seems that the thing that is *need not be*. . . . the Princess dares to substitute herself for destiny, to decide that a thing *may be*, instead of being."[45]

Guided by Heurtebise, Orphée descends to the underworld through "the zone." To separate this No Man's Land between life and death visually from the upper world, Cocteau makes imaginative use of a film technology that to us looks rather simple, although it was not. It includes double exposures, back projections, changes from positive to negative images, running film backwards, and slow motion. Technical limitations were the very inspiration for Cocteau to create a work of unrivaled visual poetry.[46]

Cocteau's conception of death and the underworld is more complex than it was in the original myth. Heurtebise, for instance, not only is an equivalent of Charon but also is more important for the story than even Eurydice. (He also loves her more than Orphée does.) The narrator, whose voice Cocteau provided himself, calls the Princess who falls in love with Orphée "his death"; Cocteau was adamant that she is not Death as such.[47] Since she has no power over the underworld, she is not an equivalent of Persephone. The underworld also carries overtones of modern bureaucracy. Three judges who form a tribunal that is loosely patterned on the three underworld judges in Greek myth wear dark business suits and sit behind an office table with files before them; they are joined by a kind of clerk who takes minutes and types out their paperwork. A partially analogous view appears in Marcel Camus' *Orfeu Negro* (*Black Orpheus* 1959), set during and shortly after the Brazilian carnival and fittingly shot in ravishing colors. Orfeu begins his descent from an office building that, as a kind of bureaucratic necropolis, stores vast amounts of personal files in disarray and neglect. "Fifteen floors of paper for nothing," Orfeu is told by his Charon. This film is the cinema's second poetic retelling of the Orpheus myth and forms an instructive contrast to Cocteau's, although to both directors creative reimagining of a myth's underlying themes is more important than merely modernizing it. With its unique visual and emotional poetry, their kind of neo-mythologism is different from that of all other films.

THE POWER OF CONVICTION

The survival of classical myth in modern society depends not only on educational institutions that preserve the tradition of the humanities in teaching and research but also, and probably much more, on the presence of myth in popular culture. So it is appropriate to conclude with statements by two epic-mythic filmmakers who point us back to Homer and Greek myth. Viewers who respond chiefly to the computerized special effects, graphic violence, rapid editing, and cranked-up sound deemed indispensable for today's blockbusters are likely to find in their words echoes of a distant age of innocence and in their films period pieces that are no longer "cool." But others will find more, for these directors' words make clear that their films are really discoveries about the nature of historical and mythological storytelling in moving images.

Italian writer-director Riccardo Freda, who was a sculptor before turning to film, addresses the difficulties and the appeal inherent in making films set in the distant past:

> The chief difficulty is ... to tell [the audience] something exceptional in a believable and acceptable manner, just like Homer, who is one of the greatest poets in the world. He did nothing but tell about heroic exploits and, if he hadn't had his power of conviction, these would be events, legends, which no one would accept. So for this reason it's much more difficult to make a costume film than a modern film – more difficult and more interesting. . . . The difficulty is to render plausible and close to ourselves characters who proceed in very different costumes, in an altogether strange décor. So it is necessary to reach the point to give them a way of saying and doing things that would at the same time be suitable to our own sensibilities and to these decorative elements. From that point on, instead of playing against the heroes, these aspects only enhance the appropriateness of the environment in which the characters develop. The secret of cinema is the gradual discovery of décor, of the world that surrounds the characters. The image must be a continual surprise to the eye.[48]

Ray Harryhausen corroborates Freda's observations. Under the heading "The Simulacrum of Life," an apt definition of cinema, he observes:

> Fantasy in art and literature is as old as mythology itself. Film fantasy, being a more recent form of expression, has the added excitement of utilizing a flowing image and being in a state of constant motion; of combining sight, sound and imagination. No other medium of expression can project the complications of the imaginative, the wondrous or the bizarre as well as the motion picture.[49]

These are heartfelt appreciations of mythological cinema. It is safe to assume that films based on Greek mythology will continue to be made and to find receptive audiences. The last words of Zeus spoken to Hera over their Olympian screen at the end of *Jason and the Argonauts* already predicted as much: "Let us continue the game another day."

FURTHER READING

The works here mentioned, together with those referred to in my notes, may aid readers in pursuing some of the aspects of mythological cinema addressed above in more detail: Mulvey (1975), often reprinted, for example, in Mulvey (1989) 14–26, is highly influential on the visual pleasures of cinema. Lucanio (1994) provides filmographic information and brief plot outlines of Italian epics. Ahl (1991) examines the appearances of gods on the screen, while Holtsmark (2001) discusses archetypes of the hero's descent to the Underworld in films set in antiquity and in recent or modern times. Durgnat (1963) is a well-known film scholar's brief appreciation of Hercules epics during their heyday; Wyke (1997) traces the modern body-builder tradition and its impact on cinema to the ancient Hercules. Passman (1991) and Futrell (2003) deal with film and television heroines. MacKinnon (1986) is a basic introduction to the best-known films of Greek tragedy, by now somewhat outdated. Evans (1977) provides information on Cocteau's Orphic films. Winkler (2005) applies Cottafavi's neo-mythologist perspective to Apollo and the Muses. Winkler (1985, 1996, 2004) examine basic features of classical hero myths and Homeric epic in the Western, the most archetypal film genre. Winkler (2006) deals with cinematic contexts of the *Iliad*.

NOTES

1   Foremost among these are Solomon (2001) 100–131 and Elley (1984) 52–66. Cf. also De España (1998) 103–63.
2   Hainsworth (1991) 148.
3   Sorlin (1980) ix.
4   The classic account of this is Stanford (1954).
5   Leprohon (1972) 174–9 discusses Cottafavi and his term "neo-mythologism." Cf. also Elley (1984) 13–24 (chapter entitled "Epic into Film").
6   Locatelli (1960) 14.
7   Locatelli (1960) 14–15 provides Tessari's points under the heading "Ten [!] Pieces of Advice for Those Who Want to Make a Historical Film." I have omitted the names of Italian stage actors in Point 4 and slightly corrected Tessari on personal names in Point 10. Here and throughout this chapter, all quotations from originally French, German, and Italian sources appear in my translations.
8   The three quotations are taken from interviews published in *Kölner Stadt-anzeiger* (May 14, 2004; http://www.ksta.de/artikel.jsp/id=1084203219381),

Berliner Morgenpost (May 12, 2004; http://morgenpost.berlin1.de/archiv2004/040512/feuilleton/story677622.html), and *Süddeutsche Zeitung* (May 10, 2004; http://www.sueddeutsche.de/kultur/artikel/607/31576). For the record, Zeus does not descend from the clouds in *Clash of the Titans*.

9   Quoted from Harryhausen and Dalton (2003) 155 and 261.

10 Harryhausen and Dalton (2003) 261–2.

11 *Iliad* 8.41–52; the last line of this passage is quoted from Lattimore (1951) 183.

12 On this cf. Edwards (1987) 135.

13 *Iliad* 16.849–50.

14 This rationalizing aspect goes further back. For example, in chapter 28 of *The Age of Fable* (1855), Thomas Bulfinch explained that Achilles died from a poisoned arrow.

15 Quoted from Harryhausen and Dalton (2003) 7–8 and 282. Cf. Harryhausen's further comment on the rise of computer animation in the 1980s at Harryhausen and Dalton (2003) 280: "The age of the hero was dead."

16 Quoted from a 2006 conversation with Harryhausen included on the DVD edition of Ernest B. Schoedsack's *Mighty Joe Young* (1949), a film on which Harryhausen worked.

17 Harryhausen in Harryhausen and Dalton (2003) 151. Cf. also this observation: "we do take 'liberties' because [such a] film has to appeal to general audiences, and you can't do that if you stick to every exact detail, as if Greek scholars were the only ones to view the picture" (174). Harryhausen remarks on the extensive manipulation of ancient myth in *Clash of the Titans* in Harryhausen and Dalton (2003) 261.

18 Harryhausen in Harryhausen and Dalton (2003) 261.

19 Apollonius, *Argonautica* 4.1638–88.

20 A detailed description with film stills, storyboard drawings, and models is at Harryhausen and Dalton (2003) 156–9. Harryhausen's inspiration for Talos had been the Colossus of Rhodes.

21 Apollonius, *Argonautica*, 4.1686–8. The quotation is from Hunter (1993) 138.

22 We may compare the psychological effect of masked acting in ancient tragedy; cf. Winkler (2002).

23 See in particular "Herakles: The Supermale and the Feminine" in Loraux (1995) 116–39 and 294–303 (notes). A classic of its kind, dealing chiefly with Perseus and Heracles, is Slater (1992). Cf. Rose (2001).

24 D'Annunzio, Italy's foremost man of letters, was involved in the film's production and changed Pastrone's original name from Ercole (Hercules) to Maciste. To D'Annunzio, Maciste's name was "a most ancient epithet of the demigod Hercules." This statement is based on the mention by Strabo, *Geography* 8.3.21, of a temple of Macistian Heracles (in Latin, *Macistus Hercules*) in the town of Makiston or Makistos (Latinized to Macistus) on the Peloponnesus. Stephanus of Byzantium, however, derives the town's name from an obscure figure in Greek mythology: Makistos (Latinized: Macistus), son of King Athamas and brother of Phrixus; see Meineke (1849) 428 (lines 11–15). Another, if less probable, explanation of the name Maciste is from Greek *mêchanê* (cf. Latin *machina*), which points to its bearer's strength.

25 The chief topic of Locatelli (1960) is an account of the origin and worldwide success of Francisci's Hercules films. My quotations are from Locatelli (1960) 13 and 17.

26 Locatelli (1960) 12.

27 Whitehall (1963) gives a critical, appreciative, and aptly titled introduction to the genre. Solomon (2001) 306–23 provides a convenient overview. Cf. also De España (1998) 431–52. A visual appreciation is the hour-long documentary *Kino Kolossal: Hercules, Maciste & Co.* (2000), directed by Hans-Jürgen Panitz and Inga Seyric.

28 Both quotations are from Whitehall (1963) 14 in the context of a highly favorable assessment of the film. For other examples, see Barr (1962), with reference to Cottafavi's Hercules as embodying the classical "Greek ideal of the *kaloskagathos*" (the man possessing physical and spiritual beauty as indications of his ethical perfection); Elley (1984) 58 (including the statement that the film has "the best-realised portrayal of Hercules in the cinema, perfectly capturing the essence of Greek mythology's most fallible yet constant hero"); Smith (2004) 129; and De España (1998) 114–15. I have used and here quote from a German-dubbed version of Cottafavi's film. The American one is shortened, has a different music score, adds a superfluous narrator, omits almost all the credits, and misspells the director's name. The film is loosely based on *L'Atlantide* (1919) by Pierre Benoît, a member of the French Academy. His novel, set in contemporary North Africa, was more or less faithfully adapted for cinema and television seven times between 1920 and 1992.

29 For testimony of Cottafavi's high reputation see, for example, Leprohon (1972) 178–9. Writer-director Riccardo Freda called Cottafavi "a man of astonishing intelligence and culture" at Lourcelles and Mizrahi (1963) 30. Rondolino (1980) makes it evident that these are not overstatements; he discusses Cottafavi's mythic-heroic films in detail at 62–74. Cottafavi later directed a number of highly regarded adaptations of Greek tragedy for Italian public television.

30 This is the only bad sequence in the film, fortunately very short. The forms of Proteus that Hercules battles include lion and dragon. But the lion seems to be on loan from a taxidermist, and the dragon is too small and too fake (a man in a scaly suit) to convey any menace. Cottafavi may have intended to parody Hercules a little; cf. his comments quoted below.

31 "It is supposed [in the film] that the blood of Uranus, killed by his son, forms uranium when falling to Earth." Quoted from Tavernier (1968–9) 61.

32 Quoted from Panitz and Seyric's film *Kino Kolossal.*

33 Quoted from Tavernier (1968–9) 64 (first ellipsis in original). Rondolino (1980) 72 discusses and quotes Tessari on bringing irony and satire to the subject.

34 Quoted from Guarner (1965) 20. This article is on Cottafavi's epic *I cento cavalieri* (1965), set in medieval Spain.

35 Solomon (2001) 259–74 surveys films of Greek tragedy. Cf. also De España (1998) 401–30 on various kinds of literary adaptations.

36 On this film, see Schwartz (1992) 505–17.

37 Quoted from Schwartz (1992) 509.

38 Quoted from McDonald and Winkler (2001) 81. Cacoyannis's films of Euripides are *Electra* (1962), *The Trojan Women* (1971), and *Iphigenia* (1977). The last is one of the greatest adaptations of classical tragedy.

39 Schwartz (1992) 510.

40 See Knox (1964), especially 21–7, and Knox (1957) 26–8.

41 On this cf. Pasolini's 1965 essay "The 'Cinema of Poetry,'" now in Pasolini (1988) 167–86. A comparable poetic approach, if with different stylistic expression, is to be found in Tony Harrison's *Prometheus* (1998), a "film/poem," as he calls it, of Aeschylus' *Prometheus Bound*. He describes his approach to poetry and cinema in Harrison (1998) xxiii–xxvii.

42 *Odyssey* 11.204–8; quoted from Lattimore (1967) 173.

43 The film's best-known English title (there are several) is *Hercules in the Haunted World*. Its screenplay was cowritten by Tessari.

44 Cocteau summarizes the main themes of *Orphée* in Cocteau (1992) 158; a synopsis by him appears at 197–8. On several occasions Cocteau called the cinema a modern Muse; see Cocteau (1992) 23, 123, and 56, and cf. 176–7 and 192–3. Our chief sources of the Orpheus myth in ancient poetry are Virgil, *Georgics* 4.453–527, and Ovid, *Metamorphoses* 10.1–85 and 11.1–66.

45 Quoted from Cocteau (1954) 128–9.

46 As Cocteau observed in Cocteau (1954) 102: "We had to give up our experiments . . . because they proved unusable. . . . I'll add, however, that such failures were useful in that they excited our imagination and set it going, compelling it to solve the problem of trick effects without resorting to any tricks." Cocteau describes the complex technical side of filming, especially regarding passages through the zone, in Cocteau (1954) 105–17.

47 For example, at Cocteau (1992) 155: "Death in my film is not Death represented symbolically by an elegant young woman, but the Death of Orphée. Each of us has our own which takes charge of us from the moment of birth."

48 Lourcelles and Mizrahi (1963) 20.

49 Harryhausen (1981) 127.

BIBLIOGRAPHY

Ackroyd, P. R. (1968) *Exile and Restoration*. Philadelphia.

Addison, J., R. Steele, et al. (1963) *The Spectator*, Gregory Smith. ed. 4 vols, London.

Agostini (1538) *Di Ovidio Le Metamorphosi . . . con le sue Allegorie. . . .* Venice.

Ahl, F. (1991) "Classical Gods and the Demonic in Film," in M. M. Winkler, ed., *Classics and Cinema*, 40–59. London.

Alanus de Insulis (1908) *The Complaint of Nature*, trans. D. M. Moffat. New York.

Alanus de Insulis (1935) *The Anticlaudian*, trans. W. Cornog. Philadelphia.

Alberg-Cornell, G. (1992) *Myth and Epos in Early Greek Art: Representation and Interpretation*. Jonsered.

Albricus of London (1532) *Allegoriae Poeticae*. London. Facsimile reprint: New York (1976).

Albricus of London (1681) *"De Deorum Imaginibus Libellus*, an abridgment of Albricus of London (1532)," in T. Munkerus, *Mythographi Latini*, 301–30. Amsterdam.

Alciati, Andrea (1492–1550) *The Latin Emblems, Indexes, and Lists*, trans. P. M. Daly, with V. Callahan and S. Cutler. Toronto (1985).

Alcock, S. E. (2002) *Archaeologies of the Greek Past: Landscape, Monuments, and Memories*. Cambridge.

Alcock, S. E., J. F. Cherry, and J. Elsner, eds. (2001) *Pausanias: Travel and Memory in Roman Greece*. Oxford.

Alexiou, M. 1974. *The Ritual Lament in Greek Tradition*. second ed., rev. by D. Yatromanolakis and P. Roilos (2002) Lanham MD.

Alighieri, P. (1978) *Il "Commentarium" di Pietro Alighieri*, R. della Vedova and M. T. Silvotti eds. Florence.

Allen, N. J. (1987) "The Ideology of the Indo-Europeans: Dumézil's Theory and the Idea of a Fourth Function." *International Journal of Moral and Social Studies* 2: 23–39.

Allen, N. J. (1996) "Romulus and the Fourth Function," in E. Polomé, ed., *Indo-European Religion after G. Dumézil*, 13–36. Washington, DC.

Allen, N. J. (2000) "Imra, Pentads and Catastrophes." *Ollodagos* 14: 278–308.

Allen, N. J. (2004) "Bhīṣma and Hesiod's Succession Myth." *International Journal of Hindu Studies* 8: 57–79.

Amyx, D. A. (1988) *Corinthian Vase-Painting of the Archaic Period*. Berkeley/Los Angeles.

Anderson, D. (1986) "Mythography or Historiography? The Interpretation of Theban Myths in Late Mediaeval Literature." *Florilegium* 8: 113–39.

Anderson, G. (2003) *The Athenian Experiment: Building an Imagined Political Community in Ancient Attica, 508–490 BC*. Ann Arbor, MI.

Andronikos, M. (1984) *Vergina: The Royal Tombs and the Ancient City*. Athens.

Andronikos, M. (1994) *Vergina II: The "Tomb of Persephone."* Athens.

Annas, J. (1982) "Plato's Myths of Judgment." *Phronesis* 27: 119–43.

Antonaccio, C. M. (1995) *An Archaeology of Ancestors: Tomb Cult and Hero Cult in Early Greece.* Lanham, MD.

Appadurai, A. (1981) "The Past as a Scarce Resource." *Man* 16: 201–19.

Arnold, M. (1858) *Merope.* London.

Arnold, M. (1861, reprint 1896) *On Translating Homer.* London.

Arnold, T. (1834) "Rugby School." *Quarterly Journal of Education* 7: 234–49.

Arnolphe of Orléans (11th century). "A Commentary on Ovid's *Metamorphoses*," in F. Ghisalberti, "Arnolfo d'Orléans, un cultore di secolo XII." *Memorie del R. Instituto Lombardi di Scienze e Lettere* (1932): 157–232.

Ashmole, B. (1972) *Architect and Sculptor in Classical Greece.* New York.

Athanassaki, L. (2004) "Deixis, Performance, and Poetics in Pindar's *First Olympian Ode.*" *Arethusa* 37: 317–41.

Athanassakis, A. N. (1983) *Hesiod: Theogony, Works and Days, Shield.* Baltimore.

Augustine, St. (354–430) *On Christian Doctrine*, trans. D. W. Robertson, Jr. Indianapolis (1958).

Austin, J. L. (1962) *How to Do Things with Words.* Oxford.

Bacon, Sir Francis(1561–1626) *On the Wisedome of the Ancients and On Principles and Origins, According to the Fables of Cupid and Coelum*, in *The Works of Francis Bacon*, 10 vols., ed. James Spedding et al. London (1861).

Barr, C. (1962) "*Hercules Conquers Atlantis.*" *Movie* 3: 29.

Barrett Browning, E. (1856) *Aurora Leigh.* Reprint: Oxford (1993).

Barsby, J. A. (1973) *Ovid: Amores I.* Oxford.

Bartholomaeus Anglicus (1326–1412) *On the Properties of Things*, trans. John de Trevisa, ed. M. C. Seymour et al. London (1975).

Bartowski, F. (1989) *Feminist Utopias.* Lincoln NE.

Bath, M. and D. Russell (1995) *Deviceful Settings: The English Renaissance Emblem and Its Contexts.* New York.

Batman, Stephan (1577) *The Golden Booke of the Leaden Gods.* London. Facsimile reprint: New York (1976).

Batman, Stephan (1582) *Batman uppon Bartholomae, His Booke De Proprietatibus Rerum.* . . . London.

Baumgarten, A. I. (1981) *The Phoenician History of Philo of Byblos.* Leiden.

Beard, M. (1995) "Re-reading (Vestal) virginity," in R. Hawley and B. Levick, B. (eds) *Women in Antiquity: New Assessments*, 166–77. Oxford.

Benson, J. L. (1970) *Horse, Bird and Man: The Origins of Greek Painting.* Amherst MA.

Benveniste, É. (1932) "Les classes sociales dans la tradition avestique." *Journal asiatique* 221: 117–34.

Benveniste, É. (1969) *Le vocabulaire des institutions indo-européennes*, 2 vols. Paris.

Berchorius, Petrus (d. 1362) *Ovidius Moralizatus*, trans. W. D. Reynolds. Ph.D. dissertation, Univ. of Illinois (1971).

Berg, W. (1976) "Pandora: Pathology of a Creation Myth." *Fabula* 17: 1–25.

Bergren, A. (1975) *The Etymology and Usage of <<peirar>> in Early Greek Poetry: A Study in the Interrelationship of Metrics, Linguistics and Poetics*, American Classical Studies 2. New York.

Berkoff, S. (1980) *Greek.* London.

Bernal, M. (1987/1991) *Black Athena: The Afroasiatic Roots of Classical Civilization*. 2 vols. London.

Bernardus Silvestris (fl. 1136) *Commentary on the First Six Books of Virgil's Aeneid*, trans. E. G. Schreiber and T. Maresca. Lincoln, NE (1979).

Bernardus Silverstis (fl. 1136) *The Commentary on Martianus Capella's De Nuptiis Philologiae et Mercurii*, ed. H. J. Westra. Toronto (1986).

Bernardus Silvestris (fl. 1136) *The Cosmographia*, trans. W. Wetherbee. New York (1973).

Biering, R. (1995) *Die Odysseefresken vom Esquilin*. Munich.

Bierl, A. (1990) "Dionysus, Wine, and Tragic Poetry: A Metatheatrical Reading of *P. Köln* VI 242A = *TrGF* II F646A." *Greek, Roman, and Byzantine Studies* 31: 353–91.

Bietenholz, P. (1994) *'Historia' and 'Fabula': Myths and Legends in Historical Thought from Antiquity to the Modern Age*. Leiden.

Bingen, J. and O. Reverdin, eds. (1996) *Pausanias historien: Huit exposés suivis de discussions*. Geneva.

Binns, J. W., ed. (1973) *Ovid*. London.

Birge, D. 1994. "Trees in the Landscape of Pausanias' Periegesis," in S. E. Alcock and R. Osborne, eds. *Placing the Gods: Sanctuaries and Sacred Space in Ancient Greece*, 231–45. Oxford.

Bittlestone, R. (2005) *Odysseus Unbound: The Search for Homer's Ithaca*, with J. Diggle and J. Underhill. Cambridge.

Black, J., G. Cunningham, E. Robson, and G. Zólyomi (2004) *The Literature of Ancient Sumer*. Oxford.

Blair, Hugh (1763, repr.1765) *A Critical Dissertation of the Poems of Ossian*.

Blake Tyrrell W. (1984) *Amazons: A Study in Athenian Mythmaking*. Baltimore.

Blakely, S. (2007) "Pherekydes' Daktyloi: Ritual, Technology, and the Presocratic Perspective." *Kernos* 20: 31–59.

Blum, Rudolf (1991) *Kallimachos: The Alexandrian Library and the Origins of Bibliography*, trans. H. H. Wellisch. Madison, WI.

Boardman, J. (1972) "Herakles, Peisistratos and Sons." *Revue Archeologique*: 57–72.

Boardman, J. (1975) "Herakles, Peisistratos and Eleusis." *JHS* 95: 1–12.

Boardman, J. (1978) "Exekias." *AJA* 82: 11–25.

Boardman, J. (1989) "Herakles, Peisistratos and the Unconvinced." *JHS* 109: 158–9.

Boardman, J., I. E. S. Edwards, N. G. L. Hammond, E. Sollberger, and C. B. F. Walker, eds. (1991) *The Cambridge Ancient History*, second ed., Vol. 3, Part 2. Cambridge.

Boccaccio, Giovanni (1313–75) *Genealogie Deorum Gentilium Libri*, Vincenzo Romano ed. Bari (1951).

Boedeker, D. (1993) "Hero Cult and Politics in Herodotus: The Bones of Orestes," in C. Dougherty and L. Kurke, eds., *Cultural Poetics in Archaic Greece*, 164–77. Oxford.

Boersma, J. S. (1970) *Athenian Building Policy from 561/0 to 405/4 B.C.* Groningen.

Bommelaer, J.-F. and D. Laroche (1991) *Guide de Delphes: Le site*. Paris.

Bonomii, Francis (1626–1705) *Chiron Achillis, sive Navarchus Humanae Vitae*. N.p. (1651).

Borchhardt, J. (1980) "Zur Darstellung von Objekten in der Entfernung. Beobachtungen zu den Anfängen der griechischen Landschaftsmalerei," in *Tainia* (Festschrift Roland Hampe), ed. H. A. Cahn and E. Simon, 257–67. Mainz.

Bordewich, F. M. (2006) "Odyssey's End?" *Smithsonian* 37: 92–100.

Borgeaud, P. (1988) *The Cult of Pan in Ancient Greece*, trans. K. Atlass and J. Redfield. Chicago/London.

Borgeaud, P. (1995) "The Rustic," in J.-P. Vernant, ed., C. Lambert and T. L. Fagan, trans. *The Greeks*, 285–98. Chicago.

Bothmer, D. V. (1957) *Amazons in Greek Art*. Oxford.

Bowie, A. M. (1993) *Aristophanes: Myth, Ritual and Comedy*. Cambridge.

Bowie, A. M. (1997) "Thinking with Drinking: Wine and the Symposium in Aristophanes." *JHS* 117: 1–21.

Bowie, A. M. (2000) "Myth and Ritual in the Rivals of Aristophanes," in F. D. Harvey and J. M. Wilkins, eds. *The Rivals of Aristophanes*, 317–39. London.

Bowie, E. L. (2001) "Ancestors of Historiography in Early Greek Elegiac and Iambic Poetry?" in N. Luraghi, ed., *The Historian's Craft in the Age of Herodotus* 45–66. Oxford.

Bowman, A. K., E. Champlin, and A. Lintott, eds. (1996) *Cambridge Ancient History*, second ed., Vol 10. Cambridge.

Boyce, M. (1984) "On the Antiquity of Zoroastrian Apocalyptic." *Bulletin of the School of Oriental and African Studies* 47: 57–75.

Boyce, M. (1996) *A History of Zoroastrianism*, Vol. 1. Leiden.

Boyle, A. J. (1991) "Ovid," in A. J. Boyle and J. P. Sullivan, eds. Roman Poets of the Early Empire, 1–8. Harmondsworth.

Boyle, A. J. (2003) *Ovid and the Monuments*. Bendigo.

Boyle, A. J. (2006) *An Introduction to Roman Tragedy*. London.

Boyle, A. J. and J. P. Sullivan, eds. (1991) *Roman Poets of the Early Empire*. Harmondsworth.

Boyle, A. J. and R. D. Woodard (2000) *Ovid Fasti*. Harmondsworth.

Bremer, J. M. (1975) "The Meadow of Love and Two Passages in Euripides' Hippolytus." *Mnemosyne* 28: 268–80.

Bremmer, J. N., ed. (1987) *Interpretations of Greek Mythology*. London.

Bremmer, J. N. (1997) "Why did Medea kill her brother Apsyrtos?" in J. J. Clauss and S. I. Johnston, eds. *Medea: Essays on Medea in Myth, Literature, Philosophy, and Art*, 83–100. Princeton.

Bremmer, J. N. (1998) "'Religion,' 'Ritual' and the Opposition 'Sacred vs. Profane,'" in F. Graf ed., *Ansichten Griechischer Ritale*, 9–32.

Bremmer, J. N. (1999) *Greek Religion*, second ed. Oxford.

Brewster, H. (1997) *The River Gods of Greece: Myths and Mountain Waters in the Hellenic World*. London.

Brisson, L. (1994) *Platon, les mots et les mythes: Comment et pourquoi Platon nomma le mythe?* trans. G. Naddaf, *Plato the Myth Maker*. Chicago/London (1998).

Brisson, L. (1998) *Introduction à la philosophie des mythes 1: Sauver les mythes*, trans. C. Tihanyi, *How Philosophers Saved Myth*. Chicago/London (2004).

Brommer, F. (1982) *Theseus: Die Taten des griechischen Helden in der antiken Kunst und Literatur*. Darmstadt.

Brown, S. A. (1999) *The Metamorphosis of Ovid: From Chaucer to Ted Hughes*.London.

Browning, R. (1877) *The Agamemnon of Aeschylus*. London.

Brumble, H. D. (1998) *Classical Myths and Legends in the Middle Ages and Renaissance: A Dictionary of Allegorical Meanings*. Westport, CT.

Buffière, F. (1956) *Les mythes d'Homère: La pensée grecque*. Paris.

Bundy, E. L. (1986) *Studia Pindarica*. Berkeley/Los Angeles.

Burgess, J. S. (1996) "The Non-Homeric Cypria." *TAPA* 126: 77–99.

Burian, P. (1997) "Myth into *muthos*: the shaping of tragic plot," in P. E. Easterling, ed., *The Cambridge Companion to Greek Tragedy*, 178–208. Cambridge.

Burkert, W. (1960) "Das Lied von Ares und Aphrodite. Zum Verhältnis von Odyssee und Ilias." *Rheinisches Museum für Philologie* 103:130–44.

Burkert, W. (1979) *Structure and History in Greek Mythology and Ritual.* Berkeley/Los Angeles.

Burkert, W. (1985) *Greek Religion.* Cambridge, MA.

Burkert, W. (1987) *Ancient Mystery Cults.* Cambridge, MA.

Burkert, W. (1992) *The Orientalizing Revolution: Near Eastern Influence on Greek Culture in the Early Archaic Age.* Cambridge, MA.

Burkert, W. (2004) *Babylon, Memphis, Persepolis: Eastern Contexts of Greek Culture.* Cambridge, MA.

Burn, A. R. (1960) *The Lyric Age of Greece.* New York.

Burn, L. (1985) "Honey Pots: Three White-Ground Cups by the Sotades Painter." *Antike Kunst* 28: 93–105.

Burn, L. (1987) *The Meidias Painter.* Oxford.

Burrow, T. (1955) *The Sanskrit Language.* London.

Burton, R. W. B. (1962) *Pindar's Pythian Odes: Essays in Interpretation.* Oxford.

Burton, Robert (1577–1639) *The Anatomy of Melancholy.* New York (1927).

Bush, D. (1937, reissued 1969) *Mythology and the Romantic Tradition in English Poetry.* Cambridge, MA.

Buxton, R. (1987) "Wolves and Werewolves in Greek Thought," in J. N. Bremmer, ed., *Interpretations of Greek Mythology,* 60–79. London.

Buxton, R. (1988) "Bafflement in Greek Tragedy." *Mètis* 3: 41–51.

Buxton, R. (1992) "Imaginary Greek Mountains." *JHS* 112: 1–15.

Buxton, R. (1994) *Imaginary Greece: The Contexts of Mythology.* Cambridge.

Buxton, R., ed., (1999) *From Myth to Reason: Studies in the Development of Greek Thought.* Oxford.

Buxton, R., ed. (2000) *Oxford Readings in Greek Religion.* Oxford.

Buxton, R. (2002) "Time, Space and Ideology: Tragic Myths and the Athenian Polis," in J. A. López Férez, ed., *Mitos en la literatura griega arcaica y clásica,* 175–89. Madrid.

Buxton, R. (2004) *The Complete World of Greek Mythology.* London.

Buxton, R. (2006) "Weapons and Day's White Horses: The Language of *Ajax,*" in I. J. F. de Jong and A. Rijksbaron, eds., *Sophocles and the Greek Language. Aspects of Diction, Syntax, and Pragmatics,* 13–23. Leiden.

Calame, C. (1991) "'Mythe' et 'rite' en Grèce: des catégories indigènes?'" *Kernos* 4: 179–204.

Calame, C. (1996) *Thésée et l'imaginaire athénien: légende et culte en Grèce antique,* second ed. Lausanne.

Calame, C. (1997) "*L'Hymne homérique à Déméter* comme offrande: Regard rétrospectif sur quelques catégories de l'anthropologie de la religion grecque." *Kernos* 10: 111–33.

Calame, C. (2000a) "Iô, les Danaïdes, l'extérieur et l'inflexion tragique," in C. Calame, *Poétique des mythes dans la Grèce antique,* 117–44. Paris.

Calame, C. (2000b) *Poétique des mythes dans la Grèce antique.* Paris.

Calame, C. (2001) *Choruses of Young Women in Ancient Greece: Their Morphology, Religious Role, and Social Function,* trans. D. Collins and J. Orion, second ed. Lanham, MD.

Calame, C. (2003a) "Fabrications du genre et identités politiques en comparaison: La création poétique de Thésée par Bacchylide," in U. Heidmann, ed., *Poétiques comparées des mythes,* 13–45. Lausanne.

Calame, C. (2003b) *Myth and History in Ancient Greece: The Symbolic Creation of a Colony.* Princeton.

Calame, C. (2005) *Masks of Authority. Fiction and Pragmatics in Ancient Greek Poetics.* Ithaca, NY.

Calame, C. (2006) *Pratiques poétiques de la mémoire. Représentations de l'espace-temps en Grèce ancienne.* Paris.

Caldwell, R. S. (1987) *Hesiod's Theogony.* Newburyport, MA.

Calvino, I. (1966) *Il visconte dimezzato.* Torino.

Cameron, A. (2004) *Greek Mythography in the Roman World.* Oxford.

Cantarella, E. (1991) "Homicides of Honor: The Development of Italian Adultery Law over Two Millennia," in D. I. Kertzer and R. P. Saller, eds., *The Family in Italy from Antiquity to the Present,* 229–44. New Haven, CT.

Carpenter, T. H. (1991) *Art and Myth in Ancient Greece.* London.

Carrière, J.-C. (1997) "Les métamorphoses des mythes et la crise de la cité dans la comédie ancienne," in P. Thiercy and M. Menu, eds., *Aristophane: la langue, la scène, et la cité,* 413–42. Bari.

Carroll-Spillecke, M. (1985) *Landscape Depictions in Greek Relief Sculpture: Development and Conventionalization,* European University Studies Ser. 38, Archaeology, Vol. 11. Frankfurt.

Carson, A. (1986) *Eros the Bittersweet: An Essay.* Princeton.

Cartari, Vincenzo (b. c. 1500) *Le Imagini dei Dei de Gli Antichi.* Venice (1571). Facsimile reprint: New York (1976).

Carter, A. (1979) *The Sadeian Woman.* London.

Cartledge, P. (1979) *Sparta and Lakonia: A Regional History 1300–362 BC.* London.

Cartledge, P. (1993) *The Greeks: A Portrait of Self and Others.* Oxford.

Cassirer, E. (1946) *Language and Myth,* trans. S. K. Langer. New York.

Cassirer, E. (1953–96) *Philosophy of Symbolic Forms,* trans. R. Manheim. New Haven, CT.

Castriota, D. (1992) *Myth, Ethos, and Actuality: Official Art in Fifth-Century BC Athens.* Madison WI.

Catling, H. (1986) "Excavations at the Menelaion, 1985." *Lakonikai Spoudai* 8: 205–16.

Catling, H. and H. Cavanagh (1976) "Two Inscribed Bronzes from the Menelaion, Sparta." *Kadmos* 15: 145–57.

Caxton, William (1422–91) *The Metamorphoses of Ovid,* trans. with commentary, London (1480). Facsimile ed.: New York (1968).

Chadwick, H. M and N. K. Chadwick (1986) *The Growth of Literature.* Cambridge.

Chance, J. (1975) *The Genius Figure in Antiquity and the Middle Ages.* New York.

Chance, J. (1985) "The Origins and Development of Medieval Mythography: From Homer to Dante," in J. Chance and R. O. Wells, eds., *Mapping the Cosmos.* Houston.

Chance, J. (1994) *Medieval Mythography.* Gainesville, FL.

Charlesworth Gelpi, B. and A. Gelpi, eds. (1993) *Adrienne Rich's Poetry and Prose.* New York/London.

Chaucer, Geoffrey (1989) *The Complete Poetry and Prose of Geoffrey Chaucer,* ed. J. H. Fisher. New York.

The Chess of Love (late 14th century), trans. Joan Jones. Ph.D. dissertation, University of Nebraska (1968).

Cherniss, H. (1947) "Some War-time Publications Concerning Plato II." *AJP* 68: 225–65.

Childs, P. (1999) *The Twentieth Century in Poetry*. London.

Childs, W. A. P. (1994) "The Date of the Old Temple of Athena on the Athenian Acropolis," in W. D. E. Coulson, O. Palagia, T. L. Shear Jr., H. A. Shapiro, and F. J. Frost, eds., *The Archaeology of Athens and Attica under the Democracy*, 1–6. Oxford.

Clackson, J. P. T. (2004) "Classical Armenian," in R. D. Woodard, ed., *The Cambridge Encyclopedia of the World's Ancient Languages*, 922–42. Cambridge.

Clark, K. (1949) *Landscape into Art*. London.

Clauss, J. J. and S. I. Johnston, eds. (1997) *Medea: Essays on Medea in Myth, Literature, Philosophy, and Art*. Princeton.

Clay, D. (1970) "Fragmentum Adespotum 976." *TAPA* 101: 119–29.

Clay, D. (1985) "The Art of Glaukos (*Phaedo* 108D4–9)." *AJP* 106: 230–6.

Clay, D. (1999) "The Invention of Atlantis: The Anatomy of a Fiction," in J. J. Cleary and G. M. Gurtler, S. J., eds., *Proceedings of the Boston Area Colloquium in Ancient Philosophy* 15. Leiden.

Clay, D. and A. Purvis (1999) *Four Island Utopias Being: Plato's Atlantis, Euhemeros of Messene's Panchaia, Iamboulos' Island of the Sun, Sir Francis Bacon's New Atlantis*. Newburyport, MA.

Clay, J. S. (1993) "The Generation of Monsters in Hesiod." *C Phil.* 88: 105–16.

Clay, J. S. (2003) *Hesiod's Cosmos*. Cambridge.

Clay, J. S. (2005) "The Beginning and End of the Catalogue of Women and its Relation to Hesiod," in R. Hunter, ed., *The Hesiodic Catalogue of Women: Constructions and Reconstructions*, 25–34. Cambridge.

Clogan, P. M. (1968) *The Medieval Achilleid of Statius*. Leiden.

Clogg, R. (2003) "The Classics and the Movement for Greek Independence," in M. Haagsma, P. den Boer, and E. M. Moormann, eds., *The Impact of Classical Greece on European and National Identities*, 25–46. Amsterdam.

Cocteau, J. (1954) *Cocteau on the Film: A Conversation Recorded by André Fraigneau*, trans. V. Traill. London.

Cocteau, J. (1992, reprint 1999) *The Art of Cinema*, ed. A. Bernard and C. Gauteur, trans. R. Buss. London.

Cohen, A. (2001) "Art, Myth, and Travel in the Hellenistic World," in S. E. Alcock, J. Cherry, and J. Elsner, eds., *Pausanias: Travel and Memory in Roman Greece*, 93–126. Oxford/New York.

Cohen, A. 2005. "Τοπίο και Μορφή στην Αρχαία Ελληνική Τέχνη," in P. Doukellis, ed., *The Greek Landscape* [in Greek], 105–29. Athens.

Cohen, B. (1994) "From Bowman to Clubman: Herakles and Olympia." *Art Bulletin* 76: 695–715.

Cohen, B., ed. (2000) *Not the Classical Ideal: Athens and the Construction of the Other in Greek Art*. Leiden.

Cohen, D. (1991) "The Augustan Law on Adultery: The Social and Cultural Context," in D. I. Kertzer and R. P. Saller, eds., *The Family in Italy from Antiquity to the Present* 109–26. New Haven, CT.

Cole, S. G. (2003) "Landscapes of Dionysos and Elysian Fields," in M. B. Cosmopoulos, ed., *Greek Mysteries: The Archaeology and Ritual of Ancient Greek Secret Cults*, 193–217. London/New York.

Cole, S. G. (2004) *Landscapes, Gender, and Ritual Space. The Ancient Greek Experience*. Berkeley/Los Angeles.

Compton, T. (2006) *Victim of the Muses*. Cambridge, MA.

Connor, W. R. (1970) "Theseus in Classical Athens," in A. G. Ward, ed., *The Quest for Theseus*, 143–74. New York: Praeger.

Connor, W. R. (1988) "Seized by the Nymphs: Nympholepsy and Symbolic Expression in Classical Greece." *Cl. Ant.* 7: 155–89.

Conti, Natale (1520?–1580?) *Mythologie, ou Explication des Fables*, trans. J. de Montlyard. Paris (1627). Facsimile reprint: New York (1976).

Cook, J. M. (1953) "Mycenae 1939–1952: the Agamemnoneion." *Annual of the British School at Athens* 48: 30–68.

Cooper, Thomas (1517–1594). *Dictionarium Historicum & Poeticum . . .*, appended to *Cooper's Thesaurus Linguae Romanae & Britannicae. . . .* London (1573).

Cornell, T. J. (1995) *The Beginnings of Rome*. London.

Cornford, F. M. (1914). *The Origin of Attic Comedy*. Cambridge.

Crane, G. (1988) *Calypso: Backgrounds and Conventions of the Odyssey*. Frankfurt.

Creason, S. (2004) "Aramaic," in R. D. Woodard, ed., *The Cambridge Encyclopedia of the World's Ancient Languages*, 391–426. Cambridge.

Cribiore, R. (2001) *Gymnastics of the Mind: Greek Education in Hellenistic and Roman Egypt*. Princeton.

Crotty, K. (1982) *Song and Action: The Victory Odes of Pindar*. Baltimore.

Csapo, E. (2005) *Theories of Mythology*. Oxford.

Csapo, E. and W. J. Slater (1994) *The Context of Ancient Drama*. Ann Arbor, MI.

Curti, L. (1998) *Female Stories, Female Bodies: Narrative, Identity and Representation*. Basingstoke and London.

Curty, O. (1995) *Les parentés légendaires entre cités grecques: Catalogue raisonné des inscriptions contenant le terme ΣΥΓΓΕΝΕΙΑ et analyse critique*. Geneva.

D'Alessio, G. B. (1994) "First-Person Problems in Pindar." *Bulletin of the Institute of Classical Studies* 39: 117–39.

Daly, P. J. and M. V. Silcox (1990) *The English Emblem: Bibliography of Secondary Literature*. New York.

Dalley, S., ed. (1998) *The Legacy of Mesopotamia*. Oxford.

Dandamaev, M. A. (1991) "Neo-Babylonian Society and Economy," in J. Boardman, I. E. S. Edwards, N. G. L. Hammond, E. Sollberger, and C. B. F. Walker, eds., *The Cambridge Ancient History*, second ed., Vol. 3, Part 2, 252–75. Cambridge.

Davies, D. (1988) "The Evocative Symbolism of Trees," in D. Cosgrove and S. Daniels, eds. *The Iconography of Landscape: Essays on the Symbolic Representation, Design and Use of Past Environments*, 32–42. Cambridge.

Davies, M. (1986) "A Convention of Metamorphosis in Greek Art." *JHS* 106: 182–3.

Davies, M. (1988) "Monody, Choral Lyric, and the Tyranny of the Handbook." *CQ* 38: 52–64.

Davies, P. R. (1976) "Daniel Chapter Two." *Journal of Theological Studies* 27: 392–401.

Davis, P. J. (1995) "*Praeceptor Amoris*: Ovid's *Ars Amatoria* and the Augustan Idea of Rome." *Ramus* 24: 181–95.

Dawson, C. M. (1944) *Romano-Campanian Mythological Landscape Painting*, YClS 9. New Haven, CT.

De España, R. (1998) *El Peplum: La antigüedad en el cine*. Barcelona.

Degrassi, A. (1963) *Inscriptiones Italiae,* 13 vols. Rome.

Delattre, C. (2005) *Manuel de mythologie grecque*. Paris.

Derrida, J. (1972) "La Pharmacie de Platon," in *La dissémination*, Paris. B. Johnson, *Dissemination*, trans. 63–171. Chicago (1981).

Dessau, H. (1892–1916) *Inscriptiones Latinae Selectae,* 3 vols. Berlin.

Detienne, M. (1981) *L'invention de la mythologie.* Paris.

Detienne, M. (1986) *The Creation of Mythology,* trans. M. Cook. Chicago.

Detienne, M. (1998) *Apollon le couteau à la main. Une approche expérimentale du polythéisme grec.* Paris.

DeVries, K. (2000) "The Nearly Other: The Attic Vision of Phrygians and Lydians," in B. Cohen, ed., *Not the Classical Ideal: Athens and the Construction of the Other in Greek Art,* 338–63. Leiden.

Dickinson, E. (1970) *Complete Poems,* ed. T. H. Johnson. London.

Diller, A. (1935) "The Text History of the Bibliotheca of Pseudo-Apollodorus." *TAPA* 66: 296–313.

Doherty, L. (2001) *Gender and the Interpretation of Classical Myth.* London.

Doherty, L. (2006) "Putting the Women Back into the Hesiodic Catalogue of Women," in V. Zajko and M. Leonard, eds., *Laughing with Medusa,* 421–62. Oxford.

Dolce, Lodovico (1508–68) *Le Transformationi.* Venice (1561).

Donatus, Tiberius Claudius (fl. mid. fourth century). *Interpretationes Vergilianae,* ed. H. Georges. Leipzig (1905).

Doniger, W. and B. K. Smith (1991) *The Laws of Manu.* Harmondsworth.

Douglas, Gawain (1474?–1522) "Preface" to Virgil, *xii Bukes of Eneados . . . tr. into Scottish metir, bi . . . Gawain Douglas.* London (1553).

Doukellis, P., ed. (2005) *The Greek Landscape* [in Greek]. Athens.

Doumas, C. (1992) *The Wall Paintings of Thera.* Athens.

Dowden, K. (1989) *Death and the Maiden. Girls' Initiation Rites in Greek Mythology.* London.

Dowden, K. (1992) *The Uses of Greek Mythology.* London.

Dowden, K. (1995) "Approaching Women through Myth: Vital Tool or Self-Delusion?" in R. Hawley and B. Levick, eds., *Women in Antiquity: New Assessments,* 44–57. Oxford.

DuBois, P. (1988) *Sowing the Body: Psychoanalysis and Ancient Representations of Women.* Chicago.

Dué, C. (2002). *Homeric Variations on a Lament by Briseis.* Lanham, MD.

Dué, C. (2006) *The Captive Woman's Lament in Greek Tragedy.* Austin.

Duffy, C. A. (1999) *The World's Wife.* London.

Dumézil, G. (1930) "La préhistoire indo-iranienne des castes." *Journal asiatique* 216: 109–30.

Dumézil, G. (1970) *The Destiny of the Warrior,* trans. A. Hiltebeitel. Chicago.

Dumézil, G. (1973) *Gods of the Ancient Northmen.* Berkeley/Los Angeles.

Dumézil, G. (1983) *The Stakes of the Warrior,* trans. D. Weeks. Berkeley/Los Angeles.

Dumézil, G. (1987) *Entretiens avec Didier Eribon.* Paris.

Dumézil, G. (1992) *Mythes et dieux des Indo-Européens,* with editorial contributions by H. Coutau-Bégarie. Paris.

Dumézil, G. (1995) *Mythe et épopée I. II. III.* Paris.

Dumézil, G. (2003) *Esquisses de mythologie.* Paris.

Durgnat, R. (1963) "Homage to Hercules." *Motion* 6: 48–50.

Early, F. and K. Kennedy, eds. (2003) *Athena's Daughters: Television's New Women Warriors.* Syracuse.

Easterling, P., (1997) "A Show for Dionysus," in P. Easterling, ed., *The Cambridge Companion to Greek Tragedy,* 36–53. Cambridge.

Ebeling, E. (1927) *Die babylonische Fabel und ihre Bedeutung für die Literaturgeschichte*. Leipzig.

Eckstein, A. M. and P. Lehman, eds. (2004) *The Searchers: Essays and Reflections on John Ford's Classic Western*. Detroit.

Edelstein, L. (1949) "The Function of Myth in Plato's Philosophy." *Journal of the History of Ideas* 10: 463–81.

Edmonds, L., ed. (1990) *Approaches to Greek Mythology*. Baltimore.

Edmonds, R. G. III (2004) *Myths of the Underworld Journey: Plato, Aristophanes, and the 'Orphic' Gold Tablets*. Cambridge.

Edwards, A. T. (2004) *Hesiod's Ascra*. Berkeley/Los Angeles.

Edwards, M. W. (1987, reprint 1990) *Homer: Poet of the Iliad*. Baltimore.

Eissfeldt, O. (1965) *The Old Testament: An Introduction*, trans. P. R. Ackroyd. New York.

Eliot, T. S. (1932, reprint 1972) *Selected Essays*. London.

Eliot, T. S. (1971) *The Waste Land*. London.

Elley, D. (1984) *The Epic Film: Myth and History*. London.

Elliger, W. (1975) *Die Darstellung der Landschaft in der griechischen Dichtung*. Berlin/New York.

Elmer, D. F. (2005) "Helen *Epigrammatopoios*." *Cl. Ant*. 24: 1–39.

Elson, R. (2001) *A Responsibility to Awe*. Manchester.

Erasmus, Desiderius (1466–1536) *The Enchiridion*, trans. R. Himelick. Bloomington, IN (1963).

Erskine, A. (2001) *Troy Between Greece and Rome: Local Tradition and Imperial Power*. Oxford.

Eustathius, Archbishop of Thessalonica (d. c. 1194). *Commentarii ad Homeri Iliadem et Odysseam*, 3 vols. Hildesheim (1960).

Evans, A. B. (1977) *Jean Cocteau and His Films of Orphic Identity*. London.

Fairclough, H. R. ed. and trans. (1978) *Virgil: Works*, Vol. 1. Cambridge, MA.

Faraone, C. A. (1997) "Salvation and Female Heroics in the Parodos of Aristophanes' *Lysistrata*." *JHS* 117: 38–59.

Farnoux, A. (1996) "Image et paysage: l'exemple des fresques de la Maison Ouest de Théra," in G. Siebert, ed., *Nature et paysage dans la pensée et l'environnement des civilisations antiques*, Actes du Colloque de Strasbourg 11–12 juin 1992, 21–30. Paris.

Feeney, D. C. (1991) *The Gods in Epic: Poets and Critics of the Classical Tradition*. Oxford.

Ferrari, G. P. (forthcoming) "The Frescoes of the West House at Akrotiri." *AJA*.

Ficino, Marsilio (1433–99) *Commentary on Plato's Symposium on Love*, trans. S. Jayne. Dallas (1985).

Figueira, T. J. and G. Nagy, eds. (1985) *Theognis of Megara: Poetry and the Polis*. Baltimore.

Filedt Kok, J. P. (1985) *Livelier Than Life: The Master of the Amsterdam Cabinet . . . , c. 1470–1500*. Amsterdam.

Finley, M. I. (2002) *The World of Odysseus*. Reprint edition with minor emendations. London.

Finkelberg, M. (2000) "The *Cypria*, the *Iliad*, and the Problem of Multiformity in Oral and Written Tradition." *C Phil*. 95: 1–11.

Fittschen, K. (1969) *Untersuchungen zum beginn der Sagendarstellung bei den Griechen*. Berlin.

Foley, H. P. (1988) "Tragedy and politics in Aristophanes' *Acharnians*." *JHS* 108: 33–47.

Fontenrose, J. (1974) "Work, Justice, and Hesiod's Five Ages." *C. Phil.* 69: 1–16.

Forbes Irving, P. M. C. (1990) *Metamorphosis in Greek Myths.* Oxford.

Fornara, C. L., ed. and trans. (1997) *Archaic Times to the End of the Pelopponesian War*, No. 3. Cambridge.

Forster, E. M. (1971) *Maurice.* London.

Forster, E. M. (2002) *Collected Short Stories.* London.

Foster, B. R. (2005) *Before the Muses: An Anthology of Akkadian Literature*, third ed. Bethesda, MD.

Fowler, B. H. (1989) *The Hellenistic Aesthetic.* Madison, WI.

Fowler, B. H. (1992) *Archaic Greek Poetry.* Madison, WI.

Fowler, R. L. (2000) *Early Greek Mythography*, Vol. 1. Oxford.

Frame, D. (1978) *The Myth of Return in Early Greek Epic.* New Haven, CT.

Fränkel, H. (1938) "A Thought Pattern in Heraclitus." *AJP* 59: 309–37.

Fraunce, Abraham (fl. 1582–1633). *Third Part of the Countesse of Pembrokes Yvychurch. . . .* London (1592). Facsimile reprint: New York (1976).

Froning, H. (1971) *Dithyrambos und Vasenmalerei in Athen.* Würzburg.

Frutiger, P. (1930) *Les mythes de Platon. Étude philosophique et litteraire.* Paris.

Fulgentius, Fabius Planciades (fl. early 6th century) *On the Ages of the World and of Man; The Exposition on the Content of Virgil; The Mythologies; and Super Thebaiden, in Fulgentius the Mythographer*, trans. L. G. Whitbread. Columbus, OH (1971).

Furley, W. D. and J. M. Bremer (2001) *Greek Hymns II. Greek Texts and Commentary.* Tübingen.

Futrell, A. (2003) "The Baby, the Mother, and the Empire: Xena as Ancient Hero," in F. Early and K. Kennedy, eds., *Athena's Daughters: Television's New Women Warriors*, 13–26 and 137–8. Syracuse.

Gagarin, M. (1974) "Hesiod's Dispute with Perses." *TAPA* 104: 103–11.

Gagarin, M. (1986) *Early Greek Law.* Berkeley/Los Angeles.

Gagarin, M. and D. Cohen, eds. (2005) *The Cambridge Companion to Ancient Greek Law.* Cambridge.

Gais, R. M. (1978) "Some Problems of River-God Iconography." *AJA* 82:355–77.

Galinsky, K. (1975) *Ovid's Metamorphoses: An Introduction to the Basic Aspects.* Berkeley/ Los Angeles.

Gamble, S., ed. (2001) *The Routledge Companion to Feminism and Postfeminism.* London.

Gantz, T. (1993) *Early Greek Myth: A Guide to Literary and Artistic Sources.* Baltimore/ London.

Gardner, P. (1888) "Countries and Cities in Ancient Art." *JHS* 9: 47–81.

Garland, R. (1995) *The Eye of the Beholder: Deformity and Disability in the Graeco-Roman World.* London.

Gentili, B., P. Angeli Bernardini, E. Cingano, and P. Giannini (1995) *Pindaro. Le Pitiche.* Milan.

Gerber, D. E. (1999) *Greek Elegaic Poetry.* Cambridge, MA.

Gershevitch, I., ed. (1985) *The Cambridge History of Iran*, Vol. 2. Cambridge.

Giannini, A. (1965) *Paradoxographorum Graecorum Reliquiae.* Milan.

Giesecke, A. L. (1999) "Elpenor, Amymone, and the Truth in the Lykaon Painter's Painting." *BABesch* 74: 63–78.

Gilligan, C. (2002) *The Birth of Pleasure.* New York.

Giovanni del Virgilio (fl. c. 1330). "Giovanni del Virgilio espositore delle 'Metamorfosi.'" *Il Giornale Dantesco* 34, N.S. 4 (1933): 1–110.

Giuliani, L. (2004) "Odysseus and Kirke. Iconography in a Pre-literate Culture," in C. Marconi, ed., *Greek Vases: Images, Contexts and Controversies*, 85–96. Leiden.

Goldhill, S. (1991) *The Poet's Voice: Essays on Poetics and Greek Literature*. Cambridge.

Goldhill, S. (2004) *Love, Sex and Tragedy*. London.

Gould, J. (2001) *Myth, Ritual, Memory and Exchange: Essays in Greek Literature and Culture*. Oxford.

Gow, A. S. F. and A. F. Scholfield (1953) *Nicander: The Poems and Poetical Fragments*. Cambridge.

Gower, John (c. 1325–1408) *Confessio Amantis*, in *The English Works of John Gower*, vols. 1–2, ed. G. C. Macaulay. Oxford (1957).

Graf, F. (1993) *Greek Mythology: An Introduction*, trans. Thomas Marier. Baltimore.

Graf, F., ed. (1998) *Ansichten griechischer Rituale. Für Walter Burkert*. Stuttgart/Leipzig.

Graf, F. (2002) "Myth in Ovid," in P. Hardie, ed., *Cambridge Companion to Ovid*, 108–21. Cambridge.

Grant, M., trans. (1960) "Fabulae; Poetica Astronomica," in *The Myths of Hyginus*. Lawrence KS.

Graves, Robert (1944) *The Golden Fleece*. Reprint: London (2003).

Greene, E., ed. (1996) *Re-reading Sappho: Contemporary Approaches*. Berkeley/Los Angeles.

Greenfield, J. C. (1995) "The Wisdom of Ahiqar," in J. D. Ray, R. P. Gordon, and H. G. M. Williamson, eds., *Wisdom in Ancient Israel: Essays in Honour of J. A. Emerson*, 43–52. Cambridge.

Griffin, J. (1980) *Homer on Life and Death*. Oxford.

Griffith, M. (1983) "Personality in Hesiod." *Cl. Ant.* 2: 37–65.

Guarner, J. L. (1965) "*The Hundred Horsemen.*" *Movie* 12: 18–20.

Guillaume de Conches (c. 1080–c. 1150) "Commentary on Boethius's *Consolation of Philosophy*," in J. M. Parent, *La Doctrine de la Creation dans l'Ecole de Chartres*, 124–36. Paris (1938).

Guillaume de Conches. "Selections from William of Conches's Commentary on Macrobius," in P. Dronke, *Fabula: Explorations into the Uses of Myth in Medieval Platonism*, 68–78. Leiden (1974).

Güterbock, H. G. (1997) "Boğazköy," in E. M. Myers, ed., *The Oxford Encyclopedia of Archaeology in the Near East*, Vol. 1, 333–5. Oxford.

Hainsworth, J. B. (1991) *The Idea of Epic*. Berkeley/Los Angeles.

Hall, E. (1989) *Inventing the Barbarian: Greek Self-Definition through Tragedy*. Oxford.

Hall, J. M. (1995) "How Argive was the 'Argive' Heraion? The Political and Cultic Geography of the Argive Plain, 900–400 BC." *AJA* 99: 577–613.

Hall, J. M. (1997) *Ethnic Identity in Greek Antiquity*. Cambridge.

Hall, J. M. (1999) "Beyond the *polis*: The Multilocality of Heroes," in R. Hägg, ed., *Ancient Greek Hero Cult*, 49–59. Stockholm.

Hall, J. M. (2002) *Hellenicity: Between Ethnicity and Culture*. Chicago.

Hall, Thomas (1610–65) *Wisdoms Conquest. or, An explanation and . . . Translation of the thirteenth Book of Ovids Metamorphoses*. London (1651).

Halliwell, S. (2002) "Mimesis and the Best Life," in *The Aesthetics of Mimesis: Ancient Texts and Modern Problems*, 98–117. Princeton.

Halm-Tisserant, M. (1999) "Le paysage sacré dans la peinture de vases grecque." *Ktema* 24:243–50.

Halperin, D. (1983) *Before Pastoral: Theocritus and the Ancient Tradition of Bucolic Poetry.* New Haven, CT.

Hansen, W. (1996) *Phlegon of Tralles' Book of Marvels.* Exeter.

Hansen, W., ed. (1998) *Anthology of Ancient Greek Popular Literature.* Bloomington IN.

Hardie, P., ed. (2002a) *Cambridge Companion to Ovid.* Cambridge.

Hardie, P. (2002b) *Ovid's Poetics of Illusion.* Cambridge.

Hardy, Thomas (1891, repr. 1974) *Tess of the d'Urbervilles.* London.

Hardy, Thomas (1895, repr. 1978) *Jude the Obscure.* New York.

Harington, John (1561–1612). *An Apologie of Poetrie*, included as a preface to Harington's trans. of, and commentary on, Ariosto's *Orlando Furioso.* London (1591).

Harris, J. R., F. C. Conybeare, and A. S. Lewis (1913) *The Story of Ahikar*, second ed. Cambridge.

Harrison, J. (1927) *Epilegomena to the Study of Greek Religion.* Cambridge.

Harrison, T. (1992) *The Common Chorus.* London.

Harrison, T. (1998) *Prometheus.* London.

Harryhausen, R. (1981) *Film Fantasy Scrapbook*, third ed. San Diego.

Harryhausen, R. and T. Dalton (2003) *Ray Harryhausen: An Animated Life: Adventures in Fantasy.* London.

Hartmen, L. F. and A. A. Di Lella (1978) *The Book of Daniel.* Garden City, NJ.

Harvey, A. E. (1955) "The Classification of Greek Lyric Poetry." *CQ* 5: 157–75.

Hawley, R. and B. Levick, eds. (1995) *Women in Antiquity: New Assessments.* Oxford.

Hawthorne, Nathaniel (1853) *A Wonder Book.* Reprint, n.d.

Hawthorne, Nathaniel (1918) *Tanglewood Tales.* Reprint: London (2002).

Hawthorne, Nathaniel (1982) *Tales and Sketches.* New York.

Hayashi, T. (1992) *Bedeutung und Wandel des Triptolemosbildes vom 6.–4. Jh. v. Chr.* Würzburg.

Heath, M. (1988) "Receiving the *kômos*: The Context and Performance of Epinician." *AJP* 109: 1–11.

Hedreen, G. (2001) *Capturing Troy: The Narrative Functions of Landscape in Archaic and Early Classical Greek Art.* Ann Arbor, MI.

Heidmann, U., ed. (2003) *Poétiques comparées des mythes.* Lausanne.

Heitsch, E., ed. (1966) *Hesiod.* Darmstadt.

Henrichs, A. (1987) "Three Approaches to Greek Mythography," in J. Bremmer, ed., *Interpretations of Greek Mythology*, 242–77. London.

Henry, R. (1997) *Photius, Bibliothéque*, 3 vols. Paris.

Heraclitus (sometimes Heraclides, probably 1st century AD) *Allégories d'Homère*, trans. F. Buffière. Paris (1962).

Herbert, W. N. and M. Hollis (2000) *Strong Words: Modern Poets on Modern Poetry.* Tarset.

Heubeck, A. and A. Hoekstra (1989) *A Commentary on Homer's Odyssey*, Vol. 2. Oxford.

Heubeck, A., S. West, and J. B. Hainsworth (1988) *A Commentary on Homer's Odyssey*, Vol. 1. Oxford.

Higbie, C. (1997) "The Bones of a Hero, the Ashes of a Politician: Athens, Salamis, and the Usable Past." *Cl. Ant.* 16: 279–308.

Higbie, C. (1999) "Craterus and the Use of Inscriptions in Ancient Scholarship." *TAPA* 129: 43–83.

Higbie, C. (2003) *The Lindian Chronicle and the Greek Creation of Their Past.* Oxford.

Hill, B. H. (1964) *The Springs: Peirene, Sacred Spring, Glauke* (Corinth, vol. 1, pt. 6). Princeton.

Himmelmann, N. (1959) *Zur Eigenart des klassischen Götterbildes*. Munich. Translated and reprinted in *Reading Greek Art*, ed. W. Childs, 103–38. Princeton (1998).

Hinds, S. (1985) "Booking the Return Trip: Ovid and *Tristia* I." *PCPS* n.s. 31:13–32.

Hirsch, E. and M. O'Hanlon, eds. (1995) *The Anthropology of Landscape: Perspectives on Place and Space*. Oxford.

Hofmann, H. (1976) *Mythos und Komödie: Untersuchungen zu den Vögeln des Aristophanes*. Hildesheim/New York.

Hoffmann, H. (1997) *Sotades: Symbols of Immortality on Greek Vases*. Oxford.

Hoffner, H. A., Jr. (1975) "Hittite Mythological Texts: A Survey," in H. Goedicke and J. J. M. Roberts, eds., *Unity and Diversity: Essays in the History, Literature, and Religion of the Ancient Near East*, 136–45. Baltimore.

Hoffner, H. A., Jr. (1988) "The Song of Silver," in E. Neu and C. Rüster, eds., *Documentum Asiae Minoris Antiquae*, 143–66. Wiesbaden.

Hoffner, H. A., Jr. (1990) *Hittite Myths*. Atlanta.

Hollander, R. (1969) *Allegory in Dante's Commedia*. Princeton.

Hollis, A. (1973) "The *Ars Amatoria* and *Remedia Amoris*," in J. W. Binns, ed., *Ovid*, 84–115. London.

Holtsmark, E. B. (2001) "The Katabasis Theme in Modern Cinema," in M. M. Winkler, ed., *Classical Myth and Culture in the Cinema*, 23–50. New York.

Hooker, J. T. (1980) *The Ancient Spartans*. London: Dent.

Hornblower, S. (1991) *A Commentary on Thucydides I. Books I–III*. Oxford.

Hughes, T. (1997) *Tales from Ovid*. London.

Hunter, R. (1993, reprint 1995) *Apollonius of Rhodes: Jason and the Golden Fleece*. Oxford.

Hunter, R., ed. (2005) *The Hesiodic Catalogue of Women: Constructions and Reconstructions*. Cambridge.

Hurwit, J. M. (1982) "Palm Trees and the Pathetic Fallacy in Archaic Greek Poetry and Art." *CJ* 77:193–9.

Hurwit, J. M. (1985) "The Dipylon Shield Once More." *Cl. Ant.* 4: 121–6.

Hurwit, J. M. (1991) "The Representation of Nature in Early Greek Art," in D. Buitron-Oliver, ed., *New Perspectives in Early Greek Art* (Studies in the History of Art 32), 33–62. Hanover/London.

Huys, M. (1997) "100 Years of Scholarship on Apollodoros the Mythographer: A Bibliographical Survey." *Ant. Class.* 66: 319–51.

Hyde, W. W. (1915–16) "The Ancient Appreciation of Mountain Scenery." *CJ* 11:70–84.

Ieranò, G. (1997) *Il ditirambo di Dioniso. Le testimonianze antiche*. Pisa/Rome.

Isidore of Seville (c. 560–636). *Etymologiarum sive originum*, ed. W. M. Lindsay. Oxford (1985) [1911].

James, Henry (1999) *Complete Stories 1874–84*. New York.

Jameson, M. H. (1990) "Perseus, the Hero of Mykenai," in R. Hägg and G. Nordquist, eds., *Celebrations of Death and Divinity in the Bronze Age Argolid*, 213–23. Stockholm.

Janko, R. (1982) *Homer, Hesiod and the Hymns: Diachronic Development in the Epic Diction*. Cambridge.

Janko, R. (1994) *The Iliad: A Commentary*, Vol. 4. Cambridge.

Janko, R. (2001) "The Derveni Papyrus ('Diagoras of Melos, Apopyrgizontes Logoi?'): A New Translation." *C. Phil.* 96: 1–32.

Jeffery, L. H. (1990) *The Local Scripts of Archaic Greece: A Study of the Origin of the Greek Alphabet and Its Development from the Eighth to the Fifth Centuries BC*, rev. ed. Oxford.

Jenkyns, R. (1980) *The Victorians and Ancient Greece.* Oxford.

John of Salisbury (1120?–1180?) *Policraticus: The Statesman's Book*, trans. M. F. Markland. New York (1979).

John the Scot (815?–877?) *Iohannis Scotti annotationes in Marcianum*, ed. C. E. Lutz. Cambridge (1942).

Johnson, Samuel (1984) *The Oxford Authors*, D. Greene. ed. Oxford.

Jones, C. P. (1999) *Kinship Diplomacy in the Ancient World.* Cambridge, MA.

Jones, J. (1962) *On Aristotle and Greek Tragedy.* London.

Joseph, J. (1986) *Persephone.* Newcastle-upon-Tyne.

Joshua, E. (2001). *Pygmalion and Galatea: The History of a Narrative in English Literature.* Aldershot.

Jüthner, J. (1923) *Hellenen und Barbaren aus der Geschichte des Nationalbewußtseins.* Leipzig.

Kaempf-Dimitriadou, S. (1969) *Die Liebe der Götter in der attischen Kunst des 5. Jahrhunderts v. Chr.* Bern.

Kahn, C. (2007) "The Myth of Plato's Statesman," in C. Parthenic, ed., *Plato's Myths.* Cambridge.

Kaltsas, N. (2002) *Sculpture in the National Archaeological Museum, Athens*, trans. D. Hardy. Los Angeles.

Käppel, L. (1992) *Paian. Studien zur Geschichte einer Gattung.* Berlin/New York.

Karageorghis, V. (2002) *Early Cyprus: Crossroads of the Mediterranean.* Los Angeles.

Kay, R. (1994). *Dante's Christian Astrology.* Philadelphia.

Kearns, E. (1989) *The Heroes of Attica, BICS* Suppl. 57. London.

Kearns, E. (2004) "The gods in the Homeric epics," in R. Fowler, ed., *The Cambridge Companion to Homer*, 59–73. Cambridge.

Keats, John (1970) *The Complete Poems*, ed. M. Allott. Harlow.

Kennedy, D. F. (2002) "Epistolarity: The *Heroides*," in P. Hardie, ed., *Cambridge Companion to Ovid*, 217–32. Cambridge.

Kertzer, D. I. and R. P. Saller, eds. (1991) *The Family in Italy from Antiquity to the Present.* New Haven, CT.

Kidd, D. (1997) *Aratus: Phaenomena.* Cambridge.

Kirk, G. S. (1990) *The Iliad: A Commentary*, Vol. 2. Cambridge.

Klementa, S. (1993) *Gelagerte Flussgötter des Späthellenismus und der römischen Kaiserzeit.* Cologne.

Knox, B. M. W. (1957) *Oedipus at Thebes: Sophocles' Tragic Hero and His Time.* New edition. New Haven, CT (1998).

Knox, B. M. W. (1964) *The Heroic Temper: Studies in Sophoclean Tragedy.* Reprint. Berkeley/Los Angeles (1983).

Knox, Vicesimus (1781) *Liberal Education, or a Practical Treatise on the Methods of Acquiring Useful and Polite Learning.*

Koenen, L. (1994) "Greece, the Near East, and Egypt: Cyclic Destruction in Hesiod and the *Catalogue of Women.*" *TAPA* 124: 1–34.

Kosmopoulou, A. (2002) *The Iconography of Sculptured Statue Bases in the Archaic and Classical Periods.* Madison, WI.

Kosofsky Sedgwick, E. (1985) *Between Men: English Literature and Male Homosocial Desire.* New York.

Kowalzig, B. (2004) "Changing Choral Worlds: Song-Dance and Society in Athens and Beyond," in P. Murray and P. Wilson, eds., *Music and the Muses: The Culture of Mousike in the Classical Athenian City*, 39–65. Oxford.

Kraus, W. (1984) "Götter und Menschen bei Homer," in *Aus Allem Eines. Studien zur antiken Geistesgeschichte*, 15–27. Heidelberg. (Reprinted from *Wiener Humanistische Blätter* 18 [1976]: 20–32.)

Krummen, E. (1990) *Pursos humnon. Festliche und mythisch-rituelle Tradition als Voraussetzungen einer Pindarinterpretation (Isthmie 4, Pythie 5, Olympie 1 und 3)*. Berlin/New York.

Kullmann, W. (1992) "Gods and Men in the *Iliad* and *Odyssey*," in *Homerische Motive: Beiträge zur Entstehung, Eigenart und Wirkung von Ilias und Odyssee*, 243–63. Stuttgart. (Reprinted from *Harv. Stud.* 89 [1985]: 1–23.)

Kurke, L. (1991) *The Traffic in Praise: Pindar and the Poetics of Social Economy*. Ithaca NY.

Kurke, L. (1992) "The politics of ἁβροσύνη in Archaic Greece," *Cl. Ant.* 11: 91–120.

Kutscher, E. Y. (1970) "Aramaic," in *Current Trends in Linguistics*, Vol. 4, 347–412. The Hague.

Lactantius Placidus (sixth century) *Commentarium in Statii Thebaida*, ed. R. Jahnke. Leipzig (1879).

Lactantius Placidus (sixth century) *Narrationes Fabularum Quae in P. Ovidii Nasonis Libris XV Metamorphoseon occurrunt*, in Thomas Munckerus, *Mythographi Latini*, 185–300. Amsterdam (1681).

Lada-Richards, I. (1999) *Initiating Dionysus: Ritual and Theatre in Aristophanes' Frogs*. Oxford.

Lambert, W. G. and Walcot, P. (1965) "A New Babylonian Theogony and Hesiod." *Kadmos* 4: 64–72.

Lamberton, R. (1988) *Hesiod*. New Haven, CT.

Landino, Cristoforo (1424–1498) *Disputationes Camuldenses*, ed. P. Lohe. Florence: Sansoni (1980). For a translation of Books 3 and 4, see P. Stahel, *Cristoforo Landino's Allegorization of the Aeneid: Books III and IV of the Camaldolese Disputations*. Ph.D. dissertation, Johns Hopkins University (1968).

Larrington, C., ed. (1992) *A Feminist Companion to Mythology*. London.

Larson, J. (2001) *Greek Nymphs: Myth, Cult, Lore*. Oxford/New York.

Lattimore, R., trans. (1951) *The Iliad of Homer*. Chicago.

Lattimore, R., trans. (1967) *The Odyssey of Homer*. New York.

Lavelle, B. M. (1993) *The Sorrow and the Pity: A Prolegomenon to a History of Athens under the Peisistratids, c. 560–510 BC*. Stuttgart.

Lavelle, B. M. (2005) *Fame, Money, and Power: The Rise of Peisistratos and 'Democratic' Tyranny at Athens*. Ann Arbor, MI.

Lavinius, Petrus (fl. first half of 16th century). *Metamorphoses*. Venice (1540).

Leahy, D. M. (1955) "The bones of Tisamenus." *Historia* 4: 26–38.

Lebeck, A. (1972) "The Central Myth of Plato's Phaedrus." *Greek, Roman, and Byzantine Studies* 13: 267–90.

Lefkowitz, M. (1988) "Who Sang Pindar's Victory Odes?" *AJP* 109: 1–11. Revised and reprinted in M. Lefkowitz, *First Person Fictions: Pindar's Poetic "I,"* 191–201. Oxford (1991).

Lefkowitz, M. (2002) "Predatory Goddesses." *Hesperia* 71: 325–44.

Leigh, M. (1996) "Varius Rufus, Thyestes and the Appetites of Antony." *PCPS* 42: 171–97.

Leprohon, P. (1972) *The Italian Cinema*, trans. R. Greaves and O. Stallybrass. New York.

Levaniouk, O. (2000) "Aithōn, Aithon, and Odysseus." *Harv. Stud.* 100: 25–51.

Lévi, S. (1966) *La doctrine du sacrifice dans les Brāhmaṇas*. Reprint. Paris.

Lexicon Iconographicum Mythologiae Classicae (1981–99). Zürich/Munich.

Lichteim, M. (1983) *Late Egyptian Wisdom Literature in the International Context*. Freiburg/Göttingen.

Lightfoot, J. L. (1999) *Parthenius of Nicaea*. Oxford.

Lincoln, B. (1986) *Myth, Cosmos and Society*. Cambridge, MA.

Lincoln, B. (1997) "Pahlavi *kirrēnīdan*: Traces of Iranian Creation Mythology." *JAOS* 117: 681–5.

Lincoln, B. (1999) *Theorizing Myth: Narrative, Ideology, and Scholarship*. Chicago.

Lindenberger, J. M. (1983) *The Aramaic Proverbs of Ahiqar*. Baltimore.

Lindheim, S. (2003) *Mail and Female*. Madison, WI.

Littleton, C. S. (1970) "The 'Kingship in Heaven' Theme," in J. Puhvel, ed., *Myth and Law Among the Indo-Europeans*, 83–121. Berkeley/Los Angeles.

Locatelli, L. (1960) "Come ai tempi di Cabiria." *La Fiera del Cinema*, 2: 10–17.

Loftis, N. (1973) *Black Anima*. New York.

Loraux, N. (1981) *Les enfants d'Athéna. Idées athéniennes sur la citoyenneté et la division des sexes*. Paris.

Loraux, N. (1995) *The Experiences of Tiresias: The Feminine and the Greek Man*, trans. P. Wissing. Princeton.

Lord, A. B. 1960. (2000) *The Singer of Tales*, second ed., eds. S. Mitchell and G. Nagy. Cambridge, MA.

Lord, A. B. (1991) *Epic Singers and Oral Tradition*. Ithaca, NY.

Lord, A. B. (1995) *The Singer Resumes the Tale*, ed. M. L. Lord. Ithaca, NY.

Lourcelles, J. and S. Mizrahi (1963) "Entretien avec Riccardo Freda." *Présence du cinéma* 17: 11–30.

Lowenstam, S. (1997) "Talking Vases: The Relationship between the Homeric Poems and Archaic Representations of Epic Myth." *TAPA* 127: 21–76.

Lubac, H. de (1959) *Exégèse médiévale: les quatre sens de l'ecriture*. Paris.

Lucanio, P. (1994) *With Fire and Sword: Italian Spectacles on American Screens 1958–1968*. Metuchen NJ.

Luce, J. V. (1998) *Celebrating Homer's Landscapes: Troy and Ithaca Revisited*. New Haven, CT.

Luraghi, N. ed. (2001) *The Historian's Craft in the Age of Herodotus*. Oxford.

Lurje, M. (2004) *Die Suche nach der Schuld: Sophokles' Oedipus Rex, Aristoteles' Poetik und das Tragödienverständnis der Neuzeit*. Munich/Leipzig.

Lynche, Richard (fl. 1600) *The Fountaine of Ancient Fiction*. London (1599). Facsimile reprint: New York (1976).

Mackie, H. S. (1996) *Talking Trojan: Speech and Community in the Iliad*. Lanham, MD.

MacKinnon, K. (1986) *Greek Tragedy into Film*. Rutherford.

Macneice, L. (1939) *Autumn Journal*. London.

Macrobius (fl. c. 430). *The Saturnalia*, trans. P. V. Davies. New York (1969).

Madden, J. D. (1983) "The Palms Do Not Weep: A Reply to Professor Hurwit and a Note on the Death of Priam in Greek Art." *CJ* 78: 193–201.

Maehler, H. (1997) *Die Lieder des Bakchylides II. Die Dithyramben und Fragmente.* Leiden/New York/Cologne.

Malkin, I. (1994) *Myth and Territory in the Spartan Mediterranean.* Cambridge.

Malkin, I. (1998) *The Returns of Odysseus: Colonization and Ethnicity.* Berkeley/Los Angeles.

Mallory, J. P. and D. Q. Adams, eds. (1997) *Encyclopedia of Indo-European Culture.* London.

Mallowan, M. (1985) "Cyrus the Great," in I. Gershevitch, ed., *The Cambridge History of Iran,* Vol. 2, 392–419. Cambridge.

Mander, Carel van (1548–1606). *Wtlegginghe op den Metamorphosis . . . and Uytbeeldinghe der Figuren . . . , in van Mander, Het Schilderboeck.* Amsterdam (1616).

Marinatos, S. (1953) "Peri tous neous basilikous taphous ton Mukenon," in *Geras Antoniou Keramopoullou,* 54–88. Athens.

Marquardt, P. (1982) "Hesiod's Ambiguous View of Woman." *C. Phil.* 77: 283–91.

Martianus Felix Capella (fl. probably first quarter of 5th century) *The Marriage of Philology and Mercury,* vol. 2 of W. H. Stahl, R. Johnson, and E. L. Burge, *Martianus Capella and the Seven Liberal Arts.* New York (1971).

Martin, R. P. (1987) "Fire on the Mountain: *Lysistrata* and the Lemnian Women." *Cl. Ant.* 6: 77–105.

Martin, R. P. (1989) *The Language of Heroes: Speech and Performance in the Iliad.* Ithaca, NY.

Martin, R. P. (1997) "Similes and Performance." E. Bakker and A. Kahane, eds. *Written Voices, Spoken Signs,* 138–66. Cambridge, MA.

Martin, R. P. (2005) "Pulp Epic: The *Catalogue* and the *Shield,*" in R. Hunter, ed., *The Hesiodic Catalogue of Women: Constructions and Reconstructions,* 153–75. Cambridge.

Marvell, A. (1996) *Complete Poems,* ed. E Story Donno. London.

Mason, H. J. (2004) "Sappho's Apples." in M. Zimmerman and R. Van Der Paardt, eds., *Metamorphic Reflections: Essays presented to Ben Hijmans at his 75th Birthday,* 243–53. Leuven.

Mayor, A. (2000) *The First Fossil Hunters.* Princeton.

McCauley, B. (1999) "Heroes and Power: The Politics of Bone Transferral," in R. Hägg, ed., *Ancient Greek Hero Cult,* 85–98. Stockholm.

McDonald, M. and M. M. Winkler (2001) "Michael Cacoyannis and Irene Papas on Greek Tragedy," in M. M. Winkler, ed., *Classical Myth and Culture in the Cinema,* 72–89. New York.

McGlew, J. F. (1993) *Tyranny and Political Culture in Ancient Greece.* Ithaca, NY.

McKay, K. J. (1963) "Ambivalent ΑΙΔΩΣ in Hesiod." *AJP* 84: 17–27.

McLane, P. E. (1968) *Spenser's Shepheardes Calender: A Study in Elizabethan Allegory.* Notre Dame, IN.

McNiven, T. J. (2000) "Behaving Like an Other: Telltale Gestures in Athenian Vase Painting," in B. Cohen, ed., *Not the Classical Ideal: Athens and the Construction of the Other in Greek Art,* 71–97. Leiden.

Meiggs, R. and D. Lewis (1969) *A Selection of Greek Historical Inscriptions to the End of the Fifth Century BC.* Oxford.

Meineke, A., ed. (1849) *Stephani Byzantini Ethnicorum quae supersunt.* Berlin.

Melandra, W. W. (1983) *An Introduction to Ancient Iranian Religion.* Minneapolis.

Meltzer, E. (1974) "Egyptian Parallels for an Incident in Hesiod's *Theogony* and an Episode in the Kumarbi Myth." *JNES* 33: 154–7.

Melville, A. D. (1998) *Ovid Metamorphoses*. Oxford.

Melville, A. D. (1999) *Ovid The Love Poems*. Oxford.

Miles, G. (1999) *Classical Mythology in English Literature: A Critical Anthology*. London/New York.

Miles, M. (1998) *The Athenian Agora 31: The City Eleusinion*. Princeton.

Miller, Arthur (2000) *A View from the Bridge/All My Sons*. London.

Miller, M. C. (2000) "The Myth of Bousiris: Ethnicity and Art," in B. Cohen, ed., *Not the Classical Ideal: Athens and the Construction of the Other in Greek Art*, 413–42. Leiden.

Minnis, A. J. and A. B. Scott, with D. Wallace (1988) *Medieval Literary Theory and Criticism, c. 1100–c. 1375*. Oxford.

Mitchell, T. C. (1991) "The Babylonian Exile and the Restoration of the Jews in Palestine," in J. Boardman, I. E. S. Edwards, N. G. L. Hammond, E. Sollberger, and C. B. F. Walker, eds., *The Cambridge Ancient History*, second ed., Vol. 3, Part 2, 410–60. Cambridge.

Mitchell, W. J. T., ed. (1984) *Landscape and Power*. Chicago.

Moessner, O. (1907) "Die Mythologie in der dorischen und altattischen Komödie." Ph.D. dissertation, Erlangen.

Mondi, R. (1990) "Greek Mythic Thought in the Light of the Near East," in L. Edmunds, ed., *Approaches to Greek Myth*, 141–98. Baltimore.

Montanari, F. (1995) "The Mythographus Homericus," in J. G. J. Abbenes, S. R. Slings, and I. Sluiter, eds., *Greek Literary Theory after Aristotle*. Amsterdam.

Montgomery, J. A. (1979) *The Book of Daniel*. Edinburgh.

Moon, W. G. (1983) "The Priam Painter: Some Iconographic and Stylistic Considerations," in W. G. Moon, ed., *Ancient Greek Art and Iconography*, 97–118. Madison WI.

Moon, W. G. (1985) "Some New and Little-Known Vases by the Rycroft and Priam Painters," in *Greek Vases in the J. Paul Getty Museum* 2: 41–70. Malibu.

Moore, M. (1980) "Exekias and Telamonian Ajax." *AJA* 84: 417–34.

Moreau, A. (1994) *Le Mythe de Jason et Médée: Le va-nu-pied et la sorcière*. Paris.

Morgan, C. and T. Whitelaw (1991) "Pots and Politics: Ceramic Evidence for the Rise of the Argive State." *AJA* 95: 79–108.

Morgan, K. (2000) *Myth and Philosophy from the Presocratics to Plato*. Cambridge.

Morgan, L. (1988) *The Miniature Wall Paintings of Thera: A Study in Aegean Culture and Iconography*. Cambridge.

Morgan, T. (1998) *Literate Education in the Hellenistic and Roman Worlds*. Cambridge.

Morris, S. P. (1989) "A Tale of Two Cities: The Miniature Frescoes from Thera and the Origins of Greek Poetry." *AJA* 93: 511–35.

Morris, S. P. (1992) *Daidalos and the Origins of Greek Art*. Princeton.

Mozley, J. H., trans. (1928) *Statius: Thebaid*, 2 vols. Cambridge MA.

Muellner, L. (1976) *The Meaning of Homeric EYXOMAI through Its Formulas*. Innsbruck.

Muellner, L. (1990) "The Simile of the Cranes and Pygmies: A Study of Homeric Metaphor." *Harv. Stud.* 93: 59–101.

Muellner, L. (1996) *The Anger of Achilles: Mênis in Greek Epic*. Ithaca, NY.

Mulroy, D. (1992) *Early Greek Lyric Poetry*. Ann Arbor, MI.

Mulvey, L. (1975) "Visual Pleasure and Narrative Cinema." *Screen* 16: 6–18.

Mulvey, L. (1989) *Visual and Other Pleasures*. Bloomington, IN.

Munich, A. (1989) *Andromeda's Chains: Gender and Interpretation in Victorian Literature and Art.* New York.

Munkerus, Thomas (fl. 17th century) *Mythographi Latini.* Amsterdam (1681).

Murray, P. and P. Wilson, eds. (2004) *Music and the Muses. The Culture of Mousike in the Classical Athenian City.* Oxford.

Musti, D. (1963) "Sull'idea di συγγένεια in iscrizioni greche." *Annali della Scuola Normale Superiore di Pisa* 32: 225–39.

Myers, E. M., ed. (1997) *The Oxford Encyclopedia of Archaeology in the Near East*, 5 vols. Oxford.

Myers, K. S. (1994) *Ovid's Causes: Cosmogony and Aetiology in the Metamorphoses.* Ann Arbor, MI.

Nafissi, M. (1991) *La nascita del Kosmos. Studi sulla storia e la società di Sparta.* Naples.

Nagy, G. (1974) *Comparative Studies in Greek and Indic Meter*, Harvard Studies in Comparative Literature 33. Cambridge, MA.

Nagy, G. (1979) *The Best of the Achaeans.* Second ed., with new introduction: Baltimore (1999). http://www.press.jhu.edu/books/nagy/BofA.html

Nagy, G. (1982) "Hesiod," in T. J. Luce, ed., *Ancient Greek Authors*, 48–67. New York.

Nagy, G. (1985) "Theognis and Megara: A Poet's Vision of His City." In T. J. Figueira and G. Nagy, eds., *Theognis of Megara: Poetry and the Polis*, 22–81. Baltimore.

Nagy, G. (1990a) *Pindar's Homer: The Lyric Possession of an Epic Past.* Baltimore. http://www.press.jhu.edu/books/nagy/PHTL/toc.html (1997).

Nagy, G. (1990b) *Greek Mythology and Poetics.* Ithaca, NY.

Nagy, G. (1993) "Alcaeus in Sacred Space," in R. Pretagostini, ed., *Tradizione e innovazione nella cultura greca da Omero all' età ellenistica: Scritti in onore di Bruno Gentili*, 221–5. Rome.

Nagy, G. (1994) "The Name of Achilles: Questions of Etymology and 'Folk Etymology,'" *Illinois Classical Studies* 19 (*Studies in Honor of Miroslav Marcovich*), Vol. 2: 3–9.

Nagy, G. (1994/1995) "Genre and Occasion." *Metis: Revue d'Anthropologie du Monde Grec Ancien* 9–10: 11–25.

Nagy, G. (1996a) *Poetry as Performance: Homer and Beyond.* Cambridge.

Nagy, G. (1996b) *Homeric Questions.* Austin.

Nagy, G. (1999) *The Best of the Achaeans*, revised ed. Baltimore.

Nagy, G. (2000) "'Dream of a Shade': Refractions of Epic Vision in Pindar's *Pythian* 8 and Aeschylus' *Seven against Thebes.*" *Harv. Stud.* 100: 97–118.

Nagy, G. (2002) *Plato's Rhapsody and Homer's Music: The Poetics of the Panathenaic Festival in Classical Athens.* Cambridge, MA/Athens.

Nagy, G. (2003) *Homeric Responses.* Austin.

Nagy, G. (2004a) *Homer's Text and Language.* Urbana/Chicago.

Nagy, G. (2004b) "Transmission of Archaic Greek Sympotic Songs: From Lesbos to Alexandria." *Critical Inquiry* 31: 26–48.

Nagy, G. (2005) "The Epic Hero," in J. M. Foley, ed., *A Companion to Ancient Epic*, 71–89. Oxford. http://chs.harvard.edu/chs/online_books

Nagy, G. (2007) *Homer the Classic.* Forthcoming.

Nagy, G. (2008) *Homer the Preclassic.* Forthcoming.

Neckam, Alexander (c. 1157–1217) *De Naturis Rerum . . . with the poem of the same author . . . De Laudibus Divinae Sapientiae*, ed. T. Wright. London (1863).

Neils, J. (1987) *The Youthful Deeds of Theseus.* Rome.

Neils, J., ed. (1992) *Goddess and Polis: The Panathenaic Festival in Ancient Athens.* Princeton.

Neils, J. (1993) "A Greek Nativity by the Meidias Painter." *Bulletin of the Cleveland Museum of Art* 70: 274–89.

Neils, J. (1994) "Reflections of Immortality: The Myth of Jason on Etruscan Mirrors," in R. D. de Puma and J. P. Small, eds., *Murlo and the Etruscans*, 190–95. Madison, WI.

Neils, J. and J. Oakley, eds. (2003) *Coming of Age in Ancient Greece: Images of Childhood from the Classical Past.* New Haven, CT.

Nelson, S. (1998) *God and the Land: The Metaphysics of Farming in Hesiod and Virgil.* Oxford.

Nesselrath, H.-G. (1990) *Die attische Mittlere Komödie: Ihre Stellung in der antiken Literaturkritik und Literaturgeschichte.* Berlin/New York.

Nesselrath, H.-G. (1995) "Myth, Parody, and Comic Poets," in G. Dobrov, ed., *Beyond Aristophanes: Transition and Diversity in Greek Comedy*, 1–27. Atlanta.

The New English Bible (1970) Oxford/Cambridge.

Nightingale, A. (1992) "Plato's *Gorgias* and Euripides' *Antiope*: A Study in Generic Transformation." *California Studies in Classical Antiquity* 11: 121–41.

Nilsson, M. P. (1951) *Cults, Myths, Oracles and Politics in Ancient Greece.* Lund.

Nilsson, M. P. (1972) *The Mycenaean Origin of Greek Mythology*, second ed. Berkeley/Los Angeles.

Nisbet, R. G. M. and M. Hubbard (1978), *A Commentary on Horace: Odes Book II.* Oxford.

Nishimura-Jensen, J. (2000) "Unstable Geographies: The Moving Landscape in Apollonius' *Argonautica* and Callimachus' *Hymn to Delos*." *TAPA* 130: 287–317.

Northrup, M. (1983) "Where Did the *Theogony* End?" *Symbolae Osloenses* 58:7–13.

Oakley, J. H. (2004) *Picturing Death in Classical Athens: The Evidence of the White Lekythoi.* Cambridge.

Ober, J. (2005) "Law and Political Theory," in M. Gagarin and D. Cohen, eds., *The Cambridge Companion to Ancient Greek Law*, 394–411. Cambridge.

O'Higgins, D. M. (1997) "Medea as Muse: Pindar's *Pythian* 4," in J. J. Clauss and S. I. Johnston, eds., *Medea: Essays on Medea in Myth, Literature, Philosophy, and Art*, 103–26. Princeton.

Olivelle, P. (2005) *Manu's Code of Law.* Oxford.

O'Neill, Eugene (1988) *Complete Plays 1920–31.* New York.

Oppenheim, A. L. (1977) *Ancient Mesopotamia*, revised ed. Chicago.

Osborne, R. (1987) *Classical Landscape with Figures: The Ancient Greek City and its Countryside.* London.

Oudemans, T. C. W. and A. P. M. H. Lardinois (1987) *Tragic Ambiguity: Anthropology, Philosophy and Sophocles' Antigone.* Leiden.

Ovide Moralisé (probably between 1316 and 1328), 5 vols., ed. L. de Boer. *Verhandelingen der Koninklijke Akademie van Wetenschappen.* Amsterdam (1915–38).

Padgett, J. M. (2003) *The Centaur's Smile. The Human Animal in Early Greek Art.* New Haven, CT.

Page, D. L. (1955) *Sappho and Alcaeus: An Introduction to the Study of Ancient Lesbian Poetry.* Oxford.

Page, D. L. (1957) *Euripides*: Medea. Oxford.

Palmer, L. R. (1979) "A Mycenaean 'Akhilleid'?" in R. Muth and G. Pfohl, eds., *Serta Philologica Aenipontana* III, 255–61. Innsbruck.

Papathomopoulos, M. (1968) *Antoninus Liberalis, Les Métamorphoses*. Paris.

Pariente, A. (1992) "Le monument argien des 'sept contre Thèbes,'" in M. Piérart, ed., *Polydipsion Argos: Argos de la fin des palais mycéniens à la constitution de l'état classique, BCH* Suppl. 22, 195–229. Paris.

Parker, R. (1987) "Myths of Early Athens," in J. M. Bremmer, ed., *Interpretations of Greek Mythology*, 187–214. London.

Parker, R. (1996) *Athenian Religion: A History*. Oxford.

Parker, R. (1999) "Through a Glass Darkly: Sophocles and the Divine," in J. Griffin, ed., *Sophocles Revisited. Essays Presented to Sir Hugh Lloyd-Jones*, 11–30. Oxford.

Parry, A. (1957) "Landscape in Greek Poetry." *YClS* 15:3–29.

Parry, A. (1966) "Have We Homer's *Iliad*?" *YClS* 20: 177–216.

Parry, A., ed. (1971) *The Making of Homeric Verse: The Collected Papers of Milman Parry*. Oxford.

Parry, M. (1932) "Studies in the Epic Technique of Oral Versemaking. II. The Homeric Language as the Language of Oral Poetry." *Harv. Stud.* 43: 1–50. Reprinted in A. Parry 1971: 325–64.

Pasolini, P. P. (1988) *Heretical Empiricism*, ed. L. K. Barnett, trans. B. Lawton and L. K. Barnett. Bloomington, IN.

Passman, K. M. (1991) "The Classical Amazon in Contemporary Cinema," in M. M. Winkler, ed., *Classics and Cinema*, 81–105. London.

Pattichis, P. (2001) "Fictional and Mythological Landscapes in Ancient Greek Literature," in G. L. Anagnostopoulos, ed., *Art and Landscape*, Vol. 2, 663–74. Athens.

Peacham, Henry (1578?–1642?) *Garden of Eloquence*. Menston (1971).

Pellizer, E. (1993) "La mitografia," in G. Cambiano, L. Canfora, and D. Lanza, eds., *Lo spazio letterario della Grecia antica I. La produzione e la circolazione del testo II. L'Ellenismo*, 283–303. Rome.

Peppas-Delmousou, D. (1988) "The *Theoria* of Brauron," in R. Hägg, N. Marinatos, and G. Nordquist, eds., *Early Greek Cult Practice*, 255–8. Uppsala.

Perry, B. E. (1965) *Babrius and Phaedrus*. Cambridge, MA.

Petropoulos, J. C. B. (1993) "Sappho the Sorceress: Another Look at fr. 1 (LP)." *ZPE* 97: 43–56.

Petropoulos, J. C. B. (1994) *Heat and Lust: Hesiod's Midsummer Festival Scene Revisited*. Lanham, MD.

Philips, D. D. (2003) "The Bones of Orestes," in G. W. Bakewell and J. P. Sickinger, eds., *Gestures: Essays in Ancient History, Literature, and Philosophy Presented to Alan L. Boegehold*, 301–16. Oxford.

Phinney, E., Jr. (1967) "Hellenistic Painting and the Poetic Style of Apollonius." *CJ* 62: 145–9.

Pickard-Cambridge, A. (1968) *The Dramatic Festivals of Athens*, second ed., revised by J. Gould and D. M. Lewis. Oxford.

Pictorius, Georgius (c. 1500–69) *Apotheoseos*. Basel (1554). Facsimile reprint: New York (1976).

Pictorius, Georgius (c. 1500–69) *Theologia Mythologica*. Antwerp (1532). Facsimile reprint: New York (1976).

Pipili, M. (1987) *Laconian Iconography of the Sixth Century B.C.* Oxford.

Plaskow, J. (1979) "The Coming of Lilith: Toward a Feminist Theology," in C. Christ and J. Plaskow, eds., *Womanspirit Rising: A Feminist Reader in Religion*, 198–209. New York.

Pochat, G. (1973) *Figur und Landschaft. Eine historische Interpretation der Landschaftsmalerei von der Antike bis zur Renaissance.* Berlin/New York.

Podlecki, A. J. (1971) "Stesichoreia." *Athenaeum* 49: 313–27.

Podlecki, A. J. (1984) *The Early Greek Poets and Their Times.* Vancouver.

Polignac, F. de (1995) *Cults, Territory, and the Origins of the Greek City-State*, trans. J. Lloyd. Chicago.

Pollitt, J. J. (1990) *The Art of Ancient Greece: Sources and Documents.* Cambridge.

Pope, Alexander (1963) *The Poems*, ed. J. Butt. London.

Pound, Ezra (1975) *The Cantos.* London.

Power, T. (2000) "The *Parthenoi* of Bacchylides 13." *Harv. Stud.* 100: 67–81.

Prenowitz, E., ed. (2004) *Selected Plays of Hélène Cixous.* London/New York.

Pritchard, J. B. (1969) *Ancient Near Eastern Texts Relating to the Old Testament*, third edition. Princeton.

Puttenham, George (1530?–1590) *The Arte of English Poesie.* London (1589).

Quarles, Francis (1592–1644) *Emblemes.* Cambridge (1643).

Rabanus Maurus (c. 784–856) *De Universo. PL* 111.

Rackham, O. (1990) "Ancient Landscapes," in O. Murray and S. Price, eds., *The Greek City: From Homer to Alexander*, 85–111. Oxford/New York.

Ray, J. D. (1995) "Egyptian Wisdom Literature," in J. D. Ray, R. P. Gordon, and H. G. M. Williamson, eds., *Wisdom in Ancient Israel: Essays in Honour of J. A. Emerton*, 17–29. Cambridge.

Redfield, J. M. (1975) *Nature and Culture in the Iliad: The Tragedy of Hector.* Chicago.

Redfield, J. M. (1982) "Notes on the Greek Wedding." *Arethusa* 15:181–201.

Rees, A. and B. Rees (1989) *Celtic Heritage.* Reprint. London.

Reinhardt, K. (1960) "Platons Mythen," in *Vermächtnis der Antike*, 291–5. Goettingen. Originally published as a monograph in 1927.

Reinhold, M. (1984) *Classica Americana: The Greek and Roman Heritage in the United States.* Detroit.

Renouard, Nicolas (fl. early 17th century) *Les Metamorphoses d'Ovide traduittes en Prose Francoise . . . Avec XV Discours contenans l'explication moralé des Fables.* Paris (1614).

Revermann, M. (1997) "Cratinus' Διονυσαλέξανδρος and the Head of Pericles." *JHS* 117: 197–200.

Reyes, D. (1994) *Archaic Cyprus.* Oxford.

Reynolds, Henry (fl. 1627–1633) "Mythomystes, Wherein a Short Survay is Taken of the Nature and Value of True Poesie . . . ," in J. E. Spingarn, *Critical Essays of the Seventeenth Century*, Vol. 1, 144–79. Bloomington, IN (1957).

Reynolds, M. (2000) *The Sappho Companion.* London.

Richardson, M. (1989) *Astrological Symbolism in Spenser's* The Shepheardes Calender. Mellen.

Richardson, N. J. (1974) *The Homeric Hymn to Demeter.* Oxford.

Richardson, N. J. (1993) *The Iliad: A Commentary*, Vol. 6. Cambridge.

Richlin, A., ed. (1992a) *Pornography and Representation in Greece and Rome.* Oxford/New York.

Richlin, A. (1992b) "Reading Ovid's Rapes," in A. Richlin, ed., *Pornography and Representation in Greece and Rome*, 158–79. Oxford/New York.

Ridewall, John (mid-14th century) *Fulgentius metaforalis*, in H. Liebschütz, ed. *Studien der Bibliothek Warburg*, 4 (1926).

Ripa, Cesare (fl. 1600). *Iconologie*. Paris (1644). Facsimile reprint: New York (1976).

Riu, X. (1999) *Dionysism and Comedy*. Lanham, MD.

Robert, L. (1960) "Recherches épigraphiques, V: inscriptions de Lesbos." *Rev. Ét. Grec.* 73: 285–315.

Roger, A. (1995) "Histoire d'une passion théorique ou comment on devient un Raboliot du Paysage," in *La théorie du paysage en France 1974–1994*, 438–51. Seyssel.

Roger, A. (2001) "Was Ancient Greece a Landscape Society?" in G. L. Anagnostopoulos, ed., *Art and Landscape*, Vol. 1, 44–54. Athens.

Rondolino, G. (1980) *Vittorio Cottafavi: Cinema e televisione*. Bologna.

Rose, P. W. (2001) "Teaching Classical Myth and Confronting Contemporary Myths," in M. M. Winkler, ed., *Classical Myth and Culture in the Cinema*, 291–318. New York.

Rosenberg, F. (1904) *Le livre de Zoroastre*. St. Petersburg.

Roskill, M. (1997) *The Languages of Landscape*. University Park, PA.

Rösler, W. (1980) *Dichter und Gruppe: Eine Untersuchung zu den Bedingungen und zur historischen Funktion früher Lyrik am Beispiel Alkaios*. Munich.

Ross, Alexander (1590–1654) *Mystagogus Poeticus, or The Muses Interpreter. . . . The second edition much enlarged*. London (1648). Facsimile reprint: New York (1976).

Roth, R. (1966) "Der Mythus von den fünf Menschengeschlechtern und die indische Lehre von den vier Weltaltern," in E. Heitsch, ed., *Hesiod*, 450–70. Darmstadt.

Rouveret, A. (1989) *Histoire et imaginaire de la peinture ancienne (Ve siècle av. J.-C.-Ier siècle ap. J.-C.)*, Bibliothèque des Écoles Françaises d'Athènes et de Rome 274. Paris/Rome.

Rouveret, A. (2004) "*Pictos ediscere mundos*. Perception et imaginaire du paysage dans la peinture hellénistique et romaine." *Ktema* 29:325–44.

Rühfel, H. 2003. *Begleitet von Baum und Strauch. Griechische Vasenbilder*. Dettelbach.

Ruskin, John (1903–12) *The Works of John Ruskin*, ed. E. T. Cook and A. Wedderburn, 39 vols. London.

Russell, D. S. (1964) *The Method and Message of Jewish Apocalyptic*. Philadelphia.

Saïd, E. W. (1978) *Orientalism*. New York.

Saïd, S. (1993) *Approches de la mythologie grecque*. Paris.

Saïd, S. (2002) "Greeks and Barbarians in Euripides' Tragedies: The End of Differences?" in T. Harrison, ed., *Greeks and Barbarians*, 62–99. New York.

Sallustius (fl. second half of the fourth century). *Concerning the Gods and the Universe*, trans. A. D. Nock. Hildesheim (1966).

Salutati, Coluccio (1331–1406). *De Laboribus Herculis*, ed. B. L. Ullman. Turici, n.d. (c. 1947).

Salvesen, A. (1998) "The Legacy of Babylon and Nineveh in Aramaic Sources," in S. Dalley, ed., *The Legacy of Mesopotamia*, 139–61. Oxford.

Sancisi-Weerdenburg, H. (2000) "Cultural politics and chronology," in H. Sancisi-Weerdenburg, ed., *Peisistratos and the Tyranny: A Reappraisal of the Evidence*, 79–106. Amsterdam.

Sandys, George (1578–1644) *Ovid's Metamorphosis, Englished, Mythologized, and Represented in Figures*, ed. K. Hulley and S. Vandersall. Lincoln, NE (1970; based on the edition of 1632).

Schefold, K. (1960) "Origins of Roman Landscape Painting." *Art Bulletin* 42: 87–96.

Schefold, K. (1966) *Myth and Legend in Early Greek Art*. New York.

Schefold, K. (1992) *Gods and Heroes in Late Archaic Greek Art*. Cambridge.

Schmitt-Pantel P. and L. Bruit-Zaidman (1992) *Religion in the Ancient Greek City*. Cambridge.

Schnapp, A. (1994/95) "De la cité des images à la cité dans l'image." *Metis: Revue d'Anthropologie du Monde Grec Ancien* 9–10: 209–18.

Schörner, G. and H. R. Goette (2004) *Die Pan-Grotte von Vari*. Mainz am Rhein.

Schretlen, M. J. (1929–1931) "Blokbogen 'de Syv Planeter,'" *Kunstmuseets Aarskrift*, 1–15.

Schwartz, B. D. (1992; reprint 1995) *Pasolini Requiem*. New York.

Schwarze, J. (1971) *Die Beurteilung des Perikles durch die attische Komödie und ihre historische und historiographische Bedeutung*. Munich.

Seaford, R. A. S. (1984) *Euripides*: Cyclops. Oxford.

Segal, C. (1986) *Pindar's Mythmaking: The Fourth Pythian Ode*. Princeton.

Segal, C. (1996) "Catharsis, Audience, and Closure in Greek Tragedy," in M. S. Silk, ed., *Tragedy and the Tragic. Greek Theatre and Beyond*, 149–72. Oxford.

Servius, Grammarian (fl. c. 400). *In Virgilii Aeneidos; In Bucolica et Georgica commentarii*, in *In Virgilii Carmina Commentarii*, 3 vols., ed. G. Thilo and H. Hagen. Leipzig (1881–1902).

Shakespeare, William (1564–1616) *The Riverside Shakespeare*, ed. G. B. Evans. Boston (1974).

Shapiro, H. A. (1989) *Art and Cult under the Tyrants in Athens*. Mainz.

Shapiro, H. A. (1992) "*Mousikoi Agones*: Music and Poetry in the Panathenaic Festival," in J. Neils, ed., *Goddess and Polis: The Panathenaic Festival in Ancient Athens*, 53–75. Princeton.

Shapiro, H. A. (1993) *Personifications in Greek Art*. Kilchberg.

Shapiro, H. A. (1994) *Myth into Art: Poet and Painter in Classical Greece*. London.

Shapiro, H. A. (1995) "Coming of Age in Phaiakia: The Meeting of Odysseus and Nausikaa," in B. Cohen, ed., *The Distaff Side: Representing the Female in Homer's Odyssey*, 155–64. Oxford/New York.

Shapiro, H. A. (1998) "Autochthony and the Visual Arts in Fifth-Century Athens," in D. Boedeker and K. A. Raaflaub, eds., *Democracy, Empire, and the Arts in Fifth-Century Athens*, 127–51. Cambridge, MA.

Shelley, Percy Bysshe (1977) *Shelley's Poetry and Prose*, ed. D. H. Reiman and S. B. Powers. New York/London.

Sherratt, E. S. (1990) "'Reading the Texts: Archaeology and the Homeric Question."*Antiquity* 64: 807–24.

Siebert, G. (1990) "Imaginaire et images de la grotte dans la Grèce archaïque et classique." *Ktema* 15: 151–61.

Siebert, G., ed. (1996) *Nature et paysage dans la pensée et l'environnement des civilisations antiques*, Actes du Colloque de Strasbourg 11–12 juin 1992. Paris.

Silk, M. S., ed. (1996) *Tragedy and the Tragic. Greek Theatre and Beyond*. Oxford.

Silk, M. S. (2000) *Aristophanes and the Definition of Comedy*. Oxford.

Simpson, M., trans. (1976) *Gods and Heroes of the Greeks: The Library of Apollodorus*. Amherst MA.

Sinos, D. (1980) *Achilles, Patroklos, and the Meaning of Philos*. Innsbruck-Sinos, D. (1975) *The Entry of Achilles into Greek Epic*. Ph.D. dissertation, Johns Hopkins University.

Slater, P. E. (1968) *The Glory of Hera: Greek Mythology and the Greek Family*. Princeton.

Slatkin, L. (1991) *The Power of Thetis: Allusion and Interpretation in the Iliad*. Berkeley/Los Angeles.

Small, J. P. (2003) *The Parallel Worlds of Classical Art and Text*. Cambridge.

Smith, G. A. (2004) *Epic Films: Casts, Credits and Commentary on over 250 Historical Spectacle Movies*. Jefferson, NC.

Smith, Horace (1846) *The Poetical Works*. London.

Snodgrass, A. (1987) *An Archaeology of Greece. Towards the History of a Discipline*. Berkeley/Los Angeles.

Snodgrass, A. (1998) *Homer and the Artists*. Cambridge.

Solodow, J. B. (1988) *The World of Ovid's Metamorphoses*. Chapel Hill, NC/London.

Solomon, J. (2001) *The Ancient World in the Cinema*, second ed. New Haven, CT.

Sorlin, P. (1980) *The Film in History: Restaging the Past*. Totowa, NJ.

Sourvinou-Inwood, C. (1990) "What is *polis* Religion?," in O. Murray and S. Price, eds., *The Greek City from Homer to Alexander*, 295–322. Oxford; now in R. Buxton, ed., *Oxford Readings in Greek Religion*, 19–37. Oxford.

Sourvinou-Inwood, C. (2002) *Tragedy and Athenian Religion*. Lanham, MD.

Spenser, Edmund (c. 1552–99) *Spenser: Poetical Works*, ed. J. C. Smith and E. de Selincourt. Oxford (1966).

Stafford, F. (1994) *The Last of the Race: The Growth of a Myth from Milton to Darwin*. Oxford.

Stanford, W. B. (1954) *The Ulysses Theme: A Study in the Adaptability of a Traditional Hero*. Reprint. Ann Arbor, MI (1968).

Stansbury-O'Donnell, M. D. (1990) "Polygnotos' *Nekyia*: A Reconstruction and Analysis." *AJA* 94: 213–35.

Stein, E. (1990) *Autorbewußtsein in der frühen griechischen Literatur*. Tübingen.

Stephanus, Charles (d. 1559). *Dictionarium Historicum Geographicum, Poeticum. . . .* London (1595).

Steuben, H. von (1968) *Frühe Sagendarstellungen in Korinth und Athen*. Berlin.

Stewart, A. (1990) *Greek Sculpture: An Exploration*. New Haven, CT.

Stewart, A. (2004) *Attalos, Athens, and the Akropolis*. Cambridge.

Stewart, J. A. (1905) *The Myths of Plato*, reprint edited by G. R. Levy. London (1970).

Stoddard, K. (2004) *The Narrative Voice in the Theogony of Hesiod*. Leiden.

Taplin, O. (1990) *Greek Fire*. New York.

Tartt, D. (1992) *The Secret History*. London.

Tavernier, B., ed. (1968–9) "Vittorio Cottafavi – 2. Entretien." *Positif* 100–101: 59–71.

Taylor, M. W. (1991) *The Tyrant Slayers: The Heroic Image in Fifth Century BC Art and Politics*, second ed. Salem, NH.

Televantou, C. A. (1994) Ακρωτήρι Θήρας· Οι Τοιχογραφίες της Δυτικής Οικίας. Athens.

Theodulph, Bishop of Orléans (c. 760–821) *Ecloga*, with commentary by O. Picardus. Lyons (c. 1487–8).

Thesleff, H. (1981) "Man and Locus Amoenus in Early Greek Poetry," in G. Kurz, D. Müller, and W. Nicolai, eds., *Gnomosyne: Menschliches Denken und Handeln in der frühgriechischen Literatur*, Festschrift für Walter Marg zum 70. Geburtstag, 31–45. Munich.

Thomas, R. (1989) *Oral Tradition and Written Record in Classical Athens*. Cambridge.

Tomlinson, R. A. (1992) "The Menelaion and Spartan Architecture," in J. Sanders, ed., *ΦΙΛΟΛΑΚΩΝ: Lakonian Studies in Honour of Hector Catling*, 247–55. London.

Treggiari, S. (1996) "Social Status and Social Legislation," in A. K. Bowman, E. Champlin, and A. Lintott, eds., *Cambridge Ancient History*, second ed., Vol. 10, 873–904. Cambridge.

Tritonio, M. Antonio (sixteenth century). *Mythologia*. Padua (1616). Facsimile reprint: New York (1979).

Turner, F. M. (1981) *The Greek Heritage in Victorian Britain*. New Haven, CT.

Tyrrell, W. B. and F. S. Brown (1991) *Athenian Myths and Institutions: Words in Action*. Oxford.

Vamvouri Ruffy, M. (2004) *La fabrique du divin. Les hymnes de Callimaque à la lumière des hymnes homériques et des hymnes épigraphiques*, Kernos Suppl. 14. Liège.

Van der Valk, M. H. A. L. H. (1958) "On Apollodori Bibliotheca." *REG* 71: 100–168.

Vatican Mythographers I (8th or 9th century), II (9th or 10th century), and III (12th century). In *Scriptores Rerum Mythicarum Latini Tres*, ed. G. H. Bode. Cellis (1834).

Venit, S. M. (2002) *Monumental Tombs of Ancient Alexandria: The Theater of the Dead*. Cambridge.

Verburg, Isaak (fl. 1732). *De Gedaant-wisselingen van P. Ovidius Naso, in het Latyn en Nederduitsch. . . .* Amsterdam (1732).

Vernant, J.-P. (1980) *Myth and Society in Ancient Greece*, trans. J. Lloyd. Cambridge, MA.

Vernant, J.-P. (1982) "La belle mort et le cadavre outragé," in G. Gnoli and J.-P. Vernant, eds., *La mort, les morts dans les sociétés anciennes*, 45–76. Cambridge/Paris. Reprinted in J.-P. Vernant, *L'individu, la mort, l'amour: Soi-même et autre en Grèce ancienne*, 41–79. Paris (1989).

Vernant, J.-P. (1983a) "Hesiod's Myth of the Races: An Essay in Structural Analysis," in *Myth and Thought among the Greeks*, 3–32. London/Boston. Republished New York (2006): 25–51.

Vernant, J.-P. (1983b) *Myth and Thought among the Greeks*, trans. J. Lloyd. London.

Vernant, J.-P. and Vidal-Naquet, P. (1988) *Myth and Tragedy in Ancient Greece*. New York. Originally *Mythe et tragédie en Grèce ancienne*, 2 vols. Paris (1972, 1986).

Versnel, H. (1990) "What's Sauce for the Goose Is Sauce for the Gander: Myth and Ritual, Old and New," in L. Edmunds, ed., *Approaches to Greek Mythology*, 23–90. Baltimore.

Veyne, P. (1988) *Did the Greeks Believe their Myths?* trans. P. Wissing. Chicago.

Viana, Sanchez de (fl. 1589). *Las transformaciones de Ovidio. . . . Con el comento, y explicación de las fabulas. . . .* Cordova (1589).

Vickers, B. (1973) *Towards Greek Tragedy: Drama, Myth, Society*. London.

Vidal-Naquet, P. (1986) *The Black Hunter: Forms of Society in the Greek World*, trans. A. Szegedy-Maszak. Baltimore.

Vollkommer, R. (1988) *Herakles in the Art of Classical Greece*. Oxford.

von Blanckenhagen, P. H. (1963) "The Odyssey Frieze." *Mitteilungen des Deutschen Archäologischen Instituts, Römische Abteilung* 70: 100–46.

Walcot, P. (1966) *Hesiod and the Near East*. Cardiff.

Waleys, Thomas (fl. 1320–40) *Metamorphosis Ovidiana moraliter explanata*. Paris (1515).

Wallace, J. (1996) *Shelley and Greece: Rethinking Romantic Hellenism*. Basingstoke.

Walsh, T. R. (2005) *Fighting Words and Feuding Words: Anger and the Homeric Poems*. Lanham, MD.

Walz, C. A. (1997) "Black Athena and the Role of Cyprus in Near Eastern/Mycenaean Contact," in J. E. Coleman and C. A. Walz, eds., *Greeks and Barbarians*, 1–27. Bethesda, MD.

Warren, P. (1979) "The Miniature Fresco from the West House at Akrotiri, Thera, and its Aegean Setting." *JHS* 99: 115–29.

Watkins, C. (1995) *How to Kill a Dragon: Aspects of Indo-European Poetics*. Oxford/New York.

Watkins, C. (2004) "Hittite," in R. D. Woodard, ed., *The Cambridge Encyclopedia of the World's Ancient Languages*, 551–75. Cambridge.

Webb, P. A. (1996) *Hellenistic Architectural Sculpture*. Madison, WI.

Webster, T. B. L. (1954) "Personification as a Mode of Greek Thought." *Journal of the Warburg and Courtauld Institutes* 17: 10–21.

Wegener, S. (1985) *Funktion und Bedeutung landschaftlicher Elemente in der griechischen Reliefkunst archaischer bis hellenistischer Zeit*, Europäische Hochschulschriften Reihe 38, Archäologie Vol. 6. Frankfurt.

Weinstock, S. (1971) *Divus Iulius*. Oxford.

Weller, C. H., et al. (1903) "The Cave at Vari." *AJA* 7: 263–349.

Welter, J. T. (1927) *L'Exemplum dans la littérature religieuse et didactique du moyen age*. Paris. Reprint. Geneva (1973).

Wender, D. (1973) *Hesiod; Theognis*. Harmondsworth.

West, E. W. (1995) *Pahlavi Texts*. Reprint. Delhi.

West, M. L. (1966) *Hesiod: Theogony*. Oxford.

West, M. L. (1974) *Studies in Greek Elegy and Iambus*. Berlin.

West, M. L. (1978) *Hesiod: Works and Days*. Oxford.

West, M. L. (1983) *The Orphic Poems*. Oxford.

West, M. L. (1985) *The Hesiodic Catalogue of Women: Its Nature, Structure, and Origins*. Oxford.

West, M. L. (1988) "The Rise of the Greek Epic." *JHS* 108: 151–72.

West, M. L. (1992) "The Descent of the Greek Epic: A Reply." *JHS* 112: 173–5.

West, M. L. (1993) *Greek Lyric Poetry*. Oxford.

West, M. L. (1994) "Ab Ovo." *CQ* 44: 289–307.

West, M. L. (1997) *The East Face of Helicon: West Asiatic Elements in Greek Poetry and Myth*. Oxford.

Wheatley, Phillis (1973) *Poems*. Boston.

Whitehall, R. (1963) "Days of Strife and Nights of Orgy." *Films and Filming* 9 no.6: 8–14

Whitley, A. J. (1994) "The Monuments That Stood before Marathon: Tomb Cult and Hero Cult in Archaic Attica." *AJA* 98: 213–30.

Whitman, J. (1987) *Allegory: The Dynamics of an Ancient and Medieval Technique*. Oxford.

Whitman, Walt (1855) *Leaves of Grass*. New York.

Whitney, Geffrey (1548–1603). *A Choice Book of Emblemes*. London (1586). Facsimile reprint, ed. Henry Green. New York (1967).

Wickersham, J. M. (1986) "The Corpse Who Calls Theognis." *TAPA* 116: 65–70.

Wickram, Georg (fl. 1545). *Ovidii Nasonis des aller sinnreichten Poeten Metamorphoses....* Meinz (1545).

Wikander, Stig. (1947). "Pāṇḍava-sagan och Mahabharatas mytiska förutsättningar." *Religion och Bibel* 6:27–39.

Wilamowitz-Moellendorff, U. von. (1900) *Textgeschichte der griechischen Lyriker*. Berlin.

Wilde, Oscar (1990) *Complete Stories, Plays and Poems*. London.

Wilhelm, G. (2004) "Hurrian," in R. D. Woodard, ed., *The Cambridge Encyclopedia of the World's Ancient Languages*, 95–118. Cambridge.

Williams, F. (1978) *Callimachus. Hymn to Apollo*. Oxford.

Williams, G. D. (1996) *The Curse of Exile: A Study of Ovid's Ibis, CPS* Supplement 19. Cambridge.

Williams, M. F. (1991) *Landscape in the ARGONAUTICA of Apollonius Rhodius*, Studien zur klassischen Philologie 63. Frankfurt am Main.

Wilson, D. F. (2002) *Ransom, Revenge, and Heroic Identity in the Iliad*. Cambridge, MA.

Wind, E. (1968) *Pagan Mysteries of the Renaissance*. New York.

Winkler, M. M. (1985) "Classical Mythology and the Western Film." *Comparative Literature Studies* 22: 516–40.

Winkler, M. M., ed. (1991) *Classics and Cinema*. London.

Winkler, M. M. (1996) "Homeric *kleos* and the Western Film." *Syllecta Classica* 7: 43–54.

Winkler, M. M., ed. (2001) *Classical Myth and Culture in the Cinema*. New York.

Winkler, M. M. (2002) "The Face of Tragedy: From Theatrical Mask to Cinematic Close-Up." *Mouseion* 3: 43–70.

Winkler, M. M. (2004) "Homer's *Iliad* and John Ford's *The Searchers*," in A. M. Eckstein and P. Lehman, eds., *The Searchers: Essays and Reflections on John Ford's Classic Western*, 145–70. Detroit.

Winkler, M. M. (2005) "Neo-Mythologism: Apollo and the Muses on the Screen." *International Journal of the Classical Tradition* 11: 383–423.

Winkler, M. M., ed. (2006) *Troy: From Homer's Iliad to Hollywood Epic*. Oxford.

Wiseman, D. J. (1991) "Babylonia 605–539 B.C.," in J. Boardman, I. E. S. Edwards, N. G. L. Hammond, E. Sollberger, and C. B. F. Walker, eds., *The Cambridge Ancient History*, second ed., Vol. 3, Part 2, 229–51. Cambridge.

Wood, C. (1970). *Chaucer and the Country of the Stars*. Princeton.

Wood, R. (1769) *An Essay on the Original Genius and Writings of Homer*. London.

Woodard, R. D. (1997) *Greek Writing from Knossos to Homer: A Linguistic Interpretation of the Origin of the Greek Alphabet and the Continuity of Ancient Greek Literacy*. Oxford/New York.

Woodard, R. D., ed. (2004) *The Cambridge Encyclopedia of the World's Ancient Languages*. Cambridge.

Woodard, R. D. (2006) *Indo-European Sacred Space: Vedic and Roman Cult*. Urbana/Chicago.

Woodard, R. D. (In press) *The Penguin Anthology of Classical Mythology*. Harmondsworth.

Woodford, S. (2003) *Images of Myths in Classical Antiquity*. Cambridge.

Woodford, S. and M. Loudon (1980) "Two Trojan Themes: The Iconography of Ajax Carrying the Body of Achilles and of Aeneas Carrying Anchises in Black Figure Vase Painting." *AJA* 84: 25–40.

Woolf, Virginia (1929) *A Room of One's Own*. London.

Wünsche, R., ed. (2003) *Herakles Herkules*. Munich.

Wyke, M. (1997) "Herculean Muscle! The Classicizing Rhetoric of Bodybuilding." *Arion*, third series 4: 51–79.

Yatromanolakis, D. (2003) "Ritual Poetics in Archaic Lesbos: Contextualizing Genre in Sappho," in D. Yatromanolakis and P. Roilos, eds., *Towards a Ritual Poetics*, 43–59. Athens.

Yatromanolakis, D. and P. Roilos, eds. (2003) *Greek Ritual Poetics*. Washington, DC.

Yoshida, A. (1964) "La structure de l'illustration du bouclier d'Achille." *Revue Belge de Philologie et d'Histoire* 42: 5–15.

Zacharia, K. (2003) *Converging Truths: Euripides' Ion and the Athenian Quest for Self-Definition*. Leiden.

Zajko, V. (1998) "Myth as Archive." *History of the Human Sciences* 11: 103–19.

Zajko, V. and M. Leonard (2006a) "Introduction," in V. Zajko and M. Leonard, eds., *Laughing with Medusa: Classical Myth and Feminist Thought*, 1–20. Oxford.

Zajko, V. and M. Leonard, eds. (2006b) *Laughing with Medusa: Classical Myth and Feminist Thought*. Oxford.

Zanker, P. (1988) *The Power of Images in the Age of Augustus*. Ann Arbor MI.

Zeitlin, F. (1995) *Playing the Other: Gender and Society in Classical Greek Literature*. Chicago.

INDEX

*A Collection of Wonders from the Entire
  Earth Arranged by Locality*, 238, 247
A Common Chorus, 446
A Streetcar Named Desire, 444
A View from the Bridge, 444
A Wonder Book, 11, 384
Abas, 373
Abdera, 216
Acarnania, 326
Accius, 83, 146, 355
Achaea, 280, 334
Achaeans, 24, 37, 56–9, 61–2, 73, 78,
  147, 191, 280, 335–6, 346–7; *see also*
  Achaians
Achaeus, 280
Achaians, 458; *see also* Achaeans
Acharnians, 193, 199–200, 202,
  325
Achelous, 326
Acheron, 319, 322, 417
Achilles, 25, 31, 33-8, 48, 54–9, 63–71,
  78–9, 81–2, 84, 91, 105, 123, 138,
  147, 167, 169, 199, 201, 291, 296,
  302, 310, 323, 325, 335, 350, 359, 361,
  404, 408, 433, 457–8, 460
Acrisius, 331
Acropolis, 203, 206, 258, 260, 280, 295,
  298–301, 313, 315, 338–41, 347
Actaeon, 293, 366–7, 441
Actorione, 290
Acusilaus, 242, 244–5, 281
Ad Familiares, 246
Adam Bede, 436
Addison, Joseph, 427, 435, 440, 444
Adeimantus, 215
adharma, 129

Admetus, 449
Adonis, 441, 450
Adrastia, 232
Adrastus, 337
adultery, 8, 362, 417
Aeacus, 215, 230, 232, 242
Aeetes, 17, 18
Aegean Sea, 269–70, 279–80
Aegeus, 26, 255, 257–8, 270, 273–4; *see
  also* Aigeus
Aegeus, 194
Aegicores, 279
Aegids, 272–4
Aegina, 58, 349
Aegipan, 98
aegis, 146, 264, 269, 272, 385
Aegisthus, 192
Aegyptus, 173
Aelius Theon, 356
Aenea, 348
Aeneaden, 359
Aeneas, 91, 291, 347–8, 355–6, 359, 369,
  378–9, 417, 433
Aeneid, 346, 357–9, 379, 410, 413, 415,
  417, 422
Aeolians, 280
Aeolic (traditions, lands, etc.), 33–5, 38,
  41, 48, 68, 83
Aeolic meter, 275, 277; *see also* meter
Aeolosicon, 194, 197
Aeolus, 197, 247, 280, 373
Aeolus, 197
Aerope, 221
Aeschylus, 19, 167, 172, 174–5, 178, 185,
  196, 204, 230, 336, 351, 430–1, 436–7,
  440, 443–4

Aesculapius, 413
Aeson, 16
Aesop, 63, 198, 211
Aether, 86, 364; see also aither
aetiology, 62, 215, 261–2, 265, 267,
    269–72, 274, 278–81, 363, 366, 368
Aetolia, 337
Agamemnon, 24, 54, 63, 68, 147, 166,
    167, 171, 173, 184–5, 221, 233, 333–6,
    338, 345, 349, 351, 361, 436
Agamemnon, 167, 174–5, 184–5, 336, 438
Agathon, 202, 224
Agave, 175-6
Agesilaus II of Sparta, 349
Aglauros, 366
Aglaurus, 280
agōnes, 20
Agora, 288, 340, 344–5, 349, 445
Agoracritus, 205
agriculturalism, 203, 264, 316
agriculturalist class, 135
agriculturalists, 118–19, 122–3, 131, 135;
    see also farmers, herders, pastoralists,
    shepherds
Ahura Mazdāh, 115, 129, 148
Aidoneus, 263
Aidos, 107, 120, 137
Aigeus, 171; see also Aegeus
ainos, 63–8, 78–9, 107, 211
aither, 228; see also Aether
Aithiopis, 37
Aitia, 358
aition, 265, 269
Ajax, 2, 58–9, 64, 69, 172, 182–4, 186,
    233, 242, 291, 296–7, 310, 323–4, 361
Akkadian, 110, 126
Akrotiri frescoes, 307–8
Alalu, 93, 96
Alanus de Insulis, 412–3
Alcaeus, 2, 22–5, 42–7, 53
Alcestis, 322
Alcestis, 449
Alcibiades, 216, 224, 437
Alcinous, 146–7, 169, 232, 315–6
Alcman, 21–2, 40
Alcmene, 204
Alcmeon, 309
Alcyoneus, 293

Alexander the Aetolian, 247
Alexander the Great, 112, 295, 350
Alexandra, 333–4
Alexandria, 237, 306
allegory, 9, 388, 395, 401, 407–13,
    415–18, 420–2
alphabet, 104, 219
Alpheius River, 327
Altar of the Twelve Gods, 344
Althaea, 361
Amakandu, 101
Amazonomachy, 298, 300
Amazons, 206, 294, 298, 302, 338, 342,
    345, 349, 411, 464
ambrosia, 89, 263
Amel-Marduk, 127
Ammon, 102, 218
Amores, 357, 361, 371–3, 376
Amphiaraus, 337
Amphiaraus, 194
Amphictyons, 275, 276–8
Amphictyons, 194
Amphion, 229
Amphitheus, 199
Amphitrite, 268-9
Amphitryon, 167, 175, 190, 204
Amphitryon, 190, 192
Amyclae, 333–4, 346
An Essay on Criticism, 434
An Essay on the Original Genius and
    Writings of Homer, 429
Anacreon, 22, 40, 46–8
Anagyrus, 194
Anatolia, 92, 104
Anatolian, 118
Anaxagoras, 334
Anchimolus, 343
Anchises, 291, 348
Andromache, 28, 36–8, 69, 173, 347, 378
Andromache, 184, 348
Andromeda, 435
Andromeda, 196, 197, 202
Anglo-Saxons, 432
Angra Mainyu, 129
Anna Perenna, 371
Annales, 355
Anshar, 99
Ant Men, 194

Antaeus, 288, 294, 449
Antenor, 273–4
Antenorids, 273–4
Antheus, 247
Anthropheracles, 197
anthropomorphism, 324, 328, 374
Anthroporestes, 197
Anticleia, 472
Antigone, 182, 310
Antigone, 182, 311
Antigonus of Carystus, 239
Antiochus Epiphanes, 125
Antiope, 298, 342–3
Antiope, 229
Antiphanes, 309
Antiphates, 78
Antoninus Liberalis, 245, 248, 251
Anu, 92–3, 95–6, 99–100, 103
Aphaea, 349
Aphareus, 240
Aphrodite, 26–34, 36, 39–41, 87, 91,
    167-8, 179–80, 182, 191, 193, 206,
    226, 262, 267, 273, 292, 300–1, 311,
    316, 318, 402, 450, 459
apocalyptic motifs, 89, 116, 125, 135, 148,
    396, 467
Apollo, 21, 36–9, 90, 173, 175, 177–81,
    183–4, 195, 225, 238, 240, 249, 251,
    268–9, 270–81, 290, 294, 297–8,
    301–2, 313–14, 316, 323–4, 341, 343,
    356, 367, 368–9, 373, 409, 412, 419,
    436, 458–60, 470, 476
Apollodorus, 6, 11, 18, 97–8, 238, 240–1,
    243–5, 252, 258–9, 320, 388–9
Apollonius (paradoxographer), 239
Apollonius of Rhodes, 168–9, 242, 245,
    312, 316, 357, 389, 462–3
Apology, 67, 211
apotheosis, 295, 300, 369, 370
apragmosune, 207
Apsu, 99–100
Apsyrtus, 18, 169
Arachne, 367, 375, 411, 416
Aramaic, 112, 126
Aranzaḫ, 93, 96
Aratus, 133, 245
Arcadia, 238, 313, 333, 347, 355, 427
Arcadians, 337

Arcesilas of Cyrene, 168, 272–4
archaeology, 81, 331
Archaic period, 2, 19, 21–4, 28, 52,
    306–7, 314, 329, 349
Archedemus of Thera, 313
Archelaus of Thessaly, 230
Archilaus of Cappadocia, 249
Archilochus, 22, 37–8, 48
Arcite, 411
Areimanius, 129
Areopagus, 213
Ares, 17, 28, 31–3, 37, 84, 90–1, 122,
    273, 410
Arestor, 244
Arete, 315
Argades, 279
Argive Heraion, 243
Argives, 57, 336–7, 343
Argo, 1, 17–18, 168–9, 302, 458, 463
Argonautica, 168, 242, 312, 316, 357, 462
Argonauts, 17–18, 168, 195, 272, 462
Argos, 8, 172, 174, 185, 200, 281, 331,
    334, 336–7
Argos (guardian of Io), 294, 385
Ariadne, 169, 257–8, 290, 361, 408,
    449
Arianna, 398
Arion, 48, 408–9
Ariosto, Ludovico, 416, 422
Aristides, 230
Aristogeiton, 288–9
Aristonymus, 194
Aristophanes, 4, 22, 105, 177, 192–7,
    200, 202, 204–7, 216, 218, 223–5,
    261, 319, 325, 392, 446
Aristotle, 38, 42, 44–5, 186, 192, 195,
    210–11, 243, 325, 339, 345, 418
Arjuna, 123
arkhaia, 259
Armenian, 118, 127, 134
Armenians, 133
Armenius of Pamphylia, 233
Arnold, Matthew, 437-8
Arnold, Thomas, 432
Arnolphe of Orléans, 410
Ars Amatoria, 357, 362–3, 371, 411
art history, 81
Art of English Poesy, 409

Artemis, 36, 73, 90, 179-80, 184–5, 195, 248, 262, 269, 279, 301, 323, 339, 343, 345, 392
aša, 129
Ascalon, 24
Asclepiades, 244–5
Asclepius, 298, 313
Ascra, 83
Asia Minor, 3, 24, 33, 41, 46, 83, 126, 233, 343
Asopus, 244
Aspasia, 193
Assyria, 112
Assyrians, 110
Astarte, 103
Asteria, 88
Asterope, 317
Astraeus, 88, 90
astrology, 412–13
Astronomy, 105
Astyanax, 173, 291
Atalanta, 198, 361, 388
Atalanta in Calydon, 438
Athanasia, 293
Atharva Veda, 128–9
athemis, 168
Athena, 17, 42, 71, 90, 167, 173, 178–9, 181–4, 191, 206, 224, 250, 267, 279, 280–1, 292, 293, 298–302, 315, 323, 339–41, 385, 460
Athenaeus, 309
Athenians, 7, 191, 194, 198, 200, 207, 216–18, 223–4, 267–70, 279, 288–9, 299, 337–8, 340, 349–50
Athens, 7, 8, 20–2, 43, 45, 47–8, 166, 170, 172–3, 184, 193–4, 198, 200, 203, 207, 212–13, 216–18, 220–4, 227–8, 243, 247, 255–8, 260, 262, 264, 266–70, 278–82, 287–9, 292–5, 297–301, 313, 315, 320, 322–3, 336, 338–45, 347, 349–51, 392, 411, 432, 435, 446, 454
Atlantis, 5, 216, 218, 220, 222–4, 466–8
Atlas, 88, 94, 102, 413
Atreids, 334, 336
Atreus, 196, 221, 334, 336, 355, 373, 436
Atropus, 232–3
Attic Nights, 83

Attica, 192, 194, 206, 212–13, 221, 224, 227, 257, 261, 280, 289, 293, 295–6, 299, 301, 311, 313–14, 326, 338–9, 342–4, 347–8
audience, 5, 7, 8, 49, 108, 146, 184–5, 191, 201, 205, 212, 216, 238, 250, 279–80, 286, 294, 311, 332, 359, 392, 409, 412, 454, 457–8, 460, 462–3, 467, 475
Augean stables, 297
Augias, 297, 469
Augustan Forum, 362
Augustine, 408
Augustus, 8, 249, 356, 359, 362, 368–71, 375, 378–9
Augustus Diuus, 368
Aulis, 169, 185, 349
aulodes, 20, 47
Aulus Gellius, 83
Aurora Leigh, 436
autochthony, 217–18, 221, 224, 280–1, 299; *see also* chthonic beings
Autolycus, 412
Autumn Journal, 445
Avesta, 115, 128
Avestan, 115, 141
Až Dahāk, 116

Baal, 103
Babylon, 24, 100, 113, 125, 133
Babylonia, 98, 100–1, 108, 113, 125–7, 139
Babylonian Exile, 125
Babylonians, 92, 110
Bacchae, 47, 174–6, 184, 192
Bacchus, 275–8, 436
Bacchylides, 22, 42, 48, 50, 260, 267–70, 279
Baitylos, 102
Balaustion's Adventure, 449
Balto-Slavic, 118
barbarians, 174, 299, 348–9
Battle of Salamis, 348–9
Battus, 271–2, 274, 366
Bava, Mario, 472
Bdelycleon, 206
Behn, Aphra, 427
Bellerophon, 295, 335

Bellum Poenicum, 355
Beloved, 446
Belshazzar, 125
Benveniste, Émile, 119, 145
Berchorius, Petrus, 410, 413–14, 416, 419–20
Berkoff, Steven, 445
Bernardus Silvestris, 410–12, 415, 417–18, 420-1
Berouth, 102
Bhima, 116, 123
biaios, 168
Bias, 334
Bible, 3, 102, 109–11, 113, 124–7, 131–2, 136, 397, 407–8, 412, 419–20, 423, 426
Bibliotheca, 6, 18, 97, 243–5, 258–9, 320
Biblis, 366
Birds, 207
Black Anima, 447-8
black-figure painting, 291, 295, 300, 302, 322–3, 339, 342, 468
Blair, Hugh, 429
Boccaccio, Giovanni, 410, 420
Boeotia, 83, 201, 346, 349
Boeotians, 341
Boğazköy, 92
Boios, 358
Boreads, 290
Boreas, 88, 90, 213, 227, 301, 316, 327
Bosphorus, 311
Botticelli, Sandro, 410, 413
boundaries, 172–5
Brahma, 129
brāhmaṇa class, 117, 130, 135–6
brahmins, 117, 135
Braine, John, 444
Brangas, 249
Brauron, 339, 343–4, 392
Brignone, Guido, 471
Briseis, 34, 68–9, 147, 357, 377
Bromius, 275
Brontë, Emily, 437
Brontës, the, 435
bronze age/*genos*, 106, 114–15, 122, 132–4, 141, 143
Browning, Elizabeth Barrett, 436, 438, 443
Browning, Robert, 449

Bull of Marathon, 287, 338, 342–3
Busiris, 291
Byblis, 247
Byron, Lord, 430

Cabiria, 464
Cacoyannis, Michael, 470
Cadmus, 17, 176, 275, 278, 366
Calchas, 185
calendar, 261, 282
Callias, 216
Callicles, 211, 214, 229–31
Callimachus, 237–9, 247, 271–3, 326, 358, 376
Callimachus (the polemarch), 289
Callinus, 22, 48
Calliope, 219
Callisto, 367, 370
Calydon, 240
Calydonian Boar Hunt, 240, 294
Calypso, 72–3, 79, 312–13
Cambyses II, 126
Camerini, Mario, 464
Camus, Marcel, 474
Canace, 197
cannibalism, 78, 88, 196, 221, 314, 415
Cape Malea, 335
Caria, 298
Carians, 270
Carmentalia, 371
Carnea, 243
Carneia, 271, 273–4
Cassandra, 173, 175, 186, 300, 333–4, 346, 361
Cassirer, Ernst, 210, 261
Castor, 184
cataclysm, 62
Catalogue of Monsters, 87, 90, 120–1
Catalogue of Ships, 334
Catalogue of Women, 91, 151, 241, 244, 335, 358, 366, 388, 391
Catasterisms, 245; *see also Katasterismoi*
Catullus, 356, 361
Caucasus, 17, 178
caves, 72–3, 312–14, 316, 321, 326, 401, 409
Cebes of Thebes, 215, 228
Cecrops, 169, 194, 280, 299, 373

Celeus, 263
Celtic, 118
Celts, 119, 429
Cenaeum, 181
Centauromachy, 297–8, 300, 342
Centaurs, 54, 105, 195, 213–14, 240,
    286, 297–9, 301–2, 342, 349
Ceos, 267, 269–70
Cephalus, 301
Cephis(s)us River, 311, 326
Cer, 87
Cerberus, 89–90, 167, 288, 290, 462,
    471
Cercopes, 290
Cercops, 244
Cercyon, 193, 287–8, 338
Ceres, 375
Cerynitan hind, 295
Ceto, 87, 121
Chaffey, Don, 458
Chalcidians, 341
Chaos, 86–7, 100, 199
Chapman, George, 430
Charities, 90, 385
Charon, 319, 322, 417, 471, 474
Chaucer, Geoffrey, 9, 10, 408, 410–12,
    419, 426
Cheiron, 313; see also Chiron
Chimaeras, 90, 213
Chimeras, 290, 295
Chios, 46
Chiron, 105, 290; see also Cheiron
Chloris, 316
choral dance, 268, 269–71, 275,
    277–8
choral lyric, 20
choral performances, 21, 25, 27, 44
choral poetry, 46
choruses, 20–2, 25, 28, 35, 38–40, 44, 49,
    172–3, 183–5, 191, 196, 198, 200–1,
    203, 219, 273–4, 277–8, 281, 311, 325
Christabel, 430
Christianity, 10, 231, 296, 407, 409–12,
    414, 416, 423, 426–7, 468, 471
Christine de Pizan, 408
chronography, 241, 243
Chrysippus, 197
Chrysothemis, 317

chthonic beings, 97–8, 102, 120, 280; see
    also autochthony, hupokhthonioi
cicadas, 194, 218–19, 310
Cicero, 246, 356
Cilicia, 98, 331
Cimon, 198
Cineas, 344
Cinyras, 374
Circe, 73, 74, 77, 91, 169, 293, 318,
    437
citharodes, 20, 45, 47
City Dionysia, 3, 4, 21, 43, 48, 166, 177,
    261, 279, 281
Cladeus River, 327
"Claremont," 428
Clash of the Titans, 457, 458–9, 471
Classical period, 19–23, 52, 80, 270, 281,
    298, 302, 306–7, 313–14, 324, 327,
    329
Cleanthes, 364
Cleisthenes, 299, 338, 340–2, 344–5
Clement of Alexandria, 334
Cleomenes, 336, 340
Cleon, 204
Cleopatra, 356, 442
Clito, 224
Cloris, 427
Clotho, 233
Clouds, 22, 199
Clymene, 88
Clytaemnestra, 333
Clytemnestra, 167, 171, 174, 443
Clytius, 317
Cnossus, 267, 270; see also Knossos
Cocalus, 194–5
Cocteau, Jean, 473–4, 476
Codrus Painter, 7, 287, 289
Coesyra, 343
Coeus, 86, 88
Colchians, 18, 169
Colchis, 1, 17, 168–71
Coleridge, Samuel Taylor, 417–18, 430
color symbolism, 116–17
colossus of Nebuchadnezzar, 113, 127, 131
comedians, 194, 237
comedy, 4, 48, 177, 190–200, 202–3,
    205, 208, 468
Complaint of Nature, 412, 420

composition, 2, 19, 21, 23–4, 28, 39, 51, 53, 84–5, 99, 112, 202, 245, 265, 277–8, 292
Confessio Amantis, 412
Conon, 60, 239, 243, 249
Constitution of the Athenians, 345
Conti, Natale, 410, 420
Convivio, 417
Corinna, 22
Corinth, 40, 48, 170–1, 295, 337, 409, 468
Corinthians, 335
Cornelius Gallus, 246
Corythus, 247
cosmic conflagration, 62
cosmic flood, 62
cosmogony, 85, 130–1, 133, 135, 149–50, 198
Cosmographia, 411–12, 420, 421
cosmology, 130, 131, 133, 148, 150, 228
Cottafavi, Vittorio, 11, 454, 461, 466, 468–9, 476
Counsels of Wisdom, 110
Countesse of Pembrokes Yvychurch, 412, 420
Cowper, William, 429
Cranach, Lucas, 410
Craterus of Macedon, 243
Cratinus, 4, 190, 192–5
creation, 98, 100, 117, 130–31, 135, 149, 194, 216–17, 222, 365, 374, 395
Creon, 170, 172, 182, 446
Cretan Sea, 267, 269–70
Crete, 88, 257, 268–70, 295, 347, 462
Creusa, 180–1, 279–81, 313, 316, 403
Critias, 216, 218, 222
Critias, 223; *see also Timaeus/Critias*
Critius, 345; *see also* Kritios
Crius, 86–7
Crommyon, 287
Cromwell, Oliver, 427
Cronus, 87, 88, 92, 95, 97–8, 100, 102–4, 106, 204, 213, 221, 230, 385
Croton, 347
cult, 6, 31, 33, 35, 194, 227, 248–9, 259–62, 264–71, 273–5, 277–9, 281, 300, 334, 343–4, 346, 351, 364, 393, 403, 466
Cupid, 371, 373, 401, 412

Cyclades, 270, 279, 281
Cyclopes, 62, 71–3, 77–8, 87–8, 145–6, 192, 314, 325, 462
Cycnus, 84; *see also* Kyknos
Cygnus, 359
Cymbeline, 441
Cypria, 53
Cyprus, 104
Cyre, 271
Cyrene, 271–4, 282, 351
Cyrene (a nymph), 271–2
Cyrus the Great, 125–6

Daedalus, 194–5, 257, 366
Dagon, 102
daimones, 121–6, 221, 226
Damkina, 99
Danaans, 57
Danae, 331, 355
Danaids, 173, 356, 360
Danaus, 172, 196, 331
dance, 21, 26, 47; *see also* choral dance
dancers, 39, 278, 468
Daniel, 113–14, 118, 124–7, 131–4, 136
Dante Alighieri, 9, 214, 226, 231, 413, 415, 417, 421, 471
Daphne, 367–8
Darius I, 126
Dark Ages, 286
darkness, 72–6
Daughters of Danaus, 194, 196
Davis, Desmond, 457
De Concini, Ennio, 464
De Mirabilium Libellus, 239
De Rerum Natura, 356
Dead Sea Scrolls, 125
deiknumena, 266
Deleia, 343
Delia, 267–8
Deliads, 269
Delian League, 270
Delos, 267–70, 272, 282, 323–4, 326, 342–3
Delphi, 88, 95, 168, 180, 243, 260, 272, 275–9, 281–2, 293, 298–9, 301, 319, 323, 333, 338, 341, 347, 445, 470
Demarous, 102
Demeter, 4, 88, 90–1, 203, 263–5, 267

demigods, 107, 142, 144
Demiurge, 222
democracy, 217, 288, 299, 338–46
Demodokos, 33
Demogorgon, 431
demokratia, 349
Demophon, 263, 267
Demos, 204–5
Dēnkard, 115, 136
Derveni papyrus, 85
destruction, 114, 117, 135, 143, 148, 222, 365
Deucalion, 9, 241, 242, 244, 365, 373, 412
dharma, 116–17, 129, 130, 135, 148–9
Diana, 411, 427
Dicaeopolis, 199–201
dichotomies, 119–21, 123–4, 129, 132, 143–4
Dickens, Charles, 435
Dickinson, Emily, 437
didactic literature, 109, 112, 149–50; *see also* wisdom literature
Dido, 357–8, 361, 417, 449
Didyma, 249
Didymus, 251
Diegesis, 239, 243, 249
dikaios, 116
Dike, 133, 232
dikē, 105, 109, 122, 124, 143, 145–6, 149
Diodorus Siculus, 1
Diomedes, 24, 249, 334, 337, 346
Dionysalexandrus, 4, 190, 193, 197
Dionysius of Halicarnassus, 42
Dionysus, 4, 24, 43, 45–6, 166, 174–76, 182, 184, 190–91, 193–4, 200, 204, 257, 260–62, 269, 275–8, 280, 291–3, 302, 311, 314, 322–3, 444
Dioscuri, 290, 334
Dioskouroi, 43
Diotima, 216, 224–7
Dirce, 311
Disputationes Camuldenses, 417
dithyrambs, 260, 267–70, 277, 279
Divine Comedy, 421
do ut des, 266, 271
Dodecanese, 347
Dodona, 17, 181

Doré, Gustave, 471
Dorian (traditions, territory), 60, 280, 335
Dorians, 271–2, 280, 336
Doris, 87
Dorus, 280
Dramata or Niobos, 194–5
Dramata or the Centaur, 194–5
drōmena, 266
"Drowne's Wooden Image," 434
drug, 129
druh, 129
Dryden, John, 426, 428
Dryope, 359
Duffy, Carol Ann, 10, 426, 448, 449
Dumézil, Georges, 3, 118–19, 123, 332
Dunciad, 428, 441
Dunnu, 101
Duris of Samos, 238
dvāparayuga, 117

Ea, 92–4, 97–100
Earth, 101
Ecclesiazusae, 207
Echidna, 87, 90
Echion, 176
Echo, 202
Eclogues, 356
ecpyrosis, 62
Edipo re, 469–70
Eëtion, 38
Egypt, 92, 104, 111–12, 118, 134, 196, 218–19, 222–3, 290–1, 306, 356, 415, 449
Egyptians, 102, 408
Ehoiai, 92
Eileithyia, 90
El, 102
Elamites, 126
Electra, 184
elegiac, 20, 22–3, 140, 358, 361
elegy, 373
Eleusis, 4, 275, 288, 337, 339, 344–5
Eliot, George, 435–7, 442
Eliot, T. S., 425, 441–3, 445, 447–8
Elioun, 102
Elpenor, 318–19
Elymians, 347

Elysian Fields, 169, 320, 471
Elysian Isles, 107; *see also* Islands of the
    Blessed, Islands of the Blest, Isles of
    the Blessed
Elysium, 417, 427
Emathides, 375
Emblemes, 412
Empedocles, 22, 210
Enceladus, 301, 373
Endimion, 413
Endymion, 41, 413
Enki, 109
Ennius, 355
Enūma Eliš, 98, 100–1
enunciation, 272, 274
Eos, 41, 73–4, 87, 90–1, 301–2
Ephesus, 26, 47, 249
Ephialtes, 225
Ephyre, 335
epic, 2, 3, 5, 19, 20, 23, 31–3, 36–9, 49,
    51–64, 66–7, 69–72, 75, 77, 79–81,
    84, 86, 98, 100, 103–5, 116–18, 124,
    149, 168–9, 176, 197, 210, 222, 237,
    240, 250, 260–2, 264–6, 271, 275, 299,
    308, 332, 337, 346, 355, 358, 363, 366,
    368–9, 373, 375, 377, 379, 402, 429,
    441, 454, 462, 464, 466, 471, 474, 476
epic cycle, 37, 53, 82, 260
epic frame, 54
Epidaurus, 260, 298
Epigeios, 102–3
epiklēros, 281
Epimetheus, 88, 216–17, 219, 383–85
Epinicia, 260, 270, 273
epinikia, 49
epiphanies, 27–30, 185, 263, 267–8, 277,
    281, 301
Epirus, 247
Epistulae ex Ponto, 372
Epithalamia, 260
Epodes, 356
Er, 212, 215, 230, 232–3
Erasmus, 407–8, 426
Erato, 219
Eratosthenes, 245, 358
Ercole al centro della terra, 472
Ercole alla conquista di Atlantide, 466
Ercole e la regina di Lidia, 464

Erebus, 86, 198
Erechtheids, 280
Erechtheus, 194, 279–80
Eretria, 343
Eretrians, 343
Erichthonius, 280, 299–300
Erinyes, 87
Eris, 87, 106–7, 120, 123
Eros, 32, 86, 199, 218–19, 224–7, 231–2,
    302
Erotica Pathemata, 358
Erotika Pathemata, 246–8
Erymanthian boar, 295
Erysichthon, 359, 366
Esarhaddon, 112
eschatology, 136, 214–15
Esquiline, 308
esthlon, 141
esthlos, 138–9, 141
Eteocles, 411
Etruscans, 293–4
Euboea, 169, 231, 275, 343, 347, 440
Euhemerism, 102, 388, 413, 415
Euhemerus, 413
Euius, 275
Eumaeus, 138, 146
Eumaios, 57, 79
Eumelus, 245
Eumenides, 184
Eumolpus, 263
Euphorbus, 325
Euphrates River, 100
Euphronius, 342
Euripides, 10, 35, 47, 167, 169, 171, 173,
    177, 180, 184–5, 192, 194, 196–7, 199,
    200, 202–4, 221, 227, 229, 245, 261,
    267, 279–81, 313, 316–17, 321, 336,
    348, 357, 397, 426, 436, 444, 449, 470
Europa, 242, 316, 361, 367, 373, 398
Eurotas River, 334
Euryalus, 247–8, 334
Eurybia, 87
Eurydice, 360, 473, 474
Eurynome, 90
Eurytos, 294
Eusebius, 339
Evander, 347, 355, 371
Evenus, 240

Evippe, 247
exarkhōn, 38
Exekias, 296–7, 323
Ezra, 126

fables, 5, 12, 63, 107–9, 112, 128, 211
fabula praetexta, 355
fabulae, 8, 332, 356, 357
Fabulae, 320
falsehoods, 2, 50, 58–9, 129
farmers, 83, 105, 123–4, 148, 194, 201,
  279; *see also* agriculturalists
Fasti, 357, 370–1, 377
fate goddesses, 93, 95
Fates, 87, 98, 233, 290, 447; *see also*
  Moerae
Ferroni, Giorgio, 460
festivals, 2–4, 20–1, 24–7, 40, 43–8, 88,
  99, 166, 191–2, 194, 202–3, 206, 261,
  267–9, 271, 273, 277, 292, 301, 339,
  343–4, 422
fiction, 5, 8, 222, 224, 357, 370, 372, 374,
  378, 397–8, 441, 443, 450, 455–6
first function, 119, 121, 131, 143–4, 147
Floralia, 371
folk etymology, 244
formulae, 27, 145, 216, 266, 291
Forster, E. M., 439–40
framed myth, 64
framing myth, 64
Francisci, Pietro, 464, 465
François Vase, 342
Frankenstein, 431, 443
Fraunce, Abraham, 411, 420
Frazer, James, 1, 388
Freda, Riccardo, 471, 475
Freud, Sigmund, 441
Frogs, 105, 192, 209, 319
Fulgentius, 410, 413, 415, 417, 420–1
Furies, 178–9, 184, 290, 374
furor, 360, 378

Gaea, 86–90, 95, 97, 100–2; *see also* Ge
Gallus, 376
Gandy, Joseph, 432
Ganymede, 301, 370
Garden of Eloquence, 417
Garth, Samuel, 428

Gauls, 299
Ge, 102, 225, 299, 301; *see also* Gaea
Geleontes, 279
Gelon, 338
gender, 268, 315, 396, 398–401, 404,
  427
Genealogia Deorum Gentillium, 410
Genealogies, 244
genos, 141–3, 148
Geometric period, 294, 297, 328
Georgics, 359, 433
geranos, 342–3
Geras, 87, 294
Germanic, 118, 130
Geryon, 290, 294, 338
Geryoneus, 87
Getic, 377
giants, 87, 98, 214, 225, 293, 349, 375,
  462–3
Gigantomachy, 98, 103, 204–5, 293,
  300–1, 356
Giovanni del Virgilio, 411
Glauce, 436
Glaucon, 215, 231, 233, 346
Glaucus, 196, 320
Glaucus, 196
Glaucus of Anthedon, 231
Gli amori di Ercole, 464
Goethe, Johann Wolfgang von, 429
Golden Age, 12, 356, 413
golden age/*genos*, 106, 115, 121, 123,
  133–4, 141, 143, 148, 212, 365
Golden Apples of the Hesperides, 317
Golden Fleece, 1, 15–16, 168
Gorgias, 5, 211, 214, 227–9, 231
Gorgons, 87, 121, 213, 290, 331
Gower, John, 410, 412
Gracchus, 356
Graces, 42, 90
Graeae, 87, 120, 290
Graiai, 394
Graves, Robert, 1
Great Works, 105
Greek Anthology, 25
Greek religion, 282
Grímnismál, 130
group, 49
gynaecocracy, 206, 208

(h)abrosuna, 47
habrosyne, 347
Hadad, 103
Hades, 73–5, 79, 88–90, 122, 143,
    203, 214, 230, 263–4, 288, 301,
    471–3
Hagnon, 193
Ḥain, 101
Halicarnassus, 298
Hall, Thomas, 410, 419
Hamlet, 441
Hanuman, 116–17
Hardy, Thomas, 435, 437, 442
Harington, John, 416
Harmodios, 288–9
Harpies, 290, 462
Harrison, John Kent, 459
Harrison, Tony, 445–6
Harryhausen, Ray, 458–63, 471, 475
Ḥattuša, 92
Hawthorne, Nathaniel, 11, 12, 16, 257,
    384, 434, 439
Hebe, 90
Hebrew, 102, 109, 126
Hecataeus, 5, 210, 242, 244
Hecate, 88, 263, 290
Hecatoncheires, 87, 89
Hector, 28, 36–8, 57, 68–9, 78, 138, 167,
    346–7, 361, 457, 459–60
Hecuba, 57, 173
Ḥedammu, 95–6, 98
Hegel, Georg Wilhelm Friedrich, 450
Hegelochus, 197
Helen, 8, 60, 167, 191, 192, 194, 218,
    242, 273, 290, 300, 302, 325, 334–5,
    362–3, 398, 408, 449
Helen, 60, 196, 202, 449
Helen of Troy, 459
Helice, 334
Helios, 74, 87, 225, 263, 292, 300, 403
Hellanicus, 242–3, 347, 348
Hellen, 241–2
Hellenistic period, 5, 6, 85, 103, 125,
    168, 238, 242, 250–2, 286, 294–5,
    298, 301, 306–7, 312, 325–9, 331–2,
    336, 462
Hemera, 86, 89
Hephaesteum, 299–300

Hephaestus, 17, 89–90, 225, 280, 291–2,
    294, 299, 326, 345
Hephaisteia, 292
Hera, 17, 24–5, 44, 88, 90, 167, 169, 175,
    182, 191, 248, 250, 291–2, 295, 317,
    321, 337, 457–8, 463, 475
Heracles, 84, 98, 123, 166, 175–6, 181–2,
    184–6, 195, 199, 204, 210, 267, 287,
    290–1, 294–5, 298–301, 313, 317, 323,
    326, 336–7, 339, 349, 464, 469
Heracles Ablaze, 197
Heraclids, 336
Heraclitus, 410
Herculanium, 190
Hercules, 9, 11, 355, 366, 369, 371, 413,
    422, 462–9, 473, 476
Hercules (Disney film), 453, 473
Hercules Conquers Atlantis, 11
Hercules Unchained, 464
Hercules: The Legendary Journeys, 453
herders, 83, 150; *see also* pastoralists,
    shepherds
here-and-now, 45, 50; *see also hic et nunc*
Hermaphroditus, 290, 450
Hermes, 73, 98, 102, 178, 184, 191,
    217–18, 221, 229, 238, 263, 280,
    301–2, 312–14, 318–19, 344, 450
Hermione, 348
Hermocrates, 223
herms, 344
Hero and Leander, 428
Herodotus, 5, 23, 46, 52, 85, 177, 210,
    213, 238, 242, 259, 274, 279, 288–9,
    300, 333–4, 336, 338–9, 341, 349
Heroes, 194
heroic age/*genos*, 107, 114, 119, 122,
    142–4
Heroides, 9, 357–8, 365, 397, 449
heroism, 167–8, 171
heroon, 337
Herse, 301
Hesiod, 3, 10, 11, 19, 23, 34, 52, 60, 62,
    83–92, 95–124, 128–9, 132–4, 137–51,
    176, 178, 195, 212–14, 217, 221, 224,
    229, 241–2, 244–5, 305, 310–11,
    316–17, 320, 335, 358, 364, 366, 376,
    386, 388, 391, 426
Hesperides, 295, 317, 318, 320–1

Hestia, 88
hetairos (plural, hetairoi), 42, 147
Heteroioumena, 358, 368
hexameter, 20, 23, 56, 105, 193, 241, 267; see also meter
hic et nunc, 260, 266, 268, 271; see also here-and-now
hieroglyphics, 219, 223
hippalektryon, 290
Hipparchus, 340, 341, 344
Hipparkhos, 47
Hipparkhos, 47
Hippias, 207, 339, 340–1, 343
Hippias Minor, 23
Hippias of Elis, 243
Hippocrates, 216
Hippodameia, 298
Hippolyta, 411
Hippolytus, 9, 35, 167, 179, 247, 262, 413, 418
Hippolytus, 35, 167, 179, 184, 185, 194, 227, 261, 267, 279, 317
Hipponax, 22, 48
Historia Plantarum, 323
Historiae Mirabiles, 239
historical linguistics, 82
Hittites, 92–8, 100–1, 103–4, 134
Homer, 2, 3, 5, 10–11, 19, 23, 46, 52–3, 58–60, 66, 82–5, 90, 105, 138, 145–7, 176, 192, 197, 199, 210, 212–13, 221, 229–30, 232, 237, 240, 245, 250–1, 260, 266, 269, 291, 305, 308, 310–12, 315, 318–19, 326, 334–6, 346, 350, 357–60, 376, 378–9, 388, 402, 410, 422, 426, 428–30, 441, 449, 454, 457–9, 461, 472, 474–6
Homeric Hymns, 38, 178, 195, 260, 264–6, 268, 271, 275–6, 316, 323
Homeric poetry, 2, 53–7, 60–2, 74–5, 80–2
Hopletes, 279
Horace, 356, 360, 377
Horae, 90, 314, 385
Horkus, 87
"How Many Bards Gild the Lapses of Time," 430
hubris, 105, 109, 116, 121–4, 143–6, 168, 267

Hughes, Ted, 448, 450
hūiti class, 131
humanitas, 363
humnos, 39, 40, 43–4
hupokhthonioi, 122; see also chthonic beings
Hurrians, 92, 95, 104
Hyacinthus, 301
Hydrophoroi, 204
Hygeia, 313, 317
Hyginus, 320, 389
Hylas, 462–3
Hyllus, 181, 336, 467–8
hymenaeus, 28
Hymenaeus, 260
Hymn to Apollo, 195, 268, 323
Hymn to Delos, 326
Hymn to Demeter, 266–7, 271, 276, 316
Hymn to Hermes, 23, 38, 178
Hymn to Zeus, 364
Hyperboreans, 308
Hyperion, 86–7
Hypermestra, 196
Hypermnestra, 331
Hypnos, 89, 293
hypothesis, 190, 193
Hypsipyle, 195, 197, 357

Ištar, 94
Iacchus, 275
Iapetus, 86, 88, 364
Iasus, 244
Ibis, 361
Ibycus, 22, 36, 48
Idas, 240–1, 247
ideology, myth as, 332, 340, 350
Ilia, 361
Iliad, 20, 25, 31–8, 52–8, 60–1, 63–4, 66–74, 78–9, 81–2, 84, 90, 105, 138, 147, 167, 178, 218, 221, 229, 230, 237, 250, 260, 311, 313, 325, 326, 334–5, 346, 357–8, 410, 428, 457–8, 460, 476
Ilion, 70
Ilissus River, 213, 218, 310, 316, 327, 341
Imagines, 311, 326
Imperial Aramaic, 126
"In a Library," 437
Inachus, 244

incest, 101
India, 80, 116, 118, 123–4, 128–9, 131–2, 134–7, 140, 142, 143, 148–50
Indo-Aryans, 127
Indo-European, 3, 92, 118, 129–31, 134; *see also* Proto-Indo-European
Indo-Europeans, 103, 118–19, 121, 123–4, 127, 131–3, 135, 137, 144, 147–50; *see also* Proto-Indo-Europeans
Indo-Iranian, 118, 127
Indo-Iranians, 119, 129, 131–6, 140, 142, 148; *see also* Proto-Indo-Iranians
Inferno, 226, 471
Instruction of Amen-em-Opet, 111–12
Instructions of Ankhsheshonqy, 112
Io, 175, 242, 244, 294, 361, 367, 369, 398, 414
Iocasta, 309; *see also* Jocasta
Iolaus, 317
Iolcus, 16, 169–70
Ion, 180, 202, 279–81
Ion, 23, 180–1, 184, 202, 313, 316
Ionia, 26, 47, 269, 279–80, 343, 433
Ionians, 126, 280–1, 334, 343
Ionic meter, 277
Ionic traditions, 48
Iphigeneia, 293
Iphigenia, 184, 361
Iphigenia in Tauris, 184
Iphis, 359, 366
Iran, 92, 115, 132, 134–7, 140, 150
Iranians, 127, 134
Iris, 184, 290
iron age/*genos*, 107, 114, 116, 123, 132, 138, 140, 142–4, 147–8, 221, 365
iron production, 134
irony, 358, 377, 379
Isaiah, 126
Isimud, 109
Isis, 369
Isis and Osiris, 129
Islands of the Blessed, 320; *see also* Elysian Isles
Islands of the Blest, 221, 229–30; *see also* Elysian Isles
Isles of the Blessed, 356, 471; *see also* Elysian Isles
Ismene, 244

Isocrates, 60, 349
Isthmian Odes, 348
Italic, 118–19
Ithaca, 69, 70, 73, 75–7, 79–80, 145, 238, 247, 308, 312
Itys, 373, 441
Ixion, 360, 471

James, Henry, 439
Janus, 294
Jason, 1, 15–17, 167–71, 174, 195, 205, 290, 295, 301, 365, 436, 462–3
Jason and the Argonauts, 458, 462, 476
Jean de Meun, 410, 412, 421
Jerusalem, 125–6, 433
Jocasta, 470; *see also* Iocasta
John of Salisbury, 418
Johnson, Samuel, 427, 435, 440, 444
Jove, 368, 376, 378, 415, 431
Joyce, James, 441
Judah, 125
Judaism, 127, 132
Jude the Obscure, 436
Judgment of Paris, 191, 321, 459
Julius Caesar, 356, 359, 369–70
Jung, Carl, 441
Juno, 367, 414, 428
Jupiter, 190, 356, 359, 365, 367–8, 370, 373–4, 376, 378, 412, 414, 428, 431
Justice, 232

kakon, 141, 169
kakos, 138–9, 141, 150
kaliyuga, 117, 130, 136, 142
Kallisteia, 2, 25, 27, 40, 45
kalon kakon, 120, 123
Karšāsp, 116
katabasis, 471–2
Katasterismoi, 358; *see also* Catasterisms
Keats, John, 10, 425, 426, 430, 432, 439
Kefalonia, 80
kēres, 67–8
kharis, 50, 51, 59
khorēgos, 21, 39, 40, 276
khoros, 20, 21, 25, 39, 49; *see also* choruses
kingship-in-heaven, 3, 92, 101–4
Kingu, 99–101
Kishar, 99

Kleopatra, 65, 67–9
Kleophrades Painter, 310, 324
kleos, 36–8, 48–9, 55–6, 60, 65–72
Knights, 204–5
Knossos, 468. *see also* Cnossus
Knox, Vicesimus, 432
kōmos, 49, 273
Kritios, 288; *see also* Critius
Kṛṣṇa, 116
kṛtayuga, 116, 135
kṣatriya class, 117, 130, 135, 142
Kumarbi, 93–8, 100–1, 103
Kyknos, 294; *see also* Cycnus

L'Odissea, 471
La guerra di Troia, 460
Labors of Heracles, 167, 296–7, 338, 465
Labors of Hercules, 464
labyrinth, 27, 257, 269–70, 288, 409, 412, 413
Lachesis, 233
Laconia, 295, 333, 335, 346
Lactantius Placidus, 410, 419, 422
Laertes, 238
Laestrygonians, 78
Lahamu, 99–100
Lahar, 101
Lahmu, 99, 100
Laius, 309, 321, 470
Lake of Acheron, 229
Lamachus, 201
Lamia, 430
LAMMA, 94, 98
Lampon, 193
Landino, Cristoforo, 410, 417
landscape, 7, 174, 291–2, 305–19, 321–9, 440, 470
langue, 333
Laocoon, 286
Laodamia, 378, 430
Lapiths, 54, 343, 349
Larkin, Philip, 444
Last Judgment, 471
Lasus, 48
Lavinia, 418
law, 117–19, 124, 135, 149, 174, 179, 182, 206, 208, 222–3, 281, 314, 362, 376, 416

Laws, 229, 314
Laws of Manu, 117, 129, 130, 135, 149
Le fatiche di Ercole, 464
Leda, 192, 361
legomena, 266
Lemnian Women, 194–5
Lemnians, 206
Lemnomeda, 197
Lemnos, 172, 195, 206, 257
Lenaea, 194
Lernaean Hydra, 87, 90, 290, 295, 449, 462
Lesbos, 2, 3, 24–8, 33–4, 37, 40, 41, 43–7, 393
Lethe, 233
Leto, 88, 90, 195, 302, 323, 343
Leucippides, 317; *see also* Leukippides
Leuctra, 346
Leukippides, 40; *see also* Leucippides
Levine, Joseph E., 465
Lévi-Strauss, Claude, 121, 332, 388
Libya, 271–4, 351
Liches, 333
Life of Aesop, 63
Life of Aristides, 26
Life of Homer, 23, 60
Life of Solon, 279
light, 72–6
liminality, 4, 172, 176, 205, 393, 399
Linear B, 81
Lipara, 317
literary persona, 83–4, 379
Lives, Plutarch's, 267
Livius Andronicus, 355
local traditions, 2, 26, 28, 33, 35, 41, 58–60, 194, 241, 252, 260, 287, 295, 331–3
Locri, 222, 301
Locrians, 169
Loftis, Norman, 447–8
logos (plural, *logoi*), 5, 50, 59, 106, 114, 115, 123–4, 134, 142, 149, 210–14, 216–17, 222, 224, 230, 389
Look Back in Anger, 444
Lord, Albert, 52–3
Lotus-Eaters, 76
Lucceius, 246
Lucian, 177, 311, 320

Lucretia, 371
Lucretius, 356, 361
Lucurgus, 355
Ludlul Bēl Nēmeqi, 139
Lupercalia, 371
Lycaon, 365, 368
"Lycidas," 427
Lycormas River, 240
Lydgate, John, 410, 419
Lydia, 26, 46–7, 347, 464
Lydians, 3, 26, 46–7, 347
Lykaon Painter, 318–19
Lyly, John, 413
Lynceus, 196, 331
lyric, 2, 3, 19–24, 28, 31–4, 36–9, 41, 44, 46–53, 57–61, 63, 66–7, 69, 72, 75, 237, 245, 316, 426, 454
Lysander, 427
Lysias, 213, 218, 226
Lysippus, 297, 465
Lysistrata, 195, 198, 203–4, 206–7, 446
Lyssa, 175, 184–5

Macareus, 197
Macedonia, 85, 112
Machae, 87
Maciste all'inferno, 471
Macneice, Louis, 445
Macpherson, James, 429
Macrobius, 422
madness, 172, 175, 177, 185, 219, 309, 360
maenads, 45, 182, 292, 321
Mahābhārata, 80, 116–17, 130, 135, 136
makarismos, 264–6, 277
Mānavadharmaśātra, 117
Mantinea, 224, 238
Mantineans, 238
Marathon, 288–9, 298, 339, 340, 343, 349, 440
Marduk, 99–100, 139
Mari, 134
Mark Antony, 356
Mārkaṇḍeya, 117, 130
Marlowe, Christopher, 428, 430
Marmor Parium, 281

Marpessa, 240
Mars, 356, 361, 412
Marsyas, 366
Marvell, Andrew, 426
master myth, 2, 50, 59–64, 66–70, 73, 76, 79
master narrator, 2, 56–7, 59–60, 63–6, 79
Maurice, 439
Medea, 15–18, 167–71, 174, 186, 247, 290, 365–6, 398, 436, 446, 462
Medea, 171, 174, 366, 397, 436
Media, 126, 133
Medieval literature, 9
Medusa, 121, 290, 295, 302, 316, 324, 331, 360, 402, 404, 462, 471
Megalensia, 371
Megara, 204
Megara (city), 140, 345
Megarians, 193, 345
Meidias Painter, 299, 317
Melampus, 334
Melanion, 198
Melanthus, 345
Meleager, 55–7, 63–9, 361, 366
Meliae, 87
melic, 20–3, 47–8, 260, 262, 275
Méliès, Georges, 453
melos, 260
Memnon, 91, 302
Menelaion, 334
Menelaos, 24, 57
Menelaus, 8, 202, 227, 312, 334, 335, 362, 459
Meno, 222, 232
Menoetius, 88
Mercury, 190, 412, 417
Merope, 437
Mesopotamia, 3, 92–5, 104, 108, 118, 125–6
Messene, 239–40
Messenia, 335
Messenians, 198, 240
Messon, 2, 24, 43–6
metallic symbolism, 107, 113–16, 119, 121–2, 124, 127, 131, 133–4, 136, 142, 212

metamorphoses, 175, 192, 214, 245, 248, 293, 357–8, 365, 368–70, 375, 379, 414, 439, 442

Metamorphoses, 8, 133, 248, 358, 359, 361, 363–70, 374–9, 410, 413–14, 419, 426, 450–1

Metaneira, 263

Metaphysics, 210–11

meteorites, 134

meter, 20, 42, 56, 250; *see also* elegiac, hexameter

Metis, 90–1

mētis, 71, 77

Michelangelo, 471

Micon, 267; *see also* Mikon

Midas, 366, 461

Mikon, 298; *see also* Micon

Miletus, 5, 210, 343

Miller, Arthur, 444

Miltiades, 243, 289

Milton, John, 10, 408, 410, 426–8, 431

mimesis, 43, 44

mimēsis, 39

Mimnermus, 22, 48

Minerva, 367, 375, 411, 416, 418

Minoans, 468

Minos, 195–6, 214, 230, 232, 256–7, 267, 270, 320, 366, 471

Minotaur, 166, 255–7, 267, 287–8, 290, 295, 299, 338, 342–3, 411

misogyny, 89, 106, 138, 390

Mithra, 128–9

Mitra, 128

mixed iron, 115, 127, 131, 133–4, 136–7

Mnemosyne, 87, 90

Mnesilochus, 202–3

Moerae, 87, 233, 268; *see also* Fates

Molione, 290

monody, 20, 45

monsters, 78, 87, 89, 95, 97, 99–101, 120, 166, 204, 267, 290–1, 294, 314, 325, 453, 460–2, 471

Mopsus, 248

Morrison, Toni, 10, 426, 446

mother goddesses, 93, 95, 403

Mother Hubur, 99

Mourning Becomes Electra, 443

Mt. Cithaeron, 174, 182, 321

Mt. Helicon, 83, 86

Mt. Hymettus, 313

Mt. Ida, 191, 321, 458

Mt. Nysa, 314

Mt. Oeta, 181

Mt. Olympus, 86, 89, 90, 96, 107, 225, 263–5, 275–6, 278, 300, 321, 339, 367, 385, 457–9, 461

Mt. Othrys, 89

Mt. Parnassus, 275

Mummu, 99

murder, 100, 168–9, 171, 192, 195, 206, 300

Musaeus, 104

Muses, 20, 21, 36, 38, 39, 42, 56–7, 60, 70, 83, 86, 90–1, 149, 218, 275–6, 278, 311, 375, 419, 433–4, 476

music, 278

musicians, 229

Musomachia, 375

muthos (plural *muthoi*), 2, 4, 5, 9, 11, 50, 54, 57–61, 107, 137, 150, 186, 198, 259, 260, 356, 389; *see also* mythos

Mycale, 343

Mycenae, 334–6, 468

Mycenaean epic, 81

Mycenaean Greek, 81

Mycenaeans, 334

Myrmidons, 147, 242

Myrrha, 366, 374

Mysia, 199, 321

Mystagogus Poeticus, 416, 418, 421

Mysteries of Eleusis, 264–6, 295

mystery cult, 264

myth of ages, 112–13, 118–19, 131, 133, 135

mythographers, 5, 97, 244–5, 250–1, 379, 408, 410–11, 413, 419, 441, 454

Mythographus Homericus, 250

mythography, 5, 6, 238–41, 243, 245–7, 252, 259, 271, 358, 388, 402, 421

Mythologies, 415, 420

mythopoeia, 5, 212, 220, 234, 402

mythos (plural, *mythoi*), 5, 210–14, 216, 224, 230, 332; *see also* muthos

myths of judgment, 212, 214–16, 227–8, 231–2

Mytilene, 24, 45

Nabonidus, 125–6
Naevius, 355
Nārāyaṇa, 130
Narcissus, 227, 366, 428
naukrariai, 344
Nausicaa, 139, 145–6, 315–16, 324, 441
Naxos, 257
Near East, 3, 32, 82, 92, 101–4, 108–10, 112, 118, 124, 128, 138, 149–50, 290, 306
Nebuchadnezzar, 24, 113–14, 125–7, 131, 133–4
Nekuia, 212, 230
Neleus, 343, 345
Nemean lion, 295, 297
Nemean Odes, 36, 49, 58–9, 242
Nemesis, 87, 107, 137, 192, 194–5, 300
neo-mythologisms, 11, 454, 461, 466, 468, 473–4, 476
Neoplatonism, 144, 411
Neoptolemos, 291
Neoptolemus, 173, 186, 324
Nephelococcygia, 199, 207
Neptune, 378
Nereids, 35–6, 87, 268–9
Nereus, 87, 268
Neriglissar, 127
Nesiotes, 288, 345
Nessus, 290
Nestor, 24, 54–5, 199
Netherworld, 89–90, 93, 96–7, 99, 101; *see also* Underworld
New Comedy, 190
New Testament, 426
Nicaenetus, 247
Nicander, 247–8, 358, 368
Nicias, 193
Nike, 290, 301–2
NINURTA, 94
Niobe, 195, 373, 446
Niobids, 300
Niobos, 195
Noah, 9, 413
Nonnus, 176
noos, 75–6, 78–9
nostos, 67–70, 72–3, 75–9
Notus, 88, 90

nymphs, 72, 87, 213, 271–2, 312–14, 321–2, 427, 436, 442, 450
Nyx, 86–7, 89, 106

O'Neill, Eugene, 443
Oceanids, 87–8, 90
Oceanus, 17, 86–7, 101, 210, 229; *see also* Okeanos
Octavian, 356
"Ode on a Grecian Urn," 425
Odes, 356, 360
Odin, 130
Odissea, 473
Odusia, 355
Odysses, 192
Odysseus, 2, 58–9, 62, 64, 69–80, 138–9, 145–7, 167, 173, 178, 183, 192, 200, 230, 232–3, 238, 244, 247–8, 293–4, 308, 312, 314–16, 318–19, 323–4, 348, 433, 441, 454, 472–3
Odyssey, 2, 20, 24, 33, 36, 52–4, 57, 59, 62, 69–82, 105, 138–9, 145–7, 167, 178, 192, 197, 212, 221, 223, 230, 237–8, 250, 260, 308, 311–15, 317–18, 321, 324, 335, 346, 357–8, 379, 418, 454, 471–2
Oedipus, 166, 172, 183, 185–6, 208, 271, 309, 321, 337, 441, 446, 459, 470
Oedipus at Colonus, 172, 310, 470
Oedipus Rex, 469
Oedipus Tyrannus, 167, 172, 174, 182, 185
Oenoe, 248
Oenopion, 258
Ogygia, 312
Ohrmazd, 115–16, 129, 131
Oinomaus, 297
Okeanos, 74; *see also* Oceanus
Old Comedy, 4, 190–2, 194–5, 198, 203, 208
Old English, 141
Old Man of the Sea, 87
Old Testament, 9, 109, 126, 412
Olivier, Laurence, 457
Olympia, 296–8, 300, 340
Olympian Odes, 50, 59–61, 311, 320
Olympians, 73, 89, 97, 101, 122, 179, 192, 292, 295, 300, 310, 375, 431, 457, 466

Olympias, 350
Olympic Games, 50, 243
Olynthus, 249
"On a Stupendous Leg of Granite,"
    432
On Imitation, 42
On the Content of Virgil, 417
"On the Nymph Complaining for the
    Death of her Fawn," 427
On Virgil's Aeneid, 417
oral poetry, 1–2, 19, 52–3, 82, 91
oral tradition, 81
Orchomenus, 275
Oreithyia, 213, 227, 301, 316, 327
Oresteia, 178–9, 185, 443
Orestes, 171, 179, 192, 200, 333–4, 336,
    361
Orestes, 184, 197, 221
Orfeu Negro, 474
orientalization, 8, 46, 348
orientalizing, 3, 47–8, 92
Orion, 73
Orlando Furioso, 416, 422
Ornithogonia, 248, 358
Oromazes, 129
Orphée, 473
Orpheus, 9, 16, 85, 104, 359–60, 413,
    473–4, 476
Orphism, 85, 198, 233, 319
Orthus, 87, 90, 290
Osborne, John, 444
Ossian poems, 429
Otus, 225
outidanos, 72
Outis, 71–2, 79
Ovid, 8–10, 133, 355–8, 360–1, 363,
    365–71, 373–9, 388–9, 397, 410–11,
    413–14, 416, 419–20, 426, 429, 441–2,
    446, 448–51
Ovide Moralisé, 410, 419
Ovidius Moralizatus, 414, 419
"Ozymandias," 432

Paean, 36, 276, 277
paeans, 37, 50, 260, 268–9, 275–8
Paestum, 220
Pagasae, 169
Pahlavi, 115, 129, 131, 133

Paine, Thomas, 433
painters, 286–8, 291–3, 296, 298, 317,
    319, 322–4, 408, 429, 434, 454
palaia, 259
Palamedes, 219
Palamedes, 196
Palamon, 411
Palatine, 356, 368–9, 374, 376
Palestine, 126
Paliki, 80
palinodes, 60, 218, 224, 227, 449
Pallas (Athena), 385, 416
Pallas (Athenian king), 258
Pallas (Titan), 88
Pan, 227, 238, 313–14, 326, 436
Panathenaea, 193
Panathenaia, 8, 20, 45, 47, 267, 301, 339,
    345
Panathenaicus, 350
Pandavas, 116–17
Pandion, 194
Pandora, 89, 106, 120, 123, 177, 300,
    383–5, 395
Pandu, 116
Panhellenism, 40, 48, 84, 194, 241, 252,
    260, 276, 287, 294, 338, 349–50
Pantalces, 313
Pantheon, 428
Panyassis, 245
Paphlagonia, 204–5
Paradise Lost, 410, 431
Paradiso, 214, 231, 413
paradoxography, 6, 238–9, 241, 247, 249,
    251
Parilia, 371
Paris, 4, 60, 167, 190–1, 290, 321, 346,
    361, 408, 457, 459–60
Parker, Dorothy, 402
Parmenides, 22, 224
parodos, 280
parody, 4, 191, 193–4, 196–8, 202,
    448
parole, 333
Parry, Adam, 53
Parry, Milman, 52–3
partheneion, 50
Parthenius of Nicaea, 245–6, 249, 251,
    358

Parthenon, 287, 292, 298, 300, 326, 340, 349
Parthenos, 133, 281, 298, 300, 394
Pasiphae, 195, 361, 398
Pasolini, Pier Paolo, 470
pastoralists, 119; *see also* herders, shepherds
Pastrone, Giovanni, 464
Pater, Walter, 438, 440
Patroclus, 147, 294, 459; *see also* Patroklos
Patrokleēs, 65, 68
Patroklos, 31, 33–4, 37, 57, 61, 64–9; *see also* Patroclus
Paulin, Tom, 445
Pausanias, 7, 23, 60, 88, 238, 262, 278, 309, 315, 319, 327–8, 331–4, 337, 339
Peacham, Henry, 417
Pegasus, 87, 213, 290, 373
Peisetaerus, 198–9, 207
Pelasgus, 172
Peleus, 199, 293, 361, 366
Peleus, 356
Pelias, 16–17, 168–9, 294
Peloponnesian League, 335
Peloponnesian Peninsula, 8, 238, 314, 333–7, 339, 350
Peloponnesian Wars, 193, 211, 261, 280, 289, 299
Peloponnesians, 270, 280
Pelops, 50, 221, 297, 366
penates, 369
Penelope, 74, 238, 247, 302, 357–8, 378, 402, 472
Penia, 226
Penthesilea, 296
Pentheus, 47, 175–6, 182, 294, 321, 366
Peparethus, 257
pepla, 453
peplos (of Athena), 301
peplums, 453, 456, 458, 471
performance, 2–6, 19–25, 27–8, 38–41, 43–5, 48–51, 53–4, 61, 63, 71, 84, 86, 139, 149, 238, 261–2, 265–6, 268–73, 276–8, 281, 332, 350
Pergamon, 293, 327
Pergamum, 237
Pericles, 191, 193, 267, 341–2
Peripatetic monographs, 246

Periphetes, 288
Persephone, 90, 203, 263–7, 301, 316, 375, 402, 473–4; *see also* Proserpina
Perses, 105–6, 109, 123, 148–9
Perses (Titan), 88
Perseus, 295, 301, 331, 337, 366, 373, 394, 471
Persia, 46, 125–7, 129, 134, 298, 339, 348–50
Persian, 126
Persian Wars, 8, 177, 207, 242, 267, 270, 279, 288, 296, 298, 301, 348
Persians, 47, 125–7, 206, 243, 288, 296, 298–9, 338, 344, 349, 351
Petersen, Wolfgang, 11, 457, 459, 461
Petrarch (Francesco Petrarca), 408, 413
Phaeacia, 169, 232, 315–16
Phaeacians, 76, 79, 139, 145–7, 312, 315
Phaedo, 215, 269
Phaedo, 23, 211, 214–15, 222, 227, 231, 320
Phaedra, 167, 182, 194, 247, 261, 357, 361, 398
Phaedra, 357
Phaedrus, 212–14, 216, 218–20, 224, 226, 327
Phaedrus, 60, 212–15, 218–20, 222, 224, 226–7, 232, 310, 316, 326
Phaenomena, 133, 245
Phaethon, 366, 374
Phaon, 41, 413
Pharmacea, 213
Pharsalus, 313
phēmē, 79
Pheraios, Rigas, 351
Pherecrates, 194, 197
Pherecydes, 242–5, 281
Phidias, 298, 342
Philaeus, 243
Philemon, 190, 366
Philip II of Macedon, 350
Philo, 102–4
Philocleon, 205–6
Philoctetes, 186
Philoctetes, 172, 197
Philodamus, 275–8
Philomela, 441
philomythos, 211

philos (plural, *philoi*), 49, 64–6,
    144–8
Philosopher, 220
philosophers, 5, 144, 210–13, 219, 226,
    230, 232, 237, 310, 412
philosophia, 226
philosophos, 211
philosophy, 219, 222
Philostratus, 311, 326
philotēs, 145, 147
philoxenos, 145–6
philtatos, 64–5
Philyllius, 194
Phlegon of Tralles, 239–41, 247, 252
Phoebe, 87–8
Phoebus, 240, 369
Phoenicia, 3, 102–4, 219
Phoenician History, 103
Phoenician Women (by Aristophanes), 194,
    196
Phoenician Women (by Strattis), 197
Phoenicians, 102, 104, 270, 447
Phoenissae (by Euripides), 321
Phoenix, 55–7, 63–8
Pholus, 195, 290
Phorcys, 87, 121
Photius, 239, 243–4, 249
Phrygians, 348
Phye, 339
Phyllis, 361
Physics, 325
Pieria, 275, 278
Pierides, 375
Pierus, 375
Pindar, 2, 19, 22, 36, 48–50, 58–61, 63,
    66–7, 72, 168–9, 177, 238, 242, 245,
    260, 272–4, 311, 320, 333, 348, 389
Pisistratids, 338–41, 343–4
Pisistratus, 8, 300, 339, 342–5, 351
Plato, 4, 23, 47, 60, 67, 211–16, 218–22,
    224–5, 227–34, 269, 305, 310, 314, 316,
    320, 326, 356, 401, 409, 411, 422
Plautus, 190
Plutarch, 26, 129, 267, 279
Pluti, 193
Pluto, 230, 316, 367
Plutus, 193
Poe, Edgar Allan, 443

Poetics, 38, 42
poets, 2, 5, 9, 11–12, 19, 21–3, 38, 45–7,
    49–50, 52, 57, 60, 84, 91, 103–4, 138,
    177, 191, 205, 210, 213, 218, 229,
    245–6, 251, 260, 286, 305–7, 326, 356,
    359, 372–3, 377, 397, 408, 412, 416,
    429–30, 434, 438, 444, 447, 454, 461,
    475
Policraticus, 418
Polion, 292
polis, 5, 7, 42, 173–4, 201, 208, 213, 287,
    289, 331, 343, 346
politics, 4, 6–8, 24, 27, 40, 42, 47, 104,
    131–2, 166, 173, 193, 200, 203, 208,
    218, 229, 242, 259–62, 270, 279, 281,
    287–8, 298–300, 309, 331–3, 336, 344,
    346, 349–51, 355–6, 361–3, 367–71,
    374, 376–7, 391, 401, 427, 469
poluphēmos, 79
Polus, 230
Polycrates, 46–8, 243
Polygnotus, 315, 319
Polyidus, 196, 320
Polyidus, 194, 196
Polymetis, 428
Polynices, 172, 182, 337, 411
Polyphemus, 62, 71, 73, 78, 146, 294,
    314–15, 473
Polyxena, 294
Pontus, 86–7, 101
Ponus, 87
Pope, Alexander, 10, 426, 428, 434,
    441
Poros, 226
Poseidon, 16, 76, 88, 90–1, 173, 177–8,
    184, 224, 230, 240, 250, 262, 267, 270,
    316, 343, 446
Postclassical period, 22–3
Post-Renaissance literature, 10, 440
pothos, 225
potnia theron, 290
Pound, Ezra, 10, 426, 441, 443, 445
pragmata, 207
prayer, 27–8, 32, 39, 40, 54, 227, 266,
    275, 277–8, 450
Pre', 112
Precepts of Chiron, 105
Presocratics, 228

Priam, 138, 167, 174, 199, 249, 291, 322, 324, 346, 408
Priapus, 436
priestly class, 117, 135
priestly function, 119
primeval giant, 130–1, 135, 149
Proagon, 195
Proclus, 144
Procrustes, 287, 338
profane (vs. sacred), 43
Progymnasmata, 356
promanteia, 275
Prometheus, 88, 106, 123, 177–8, 204, 216–17, 219, 230, 241, 300, 364, 385, 430–1, 471
Prometheus Bound, 175, 178–9, 230, 430
Prometheus Unbound, 430–1
Pronoea, 241
Propertius, 360–1
prophecy, 12, 54, 79, 107, 113–14, 116, 132–3, 141–4, 147–8, 194, 227, 272, 313, 376
prophets, 17, 115, 126, 136, 233
Propylaea, 315
Prose Edda, 130
Proserpina, 367; see also Persephone
Protagoras, 216–17
Protagoras, 215–16, 218–20, 222, 230
Proteus, 312, 373, 466
Proto-Indo-Europeans, 82, 118–19; see also Indo-Europeans
Proto-Indo-Iranians, 137; see also Indo-Iranians
Proverbs, 3, 109–11
proxenia, 275
Pseudea, 87
psukhē, 74–5, 80
Psyche, 401
Ptolemies, 112
Puruṣa, 130–2
Puttenham, George, 409
Pygmalion, 374, 434–5, 447–8
Pygmalion et Galathée, 453
Pylos, 343, 345
Pyramus, 366, 412
Pyrrha, 241, 365, 373

Pythagoreanism, 429
Pythagoreans, 215
Pythia, 277, 470
Pythian games, 243, 272, 274, 277–8
Pythian Odes, 72, 168–9, 272–4, 333
Pytho, 88

Quarles, Frances, 412
Qumran, 125–6

Rabanus, Maurus, 413
Rāmāyaṇa, 116
rape, 135, 167, 180, 197, 203, 265, 300–1, 316, 343, 360, 363, 367, 369–71, 375, 377, 398, 444
Rape of the Sabine Women, 371
"Ravenna," 440
recitation, 20
red-figure painting, 45, 211, 291, 295, 298, 301–2, 315–17, 324, 338, 342, 345
Reeves, Steve, 464
religion, 4, 6, 115, 119, 129, 131, 136, 180, 185, 203, 259, 369, 426; see also Greek religion
Remedia Amoris, 361
Remus, 347, 371
Renaissance literature, 9, 428
Renault, Mary, 446
Republic, 23, 212–15, 219, 222, 228–33, 305, 401, 409
Rhadamanthus, 215
Rhadamanthys, 230, 232
Rhamnus, 300
rhapsodes, 20, 48, 260, 264, 266
Rhea, 86, 88, 95
Rhesus, 249
rhetoric, 42, 66, 182, 200, 218, 226, 230, 361
Rhetoric, 44
Rhetorica ad Herennium, 356
Rich, Adrienne, 401
Rig Veda, 128, 130–1
ritual, 2, 6, 8, 19, 28, 31–2, 34–5, 40, 45, 53, 72, 134, 136, 149–50, 172, 175, 181, 184, 259–62, 264–70, 272–9, 281, 292, 301, 328, 356–7, 392, 395

rituals, 2, 24, 27–8, 34, 50, 58, 251, 349, 392–3
River, 101, 447
Rochester, John Wilmot, 427
Roman frescoes, 308
Roman period, 306, 331, 337
Romance of the Rose, 412
romanitas, 367, 369, 371
Romanticism, 429
Rome, 8, 246, 306, 308, 331, 346–7, 355–6, 360, 362, 364, 367–70, 377–9, 399–400, 426, 432, 435, 446
Romulus, 347, 355–6, 369, 371
Room at the Top, 444
Ross, Alexander, 416, 418, 421
Rossi, Franco, 471, 473
ṛta, 129
Runaways, 193–4
Ruskin, John, 435, 444
Rycroft Painter, 323

Sabines, 363, 371
sacred (vs. profane), 43
sacred groves, 229
sacred moment, 40
sacred space, 24–7, 40, 43–6, 202
Salamis, 242, 440
Salmacis, 450
Šamaš, 111
Samos, 46–8, 238
Sanchuniathon, 102–3
Sandys, George, 410, 413, 416, 420
Sanskrit, 116, 129, 141
Santorini, 271
"Sapho and Phao," 413
Sappho, 2, 22–33, 35–48, 53, 260, 346, 393, 402, 413
Sargossa Sea, 224
Sarmatian, 377
Saturn, 221–2, 413, 415
Saturnalia, 422
satyrs, 191–2, 290–2, 322, 430, 436
Šauška, 94–5
Scaean Gate, 218
Scamander, 326
Scamander River, 325
Scandinavia, 123, 130
Scarphea, 275

Scheria, 315
scholia, 24–5, 61, 144, 221, 242, 245, 250–1
Scholiast to Lycophron, 334
Sciron, 287–8, 338
sculptors, 286, 288, 454
Scylla, 361, 373; *see also* Skylla
Scythians, 347
Sea, 101
second function, 119, 121, 131, 143, 147
seers, 75, 117, 130, 182, 185, 194, 297, 320
Selanna, 41
Selene, 41, 87, 225, 292, 300
Seleucids, 125
Semele, 204, 275, 367
Semitic, 102, 126, 132
Semonides, 22
Seneca, 366
Sennacherib, 112
Šertapšuruḫi, 95–6
Servius, 388–9, 410
Seven against Thebes, 107, 115, 194, 293, 337–8, 351
sexuality, 33, 179–80, 191, 193, 203, 206, 221, 316, 361, 366, 393, 395, 426–7, 439, 441
Shakespeare, William, 10, 408–10, 412, 419, 426, 428, 430, 449–50
Shelley, Mary, 431
Shelley, Percy Bysshe, 430–2, 443
Shepheardes Calender, 413
shepherds, 279; *see also* herders, pastoralists
Shield of Heracles, 84, 151
Sicily, 48, 347
Sicon, 197
Sigurðr, 123
Silver, 95–6, 98
silver age/*genos*, 106, 115, 121–2, 133–4, 141, 143
Silvia, 371
similes, 61–2, 120, 239, 374
Simmias, 215, 228–9
Simonides, 22–3, 48, 245
Sin, 125
singers, 20, 22, 25, 27, 38–9, 44–5, 49, 69, 79, 218, 274, 359, 409

Sinis, 287, 338

Sirens, 70, 78, 233, 290, 292, 302

Siris, 347

Sisyphus, 230, 360, 471

Sithonia, 249

Škend Gumānīg Vizār, 131

skene, 174, 229

Skylla, 290; *see also* Scylla

slave class, 117

Slavic, 130

Smith, Horace, 432, 443

social classes, 133, 135–6, 142

Socrates, 5, 210–20, 222–33, 269, 305–6, 310, 326–7

Solon, 22, 222–3, 267

song, 16, 20–2, 24, 26–39, 41–4, 46, 48–50, 56, 58, 60–1, 65–6, 69–70, 73, 78, 86, 94–5, 261, 266–70, 274–6, 278, 280, 311, 359–60, 375, 409, 442

Song of Kumarbi, 93, 95

Song of LAMMA, 93–4

Song of Hedammu, 93, 95

Song of Silver, 93, 95

"Song of the Exposition," 433

Song of Ullikummi, 93–5, 97

sophia, 226

Sophist, 220

sophistes, 216–18

sophists, 220, 230

Sophocles, 167, 172, 177, 181–2, 185, 197, 204, 248, 310, 323, 326, 336, 449, 469–70

Sosia, 190

sōšyants, 116

Sotades Painter, 320–1

Sow of Crommyon, 338, 342

Spənta Mainyu, 129

Sparta, 8, 26, 40, 47–8, 60, 191, 198–200, 238, 271–4, 282, 312, 325, 333–8, 340, 343, 345, 349, 351, 438, 445, 448

Spartans, 198, 295, 333–7, 345, 350–1

speech-acts, 2, 54, 57, 61

Spence, Joseph, 428

Spenser, Edmund, 408–10, 412–13, 418–19

Sphinx, 87, 167, 290

Spintharus, 197

Staphylus, 258

Star Wars, 438

Starkaðr, 123

Statesman, 211–12, 215–17, 220–2

Statius, 389, 410, 421

Stesichorus, 22, 48, 60, 333, 347, 449

Sthenelus, 334, 336

Stič o golubinoj knig, 131

Stoa Poikile, 298, 349

Stoics, 364, 412

Strabo, 211

Strattis, 196

Strymon, 249

Sturluson, Snorri, 130

Stymphalian birds, 295, 297

Styx, 88–9, 471

Šubši-mešre-Šakkan, 139

succession myths, 88–90, 92, 95, 204

śudra class, 117, 130–1, 135, 142

Suetonius, 368

suicide, 58, 167, 173, 183, 194, 197, 270, 296–7, 310, 323

Sūdkar Nask, 115

Sumer, 95, 108, 110, 118

Sumerians, 108

Sun God of the Sky, 94

Suppliant Maidens, 172

Swinburne, Algernon, 437, 446

symmetry (poetic), 42–5

symposium, 22, 42–7, 206, 289, 292

Symposium, 67, 215–16, 218, 223–7

sympotic poetry, 45–7, 61

Synoikia, 344

Syracuse, 223, 338

Syria, 347

Syria-Palestine, 92, 104

Syrinx, 436

Taautos, 102

Tables of Illustrious Persons in Every Branch of Learning Together with a List of their Works, 237

Tablets of Fate, 99–100

Tales from Ovid, 448

Talos, 462–3

Tanglewood Tales, 11–12, 16, 257

Tantalus, 230, 360, 373, 471

Tartarus, 86, 89, 97, 100, 107, 193, 205, 215, 228–30, 233, 360, 471
Tašmišu, 93–4, 96
technology, 62, 134, 459, 471, 473
Tegea, 333, 335–6
Tegeans, 333, 335
Teiresias, 75; *see also* Tiresias
Telecleides, 194
Telemachus, 473
Telemakhos, 70
Telephos, 294
Telephus, 199–201, 327
Telephus, 196, 202
Tema, 125
temenos, 25
temporal cyclicity, 148, 233
Tereus, 361, 366
Terpander, 47–8
Terpsichore, 219
Tess of the d'Urbervilles, 436
Teššub, 92–8, 100, 104
Tessari, Duccio, 455, 461, 464, 468
Tethys, 87
Thalamae, 346
Thamus, 214, 218–19
Thanatos, 89, 224
Thaumas, 87
"The Author of 'Beltraffio,'" 439
The Divine Comedy, 410
The Excursion, 430
The Faerie Queene, 409, 412
The Heron and the Turtle, 108
The Instructions of Šuruppag, 110
"The Knight's Tale," 411
The Long Night, 190
The Madness of Heracles, 167, 175
"The Other Kingdom," 439
The Peloponnesian War, 210
The Sorrows of Young Werther, 429
"The Wanderer," 432
The Waste Land, 441, 447–8
"The Wife of Bath's Tale," 412
The Winter's Tale, 412, 450
The World's Wife, 448–9
Theaetetus, 220
theater, 43, 47–8, 166, 262, 280, 412, 459
Thebaid, 421
Thebais, 337

Thebes, 17, 167, 172, 174, 186, 215, 228–9, 273–6, 311, 321, 337, 346, 373, 411, 466, 468
Thebes (in Egypt), 218–19
Theia, 86–7
Themis, 87, 90, 301
Themistocles, 267
Theocritus, 306, 325, 389
Theognis, 22, 46, 61, 75, 140–1, 150
theogoniē, 85
theogony, 85–6, 101–4
Theogony, 3, 60, 62, 84–6, 89, 91–2, 96–8, 100–2, 105–6, 120–2, 138, 144, 149, 151, 176, 178, 221, 229, 244, 311, 316–17, 358
Theophrastus, 323
Theopompus, 194
theōria, 269
theoudēs, 145–6
Theoxenia, 275–8
Thera, 81, 271–4, 307–8
Therapne, 334
Theras, 271, 274
Thermopylae, 440
Theseum, 298
Theseus, 7–9, 166, 169, 173, 179, 186, 193–4, 205, 245, 247, 255–8, 262, 267, 269–70, 287–92, 295, 298–9, 301, 337–9, 341–5, 366, 411, 413, 446, 473
Thesmophoria, 4, 202–3
Thesmophoriazusae, 4, 196, 199, 202
Thessalos, 343
Thessaly, 271–2, 343
Thetis, 35–6, 68, 91, 169, 184, 199, 293, 302, 361, 430–1, 458
Thetis, 356
Theuth, 214, 218, 219
third function, 119, 121, 123, 131, 143, 148, 150
Thisbe, 412
Thoas, 257
Thoth, 102
Thourios, 351
Thrace, 195, 216, 348
Thracians, 249, 347
Thucydides, 5, 24, 198, 210, 243, 266, 269–70, 344, 347
Thurii, 193

Thyestes, 196, 221, 356
Thyiades, 278
Thymoetes, 345
Thyone, 275
thyrsus, 291
Tiamat, 99–100
Tiberius, 370
Tibullus, 376
Tigris River, 93, 96, 100
Timaeus, 220, 222
Timaeus, 220, 222–3, 229, 356
Timaeus/Critias, 215–16, 220, 222–4
Timon, 198
Timonassa, 342
Tiresias, 182, 318, 366–7, 472; *see also* Teiresias
Tiryns, 337
Tisamenus, 334
Titanomachy, 89–90, 103, 204
Titans, 86–90, 96, 98, 101, 122, 178, 193, 214, 431, 466
Tithonos, 41
Tithonus, 301
Titian (Tiziano Vecellio), 410
Titus Andronicus, 441
Tityos, 373
Tityus, 230, 360
Tmolus, 374
Tomis, 369, 377
Tooke, Andrew, 428
topia, 306
Toth, 218
Trachiniae, 326; *see also Women of Trachis*
tragedians, 12, 169, 177, 184–5, 197, 202, 237, 244–5, 355, 366, 431
tragedy, 3, 166–7, 169, 171–2, 174–8, 181–2, 185–7, 194, 196, 198–203, 227, 260–1, 278–81, 309–10, 313, 316, 319, 336, 352, 366, 431, 436, 438, 444, 469–70, 476
tretāyuga, 117
tripartite ideology, 119, 124, 148, 150
tripartition, 119, 124, 150
Triptolemus, 194, 263, 366
Tristia, 357–8, 361, 376–9
Triton, 290
Troezen, 262, 282, 338, 341–2
Trojan Horse, 71, 244, 302

Trojan War, 4, 79, 81, 102, 107, 115, 242, 244, 274, 291, 294, 296, 302, 312, 329, 348, 366, 458, 460
Trojan Women, 173, 184
Trojans, 8, 62, 200, 218, 273, 346–9, 351–2, 458, 460
Troy, 4, 11, 24–5, 33–4, 56, 62, 67–8, 70–3, 75, 77–9, 138, 147, 167, 173–4, 185, 191–2, 199, 244, 249, 273–4, 291, 301, 308, 321, 323–6, 333, 335, 346–8, 350, 370, 378–9, 433, 446, 449, 453, 457–60
truth, 2, 5, 50, 58–60, 72, 103, 105, 117, 129, 137, 176, 183, 186, 211, 222, 232, 332, 356, 359, 372–6, 415, 423, 428, 438
Twelfth Night, 409
Tydeus, 293, 337
Typhoeus, 89–90, 97–8, 101, 204; *see also* Typhon
Typhon, 97–8, 214; *see also* Typhoeus
Tyrannicides, 288–9, 340, 345
Tyrimmas, 247
Tyrrhenian pirates, 293
Tyrtaeus, 22, 35, 335

Ubelluri, 93–4, 96–7
Ugaritic, 102
Ulisse, 464
Ullikummi, 93–8
Ulysses, 357, 377–8
Ulysses, 441
underworld, 97, 228, 230
Underworld, 7, 212, 229, 232, 310–11, 316, 318–20, 322, 471, 476; *see also* Netherworld
Urania, 219
Uranus, 86–8, 90, 92, 95, 97–8, 100, 102–4, 204, 213, 221, 466–7
Urea, 86
Ušēdar, 116
Ušēdarmah, 116

Vahman Yašt, 115–16, 136
vaiśya class, 117, 130, 135–6
Varius, 356
varṇas, 130, 134, 142
Varro, 356

Varuṇa, 128–9
Vatican Mythographer, 389
Vedas, 117, 128–31, 135
Velia, 212, 220
Velleius, 363
Venus, 41, 355–6, 359, 361, 370–1, 408, 411–12, 436, 450
Venus and Adonis, 428, 450
Verae Historiae, 311, 320
Vergil, 347; *see also* Virgil
Vernant, Jean-Pierre, 3, 35, 119, 121–3, 143, 186, 395
Vesta, 369
Vestal Virgins, 399–401
Vestalia, 371
Vestals, 399–400
Vi, 17, 20
Virgil, 356–7, 359–60, 376–7, 379, 410, 413, 415, 417–18, 426, 429, 433; *see also* Vergil
Virgo, 133
Viṣṇu, 116–17, 130

warp and woof, 84, 150
warrior class, 117, 135
warrior function, 119
Wasps, 205
weaving, 5, 26, 84, 150, 222
West Semitic, 102
Wheatley, Phillis, 447
white-ground painting, 320–2, 324
Whitman, Walt, 433–4, 436, 439, 446
Wilde, Oscar, 440
Williams College, 12
Williams, Tennessee, 444
Willing, Nick, 462
wisdom literature, 109–11, 113; *see also* didactic literature
Wisdoms Conquest, or, An explanation and . . . Translation of the thirteenth Book of Ovids Metamorphoses, 410
Wise, Robert, 459
Women of Trachis, 181; *see also* Trachiniae
Wood, Robert, 429

Woolf, Virginia, 398
Words of Ahiqar, 112
Wordsworth, William, 430, 444
worker class, 117
worker function, 119
Works and Days, 3, 84–5, 89, 105–12, 116, 118, 120–4, 128, 133, 137, 139, 141, 143, 148–9, 151, 177, 212, 221, 310, 320, 358, 386
writing, 23, 81, 102, 218–19, 247
Wuthering Heights, 437

Xanthus River, 325
Xena: Warrior Princess, 453
xenia, 276
xenodokos, 144, 146
Xenophanes, 22, 47, 213, 347
xenos, 49, 144–6
Xerxes, 280, 350
Xuthus, 280

Ymir, 130
Yudhiṣthira, 117, 130
yugas, 116–17, 130, 132, 142

Zarathuštra, 115, 129, 148
Zarduš t, 115–16, 131, 134, 136
Zechariah, 127
Zelos, 106–7, 120, 137
Zephyr, 408
Zephyrus, 88, 90, 301
Zethus, 229
Zeus, 24, 26, 44, 61–2, 72, 86, 88–92, 95–8, 100, 103–7, 120, 122–3, 128–9, 137–9, 143, 146, 173, 177–8, 181, 192–3, 195, 204, 216–17, 219, 221–3, 225, 230, 240, 243, 250, 263, 268, 274–5, 293, 296–302, 316–17, 327, 334, 337, 340–1, 385–6, 430–1, 457–8, 461, 475
Zopyrus Ablaze, 197
Zoroaster, 129
Zoroastrianism, 115–16, 124, 127, 129, 134–6, 148